Frommer's®

POSTCARDS

FROM

NEW YORK CITY

No matter how many times you've seen it, the Manhattan skyline is simply astounding. See chapter 7 for details on all the architectural landmarks. © Greg Pease/Tony Stone Images.

MoMA boasts masterworks by Picasso and just about every other major artist of the 20th century. See chapter 7. © Catherine Karnow Photography.

Discover the art and architecture of medieval Europe at The Cloisters. See chapter 7. © Rudi von Briel Photography.

The Met is the nation's premier art museum. See chapter 7. © Bob Krist Photography.

Downtown in the Village and SoHo, you can still find lots of mom-and-pop shops and unique stores, though many shoppers head straight for the big names like Bloomingdale's. See chapter 8. Both images © Catherine Karnow Photography.

View of the twin towers of the World Trade Center as seen from beneath the Brooklyn Bridge. See chapter 7. © Rudi Von Briel Photography.

Central Park is New York's most famous place to play. See chapter 7. © *Kelly/Mooney Photography.*

Tavern on the Green is known for its spectacular setting and décor. See chapter 6 for a complete review. © Catherine Karnow Photography.

Delis are one of the quintessential New York dining experiences. See chapter 6. © Catherine Karnow Photography.

There's no place more festive than New York during the holidays. Shoppers flock to the stores, and thousands of visitors attend Radio City's annual Christmas Spectacular. See chapter 9.
© *Color Day/The Image Bank.*

New York has become a great place for a family vacation. Your kids will love the newly revitalized Times Square and the dinosaurs at the Museum of Natural History. See chapter 7. Both photos © Rudi Von Briel Photography.

Walking across the Brooklyn Bridge is one of our all-time favorite New York experiences. See chapter 7. © Kelly/Mooney Photography.

Mulberry Street, lined with restaurants and cafes, is the heart of Little Italy. See chapters 4 and 6. © Rudi Von Briel Photography.

The Chrysler Building is perhaps the city's most romantic architectural achievement.
See chapter 7. © Andrea Pistolesi Photography.

New York cabbies hail from all over the world. See chapter 4 for helpful tips. © Catherine Karnow Photography.

Wall Street is the hub of the financial world. See chapter 7 for details on how to tour the Stock Exchange. © Rudi Von Briel Photography.

St. Patrick's is the largest Catholic cathedral in the United States. See chapter 7. © Robert Landau Photography.

The Flatiron Building, a triangular masterpiece, was one of the city's first skyscrapers. See chapter 7. © Rudi Von Briel Photography.

The Guggenheim Museum, the only Frank Lloyd Wright building in the city, is more noted for its controversial design than for the collection of modern art it houses. See chapter 7.
© John Carucci Photography.

No other monument so embodies the nation's ideals of political freedom and economic prosperity as the Statue of Liberty. See chapter 7. © Jon Ortner/Tony Stone Images.

Other Great Guides for Your Trip:

Frommer's New York City from $80 a Day

Frommer's Portable New York City

Frommer's Portable New York City from $80 a Day

Frommer's Memorable Walks in New York City

Frommer's Irreverent Guide to Manhattan

The Unofficial Guide to New York City

Frommer's Born to Shop New York City

Here's what the critics say about Frommer's:

"Amazingly easy to use. Very portable, very complete."
—Booklist

♦

"The only mainstream guide to list specific prices. The Walter Cronkite of guidebooks—with all that implies."
—Travel & Leisure

♦

"Complete, concise, and filled with useful information."
—New York Daily News

♦

"Hotel information is close to encyclopedic."
—Des Moines Sunday Register

♦

"Detailed, accurate and easy-to-read information for all price ranges."
—Glamour Magazine

Frommer's® 2001

New York City

by Cheryl Farr Leas

with research assistance from Nathaniel R. Leas

IDG Books Worldwide, Inc.
An International Data Group Company
Foster City, CA • Chicago, IL • Indianapolis, IN • New York, NY

ABOUT THE AUTHOR

Cheryl Farr Leas was a senior editor at Frommer's before embarking on a freelance writing career. She also authors *Frommer's New York City from $80 a Day, California for Dummies,* and *Hawaii for Dummies* (the last two IDG titles are brand-new in late 2000). She has also contributed to *Frommer's USA,* Continental Airlines' in-flight magazine, *Daily Variety,* and other publications. When she's not traveling, she's at home in Park Slope, Brooklyn, with her groovy husband, Rob, and their happy dog, Monty. Feel free to write her directly at rncleas@yahoo.com.

IDG BOOKS WORLDWIDE, INC.

An International Data Group Company
919 E. Hillsdale Blvd.
Suite 400
Foster City, CA 94404

Find us online at **www.frommers.com**

ISBN 0-02-863786-0
ISSN 1090-7335

Editor: Lisa Renaud/Dog-Eared Pages
Production Editor: Carol Sheehan
Photo Editor: Richard Fox
Design by Michele Laseau
Staff Cartographers: John Decamillis, Elizabeth Puhl, Roberta Stockwell
Page creation by: IDG Books Indianapolis Production Department

SPECIAL SALES

For general information on IDG Books Worldwide's books in the U.S., please call our Consumer Customer Service department at 1-800-762-2974. For reseller information, including discounts, bulk sales, customized editions, and premium sales, please call our Reseller Customer Service department at 1-800-434-3422.

Manufactured in the United States of America

5 4 3 2 1

Contents

List of Maps

AN INVITATION TO THE READER

In researching this book, we discovered many wonderful places—hotels, restaurants, shops, and more. We're sure you'll find others. Please tell us about them, so we can share the information with your fellow travelers in upcoming editions. If you were disappointed with a recommendation, we'd love to know that, too. Please write to:

Frommer's New York City 2001
IDG Books Worldwide, Inc.
909 Third Avenue
New York, NY 10022

AN ADDITIONAL NOTE

Please be advised that travel information is subject to change at any time—and this is especially true of prices. We therefore suggest that you write or call ahead for confirmation when making your travel plans. The authors, editors, and publisher cannot be held responsible for the experiences of readers while traveling. Your safety is important to us, however, so we encourage you to stay alert and be aware of your surroundings. Keep a close eye on cameras, purses, and wallets, all favorite targets of thieves and pickpockets.

WHAT THE SYMBOLS MEAN

✪ Frommer's Favorites

Our favorite places and experiences—outstanding for quality, value, or both.

The following abbreviations are used for credit cards:

AE	American Express	EURO	Eurocard
CB	Carte Blanche	JCB	Japan Credit Bank
DC	Diners Club	MC	MasterCard
DISC	Discover	V	Visa
ER	EnRoute		

FIND FROMMER'S ONLINE

www.frommers.com offers up-to-the-minute listings on almost 200 cities around the globe—including the latest bargains and candid, personal articles updated daily by Arthur Frommer himself. No other Web site offers such comprehensive and timely coverage of the world of travel.

The Best of the Big Apple

Welcome to New York City—the only city on the planet brazen enough to call itself "The Capital of the World." New York has never been subtle, self-effacing, or coy. This is the Muhammad Ali of cities: We Are the Greatest!

It's precisely this kind of urban machismo that makes people either love New York or hate it—or both. Either you'll be enthralled by the tempo, glamour, and sheer excitement of it all, or you'll be stunned by the noise, the juxtaposition of inhuman poverty and unimaginable wealth, the smog, and the callousness that's an everyday occurrence on these city streets. If your emotional metronome swings back and forth from one moment to the next, take heart: We New Yorkers have a never-ending love-hate relationship with this awful, wonderful town. We talk endlessly about escaping for the weekend, commiserate about subways that arrive late, and bemoan the noise, the rents, the crowds, the cab drivers who don't seem to know Lincoln Center from the Lower East Side. Yet still we stay.

The questions beg to be asked: Why do we stay? And what is it about New York City that makes you, dear reader, want to join us?

Any attempt to define New York today recalls the Zen wisdom that you can't step in the same stream twice. The city is so mutable, so constantly changing, that it's almost impossible to get a fix on. Restaurants and nightclubs become trendy overnight, then die under the weight of their own popularity. (Yogi Berra had the perfect phrase for that very phenomenon: "Nobody goes there anymore; it's too crowded.") Fashions, almost by definition, change in the time it takes to try on a pair of vinyl pants. Broadway shows, exercise fads, even neighborhoods are all subject to the same Big Apple fickleness. But within this ebb and flow lies the answer: No other place keeps you on your toes quite like New York City. Nowhere else is the challenge so tough, the pace so relentless, the stimuli so everchanging and insistent—and the payoff so rewarding. Simply put, New York never gets boring. Anything can happen here.

The city has a special magnetism—a charisma, if you will—that pulls in the intelligent, the creative, the determined, the overbearing, and the overblown from all over the world. Just about any language and any dialect is spoken here, from Mandarin to Brooklynese; no other dot on the map is quite so ethnically, culturally, socially, and economically diverse. This is the nerve center of world finance and trade.

The international hub of advertising, publishing, entertainment, and fashion. The creative core for the arts. The top showcase for pure celebrity. And, now as never before, a huge magnet for travelers from all over the country and around the globe, in search of a brief glimpse of it all.

You've probably heard the good news: The city is in top form, its finest in more than 50 years. The economy is up, and crime is down. Everywhere you look, things are being refurbished and the city is steadily improving. It has even become, believe it or not, *family-friendly*—just look at the new peep show– and porn-free Times Square. Few alive today have ever seen the city so radiant, so manageable. New Yorkers love to wax nostalgic about the good-old, bad-old days, but the fact is that we're reveling in our own good fortune—and the success of the world's largest millennium celebration and the defeat of the Y2K bug has lent an air of invincibility to the whole package. Now is a great time to be in New York.

Visitors, pumped with curiosity about this "new" New York, are arriving by the millions, swarming the city's streets, sights, hotels, restaurants, nightclubs, and theaters. The city, aglow in its millennial optimism, is welcoming them, and you, with open arms. So come—and be prepared to be overwhelmed, exasperated, delighted, and utterly charmed. That's what the Big Apple is all about.

1 Frommer's Favorite New York City Experiences

- **Sailing to the Statue of Liberty.** If you have time to do only one thing on your visit to New York, this is what to choose. No other monument so embodies the nation's, and the world's, notion of political freedom and economic potential more than Lady Liberty. As silly as this may sound, the view never loses its power—and neither do the skyline views of Manhattan, which are breathtaking from this perspective. The ferry that takes you out to **Liberty Island** also stops at the historic federal immigration station on **Ellis Island,** gateway to America for nearly half of the nation's forefathers. The museum's exhibits illustrate with moving simplicity what coming to the promised land was all about. If you want the view but prefer to skip the tourist crowds, consider catching the free Staten Island ferry, a city icon unto itself, instead. See chapter 7.
- **Visiting the Museums.** The Metropolitan Museum of Art, the American Museum of Natural History, the Museum of Modern Art, the Whitney Museum of American Art, the Guggenheim—museum hopping just doesn't get any better than this. The number of masterworks housed in this city is mind-boggling. But don't just stick to the biggies; New York boasts a wealth of smaller, lower-profile museums that speak to specific interests—from folk art to photography to financial history—and house some phenomenal treasures. For a complete rundown, see chapter 7.

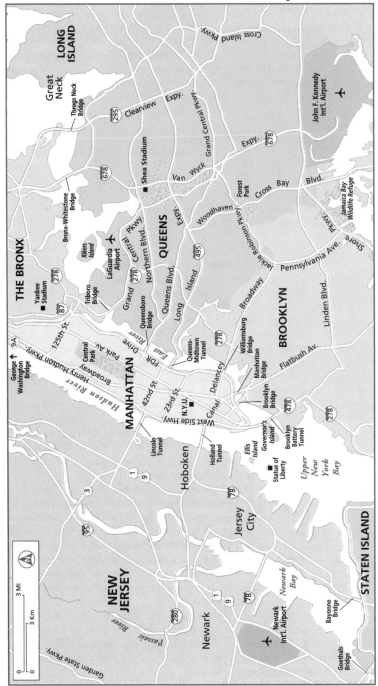

- **Strolling the Neighborhoods.** One of the greatest things about New York is the distinct character of each of its neighborhoods. Rather than trying to quick-scan them all, I highly recommend picking one and really getting to know it. Wend your way through the historic streets of **Greenwich Village,** saunter the cast-iron canyons of **SoHo,** or explore the lovely, trendy **Flatiron District.** All you really need is a map and a sense of adventure. If you prefer a little structure, consider taking one of the many excellent guided walking tours that are available—there's no better way to get to know a neighborhood than with an expert at the helm. See chapters 4 and 7.

- **Walking the Brooklyn Bridge.** A marvel of civic engineering when it first connected Brooklyn to Manhattan in 1883, the **Brooklyn Bridge** is still able to inspire awe even in jaded New Yorkers. I never tire of admiring its Gothic-inspired stone pylons and intricate steel-cable webs. Get an up-close look, and some marvelous views of Manhattan, by taking the easy stroll from end to end. Start at the Brooklyn end for best effect, and consider preceding your walk with a stroll through historic Brooklyn Heights for a leafy, lovely afternoon. See chapter 7.

- **Being on Top of the World.** Go to the top. Straight to the top—higher than you've ever been before. New York is made to be seen from above, in the full light of day or in the full glitter of night—it's your choice. Better yet, get both perspectives. Head up to the Top of the World observation deck at the **World Trade Center** where, if you're lucky, you'll be able to go out on the rooftop promenade, the world's highest open-air observation deck. If you'd rather avoid the tourist crowds, book a table at Windows on the World or Wild Blue, or order up a cocktail at the Greatest Bar on Earth, all of which boast the same incredible views. And don't forget about the **Empire State Building**—not quite as high up, but doubly romantic. See chapters 6, 7, and 9.

- **Star Gazing at Grand Central Terminal.** Always a beaux arts gem, this majestic 1913 railroad station has gotten a remarkable face-lift that has made it a must-see. Every surface glitters with renewed optimism—but none more than the masterful ceiling, once again brilliant with 24-karat gold zodiac constellations against a gorgeous blue-green sky. Walk in, throw your head back, and watch the stars gleam. Or consider dining at Michael Jordan's—The Steak House, which opens onto the stellar view. See chapters 6 and 7.

- **Ogling the City's Art Deco Marvels.** Nothing embodies the city's historic sense of optimism more than its streamline masterpieces. And nowhere is the art deco style more passionately realized than at **Rockefeller Center,** the business-and-entertainment center at the heart of Midtown. The most romantic of the city's skyscrapers, the chrome-topped **Chrysler Building,** is another art deco gem; look for the gargoyles, looking suspiciously like streamline-Gothic hood ornaments, jutting out from the upper floors. And when you visit the marvelous **Empire State Building,** don't miss the streamline mural in the lobby in your rush to get to the top. See chapter 7.

- **Wandering Central Park.** This beautiful accident of civic planning makes the otherwise uninterrupted urban jungle tolerable for workaday New Yorkers. Without this great green park, I couldn't imagine life in the city. Be sure to seek out Strawberry Fields, the living memorial to John Lennon, which exhorts us all to IMAGINE. See chapters 6 and 7.

- **Watching Your Favorite Talk Show Being Taped.** If you have the forethought (to send away months in advance) or the patience (to wait in the standby line), you can watch Dave, Conan, Rosie, Jon Stewart, the ladies of *The View,* or even Regis work their TV magic. If sketch comedy is more your speed, think the holy grail of TV audience wannabes: *Saturday Night Live.* To start planning, see chapter 7.

- **Dining Out.** New York is the world capital of great eating, with the finest fine dining in the entire world. Consider splurging on a meal at Chanterelle, Le Cirque, Nobu, La Grenouille, or one of the city's other top-flight restaurants, a surprising number of which are capable of creating lifelong culinary memories. But the true beauty of New York's restaurant scene is that you don't have to spend a fortune to eat well. You'll find cheap but dazzling Chinese in Chinatown, pastrami to die for at any number of Jewish delis, pasta that even your Italian grandmother could love . . . the list goes on and on. See chapter 6.
- **Shopping 'til You Drop.** There's no more glorious shoppers' paradise in the country—maybe even the world—than New York City. You want it? New York's got it. Check out chapter 8 to find it.
- **Watching the Curtain Rise on a Play.** There's nothing like the immediacy and excitement of a stage production in action. Movie and TV stars know it, which is why more and more are strutting their stuff on the New York stages. Make it a priority to catch a live theater production while you're in town. If musicals are your thing, stick to the Great White Way; if you prefer cutting-edge drama, try Off Broadway. See chapter 9 for tips on getting tickets.
- **Bar Hopping & Nightclubbing.** It doesn't matter whether you're the Ketel One martini or the draft beer type, whether cabaret or stand-up comedy or electronica is your thing, New York has the after-dark hangout for you. They don't call this "The City That Never Sleeps" for nothing. See chapter 9 for all the options.
- **Celebrating the Holidays in the City.** As millions of my neighbors head out of town to the shores and the mountains, I love to stay behind. On July 4, a peaceful hush comes over the city—until the fireworks explode overhead, lighting up the night sky with patriotic flair. Nobody does Labor Day like the "ladies" of Wigstock. On Halloween, more than the usual ghouls walk among us in Greenwich Village. The huge hot-air balloons of the Macy's Thanksgiving Day Parade bring out the kid in all of us. No place is more festive than Rockefeller Center at Christmastime. And on Chinese New Year, a bright dragon promises great fortune ahead. For details on these events and others, see the "Calendar of Events" in chapter 2.

2 Best Hotel Bets

This city boasts some of the best hotels in the world—and, believe it or not, some great affordable choices, too. For the details on these and other New York City hotels, see chapter 5.

- **Best Landmark Hotel:** Hands down, the newly and exquisitely restored **Algonquin,** 59 W. 44th St. (☎ **800/555-3000**), is the winner. The birthplace of the *New Yorker* and home to Dorothy Parker's legendary Round Table in the '20s, this venerable beauty has managed to re-create the glamour of the past without pricing itself out of the reach of regular folks. Even if you don't stay here, stop into the wonderful oak-paneled and velvet-seated lobby—one of the most comfortable and welcoming in the city—for afternoon tea or a posttheater cocktail.
- **Best for Classic New York Elegance:** There's lots of competition in this category, but the low-key **Sherry-Netherland,** 781 Fifth Ave. (☎ **800/247-4377**), steals

the show. This gargoyled neo-Romanesque residence hotel is the epitome of understated service and elegance. The rooms and suites provide a chance to experience the glamour of uptown apartment living, and the location—at the southeast of Central Park, presiding grandly over Fifth Avenue at its most fabulous—couldn't be more spectacular. Quintessentially New York in every way.

- **Best Trendy Hotel:** Ian Schrager's endlessly hip **Royalton,** 44 W. 44th St. (☎ **800/635-9013**), is primed to transcend yet another decade with its trendiness still intact.

- **Best Service If Money Is No Object:** For the ultimate pampering, you'd be hard-pressed to do better than the **Carlyle,** 35 E. 76th St. (☎ **800/227-5737**), where the staff-to-guest ratio is a phenomenal two-to-one; you won't want for anything here. But these days, the Carlyle is getting a run for its money from **Trump International Hotel & Tower,** 1 Central Park West (☎ **888/44-TRUMP**). Your very own Trump Attaché will fulfill your every whim, keeping meticulous notes all the while for your next stay, when you won't even have to *ask*. Of course, such personal attention in Manhattan doesn't come cheap—but you'll be in supreme comfort as you max out that platinum card!

- **Best Service for the Budget-Minded:** The professional staff at the **Broadway Inn,** 264 W. 46th St. (☎ **800/826-6300**), just may be the most helpful in the city. They're so committed to making their guests feel welcome and at home in New York that they give you a hotline number upon check-in so you can call when you're out and about if you need directions, advice on where to eat, or any other assistance. When you come home from your long day of sightseeing, they'll be happy to order in delivery from any of the nearby restaurants for you. And you thought New York wasn't friendly!

- **Best for Business Travelers:** The **Millenium Hilton,** 55 Church St. (☎ **800/835-2220**), is the best hotel in the Financial District, with an ideal location (just across the street from the World Trade Center), first-rate amenities, and stellar views. In Midtown, the **Peninsula–New York,** 700 Fifth Ave. (☎ **800/262-9467**), is the ultimate address for power brokers; each room has a terrific L-shaped executive workstation with desk-level inputs, direct-line fax, and dual-line speakerphones, plus other high-tech amenities for ladder-climbing execs. If your expense account isn't quite that big, book in at the brand-new **Benjamin,** 125 E. 50th St. (☎ **888/4-BENJAMIN**), which offers similar 21st-century technology and luxury-level comforts for a lot less. Or stay at the **Doubletree Guest Suites,** 1568 Broadway (☎ **800/222-TREE**), where you can get a two-room suite with all the comforts of home *and* office for the same money you'd pay for a standard hotel room; there are even some conference suites available if you want to hold an ensuite meeting.

- **Best Unique Inn:** If you're looking for something special, book into **Country Inn the City,** on West 77th Street (☎ **212/580-4183**), one of the most impeccably done guesthouses I've ever seen—and superbly located in prime Upper West Side territory. Another marvelous choice is Chelsea's brand-new charmer, the **Inn on 23rd,** 131 W. 23rd St. (☎ **877/387-2323**), one of New York's few genuine bed-and-breakfasts—and its best, by far.

- **Best for Families:** The **Doubletree Guest Suites,** 1568 Broadway (☎ **800/222-TREE**), isn't just for business travelers—it's great for families, too. There's an entire floor of childproof suites, complete with living rooms for spreading out and kitchenettes for preparing light meals. And your young ones will love the Kids Club (for ages 3 to 12), which boasts a playroom, an arts-and-crafts center, and computer and video games. For more kid-friendly suggestions, see "Family-Friendly Hotels" in chapter 5.

- **Best Moderately Priced Hotel:** The **Hotel Metro,** 45 W. 35th St. (☎ **800/356-3870**), is a Midtown gem that gives you a surprisingly good deal, including a marble bath. I also love the **Wyndham,** 42 W. 58th St. (☎ **800/257-1111**), a family-owned charmer with simply enormous rooms on a great block and only steps away from Fifth Avenue shopping and Central Park. And on the Upper West Side, it's hard to choose between the **Lucerne,** 201 W. 79th St. (☎ **800/492-8122**), and the **Excelsior Hotel,** 45 W. 81st St. (☎ **800/368-4575**), both big on comforts but not on price.

- **Best Budget Hotel:** If you don't mind sharing a bathroom, the charming **Larchmont Hotel,** in the heart of Greenwich Village at 27 W. 11th St. (☎ **212/989-9333**), is the best budget deal in town. If you want your very own facilities, you can't lose with the **Cosmopolitan Hotel–Tribeca,** 95 W. Broadway (☎ **888/895-9400**), whose small but comfy IKEA-ish rooms boast petite but immaculate private bathrooms. Or head uptown to the **Hotel Newton,** 2528 Broadway (☎ **888/HOTEL58**), the one budget hotel in the city that doesn't expect you to put up with a minuscule room, myriad inconveniences, or a just-graduated-from–Burger King staff just because you don't have a king's ransom to spend.

- **Best New Year's Eve Lookouts:** Hotels boasting great views of the Times Square action include the **Crowne Plaza Manhattan,** 1605 Broadway (☎ **800/243-NYNY**); the **Millennium Broadway,** 145 W. 44th St. (☎ **800/622-5569**); and the **New York Marriott Marquis,** 1535 Broadway (☎ **800/843-4898**). But none of these monoliths can beat the intimate **Casablanca Hotel,** 147 W. 43rd St. (☎ **888/922-7225**), for vantage. This charming Moroccan-themed hotel has a wonderful rooftop deck (for guests only, natch) that couldn't be better situated for watching the ball drop—it's practically a private show.

- **Best for Gay & Lesbian Travelers:** New York is such an important center of gay life that virtually all of the city's hotels welcome gay and lesbian visitors. But if you're looking for like-minded folks, try the **Colonial House Inn,** 318 W. 22nd St. (☎ **800/262-9467**). In the heart of gay-friendly Chelsea, this friendly B&B caters predominantly to gays and lesbians, but it extends hospitality to straight travelers, too.

- **Best Health Club:** It's hard to beat the **Peninsula–New York,** 700 Fifth Ave. (☎ **800/759-3000**), which boasts a tri-level 35,000-square-foot fitness center with a gorgeous pool and complete spa services. But **Le Parker Meridien,** 118 W. 57th St. (☎ **800/543-4300**), comes close: The mammoth 15,000-square-foot-plus Gravity is a comprehensive fitness center, with state-of-the-art equipment on two levels (including a dedicated free-weight room), squash and racquetball courts, spa-treatment rooms, and more—including personal trainers, aerobics classes, and nutritional counseling. If that's not enough to occupy you, head up to the 42nd floor, where the pool has marvelous skyline views, or to the rooftop sundeck or jogging track.

- **Best Packages:** Le Parker Meridien, 118 W. 57th St. (☎ **800/543-4300**), gets points for creativity: At press time, their "Afternoon Delight" package included a bottle of champagne, room-service lunch, a deluxe room (from 11am to 4pm), and an issue of *Cosmopolitan* for inspiration. But don't overlook their more serious offers, which can range from weekend romance packages to $175 winter Sundays. Also see what's on offer from the **Avalon,** 16 E. 32nd St. (☎ **888/**

HI-AVALON), which sometimes has a 2-night package for as little as $450, including dinner at the highly regarded Coach House restaurant and free museum passes; and the **Millennium Broadway,** 145 W. 44th St. (☎ **800/ 622-5569**), which usually offers the best packages in the Theater District (be sure to check for Internet-only deals). At the **Millenium Hilton** (no relation to the Millennium Broadway), across from the World Trade Center at 55 Church St. (☎ **800/835-2220**), vacationers can make phenomenal deals on luxury rooms abandoned for the weekend by Wall Street types.

- **Best Suite Deals:** The **Kimberly,** 145 E. 50th St. (☎ **800/683-0400**), offers full-fledged one- and two-bedroom apartments—complete with full kitchens— for the same price as most standard Midtown hotels. Free access to a fabulous full-service health club and complimentary sunset cruises in summer add to the fabulous value; visit in the off-season, and the suites are so cheap that you'll feel like you're stealing. On the Upper West Side, one of the city's most desirable residential neighborhoods, the **Hotel Beacon,** 2130 Broadway (☎ **800/ 572-4969**), also has spacious suites that boast all the comforts, including microwaves in the kitchenettes and well-furnished living rooms with pullout sofas. Most New York families don't live in two-bedroom apartments as big as these.

- **Best for Disabled Travelers:** Disabled travelers no longer have to spend a fortune to stay in a hotel that can accommodate them. The affordable **Gorham,** 136 W. 55th St. (☎ **800/735-0710**), features rooms equipped for the wheelchair bound, smoke detectors for the hearing impaired, braille and audible floor indicators in elevators, and braille electronic key cards. The comfortable, budget-minded **Skyline Hotel,** 725 Tenth Ave. (☎ **800/433-1982**), has seven wheelchair-accessible rooms, ramps, and fire-safety alarms for deaf and blind visitors, plus free parking. If you want luxury, head to the **Fitzpatrick Grand Central,** 141 E. 44th St. (☎ **800/367-7701**), which has 10 rooms specifically designed for the physically challenged; or the brand-new **Benjamin,** 125 E. 50th St. (☎ **888/4-BENJAMIN**), whose 10 ADA-compliant corner suites have lots of space for wheelchair negotiating, including huge bathrooms.

3 Best Dining Bets

One of the great joys of being in New York is that there's fabulous food at nearly every turn. You can flex your gold card on some of the most memorable fine dining in the world, or go ethnic to indulge in the best cheap eats you'll find anywhere. For the details on these and other terrific New York City restaurants, see chapter 6.

- **Best Spot for a Break-the-Bank Celebration:** For understated elegance, perfect service, and sublime New French cuisine, there's **Chanterelle,** 2 Harrison St. (☎ **212/966-6960**), which can cause even the most jaded gourmands to swoon. For pure New York excitement, the choice is **Le Cirque 2000,** 455 Madison Ave. (☎ **212/303-7788**), whose legendary panache simply can't be beat. For the ultimate in classic French tradition, book a table at **La Grenouille,** 3 E. 52nd St. (☎ **212/752-1495**), which has been hosting celebratory parties since 1962.

- **Best for Romance:** Downtown, reserve at **One If By Land, Two If By Sea,** 14 Barrow St. (☎ **212/228-0822**), where candlelight, lush piano music, and tuxedoed service in a pre-Revolutionary Greenwich Village town house take you back in time and put you in the mood. In Midtown, try **March,** 405 E. 58th St. (☎ **212/754-6272**), for a sublime multicourse meal elegantly served in a cozy, firelit town house.

On New York

It's a city where everyone mutinies but no one deserts.

—Harry Hershfield

The end [of the world] wouldn't come as a surprise here. Many people already bank on it.

—Saul Bellow

- **Best View:** Without a doubt, the winners are sister restaurants **Windows on the World** and **Wild Blue,** high atop 1 World Trade Center (☎ **212/524-7000**). No matter how many years I live in this city, the views never fail to take my breath away. Windows is your formal jacket–and–cocktail dress option; Wild Blue is warmer, more relaxed, and slightly less expensive. For a different perspective on the spectacular Lower Manhattan skyline, head to Brooklyn Heights and the **River Café,** 1 Water St. (☎ **718/522-5200**).
- **Best Spot for a Business Lunch:** The landmark **"21" Club,** 21 W. 52nd St. (☎ **212/582-7200**), is the classic choice of New York's old-school power set. If you prefer more casual and want to impress with your New York acumen, head to the **Oyster Bar,** in Grand Central Terminal (☎ **212/490-6650**), another New York classic that's a perfect spot to seal the deal.
- **Best Spot for a Ladies-Who-Lunch Lunch:** What's more decadent than lingering over three courses —with wine—in the middle of the day, when regular folks are hard at work? **Daniel,** 60 E. 65th St. (☎ **212/288-0033**), is the ideal place to rub elbows with the Upper East Side society dames who've made this meal a way of life.
- **Best Spot for Breakfast and Brunch:** Uptown, head to **Sarabeth's Kitchen,** 423 Amsterdam Ave. (☎ **212/496-6280**), whose sophisticated home-style cooking and sigh-inducing pastries inspire lines around the block (go early on weekends to avoid the wait). Downtown, intimate **Le Gigot,** 18 Cornelia St. (☎ **212/627-3737**), is the Village's best-kept brunch secret—until now, that is. For everyday breakfast, head to TriBeCa favorite **Bubby's,** 120 Hudson St. (☎ **212/219-0666**)—and don't be surprised if Harvey Keitel is chowing down on a monster-size omelet at the next table.
- **Best for Pre- (or Post-) Theater: Molyvos,** 871 Seventh Ave. (☎ **212/582-7500**), a warm and inviting Greek taverna that feels like it was transplanted wholesale from Crete, offers a wonderful pretheater dinner for $34.50 (weekdays only). Caviar lovers shouldn't miss the terrific prix-fixe value at legendary sturgeon importer **Petrossian,** 182 W. 58th St. (☎ **212/245-2214**). Lincoln Center–goers have sublime **Jean Georges,** in the Trump International Hotel & Tower, 1 Central Park West (☎ **212/299-3900**), where the faultless wait staff will make sure you're wowed well before curtain time. After the show, **Joe Allen,** 326 W. 46th St. (☎ **212/581-6464**), is the ultimate Broadway pub—and the meat loaf is marvelous.
- **Best Dessert:** There are many impressive pastry chefs in town, but few of them can top the remarkable confections at **Payard Pâtisserie & Bistro,** 1032 Lexington Ave. (☎ **212/717-5252**), which is well located for a pick-me-up during a day of Upper East Side museum-hopping or shopping. For down-home indulgence, head to **Bubby's,** 120 Hudson St. (☎ **212/219-0666**), where the classic home-style pies are to die for.

- **Best Contemporary American Cuisine:** David Bouley has long been considered New York's best chef, and **Bouley Bakery,** 120 W. Broadway (☎ **212/964-2525**), is the place to indulge in his sublime French-accented New American fare. Only intended as a stopgap between higher-profile restaurant projects, this intimate gem has blossomed into a four-star jewel, courtesy of the *New York Times*—and the glorious praise is fully deserved.
- **Best Chinese Cuisine:** With all the culinary wonders that Chinatown has to offer, this is a tough choice. But I can't stop thinking about those steamy soup dumplings at **Joe's Shanghai,** 9 Pell St. (☎ **212/233-8888**).
- **Best French Cuisine:** Downtown, magical **Chanterelle,** 2 Harrison St. (☎ **212/966-6960**), is the obvious choice, serving ethereal French with welcome contemporary twists. Uptown, longtime favorite **La Grenouille,** 3 E. 52nd St. (☎ **212/752-1495**), serves the classics with elegant perfection. For more affordable French, your best bet is **Le Gigot,** a true slice of St-Germain at 18 Cornelia St. (☎ **212/627-3737**).
- **Best Italian Cuisine:** With **Babbo,** 110 Waverly Place (☎ **212/777-0303**), Food Network chef Mario Batali has created the ideal setting for his exciting northern Italian cooking. The room is beautiful, the service warm and gracious, and the food excellent. Nobody does pasta better. If you're watching your wallet, head to Molto Mario's brand-new budget-friendly outpost, **Lupa,** 170 Thompson St. (☎ **212/982-5089**), one of the city's best dining values.
- **Best Japanese Cuisine:** In a category all its own is inventive **Nobu,** 105 Hudson St. (☎ **212/219-0500**), where unusual textures, daring combinations, and surprising flavors add up to a first-rate dining adventure that you won't soon forget. For sushi as high art, head to super-fashionable **BondSt,** 6 Bond St. (☎ **212/777-2500**), where you'll find faultlessly fresh, beautifully prepared raw fish, some of it flown in from Japan daily.
- **Best Home-Style Cooking:** No other restaurant warms my heart more than the aptly named **Home,** 20 Cornelia St. (☎ **212/243-9579**), where the cumin-crusted pork chop sits in a bed of homemade barbecue sauce that's better than Dad used to make, and even Mom would tip her hat to the silky smooth chocolate pudding.
- **Best Jewish Deli:** Kosher **Second Avenue Deli,** 156 Second Ave. (☎ **212/677-0606**), is the choice among those who know their kreplach, matzo, and pastrami. No cutesy sandwiches named for celebrities here—just top-notch Jewish classics.
- **Best Burger and Beer:** Ask a hundred New Yorkers, and you'll get a hundred opinions. But for my money, there's no better choice than **Old Town Bar & Restaurant,** 45 E. 18th St. (☎ **212/529-6732**). Whether you go low-fat turkey or bacon-chili-cheddar, the burgers at this venerable 19th-century pub are perfect every time. The fries are addictively crisp, the Buffalo wings are slathered in spicy sauce, and there's a whole selection of great beers on tap.
- **Best Pizza:** Pizza doesn't get any better than the coal oven–baked, fresh mozzarella-topped pies at **Grimaldi's Pizzeria,** 19 Old Fulton St., Brooklyn Heights (☎ **718/858-4300**). If you're unwilling to travel across the river for real Noo Yawk pizza, head to **Lombardi's,** 32 Spring St. (☎ **212/941-7994**), which has been baking up its own coal-oven pies since 1905.
- **Best Seafood:** The black bass ceviche alone—not to mention everything else that comes out of its blue-ribbon kitchen—keeps **Le Bernardin,** 155 W. 51st St. (☎ **212/489-1515**), at the top of the world's great fish restaurants. If your budget isn't quite big enough to handle such a splurge, head instead to the venerable

Oyster Bar & Restaurant, on Grand Central Terminal's lower-level restaurant concourse, 23 Vanderbilt Ave. (☎ **212/490-6650**), or SoHo's **Aquagrill,** 210 Spring St. (☎ **212/274-0505**).

- **Best for Celebrity Spotting:** It's the luck of the draw, really. But for the best odds, head to **Le Cirque 2000,** 455 Madison Ave. (☎ **212/303-7788**), where the crowd is full of big-name movie stars, politicos, and socialites; I spotted Whoopi just moments after walking through the front door. Your other best bet is **Mr. Chow,** 324 E. 57th St. (☎ **212/751-9030**), a favorite among Uptown celebs like Puffy, Madonna, and the latest names in hip hop—and where you'll be treated like a star, too. If your budget is limited, I suggest trying one of the newest downtown hot spots, such as **Pastis,** 9 Ninth Ave. (☎ **212/929-4844**), where I just sighted longtime marrieds Kevin Kline and Phoebe Cates.
- **Best Late-Night Hangout:** Half authentic French bistro, half all-American diner, **Florent,** 69 Gansevoort St. (☎ **212/989-5779**), is the hipster crowd's favorite after-hours hangout. Thanks to its good food, great people-watching, and wonderful sense of humor, it's mine, too.
- **Best Wine List:** Newcomer **Veritas,** 43 E. 20th St. (☎ **212/353-3700**), boasts what must be the most enthralling wine cellar in town; serious oenophiles can download the full list—market *and* reserve—for advance study, and then call up to have their choice opened and decanted for dinnertime.
- **Best Wine Deal: Cité,** 120 W. 51st St. (☎ **212/956-7100**), offers a nightly deal after 8pm that's almost too good to be true: For $59.50, you get a three-course meal—your choice of appetizer, main course, and dessert—and you can enjoy unlimited quantities of the four wines on offer *at no extra charge.* And you're not getting the cheap stuff: Recent choices included a '90 Mondavi cabernet, a '97 Acacia chardonnay, a '94 Chalone Vineyard pinot noir reserve, and Taittinger brut for celebrating. These deals should still be on while you're in town, but call ahead to be sure.
- **Best Newcomer:** There have been a number of stellar openings this year, but the winner must be **Veritas,** 43 E. 20th St. (☎ **212/353-3700**); the epitome of contemporary style and unpretentious grace, this low-profile 65-seat restaurant is the ideal showcase of Chef Scott Bryan's unfussy cooking, which bursts with clean flavors, and owners Park B. Smith and Steve Verlin's mind-boggling wine collection. For more casual (read: affordable) dining, the winner is **Lupa,** 170 Thompson St. (☎ **212/982-5089**), the brainchild of TV chef Mario Batali, serving shockingly good northern Italian at bargain-basement prices.
- **Best Service:** With an almost-unheard-of 27 (out of a possible 30) rating for service from Zagat's, **Chanterelle,** 2 Harrison St. (☎ **212/966-6960**), simply can't be beat. The service somehow manages to be impeccable without being too formal or stuffy. Other restaurants try, but this is how it's supposed to be. A magical experience, and worth every penny.

2 Planning Your Trip: The Basics

In the pages that follow, you'll find everything you need to know to handle the practical details of planning your trip in advance: airlines and area airports, a calendar of events, resources for those of you with special needs, and much more.

Note that there's no need to rent a car. Driving is a nightmare and parking is ridiculously expensive (or near-to-impossible in some neighborhoods). It's much easier to get around using public transportation and taxis. If you're going to visit Aunt Erma on Long Island or you have some other need to travel beyond the five boroughs, call one of the major car-rental companies, such as **National** (☎ 800/227-7368; www.nationalcar.com), **Hertz** (☎ 800/654-3131; www.hertz.com), or **Avis** (☎ 800/230-4898; www.avis.com), all of which have airport and Manhattan locations.

1 Visitor Information

For information before you leave home, your best source (besides this book, of course) is NYC & Company, the organization behind the **New York Convention & Visitors Bureau (NYCVB),** 810 Seventh Ave., New York, NY 10019. You can call ☎ 800/NYC-VISIT or 212/397-8222 to order the **Official NYC Visitor Kit,** detailing hotels, restaurants, theaters, attractions, events, and more. It costs $5.95 to receive the packet (payable by credit card) in 7 to 10 days, $9.95 for rush delivery (3 to 4 business days) to U.S. addresses and international orders. You can also order the guide that's the heart of the kit for free on the bureau's Web site, **www.nycvisit.com**. The Web site itself is also a terrific source of information. To speak to a travel counselor who can answer specific questions, call ☎ 212/484-1222.

For visitor center and information desk locations once you arrive, see "Visitor Information" in chapter 4.

FOR U.K. VISITORS There is an **NYCVB Visitor Information Center** at 33–34 Carnaby St., London W1V 1PA (☎ 0207/437-8300). You can order the Official NYC Visitor Kit by sending an A5-size self-addressed envelope and 52p postage to the above address. For New York–bound travelers in the London area, the center also offers free one-on-one travel-planning assistance.

2 Money

You never have to carry too much cash in New York, and while the city's pretty safe these days, it's best not to overstuff your wallet (although always make sure you have at least $20 in taxi fare on hand). Credit cards and traveler's checks are accepted almost everywhere—plastic is even accepted in the subway system now—and ATMs are almost always on hand in case you need the green stuff.

ATMS

Almost all New York City ATMs are linked to a national network that most likely includes your bank at home. **Cirrus** (☎ **800/424-7787;** www.mastercard. com/atm) and **PLUS** (☎ **800/843-7587;** www.visa.com/atms) are the two most popular networks; check the back of your ATM card to see which network your bank belongs to (most banks belong to both these days). The city's biggest banks are Citibank, Chase, Fleet, and HSBC, which belong to both networks.

In the most popular Manhattan neighborhoods, there's a bank with ATM machines on every other corner or so. The only places you may have some difficulty are in more far-flung neighborhoods, like the far East Village or far uptown in Harlem. If you don't easily spot an ATM, use the 800 numbers to find one in your location.

New York's Consumer Affairs chief has tried to ward off additional ATM charges for consumers, but it has proven to be a losing battle. Expect to pay $1 to $2 each time you withdraw money from an ATM, in addition to what your home bank charges. Try to stay away from commercial machines, like those in hotel lobbies and corner delis, which often charge $3 or more per transaction.

TRAVELER'S CHECKS

Traveler's checks are something of an anachronism from the days before the ATM made cash accessible at any time. These days, they seem less necessary because 24-hour ATMs allow you to withdraw as needed. But New York is an expensive city, capable of sucking money right out of your pocket. If you're withdrawing money every day, you can really rack up those withdrawal charges, so you might be better off with traveler's checks—provided you don't mind showing identification every time you want to cash one.

Site Seeing: The Big Apple on the Web

The NYCVB's official site, **www.nycvisit.com**, is an excellent online resource offering tons of information on the city, from trip-planning basics to tips on where to take the kids. Other privately run general information sites also serve top-flight trip-planning tools, providing everything from a current calendar of events to the latest club schedules. The best of the bunch, by far, are **Citysearch** (**www.newyork.citysearch.com**); the *New York Times*'s **New York Today** (**www.nytoday.com**); and the Web site from the legendary weekly **Village Voice** (**www.villagevoice.com**).

For more details on these and other useful Web sites, see "Planning Your Trip: An Online Directory," p. 38.

Avoid poorly lit or out-of-the-way ATMs, especially at night. Use an indoor machine, or one at a well-trafficked, well-lit location. Put your money away discreetly; don't flash it around or count it in a way that could attract the attention of thieves.

You can get traveler's checks at almost any bank. **American Express** offers checks in denominations of $10, $20, $50, $100, $500, and $1,000. You'll pay a service charge ranging from 1 to 4%. You can also get American Express traveler's checks over the phone by calling ☎ **800/221-7282** or 800/721-9768; you can also purchase checks online at **www.americanexpress.com**. AmEx gold or platinum cardholders can avoid paying the fee by ordering over the telephone; platinum cardholders can also purchase checks with no fee in person at AmEx Travel Service locations (check the Web site for the office nearest you). American Automobile Association members can obtain checks with no fee at most AAA offices.

Visa offers traveler's checks at Citibank branches and other financial institutions nationwide; call ☎ **800/227-6811** to locate the purchase location near you. **MasterCard** also offers traveler's checks through **Thomas Cook Currency Services;** call ☎ **800/223-9920** for a location near you.

If you carry traveler's checks, be sure to keep a record of their serial numbers (separately from the checks, of course) so you're ensured a refund in case they're lost or stolen.

CREDIT CARDS

Credit cards are the way to pay in New York. They're a safe way to carry money and keep track of your expenses. **American Express, MasterCard,** and **Visa** are accepted virtually everywhere in New York. **Carte Blanche** and **Diner's Club** have made quite a comeback, especially in hotel circles, and **Discover** is also quite popular (although don't count on it being accepted everywhere). Since New York has such a heavy influx of international visitors, cards like **enRoute, Eurocard,** and **JCB** are also widely accepted, particularly at hotels.

Still, be sure to keep some cash on hand for small expenses, like cab rides, or for that rare occasion when a restaurant or small shop doesn't take plastic, which can happen if you're dining at a neighborhood joint or buying from a small vendor.

THEFT Almost every credit-card company has an emergency 800 number that you can call if your wallet or purse is stolen. They may be able to wire you a cash advance off your credit card immediately, and in many places, they can deliver an emergency credit card in a day or two. **Visa's** U.S. emergency number is ☎ **800/847-2911. American Express** cardholders should call ☎ **800/233-5432** to report a lost card, while traveler's check holders should call ☎ **800/221-7282** if they have a money emergency. **MasterCard** holders should call ☎ **800/307-7309.**

Odds are that if your wallet is gone, the police won't be able to recover it for you. However, after you realize that it's gone and you cancel your credit cards, it's still worth informing the authorities. Your credit-card company or insurer may require a police report number.

Summer or winter, rain or shine, there's always great stuff going on in New York City, so there's no real "best" time to go.

If you're planning a visit with specific interests in mind, certain times of year may be better than others. Culture hounds might come in fall, winter, and early spring, when the theater and performing arts seasons reach their heights. During summer, many of the top cultural institutions, especially Lincoln Center, offer alfresco entertainment. Those who want to see the biggest hits on Broadway usually have the best luck getting tickets in the slower months of January and February.

Gourmands might find it easier to get the best tables during July and August, when New Yorkers escape the city on weekends. If you prefer to walk every city block to take in the sights, spring and fall usually offer the mildest and most pleasant weather.

New York is a nonstop holiday party from early December through the start of the new year. Celebrations of the season abound in festive holiday windows and events like the lighting of the Rockefeller Center tree and the Radio City Christmas Spectacular—not to mention those terrific seasonal sales that take over the city, making New York a holiday shopping bonanza. However, keep in mind that hotel prices go sky high (more on that below), and the crowds are almost intolerable. If you'd rather have more of the city to yourself—better chances at restaurant reservations and show tickets, easier access to museums and other attractions—choose another time of year to visit.

MONEY MATTERS   If money is your biggest concern, you might want to visit in winter, between the first of the year and early April. Sure, the weather can suck, but hotels are suffering from the postholiday blues, and rooms often go for a relative song. In the winter of 2000, you could even get a room at the legendary Waldorf-Astoria for as little as $199 on select nights, and rooms at the truly comfortable Comfort Inn Midtown were going for as little as $79.

Spring and fall are the busiest, and most expensive, seasons after holiday time. Don't expect hotels to be handing you deals, but you may be able to negotiate a decent rate.

New York's spit-shined image means that the city is drawing more families these days, and they usually visit in the summer. Still, the prospect of heat and humidity keeps some people away, making July and the first half of August a significantly cheaper time to visit than later in the year; good hotel deals are often available.

At Christmas, all bets are off—expect to pay top dollar for everything. The first 2 weeks of December—the shopping weeks—are the absolute worst when it comes to scoring an affordable hotel room; that's when shoppers from around the world converge on the town to catch the holiday spirit and spend, spend, spend. But Thanksgiving can be a great time to come, believe it or not: Business travelers have gone home for the holiday, and the holiday shoppers haven't yet arrived. It's a little-known secret that most hotels away from the Thanksgiving Day Parade route have empty rooms sitting, and they're usually willing to make great deals to fill them.

WEATHER   The worst weather in New York is during that long week or 10 days that arrives each summer between mid-July and mid-August, when temperatures go up to around 100°F with 90% humidity. You feel sticky all day, the streets smell horrible, everyone's cranky, and the concrete canyons become furnaces. It can be no fun walking around in this weather. Don't get put off by this—summer has its compensations, such as wonderful free open-air concerts and other events, as I've already mentioned—but bear it in mind. And you may luck out, as the last few summers have been downright lovely. But if you are at all temperature sensitive, your odds of getting comfortable weather are better in June or September.

Another period when you might not like to stroll around the city is during January or February, when temperatures are commonly in the 20s and those concrete canyons turn into wind tunnels. The city looks gorgeous for about a day after a snowfall, but the streets soon become an ugly, slushy mess. Again, you never know—temperatures have regularly been in the 30s and mild 40s during the past few winters. If you hit the weather jackpot, you could have a bargain bonanza (see "Money Matters" directly above).

Fall and spring are the best times in New York. From April to June and September to November, temperatures are mild and pleasant, and the light is beautiful. With the leaves changing in Central Park and just the hint of crispness in the air, October is a fabulous time to be here—but expect to pay for the privilege.

If you want to know how to pack just before you go, check the Weather Channel's online 5-day forecast at **www.weather.com**, or call ☎ **900-WEATHER,** for 95¢ per minute. You can also get the local weather by calling ☎ **212/976-1212.**

New York's Average Temperature & Rainfall

	Jan	Feb	Mar	Apr	May	June	July	Aug	Sept	Oct	Nov	Dec
Daily Temp. (°F)	38	40	48	61	71	80	85	84	77	67	54	42
Daily Temp. (°C)	3	4	9	16	22	27	29	29	25	19	12	6
Days of Precipitation	11	10	11	11	11	10	11	10	8	8	9	10

New York City Calendar of Events

As with any schedule of events, the following information is always subject to change. Always confirm information before you make plans around an event. Call the venue or the NYCVB at ☎ **212/484-1222,** go to **www.nycvisit.com** or **www.newyork.citysearch.com**, or pick up a copy of *Time Out New York* once you arrive in the city for the latest details on these or other events taking place during your visit.

January

- **New York National Boat Show.** Slip on your docksiders and head to the **Jacob K. Javits Convention Center** for the 91st edition, which promises a leviathan fleet of boats and marine products from the world's leading manufacturers. Call ☎ **212/922-1212,** or point your Web browser to **www.boatshows.com** or **www.javitscenter.com**. One week in early or mid-January.

- **Chinese New Year.** Every year Chinatown rings in its own New Year (based on a lunar calendar) with 2 weeks of celebrations, including parades with dragon and lion dancers, vivid costumes of all kinds, and fireworks (though the city has been cracking down on fireworks in recent years). The year 2001 (4699 in the Chinese designation) is the Year of the Snake, and the Chinese New Year falls on January 24. Call the NYCVB hotline at ☎ **212/484-1222** or the Chinese Center at 212/373-1800.

✪ **Restaurant Week.** Look for the new winter version of the favorite summer event, which allows you to lunch for only $20 at some of New York's finest restaurants. Call ☎ **212/484-1222** or check **www.restaurantweek.com** to see if the winter event is repeated in 2001. *Reserve instantly.* Late January or early February.

February

• **Valentine's Day Marriage Marathon at the World Trade Center.** Once again, 110 people will be married at the top of the city's tallest skyscraper during the annual Valentine's Day Marriage Marathon. Applicants for "marrying slots" will be accepted from January 1, 2000; a maximum of 55 couples will be selected by February 1, 2001. To be considered, contestants are usually required to write a one-page typewritten essay entitled "Why We Want to Get Married at the Highest Place in New York"; call ☎ **212/323-2340.** A similar event for just 15 lucky couples is held on the 80th-floor observation deck at the **Empire State Building;** the deadline for submissions is December 31; call ☎ **212/736-3100** or visit **www.esbnyc.com** for details.

✪ **Westminster Kennel Club Dog Show.** The ultimate purebred pooch fest. Some 30,000 dog fanciers from the world over congregate at **Madison Square Garden** for the 125th "World Series of Dogdom." All 2,500 dogs are American Kennel Club Champions of Record, competing for the Best in Show trophy. Call ☎ **800/ 455-3647** or visit **www.westminsterkennelclub.org** for this year's exact dates (usually second or third weekend in Feb). Tickets become available after January 1 through **TicketMaster** (☎ **212/307-7171** or 212/307-1212; **www.ticketmaster.com**).

March

✪ **Manhattan Antiques and Collectibles Triple Pier Expo.** The city's largest and most comprehensive antiques show takes place over two consecutive weekends, as more than 600 dealers exhibit their treasures, ranging from ephemera to jewelry to home furnishings, on three piers along the Hudson River between 48th and 51st streets. **Pier 88** features 20th-century modern collectibles; **Pier 90** has all manner of Americana, including country rustic, folk art, and Arts and Crafts; and **Pier 92** houses 18th- and 19th-century formal European antiques. Call ☎ **212/255-0020** or visit **www.antiqnet.com/Stella** for this year's dates, plus a calendar of additional shows. Usually mid-March, and again in mid-November.

• **St. Patrick's Day Parade.** More than 150,000 marchers join in the world's largest civilian parade, as Fifth Avenue from 44th to 86th streets rings with the sounds of bands and bagpipes, and an inordinate amount of beer is consumed (much of it green). The parade usually starts at 11am, but go extra early if you want a good spot. Call ☎ **212/484-1222.** March 17.

April

✪ **Easter Parade.** This isn't a traditional parade, per se: There are no marching bands, no baton twirlers, no protesters. Once upon a time, New York's gentry came out to show off their tasteful but discreet toppings. Today, if you were planning to slip on a tasteful little number—say something delicately woven in straw with a simple flower or two that matches your gloves—you will *not* be the grandest lady in this springtime hike along Fifth Avenue from 48th to 57th streets. It's more about flamboyant exhibitionism, with hats and costumes that get more outrageous every year—and anybody can join right in for free. The parade generally runs Easter Sunday from about 10am to 3 or 4pm. Call ☎ 212/484-1222. April 15.

- **New York International Auto Show.** Hot wheels from all over the world whirl into the **Jacob K. Javits Convention Center** for the largest auto show in the United States. Many concept cars show up that will never roll off the assembly line, but are fun to dream about nonetheless. Call ☎ 800/282-3336 or 212/216-2000, or point your browser to **www.auto.com** or **www.javitscenter.com**. One week in early or mid-April.

May

○ **Bike New York: The Great Five Boro Bike Tour.** The largest mass-participation cycling event in the United States attracts about 30,000 cyclists from all over the world. After a 42-mile ride through the five boroughs, finalists are greeted with a traditional New York–style celebration of food and music. The starting line is at Battery Park in Manhattan; the finish line is at Fort Wadsworth Naval Station on Staten Island. Call ☎ 212/932-BIKE or visit **www.bikenewyork.org** to register. First or second Sunday in May.

- **Ninth Avenue International Food Festival.** Cancel dinner reservations and spend the day sampling sizzling Italian sausages, homemade pierogi, spicy curries, and an assortment of other ethnic dishes. Street musicians, bands, and vendors add to the festive atmosphere at one of the city's best street fairs, stretching along Ninth Avenue from 37th to 57th streets. Call ☎ 212/581-7217. One weekend in mid-May.

○ **Fleet Week.** About 10,000 Navy and Coast Guard personnel are "at liberty" in New York for the annual Fleet Week at the end of May. Usually from 1 to 4pm daily, you can visit the ships and aircraft carriers as they dock at the piers on the west side of Manhattan, and watch some dramatic exhibitions by the U.S. Marines. The whole celebration is hosted by the *Intrepid* Sea-Air-Space Museum, and kids love it. But even if you don't take in any of the events, you'll know it's Fleet Week, since those 10,000 sailors invade Midtown in their starched white uniforms. It's simply wonderful—just like *On the Town* come to life. Call ☎ 212/245-0072, or visit **www.uss-intrepid.com**. Late May.

June

- **Belmont Stakes.** The third jewel in the Triple Crown is held at the **Belmont Park Race Track** in Elmont, Long Island. If a triple crown winner is to be named, it will happen here. For information, call ☎ 516/488-6000, or visit **www.nyracing.com/belmont**. Early June.

- **Museum Mile Festival.** Fifth Avenue from 82nd to 102nd streets is closed to cars from 6 to 9pm as 20,000-plus strollers enjoy live music from Broadway tunes to string quartets, street entertainers from juggling to giant puppets, and free admission to nine Museum Mile institutions, including the Metropolitan Museum of Art and the Guggenheim. Visit **www.museummile.org** or call any of the participating institutions for details. Usually the second Tuesday in June (June 12 in 2001).

○ **Lesbian and Gay Pride Week and March.** A week of cheerful happenings, from simple parties to major political fund-raisers, precedes a zany parade commemorating the Stonewall Riot of June 27, 1969, which for many marks the beginning of the gay liberation movement. Fifth Avenue goes wild as the gay/lesbian community celebrates with bands, marching groups, floats, and plenty of panache. The parade starts on upper Fifth Avenue around 52nd Street and continues into the Village, where a street festival and a waterfront dance party with fireworks cap the day. Call ☎ **212/807-7433.** Mid- to late June.

- **Metropolitan Opera in the Parks.** Free evening performances are given in the city parks. Past performers have included the likes of Luciano Pavarotti and Kathleen Battle. Call ☎ **212/362-6000** or visit **www. metopera.org**. June through July.

✪ **SummerStage.** A summer-long festival of free or low-cost outdoor concerts in **Central Park,** featuring world music, pop, folk, and jazz artists ranging from Ziggy Marley to Yoko Ono to Morrissey. Call ☎ **212/ 360-2777** or visit **www.summerstage.com**. June through August.

✪ **Shakespeare in the Park.** The Delacorte Theater in **Central Park** is the setting for first-rate free performances under the stars—including at least one Shakespeare production each season—often with stars on the stage. For details, see "Park It! Shakespeare, Music & Other Free Fun" in chapter 9. Call ☎ **212/539-8750,** or point your browser to **www. publictheater.org**. June through August.

✪ **Restaurant Week.** Lunch for only $20 at some of New York's finest restaurants. Participating places vary each year, so watch for the full-page ads in the *New York Times,* call the NYCVB at ☎ **212/484-1222,** or check **www.restaurantweek.com** for the current schedule and list of participants, usually available by mid- or late May. *Reserve instantly.* One week in late June; some restaurants extend their offers through summer to Labor Day.

July

✪ **Independence Day Harbor Festival and Fourth of July Fireworks Spectacular.** Start the day amid the patriotic crowds at the Great July Fourth Festival in Lower Manhattan, and then catch Macy's great fireworks extravaganza (one of the country's most fantastic) over the East River (the best vantage point is from the FDR Drive, which closes to traffic several hours before sunset). Call ☎ **212/484-1222,** or Macy's Visitor Center at 212/494-2922. July 4.

✪ **Lincoln Center Festival 2001.** This festival celebrates the best of the performing arts from all over the world—theater, ballet, contemporary dance, opera, even puppet and media-based art. Recent editions have featured performances by Ornette Coleman, the Royal Opera, the Royal Ballet, and the New York Philharmonic. Schedules are usually available in mid-March, and tickets go on sale in late May or early June. Call ☎ **212/546-2656,** or visit **www.lincolncenter.org**. July.

✪ **Midsummer Night's Swing.** Dancing duos head to the **Lincoln Center Fountain Plaza** for romantic evenings of big-band swing, salsa, and tango under the stars to the sounds of top-flight bands. Dance lessons are offered with the purchase of a ticket. Call ☎ **212/875-5766,** or visit **www.lincolncenter.org**. July and August.

- **Mostly Mozart.** World-renowned ensembles and soloists (Alicia de Larrocha and André Watts have performed in the past) are featured at this monthlong series at **Avery Fisher Hall.** Schedules are usually available in mid-April, and tickets in early May. Call ☎ **212/875-5030** for information or 212/721-6500 to order tickets, or visit **www.lincolncenter. org/mostlymozart**. Late July through August.

- **Lincoln Center Out-of-Doors.** This series of free music and dance performances is held outdoors at **Lincoln Center.** Call ☎ **212/875-5108** or visit **www.lincolncenter.org** for this year's schedule (usually available in mid-July). August to September.

- **New York Fringe Festival.** Held in a variety of tiny Lower East Side venues for a mainly hipster crowd, this arts festival presents alternative as well as traditional theater, musicals, dance, comedy, and all manner of performance art, including new media. Literally hundreds of events are held at all hours over about 10 days in late August. The quality can vary wildly (lots of performers use Fringe as a workshop to develop their acts and shows) and some performances really push the envelope, but you'd be surprised at how many shows are actually *good.* Call ☎ **888/FRINGENYC** or 212/420-8777, or point your browser to **www.fringenyc.org**. Mid- to late August.

- ✪ **U.S. Open Tennis Championships.** The final Grand Slam event of the tennis season is held at the slick new facilities at **Flushing Meadows Park** in Queens. Tickets go on sale in May or early June. The event sells out immediately, since many of the tickets are held by corporate sponsors who hand them out to customers. (It's worth it to check the list of sponsors to determine if anyone you know has a connection for getting tickets.) You can usually scalp tickets outside the complex (an illegal practice, of course), which is right next to **Shea Stadium.** The last few matches of the tournament are the most expensive, but you'll see a lot more tennis early on, when your ticket allows you to wander the outside courts and view several different matches. Call ☎ **888/OPEN-TIX** or 718/760-6200 well in advance; visit **www.usopen.org** or www.usta.com for additional information. Two weeks surrounding Labor Day.

- **Harlem Week.** The world's largest black and Hispanic cultural festival actually spans almost the whole month, including the Black Film Festival, the Harlem Jazz and Music Festival, and the Taste of Harlem Food Festival. Expect a full slate of music, from gospel to hip hop, and lots of other festivities. Visit **www.harlemweek.com** or www.discoverharlem.com (where you'll find contact numbers relating to specific events) or call ☎ **212/484-1222** for this year's schedule of events and locations. Throughout August.

September

- **West Indian–American Day Parade.** This annual Brooklyn event is New York's largest street celebration. Come for the extravagant costumes, pulsating rhythms (soca, calypso, reggae), bright colors, folklore, food (jerk chicken, oxtail soup, Caribbean soul food), and 2 million hip-shaking revelers. The parade runs down Eastern Parkway in Brooklyn. Call ☎ **212/484-1222** or 718/625-1515. Labor Day.

- ✪ **Wigstock.** Come see the Lady Bunny, Hedda Lettuce, Lypsinka, even RuPaul—plus hundreds of other fabulous drag queens—strut their stuff. The crowd is usually wilder than the stage acts. A true East Village event, Wigstock outgrew its original location, Tompkins Square Park, and has been held on the pier at 11th Street on the Hudson River in recent years, but another move could be in the offing. For a preview, see Goldwyn's *Wigstock: The Movie.* For this year's information, point your Web browser to **www.wigstock.nu**, or call ☎ **800/494-TIXS** (www.boxofficetickets.com) or the Lesbian and Gay Community Services Center at ☎ **212/620-7310** (www.gaycenter.org). Labor Day weekend.

- **Broadway on Broadway.** This free afternoon show features the songs and casts from virtually every Broadway production performing on a stage erected in the middle of Times Square. Call ☎ **212/768-1560,** or visit **www.timessquarebid.org** and click on EVENTS. Early or mid-September.

- **Feast of San Gennaro.** An atmospheric Little Italy street fair honoring the patron saint of Naples, with great food, traditional music, carnival rides, games, and vendors set up along Mulberry Street north of Canal Street. Expect big crowds. And who knows? You may even spot a Godfather or two. Call **212/768-9320** or visit **www.sangennaro.org** for this year's schedule. Usually 10 days in mid-September.

- ✪ **New York Film Festival.** Legendary hits *Pulp Fiction* and *Mean Streets* both had their U.S. premieres at the Film Society of Lincoln Center's 2-week festival, a major stop on the film fest circuit. Schedules in recent years have included advance looks at *The Sweet Hereafter, Rushmore,* and *All About My Mother.* Screenings are held in various Lincoln Center venues; advance tickets are a good bet always, and a necessity for certain events (especially evening and weekend screenings). Call ☎ **212/875-5601,** or check out **www.filmlinc.com**. Two weeks from late September to early October.

- ✪ **BAM Next Wave Festival.** One of the city's most important cultural events takes place at the **Brooklyn Academy of Music.** The monthslong festival showcases experimental new dance, theater, and music works by both renowned and lesser-known international artists. Recent celebrated performances have included Astor Piazzolla's *Maria de Buenos Aires* (featuring Piazzolla disciple Gidon Kremer), the 25th anniversary of the Kronos Quartet, and choreographer Bill T. Jones's *We Set Out Early . . . Visibility Was Poor* (set to the music of Igor Stravinsky, John Cage, and Peteris Vask). Call ☎ **718/636-4100** or visit **www.bam.org**. September through December.

October

- ✪ **Feast of St. Francis.** Animals from goldfish to elephants are blessed as thousands of Homo sapiens look on at the **Cathedral of St. John the Divine.** A magical experience; pets, of course, are welcome. A festive fair follows the blessing and music events. Buy tickets in advance because they can be hard to come by. Call ☎ **212/316-7540** or 212/662-7133 for tickets, or visit **www.stjohndivine.org**. First Sunday in October.

- **Ice-Skating.** Show off your skating style in the limelight at the diminutive **Rockefeller Center** rink (☎ **212/332-7654**), open from mid-October to mid-March (you'll skate under the magnificent Christmas tree for the month of Dec), or at the larger **Wollman Rink** in Central Park, at 59th Street and Sixth Avenue (☎ **212/396-1010**), which usually closes in early April.

- ✪ **Greenwich Village Halloween Parade.** This is Halloween at its most outrageous. You may have heard Lou Reed singing about it on his classic album *New York*—he wasn't exaggerating. Drag queens and assorted other flamboyant types parade through the Village in wildly creative costumes. The parade route has changed over the years, but most recently it has started after sunset at Spring Street and marched up Sixth Avenue to 23rd Street or Union Square. Point your Web browser to **www.halloween-nyc.com** or check the papers for the exact route so you can watch—or participate, if you have the threads and the imagination. October 31.

November

✪ **New York City Marathon.** Some 30,000 hopefuls from around the world participate in the largest U.S. marathon, and more than a million fans will cheer them on as they follow a route that touches on all five New York boroughs and finishes at Central Park. Call ☎ **212/860-4455,** or point your Web browser to **www.nyrrc.org**. November 5 in 2000; call for the 2001 date.

• **Radio City Music Hall Christmas Spectacular.** A rather gaudy extravaganza, but lots of fun nonetheless. Starring the Radio City Rockettes and a cast that includes live animals (just try to picture the camels sauntering in the Sixth Avenue entrance!). After undergoing an extensive restoration for most of 1999, spectacular Radio City itself is a sight to see. For information, call ☎ **212/247-4777** or visit **www.radiocity. com**; buy tickets at the box office or via TicketMaster's **Radio City Hotline** (☎ **212/307-1000**), or visit **www.ticketmaster.com**. Mid-November through early January.

✪ **Manhattan Antiques and Collectibles Triple Pier Expo.** The city's largest antiques show takes place over 2 consecutive weekends, usually just before Thanksgiving; for details, see March, above. Call ☎ **212/ 255-0020** or visit **www.antiqnet.com/Stella** for this year's dates.

✪ **Macy's Thanksgiving Day Parade.** The procession from Central Park West and 77th Street and down Broadway to Herald Square at 34th Street continues to be a national tradition. Huge hot-air balloons in the forms of Rocky and Bullwinkle, Snoopy, Underdog, the Pink Panther, Bart Simpson, and other cartoon favorites are the best part of the fun. The night before, you can usually see the big blow-up on Central Park West at 79th Street; call in advance to see if it will be open to the public again this year. Call ☎ **212/484-1222,** or Macy's Visitor Center at 212/494-2922. November 23 in 2000, November 22 in 2001.

✪ **Big Apple Circus.** New York City's homegrown, not-for-profit circus is a favorite with children and everyone who's young at heart. Big Apple is committed to maintaining the classical circus tradition with sensitivity, and only features animals that have a traditional working relationship with humans. A tent is pitched in **Damrosch Park** at **Lincoln Center.** Call ☎ **212/268-2500,** or visit **www.bigapplecircus.org**. November to January.

• *The Nutcracker.* Tchaikovsky's holiday favorite is performed by the New York City Ballet at **Lincoln Center.** The annual schedule is available from mid-July, and tickets usually go on sale in early October. Call ☎ **212/870-5570,** or point your Web browser to **www.nycballet.com**. Late November through early January.

December

✪ **Lighting of the Rockefeller Center Christmas Tree.** The annual lighting ceremony is accompanied by an ice-skating show, singing, entertainment, and a huge crowd. The tree stays lit around the clock until after the new year. Call ☎ **212/632-3975** for this year's date. Early December.

✪ **Holiday Trimmings.** Stroll down festive Fifth Avenue, and you'll see doormen dressed as wooden soldiers at **FAO Schwarz,** a 27-foot sparkling snowflake floating over the intersection outside **Tiffany's,** the **Cartier** building ribboned and bowed in red, wreaths warming the necks of the **New York Public Library's** lions, and fanciful figurines in the windows of **Saks Fifth Avenue** and **Lord & Taylor.** Throughout December.

- **Christmas Traditions.** In addition to the **Radio City Music Hall Christmas Spectacular** and the New York City Ballet's staging of *The Nutcracker* (see Nov, above), traditional holiday events include *A Christmas Carol* at **The Theater at Madison Square Garden** (☎ 212/ 465-6741 or www.thegarden.com, ☎ 212/307-7171 or www.ticketmaster.com for tickets), usually featuring a big name or two to draw in the crowds (Roger Daltrey in 1998). At **Avery Fisher Hall** is the National Chorale's sing-along performances of Handel's *Messiah* (☎ 212/875-5030; www.lincolncenter.org) for a week before Christmas. Don't worry if the only words you know are "Alleluia, Alleluia!"—a lyrics sheet is given to ticket holders.
- **Lighting of the Hanukkah Menorah.** Everything is done on a grand scale in New York, so it's no surprise that the world's largest menorah (32 ft. high) is at Manhattan's **Grand Army Plaza,** Fifth Avenue and 59th Street. Hanukkah celebrations begin at sunset on December 21, 2000, and December 8, 2001, with the lighting of the first of the giant electric candles.
- ✪ **New Year's Eve.** The biggest party of them all happens in **Times Square,** where hundreds of thousands of raucous revelers count down in unison the year's final seconds until the new lighted ball drops at midnight at 1 Times Square. I personally don't understand it, since it's always a crowded, cold, boozy madhouse, but hey! Call ☎ 212/768-1560 or 212/484-1222, or visit **www.timessquarebid.org**. December 31.

  Other unique events include **fireworks** followed by the New York Road Runner's Club's annual **5K Midnight Run** in **Central Park,** which is fun for runners and spectators alike; call ☎ 212/860-4455 or visit **www.nyrrc.org**. Head to Brooklyn for the city's largest New Year's Eve **fireworks** celebration at Prospect Park; call **718/965-8951** or visit **www.prospectpark.org**.

  The Cathedral of St. John the Divine is known for its annual **New Year's Eve Concert for Peace.** Past performers have included the Manhattan School of Music Chamber Sinfonia, Tony award–winning composer Jason Robert Brown *(Parade),* American soprano Lauren Flanigan, and the Forces of Nature Dance Company. Call ☎ 212/316-7540 for information or 212/622-2133 for tickets, or go online to **www.stjohn divine.org**.

4 Health & Insurance

WHAT TO DO IF YOU GET SICK AWAY FROM HOME

If you worry about getting sick away from home, you may want to consider **medical travel insurance** (see "Travel Insurance," below). In most cases, however, your existing health plan will provide all the coverage you need. Be sure to carry your identification card in your wallet.

If you suffer from a chronic illness, consult your doctor before your departure. For conditions like epilepsy, diabetes, or heart problems, wear a **Medic Alert Identification Tag** (☎ 800/ID-ALERT; www.medicalert.org), which will immediately alert doctors to your condition and give them access to your records through Medic Alert's 24-hour hotline.

Pack prescription medications in your carry-on luggage. Carry written prescriptions in generic, not brand-name form, and dispense all prescription medications from their original labeled vials. If you wear contact lenses, pack an extra pair in case you lose one.

FINDING A DOCTOR   If you do get sick, ask the concierge at your hotel to recommend a local doctor, even his or her own. This will probably yield a better recommendation than any 800 number would. There are also several walk-in medical centers, like **DOCS at New York Healthcare,** 55 E. 34th St., between Park and Madison avenues (☎ **212/252-6001**), for nonemergency illnesses. The clinic, affiliated with Beth Israel Medical Center, is open Monday through Thursday from 8am to 8pm, Friday from 8am to 7pm, Saturday from 9am to 3pm, and Sunday from 9am to 2pm. A 24-hour referral service for doctors who make house calls can be reached by calling ☎ **212/ 737-2333.**

If you have dental problems, a nationwide referral service known as **1-800-DENTIST** (☎ **800/336-8478**) will provide the name of a nearby dentist or clinic.

If you can't find a doctor who can help you right away, try the emergency room at the local hospital. Many emergency rooms have walk-in-clinics for emergency cases that are not life-threatening. You may not get immediate attention, but you won't pay the high price of an emergency room visit (usually a minimum of $300 just for signing your name, plus the price of whatever treatment you receive). For a list of local hospitals, see "Fast Facts: New York City," in chapter 4.

TRAVEL INSURANCE

There are three kinds of travel insurance: trip-cancellation, medical, and lost-luggage coverage. Rule number one: Check your existing policies and credit-card agreements before you buy additional coverage you may not need. Some credit- and charge-card companies may insure you against travel accidents if you buy plane, train, or bus tickets with their cards. Call your insurers or credit-card companies if you have any questions.

Trip-cancellation insurance is a good idea if you have paid a large portion of your vacation expenses up front (say, by purchasing a package deal). But don't buy it from your tour operator—talk about putting all of your eggs in one basket! Buy it from an outside vendor instead. It should cost approximately 6% to 8% of the total value of your tour package. Your existing health insurance should cover you if you get sick while on vacation—though if you belong to an HMO, you should check to see whether you are fully covered when away from home. For independent travel health insurance providers, see below.

Your homeowner's or renter's insurance should cover stolen luggage. The airlines are responsible for losses up to $2,500 on domestic flights if they lose your luggage (finally upped in early 2000 from the old 1984 limit of $1,250); if you plan to carry anything more valuable than that, keep it in your carry-on bag.

Among the reputable issuers of travel insurance are **Access America** (☎ **800/284-8300;** www.accessamerica.com); **Travel Guard International** (☎ **800/826-1300;** www.travel-guard.com); and **Travelex Insurance Services** (☎ **888/457-4602;** www.travelex-insurance.com).

5 Tips for Travelers with Special Needs

FOR FAMILIES

For the last few years, as a result of the startling decrease in crime and the sudden increase in family-oriented entertainment (exemplified by the "new"

Times Square), the city's sidewalks have been full of pint-sized visitors who love its eye-popping delights. There are hundreds of ways to keep the kids entertained, from kid-oriented museums and theater to theme park–style shopping and restaurants.

For the best places to stay and eat, see "Family-Friendly Hotels" in chapter 5 and "Family-Friendly Restaurants" in chapter 6. For details on sightseeing, check out the section called "Especially for Kids" in chapter 7.

Those of you who want a guide devoted exclusively to travel with children might buy a copy of *Frommer's New York City with Kids.*

Good bets for the most timely information include the "Weekend" section of Friday's *New York Times,* which has a whole section dedicated to the week's best kid-friendly activities; the weekly *New York* magazine, which has a full calendar of children's events in its "Cue" section; and *Time Out New York,* which also has a great weekly kids section with a bit of an alternative bent. Good Web sources for up-to-date information, advice, and yellow-pages links to family-related services include **New York Family** (**www.family.go. com/Local/nyfm**). Both *New York Family* and the *Big Apple Parents' Paper* are usually available for free at children's stores and other locations in Manhattan.

FINDING A BABY-SITTER   The first place to look for baby-sitting is in your hotel (better yet, ask about baby-sitting when you reserve). Many hotels have baby-sitting services or will provide you with lists of reliable sitters. If this doesn't pan out, call the **Baby Sitters' Guild** (☎ **212/682-0227;** www. babysittersguild.com). The sitters are licensed, insured, and bonded, and can even take your child on outings.

FOR TRAVELERS WITH DISABILITIES

New York is more accessible to disabled travelers than ever before. The city's bus system is wheelchair-friendly, and most of the major sightseeing attractions are easily accessible. Even so, always call first to be sure that the places you want to go to are fully accessible.

Most hotels are ADA compliant, with suitable rooms for wheelchair-bound travelers as well as those with other disabilities. But before you book, **ask lots of questions** based on your needs. Many city hotels are housed in older buildings that have had to be modified to meet requirements; still, elevators and bathrooms can both be on the small side, and other impediments may exist. If you have mobility issues, you'll probably do best to book into one of the city's newer hotels, which tend to be more spacious and accommodating. Check out "Best for Disabled Travelers" under **"Best Hotel Bets"** in chapter 1.

Some Broadway theaters and other performance venues provide total wheelchair accessibility; others provide partial accessibility. Many also offer lower-priced tickets for disabled theatergoers and their companions, though you'll need to check individual policies and reserve in advance.

GENERAL TRAVEL INFORMATION   **Moss Rehab ResourceNet** (**www. mossresourcenet.org**) is a great source for information, tips, and resources relating to accessible travel. You'll find links to a number of travel agents who specialize in planning trips for disabled travelers here and through **Access-Able Travel Source** (**www.access-able.com**), another excellent online source. You'll also find relay and voice numbers for hotels, airlines, and car-rental companies on Access-Able's user-friendly site, as well as links to accessible accommodations, attractions, transportation, tours, local medical resources and equipment repair, and much more.

You can join the **Society for the Advancement of Travelers with Handicaps** (SATH), 347 Fifth Ave., Suite 610, New York, NY 10016 (☎ **212/447-7284;** fax 212-725-8253; www.sath.org), to gain access to their vast network of connections in the travel industry. They provide information sheets on destinations and referrals to tour operators that specialize in traveling with disabilities. Their quarterly magazine, *Open World,* is full of good information and resources.

CITY-SPECIFIC INFORMATION Hospital Audiences, Inc., 548 Broadway, 3rd Floor, New York, NY 10012-3950 (☎ **212/575-7676** or 212/575-7660; TTY 212/575-7673; www.hospitalaudiences.org), arranges attendance and provides details about accessibility at cultural institutions as well as cultural events adapted for people with disabilities. Services include "Describe!" which allows visually impaired theatergoers to enjoy theater events, and an omnibus program that transports the disabled to cultural events. This nonprofit organization also publishes *Access for All,* a guidebook on accessibility at many of the city's cultural institutions, available by calling ☎ **212/575-7663** or by sending a $5 check to the above address.

Another terrific source for disabled travelers coming to New York City is **Big Apple Greeter** (☎ **212/669-8159;** www.bigapplegreeter.org). Their Greeter Access Project is geared to travelers with disabilities interested in getting to know the Big Apple. All of their employees are extremely well versed in accessibility issues. They can provide a resource list of agencies that serve the city's disabled community, and sometimes have special discounts available to theater and music performances. Big Apple Greeter even offers one-to-one tours that pair volunteers with disabled visitors; they can even introduce you to the public transportation system if you like. Reserve at least 1 week ahead.

Other helpful organizations are the **American Foundation for the Blind,** 11 Penn Plaza, Suite 300, New York, NY 10001 (☎ **800/232-5463** or 212/502-7600); **Lighthouse, Inc.,** 111 E. 59th St., New York, NY 10022 (☎ **800/829-0500** or 212/821-9200; www.lighthouse.org); and the **New York Society for the Deaf,** 817 Broadway, 7th floor, New York, NY 10003 (☎ TTY/voice **212/777-3900;** www.nysd.org).

GETTING AROUND Gray Line Air Shuttle (☎ **800/451-0455** or 212/315-3006; www.graylinenewyork.com) operates minibuses with lifts from JFK, LaGuardia, and Newark airports to Midtown hotels by reservation; arrange pickup 3 or 4 days in advance. **Olympia Airport Express** (☎ **888/662-7700** or 212/964-6233; www.olympiabus.com) provides service from Newark Airport, with half-price fares for disabled travelers.

A licensed ambulette company, **Upward Mobility Limousine Service** (☎ **718/645-7774;** www.brainlink.com/~phil) is a wheelchair-accessible car service that can provide door-to-door airport shuttle service as well as taxi service anywhere in the metropolitan area. Arrange airport pickups with as much advance notice as possible.

Taxis are required to carry people who have folding wheelchairs and guide or therapy dogs. However, don't be surprised if they don't run each other down trying to get to you; even though you shouldn't have to, you may have to wait a bit for a friendly (or fare-desperate) driver to come along.

Public buses are an inexpensive and easy way to get around New York. All buses' back doors are supposed to be equipped with wheelchair lifts (though the city has had complaints that not all are in working order). Buses also "kneel," lowering their front steps for people who have difficulty boarding.

Passengers with disabilities pay half-price fares (75¢). The **subway** isn't yet fully wheelchair accessible, but a list of about 30 accessible subway stations and a guide to wheelchair-accessible subway itineraries is on the MTA Web site. Call ☎ **718/596-8585** for bus and subway transit info, or point your browser to **www.mta.nyc.ny.us/nyct**; click on CUSTOMERS WITH SPECIAL NEEDS under GENERAL INFORMATION.

You're better off not trying to rent your own car to get around the city. But if you consider it the best mode of transportation for you, **Wheelchair Getaways** (☎ **800/379-3750** or 800/344-5005; www.wheelchair-getaways.com) rents specialized vans with wheelchair lifts and other features for travelers with disabilities throughout the New York metropolitan area.

FOR SENIOR TRAVELERS

One of the benefits of age is that travel often costs less. New York subway and bus fares are half price (75¢) for people 65 and older. Many museums and sights (and some theaters and performance halls) offer discounted entrance and tickets to seniors, so don't be shy about asking. Always bring an ID card, especially if you've kept your youthful glow.

Also mention the fact that you're a senior when you first make your travel reservations. Both **Amtrak** (☎ **800/USA-RAIL;** www.amtrak.com) and **Greyhound** (☎ **800/231-2222;** www.greyhound.com) offer discounts to persons over 62, and most of the major domestic airlines offer discount programs for senior travelers.

Many hotels offer senior discounts; **Choice Hotels** (which include Comfort Inns, some of my favorite affordable Midtown hotels; see chapter 5), for example, gives 30% off their published rates to anyone over 50, provided you book your room through their nationwide toll-free reservations number (that is, not directly with the hotels or through a travel agent). For a complete list of Choice Hotels, visit **www.hotelchoice.com**.

Members of the **American Association of Retired Persons (AARP)**, 601 E St. NW, Washington, DC 20049 (☎ **800/424-3410;** www.aarp.org), get discounts on hotels, airfares, and car rentals. AARP offers members a wide range of special benefits, including *Modern Maturity* magazine and a monthly newsletter. If you're not already a member, do yourself a favor and join.

Some thugs and unscrupulous tricksters try to take advantage of seniors. Be as skeptical as a New Yorker whenever you're approached, especially by someone who has a long story that promises to give you something for nothing. For safety tips, see "Playing It Safe" in chapter 4.

FOR GAY & LESBIAN TRAVELERS

Gay and lesbian culture is as much a part of New York's basic identity as yellow cabs, high-rises, and Broadway theater. Indeed, in a city with one of the world's largest, loudest, and most powerful gay and lesbian populations, homosexuality is hardly seen as "alternative" these days—it's squarely in the urban mainstream. So city hotels tend to be neutral on the issue, and gay couples shouldn't have a problem; for particularly gay-friendly accommodations, see "Best for Gay & Lesbian Travelers" under **"Best Hotel Bets"** in chapter 1. You'll want to see "The Gay & Lesbian Scene" in chapter 9 for nightlife suggestions.

If you want help planning your trip, the **International Gay & Lesbian Travel Association** (**IGLTA;** ☎ **800/448-8550** or 954/776-2626; www.iglta. org), can link you up with the appropriate gay-friendly service organization or

Many gay visitors will want to visit the **Stonewall Bar,** 53 Christopher St., at Seventh Avenue (☎ **212/463-0950**), in nearly the same location as where the famed Stonewall Inn once stood. On the night of June 27, 1969, customers at the original Stonewall, tired of constant police harassment, decided to fight back. That milestone marked the beginnings of the contemporary gay liberation movement. The usually celebratory, always engaging Lesbian and Gay Pride March is held in late June to commemorate the Stonewall "Riots"—see the "Calendar of Events," earlier in this chapter.

tour specialist. With around 1,200 members, it offers quarterly newsletters, marketing mailings, and a membership directory that's updated quarterly. Members are kept informed of gay and gay-friendly hoteliers, tour operators, and airline and cruise-line representatives.

Out and About (☎ **800/929-2268** or 212/645-6922; www.outandabout. com) offers a monthly newsletter packed with good information on the global gay and lesbian scene. Out and About's guidebooks are available at most major bookstores and through **A Different Light Bookstore,** 151 W. 19th St. (☎ **800/343-4002** or 212/989-4850; www.adlbooks.com), while its Web site features links to gay and lesbian tour operators and other gay-themed travel links.

All over Manhattan, but especially in neighborhoods like the **West Village** (particularly Christopher St., famous the world over as the main drag of New York gay male life) and **Chelsea** (especially Eighth Ave. from 16th to 23rd sts. and West 17th to 19th sts. from Fifth to Eighth aves.), shops, services, and restaurants have a lesbian and gay flavor. A Different Light (above) and the **Oscar Wilde Bookshop,** 15 Christopher St. (☎ **212/255-8097;** www. oscarwildebooks.com), are the city's best two gay and lesbian bookstores; both are good sources for information on the city's gay community.

The **Lesbian and Gay Community Services Center** is at 1 Little W. 12th St., at Hudson and Gansevoort streets, 1 block south of West 13th Street (☎ **212/620-7310;** www.gaycenter.org). (This is its temporary home while its headquarters at 208 W. 13th St. is being renovated, so call and check the address before you go.) The center is the meeting place for more than 400 lesbian, gay, and bisexual organizations. The center also runs many programs of its own, and there's always something going on. You can check the online events calendar, which lists hundreds of happenings—lectures, dances, concerts, readings, films—or call for the latest. Their site offers links to additional gay-friendly hotels and guesthouses in and around New York, plus tons of other information; they're also exceedingly friendly and helpful in person or over the phone. A great place to start, whether you're just visiting or contemplating a move to the Big Apple.

Another good source for lesbian and gay events is *Homo Xtra (HX),* a weekly magazine you can pick up in appropriate bars, clubs, and stores throughout town. Lesbians now have their own version, *HX for Her.* Both mags have lots of information online at **www.hx.com**. In addition, the weekly *Time Out New York* boasts a terrific gay and lesbian section. For other online information sources, see "Planning Your Trip: An Online Directory," p. 38.

In addition, there are lesbian and gay musical events, such as performances by the **Gay Men's Chorus** (☎ **212/398-5888;** www.nycgmc.org); health programs sponsored by the **Gay Men's Health Crisis (GMHC; ☎ 800/ AIDS-NYC** or 212/807-6655; www.gmhc.org); the **Gay and Lesbian Switchboard of New York** (☎ **888/843-4564** or 212/989-0999; www. glnh.org), offering peer counseling and information on upcoming events; and many other organizations. If you're a traveler with HIV, this city just might be the best place to visit. Its support and medical services are unrivaled.

FOR STUDENTS

Many museums, sights, and theaters offer reduced admission to students, so don't forget to bring your student ID and valid proof of age.

Your best resource is the **Council on International Educational Exchange,** or **CIEE.** They can set you up with an International Student ID card, and their travel branch, **Council Travel** (☎ **800/226-8624;** www. counciltravel.com), the world's biggest student travel agency, can get you discounts on plane tickets and the like. In New York City, they have offices at 254 Greene St., in Greenwich Village (☎ **212/254-2525**); in Midtown at 205 E. 42nd St. (☎ **212/822-2700**); and on the Upper West Side at 895 Amsterdam Ave. (☎ **212/666-4177**).

Hostelling International–American Youth Hostels (☎ **202/783-6161;** www.hiayh.org), has their largest hostel in New York City at 891 Amsterdam Ave, at 103rd Street (☎ **212/932-2300;** www.hinewyork.org). Reserve well ahead because this place is always booked.

For a wider selection of budget accommodations and dining than you'll find in this book, see *Frommer's New York City from $80 a Day.*

6 Getting There

BY PLANE

Three major airports serve New York City: **John F. Kennedy International Airport** (☎ **718/244-4444**) in Queens, about 15 miles (or 1 hour's driving time) from Midtown Manhattan; **LaGuardia Airport** (☎ **718/533-3400**), also in Queens, about 8 miles (or 30 min.) from Midtown; and **Newark International Airport** (☎ **973/961-6000**) in nearby New Jersey, about 16 miles (or 45 min.) from Midtown. Information about all three airports is available online at **www.panynj.gov.**

Almost every major domestic carrier serves at least one of these airports; most serve two or all three. Among them are **America West** (☎ **800/ 235-9292;** www.americawest.com), **American** (☎ **800/433-7300;** www. americanair.com), **Continental** (☎ **800/525-0280;** www.continental.com), **Delta** (☎ **800/221-1212;** www.delta-air.com), **Northwest** (☎ **800/ 225-2525;** www.nwa.com), **TWA** (☎ **800/221-2000;** www.twa.com), **US Airways** (☎ **800/428-4322;** www.usairways.com), and **United** (☎ **800/ 241-6522;** www.ual.com).

In recent years there has been rapid growth in the number of start-up, no-frills airlines serving New York. These smaller, sometimes struggling airlines may offer lower fares—but don't expect the same kind of service you get from the majors. You might check out Atlanta-based **AirTran** (☎ 800/AIRTRAN; www.airtran.com); Denver-based **Frontier** (☎ 800/4321-FLY; www.flyfrontier. com); Detroit-based **Spirit Airlines** (☎ 800/772-7117; www.spiritair.com); Raleigh-Durham-based **Midway** (☎ 888/22-MIDWAY; www.midwayair. com); Milwaukee- and Omaha-based **Midwest Express** (☎ 800/452-2022; www.midwestexpress.com); Chicago-based **ATA** (☎ 800/I-FLY-ATA; www. ata.com); Las Vegas–based **National Airlines** (☎ 888/757-JETS;

It's more convenient to fly into Newark than Kennedy if your destination is Manhattan, and consider that fares to Newark are often cheaper than the other airports. Newark can also be the most convenient if your hotel is in Midtown West or downtown near the World Trade Center.

www.nationalairlines.com); and Minneapolis-based **Sun Country** (☎ 800/752-1218; www.suncountry.com). After a much-lauded launch in early 2000, the new cheap-chic airline **jetBlue** (☎ 800/JETBLUE; www.jetblue.com) has taken New York by storm with its low fares and high-end service to Buffalo, New York, and Florida; expect a significantly expanded route map by the time you're ready to fly. The nation's leading discount airline, **Southwest** (☎ 800/435-9792; www.iflyswa.com), announced flights to MacArthur (Islip) Airport on Long Island, 40 miles east of Manhattan, but there are no current plans to fly into the city's airports.

Most major international carriers also serve New York; see chapter 3 for details.

FLY FOR LESS: TIPS FOR GETTING THE BEST AIRFARES

- Keep your eye out for periodic sales. Check your newspaper for advertised discounts or call the airlines directly and ask if any **promotional rates or special fares** are available. You'll almost never see a sale during the peak summer vacation months of July and August, or during the Thanksgiving or Christmas seasons; in periods of low-volume travel, however, you should pay no more than $400 for a cross-country flight.

  Note, however, that the lowest-priced fares are often nonrefundable, require advance purchase of 1 to 3 weeks and a certain length of stay, and carry penalties for changing dates of travel. So, when you're quoted a fare, make sure you know exactly what the restrictions are before you commit.

- **Consolidators,** also known as bucket shops, are a good place to find low fares, often below even the airlines' discounted rates. Basically, they're just big travel agents that get discounts for buying in bulk and pass some of the savings on to you. Before you pay, however, ask for a confirmation number from the consolidator and then call the airline itself to confirm your seat. Be prepared to book your ticket with a different consolidator—there are many to choose from—if the airline can't confirm your reservation. Also be aware that consolidator tickets are usually nonrefundable or come with stiff cancellation penalties.

  I've gotten great deals on many occasions from ✪ **Cheap Tickets** (☎ 800/377-1000; www.cheaptickets.com). **Council Travel** (☎ 800/226-8624; www.counciltravel.com) and **STA Travel** (☎ 800/781-4040; www.startravel.com) cater especially to young travelers, but their bargain-basement prices are available to people of all ages. Other reliable consolidators include **Lowestfare.com** (☎ 888/278-8830; www.lowestfare.com); **1-800-AIRFARE** (www.1800airfare.com); **Cheap Seats** (☎ 800/451-7200; www.cheapseatstravel.com); and **1-800-FLY-CHEAP** (www.flycheap.com).

- Search the **Internet** for cheap fares—though it's still best to compare your findings with the research of a dedicated travel agent, if you're lucky enough to have one, especially when you're booking more than just a flight. A few of the better-respected virtual travel agents are **Travelocity** (**www.travelocity.com**) and **Microsoft Expedia** (**www.expedia.com**).

Smarter Living (**www.smarterliving.com**) is a great source for last-minute deals. Take a moment to register, and every week you'll get an e-mail summarizing the discount fares available from your departure city. The site also features concise lists of links to hotel, car-rental, and other hot travel deals.

See "Planning Your Trip: An Online Directory" on p. 38 for further discussion on this topic and other recommendable sites.

TRANSPORTATION TO & FROM THE NEW YORK AREA AIRPORTS

Since there's no need to rent a car in New York, you're going to have to figure out how you want to get from the airport to your hotel and back.

For complete transportation information for all three airports (JFK, LaGuardia, and Newark), call **Air-Ride** (☎ **800/247-7433**); it gives recorded details on bus and shuttle companies and private car services registered with the New York and New Jersey Port Authority. Similar information is available online at **www.panynj.gov**; just click on the airport at which you'll be arriving.

On the arrivals level at each airport, the Port Authority also has Ground Transportation Information counters where you can get information and book on all manner of transport once you land. Most transportation companies also have courtesy phones near the baggage-claim area.

Generally, travel time between the airports and Midtown Manhattan by taxi or car is 1 hour for JFK, 45 minutes for LaGuardia, and 50 minutes for Newark. Always allow extra time, though, especially during rush hour, peak holiday travel times, and if you're taking a bus.

SUBWAYS & PUBLIC BUSES   For the most part, your best bet is to stay away from the MTA when traveling to and from the airport. You might save a few dollars, but subways and buses that currently serve the airports involve multiple transfers, and you'll have to drag your luggage up and down staircases. On some subways you'd be traveling through undesirable neighborhoods. Spare yourself the drama.

The only exception to this rule that I feel comfortable with is the subway service to and from JFK—but you should only consider it if money is extremely tight *and* you're already well versed in the ways of New York. It's a huge hassle, and you should expect it to take 90 minutes or more, but you can take the **A train,** which connects to one of two free **shuttle buses** that serve all the JFK terminals. Upon exiting the terminal, pick up the shuttle bus (marked **LONG-TERM PARKING LOT**) out front; it takes you to the **Howard Beach station,** where you pick up the A train to the west side of Manhattan. Service is every 10 to 15 minutes during rush hour and every 20 minutes at midday, and the subway fare is $1.50. If you're traveling to JFK from Manhattan, be sure to take the A train that says **FAR ROCKAWAY** or **ROCKAWAY PARK**—*not* **LEFFERTS BOULEVARD**. Get off at the Howard

Money-Saving Tip

If your schedule is flexible, you can almost always get a cheaper fare by staying over a Saturday night or by flying during midweek. Many airlines won't volunteer this information, so be sure to ask.

Money-Saving Package Deals

Before you start your search for the lowest airfare, you may want to consider booking your flight as part of a travel package.

Package tours are not the same as escorted tours. They are simply a way to buy airfare and accommodations (and sometimes extras like sightseeing tours and hard-to-get theater tickets) at the same time. When you're visiting New York, a package can be a smart way to go. In many cases, a package that includes airfare, hotel, and transportation to and from the airport will cost you less than your hotel bill alone would have had you booked it yourself. That's because packages are sold in bulk to tour operators, who then resell them to the public at a cost that drastically undercuts standard rates.

Packages, however, vary widely. Some offer a better class of hotels than others. Some offer the same hotels for lower prices. With some packagers, your choice of accommodations and travel days may be limited. Which package is right for you depends entirely on what you want.

Here are a few tips to help you tell one package from another, and figure out which one is right for you:

- **Read this guide.** Do a little homework; read up on New York. Compare the rack rates that we've published to the discounted rates being offered by the packagers to see what kinds of deals they're offering—if you're actually being offered a substantial savings, or if they've just gussied up the rack rates to make their offer *sound* like a deal. If you're being offered a stay in a hotel that we haven't recommended, do more research to learn about it, especially if it isn't a reliable franchise like Holiday Inn or Hyatt. It's not a deal if you end up at a dump.

- **Read the fine print.** Make sure you know *exactly* what's included in the price you're being quoted, and what's not. Are hotel taxes and airport transfers included, or will you have to pay extra? Conversely, don't pay for a rental car you don't need—and you won't need one in New York. Before you commit to a package, make sure you know how much flexibility you have, say, if your kid gets sick or your boss suddenly asks you to adjust your vacation schedule. Some packagers require ironclad commitments, while others are will go with the flow, charging only minimal fees for changes or cancellations.

- **Use your best judgment.** Stay away from fly-by-nights and shady packagers. If a deal appears to be too good to be true, it probably is. Go with a reputable firm with a proven track record. This is where your travel agent can come in handy; he or she should be knowledgeable about different packagers, the deals they offer, and the general rate of satisfaction among their customers.

So how do you find a package deal?

Beach/JFK Airport station and connect to the shuttle bus, A or B, that goes to your terminal (they're clearly marked, and there's usually a guide to point you to the right one). The subway can actually be more reliable than taking a car or taxi at the height of rush hour, but *a few words of warning:* This isn't the right option for you if you're bringing more than a single piece of luggage,

The best place to start your search is the travel section of your local Sunday newspaper. Also check the ads in the back of national travel magazines like *Travel Holiday, National Geographic Traveler,* and *Arthur Frommer's Budget Travel.*

One of the biggest packagers in the Northeast, **Liberty Travel** (☎ **888/271-1584;** www.libertytravel.com) boasts a full-page ad in many Sunday papers. You won't get much in the way of service, but you will get a good deal. They offer great-value 2- to 7-night New York packages that usually include such freebies as a Circle Line cruise, a guided city tour, and discounts at Planet Hollywood, plus lots of good hotels to choose from.

The major airlines offering good-value packages to New York include **Continental Airlines Vacations** (☎ **800/634-5555;** www.coolvacations. com), which featured a short but strong selection of hotels at press time, among them the Hotel Metro, one of my midpriced favorites; the Doubletree Guest Suites, a great family choice; and the luxurious (and legendary) Waldorf Astoria. **Delta Vacations** (☎ **800/872-7786;** www. deltavacations.com), boasts a similarly good selection of hotels. **US Airways Vacations** (☎ **800/455-0123;** www.usairwaysvacations.com) offers a pleasing range of hotels, plus Broadway tickets as part of its list of add-on options (watch for the rental car you don't need, however). Both **United Vacations** (☎ **800/328-6877;** www.unitedvacations.com) and **American Airlines Vacations** (☎ **800/321-2121;** www.aavacations. com) have an extensive but mixed selection of hotels, so be careful where you book. **Northwest WorldVacations** (☎ **800/800-1504;** www.nwa. com/vacpkg) is another option. You may want to choose the airline that has frequent service to your hometown or the one on which you accumulate frequent-flyer miles (you may even be able to pay with your trip using miles).

For one-stop shopping on the Web, go to **www.vacationpackager. com**, a search engine that will link you to many different package-tour operators offering New York City vacations, often with a company profile summarizing the company's basic booking and cancellation terms.

A terrific source specifically for Big Apple packages is **New York City Vacations** (☎ **888/692-8701;** www.nycvp.com), which can sell you a complete vacation package including hotel stay, theater tickets, and more.

In New York, many **hotels** also offer package deals, especially for weekend stays. Some of the best deals in town are those that include theater tickets, sometimes for otherwise sold-out shows like *The Lion King.* (Most aren't air/land combos, however; you'll have to book your airfare separately.) I've included tips on hotels that regularly offer them in chapter 5, but always ask about available packages when you call any hotel.

since there's a good amount of walking and some stairs involved in the trip, and you'll have nowhere to put it on the subway train. And *do not* use this method if you're traveling to or from the airport after dark, or too early in the morning—it's just not safe. For additional subway information, see "Getting Around" in chapter 4.

Planning Basics

TAXIS Taxis are a quick and convenient way to travel to and from the airports. They're available at designated taxi stands outside the terminals, with uniformed dispatchers on hand during peak hours (follow the **GROUND TRANSPORTATION** or **TAXI** signs). There may be a long line, but it generally moves pretty quickly. Fares, whether fixed or metered, do not include bridge and tunnel tolls ($3.50 to $4) or a tip for the cabbie (15 to 20% is customary). They do include all passengers in the cab and luggage—never pay more than the metered or flat rate, except for tolls and a tip (from 8pm to 6am a 50¢ surcharge also applies on New York yellow cabs). Taxis have a limit of four passengers, so if there are more in your group, you'll have to take more than one cab. For more on taxis, see "Getting Around" in chapter 4.

- **From JFK:** A flat rate of $30 to and from Manhattan (plus any tolls and tip) is charged. The meter will not be turned on and the surcharge will not be added.
- **From LaGuardia:** $20 to $25, metered.
- **From Newark:** The dispatcher for New Jersey taxis gives you a slip of paper with a flat rate ranging from $30 to $45 (toll and tip extra), depending on where you're going in Manhattan, so you'll have to be precise about your destination. New York yellow cabs aren't permitted to pick up passengers at Newark. The yellow-cab fare from Manhattan to Newark is the meter amount plus $10 and tolls (about $40 to $50, perhaps a few dollars more with tip). New Jersey taxis aren't permitted to take passengers from Manhattan to Newark.

PRIVATE CAR & LIMOUSINE SERVICES Private car and limousine companies provide convenient 24-hour door-to-door airport transfers. The advantage they offer over taking a taxi is that you can arrange your pickup in advance and avoid the hassles of the taxi line. Call at least 24 hours in advance (even earlier on holidays), and a driver will meet you near baggage claim (or at your hotel for a return trip). You'll probably be asked to leave a credit-card number to guarantee your ride; you'll likely be offered the choice of indoor or curbside pickup. Vehicles range from sedans to vans to limousines and tend to be relatively clean and comfortable. Prices vary slightly by company and the size of car reserved, but expect to pay around the same as you would for a taxi if you request a basic sedan and have only one stop; toll and tip policies are the same. (Note that car services are not subject to the flat-rate rule that taxis have for rides to and from JFK.) Ask when booking what the fare will be and if you can use your credit card to pay for the ride so there are no surprises at drop-off time. There may be waiting charges tacked on if the driver has to wait an excessive amount of time for your plane to land when picking you up, but the car companies will usually check on your flight beforehand to get an accurate landing time.

I've had the best luck with **Carmel** (☎ **800/922-7635** or 212/666-6666) and **Legends** (☎ **888/LEGENDS** or 718/788-1234); **Allstate** (☎ **800/**

An Airport Warning

Never accept a car ride from the hustlers who hang out in the terminal halls. They're illegal, don't have proper insurance, and aren't safe. You can tell who they are because they'll approach you with a suspicious conspiratorial air and ask if you need a ride. Not from them, you don't. Sanctioned city cabs and car services wait outside the terminals.

Southwest Airlines, the nation's leading discount carrier, now flies into the New York area via Long Island's Islip Airport, 50 miles east of Manhattan. If you're on one of these flights, here are your options for getting into the city:

Classic Transportation (☎ 800/666-4949 or 516/567-5100; www. classictrans.com) and **Legends** (☎ 888/LEGENDS or 718/788-1234) will pick you up at Islip Airport and deliver you to Manhattan via private sedan, but expect to pay $100 plus tolls and tip for door-to-door service. Be sure to arrange for it 24 hours in advance.

Or call **Village Taxi** when you land (☎ 516/563-4611), and they'll send over a driver to take you 3 miles to the Ronkonkoma Long Island Rail Road Station, where you can pick up an LIRR (Long Island Rail Road) train to Manhattan. The taxi fare is $5 to $8, plus tip. From Ronkonkoma, it's about a 1¹/₂-hour train ride to Manhattan's Penn Station; the one-way fare is $9.50 at peak hours, $6.50 off-peak (half fare for seniors 65 or older and kids 5 to 11). Trains usually leave Ronkonkoma once or twice every hour, depending on the day and time. For more information, call ☎ 718/217-5477 or go online to **www.mta.nyc.ny.us/lirr**.

453-4099 or 212/741-7440) and **Tel-Aviv** (☎ 800/222-9888 or 212/777-7777) are also reliable bets.

If you call in advance, you can have the nicety of the driver meeting you with a sign and walking you right to your car, but you'll have to pay an extra $5 to $10 to cover the driver's airport parking charges. You can save a few dollars and usually only have to wait an extra 5 to 10 minutes if you call as soon as you land, and then take your luggage out to the waiting area; the driver will pull up with your name on a sign and never has to park.

These car services are good for rush hour (no ticking meters in rush-hour traffic), but if you're arriving at a quieter time of day, taxis are a fine option. Especially if you're landing at JFK, the flat taxi fare to Manhattan is cheaper than what a car service charges.

PRIVATE BUSES & SHUTTLES Buses and shuttle services provide a comfortable and less expensive (but usually more time-consuming) option for airport transfers than do taxis and car services.

Gray Line Air Shuttle and **Super Shuttle** serve all three airports; **New York Airport Service** serves JFK and LaGuardia; **Olympia Trails** serves Newark. These services are my favorite option for getting to and from Newark during peak travel times because the drivers usually take lesser-known surface streets that make the ride much quicker than if you go with a taxi or car, which will virtually always stick to the traffic-clogged main route.

Gray Line Express Shuttle USA (☎ 800/451-0455 or 212/315-3006; www.graylinenewyork.com) vans depart JFK, LaGuardia, and Newark every 20 minutes between 7am and 11:30pm. They will drop you off at most hotels between 23rd and 63rd streets in Manhattan, or Port Authority (34th St. and Seventh Ave.) or Grand Central (42nd St. and Park Ave.) terminals if you need to catch a subway to another part of town or a train to the 'burbs. No reservation is required; just go to the ground-transportation desk or use the courtesy phone in the baggage-claim area and ask for Gray Line. Service from most major mid-Manhattan hotels to all three airports operates from 5am to 9pm;

you must call a day in advance to arrange a hotel pickup. The regular one-way fare to and from JFK is $19, to and from LaGuardia is $16, and to and from Newark is $19, but you can save a few bucks by prepaying your round-trip at the airport ($28 for JFK and Newark, $26 for LaGuardia).

The familiar blue vans of **Super Shuttle** (☎ 800/258-3826 or 212/258-3826; www.supershuttle.com) serve all three area airports, providing door-to-door service to Manhattan and points on Long Island every 15 to 30 minutes around the clock. As with Gray Line, you don't need to reserve your airport-to-Manhattan ride; just go to the ground-transportation desk or use the courtesy phone in the baggage-claim area and ask for Super Shuttle. Hotel pickups for your return trip require 24 to 48 hours' advance booking; reservations can be made online. One-way fares are $16 to and from JFK, $15 to and from LaGuardia, and $19 to and from Newark; you'll pay full fare for the first passenger, and $9 for each additional passenger.

New York Airport Service (☎ 718/875-8200) buses travel from JFK and LaGuardia to the Port Authority Bus Terminal (42nd St. and Eighth Ave.), Penn Station (34th St. and Seventh Ave.), Grand Central Terminal (Park Ave. between 41st and 42nd sts.), or your Midtown hotel, plus the Jamaica **LIRR** Station in Queens, where you can pick up a train for Long Island. Follow the **GROUND TRANSPORTATION** signs to the curbside pickup or look for the uniformed agent. Buses depart the airport every 20 to 70 minutes (depending on your departure point and destination) between 6:30am and midnight. Buses to JFK and LaGuardia depart the Port Authority and Grand Central Terminal on the Park Avenue side every 15 to 30 minutes, depending on the time of day and the day of the week. To request direct shuttle service from your hotel, call the above number at least 24 hours in advance. One-way fare for JFK is $13, and $10 to and from LaGuardia; children under 12 ride free with a parent.

Olympia Airport Express (☎ 888/662-7700 or 212/964-6233; www.olympiabus.com) provides service every 5 to 10 minutes (less frequently during off hours) from Newark Airport to four Manhattan locations: 1 World Trade Center (on West St., next to the Marriott World Trade Center Hotel), Penn Station (the pickup point is the northwest corner of 34th St. and Eighth Ave. and the drop-off point is the southwest corner), the Port Authority Bus Terminal (on 42nd St. between Eighth and Ninth aves.), and Grand Central Terminal (on 41st St. between Park and Lexington aves.). Passengers to and from the Grand Central Terminal location can connect to Olympia's Midtown shuttle vans, which service most hotels between 30th and 65th streets. From the above departure points in Manhattan, service runs every 15 to 30 minutes depending on your pickup point; call for the exact schedule. The one-way fare is $10, or $15 if you connect to the hotel shuttle; senior and disabled citizens ride for half price.

BY TRAIN

Amtrak (☎ 800/USA-RAIL; www.amtrak.com) runs frequent service to New York City's **Penn Station,** on Seventh Avenue between 31st and 33rd streets, where you can easily pick up a taxi, subway, or bus to your hotel. To get the best rates, book early (as much as 6 months in advance) and travel on weekends.

If you're traveling to New York from a city along Amtrak's Northeast Corridor—such as Boston, Philadelphia, Baltimore, or Washington, D.C.—Amtrak may be your best travel bet now that they've rolled out their new high-speed Acela trains, which will have replaced all the old Metroliners by the time

If you're traveling to a borough other than Manhattan, call **ETS Air Service** (☎ 718/221-5341) for shared door-to-door service. For Long Island service, call **Classic Transportation** (☎ 800/666-4949 or 516/567-5100; www.classictrans.com) above. For service to Westchester County or Connecticut, contact **Connecticut Limousine** (☎ 800/472-5466 or 203/878-6867; www.ctlimo.com) or **Prime Time Shuttle of Connecticut** (☎ 800/733-8267; www.primetimeshuttle.com).

If you're traveling to points in New Jersey from Newark Airport, call **Olympic Limousine** (☎ **800/822-9797** or 908/938-4300) for Ocean and Monmouth counties; the **Airporter** (☎ **800/385-4000** or 609/587-6600; www.goairporter) to Middlesex and Mercer counties; or **State Shuttle** (☎ **800/427-3207** or 973/729-0030) for other Jersey destinations.

you read this. The Acela Express trains cut travel time from D.C. down to $2^1/_2$ hours, and travel time from Boston to a lightning-quick 3 hours.

BY BUS

Buses arrive at the **Port Authority Terminal,** on Eighth Avenue between 40th and 42nd streets, where you can easily transfer to your hotel by taxi, subway, or bus. I don't suggest taking the bus because the ride is long and uncomfortable, and fares are usually no cheaper than the much quicker and more comfortable train. But if for some reason bus is your preferred mode of transportation, call **Greyhound Bus Lines** (☎ **800/231-2222** or 402/330-8552; www.greyhound.com).

BY CAR

From the **New Jersey Turnpike** (I-95) and points west, there are three Hudson River crossings into the city's west side: the **Holland Tunnel** (lower Manhattan), the **Lincoln Tunnel** (Midtown), and the **George Washington Bridge** (upper Manhattan).

From **upstate New York,** take the **New York State Thruway** (I-87), which crosses the Hudson on the Tappan Zee Bridge and becomes the **Major Deegan Expressway** (I-87) through the Bronx. For the east side, continue to the Triborough Bridge and then down the FDR Drive. For the west side, take the Cross Bronx Expressway (I-95) to the Henry Hudson Parkway or the Taconic State Parkway to the Saw Mill River Parkway to the Henry Hudson Parkway south.

From **New England,** the **New England Thruway** (I-95) connects with the **Bruckner Expressway** (I-278), which leads to the Triborough Bridge and the FDR on the east side. For the west side, take the Bruckner to the Cross Bronx Expressway (I-95) to the Henry Hudson Parkway south.

Note that you'll have to pay tolls along some of these roads and at most crossings.

Once you arrive in Manhattan, park your car in a garage (expect to pay at least $20 to $35 per day) and leave it there. Don't use your car for traveling within the city. Public transportation, taxis, and walking will easily get you where you want to go without the headaches of parking, gridlock, and dodging crazy cabbies.

Planning Your Trip: An Online Directory

Frommer's Online Directory will help you take better advantage of the travel-planning information available online. Part 1 lists general Internet resources that can make any trip easier, such as sites for obtaining the best possible prices on airline tickets. In Part 2 you'll find some top online guides specifically for New York.

This is not a comprehensive list, but a discriminating selection to get you started. Recognition is given to sites based on their content value and ease of use. Inclusion here is not paid for—unlike some Web-site rankings, which are based on payment. Finally, remember this is a press-time snapshot of leading Web sites; some undoubtedly will have evolved, changed, or moved by the time you read this.

1 Top Travel-Planning Web Sites

By Lynne Bairstow

Lynne Bairstow is the co-author of *Frommer's Mexico*, and the editorial director of *e-com* magazine.

WHY BOOK ONLINE?

Online agencies have come a long way over the past few years, now providing tips for finding the best fare, and giving you suggested dates or times to travel that yield the lowest price if your plans are at all flexible. Other sites even allow you to establish the price you're willing to pay, and they check the airlines' willingness to accept it. However, in some cases, these sites may not always yield the best price. Unlike a travel agent, for example, they may not have access to charter flights offered by wholesalers.

Online booking sites aren't the only places to reserve airline tickets—all major airlines have their own Web sites and often offer incentives (bonus frequent-flyer miles or net-only discounts, for example) when you buy online or buy an e-ticket.

The new trend is toward conglomerated booking sites. By mid-2000, a consortium of U.S. and European-based airlines is planning to launch an as-yet unnamed Web site that will offer fares lower than those available through travel agents. United, Delta, Northwest, and Continental have initiated this effort, based on their success at selling airline seats on their own sites.

Check Out Frommer's Site

We highly recommend **Arthur Frommer's Budget Travel Online** (**www.frommers.com**) as an excellent travel-planning resource. Of course, we're a little biased, but you'll find indispensable travel tips, reviews, monthly vacation giveaways, and online booking. Among the most popular features of this site are the regular "Ask the Expert" bulletin boards, which feature Frommer's authors answering your questions via online postings.

Subscribe to Arthur Frommer's Daily Newsletter (**www.frommers. com/newsletters**) to receive the latest travel bargains and inside travel secrets in your E-mail box every day. You'll read daily headlines and articles from the dean of travel himself, highlighting last-minute deals on airfares, accommodations, cruises, and package vacations.

Search our Destinations archive (**www.frommers.com/destinations**) of more than 200 domestic and international destinations for great places to stay and dine, and tips on sightseeing. Once you've researched your trip, the online reservation system (**www.frommers.com/booktravelnow**) takes you to Frommer's favorite sites for booking your vacation at affordable prices.

The best of the travel planning sites are now highly personalized; they store your seating preferences, meal preferences, tentative itineraries, and credit-card information, allowing you to quickly plan trips or check agendas.

In many cases, booking your trip online can be better than working with a travel agent. It gives you the widest variety of choices, control, and the 24-hour convenience of planning your trip when you choose. All you need is some time—and often a little patience—and you're likely to find the fun of online travel research will greatly enhance your trip.

WHO SHOULD BOOK ONLINE?

Online booking is best for travelers who want to know as much as possible about their travel options, for those who have flexibility in their travel dates, and for bargain hunters.

One of the biggest successes in online travel for both passengers and airlines is the offer of last-minute specials, such as American Airlines' weekend deals or other Internet-only fares that must be purchased online. Another advantage is that you can cash in on incentives for booking online, such as rebates or bonus frequent-flyer miles.

Business and other frequent travelers also have found numerous benefits in online booking, as the advances in mobile technology provide them with the ability to check flight status, change plans, or get specific directions from handheld computing devices, mobile phones, and pagers. Some sites will even E-mail or page a passenger if their flight is delayed.

Online booking is increasingly able to accommodate complex itineraries, even for international travel. The pace of evolution on the Net is rapid, so you'll probably find additional features and advancements by the time you visit these sites. The future holds ever-increasing personalization and customization for online travelers.

Online Directory

TRAVEL-PLANNING & -BOOKING SITES

The following sites offer domestic and international flight, hotel, and rental-car bookings, plus news, destination information, and deals on cruises and vacation packages. Free (one-time) registration is required for booking.

Important Note: See chapters 2 and 3 for the Web addresses of all the airlines serving New York City. These sites offer schedules and flight booking, and most have pages where you can sign up for E-mail alerts for weekend deals and other late-breaking bargains.

○ Expedia. expedia.com

Expedia is known as the fastest and most flexible online travel planner for booking flights, hotels, and rental cars. It offers several ways of obtaining the best possible fares: **Flight Price Matcher** service allows your preferred airline to match an available fare with a competitor; a comprehensive **Fare Compare** area shows the differences in fare categories and airlines; and **Fare Calendar** helps you plan your trip around the best possible fares. Its main limitation is that like many online databases, Expedia focuses on the major airlines and hotel chains, so don't expect to find too many budget airlines or one-of-a-kind B&Bs here.

Personalized features allow you to store your itineraries, and receive weekly fare reports on favorite cities. You can also check on the status of flight arrivals and departures, and through MileageMiner, track all of your frequent-flyer accounts.

Expedia also offers vacation packages, cruises, and information on specialized travel (like casino destinations, and adventure, ski, and golf travel). There are also special features for travelers accessing information on mobile devices.

Note: In early 2000, Expedia bought travelscape.com and vacationspot.com, and incorporated these sites into expedia.com.

Travelocity (incorporates Preview Travel). www.travelocity.com; www.previewtravel.com

Travelocity uses the SABRE system to offer reservations and tickets for more than 400 airlines; you can also reserve and purchase from more than 45,000 hotels and 50 car-rental companies. An exclusive feature of the SABRE system is their **Low Fare Search Engine,** which automatically searches for the three lowest-priced itineraries based on a traveler's criteria. Last-minute deals and consolidator fares are included in the search. If you book with Travelocity, you can select specific seats for your flights with online seat maps, and also view diagrams of the most popular commercial aircraft. Their hotel finder provides street-level location maps and photos of selected hotels.

Travelocity features an inviting interface for booking trips, though the wealth of graphics involved can make the site somewhat slow to load, and any adjustment in your parameters means you'll need to completely start over.

This site also has some very cool tools. With the **Fare Watcher** E-mail feature, you can select up to five routes for which you'll receive E-mail notices when the fare changes by $25 or more. If you own an alphanumeric pager with national access that can receive E-mail, Travelocity's **Flight Paging** can alert you if your flight is delayed. You can also access real-time departure and arrival information on any flight within the SABRE system.

Note to AOL Users: You can book flights, hotels, rental cars and cruises on AOL at keyword: Travel. The booking software is provided by Travelocity/Preview Travel and is similar to the Internet site. Use the AOL "Travelers Advantage" program to earn a 5% rebate on flights, hotel rooms, and car rentals.

Online Directory

More people still look online than book online, partly due to fear of putting their credit-card numbers out on the Net. Secure encryption; and increasing experienced buying online, has removed this fear for most travelers. In some cases, however, it's simply easier to buy from a local travel agent who can deliver your tickets to your door (especially if your travel is last-minute or if you have special requests). You can find a flight online and then book it by calling a toll-free number or contacting your travel agent, though this is somewhat less efficient. To be sure you're in secure mode when you book online, look for a little icon of a key (in Netscape) or a padlock (in Internet Explorer) at the bottom of your Web browser.

TRIP.com. www.trip.com
TRIP.com began as a site geared for business travelers, but its innovative features and highly personalized approach have broadened its appeal to leisure travelers as well. It is the leading travel site for those using mobile devices to access Internet travel information.

TRIP.com provides the average and lowest fare for the route requested, in addition to the current available fare. An on-site "newsstand" features breaking news on airfare sales and other travel specials. Among its most popular features are Flight TRACKER and intelliTRIP. **Flight TRACKER** allows users to track any commercial flight en-route to its destination anywhere in the U.S., while accessing real-time FAA-based flight monitoring data. **intelliTRIP** is a search tool that allows users to identify the best airline, hotel, and rental-car fares in less than 90 seconds.

In addition, trip.com offers E-mail notification of flight delays, plus city resource guides, currency converters, and a weekly E-mail newsletter of fare updates, travel tips, and traveler forums.

Yahoo Travel. www.travel.yahoo.com
Yahoo is currently the most popular of the Internet information portals, and its travel site is a comprehensive mix of online booking, daily travel news, and destination information. Their **Best Fares** area offers what it promises, and provides feedback on refining your search if you have flexibility in travel dates or times. There is also an active section of Message Boards for discussions on travel in general, and to specific destinations.

LAST-MINUTE DEALS & OTHER ONLINE BARGAINS

There's nothing airlines hate more than flying with lots of empty seats. The Net has enabled airlines to offer last-minute bargains to entice travelers to fill those seats. Most of these are announced on Tuesday or Wednesday and are valid for travel the following weekend, but some can be booked weeks or months in advance. You can sign up for weekly E-mail alerts at the airlines' own sites (see "Getting There," in "Planning Your Trip: The Basics") or check sites that compile lists of these bargains, such as **Smarter Living** or **WebFlyer** (see below). To make it easier, visit a site that will round up all the deals and send them in one convenient weekly E-mail.

Also popular are services that let you name the price you're willing to pay for a air seat or vacation package, and travel auction sites.

Cheap Tickets. www.cheaptickets.com

Cheap Tickets has exclusive deals that aren't available through more mainstream channels. One caveat about the Cheap Tickets site is that it will offer fare quotes for a route, and later show this fare is not valid for your dates of travel—most other Web sites, such as Expedia, consider your dates of travel before showing what fares are available. Despite its problems, Cheap Tickets can be worth the effort because its fares can be lower than those offered by its competitors.

✪ 1travel.com. www.1travel.com

Here you'll find deals on domestic and international flights and hotels. 1travel. com's **Saving Alert** compiles last-minute air deals so you don't have to scroll through multiple E-mail alerts. A feature called "Drive a little using low-fare airlines" helps map out strategies for using alternate airports to find lower fares. And **Farebeater** searches a database that includes published fares, consolidator bargains, and special deals exclusive to 1travel.com. *Note:* The travel agencies listed by 1travel.com have paid for placement.

Bid for Travel. www.bidfortravel.com

Bid for Travel is another of the travel auction sites, similar to Priceline (see below), which are growing in popularity. In addition to airfares, Internet users can place a bid for vacation packages and hotels.

LastMinuteTravel.com. www.lastminutetravel.com

Suppliers with excess inventory come to this online agency to distribute unsold airline seats, hotel rooms, cruises, and vacation packages. It's got great deals, but you have to put up with an excess of advertisements and slow-loading graphics.

Moment's Notice. www.moments-notice.com

As the name suggests, Moment's Notice specializes in last-minute vacation deals. You can browse for free, but if you want to purchase a trip, you have to join Moment's Notice, which costs $25.

✪ New York City Vacations. www.nycvp.com

You can buy a complete vacation—including hotel stay, theater tickets, and more—from this Big Apple–dedicated online travel agency, endorsed by the New York Convention and Visitors Bureau. They'll even handle your travel arrangements if you choose. Packages always include a few admission freebies and dining discounts.

✪ Priceline.com. travel.priceline.com

Priceline lets you "name your price" for domestic and international airline tickets and hotel rooms. You select a route and dates, guarantee with a credit card, and make a bid for what you're willing to pay. If one of the airlines in

---

Know When the Sales Start

While most people learn about last-minute weekend deals from E-mail dispatches, it can be best to find out precisely when these deals become available. Because these deals are limited, they can vanish within hours—sometimes even minutes—so it pays to log on as soon as they're available. Check the pages devoted to these deals on airlines' Web pages to get the info. An example: Southwest's specials are posted at 12:01 am Tuesdays (central time). So if you're looking for a cheap flight, stay up late and check Southwest's site to grab the best new deals.

Check Your E-mail While You're on the Road

You don't have to be out of touch just because you don't carry a laptop while you travel. Web browser–based free E-mail programs make it much easier to stay in e-touch.

Just open a freemail account at a browser-based provider, such as **MSN Hotmail** (hotmail.com) or **Yahoo! Mail** (mail.yahoo.com). AOL users should check out AOL Netmail, and USA.NET (www.usa.net) comes highly recommended for functionality and security. You can find hints, tips, and a mile-long list of freemail providers at www.emailadddress.com.

Be sure to give your freemail address to the family members, friends, and colleagues with whom you'd like to stay in touch while you're in New York. All you'll need to check your freemail account while you're away from home is a Web connection, easily available at net cafes, copy shops, and cash- and credit-card Internet-access machines (often available in hotel lobbies or business centers) throughout the Big Apple. After logging on, just point the browser to **www.hotmail.com**, **www.yahoo.com**, or the address of any other service you're using. Enter your user name and password, and you'll have access to your mail, both for receiving and sending messages to friends and family back home, for just a few dollars an hour.

The **Times Square Visitors Center,** 1560 Broadway, between 46th and 47th streets (☎ 212/768-1560), has computer terminals that you can use to send E-mails courtesy of Yahoo; you can even send an electronic postcard with a photo of yourself home to Mom.

The **Internet Cafe,** 82 E. 3rd St., between First and Second avenues in the East Village (☎ 212/614-0747; www.bigmagic.com), offers direct Internet access at $2.50 per 15 minutes. **Cybercafe** (www.cyber-cafe.com), in SoHo at 273 Lafayette St., at Prince Street (☎ 212/334-5140), and in Times Square at 250 W. 49th St., between Broadway and Eighth Avenue (☎ 212/333-4109), is more expensive at $6.40 per half hour, with a half-hour minimum (you're billed $3.20 for every subsequent 15 min.). But their T1 connectivity gives you much speedier access, and they offer a full range of other cyber and copy services; there are even Macs on hand, and AOL users can even access their accounts.

Kinko's (www.kinkos.com) charges 20¢ per minute ($12 per hr.) and has four downtown locations, all open 24 hours: 100 Wall St., at Water Street (☎ 212/269-0024); near City Hall at 105 Duane St., btw. Broadway and Church Street (☎ 212/406-1220); 250 E. Houston St., between avenues A and B (☎ 212/253-9020); and 21 Astor Place, at Lafayette Street (☎ 212/228-9511).

Priceline's database has a fare lower than your bid, your credit card will automatically be charged for a ticket.

But you can't say when you want to fly—you have to accept any flight leaving between 6am and 10pm on the dates you selected, and you may have to make a stopover. No frequent-flyer miles are awarded, and tickets are nonrefundable and can't be exchanged for another flight. So if your plans change, you're out of luck. Priceline can be good for travelers who have to take off on short notice (and who are thus unable to qualify for advance-purchase discounts). But be sure to shop around first because if you overbid, you'll be required to purchase the ticket—and Priceline will pocket the difference between what it paid for the ticket and what you bid.

Priceline says that over 35% of all reasonable offers for domestic flights are being filled on the first try, with much higher fill rates on popular routes (New York to San Francisco, for example). They define "reasonable" as not more than 30% below the lowest generally available advance-purchase fare for the same route.

Smarter Living. www.smarterliving.com
Best known for its E-mail dispatch of weekend deals on 20 airlines, Smarter Living also keeps you posted about last-minute bargains.

SkyAuction.com. www.skyauction.com
An auction site with categories for airfare, travel deals, hotels, and much more.

Travelzoo.com. www.travelzoo.com
At this Internet portal, more than 150 travel companies post special deals. It features a Top 20 list of the best deals on the site, selected by its editorial staff each Wednesday night. This list is also available via an E-mailing list, free to those who sign up.

WebFlyer. www.webflyer.com
WebFlyer is a comprehensive online resource for frequent flyers and also has an excellent listing of last-minute air deals. Click on "Deal Watch" for a roundup of weekend deals on flights, hotels, and rental cars from domestic and international suppliers.

2 The Top Web Sites for New York City

By Cheryl Farr Leas

CITY GUIDES

The **New York Convention and Visitor Bureau's www.nycvisit.com** is a terrific online resource offering tons of information on the city, from trip-planning basics to tips on where to take the kids; you can even book a hotel right online.

But there's much more to be learned about New York in cyberspace than the official line. Sure, there's a lot of junk out there—but the Net boasts some terrific sites on the city, which can supply up-to-the minute news and events information; recommendations on shopping or club hopping; or just another point of view. These are the city's best general information sites:

About.com—New York City for Visitors. www.gonyc.about.com
This network of sites has a very useful New York page, hosted by an insightful and opinionated local expert. The site is most notable for its extensive list of links to museums, attractions, guided-tour operators, and the like. Those looking for a more extensive list of bed-and-breakfasts than I could include in this book will find some helpful links under "Accommodations."

✪ CitySearch. www.newyork.citysearch.com
Done in cooperation with the *Daily News* and *Time Out New York* magazine— hands down the best weekly magazine source for what's going on in the city— CitySearch is the city's hippest and most comprehensive general-information site, with reviews and listings for restaurants, shopping, hotels and inns, attractions, and nightlife. (The only other site that gives CitySearch a run for its money is New York Today, below.) They're completely up on current happenings, from the latest museum and gallery shows to the newest restaurants to

what's happening on the club scene. CitySearch does take paid advertising and hosts Web sites for advertisers, but the text is always clearly labeled (links say "editorial profile" or "advertiser's Web site"). I've never noted any bias; you'll notice, however, that advertisers' Web sites will pop up first if you do a general search.

Digital City New York. www.digitalcity.com/newyork
Much like CitySearch, but not quite as comprehensive or quick on the uptake. Still, good for an alternative view.

New York City Reference. www.panix.com/clay/nyc
Commonly referred to as New York City Reference, this handy site is a virtual hyperlink index of New York–related sites. It's regularly updated, and at press time there were about 2,000 links covering every subject area from "The Best Public Toilets" (**www.besttoilets.com**, if you want to bypass the middleman) to "Webcams: Live Pictures of New York City."

New York Magazine. www.newyorkmag.com
Insightful features on the city. But they don't give it all away—some articles are available only in the print magazine. Especially useful are the critics and columnists archives, and the "Marketplace" section for shoppers.

The New York Times Online. www.nytimes.com
The authoritative scoop from the paper of record: news, sports, arts, and much more.

✪ New York Today. www.nytoday.com
The *New York Times* created this site as a gift to those of us who wanted access to the *Times'* cultural coverage without having to wade through the main site (above), which requires you to register and pay archiving fees on past articles. Set up in an easy-access daily calendar format, the site is an expanded version of the paper's cultural coverage. You'll find even more events listings and critics' reviews in this electronic version, including museum schedules and sports events, plus the *Times'* definitive restaurant reviews.

Paper. www.papermag.com
The online version of the glossy alterna-monthly *Paper* serves as good prep for those of you who want to experience the hipper side of the city. There's opinionated coverage on clubs and bars (including extensive gay scene coverage)—virtually all downtown, of course.

✪ The Village Voice. www.villagevoice.com
Features, columns, and reviews from New York's legendary left-leaning alternative weekly. The up-to-date cultural and entertainment calendar couldn't be more extensive, and it's much easier to search on this user-friendly site than in the rather unwieldy paper. Especially good for live music coverage.

WEATHER FORECASTS
CNN Interactive. www.cnn.com
New York 1 News. www.ny1.com
The Weather Channel. www.weather.com

GETTING AROUND
MetroCard.com. www.citysearch.metrocard.com
The only official outlet for online advance purchases of MetroCard subway and bus fare cards.

Online Directory

✪ **Metropolitan Transportation Authority (MTA). www.mta.nyc.ny.us**
The official site for transportation information. Comprehensive information on the MTA subway and bus systems, plus the Long Island Rail Road, Long Island Bus, Metro-North Railroad, and the city's bridges and tunnels.

New York Transportation. www.newyorktransportation.com
A private guide to the city's buses, subway, taxis, and car services. You'll also find parking garage locations throughout the city, towing and auto-repair companies, and other transportation-related stuff.

✪ **The Port Authority of New York & New Jersey. www.panynj.gov**
This terrific official site will tell you everything you need to know about area airports—JFK, LaGuardia, and Newark—including transportation information, the latest terminal construction advisories, and more. You'll also find information on the city's bridges and tunnels (including toll and EZ Pass info), the Port Authority Bus Terminal, the PATH trains that link Manhattan and New Jersey, and ferry services.

DINING

Don't forget to also check out **New York Today** and **CitySearch,** which have the best and most up-to-date online coverage of the city's dining scene (see "City Guides," above).

CuisineNet. www.cuisinenet.com
Listings and reviews for New York and other U.S. cities. Each restaurant has a capsule review compiled by CuisineNet and numeric ratings based on survey responses from site users. For many restaurants, only two or three people have bothered to submit ratings, so they may not be statistically significant. However, comments can be instructive and fun to browse for restaurant buffs.

Zagat Survey. www.zagat.com
Reviews of top restaurants for New York and other worldwide cities. Zagat has made a name for itself as the people's choice, as its listings are based on extensive surveys.

SHOPPING

Also check out **CitySearch,** which is beginning to improve its shopping coverage, and *New York* **Magazine** (see "City Guides," above).

InShop. www.inshop.com
NYSale. www.nysale.com
Style Shop. www.styleshop.com
These free registration sites let you in on unadvertised sales taking place throughout the city. InShop is best for detailed information on retail sales, while NYSale and Style Shop are particularly useful for letting you in on unadvertised designer sample sales (in addition to retail sales).

ARTS & ENTERTAINMENT

In addition to these specific sites, don't forget to check out those listed under "City Guides" above.

THE PERFORMING ARTS

CultureFinder. www.culturefinder.com
An excellent site for all arts and entertainment things in New York City, with an emphasis on museum shows, theater, and classical music. Direct links to ticketsellers, plus exclusive discount ticket offers.

Broadway.com. **www.broadway.com**

✪ Playbill Online. **www.playbill.com or www.playbillclub.com**

TheaterMania. **www.theatermania.com**

✪ Theatre.com. **www.theatre.com**

Each of these competing commercial sites offers complete online information to Broadway and Off-Broadway shows, with links to the ticket-buying agencies once you've selected your show. I like the user-friendliness of Theatre.com best, but they all serve fundamentally the same function.

Each offers an **online theater club** that's free to join and can yield substantial savings—from 20 to 50%—on advance-purchase theater tickets for select Broadway and Off-Broadway shows. All you have to do is register, and you'll have access to discounts that can range from a few dollars to as much as 50% off regular ticket prices. You can sign up to be notified by E-mail as offers change. (TheaterMania's club only provides information this way, which I consider a downside; both Playbill and Theatre.com allow members to access offers on their sites at any time.) I like the Playbill Club best; it was the first of the bunch and its discounts are wide ranging, often including the best Broadway and Off-Broadway shows. It also offers members excellent deals at city hotels as well as dining discounts on occasion. (Theatre.com offers hotel discounts too, in a more limited fashion).

Broadway.com had not launched at press time, but they're expected to offer a similar sign-up service.

CurtainUp. **www.curtainup.com**

New York Theatre Wire. **www.nytheatre-wire.com**

These sites provide news and reviews of what's playing on the city's stages. In addition to theater, Theatre Wire also includes dance and performance art among its reviews, and has a strong alternative bent; good for those looking for something different.

Live Broadway. **www.broadway.org**

The Live Broadway site is run by the League of American Theaters and Producers and offers information and links to official Web sites for Broadway shows exclusively.

NYC/Onstage. **www.tdf.org**

Run by the Theatre Development Fund (the same people behind the TKTS discount ticket booth in Times Square). Click on NYC/ONSTAGE under "The TDF Story." The bias is toward Broadway and Off-Broadway plays, but NYC/Onstage is also a good source for chamber and orchestral music (including all Lincoln Center events), dance, opera, cabaret, and family entertainment, too. Once you've chosen an option, you can link to the appropriate ticket-selling outlet, which may be TicketMaster or TeleCharge, or you'll be provided with contact information for the theater's box office.

LIVE MUSIC & CLUB LISTINGS

Local Music.com. **www.localmusic.com**

Metropolitan Concert Hotline. **www.concerthotline.com**

Gigmania. **www.gigmania.com**

The sources for live music schedules and news. Local Music and Gigmania cover all genres and venues ranging from tiny downtown clubs to Madison Square Garden, while Metropolitan concentrates on midsize and larger venues.

PromoNY.com. **www.promony.com**
This club resource site is most useful for its online guest lists, which can supply you with access and discounted admission to select clubs.

TICKET SOURCES

TicketMaster. **www.ticketmaster.com**
This national outlet sells tickets for sports, most concerts, and some Broadway shows—all with a hefty service charge.

TeleCharge. **www.telecharge.com**
TeleCharge handles most Broadway and Off-Broadway shows and some concerts; expect a surcharge to be added to each purchase.

TicketWeb. **www.ticketweb.com**
TicketWeb also sells theater and concert tickets, generally at smaller venues like Bowery Ballroom and the Knitting Factory. Service charges are usually substantially lower than what TicketMaster tacks on.

Theatre Direct International (TDI). **www.theatredirect.com**
Keith Prowse & Co. **www.keithprowse.com**
Ticket Depot. **www.ticketdepot.com**
These reliable ticket brokers sell tickets at a premium to sold-out shows. The first two brokers specialize in theater tickets, while Ticket Depot handles all kinds of events.

For Foreign Visitors

3

You've seen it all already—the high-rises, the bustling crowds, the glittering nightlife and shopping. New York's global media profile might make it appear familiar, but movies and TV, music videos, and news images distort as much as they reflect. The gap between image and reality can make certain situations puzzling for the foreign—or even the domestic—visitor. This chapter will help prepare you for the more common issues or problems that you may encounter.

1 Preparing for Your Trip

ENTRY REQUIREMENTS

Immigration laws are a hot political issue in the United States these days, and the following requirements may have changed somewhat by the time you plan your trip. Check at any U.S. embassy or consulate for current information and requirements, or plug into the U.S. State Department's Web site at **travel.state.gov**. Click on VISA SERVICES for the latest entry requirements, while LINKS TO FOREIGN EMBASSIES will provide you with contact information for U.S. embassies and consulates worldwide.

VISAS

The U.S. State Department has a **Visa Waiver Pilot Program** allowing citizens of certain countries to enter the United States without a visa for stays of up to 90 days. At press time, this visa waiver program applied to citizens of these countries: Andorra, Argentina, Australia, Austria, Belgium, Brunei, Denmark, Finland, France, Germany, Iceland, Ireland, Italy, Japan, Liechtenstein, Luxembourg, Monaco, the Netherlands, New Zealand, Norway, Portugal, San Marino, Singapore, Slovenia, Spain, Sweden, Switzerland, the United Kingdom, and Uruguay.

Citizens of these countries need only a valid passport and a round-trip air or cruise ticket in their possession upon arrival. (Greece has been preliminarily approved, but at press time visas were still required.) If they first enter the United States, they may also visit Mexico, Canada, Bermuda, and/or the Caribbean islands and return to the United States without a visa. Further information is available from any U.S. embassy or consulate.

Canadian citizens may enter the United States without visas; they need only proof of residence.

Citizens of all other countries must have: (1) a valid passport that expires at least 6 months later than the scheduled end of their visit to the United States, and (2) a tourist visa, which may be obtained from any U.S. consulate.

OBTAINING A VISA   To obtain a visa, you must submit a completed application form (either in person or by mail) with two 1¹/₂-inch-square photos and a U.S.$45 fee, and must demonstrate binding ties to a residence abroad. Usually you can obtain a visa at once or within 24 hours, but it may take longer during the summer rush from June through August. If you cannot go in person, contact the nearest U.S. embassy or consulate for directions on applying by mail. Your travel agent or airline office may also be able to provide you with visa applications and instructions. The U.S. consulate or embassy that issues your visa will determine if you will be issued a multiple- or single-entry visa and any restrictions regarding the length of your stay.

Inquiries about visa cases and the application process can be made by calling ☎ 202/663-1225.

MEDICAL REQUIREMENTS

Unless you're arriving from an area known to be suffering from an epidemic (particularly cholera or yellow fever), inoculations or vaccinations are not required for entry into the United States. If you have a disease that requires treatment with narcotics or syringe-administered medications, carry a valid signed prescription from your physician to allay any suspicions that you may be smuggling narcotics (a serious offense that carries severe penalties in the United States).

For HIV-positive visitors, requirements for entering the United States are confusing. If an HIV-positive noncitizen applying for a nonimmigrant visa knows that HIV is a communicable disease of public health significance but checks "no" on the question about communicable diseases, INS may deny the visa because it thinks the applicant committed fraud. If a nonimmigrant visa applicant checks "yes," or if INS suspects the person is HIV positive, it will deny the visa unless the applicant asks for a special waiver for visitors. This waiver is for people visiting the United States for a short time, to attend a conference, for instance, to visit close relatives, or to receive medical treatment.

For up-to-the-minute information concerning HIV-positive travelers, contact the **HIV/AIDS Treatment Information Service** (☎ **800/HIV-0440** or 301/519-0459; www.hivatis.org), the Center for Disease Control and Prevention's **National AIDS Hotline** (☎ **800/342-2437,** or 800/344-7432 in Spanish; www.cdc.gov), or the **Gay Men's Health Crisis** (☎ **800/AIDS-NYC** or 212/807-6655; www.gmhc.org).

DRIVER'S LICENSES

Foreign driver's licenses are mostly recognized in the United States, although you may want to get an international driver's license if your home license is not written in English.

CUSTOMS

WHAT YOU CAN BRING IN   Every visitor over 21 years of age may bring in, free of duty, the following: (1) 1 liter of wine or hard liquor; (2) 200 cigarettes, 150 cigars

Immigration Questions

Automated information and live operator assistance regarding U.S. immigration policies and laws is available from the **Immigration and Naturalization Service's Customer Information Center** (☎ **800/375-5283;** www.ins.usdoj.gov), or the **New York Immigration Hotline** (☎ **718/899-4000**).

(but not from Cuba), or 3 pounds of smoking tobacco; and (3) $100 worth of gifts. These exemptions are offered to travelers who spend at least 72 hours in the United States and who have not claimed them within the preceding 6 months. Foreign tourists may bring in or take out up to $10,000 in U.S. or foreign currency with no formalities; larger sums must be declared to U.S. Customs upon entering or leaving, which includes filing form CM 4790. For more specific information regarding U.S. Customs, contact your nearest U.S. embassy or consulate, or the **U.S. Customs** office (☎ **202/927-1770;** www.customs.ustreas.gov).

WHAT YOU CAN BRING HOME   Check with your country's Customs or Foreign Affairs department for the latest guidelines—including information on items that are not allowed to be brought into your home country—just before you leave home.

U.K. citizens should contact **HM Customs & Excise Passenger Enquiries** (☎ **020/7202 4227**), or visit **www.hmce.gov.uk**.

For a clear summary of **Canadian** rules, visit the comprehensive Web site of the **Canada Customs and Revenue Agency** at **www.ccra-adrc.gc.ca**.

Citizens of **Australia** should request the helpful Australian Customs brochure *Know Before You Go,* available by calling ☎ **1-300/363-263** from within Australia, or 61-2/6275-6666 from abroad. For additional information, go online to **www. dfat.gov.au** and click on HINTS FOR AUSTRALIAN TRAVELLERS.

For New Zealand Customs information, contact **New Zealand Customs Service** at ☎ **09/359-6655,** or go online to **www.customs.govt.nz**.

INSURANCE

Although it's not required of travelers, health insurance is highly recommended. Unlike many European countries, the United States does not usually offer free or low-cost medical care to its citizens or visitors. Doctors and hospitals are expensive, and in most cases will require advance payment or proof of coverage before they render their services. Travel insurance policies can cover everything from the loss or theft of your baggage and trip cancellation to the guarantee of bail in case you're arrested. Good policies will also cover the costs of an accident, repatriation, or death. See "Health & Insurance" in chapter 2 for more information. Packages such as **Europ Assistance** in Europe are sold by automobile clubs and travel agencies at attractive rates. **Worldwide Assistance Services, Inc.** (☎ **800/777-8710,** ext. 409, or 703/204-1897; www. worldwideassistance.com) is the agent for Europe Assistance in the United States.

Though lack of health insurance may prevent you from being admitted to a hospital in nonemergencies, don't worry about being left on a street corner to die: The American way is to fix you now and bill the living daylights out of you later.

FOR BRITISH TRAVELERS   Most big travel agents offer their own insurance and will probably try to sell you their package when you book a holiday. Think before you sign. Britain's Consumers' Association recommends that you insist on seeing the policy and reading the fine print before buying travel insurance. The **Association of British Insurers** (☎ **0171/600-3333**) gives advice by phone and publishes the free *Holiday Insurance,* a guide to policy provisions and prices. You might also shop around for better deals: Try **Columbus Direct** (☎ **0171/375-0011; www.columbusdirect. co.uk**).

FOR CANADIAN TRAVELERS   Canadians should check with their provincial health plan offices or call **HealthCanada** (☎ **613/957-2991**) to find out the extent of their coverage and what documentation and receipts they must take home in case they are treated in the United States.

MONEY

CURRENCY   The U.S. monetary system is painfully simple: The most common bills (all ugly, all green) are the $1 (colloquially, a "buck"), $5, $10, and $20 denominations. There are also $2 bills (seldom encountered), $50 bills, and $100 bills (the last two are usually not welcome as payment for small purchases). Note that redesigned $100, $50, and $20 bills were introduced in the last few years, but the old-style bills are still legal tender. Expect to see redesigned $10 and $5 notes by the time you arrive.

There are six denominations of coins: 1¢ (1 cent, or a penny); 5¢ (5 cents, or a nickel); 10¢ (10 cents, or a dime); 25¢ (25 cents, or a quarter); 50¢ (50 cents, or a half dollar); and the rare $1 piece (the older, large silver dollar and the newer, small Susan B. Anthony coin). In 2000, a new gold-toned $1 piece was introduced.

CURRENCY EXCHANGE   The foreign-exchange bureaus so common in Europe are rare even at airports in the United States and nonexistent outside major cities. You'll find them in New York's prime tourist areas like Times Square, but expect to get extorted on the exchange rate.

American Express (☎ **800/AXP-TRIP;** www.americanexpress.com) has many offices throughout the city, including at the New York Hilton, 1335 Sixth Ave., at 53rd Street (☎ 212/664-7798); the New York Marriott Marquis, 1535 Broadway, in the 8th-floor lobby (☎ 212/575-6580); on the mezzanine level at Macy's Herald Square, 34th Street and Broadway (☎ 212/695-8075); and 65 Broadway, between Exchange Place and Rector Street (☎ 212/493-6500).

Thomas Cook Currency Services (☎ **800/223-9920;** www.thomascook.com) has locations throughout the city, including JFK Airport and 41 E. 42nd St. (☎ 212/883-0400). Call for additional locations.

It's best not to expect to change foreign money (or traveler's checks denominated in a currency other than U.S. dollars) at a small-town bank, or even a bank branch in New York. In fact, it's best to just leave any currency other than U.S. dollars at home—it may prove a greater nuisance to you than it's worth.

TRAVELER'S CHECKS   Though traveler's checks are widely accepted, *make sure that they're denominated in U.S. dollars,* as foreign-currency checks are often difficult to exchange. The three traveler's checks that are most widely recognized—and least likely to be denied—are **Visa, American Express,** and **Thomas Cook/MasterCard.** Be sure to record the numbers of the checks, and keep that information separately in case they get lost or stolen. Most businesses are pretty good about taking traveler's checks, but you're better off cashing them in at a bank (in small amounts, of course) and paying in cash. Remember: You'll need identification, such as a driver's license or passport, to change a traveler's check.

CREDIT CARDS & ATMs   Credit cards are the most widely used form of payment in the United States: **Visa** (BarclayCard in Britain), **MasterCard** (Eurocard in Europe, Access in Britain, Chargex in Canada), **American Express, Diners Club, Discover,** and **Carte Blanche;** you'll also find that New York vendors may accept international cards like **enRoute, Eurocard,** and **JCB,** but not as universally as AmEx, MasterCard, or Visa. There are, however, a handful of stores and restaurants that do not take credit cards, so be sure to ask in advance. And be aware that often businesses require a minimum purchase price, usually around $10 or $15, to use a credit card.

I strongly recommend that you bring at least one major credit card. Hotels, car-rental companies, and airlines usually require a credit-card imprint as a deposit against expenses, and in an emergency a credit card can be priceless.

Travel Tip

Be sure to keep a copy of all your travel papers separate from your wallet or purse, and leave a copy with someone at home should you need it faxed in an emergency.

You'll find automated teller machines (ATMs) on just about every block in Manhattan. Some ATMs will allow you to draw U.S. currency against your bank and credit cards. Check with your bank before leaving home, and remember that you will need your personal identification number (PIN) to do so. Most accept Visa, MasterCard, and American Express, as well as ATM cards from other U.S. banks. Expect to be charged up to $3 per transaction, however, if you're not using your own bank's ATM.

SAFETY

Tourist areas in Manhattan are generally safe, and the city has experienced a dramatic drop in its crime rate in recent years. Still, crime is a national problem, and U.S. urban areas tend to be less safe than those in Europe or Japan. You should always stay alert, use common sense, and trust your instincts. If you feel you're in an unsafe area or situation, you probably are and should leave as quickly as possible.

GENERAL SAFETY SUGGESTIONS   Leave your valuables at home if you can live without them. Don't display expensive cameras or flashy jewelry as you walk around the city. If you are using a map, consult it as discreetly as possible, with one eye on what's going on around you at all times.

Remember that hotels are open to the public, and in a large hotel, security may not be able to screen everyone entering. Always lock your room door—don't assume that once inside your hotel you are automatically safe and no longer need to keep an eye on your valuables or be aware of your surroundings.

Avoid deserted areas, especially at night, and don't go into public parks at night unless there's a concert or similar occasion that will attract a crowd.

For more about personal security in Manhattan, see **"Playing It Safe"** in chapter 4.

DRIVING   An inviolable rule of thumb for New York: Don't even think of driving within the city. Like many cities, New York has its own arcane rules of the road, confusing one-way streets, incomprehensible street-parking signs, and outrageously expensive parking garages. Public transportation—whether buses, subways, or taxis—will get you anywhere you want to go quickly and easily, and that's where you'll be most comfortable.

If you do drive to New York in a rental car, return it as soon as you arrive and rent another when you're ready to leave the city. Always keep your car doors locked. Never leave any packages or valuables in sight because thieves will break car windows. If someone attempts to rob you or steal your car, don't resist. Report the incident to the police department immediately.

2 Getting to the United States

In addition to the domestic airlines listed in chapter 2, many international carriers serve John F. Kennedy International and Newark airports. **British Airways** (☎ **0345/222-111** in the U.K., 800/AIRWAYS in the U.S.; www.british-airways.com) has daily service from London as well as direct flights from Manchester and Glasgow. **Virgin Atlantic** (☎ **01293/747-747** in the U.K., 800/862-8621 in the U.S.; www.virgin-atlantic.com) flies from London's Heathrow to New York.

Canadian readers might book flights on **Air Canada** (☎ 800/776-3000; www. aircanada.ca), which offers direct service from Toronto, Montréal, Ottawa, and other cities; and **Canadian Airlines** (☎ 800/426-7000; www.cdnair.ca).

Aer Lingus flies from Ireland to New York (☎ 01/886-8888 in Dublin, 800/IRISH-AIR in the U.S.; www.aerlingus.ie). The following U.S. airlines fly to New York from most major European cities: **Continental** (☎ 01293/776-464 in the U.K., 800/525-0280 in the U.S.; www.continental.com); **TWA** (☎ 0181/815-0707 in the U.K., 800/221-2000 in the U.S.; www.twa.com); **United** (☎ 0845/ 8-444-777 in the U.K., 800/538-2929 in the U.S.; www.ual.com); **American** (☎ 0181/572-5555 in the U.K., 800/433-7300 in the U.S.; www.americanair.com); and **Delta** (☎ 0800/414-767 in the U.K., 800/221-1212 in the U.S.; www.delta-air. com).

Qantas (☎ 13-13-13 in Australia, 800/227-4500 in the U.S.; www.qantas. com.au) and **Air New Zealand** (☎ 0800/737-000 in New Zealand, 800/262-1234 in the U.S.; www.airnewzealand.co.nz) fly to the West Coast and will book you straight through to New York City on a partner airline.

AIRLINE DISCOUNTS   For more money-saving airline advice, see "Getting There" in chapter 2. For the best rates, compare fares and be flexible with the dates and times of travel.

Operated by the European Travel Network, **www.discount-tickets.com** is a great online source for regular and discounted airfares to New York and other destinations around the world. You can also use this site to compare rates and book accommodations, car rentals, and tours. Click on "Special Offers" for the latest package deals. Students should also try **Campus Travel** (☎ 0171/730-2101; www.usitcampus.co.uk).

IMMIGRATION & CUSTOMS CLEARANCE   Visitors arriving by air, no matter what the port of entry, should cultivate patience and resignation before setting foot on U.S. soil. Getting through immigration control may take as long as 2 hours on some days, especially on summer weekends, so be sure to have this guidebook or something else to read. Add the time it takes to clear Customs, and you'll see that you should make a 2- to 3-hour allowance for delays when you plan your connections between international and domestic flights.

In contrast, for the traveler arriving by car or rail from Canada, the border-crossing formalities have been streamlined to the vanishing point. People traveling by air from Canada, Bermuda, and some places in the Caribbean can sometimes clear Customs and Immigration at the point of departure, which is much quicker.

If You're Traveling Beyond New York City

Some major American carriers—including Delta and Continental—offer travelers on their transatlantic or transpacific flights special low-price tickets on U.S. continental flights under the **Discover America** program (sometimes called **Visit USA,** depending on the airline). Offering one-way travel between U.S. destinations at significantly reduced prices, this coupon-based airfare program is the best and easiest way to tour the United States at low cost.

These discounted fare coupons are not available in the United States and must be purchased abroad in conjunction with your international ticket. Ask your travel agent or the airline reservations agent about this program well in advance of your departure—preferably when you buy your international ticket—since the regulations may govern your trip planning, and conditions can change without notice.

Fast Facts: For the Foreign Traveler

Also see "Fast Facts: New York City" in chapter 4 for more New York City–specific information.

Automobile Organizations   Auto clubs will supply maps, suggested routes, guidebooks, accident and bail-bond insurance, and emergency road service. The **American Automobile Association (AAA)** is the major auto club in the United States. If you belong to an auto club in your home country, inquire about AAA reciprocity before you leave. You may be able to join AAA even if you're not a member of a reciprocal club; to inquire, call ☎ **800/222-4357**, or visit **www.aaa.com**. AAA is actually an organization of regional auto clubs, so look under "AAA Automobile Club" in the White Pages of the telephone directory. AAA has a nationwide emergency road service telephone number (☎ **800/AAA-HELP**).

Automobile Rentals   To rent a car in the United States, you need a valid driver's license, a passport, and a major credit card. The minimum age is usually 25, but some companies will rent to younger people and add a surcharge. It's a good idea to buy maximum insurance coverage unless you're positive your own auto or credit-card insurance is sufficient. All major car-rental agencies have branches in Manhattan; try **Hertz** (☎ **800/654-3131**; www.hertz.com), **National** (☎ **800/227-7368**; www.nationalcar.com), or **Avis** (☎ **800/230-4898**; www.avis.com). Stick to the major companies because what you might save with smaller companies might not be worth the headache if you have mechanical troubles on the road. Rates vary, so it pays to call around.

Business Hours   See "Fast Facts: New York City" in chapter 4.

Currency & Currency Exchange   See "Money" under "Preparing for Your Trip," earlier in this chapter. For the latest market conversion rates, point your Internet browser to **www.cnn.com/travel/currency** or **www.x-rates.com**.

Drinking Laws   The legal age for purchase and consumption of alcoholic beverages is 21; proof of age is required and often requested at bars, nightclubs, and restaurants, so it's always a good idea to bring ID when you go out. Liquor stores, the only retail outlets for wine as well as hard liquor in New York, are closed on Sunday, holidays, and election days while the polls are open. Beer can be purchased in grocery stores and delis all day Monday through Saturday and Sunday after noon.

Do not carry open containers of alcohol in your car or any public area that isn't zoned for alcohol consumption. The police can, and probably will, fine you on the spot. And nothing will ruin your trip faster than getting a citation for DUI ("driving under the influence"), so don't even think about driving while intoxicated.

Electricity   Like Canada, the United States uses 110 to 120 volts AC (60 cycles), compared to 220 to 240 volts AC (50 cycles) in most of Europe, Australia, and New Zealand. If your small appliances use 220 to 240 volts, you'll need a 110-volt transformer and a plug adapter with two flat parallel pins to operate them here. Downward converters that change 220–240 volts to 110–120 volts are difficult to find in the United States, so bring one with you.

Embassies/Consulates   All embassies are in Washington, D.C. Some countries have consulates general in major U.S. cities, and most have a mission to the

United Nations in New York City. If your country isn't listed below, call for directory information in Washington, D.C. (☎ **202/555-1212**) or point your Web browser to **www.embassy.org/embassies** for the location and phone number of your national embassy.

Australia: Embassy, 1601 Massachusetts Ave. NW, Washington, DC 20036 (☎ 202/797-3000; www.austemb.org); Consulate General, 150 E. 42nd St., New York, NY 10117 (☎ 212/351-6500). **Canada:** Embassy, 501 Pennsylvania Ave. NW, Washington, DC 20001 (☎ 202/682-1740; www.canadianembassy.org); Consulate General, 1251 Ave. of the Americas, New York, NY 10020 (☎ 212/596-1628; www.canada-ny.com). **Ireland:** Embassy, 2234 Massachusetts Ave. NW, Washington, DC 20008 (☎ 202/462-3939; www.irelandemb. org); Consulate General, 345 Park Ave., New York, NY 10154-0037 (☎ 212/ 319-2555). **Japan:** Embassy, 2520 Massachusetts Ave. NW, Washington, DC 20008 (☎ 202/238-6700; www.embjapan.org). **New Zealand:** Embassy, 37 Observatory Circle, Washington, DC 20008 (☎ 202/328-4800; www.emb. com/nzemb); Consulate General, 780 Third Ave., New York, NY, 10017 (☎ 212/832-4038). **United Kingdom:** Embassy, 3100 Massachusetts Ave. NW, Washington, DC 20008 (☎ 202/588-6500; www.britainusa.com); Consulate General, 845 Third Ave., New York, NY 10022 (☎ 212/745-0200; www. britainusa. com/bis/consular/ny/ny.stm).

Emergencies   Call ☎ **911** to report a fire, call the police, or get an ambulance anywhere in the United States. This is a toll-free call (no coins are required at public telephones).

If you have a medical emergency that doesn't require an ambulance, you can walk into a hospital's 24-hour emergency room (usually a separate entrance). For a list of hospitals, see "Fast Facts: New York City" in chapter 4. Because emergency rooms are often crowded and waits are long, one of the walk-in medical centers listed under "Finding a Doctor" under "Health & Insurance" in chapter 2 might be a better option. Otherwise, call ☎ **212/737-2333,** a referral service available from 8am to midnight, for doctors who make house calls.

Gasoline (Petrol)   Petrol is known as gasoline (or simply "gas") in the United States, and petrol stations are known as both gas stations and service stations. Gasoline costs about half as much here as it does in Europe (though prices were rising at press time), and taxes are already included in the printed price. One U.S. gallon equals 3.8 liters or .85 Imperial gallons.

Holidays   Banks, government offices, post offices, and many stores, restaurants, and museums are closed on the following legal national holidays: January 1 (New Year's Day), the third Monday in January (Martin Luther King Jr. Day), the third Monday in February (Presidents' Day, Washington's Birthday), the last Monday in May (Memorial Day), July 4 (Independence Day), the first Monday in September (Labor Day), the second Monday in October (Columbus Day), November 11 (Veterans' Day/Armistice Day), the fourth Thursday in November (Thanksgiving Day), and December 25 (Christmas). Also, the Tuesday following the first Monday in November is Election Day and is a federal government holiday in presidential-election years (held every 4 years, in 2000 and next in 2004).

Legal Aid   Most foreign tourists will probably never become involved with the American legal system. If you are stopped for a minor infraction (for example, of the highway code, such as speeding), never attempt to pay the fine directly to a police officer; this could be construed as attempted bribery, a much more serious crime. If it's a traffic infraction, do not get out of the car; stay seated with your hands on the steering wheel until the officer approaches you. Pay fines by mail, or directly into the hands of the clerk of the court. If accused of a more serious offense, say and do nothing before consulting a lawyer. Here the burden is on the state to prove a person's guilt beyond a reasonable doubt, and everyone has the right to remain silent, whether he or she is suspected of a crime or actually arrested. Once arrested, a person can make one telephone call to a party of his or her choice. Call your embassy or consulate.

Mail   Generally found at intersections, mailboxes are blue with a white eagle logo and carry the inscription U.S. MAIL. If your mail is addressed to a U.S. destination, don't forget to add the five-digit postal code (or ZIP code), after the two-letter abbreviation of the state to which the mail is addressed.

At press time, domestic postage rates were 20¢ for a postcard and 33¢ for a letter. For international mail, a first-class letter of up to one-half ounce costs 60¢ (48¢ to Canada and 40¢ to Mexico); a first-class postcard costs 55¢ (45¢ to Canada and 35¢ to Mexico); and a preprinted postal aerogramme costs 60¢. Point your Web browser to **new.usps.com** for complete U.S. postal information, or call ☎ **800/275-8777** for information on the nearest post office. Most branches are open Monday through Friday from 8am to 5 or 6pm, and Saturday from 9am to 3pm.

Newspapers/Magazines   In addition to the *New York Times* and other city papers, many newsstands carry a selection of international newspapers and magazines. For nearly all major newspapers and magazines from around the world, head to **Universal News & Magazines,** 977 Eighth Ave., at 57th Street (☎ **212/459-0932**), or **Hotalings News Agency,** inside the Times Square Visitor Center at 1560 Broadway, between 46th and 47th streets (☎ **212/ 840-1868**).

Taxes   There is no value-added tax (VAT) or other indirect tax at the national level, but every state, county, and city has the right to levy its own local tax on all purchases, including hotel and restaurant checks, airline tickets, and so on. Sales tax is usually not included in the price tags on merchandise but is added at the cash register. These taxes aren't refundable. In New York City, the **sales tax** is 8.25%, but there is no sales tax on clothing purchases under $110. The **hotel tax** is 13.25% plus $2 per room per night (including sales tax). The **parking garage tax,** added to already high basic fees, is 18.25%.

Telephone & Fax   The telephone system in the United States is run by private corporations, so rates, especially for long-distance service and operator-assisted calls, can vary widely. Generally, hotel surcharges on long-distance and local calls are astronomical, so you're usually better off using a **public pay telephone,** which you'll find clearly marked in most public buildings and private establishments as well as in hotel lobbies and on the street. Many convenience stores and newsstands sell **prepaid calling cards** in denominations up to $50; these can be the least expensive way to call home. Many public phones at airports now accept American Express, MasterCard, and Visa credit cards. **Local calls** made from public pay phones usually cost 25¢ for the first 5 minutes, but sometimes it's 35¢. Pay phones do not accept pennies, and few will take anything larger than a quarter.

Most long-distance and international calls can be dialed directly from any phone. **For calls within the United States and to Canada,** dial 1 followed by the area code and the seven-digit number. **For other international calls,** dial

011 followed by the country code, city code, and the telephone number of the person you are calling. Some country and city codes are as follows: **Australia** 61, Melbourne 3, Sydney 2; **Ireland** 353, Dublin 1; **New Zealand** 64, Auckland 9, Wellington 4; **United Kingdom** 44, Belfast 232, Birmingham 21, Glasgow 41, London 71 or 81. If you're calling the **United States** from another country, the country code is 01.

For **reversed-charge, collect, operator-assisted, and person-to-person calls,** dial 0 (the number zero) followed by the area code and number you want; an operator will then come on the line, and you should specify that you are calling collect, or person-to-person, or both. If your operator-assisted call is international, ask for the overseas operator.

For local and national directory assistance ("information"), dial ☎ 411.

Most hotels have **fax machines** available for guest use (be sure to ask about the charge to use it), and many hotel rooms even have in-room fax machines. Receiving faxes is usually free (always ask first if it matters, though), but a less expensive way to send faxes may be at stores such as **Mail Boxes Etc.,** a national chain of packing service shops (look in the Yellow Pages under "Packing Services").

There are two kinds of telephone directories in the United States. The so-called **White Pages** list private households and business subscribers in alphabetical order. The inside front cover lists emergency numbers for police, fire, ambulance, the poison-control center, crime-victims hotline, and so on. The first few pages will tell you how to make long-distance and international calls, complete with country codes and area codes. Government numbers are usually printed on blue paper within the White Pages. Printed on yellow paper, the **Yellow Pages** list all local services, businesses, industries, and houses of worship according to activity with an index at the front or back. (Drugstores/pharmacies and restaurants are also listed by geographic location.) The Yellow Pages also include city plans or detailed area maps, postal ZIP codes, and public transportation routes. A useful online "yellow pages" for finding phone numbers and addresses in New York and other U.S. cities include **www.yp.ameritech.net**.

Time The continental United States is divided into four time zones: eastern standard time (EST), the time zone New York is in, which is 5 hours behind Greenwich mean time (GMT); central standard time (CST); mountain standard time (MST); and Pacific standard time (PST). Alaska and Hawaii have their own zones. For example, noon in New York City (EST) is 11am in Chicago (CST), 10am in Denver (MST), 9am in Los Angeles (PST), 8am in Anchorage (AST), and 7am in Honolulu (HST).

Daylight saving time is in effect from 1am on the first Sunday in April through 1am on the last Sunday in October, except in Arizona, Hawaii, part of Indiana, and Puerto Rico. Daylight saving time moves the clock 1 hour ahead of standard time. When daylight saving time is in effect, New York is only 4 hours behind Greenwich mean time.

For the correct local time in New York, dial ☎ 212/976-1616.

Travel Tip
───

Calls to area codes **800, 888,** and **877** are toll-free. However, calls to numbers in area codes **700** and **900** (chat lines, bulletin boards, "dating" services, and so on) can be very expensive—usually a charge of 95¢ to $3 or more per minute, and they sometimes have minimum charges that can run as high as $15 or more.

───

Tipping   Tips are a very important part of certain workers' salaries, so it's necessary to leave appropriate gratuities. Unlike in most of Europe, tips aren't automatically added to restaurant and hotel bills. In restaurants, a tip to the wait person of 15% to 20% of the total check is customary; in New York City, just double the 8.25% tax to figure the appropriate tip.

Other tipping guidelines: 15% to 20% of the fare to taxi drivers; 10% to 15% of the tab to bartenders; $1 to $2 per bag to bellhops; at least $1 per day to hotel maids; $1 per item to checkroom attendants; $1 to valet parking attendants; and 15% to 20% to hairdressers. Tipping theater ushers, gas station attendants, and cafeteria and fast-food restaurant employees isn't expected.

Toilets   In general, you won't find public toilets or "rest rooms" on the streets in New York, but they can be found in hotel lobbies, bars, restaurants, museums, department stores, or railway and bus stations. See "Rest Rooms" under "Fast Facts: New York City" in chapter 4.

Traveler's Assistance   See "Fast Facts: New York City" in chapter 4.

4 Getting to Know New York City

This chapter gives you an insider's take on Manhattan's most distinctive neighborhoods and streets, tells you how to get around town, and serves as a handy reference to everything from personal safety to libraries and liquor.

1 Orientation

VISITOR INFORMATION
INFORMATION OFFICES

☼ The **Times Square Visitors Center,** 1560 Broadway, between 46th and 47th streets (where Broadway meets Seventh Ave.), across from the TKTS booth (☎ **212/768-1560;** www.timessquarebid.org), is the city's top info stop. This pleasant and attractive center features a helpful information desk offering loads of citywide information. There's also a tour desk selling tickets for Gray Line bus tours and Circle Line boat tours; a Metropolitan Transportation Authority (MTA) desk staffed to sell MetroCard fare cards, provide public transit maps, and answer all of your questions on the transit system; a Broadway Ticket Center providing show information and selling full-price show tickets; ATMs and currency exchange machines; computer terminals with free Internet access courtesy of Yahoo; an international newsstand; and more. It's open daily from 8am to 8pm.

• The New York Convention and Visitors Bureau runs the **NYCVB Visitor Information Center** at 810 Seventh Ave., between 52nd and 53rd streets. In addition to loads of information on citywide attractions and a multilingual information counselor on hand to answer questions, the center also has interactive terminals that provide free touch-screen access to visitor information via Citysearch and sell advance tickets to major attractions (which can save you from standing in long ticket lines once you arrive). There's also an ATM, a gift shop, and a bank of phones that connect you directly with American Express card member services. The center is open Monday through Friday from 8:30am to 6pm, Saturday and Sunday from 9am to 5pm. For over-the-phone assistance, call ☎ **212/484-1222.**

• **Grand Central Partnership** runs a staffed information window on the main concourse of Grand Central Terminal, East

42nd Street at the corner of Vanderbilt Avenue (☎ **212/883-2420;** www. grandcentralterminal.com). It's open daily from 9am to 6pm.

- **34th Street Partnership** operates a visitor information kiosk in Penn Station, Seventh Avenue between 31st and 33rd streets (☎ **212/868-0521**), that's well stocked with brochures and staffed Monday through Friday from 8:30am to 5:30pm and Saturday and Sunday from 9am to 6pm.

- The **Lower East Side Business Improvement District** operates a neighborhood visitor center at 261 Broome St., between Orchard and Allen streets (☎ **888/VALUES-4-U** or 212/226-9010), that's open Sunday through Friday from 10am to 4pm (sometimes later). Stop in for an Orchard Street Bargain District shopping guide (which they can also send you in advance), plus other information on this historic yet newly hip 'hood.

PUBLICATIONS

For comprehensive listings of films, concerts, performances, sporting events, museum and gallery exhibits, street fairs, and special events, there are many local publications to choose from. The following are your best bets:

- The *New York Times* (**www.nytimes.com** or **www.nytoday.com**) features terrific arts and entertainment coverage, particularly in the two-part Friday "Weekend" section and the Sunday "Arts & Leisure" section. Both days boast full guides to the latest happenings in Broadway and Off-Broadway theater, classical music, dance, pop and jazz, film, and the art world. Friday is particularly good for cabaret, family fun, and general-interest recreational and sightseeing events.

- *Time Out New York* (**www.timeoutny.com**) is my favorite weekly magazine. Dedicated to weekly goings-on, it's attractive, well organized, and easy to use. *TONY* features excellent coverage in all categories, from live music, theater, and clubs (gay and straight) to museum shows, dance events, book and poetry readings, and kids' stuff. The regular "Check Out" section, unequaled in any other listings magazine, will fill you in on upcoming sample and close-out sales, crafts and antiques shows, and other shopping-related scoop. A new issue hits newsstands every Thursday.

- The free weekly *Village Voice* (**www.villagevoice.com**), the city's legendary alterna-paper, is available late Tuesday downtown and early Wednesday in the rest of the city. From classical music to clubs, the arts and entertainment coverage couldn't be more extensive, and just about every live music venue advertises its shows here. But I find the paper a bit unwieldy to navigate, and the exposé tone of its features can be tiresome.

Other useful weekly rags include the glossy *New York* magazine (**www.newyorkmag. com**), whose "Cue" section is a selective guide to city arts and entertainment, and the *New Yorker,* which features an artsy "Goings On About Town" section at the front of the magazine. Monthly *Paper* (**www.papermag.com**) is a glossy alterna-mag that serves as good prep for those of you who want to experience the hipper side of the city.

CITY LAYOUT

Open the sheet map that comes free with this book and you'll see the city is comprised of five boroughs: **Manhattan,** where most of the visitor action is; the **Bronx,** the only borough connected to the mainland United States; **Queens,** where Kennedy and LaGuardia airports are located and which borders the Atlantic Ocean and occupies part of Long Island; **Brooklyn,** south of Queens, which is also on Long Island and is famed for its attitude, accent, and Atlantic-front Coney Island; and **Staten Island,** the least populous borough, bordering Upper New York Bay on one side and the Atlantic Ocean on the other.

When most visitors envision New York, they think of Manhattan, the long finger-shaped island pointing southwest off the mainland—surrounded by the Harlem River to the north, the Hudson River to the west, the East River (really an estuary) to the east, and the fabulous expanse of Upper New York Bay to the south. Despite the fact that it's the city's smallest borough ($13^1/2$ miles long, $2^1/4$ miles wide, 22 square miles), Manhattan contains the city's most famous attractions, buildings, and cultural institutions. For that reason, all of the accommodations and most of the restaurants suggested in this book are in Manhattan.

In most of Manhattan, finding your way around is a snap because of the logical, well-executed grid system by which the streets are numbered. If you can discern uptown and downtown, and East Side and West Side, you can find your way around pretty easily. In real terms, **uptown** means north of where you happen to be and **downtown** means south, although sometimes these labels have vague psychographical meanings (generally speaking, "uptown" chic vs. "downtown" bohemianism).

Avenues run north and south (uptown and downtown). Most are numbered. **Fifth Avenue** divides the East Side from the West Side of town, and serves as the eastern border of Central Park north of 59th Street. **First Avenue** is all the way east and **Twelfth Avenue** is all the way west. The three most important unnumbered avenues on the East Side you should know are between Third and Fifth avenues: **Madison** (east of Fifth), **Park** (east of Madison), and **Lexington** (east of Park, just west of Third). Important unnumbered avenues on the West Side are **Avenue of the Americas,** which all New Yorkers call Sixth Avenue; **Central Park West,** which is what Eighth Avenue north of 59th Street is called as it borders Central Park on the west (hence the name); **Columbus Avenue,** which is what Ninth Avenue is called north of 59th Street; and **Amsterdam Avenue,** or Tenth Avenue north of 59th.

Broadway is the exception to the rule—it's the only major avenue that doesn't run uptown–downtown. It cuts a diagonal path across the island, from the northwest tip down to the southeast corner. As it crosses most major avenues, it creates **squares** (Times Sq., Herald Sq., Madison Sq., and Union Sq., for example).

Streets run east–west (crosstown) and are numbered consecutively as they proceed uptown from Houston (HOUSE-ton) Street. So to go uptown, simply walk north of, or to a higher-numbered street than, where you are. Downtown is south of (or a lower-numbered street than) your current location. If you can see a major landmark like the Empire State Building or the World Trade Center, it's easy to determine uptown from downtown if you know what street you are on and remember that the former is on 34th Street and the latter near the southern tip of the island.

As I've already mentioned, Fifth Avenue is the dividing line between the **East Side** and **West Side** of town (except below Washington Sq., where Broadway serves that function). On the East Side of Fifth Avenue, streets are numbered with the distinction "East"; on the West Side of that avenue they are numbered "West." East 51st Street, for example, begins at Fifth Avenue and runs east to the East River, while West 51st Street begins at Fifth Avenue and runs west to the Hudson River.

If you're looking for a particular address, remember that even-numbered street addresses are on the south side of streets and odd-numbered addresses are on the north. Street addresses increase by about 50 per block starting at Fifth Avenue. For example, nos. 1 to 50 East are just about between Fifth and Madison avenues, while nos. 1 to 50

Orientation Tips

I've indicated the cross streets for all destinations in this book, but be sure to ask for the cross street (or avenue) if you're ever calling for an address.

When you give a taxi driver an address, always specify the cross streets. New Yorkers, even most cab drivers, probably wouldn't know where to find 994 Second Ave., but they do know where to find 51st and Second. If you're heading to the restaurant Le Bernadin, for example, tell them that it's on 51st Street between Sixth and Seventh avenues. The exact number (in this case, no. 155) is given only as a further precision.

If you have only the numbered address on an avenue and need to figure out the cross street, put new batteries in your calculator and refer to the address locator in the front of the Yellow Pages.

West are just about between Fifth and Sixth avenues. Traffic generally runs east on even-numbered streets and west on odd-numbered streets, with a few exceptions, like the major east–west thoroughfares—**14th, 23rd, 34th, 42nd, 57th, 72nd, 79th, 86th,** and so on—which have two-way traffic. Therefore 28 W. 23rd St. is a short walk west of Fifth Avenue; 325 E. 35th St. would be a few blocks east of Fifth.

Avenue addresses are irregular. For example, 994 Second Ave. is at East 51st Street, but so is 320 Park Ave. Thus, it's important to know a building's cross street to find it easily.

Unfortunately, these rules don't apply to neighborhoods in Lower Manhattan, south of 14th Street—like Wall Street, Chinatown, SoHo, TriBeCa, the Village—since they sprang up before engineers devised this brilliant grid scheme. A good map is essential when exploring these areas.

STREET MAPS   You'll find a useful pull-out map of Manhattan at the back of this book. There's also a decent one available for free as part of the **Official NYC Visitor Kit** if you write ahead for information (see "Visitor Information" in chapter 2); you can also pick it up for free at most of the visitor centers listed above.

Even with all these freebies at hand, I suggest investing in a map with more features if you really want to zip around the city like a pro. **Hagstrom** maps are my favorites because they feature block-by-block street numbering—so instead of trying to guess the cross street for 125 Prince St., you can see right on your map that it's Greene Street. Stephen Van Dam's **"New York City Unfolds,"** a pop-up map that unfolds and refolds like an origami flower, is a good idea because it's easy to handle on the run and pack away into a purse or pocket; it can also be read discreetly, which is a major deterrent to crime. These and other visitor-friendly maps are available at just about any good bookstore, including the Barnes & Noble and Borders Books & Music branches around town; see chapter 8 for locations.

Manhattan's Neighborhoods in Brief

Since they grew up over the course of hundreds of years, Manhattan neighborhoods have multiple, splintered personalities and fluid boundaries. Still, it's relatively easy to agree upon what they stand for in general terms—so if you stop a New Yorker on the street and ask them to point you to, say, the Upper West Side or the Flatiron District, they'll know where you want to go. From south to north, here is how I've defined Manhattan's neighborhoods throughout this book.

DOWNTOWN

Lower Manhattan: South Street Seaport & the Financial District   At one time, this was New York. Originally established by the Dutch in 1625 (hence the city's original name, Nieuw Amsterdam), the first settlements sprung up here, on the southern tip of Manhattan island, and everything uptown was farm country and wilderness. While all that's changed, this is still the best place in the city to search for the past. (The Wall Street and Financial District walking tour in chapter 7 can guide you.)

Lower Manhattan constitutes everything south of Chambers Street. **Battery Park,** the point of departure for the Statue of Liberty, Ellis Island, and Staten Island, is on the very south tip of the island. The **South Street Seaport,** now touristy but still a reminder of times of when shipping was the lifeblood of the city, lies a bit north on the east coast; it's just south of the Brooklyn Bridge, which stands proudly as the ultimate engineering achievement of New York's 19th-century Industrial Age.

The rest of the area is considered the **Financial District.** It's anchored by the towering **World Trade Center** (also known as the Twin Towers), with the World Financial Center complex and residential Battery Park City to the west, and Wall Street—now a state of mind much grander than the actual narrow street itself—running crosstown a little south and to the east. **City Hall** is at the northern border of the district, abutting Chambers Street (look for City Hall Park on the map). Most of the streets of this neighborhood are narrow concrete canyons, with Broadway serving as the main uptown–downtown artery.

Just about all of the major subway lines congregate here before they either end or head to Brooklyn (the Sixth Ave. B, D, F, Q line being the chief exception—it crosses into Brooklyn from the Lower East Side, over the Manhattan Bridge).

During the week this neighborhood is the heart of capitalism and city politics, and the sidewalks are crowded with the business-suit set. The neighborhood still feels rather desolate after work and on the weekends, despite the fact that some office buildings have been redeveloped into high-end apartments. This may sound like the most romantic time to explore the area, but it's actually more fun to be here at the height of the hustle and bustle, between 8am and 6pm on weekdays. Still, you might consider staying down here, especially if you're visiting on the weekend or during the holidays, when your dollars can go a lot further in the luxury hotels that business travelers have abandoned for home.

TriBeCa   Bordered by the Hudson River to the west, the area north of Chambers Street, west of Broadway, and south of Canal Street is the *Tri*angle *Be*low *Ca*nal Street, or TriBeCa. Since the 1980s, as SoHo became saturated with chic, the spillover has been quietly transforming TriBeCa into one of the city's hippest residential neighborhoods, where celebrities and families quietly coexist in cast-iron warehouses converted into spacious, expensive loft apartments. Artists' lofts and galleries as well as hip antiques and design shops pepper the area, as do as some of the city's best restaurants. Robert DeNiro gave the neighborhood a tremendous boost when he established the TriBeCa Film Center, and Miramax headquarters gave the area further capitalist-chic cachet. Still, historic streets like White (especially the Federal-style building at no. 2) and Harrison (the complete stretch west from Greenwich St.) evoke a bygone, more human-scaled New York, as do a few hold-out businesses and old-world pubs. I love this neighborhood because it seems to have brought together the old city and the new without bastardizing either. And because retail spaces are usually a few doors apart rather than right on top of one another, it also manages to be more peaceful than similarly popular neighborhoods.

Manhattan Neighborhoods

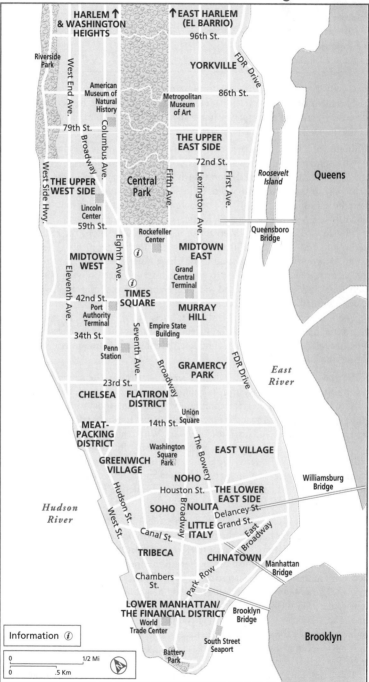

The main uptown–downtown drag is **West Broadway** (2 blocks to the west of
Broadway), and the main subway line is the 1/9, which stops at Franklin in the heart
of the 'hood. Take your map; the streets are a maze.

Chinatown   New York City's most famous ethnic enclave is bursting past its traditional boundaries and encroaching on Little Italy, much to the chagrin of civic fathers
there. The former marshlands northeast of City Hall and below Canal Street, from
Broadway to the Bowery, are where Chinese immigrants arriving from San Francisco
were forced to live in the 1870s. This booming neighborhood is now a conglomera-
tion of Asian populations. As such, it offers tasty cheap eats in cuisines from Szechuan
to Hunan to Cantonese to Vietnamese to Thai. Exotic shops offer strange foods,
herbs, and souvenirs. Bargains on clothing and leather are plenty. The area is also
home to sweatshops, however, and doesn't have quite the quaint character you'd find
in San Francisco. Still, it's a blast to walk down Canal Street, peering into the myriad
electronics and luggage stores and watching crabs cut loose from their handlers at the
exotic fish markets.

The Grand Street (B, D, Q) and Canal Street (J, M, Z, N, R, 6) stations will get
you to the heart of the action. The streets are crowded during the day and empty out
after around 9pm; they remain quite safe, but the neighborhood is more enjoyable
during the bustle.

Little Italy   Nearby is Little Italy, just as ethnic if not quite so vibrant, and compelling for its own culinary treats. Traditionally the area east of Broadway between
Houston and Canal streets, the community is shrinking today, due to the encroach-
ment of thriving Chinatown. It's now limited mainly to **Mulberry Street,** where you'll
find most restaurants, and just a few offshoots. With rents going up in the increasingly
trendy Lower East Side, a few chic spots are moving in, further intruding upon the
old-world landscape. To reach Little Italy, your best bet is to walk up Mulberry Street
from the Grand Street Station, or east from the Spring Street station on the no. 6 line.
September, when Mulberry Street comes alive during the Feast of San Gennaro, is a
great time to visit.

Lower East Side   Of all the successive waves of immigrants and refugees who passed
through this densely populated tenement neighborhood from the mid–19th century
to the 1920s, the Eastern European Jews left the most lasting impression here. Drugs
and crime ultimately supplanted the Jewish communities, which first popped up
between Houston and Canal streets, east of the Bowery, dragging the Lower East Side
into the gutter—until recently, that is. The neighborhood has experienced quite a
renaissance over the last few years; lots of hip Generation Y–targeted bars, clubs, and
boutiques have sprung up, prompting complaints from old-time residents who seem
to have preferred the desolation and crime of the old days. Still, the area can be dicey
in spots—not to mention more than a tad grungy—and should be explored with cau-
tion after dark.

There are some remnants of what was once the largest Jewish population in
America along **Orchard Street,** where you'll find great bargain hunting in its many
old-world fabric and clothing stores still thriving between the club-clothes boutiques

and trendy lounges. There's a good visitor center run by the neighborhood business improvement district, where you can get your bearings and pick up a shopping guide, just around the corner at 261 Broome St. Keep in mind that the old-world shops (and the visitor center) close early on Friday afternoon and all day on Saturday (the Jewish Sabbath). The trendy set can be found mostly along Orchard and Ludlow streets south of Houston and north of Delancey, with more new shops, bars, and restaurants popping up in the blocks to the east every day.

This area is not well served by the subway system (one cause for its years of decline), so your best bet is to take the F train to Second Avenue and walk east on Houston; when you see Katz's Deli, you'll know you've arrived.

SoHo & NoLiTa   No relation to the London neighborhood of the same name, **SoHo** got its moniker as an abbreviation of "South of Houston Street" (pronounced HOUSE-ton). This super-fashionable neighborhood extends down to Canal Street, between Sixth Avenue to the west and Lafayette Street (1 block east of Broadway) to the east. It's easily accessible by subway: Take the B, D, F, or Q train to the Broadway–Lafayette stop; the N, R to the Prince Street Station; or the C, E to Spring Street.

An industrial zone during the 19th century, SoHo retains the impressive cast-iron architecture of the era, and in many places, cobblestone peeks out from beneath the street's asphalt. In the early 1960s, cutting-edge artists began occupying the drab and deteriorating buildings, soon turning it into the trendiest neighborhood in the city. SoHo is now a prime example of urban gentrification and a major New York attraction thanks to its impeccably restored buildings, influential arts scene, fashionable restaurants, and stylish boutiques. On weekends, the cobbled streets and narrow sidewalks are crowded with gallery-goers and shoppers, with the prime action being between Broadway and Sullivan Street north of Grand Street.

Some critics claim that SoHo is becoming a victim of its own popularity—witness the recent departure of several imaginative galleries and independent boutiques that fled to TriBeCa and Chelsea as well as the influx of suburban mall-style stores like J. Crew, Victoria's Secret, and Smith & Hawken. However, SoHo is still one of the best shopping neighborhoods in the city, and few are more fun to browse. High-end street peddlers set up along the boutique-lined sidewalks, hawking silver jewelry, coffee-table books, and their own art. At night, the neighborhood is transformed into a terrific, albeit pricey, dining and bar-hopping neighborhood. You can even stay here now, thanks to the introduction of two super-trendy hotels, the Mercer and the SoHo Grand.

In recent years SoHo has been crawling its way east, taking over Mott and Mulberry streets—and white-hot Elizabeth Street in particular—north of Kenmare Street, an area now known as **NoLiTa** for its *No*rth of *Li*ttle *Ita*ly location. NoLiTa is becoming increasingly well known for its hot shopping prospects, which include a number of pricey antiques and home design stores. Taking the 6 to Spring Street will get you closest by subway, but it's just a short walk east from SoHo proper.

East Village & NoHo   The **East Village,** which extends between 14th Street and Houston Street, from Broadway east to First Avenue and beyond to Alphabet City—avenues A, B, C, and D—is where the city's real Bohemia has gone. Once, flower children tripped along St. Mark's Place and listened to music at the Fillmore East; now the East Village is a fascinating mix of affordable ethnic and trendy restaurants, upstart clothing designers and kitschy boutiques, punk-rock clubs (yep, still) and folk cafes, all of which give the neighborhood a youthful vibe. A half-dozen Off-Broadway theaters also call this place home.

The gentrification that has swept the city has made a huge impact on the East Village, but there's still a seedy element that some of you won't find appealing. Now yuppies and other ladder-climbing types make their homes alongside old-world Russian immigrants who have lived in the neighborhood forever, and the cross-dressers and squatters who settled here in between. The neighborhood still embraces great ethnic diversity, with strong elements of its Ukrainian and Irish heritage, while more recent immigrants have taken over Sixth Street between First and Second avenues, turning it into a haven of cheap eats known as **Little India.**

The East Village isn't very accessible by subway; unless you're traveling along 14th Street (the L line will drop you off at Third and First aves.), your best bet is to take the N, R to 8th Street or the 6 to Astor Place and walk east.

Until 1998 or so, Alphabet City resisted gentrification and remained a haven of drug dealers and other unsavory types. No more. Bolstered by a major real estate boom, this way-east area of the East Village has blossomed, especially among New York's young Internet industry techies, who have a few bucks to spend. French bistros and smart shops are popping up on every corner. Nevertheless, the neighborhood can get deserted late at night since it's generally the province of locals and so far off the subway line, so know where you're going if you venture out here.

The southwestern section of the East Village, around Broadway and Lafayette between Bleecker and 4th streets, is called NoHo (for *No*rth of *Ho*uston), and has a completely different character. As you might have guessed from its name, this area has developed much more like its neighbor to the south, SoHo. Here you'll find a crop of trendy lounges, stylish restaurants, cutting-edge designers, and upscale antiques shops. NoHo is wonderful fun to browse; the Bleecker Street stop on the no. 6 line will land you right in the heart of it, and the Broadway/Lafayette stop on B, D, F, Q lines will drop you right at its edge.

Greenwich Village   Tree-lined streets crisscross and wind, following ancient streams and cow paths. Each block reveals yet another row of Greek Revival town houses, a well-preserved Federal-style house, or a peaceful courtyard or square. This is "the Village," from Broadway west to the Hudson River, bordered by Houston Street to the south and 14th Street to the north. It defies Manhattan's orderly grid system with streets that predate it, virtually every one choc-a-block with activity, and unless you live here, it may be impossible to master the lay of the land—so be sure to take a map along as you explore.

The Seventh Avenue line (1, 2, 3, 9) is the area's main subway artery, while the West 4th Street stop (where the A, C, E lines meet the B, D, F, Q lines) serves as its central hub.

Nineteenth-century artists like Mark Twain, Edgar Allan Poe, Henry James, and Winslow Homer first gave the Village its reputation for embracing the unconventional. Groundbreaking artists like Edward Hopper and Jackson Pollack were drawn in, as were writers like Eugene O'Neill, e.e. cummings, and Dylan Thomas. Radical thinkers from John Reed to Upton Sinclair basked in the neighborhood's liberal ethos, and beatniks Allen Ginsberg, Jack Kerouac, and William Burroughs dug the free-swinging atmosphere. Now the Village is the roost of choice for the young celebrity set, with the likes of Gwyneth Paltrow, the Beastie Boys, and Matthew Broderick and Sarah Jessica Parker drawn by its historic, low-rise, laid-back charms. Gentrification and escalating real-estate values conspire to push out the artistic element, but culture and counterculture still rub shoulders in cafes, internationally renowned jazz clubs, neighborhood bars, Off-Broadway theaters, and an endless variety of tiny shops and restaurants.

The Village is probably the most chameleonlike of Manhattan's neighborhoods. Some of the highest-priced real estate in the city runs along lower Fifth Avenue, which dead-ends at **Washington Square Park.** Serpentine **Bleecker Street** stretches through most of the neighborhood and is emblematic of the area's historical bent. The tolerant anything-goes attitude in the Village has fostered a large gay community, which is still largely in evidence around **Christopher Street** and Sheridan Square. The streets west of Seventh Avenue, an area known as the West Village, boast a more relaxed vibe and some of the city's most charming and historic brownstones. Three colleges—New York University, Parsons School of Design, and the New School for Social Research—keep the area thinking young—hence the popularity of Eighth Street, lined with shops selling cheap, hip clothes to bridge-and-tunnel kids and the college crowd.

Streets are often crowded with weekend warriors and teenagers, especially on Bleecker, West 4th, 8th, and surrounding streets. Keep an eye on your wallet when navigating the weekend throngs. And Washington Square Park was cleaned up a couple of years back, but there's never any telling when the drug dealers will be back; stay away after dark.

MIDTOWN

Chelsea & the Meat-Packing District   Chelsea has come on strong of late as a hip address, especially for the gay community. A low-rise composite of town houses, tenements, lofts, and factories, the neighborhood comprises roughly the area west of Sixth Avenue from 14th to 30th streets. (Sixth Ave. itself below 23rd St. is actually considered part of the Flatiron District; see below.) Its main arteries are Seventh and Eighth avenues, and it's primarily served by the C, E and 1, 9 subway lines.

The **Chelsea Piers** sports complex to the far west and a host of shops (both unique boutiques and big names like Williams-Sonoma), well-priced bistros, and thriving bars along the main drags have contributed to the area's rebirth. Even the Hotel Chelsea—the neighborhood's most famous architectural and literary landmark, where Thomas Wolfe and Arthur Miller wrote, Bob Dylan composed "Sad-Eyed Lady of the Low Land," Viva and Edie Sedgwick of Andy Warhol fame lived, and Sid Vicious killed girlfriend Nancy Spungeon—has undergone a renovation. You'll find a number of very popular flea markets set up in parking lots along Sixth Avenue, between 24th and 27th streets, on the weekends.

One of the most influential trends in Chelsea has been the establishment of far **West Chelsea** (from Ninth Ave. west) and the adjacent **Meat-Packing District** (south of West Chelsea, roughly from 17th St. to Little West 12th St.) as the style-setting neighborhoods for the 21st century. What SoHo was in the '60s, this industrial west world (dubbed "the Lower West Side" by *New York* magazine) is today. New

Touring Tip

If you'd like to tour a specific neighborhood with an expert guide, call **Big Apple Greeter** (☎ **212/669-8159;** www.bigapplegreeter.org) at least 1 week ahead of your arrival. This nonprofit organization has specially trained volunteers who take visitors around town for a free 2- to 4-hour tour of a particular neighborhood. And they say New York isn't friendly! The office is open Monday through Friday from 10am to 5:30pm.

restaurants, cutting-edge shopping, and super-hot nightspots pop up daily in the still-beefy Meat-Packing District, while the area from West 22nd to West 29th streets between Tenth and Eleventh avenues is home to the cutting edge of today's New York art scene, with West 26th serving as the unofficial "gallery row." The power of art can also be found at the Joyce Theater, New York's principal modern dance venue. This area is still seriously industrial and in the early stages of transition, however, and not for everyone. With galleries and bars tucked away in converted warehouses and former meat lockers, browsing can be frustrating, and the sometimes desolate streets a tad intimidating. Your best bet is to have a specific destination (and an exact address) in mind, be it a restaurant, gallery, boutique, or nightclub, before you come.

Flatiron District, Union Square & Gramercy Park   These adjoining and at places overlapping neighborhoods are some of the city's most appealing. Their streets have been rediscovered by New Yorkers and visitors alike thanks to great shopping and dining opportunities; an impressive new hotel has been added to the mix this year. The commercial spaces are often large loftlike expanses with witty designs and graceful columns.

The **Flatiron District** lies south of 23rd Street to 14th Street, between Broadway and Sixth Avenue, and centers around the historic Flatiron Building on 23rd (so named for its triangular shape) and Park Avenue South, which has become a sophisticated new Restaurant Row. Below 23rd Street along Sixth Avenue (once known as the Ladies' Mile shopping district), mass-market discounters like Filene's Basement, Bed Bath & Beyond, Old Navy, and others have moved in. The shopping gets classier on Fifth Avenue, where you'll find a mix of national names (including Emporio Armani, Kenneth Cole, Banana Republic, and trendy Restoration Hardware) and hip boutiques. Lined with Oriental carpet dealers and high-end fixture stores, Broadway is becoming the city's home-furnishings alley; its crowning jewel is the justifiably famous ABC Carpet & Home, with 8 floors of gorgeous textiles, homewares, and gifts on one side of Broadway, and an equally dazzling display of floor coverings on the other.

Union Square is the hub of the entire area; the N, R, 4, 5, 6, and L trains stop here, making it easy to reach from most other city neighborhoods. Long in the shadows of the more bustling (Times and Herald) and high-toned (Washington) city squares, Union Square has experienced a major renaissance in the last decade. Local businesses joined forces with the city to rid the park of drug dealers a few years back, and now it's a delightful place to spend an afternoon. Union Square is best known as the setting for New York's premier green market every Monday, Wednesday, Friday, and Saturday. Musical acts often play the small pavilion at the north end of the park, and in-line skaters take over the market space in the after-work hours. A number of hip restaurants rim the square, as do superstores like Toys '[R]' Us, the city's best Barnes & Noble superstore, and a Virgin Megastore.

From about 16th to 23rd streets, east from Park Avenue South to about Second Avenue, is the leafy, largely residential district known as **Gramercy Park.** The pity of the Gramercy Park district is that so few can enjoy the park: Built by Samuel Ruggles in the 1830s to attract buyers to his property in the area, it is the only private park in the city and is locked to all but those who live on its perimeter (the rule is that your windows have to look over the park for you to have a key). Located at the southern endpoint of Lexington Avenue (at 21st St.), it is one of the most peaceful spots in the city. If you know someone who has a magic key, go there. Or better yet, book a room at the Gramercy Park Hotel, whose guests have park privileges.

At the northern edge of the area, fronting the Flatiron Building on 23rd Street and Fifth Avenue, is another of Manhattan's lovely little parks, **Madison Square.** Across from its northeastern corner once stood Stanford White's original Madison Square Garden (in whose roof garden White was murdered in 1906 by possibly deranged, but definitely jealous, millionaire Harry K. Thaw). It's now majestically presided over by the massive New York Life Insurance Building, the masterful New York State Supreme Court, and the Metropolitan Life Insurance Company, whose tower in 1909 was the tallest building in the world at 700 feet.

Times Square & Midtown West   Midtown West, the vast area from 34th to 59th streets west of Fifth Avenue to the Hudson River, encompasses several famous names: Madison Square Garden, the Garment District, Rockefeller Center, the Theater District, and Times Square. This is New York's tourism central, where you'll find the bright lights and bustle that draw people from all over the world. As such, this—along with Midtown East (see below)—is the city's biggest hotel neighborhood, with choices running the gamut from budget to deluxe.

The 1, 2, 3, 9 subway line serves the massive neon station at the heart of Times Square, at 42nd Street between Broadway and Seventh Avenue, while the B, D, F, Q line runs up Sixth Avenue to Rockefeller Center. The N, R line cuts diagonally across the neighborhood, following the path of Broadway before heading up Seventh Avenue at 42nd Street. The A, C, E line serves the west side, running along Eighth Avenue.

If you know New York but haven't been here in a few years, you'll be quite surprised by the "new" **Times Square.** Longtime New Yorkers like to kvetch nostalgic about the glory days of the old peep-show-and-porn-shop Times Square that this cleaned-up, Disney-fied version supplanted, but the truth is that it's a hugely successful regentrification. Grand old theaters have come back to life as Broadway and children's playhouses, and scores of new family-friendly restaurants and shops have opened (including the terrific Virgin Megastore on Broadway as well as Disney and Warner Bros. studio stores). Plenty of businesses have moved in—MTV studios overlook Times Square at 1515 Broadway, and, taking a key note from the far more successful *Today* show, *Good Morning America* now has its own street-facing studio at Broadway and 44th Street. The neon lights have never been brighter, and middle America has never been more welcome.

Most of the great Broadway theaters light up the streets just off Times Square, in the West 40s just east and west of Broadway. At the heart of the **Theater District,** where Broadway meets Seventh Avenue, is the TKTS booth, where crowds line up daily to buy discount tickets for tonight's shows.

Unlike neighboring Times Square, gorgeous **Rockefeller Center** has needed no renovation. Situated between 46th and 50th streets from Sixth Avenue east to Fifth, this art deco complex contains some of the city's great architectural gems, which house hundreds of offices, a number of NBC studios (including *Saturday Night Live, Late Night with Conan O'Brien,* and the famous glass-walled *Today* show studio at 48th Street), and some pleasing upscale boutiques (attention, shoppers: Saks Fifth Avenue is just on the other side of Fifth). Holiday time is a great time to be here, as ice-skaters take over the central plaza and the huge Christmas tree twinkles against the night sky.

Along Seventh Avenue south of 42nd Street is the **Garment District,** of little interest to tourists except for its sample sales, where some great new fashions are sold off

Impressions

I'm opposed to the redevelopment. I think there should be one neighborhood in New York where tourists are afraid to walk.

—Fran Lebowitz on the "new" Times Square

cheap to serious bargain hunters willing to scour the racks. Other than that, it's a pretty grim commercial area. Between Seventh and Eighth avenues and 31st and 33rd streets, **Penn Station** sits beneath **Madison Square Garden,** where the Rangers and the Knicks play. Taking up all of 34th Street between Sixth and Seventh avenues is **Macy's,** the world's largest department store; exit Macy's at the southeast corner and you'll find more famous-label shopping around **Herald Square.**

Farther north, despite the presence of grand dame Carnegie Hall, West 57th Street has become a theme restaurant bonanza, with Planet Hollywood (for now, anyway; it may move to Times Sq.), the Harley-Davidson Cafe, Brooklyn Diner USA, and the venerable Hard Rock in residence, not to mention the back-in-business Russian Tea Room. There are a good number of hotels in all price categories in this area, and their convenience to Central Park (which starts at 59th St.) is an extra plus.

If you're looking for something a little more culture-rich than an overpriced burger and a logo T-shirt, Midtown West is also home to the Museum of Modern Art, Radio City Music Hall, and the *Intrepid* Sea-Air-Space Museum.

Midtown East & Murray Hill   Midtown East, the area including Fifth Avenue and everything east from 34th to 59th streets, is the more upscale side of the Midtown map. This side of town is short of subway trains, served primarily by the Lexington Avenue 4, 5, 6 line.

Midtown East is where you'll find the city's finest collection of grand hotels, mostly along Lexington Avenue and near the park at the top of Fifth. The stretch of **Fifth Avenue** from Saks at 49th Street extending to FAO Schwarz at 59th is home to the city's most high-profile haute shopping, including Tiffany & Co., Cartier, and Bergdorf Goodman, but more midpriced names like Banana Republic and Liz Claiborne have moved their superstores in of late. The stretch of 57th Street between Fifth and Lexington avenues is also known for high-fashion boutiques (Chanel, Hermès) and high-ticket galleries, but change is underway since Warner Bros. (at the intersection with Fifth), Levi's, Niketown, and the NBA Store squeezed in. You'll find plenty of spillover along **Madison Avenue,** a great strip for shoe shopping in particular.

Magnificent architectural highlights include the recently repolished **Chrysler Building,** with its stylized gargoyles glaring down on passersby; the beaux arts tour de force that is **Grand Central Terminal;** magnificent **St. Patrick's Cathedral;** and the glorious **Empire State Building.**

Far east, swank Sutton and Beekman places are enclaves of beautiful town houses, luxury living, and tiny pocket parks that look out over the East River. Along this river is the **United Nations,** which isn't officially in New York City, or even the United States, but is on a parcel of international land belonging to member nations.

Claiming the territory east from Madison Avenue, **Murray Hill** begins somewhere north of 23rd Street (the line between it and Gramercy Park is fuzzy), and is most clearly recognizable north of 30th Street to 42nd Street. This brownstone-lined quarter is largely a quiet residential neighborhood, most notable for its handful of good budget and midpriced hotels.

UPTOWN

Upper West Side   North of 59th Street and encompassing everything west of Central Park, the Upper West Side contains **Lincoln Center,** arguably the world's premier performing arts venue; the **American Museum of Natural History,** whose renovated Dinosaur Halls garner justifiably rave reviews; and a number of midpriced hotels whose larger-than-Midtown rooms and nice residential location make them some of the best values in the entire city. Unlike the more stratified Upper East Side, the Upper West Side is home to an egalitarian mix of middle-class yuppiedom, laid-back wealth (lots of celebs and monied media types call the grand apartments along Central Park West home), and ethnic families who were here before the gentrification.

The neighborhood runs all the way up to Harlem, around 125th Street, and encompasses **Morningside Heights,** where you'll find **Columbia University** and the perennial construction project known as the **Cathedral of St. John the Divine.** But prime Upper West Side—the part you're most likely to explore—is the area running from Columbus Circle at 59th Street into the 80s, between the park and Broadway. North of 59th Street is where Eighth Avenue becomes Central Park West, the eastern border of the neighborhood (and the western border of Central Park); Ninth Avenue becomes Columbus Avenue, lined with attractive boutiques and cafes; and Tenth Avenue becomes Amsterdam Avenue, less charming than Columbus to the east and less trafficked than bustling Broadway (whose highlights are the gourmet mega-marts Zabar's and Fairway) to the west; still, Amsterdam has blossomed into quite a happening restaurant and bar strip over the last couple of years. You'll find Lincoln Center in the mid-60s, where Broadway cross-cuts Amsterdam.

Two major subway lines service the area: the 1, 2, 3, 9 line runs up Broadway, while the B and C trains run up glamorous Central Park West, stopping right at the historic Dakota apartment building (where John Lennon was shot and Yoko still lives, albeit without an all-grown-up Sean) at 72nd Street, and at the Museum of Natural History at 81st Street.

Upper East Side   North of 59th Street and east of Central Park is some of the city's most expensive residential real estate. This is New York at its most gentrified: Walk along Fifth and Park avenues, especially between 60th and 80th streets, and you're sure to encounter some of the wizened WASPs and Chanel-suited socialites that make up the most rarefied of the city's population. Madison Avenue to 79th Street is the monied crowd's main shopping strip, recently vaunting ahead of Hong Kong's Causeway Bay to become the most expensive retail real estate *in the world*—so bring your platinum card. You can also use it to stay at one of the neighborhood's remarkably luxurious hotels, such as the Carlyle or the Mark, or to dine at four-star wonders like Le Cirque 2000 and Daniel.

The main attraction of this neighborhood is **Museum Mile,** the stretch of Fifth Avenue fronting Central Park that's home to no fewer than 10 terrific cultural institutions, including Frank Lloyd Wright's Guggenheim, and anchored by the mind-boggling **Metropolitan Museum of Art.** But the elegant rows of landmark town houses are worth a look alone: East 70th Street, from Madison east to Lexington, is one of the world's most charming residential streets. If you want to see where real people live, move east to Third Avenue and beyond; that's where affordable restaurants and active street life start popping up.

A second subway line is in the works, but it's still no more than an architect's blueprint. For now, the Upper East Side is served solely by the Lexington Avenue line (4, 5, 6 trains), so wear your walking shoes (or bring taxi fare) if you're heading up here to explore.

Harlem   Harlem is really two areas. Harlem proper stretches from river to river, beginning at 125th Street on the West Side and 96th Street on the East Side. East of Fifth Avenue, Spanish Harlem (El Barrio) runs between East 100th and East 125th streets.

Parts of Harlem are benefiting from the revitalization that has swept so much of the city, with national-brand retailers moving in and visitors arriving to tour historic sites related to the Golden Age of African-American culture, when great bands like the

Count Basie and Duke Ellington orchestras played the Cotton Club and Sugar Cane Club, and literary giants like Langston Hughes and James Baldwin soaked up the scene. Some houses date back to a time when the area was something of a country retreat and represent some of the best brownstone mansions in the city. On Sugar Hill (from 143rd St. to 155th St., between St. Nicholas and Edgecombe aves.) and Striver's Row (West 139th St. between Adam Clayton Powell Jr. and Frederick Douglass blvds.) are a significant number of fine town houses. For cultural visits, there's the Morris–Jumel Mansion, the Schomburg Center, the Studio Museum, and the Apollo Theater.

By all means, come see Harlem—it's one of the city's most vital and historic neighborhoods. But your best bet is to take a guided tour (see chapter 7). Sights tend to be far apart, and neighborhoods change quickly. Don't wander thoughtlessly through Harlem, especially at night.

Washington Heights & Inwood   Located at the northern tip of Manhattan, Washington Heights (the area from 155th St. to Dyckman St., with adjacent Inwood running to the tip) is home to a large segment of Manhattan's Latino community. **Fort Tryon Park** and **the Cloisters** are the two big reasons to come up this way. The Cloisters houses the Metropolitan Museum of Art's stunning medieval collection, in a building perched atop a hill, with excellent views across the Hudson to the Palisades. Committed off-the-beaten-path sightseers might also want to visit the Dyckman Farmhouse, a historic jewel built in 1783 and the only remaining Dutch Colonial structure in Manhattan.

2 Getting Around

Frankly, Manhattan's transportation systems are a marvel. It's simply miraculous that so many people can gather on this little island and move around it. For the most part, you can get where you're going pretty quickly and easily using some combination of subways, buses, and cabs; this section will tell you how to do just that.

But between traffic gridlock and subway delays, sometimes you just can't get there from here—unless you walk. Walking can be the fastest way to navigate the island. During rush hours, you'll easily beat car traffic while on foot, as taxis and buses stop and groan at gridlocked corners (don't even *try* going crosstown in a cab or bus in Midtown at midday). You'll also just see a whole lot more by walking than you will if you ride beneath the street in the subway or fly by in a cab. So pack your most comfortable shoes and hit the pavement—it's the best, cheapest, and most appealing way to experience the city.

BY SUBWAY

The much-maligned subway system is actually the best way to travel around New York, especially during rush hours. Some 3^1/$_2$ million people a day seem to agree with me, as it's their primary mode of transportation. The subway is quick, inexpensive, relatively safe, and pretty efficient, as well as being a genuine New York experience that you really shouldn't miss.

The subway runs 24 hours a day, 7 days a week. The rush-hour crushes are roughly from 8am to 9:30am and from 5 to 6:30pm on weekdays; the rest of the time the trains are relatively uncrowded.

PAYING YOUR WAY

The subway fare is $1.50 (half price for seniors and those with disabilities), and children under 44 inches tall ride free (up to three per adult). **Tokens** still exist (although they may be phased out altogether), but most people pay fares with the **MetroCard,** a magnetically encoded card that debits the fare when swiped through the turnstile, or the fare box on any city bus. Once you're in the system, you can transfer freely to any subway line that you can reach without exiting your station. MetroCards—not tokens—also allow you **free transfers** between the bus and subway within a 2-hour period.

The MetroCard can be purchased in a few different configurations:

Pay-Per-Ride MetroCards, which can be used for up to four people by swiping up to four times (bring the whole family). You can put any amount from $3 (two rides) to $80 on your card. Every time you put $15 on your Pay-Per-Ride MetroCard, it's automatically credited 10%—that's one free ride for every $15. You can buy Pay-Per-Ride MetroCards in any denomination at any subway station; an increasing number of stations now have automated MetroCard vending machines, which allow you to buy MetroCards using your major credit card. MetroCards are also available from shops and newsstands around town in $15 and $30 values. You can refill your card at any time until the expiration date on the card, usually about a year from the date of purchase, at any subway station.

Unlimited-Use MetroCards, which can't be used for more than one person at a time or more frequently than 18-minute intervals, are available in four values: the **daily Fun Pass,** which allows you a day's worth of unlimited subway and bus rides for $4; the **7-Day MetroCard,** for $17; and the **30-Day MetroCard,** for $63. Seven-and 30-day Unlimited-Use MetroCards can be purchased at any subway station or a MetroCard merchant. Fun Passes, however, cannot be purchased at token booths—you can only buy them from a MetroCard merchant, such as most Rite Aid drugstores; at the MTA information desk at the Times Square Visitor Center, 1560 Broadway, between 46th and 47th streets; at a station that has a MetroCard vending machine (an increasing number of stations have these); or by ordering them online at **www.metrocard.citysearch.com** (more on this below). Unlimited-Use MetroCards go into effect not at the time you buy them but the first time you use them—so if you buy a card on Monday and don't begin to use it until Wednesday, Wednesday is when the clock starts ticking on your MetroCard. A Fun Pass is good from the first time you use it until 3am the next day, while 7- and 30-day MetroCards run out at midnight

On the Sidewalks

What's the primary means New Yorkers use for getting around town? The subway? Buses? Taxis? Nope. Walking. They stride across wide, crowded pavements without any regard for the light, weaving through crowds at high speeds, dodging taxis and buses whose drivers are forced to interrupt the normal flow of traffic to avoid flattening them. **Never take your walking cues from the locals.** Wait for walk signals and always use crosswalks—don't cross in the middle of the block. Do otherwise and you could quickly end up with a jaywalking ticket—or as a flattened statistic.

Always pay attention to the traffic flow. Walk as if you're driving, staying to the right. Pay attention to what's happening in the street, even if you have the right of way. At intersections, keep an eye out for drivers who don't yield, turn without looking, or think a yellow traffic light means "Hurry up!" as you cross. Unfortunately, most bicyclists seem to think that the traffic laws don't apply to them; they'll often blithely fly through red lights and dash the wrong way on one-way streets, so be on your guard.

For more important safety tips, see "Playing It Safe," later in this chapter.

on the last day. These MetroCards cannot be refilled; you throw it out once it's been used up and buy a new one.

Tips for using your MetroCard: The MetroCard swiping mechanisms at turnstiles are the source of much grousing among subway riders. If you swipe too fast or too slow, the turnstile will ask you to swipe again. If this happens, *do not move to a different turnstile,* or you may end up paying twice. If you've tried a bunch of times and really can't make your MetroCard work, tell the token booth clerk; chances are good, though, that you'll get the movement down after a couple of uses.

If you're not sure how much money you have left on your MetroCard, or what day it expires, use the station's MetroCard Reader, usually located near the station entrance or the token booth (on buses, the fare box will also provide you with this information).

To locate the nearest MetroCard merchant, or for any other MetroCard questions, call ☎ **800/METROCARD** or 212/METROCARD (212/638-7622), or go online to **www.mta.nyc.ny.us/metrocard**. MetroCards in any denomination can be ordered online at **www.metrocard.citysearch.com**. There is no additional charge or shipping fee, but be sure to place your order more than a week before your departure date so the post office has time to get it to you.

USING THE SYSTEM

As you can see from the full-color subway map on the inside front cover of this book, the subway system basically mimics the lay of the land above ground, with most lines in Manhattan running north and south, like the avenues, and a few lines east and west, like the streets.

To go up and down the east side of Manhattan (and to the Bronx and Brooklyn), take the 4, 5, or 6 train.

To travel up and down the west side (and also to the Bronx and Brooklyn), take the 1, 2, 3, or 9 line; the A, C, E, or F line; or the B or D line.

The N and R lines first cut diagonally across town from east to west and then snake under Seventh Avenue before shooting out to Queens.

The crosstown S line, the Shuttle, runs back and forth, back and forth, between Times Square and Grand Central Terminal. Farther downtown, across 14th Street, the L line works its own crosstown magic.

Lines have assigned colors on subway maps and trains—red for the 1, 2, 3, 9 line; green for the 4, 5, 6 trains; and so on—but nobody ever refers to them by color. Always refer to them by number or letter when asking questions. Within Manhattan, the distinction between different numbered trains that share the same line is usually that some are express and others are local. **Express trains** often skip about three stops for each one that they make; express stops are indicated on subway maps with a white (rather than solid) circle. Local stops usually come about 9 blocks apart.

Directions are almost always indicated using "Uptown" (northbound) and "Downtown" (southbound), so be sure to know what direction you want to head in. The outsides of some subway entrances are marked UPTOWN ONLY or DOWNTOWN ONLY; read carefully, as it's easy to head in the wrong direction. Once you're on the platform, check the signs overhead to make sure that the train you're waiting for will be traveling in the right direction. If you do make a mistake, it's a good idea to wait for an express station, like 14th Street or 42nd Street, so you can get off and change for the other direction without paying again.

The days of graffiti-covered cars are gone, but the stations—and an increasing number of trains—are not nearly as clean as they could be. Trains are air-conditioned (move to the next car if yours isn't), though during the dog days of summer the platforms can be sweltering. In theory, all subway cars have PA systems to allow you to hear the conductor's announcements, but they don't always work well. It's a good idea to move to a car with a working PA system in case sudden service changes are announced that you'll want to know about.

For **subway safety tips,** see "Playing It Safe" later in this chapter.

BY BUS

Less expensive than taxis and more pleasant than subways (they provide a mobile sightseeing window on Manhattan), buses are a good transportation option. Their very big drawback: They can get stuck in traffic, sometimes making it quicker to walk. They also stop every couple of blocks, rather than the 8 or 9 blocks that local subways traverse between stops. So for long distances, the subway is your best bet; but for short distances or traveling crosstown, try the bus.

PAYING YOUR WAY

Like the subway fare, the **bus fare** is $1.50, half price for seniors and riders with disabilities, free for children under 44 inches (up to three per adult). The fare is payable with a **MetroCard, token** (for now, anyway) or **exact change.** Bus drivers don't make change, and fare boxes don't accept dollar bills or pennies. You can't purchase MetroCards or tokens on the bus, so you'll have to have them before you board; for details on where to get them, see "Paying Your Way" under "By Subway" above.

If you pay with a MetroCard, you can transfer to another bus or to the subway for free within 2 hours. If you use a token, you must request a **free transfer** slip that allows you to change to an intersecting bus route only (legal transfer points are listed on the transfer paper) within 1 hour of issue. Transfer slips cannot be used to enter the subway.

USING THE SYSTEM

You can't flag a city bus down—you have to meet it at a bus stop. **Bus stops** are located every 2 or 3 blocks on the right-side corner of the street (facing the direction of traffic flow). They're marked by a curb painted yellow and a blue-and-white sign with

---

For More Bus & Subway Information

For additional transit information, call the **MTA/New York City Transit's Travel Information Center** at ☎ **718/330-1234.** Extensive automated information is available at this number 24 hours a day, and travel agents are on hand to answer your questions and provide directions daily from 6am to 9pm. For online information, point your Web browser to **www.mta.nyc.ny.us**.

To request system maps, call the Customer Assistance Line at ☎ 718/330-3322 Monday through Friday from 9am to 5pm. Disabled riders should direct inquiries to ☎ 718/596-8585 (recorded information 24 hours daily; staffed daily from 6am to 9pm). For MetroCard information, call ☎ 212/638-7622 (or 800/638-7622 outside of New York), or go online to www.mta.nyc.ny.us/metrocard or www.metrocard. citysearch.com.

You can get bus and subway maps and additional transit information at most tourist information centers (see "Visitor Information" earlier in this chapter); there's a particularly helpful MTA transit information desk at the Times Square Visitor Center, 1560 Broadway, between 46th and 47th streets, where you can also buy MetroCards. Maps are sometimes available in subway stations (ask at the token booth), but rarely on buses.

a bus emblem and the route number or numbers. Guide-A-Ride boxes at most stops display a route map and a hysterically optimistic schedule.

Almost every major avenue has its own **bus route.** They run either north or south: downtown on Fifth, uptown on Madison, downtown on Lexington, uptown on Third, and so on. There are **crosstown buses** at strategic locations all around town: 8th Street (eastbound); 9th (westbound); 14th, 23rd, 34th, and 42nd (east- and westbound); 49th (eastbound); 50th (westbound); 57th (east- and westbound); 65th (eastbound across the West Side, through the park, and then north on Madison, continuing east on 68th to York Ave.); 67th (westbound on the East Side to Fifth Ave. and then south on Fifth, continuing west on 66th St. through the park and across the West Side to West End Ave.); and 79th, 86th, 96th, 116th, and 125th (east- and westbound). Some bus routes, however, are erratic: The M104, for example, starts at the East River, then turns at Eighth Avenue and goes up Broadway. The buses of the Fifth Avenue line go up Madison or Sixth and follow various routes around the city. Most routes operate 24 hours a day, but service is infrequent at night. Some say that New York buses have a herding instinct: They come only in groups. During rush hour, main routes have "limited" buses, identifiable by the red card in the front window; they stop only at major cross streets.

To make sure the bus you're boarding goes where you're going, check the maps on the sign that's at every bus stop, get your hands on a route map (see "For More Bus & Subway Information," above), or **just ask.** The drivers are helpful, as long as you don't hold up the line too long.

While traveling, look out the window not only to take in the sights but also to keep track of cross streets so you know when to get off. Signal for a stop by pressing the tape strip above and beside the windows and along the metal straps, about 2 blocks before you want to stop. Exit through the pneumatic back doors (not the front door) by pushing on the yellow tape strip; the doors open automatically (pushing on the handles is useless unless you're as buffed as Hercules). Most city buses are equipped with wheelchair lifts, making buses the preferable mode of public transportation for wheelchair-bound travelers; for more on this topic, see "Tips for Travelers with Special Needs" in chapter 2. Buses also "kneel," lowering down to the curb to make boarding easier.

BY TAXI

If you don't want to deal with the hustle and bustle of public transportation, finding an address that might be a few blocks from the subway station, or sharing your ride with 3¹/₂ million other people, then take a taxi. The biggest advantages are, of course, that cabs can be hailed on any street (providing you find an empty one—often simple, yet at other times nearly impossible) and will take you right to your destination. I find they're best used at night when there's little traffic to keep them from speeding you to your destination and when the subway may seem a little daunting. In Midtown at midday, you can usually walk to where you're going more quickly.

Official New York City taxis, licensed by the Taxi and Limousine Commission, are yellow, with the rates printed on the door and a light with a medallion number on the roof. You can hail a taxi on any street. *Never* accept a ride from any other car except an official city yellow cab (private livery cars are not allowed to pick up fares on the street).

Impressions

Traffic signals in New York are just rough guidelines.
—David Letterman

Taxi-Hailing Tips

- When you're waiting on the street for an available taxi, look at the medallion light on the top of the coming cabs. If the light is out, the taxi is in use. When the center part (the number) is lit, the taxi is available—this is when you raise your hand to flag the cab. If all the lights are on, the driver is off duty.

- A taxi can't take more than four people, so expect to split up if your group is larger.

The base fare on entering the cab is $2. The cost is 30¢ for every one-fifth mile or 20¢ per minute in stopped or very slow-moving traffic (or for waiting time). There's no extra charge for each passenger or for luggage. However, you must pay bridge or tunnel tolls (sometimes the driver will front the toll and add it to your bill at the end; most times, however, you pay the driver before the toll). You'll also pay a 50¢ night surcharge after 8pm and before 6am. A 15 to 20% tip is customary.

Forget about hopping into the back seat and having some double-chinned, cigar-chomping, all-knowing driver slowly turn and ask nonchalantly, "Where to, Mac?" Nowadays most taxi drivers speak only an approximation of English and drive in engagingly exotic ways. Always wear your seat belt—taxis are required to provide them.

The TLC has posted a **Taxi Rider's Bill of Rights** sticker in every cab. Drivers are required by law to take you anywhere in the five boroughs, to Nassau or Westchester counties, or to Newark Airport. They are supposed to know how to get you to any address in Manhattan and all major points in the outer boroughs. They are also required to provide air-conditioning and turn off the radio on demand, and they cannot smoke while you're in the cab. They are required to be polite.

You are allowed to dictate the route that is taken. It's a good idea to look at a map before you get in a taxi. Taxi drivers have been known to jack up the fare on visitors who don't know better by taking a circuitous route between point A and point B. Know enough about where you're going to know that something's wrong if you hop in a cab at Sixth Avenue and 57th Street to go to the Empire State Building (Fifth Avenue and 34th Street), say, and you suddenly find yourself on Ninth Avenue.

On the other hand, listen to drivers who propose an alternate route. These guys spend 8 or 10 hours a day on these streets, and they know them well—where the worst midday traffic is, where Con Ed has dug up an intersection that should be avoided. A knowledgeable driver will know how to get you to your destination quickly and efficiently.

Another important tip: **Always make sure the meter is turned on at the start of the ride.** You'll see the red LED readout register the initial $2 and start calculating the fare as you go. I've witnessed a good number of unscrupulous drivers buzzing unsuspecting visitors around the city with the meter off, and then overcharging them at drop-off time.

Always ask for the receipt—it comes in handy if you need to make a complaint or have left something in a cab. In fact, it's a good idea to make a mental note of the driver's four-digit medallion number (usually posted on the divider between the front and back seats) just in case you need it later. You probably won't, but it's a good idea to play it safe.

For driver complaints and lost property, call the 24-hour Consumer Hotline at ☎ **212/NYC-TAXI.** For details on getting to and from the local airports by taxi, see "By Plane" under "Getting There" in chapter 2. For further taxi information—including a complete rundown of your rights as a taxi rider—point your Web browser to **www.ci. nyc.ny.us/taxi.**

BY CAR

Forget driving yourself around the city. It's not worth the headache. Traffic is horrendous; you don't know the rules of the road (written or unwritten) or the arcane alternate-side-of-the-street parking regulations (in fact, precious few New Yorkers do). You don't want to find out the monstrous price of parking violations or live the Kafka-esque tragedy of liberating a vehicle from the tow pound. Not to mention the security risks.

If you do arrive in New York City by car, park it in a garage (expect to pay at least $20 to $35 per day) and leave it there for the duration of your stay. If you drive a rental car in, return it as soon as you arrive and rent another on the day you leave. Just about all of the major car-rental companies, including **National** (☎ 800/227-7368; www.nationalcar.com), **Hertz** (☎ 800/654-3131; www.hertz.com), and **Avis** (☎ 800/ 230-4898; www.avis.com), have Manhattan locations.

TRAVELING FROM THE CITY TO THE SUBURBS

The **PATH** (☎ 800/234-7284; www.panynj.gov/path) system connects urban communities in New Jersey, including Hoboken and Newark, to Manhattan by subway-style trains. Stops in Manhattan are at the World Trade Center, Christopher and 9th streets, and along Sixth Avenue at 14th, 23rd, and 33rd streets. The fare is $1.

New Jersey Transit (☎ 973/762-5100; www.njtransit.state.nj.us) operates commuter trains from Penn Station, and buses from the Port Authority at Eighth Avenue and 42nd Street, to points throughout New Jersey.

The **Long Island Rail Road** (☎ 718/217-5477; www.mta.nyc.ny.us/lirr) runs from Penn Station, at Seventh Avenue between 31st and 33rd streets, to Queens (ocean beaches, Shea Stadium, Belmont Park) and points beyond on Long Island, to even better beaches and summer hot spots like Fire Island and the Hamptons.

Metro North (☎ 800/638-7646 or 212/532-4900; www.mta.nyc.ny.us/mnr) departs from Grand Central Terminal, at 42nd Street and Lexington Avenue, for areas north of the city, including Westchester County, the lovely Hudson Valley, and Connecticut.

3 Playing It Safe

Sure, there's crime in New York City, but millions of people spend their lives here without being robbed and assaulted. In fact, New York is safer than any other big American city, and is listed by the FBI as somewhere around 150th in the nation for total crimes. While that's quite encouraging for all of us, it's still important to take precautions. Visitors especially should remain vigilant, as swindlers and criminals are expert at spotting newcomers who appear disoriented or vulnerable.

Men should carry their wallets in their front pockets and women should keep constant hold of their purse straps. Cross camera and purse straps over one shoulder, across your front, and under the other arm. Never hang a purse on the back of a chair or on a hook in a bathroom stall; keep it in your lap or between your feet with one foot through a strap and up against the purse itself. Avoid carrying large amounts of

Impressions

I like it here in New York. I like the idea of having to keep eyes in the back of your head all the time.

—John Cale

The Top Safety Tips

Trust your instincts, because they're usually right. You'll rarely be hassled, but it's always best to walk with a sense of purpose and self-confidence, and don't stop in the middle of the sidewalk to pull out and peruse your map. Anywhere in the city, if you find yourself on a deserted street that feels unsafe, it probably is; leave as quickly as possible. If you do find yourself accosted by someone with or without a weapon, remember to keep your anger in check and that the most reasonable response (maddening though it may be) is not to resist.

cash. You might carry your money in several pockets so that if one is picked, the others might escape. Skip the flashy jewelry and keep valuables out of sight when you're on the street.

Panhandlers are seldom dangerous but should be ignored (more aggressive pleas should firmly be answered, "Not today"). I hate to be cynical, but experience teaches that if a stranger walks up to you on the street with a long sob story ("I live in the sub-urbs and was just attacked and don't have the money to get home"), you should ignore it—it's a scam. If someone approaches you with any kind of elaborate tale, it's most definitely a con game. Walk away and don't feel bad. Be wary of an individual who "accidentally" falls in front of you or causes some other commotion because he or she may be working with someone else who will take your wallet when you try to help. And remember: You *will* lose if you place a bet on a sidewalk card game or shell game.

Certain areas should be avoided late at night. I don't recommend going to the Lower East Side, Alphabet City in the far East Village, or the Meat-Packing District unless you know where you're going; don't be afraid to go, but head straight for your destination and don't wander onto side streets. The areas above 96th Street aren't the best, either. Times Square has been cleaned up, and there'll be crowds around until midnight, when theater- and moviegoers leave the area. Still, stick to the main streets, such as Broadway. The areas west and south of Times Square are not worth going to and should be avoided. Take a cab or bus when visiting the Jacob Javits Center on 34th Street and the Hudson River. Don't go wandering the parks after dark, unless you're going to a performance; if that's the case, stick with the crowd.

If you plan on visiting the outer boroughs, go only during the daylight hours. If the subway doesn't go directly to your destination, your best bet is to take a taxi. Don't wander the side streets; many areas in the outer boroughs are absolutely safe, but neighborhoods change quickly, and it's easy to get lost.

All this having been said, don't panic. New York has experienced a dramatic drop in crime and is generally safe these days, especially in the neighborhoods that visitors are prone to frequent. There's a good police presence on the street, so don't be afraid to stop an officer, or even a friendly-looking New Yorker (trust me—you can tell), if you need help getting your bearings.

SUBWAY SAFETY TIPS   In general, the subways are safe, especially in Manhattan. There are panhandlers and questionable characters like anywhere else in the city, but subway crime has gone down to 1960s levels. Still, stay alert and trust your instincts. Always keep a hand on your personal belongings.

When using the subway, don't wait for trains near the edge of the platform or on extreme ends of a station. During nonrush hours, wait for the train in view of the token booth clerk or under the yellow DURING OFF HOURS TRAINS STOP HERE signs, and ride in the train operator's or conductor's car (usually in the center of the train; you'll see his or her head stick out of the window when the doors open). Choose crowded cars over empty ones—there's safety in numbers.

Avoid subways late at night, and splurge on a cab after about 10 or 11pm—it's money well spent to avoid a long wait on a deserted platform. Or take the bus.

Fast Facts: New York City

Ambulance & Emergencies   Dial ☎ 911.

American Express   Travel service offices are at many Manhattan locations, including the New York Hilton, 1335 Sixth Ave., at 54th Street (☎ 212/664-7798); the New York Marriott Marquis, 1535 Broadway, in the 8th-floor lobby (☎ 212/575-6580); on the balcony level at Macy's Herald Square, 34th Street and Broadway (☎ 212/695-8075); and 65 Broadway, between Exchange Place and Rector Street (☎ 212/493-6500). Call ☎ **800/AXP-TRIP** or go online to **www.americanexpress.com** for other city locations or general information.

Area Codes   There are four area codes in the city: two in Manhattan, the original **212** and the new **646,** and two in the outer boroughs, the original **718** and the new **347.** Also common is the **917** area code, which is assigned to cell phones, pagers, and the like. All calls between these area codes are local calls, but you'll have to dial 1 + the area code + the 7 digits if the number you're calling is not within your area code.

Business Hours   In general, **retail stores** are open Monday through Saturday from 10am to 6pm or 7pm, Thursday from 10am to 8:30 or 9pm, and Sunday from noon to 5pm (see chapter 8). **Banks** tend to be open Monday through Friday from 9am to 3pm and sometimes Saturday mornings.

Dentists   See "Health & Insurance" in chapter 2.

Doctors   For medical emergencies requiring immediate attention, head to the nearest emergency room (see "Hospitals" below). For less urgent health problems, see "Health & Insurance" in chapter 2 for walk-in medical centers and doctor referral services.

Embassies/Consulates   See "Fast Facts: For the Foreign Traveler" in chapter 3.

Emergencies   Dial ☎ **911** for fire, police, and ambulance. The **Poison Control Center** is at ☎ **212/764-7667** or 212/340-4494.

Fire   Dial ☎ **911.**

Hospitals   Downtown: New York Downtown Hospital, 170 William St., between Beekman and Spruce streets (☎ **212/312-5063**); St. Vincent's Hospital, 153 W. 11th St., at Seventh Avenue (☎ **212/604-7000**); and Beth Israel Medical Center, First Avenue and 16th Street (☎ **212/420-2000**). **Midtown:** Bellevue Hospital Center, 462 First Ave., at 27th Street (☎ **212/562-4141**); New York University Medical Center, 560 First Ave., at 33rd Street (☎ **212/263-7300**); and Roosevelt Hospital, 425 W. 59th St., between Ninth and Tenth avenues (☎ **212/523-4000** or 212/523-6800). **Upper West Side:** St. Luke's Hospital Center, Amsterdam Avenue and 113th Street (☎ **212/523-4000** or 212/523-3335); and Columbia Presbyterian Medical Center, 622 W. 168th St., at Broadway (☎ **212/305-2500**). **Upper East Side:** New York Presbyterian Hospital's Emergency Center, 525 E. 68th St., at York Avenue (☎ **212/746-5050**); Lenox Hill Hospital, 100 E. 77th St., between Park and Lexington avenues (☎ **212/434-2000**);

and Mount Sinai Hospital, Madison Avenue between 100th and 101st streets (☎ **212/241-6500**). Don't forget your insurance card.

Hotlines   The 24-hour **Crime Victims Hot Line** is ☎ **212/577-7777.** You can reach **Alcoholics Anonymous** at ☎ **212/870-3400** (general office) or 212/647-1680 (intergroup, for alcoholics who need immediate counseling from a sober recovering alcoholic). Other useful numbers include: **Sex Crimes Report Line** ☎ 212/267-7273; **Crisis Help Line** ☎ 212/532-2400; **Samaritans' Suicide Prevention Line** ☎ 212/673-3000; local **police precincts** ☎ 212/ 374-5000; **Department of Consumer Affairs** ☎ 212/487-4444; and **Taxi complaints** ☎ 212/NYC-TAXI.

Internet Centers   See "Check Your E-Mail While You're on the Road" in "Planning Your Trip: An Online Directory" on p. 43.

Libraries   The **New York Public Library** is on Fifth Avenue at 42nd Street (☎ **212/930-0830**). This beaux arts beauty houses more than 38 million volumes, and the beautiful reading rooms have been restored to their former glory. More efficient and modern, if less charming, is the mid-Manhattan branch at 455 Fifth Ave., at 40th Street, across the street from the main library (☎ **212/340-0833**). There are other branches in almost every neighborhood; you can find a list online at **www.nypl.org**.

Liquor Laws   The minimum legal age to purchase and consume alcoholic beverages in New York is 21. Liquor and wine are sold only in licensed stores, which are closed on Sunday, holidays, and election days while the polls are open. Beer can be purchased in grocery stores and delis 24 hours a day, except Sunday before noon.

Newspapers/Magazines   There are three major daily newspapers: the *New York Times,* the *Daily News,* and the *New York Post.* For details on where to find arts and entertainment listings, see "Orientation" earlier in this chapter.

In addition to the dailies, many newsstands carry a selection of newspapers and magazines. If you want to find your hometown paper, try **Universal News & Magazines,** 977 Eighth Ave., between 57th and 58th streets (☎ **212/ 459-0932**), or **Hotalings News Agency,** inside the Times Square Visitor Center at 1560 Broadway, between 46th and 47th streets (☎ **212/840-1868**). Both have huge selections of international and domestic newspapers and magazines.

Pharmacies   **Duane Reade** has 24-hour pharmacies in Midtown at 224 W. 57th St., at Broadway (☎ **212/541-9708**); and on the Upper East Side at 1279 Third Ave., at 74th Street (☎ **212/744-2668**).

Police   Dial ☎ **911** in an emergency; otherwise, call ☎ **212/374-5000** for the number of the nearest precinct.

Post Office   The main post office is at the monumental James A. Farley Building, 421 Eighth Ave., between 31st and 33rd streets (☎ **212/967-8585**); it's open 24 hours, although services are limited after regular hours. There's a second branch with extended hours (Mon through Fri from 7am to midnight, Sat from 9am to 5pm) north of the World Trade Center at 90 Church St., between Barclay and Vesey streets (☎ **212/330-5313**). There are branches and drop boxes throughout the city; call ☎ **800/275-8777** to locate the branch nearest you. Most are open Monday through Friday from 8am to 5 or 6pm, Saturday from 9am to 3pm.

Rest Rooms   Public rest rooms are available at the visitor centers in Midtown (1560 Broadway, between 46th and 47th sts.; and 810 Seventh Ave., between

52nd and 53rd sts.). Grand Central Terminal, at 42nd Street between Park and Lexington avenues, also has clean rest rooms. Your best bet on the street is Starbucks. You can't walk more than a few blocks without seeing one, and I've found that the only good thing the evil empire has brought to the city is a plethora of clean bathrooms. I've always gotten away with using them without a purchase. (Ditto at Timothy's and New World Coffee, other city java chains.) The big chain bookstores are good for this, too (in addition to bedtime reading material). You can also head to hotel lobbies (especially the big Midtown ones) and department stores like Macy's and Bloomingdale's. On the Lower East Side, stop into the Lower East Side BID Visitor Center, 261 Broome St., between Orchard and Allen streets (open Sun through Fri from 10am to 4pm, sometimes later).

Salon Services   Need a haircut or a manicure while you're here in town? Stylish **Warren-Tricomi,** 16 W. 57th St., just west of Fifth Avenue (☎ **212/262-8899**), can meet all your salon needs.

Smoking   Smoking is prohibited on all public transportation, in the lobbies of hotels and office buildings, in taxis, and in most shops. Smoking also may be restricted or not permitted in restaurants; for more on this, see chapter 6.

Taxes   **Sales tax** is 8.25% on meals, most goods, and some services, though as of March 1, 2000, sales tax was eliminated on clothing and footwear items under $110. **Hotel tax** is 13.25% plus $2 per room per night (including sales tax). **Parking garage tax** is 18.25%.

Telephone Information   Dial ☎ **411,** or the area code of the area you wish to reach plus 555-1212.

Time   For the correct time, dial ☎ **212/976-1616.**

Transit Information   For information on getting to and from the airport, see "Getting There" in chapter 2 or call **Air-Ride** at ☎ **800/247-7433.** For information on subways and buses, see "Getting Around" earlier in this chapter.

Traveler's Assistance   **Travelers Aid** helps distressed travelers with all kinds of problems, including accidents, sickness, and lost or stolen luggage. There is an office on the second floor of the International Arrivals Building at JFK Airport (☎ **718/656-4870**), and one in Newark Airport's Terminal B (☎ **973/623-5052**).

Weather   For the current temperature and next day's forecast, look in the upper-right corner of the *New York Times* or call ☎ **212/976-1212.** If you want to know how to pack before you arrive, point your browser to **www.cnn.com/weather** or **www.weather.com** for the 4- or 5-day forecast. The Weather Channel also offers phone forecasts for 95¢ per minute at ☎ **900-WEATHER.**

Accommodations 5

As you're probably well aware, New York is more popular than it's been in decades. On one hand, that's terrific: It's a reflection of how well the city's doing, and how well it's projecting that positive image to the rest of the world. The city feels vital and self-assured; you can practically feel the excitement and energy as you walk down the street.

Now the downside: With increased demand comes higher prices—Economics 101, pure and simple. Occupancy rates have skyrocketed, and rates have responded accordingly. Average room rates are now hovering perilously close to $200, higher than ever before in the city's history. With rates at these levels—and that's just for an *average* hotel room—accommodations are likely to be the biggest financial commitment of your trip. Choose carefully.

That doesn't mean that there aren't a few bargains out there—so even if money is tight, don't give up yet. In the pages that follow, I'll tell you about some truly wonderful places to stay that won't break your bank account. And even those of you who can afford a bit (or a lot) of luxury still want to get the most for your money; I'll show you how to do that, too.

When deciding what you're willing to pay versus what you're willing to put up with, keep in mind that this is the land of $200-a-night-plus Holiday Inns and HoJos—so if you only want to spend 100 bucks a night, you're going to have to put up with some inconveniences. For the best cheap sleeps in town, you'll have to get used to the idea of sharing a bathroom. If you're willing to do so (Europeans seem to have a much easier time with this than Americans do), you can get a lot of bang for your buck.

Know it now: New York hotel rooms give everybody a whole new perspective on "small." Space is the city's biggest asset, and getting some will cost you. If you're traveling on a tight budget, don't be surprised if your room isn't much bigger than the bed that's in it and the cramped bathroom has a sink so small that it looks like it was manufactured in a gnome factory. Even expensive rooms can be on the small side, or lack closet space, or have smallish bathrooms.

PRICE CATEGORIES & RACK RATES   The **rates** quoted in the listings below are the rack rates—the maximum rates that a hotel charges for rooms. I've used these rack rates to divide the hotels into four price categories, ranging from "Very Expensive" to "Inexpensive," for easy reference. But rack rates are only guidelines,

A Note on the Listings

Many **features** come standard in most hotel rooms these days. If you stay in a hotel listed under the "Very Expensive" or "Expensive" categories below, you can assume that your room will have an alarm clock, a hair dryer in the bathroom, an in-room safe, an iron and ironing board in the closet, and voice mail and data port on the telephone unless I've noted otherwise. But in hotels listed under "Moderate" and "Inexpensive," these features aren't a given, so I've explicitly listed all in-room amenities; if it's not listed, don't expect it.

---

and there are often ways around them; see "Tips for Saving on Your Hotel Room," below.

The hotels listed below have provided us with their best rate estimates for 2001, and all quoted rates were correct at press time. Be aware, however, that **rates can change at any time.** Rates are always subject to availability, seasonal fluctuations, and plain old increases—especially with demand for hotel rooms being what it is in New York City.

PET POLICIES   I've indicated in the listings below those hotels that admitted that they would accept pets. However, understand that these policies may have limitations, such as weight and breed restrictions; may require a deposit and/or a signed waiver against damages; and may be revoked at any time. Always inquire when booking if you're bringing Bowser, Fluffy, or Spike along—*never* just show up with him or her in tow.

TIPS FOR SAVING ON YOUR HOTEL ROOM

In the listings below, I've tried to give you an idea of the kind of deals that may be available at particular hotels: which ones have the best discounted packages, which ones offer AAA and other discounts, which ones allow kids to stay with Mom and Dad for free, and so on. But there's no way of knowing what the offers will be when you're booking, so also consider these general tips:

- **Choose your season carefully.** Room rates can vary dramatically—by hundreds of dollars in some cases—depending on what time of year you visit. Winter, from January to March, is best for bargains, with summer (especially July and Aug) second-best. Fall is the busiest and most expensive season after Christmas. All bets are off at Christmas—expect to pay top dollar for everything—but Thanksgiving can be great for bargain hunters. For more on this subject, see "Money Matters" under "When to Go" in chapter 2.

- **Go uptown or downtown.** The advantages of a Midtown location are highly overrated, especially when saving money is your object. The subway can whisk you anywhere you want to go in minutes; even if you stay on the Upper East Side, you can be at the ferry launch for the Statue of Liberty in about a half hour. You'll get the best value for your money by staying outside the Theater District, in the residential neighborhoods where real New Yorkers live, like Greenwich Village, Chelsea, Murray Hill, or—my absolute favorite for space-seekers and bargain hunters—the Upper West Side. These are the neighborhoods where real New Yorkers hang out, too, so you won't want for good eats, nightlife, or Big Apple bustle. Or hoof it to the Financial District for weekend stays (see below).

- **Visit over a weekend.** If your trip includes a weekend, you might be able to save big bucks. Business hotels tend to empty out, and rooms that go for $300 or more Monday through Thursday can drop dramatically, as low as $150 or less, once the midlevel execs have headed home. These deals are especially prevalent in the Financial District, but they're often available in tourist-friendly Midtown, too. Look in the Travel section of the Sunday *New York Times* for some of the best weekend deals. They're also often advertised on the hotel's Web site. Or just ask when you call.

- **Shop online.** Hotels often offer "Internet only" deals that can save you 10% to 20% over what you'd pay if you booked over the telephone. Also, hotels often advertise all of their available deals on their Web sites, so you don't have to rely on a reservation agent to fill you in. What's more, some of the discount reservations agencies (see below) have sites that allow you to book online. And consider joining the **Playbill Online Theater Club** (**www.playbillclub.com**), a free service that offers some excellent members-only rates at select city hotels in addition to discounts on theater tickets.

- **Investigate reservation services.** These outfits usually work as consolidators, buying up or reserving rooms in bulk, and then dealing them out to customers at a profit. They do garner special deals that range from 10% to 50% off; but remember, these discounts apply to rack rates, inflated prices that people rarely end up paying. You're probably better off dealing directly with a hotel, but if you don't like bargaining, this is certainly a viable option. Most of them offer online reservation services as well. A few of the more reputable providers are **Accommodations Express** (☎ 800/906-4685; www.accommodationsxpress.com) and **Hotel Reservations Network** (☎ 800/715-7666; www.180096HOTEL.com).

  Another good bet is **Hotel ConXions** (☎ 800/522-9991 or 212/840-8686; www.hotelconxions.com), a consolidator that handles hotels in only a few select destinations, including New York. Not only can they check pricing and availability on a number of hotels with just one phone call, they can also save you up to 60% off rack rates. Also, because Hotel ConXions has guaranteed room blocks in select properties, they can often get you into a hotel that's otherwise sold out.

  Important tip: Never just rely on a reservations service. Do a little homework; compare the rack rates to the discounted rates being offered by the service to see what kind of deal they're offering—that way you'll know if you're actually being offered a substantial savings, or if they've just gussied up the rack rates to make their offer sound like a deal. If you're being offered a stay in a hotel I haven't recommended, do more research to learn about it, especially if it isn't a reliable chain name like Holiday Inn or Hyatt. It's not a deal if you end up at a dump.

- **Buy a money-saving package deal.** A travel package that gets your plane tickets and your hotel stay for one price may just be the best bargain of all. In some cases, you'll get airfare, accommodations, transportation to and from the airport, plus extras—maybe an afternoon sightseeing tour, or restaurant and shopping discount coupons—for less than the hotel alone would have cost had you booked it yourself. For more on this, see "Money-Saving Package Deals" in chapter 2.

More Important Advice on Accommodations

For an easy-to-scan introduction to the best of what the city has to offer, take a moment to check out **"Best Hotel Bets"** in chapter 1. For more help in choosing a location, take a close look at **"Manhattan's Neighborhoods in Brief"** in chapter 4.

1 South Street Seaport & the Financial District

EXPENSIVE

In addition to the choices below, you might also consider the **Marriott Financial Center,** 85 West St. (☎ 800/242-8685 or 212/385-4900), and the **Marriott World Trade Center,** 3 World Trade Center (☎ 800/228-9290 or 212/938-9100), both excellent branches of the reliable chain and both catering primarily to business travelers. Inquire when you call, or check **www.marriott.com**, for deeply discounted weekend rates and other promotions.

Millenium Hilton. 55 Church St. (btw. Fulton and Dey sts.), New York, NY 10017. ☎ **800/835-2220** or 212/693-2001. Fax 212/571-2316. www.hilton.com. 561 units. A/C MINIBAR TV TEL. $289–$509 double or junior suite; $400–$1,550 suite. Rates drop to $149–$199 double on weekends, depending on season. Corporate, senior, AAA, and other discounts may also be available. Extra person $30. Children under 18 stay free in parents' room. AE, CB, DC, DISC, JCB, MC, V. Valet or self-parking $35. Subway: N, R, 1, 9 to Cortlandt St.; C, E to World Trade Center.

This Mobil four-star, AAA four-diamond hotel is an excellent choice for bulls and bears—and vacationers, too, especially on weekends, when it becomes one of the best values in town. Facing the World Trade Center, the 58-story tinted-glass monolith opened in 1992. In 1994, Hilton took over, renaming it—obviously without running a spell check—and remaking it into the World Trade Center area's best hotel. This neighborhood goes from bustling to near-desolate on weekends, but multiple subway lines are nearby, ready to whisk you uptown in no time.

The rooms are light and bright on every floor, but the views become more and more glorious as you go up. The accommodations are extremely comfortable, with excellent platform beds fitted with cushioned quilts, firm mattresses, and down pillows. Other appealing in-room features include well-designed built-ins that maximize work and storage space; big bathrooms with lots of counter space; two-line phones; fax/printer/copiers; and cushy bathrobes. I saw some wear in the wood furnishings in some rooms, but everything else was in beautiful shape.

Dining/Diversions: Two American restaurants—one upscale, one casual—serve fine but unremarkable fare; there's also a comfortable bar.

Amenities: Business center with conference room, lots of meeting space, secretarial services, well-equipped fitness center with a great pool and a dry sauna, concierge, 24-hour room service, turndown, express checkout, complimentary car service to Midtown, gift shop and newsstand.

Wall Street Inn. 9 S. William St. (at Mill Lane, 2 blocks south of Wall St.), New York, NY 10004. ☎ **212/747-1500.** Fax 212/747-1900. www.thewallstreetinn.com. 46 units. A/C TV TEL. $215–$450 double. Rates include continental breakfast. Deeply discounted weekend rate, plus AAA and AARP rates available; also ask about corporate and group rates. Extra person $20. AE, DC, DISC, MC, V. Parking $30 nearby. Subway: 2, 3 to Wall St.; 4, 5 to Bowling Green.

New in 1999, this intimate hotel is housed in a landmark seven-story building. Its impeccable early American interiors boast a pleasing freshness. The hotel is warm, comforting, and serene; the professional staff offers personalized service. Rooms aren't huge, but the bedding is top-quality and all the conveniences are at hand: spacious new bathrooms, two-line phones with data ports, VCRs, minifridges, and irons and ironing boards conveniently hidden behind full-length mirrors. (Laptop-toting business travelers may find the work desk to be too small for comfort, however.) Rooms ending in "01" are smallest; seventh-floor rooms are best, as the bathrooms have extra

Downtown Accommodations

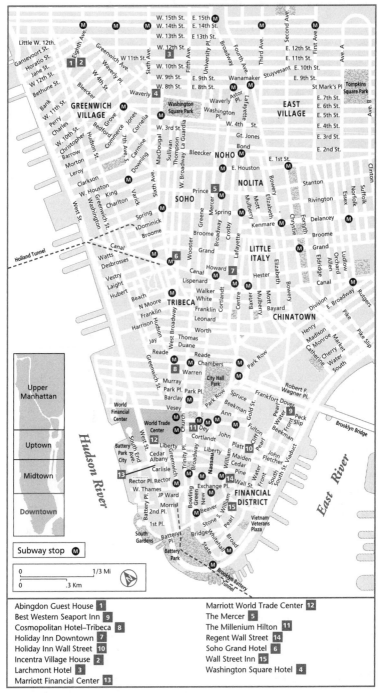

Upper Manhattan

Uptown

Midtown

Downtown

Subway stop Ⓜ

0   1/3 Mi
0   .3 Km

Abingdon Guest House **1**	Marriott World Trade Center **12**
Best Western Seaport Inn **9**	The Mercer **5**
Cosmopolitan Hotel–Tribeca **8**	The Millenium Hilton **11**
Holiday Inn Downtown **7**	Regent Wall Street **14**
Holiday Inn Wall Street **10**	Soho Grand Hotel **6**
Incentra Village House **2**	Wall Street Inn **15**
Larchmont Hotel **3**	Washington Square Hotel **4**
Marriott Financial Center **13**	

What's New on Wall Street

The recent economic boom has triggered quite a bull market for hotel developers. In addition to the **Wall Street Inn** (see below), here's what else is new in the Financial District:

The ultra-deluxe **Regent Wall Street,** 55 Wall St. (☎ 800/545-4000 or 212/845-8600; www.regenthotels.com), sets the new standard for expense-account luxury. Housed in a jaw-droppingly gorgeous 1842 Greek Revival building that formerly served as the New York Mercantile Exchange (there are even jail cells for debtors in the basement), it's geared to traveling CEOs, with mammoth rooms outfitted with every toy—including 39-inch TVs and DVD players—and rates that start at a whopping $545 a night. This is the place to stay in Lower Manhattan if somebody else is paying. Once the bulls and bears have gone home, value-seekers looking to splurge can score weekend packages starting at $375.

Also new is the more down-to-earth **Holiday Inn Wall Street,** 15 Gold St. (☎ 800/HOLIDAY or 212/232-7700; www.holidayinnwsd.com), whose comfortable rooms are stocked with everything a junior executive might need, from an ergonomic chair at the L-shaped workstation to paper clips and white out, plus Internet-access TV, Nintendo, and a CD player for those in-between-meetings moments. Expect rates to run anywhere from $169 to $345 ($269 to $450 for suites), and as low as $139 or $149 for weekenders.

In addition, expect **Embassy Suites** and **Ritz-Carlton** to add to the Lower Manhattan skyline sometime in late 2000 or 2001.

counter space and whirlpool tubs. There's no restaurant or room service, but continental breakfast is included, coffee and cookies are set out all day, and a number of restaurants dot the immediate area.

Best of all, vacationers who don't mind the weekend quiet of Wall Street will find amazing deals once the execs go home: Rates drop to as low as $150 on Friday through Sunday nights, and the staff will assign you the best available room when you check in.

Amenities: Concierge, dry-cleaning and laundry service, *Wall Street Journal* delivery, free video library, fitness room with sauna and steam, business center, two small conference rooms. Guests have access to a full kitchen with microwave.

MODERATE

Best Western Seaport Inn. 33 Peck Slip (2 blocks north of Fulton St., btw. Front and Water sts.), New York, NY 10038. ☎ **800/HOTEL-NY** or 212/766-6600. Fax 212/766-6615. www.bestwestern.com/seaportinn. 72 units. A/C TV TEL. $169–$209 double. Rates include continental breakfast. Corporate rates from $149; family, senior, and weekend discounts may also be available. Extra person $10. Children under 18 stay free in parents' room. AE, DC, DISC, MC, V. Parking $20 nearby. Subway: 2, 3 to Fulton St.

Catering primarily to business travelers, this well-kept chain hotel is also a good bet for vacationers. It's located in cobblestoned South Street Seaport, within walking distance of the ferries to the Statue of Liberty, Ellis Island, and Staten Island. Though they're housed in an 1852 building with a beautifully restored exterior, the guest rooms are what you'd expect from a Best Western, but they're quite comfortable. Each is equipped with a work desk, phone with data port, refrigerator, VCR, hair dryer, clock radio, and safe; some have small dining tables, sleeper sofas, steam baths, whirlpools, and/or terraces with fine views of the seaport. On the downside, some closets consist only of racks on the walls and the towels are motel-thin, but there are luggage-size benches in each room and the bathrooms are spacious. Ask for a corner room for extra space—they boast two queen beds and lots of windows, some with wonderful water views. Light sleepers should ask for an inside room, since the Fulton Fish Market is right next door, and it's in full swing daily from 11pm to 8am.

Video rentals and valet service are available, and a fitness room was added in 1999. There's no room service, but nearby restaurants are happy to deliver.

2 TriBeCa

INEXPENSIVE

✪ **Cosmopolitan Hotel–Tribeca.** 95 W. Broadway (at Chambers St.), New York, NY, 10007. ☎ **888/895-9400** or 212/566-1900. Fax 212/566-6909. www.cosmohotel.com. 104 units. A/C TV TEL. $99–$149 double. AE, CB, DC, EURO, JCB, MC, V. Parking $20, 1 block away. Subway: 1, 2, 3, 9 to Chambers St.

Hiding behind a plain-vanilla Tribeca awning is the best hotel deal in Manhattan for budget travelers who insist on a private bathroom. Every room comes with its own small but spotless bathroom, telephone with data port, air-conditioning, satellite TV, alarm, and ceiling fan, all for as little as 99 bucks a night. Everything is strictly budget, but nice: The modern IKEA-ish furniture includes an armoire (a few rooms have a dresser and hanging rack instead) and a work desk; for a few extra bucks, you can have a love seat, too. Beds are comfy, and sheets and towels are of good quality. Rooms are small but make the most of the limited space, and the whole place is pristine. The two-level mini-lofts have lots of character, but expect to duck on the second level: Downstairs is the bath, TV, closet, desk, and club chair, while upstairs is a low-ceilinged bedroom with a second TV and phone. The neighborhood is safe, hip, and subway-convenient; the Financial District is just a walk away. There's no room service, but a range of great restaurants will deliver. All services are kept at a bare minimum to keep costs down, so you must be a low-maintenance guest to be happy here. If you are, this place is a smokin' deal.

3 Chinatown

MODERATE

Holiday Inn Downtown. 138 Lafayette St. (at Howard St., 1 block north of Canal St.), New York, NY 10013. ☎ **800/HOLIDAY** or 212/966-8898. Fax 212/966-3933. www.holiday-inn.com/hotels/nycdt/welcome. 227 units. A/C TV TEL. $169–$289 double; $249–$309 junior suite. AAA, AARP, and other discounts may be available. Extra person $20. Children 18 and under stay free in parents' room. AE, DC, DISC, JCB, MC, V. Valet parking $26. Subway: 6 to Canal St.

This Holiday Inn is everything you'd expect from this good-value chain: clean, well outfitted, reliable, and very comfortable. The guest rooms are chain-standard but have everything you need, including a desk with easy-access data port, two phones with voice mail, an in-room safe, an iron and ironing board, and lots of counter space in the bathroom. Most junior suites have in-room fax machines as well. You'll find Asian touches throughout, a nod to the hotel's location: At the northern edge of Chinatown, just steps away from SoHo, it's safe and well situated for those who prefer downtown's shopping, dining, and club scenes. On site is a well-respected Cantonese restaurant, Pacifica, and a cocktail bar. Other amenities include a concierge, room service

(6:30am–10:30pm), dry-cleaning service, express checkout, free newspapers at the front desk, a fax machine for guests' use, a meeting room, and privileges at a nearby health club for a fee. You can't go wrong here.

4 SoHo

VERY EXPENSIVE

The Mercer. 99 Prince St. (at Mercer St.), New York, NY 10012. ☎ **888/918-6060** or 212/966-6060. Fax 212/965-3838. 75 units. A/C MINIBAR TV TEL. $350–$400 double; $460–$500 studio; from $925 suite. AE, DC, MC, V. Parking $26 nearby. Subway: N, R to Prince St.

André Balazs, a longtime Manhattan nightcrawler and owner of L.A.'s chic Château Marmont, opened the Mercer in April 1997, and the beautiful people have been keeping the place booked ever since. The lobby feels like a postmodern library lounge, with design books lining the shelves and a hip staff scurrying about in Isaac Mizrahi finery. Word is that the hotel is more service-oriented than competitors like the Royalton, but I found its ultra-cool, almost frosty air a little offputting. Even the entrance, guarded by heavy curtains, feels almost uninviting.

The high-ceilinged guest rooms, by French designer Christian Liaigre, are more welcoming, with simple, clean-lined furnishings in beautiful African wenge wood. The linens are gorgeous textured cottons. There's comfortable seating and a large work table in every room that easily can double as a dining table. The austerely beautiful tile-and-marble bathrooms have a steel cart for storage, oversize shower stalls (request one with an oversize two-person tub when booking if you want one), and Face Stockholm toiletries. Nice extras include ceiling fans, VCRs and video games, CD players, minibars stocked with goodies from Dean & Deluca, and three phones (one portable) with a direct-dial number.

Dining/Diversions: Mercer Kitchen is the downtown domain of superstar chef Jean-Georges Vongerichten, of JoJo, Vong, and Jean Georges. The French/Asian fusion cuisine is good, but not quite good enough for what they're charging. Still, it's a hip scene, and open 24 hours for guests. The Cellar Lounge, a 50-seat bar, is in the works, and seems destined to be another hot spot.

Amenities: 24-hour concierge, 24-hour room service from Mercer Kitchen, dry-cleaning/laundry/valet service, turndown, overnight shoe shine, newspaper delivery, free access to nearby David Barton Gym, meeting rooms. Cell phones, fax machines, computers, secretarial and courier services available.

Soho Grand Hotel. 310 W. Broadway (btw. Grand and Canal sts.), New York, NY 10013. ☎ **800/965-3000** or 212/965-3000. Fax 212/965-3244 (reservations) or 212/965-3200 (guests). www.sohogrand.com. 373 units. A/C MINIBAR TV TEL. $354–$534 double; from $1,099 penthouse suite. AE, CB, DC, DISC, ER, JCB, MC, V. Valet parking $25. Subway: A, C, E, N, R, 1, 9 to Canal St. Pets welcomed.

New in 1996, this haven for the image conscious was the first hotel to open in SoHo in more than a century. Built from the ground up, it was designed as a modern ode to the neighborhood's cast-iron past; the result is an Industrial Age–meets–21st-century environment that will probably have a longer shelf life than wholly modern rivals like the Mercer. Here, they got the mix right: The self-conscious modern design that overwhelms at the Mercer is toned down and warmed up with natural hues, textures, and materials, but without the contrivance that reigns at W New York.

The guest rooms boast retro-reproduction furnishings with an Asian slant, including desks that resemble artists' drafting tables and end tables that look like sculptors' stands. The natural colors are warm and soothing, William Morris fabrics abound, and there's beautiful lighting throughout. The beds are fitted with Frette linens, cushioned Naugahyde headboards, and gorgeous coverlets. Decked out in ceramic subway tile, the bathrooms are beautiful but simple. In-room conveniences include full-length mirrors, VCRs and CD players, double-paned windows that open, two-line phones with free local calls and data ports, and your very own fish in a bowl—courtesy of owners Hartz Mountain, of course.

Aesthetically speaking, the Soho Grand is a beauty—my favorite of the new breed of designer hotels—but I've heard a few minor complaints about the level of service. Indeed, considering the rates, turndown should be offered.

Dining/Diversions: Awarded two stars by the *New York Times,* Canal House serves sophisticated and satisfying New England–style tavern fare; the macaroni and cheese (made with 3-year-aged cheddar) is excellent. The Grand Bar is a clubby retro-hip spot that's so popular the action often spills out into the lobby's comfy living room–like "salon." On street level is Caviarteria, a wonderful caviar-and-champagne bar.

Amenities: Fitness center, concierge, 24-hour room service (including a menu for your pooch or kitty), valet service, weekday newspaper delivery, express checkout, conference room. Butler's pantry with complimentary coffee, tea, and hot chocolate on every floor. On street level is Privé, a chic salon.

5 Greenwich Village

MODERATE

The **Incentra Village House,** 32 Eighth Ave. (btw. W. 12th and Jane sts.; ☎ 212/ 206-0007), is a pleasant B&B that particularly welcomes gay and lesbian travelers.

✪ **Abingdon Guest House.** 13 Eighth Ave. (btw. W. 12th and Jane sts.), New York, NY 10014. ☎ **212/243-5384.** Fax 212/807-7473. www.abingdonguesthouse.com. 9 units (7 with private bathroom). A/C TV TEL. High season (Apr–June and Sept–Jan 15) $120–$145 double with shared bathroom, $165–$220 double with private bathroom; low season (Jan 16–Mar and July–Aug) $105–$130 double with shared bathroom, $145–$185 double with private bathroom. 4-night minimum on weekends, 2-night minimum on weekdays. Rates are $15 less for single travelers. Extra person $25. AE, DC, DISC, MC, V. Parking $20 nearby. Subway: A, C, E, 1, 2, 3, 9 to 14th St.

Steve Austin and his partner, Zachary Stass, run this lovely guesthouse (and its downstairs coffee bar, Brewbar) in a wonderful West Village neighborhood. Both men have an eye for style and take the guesthouse business seriously, and their commitment shows—the Abingdon is beautifully outfitted and professionally run. All the rooms are done in bold colors and equipped with well-chosen art and furnishings; each can be previewed on their Web site, so choose the one that best fits your personal style and budget. I suggest opting for one with a new bathroom (they're large and well done). But no matter which one you choose, you'll get a superior-quality mattress and linens, a hair dryer, soft polyfleece bathrobes, an alarm, a small TV, and a telephone with your own answering machine (a splitter can be provided for your laptop); five rooms also have ceiling fans. The best (and most expensive) is the Ambassador Room, which has a witty British Raj theme and a kitchenette (with microwave), VCR, and sleeper sofa for a third person.

The neighborhood is terrific, especially for those who want to be close to good restaurants and boutiques, but it's a bit off the beaten path if you're planning on lots of Midtown sightseeing. And the Abingdon is best for mature, independent-minded travelers since there's no regular staff on-site. No smoking.

INEXPENSIVE

⊗ **Larchmont Hotel.** 27 W. 11th St. (btw. Fifth and Sixth aves.), New York, NY 10011.
☎ **212/989-9333.** Fax 212/989-9496. www.larchmonthotel.citysearch.com. 57 units
(none with private bathroom). A/C TV TEL. $70–$80 single; $85–$109 double. Rates include
continental breakfast. Children under 13 stay free in parents' room. AE, CB, DC, DISC, MC, V.
Parking $18 nearby. Subway: N, R, L, 4, 5, 6 to Union Square; A, C, E, B, D, F, Q to West 4th
St. (use 8th St. exit); F to 14th St.

Excellently located on a beautiful tree-lined block in a quiet residential part of the
Village, this European-style hotel is simply a gem. If you're willing to share a bathroom, you can't do better for the money. The entire place has a wonderful air of
warmth and sophistication; the butter-yellow lobby even *smells* good. Each bright
guest room is tastefully done in rattan and outfitted with a writing desk, a wash basin,
a mini-library of books, an alarm clock, and a few extras that you normally have to
pay a lot more for, such as cotton bathrobes and ceiling fans. Every floor has two
shared bathrooms (with hair dryers) and a small, simple kitchen. The management is
constantly renovating, so everything feels clean and fresh. Free continental breakfast,
including fresh-baked goods every morning, is the crowning touch that makes the
Larchmont an unbeatable deal. And with some of the city's best shopping, dining, and
sightseeing, plus your choice of subway lines, just a walk away, you couldn't be better
situated. Book *well* in advance (the management suggests 6 to 7 weeks' lead time).

Washington Square Hotel. 103 Waverly Place (btw. Fifth and Sixth aves.), New York, NY
10011. ☎ **800/222-0418** or 212/777-9515. Fax 212/979-8373. www.wshotel.com. 180
units. A/C TV TEL. $110–$125 single; $135–$165 double; $165–$180 quad. Rates include
continental breakfast. AE, MC, JCB, V. Parking $27 nearby. Subway: A, B, C, D, E, F, Q to West
4th St.

The best thing about this hotel is its great location, right in the heart of Greenwich
Village overlooking Washington Square Park. The pretty facade and marble-and-brass
lobby come as quite a surprise—not exactly what you expect from a budget hotel.
    The tiny, plain rooms are a decent value. Each comes with a private bathroom, a
deposit-activated phone with voice mail and data port, and a small closet with a pint-
size safe; irons and hair dryers are available from the front desk. Beds are firm, but the
pillows are flat, and a little more elbow grease could go into the detailing of some of
the petite bathrooms. Still, for the money, you could do worse. It's worth paying a few
extra dollars for a south-facing room on a high floor, since others can be a bit dark.
There's a basic gym and a very good restaurant, CIII, which even draws locals with its
well-priced bistro fare, friendly staff, two-for-one happy hours (Mon through Fri from
4 to 7pm), and Sunday jazz brunch that Zagat's calls "marvelous." However, the hotel
staff has been terse on occasion, so be on your guard and let me know if you have any
problems.

6 Chelsea

The hotels in this neighborhood can be found on the "Midtown Accommodations"
map on pp. 102–103.

MODERATE

Hotel Chelsea. 222 W. 23rd St. (btw. Seventh and Eighth aves.), New York, NY 10011.
☎ **212/243-3700.** Fax 212/675-5531. www.hotelchelsea.com. 400 units, about 100
available to travelers (most with private bathroom). A/C (in most rooms) TV TEL.
$165–$300 double or junior suite; from $300 suite. AE, JCB, MC, V. Valet parking $18.
Subway: C, E, 1, 9 to 23rd St.

If you're looking for dependable, predictable comforts, book a room next door at the Chelsea Savoy. But if it's Warhol's New York you're here to discover—or Sarah Bernhardt's or Eugene O'Neill's or Lenny Bruce's—the Hotel Chelsea is the only place to stay. Thomas Wolfe wrote *You Can't Go Home Again* at the Chelsea; Arthur Miller penned *After the Fall* in its welcoming arms; William Burroughs moved in to work on *Naked Lunch;* and in a defining moment of punk history, Sid Vicious killed screechy girlfriend Nancy Spungeon here. No other hotel boasts so much genuine atmosphere. Currently, most of the 400 rooms are inhabited by long-term residents of the creative bent, so the bohemian spirit and sense of community are as strong as ever.

A designated landmark, the 1884 redbrick Victorian boasts graceful cast-iron balconies and a bustling lobby filled with museum-quality works by prominent current and former residents. A recent renovation has taken the seediness out of the allure— these days, the hotel is looking very nice. It's still very quirky, mind you, and not for everybody: Most of the individually decorated rooms and suites have air-conditioning, and they tell me that all rooms have TVs and telephones now, but otherwise it's a crapshoot. The accommodations tend to be sparsely furnished, but they're almost universally large and virtually soundproof (you can see how this would be a plus for unbridled creation). I loved no. 520, a pretty purple-painted junior suite with two double beds, a ceiling fan, a sofa, and a pantry kitchenette. Everything is clean, but don't expect new. The hotel is service-oriented, but in an appropriately fluid way: There's no room or valet service, but the bellmen will be happy to deliver takeout to your room or run your dirty clothes to the cleaners. In the basement is très hip Serena for cocktails (see chapter 9).

○ **The Inn on 23rd.** 131 W. 23rd St. (btw. Sixth and Seventh aves.), New York, NY 10011. ☎ **877/387-2323** or 212/463-0330. Fax 212/463-0302. www.bbonline.com/ny/innon23rd. 11 units. A/C TV TEL. $150–$250 double; $350 suite. Rates include generous continental breakfast. Extra person $20. Children under 12 stay free in parents' room. AE, JCB, MC, V. Parking about $20 nearby. Subway: F, 1, 9 to 23rd St.

Friendly Annette and Barry Fisherman have launched one of Manhattan's few—and one of its finest—full-service bed-and-breakfast inns. This is a marvelous find for those who love individualized accommodations and a personal touch. All guest rooms are spacious. Each has a king or queen bed outfitted with a supremely comfy pillowtop mattress and top-quality linens; a satellite TV; a new private bathroom with hair dryer and thick Turkish terry towels; a phone with data port on the desk; an iron and ironing board in the roomy closet; and a wonderfully homey vibe. The gorgeous mix of antiques, family heirlooms, and contemporary art is the product of Annette's impeccable eye. I love the coolly sophisticated Rosewood Room, with gorgeous '60s built-ins; the Bamboo Room, peacefully quiet and elegantly Asian; the '40s Room, a Heywood–Wakefield lover's dream come true; and Ken's Cabin, a large, lodgey room with cushy, well-worn leather furnishings and wonderful Americana relics. The suite has a skylight with ultra-romantic Empire State Building views.

Welcoming public spaces include a cozy library with a stereo and VCR. An elevator means you don't have to cart your luggage up multiple flights of stairs, and a number of rooms have pull-out sofas or Murphy beds to accommodate more than two travelers. A real winner!

INEXPENSIVE

○ **Chelsea Lodge.** 318 W. 20th St. (btw. Eighth and Ninth aves.), New York, NY 10011. ☎ **800/373-1116** or 212/243-4499. Fax 212/342-7852. www.chelsealodge.com. 22 units (all with semiprivate bathroom). A/C TV. $70–$90 single; $85–$105 double. AE, DC, DISC, EURO, MC, V. Parking about $20 nearby. Subway: C, E to 23rd St.

Put down this book *right now* and go book a room at Chelsea Lodge, before every other budget-minded traveler looking for the city's best new bargain gets there first. Housed in a lovely brownstone on a landmarked block, this small hotel is brand new, utterly charming, and a terrific value. The young, friendly husband-and-wife owners have put in an incredible effort: Impeccable renovations have restored original woodwork to mint condition and created a homey, country-in-the-city vibe with beautiful wallpapers and wainscotting, smartly refinished vintage furniture, and lovely little touches like Hershey's Kisses on the fluffy pillows. The beds are the finest and best outfitted I've seen in this price category. The only place with a similar grown-up sensibility for the same money is Greenwich Village's Larchmont (above), but all bathroom facilities are shared there; at Chelsea Lodge, each room has its own sink and in-room shower stall, so you only have to share a cute toilet room with your neighbors. I won't kid you—rooms are petite, the open closets are small, and beds are full-size (queens wouldn't cut it). But considering the stylishness, the amenities—which include TV (not common in this price category), a ceiling fan, a small desk, and an alarm clock—and the great neighborhood, you'd be hard-pressed to do better for the money. Best for couples rather than shares. *Tip:* Try to book 2A, which is bigger than most, or one of the first-floor rooms, whose high ceilings make them feel more spacious.

✪ Chelsea Savoy Hotel. 204 W. 23rd St. (at Seventh Ave.), New York, NY 10011. ☎ **212/ 929-9353.** Fax 212/741-6309. www.chelseasavoy.qpg.com. 90 units. A/C TV TEL. $99–$115 single; $125–$165 double; $155–$195 quad. Rates include continental breakfast. Children stay free in parents' room. AE, JCB, MC, V. Parking $18 nearby. Subway: 1, 9 to 23rd St.

This 3-year-old hotel has been a welcome addition to Chelsea, a neighborhood abloom with art galleries, restaurants, and weekend flea markets but formerly devoid of nice, affordable hotels. The six-story Savoy was built from the ground up, so it isn't subject to the eccentricities of the mostly older hotels in this price range: The hallways are attractive and wide, the elevators are swift and silent, and the generic but cheery rooms are good size and have big closets and roomy, immaculate bathrooms with tons of counter space. Creature comforts abound: The rooms boast mattresses, furniture, textiles, and linens of high quality, plus the kinds of amenities you usually have to pay more for, like hair dryers, minifridges, alarm clocks, irons and ironing boards, in-room safes, and toiletries. Most rooms are street-facing and sunny; corner rooms tend to be brightest but noisiest. Ask for a darker, back-facing room if you crave total silence. There's a plain but pleasant sitting room off the lobby where you can enjoy your morning coffee over a selection of newspapers and magazines. The staff is young and helpful, and the increasingly hip neighborhood makes a good base for exploring both Midtown and downtown.

Chelsea Star Hotel. 300 W. 30th St. (at Eighth Ave.), New York, NY 10001. ☎ **877/ 827-6969** or 212/244-7827. Fax 212/279-9018. www.chelseastarhotel.citysearch.com or www.starhotelny.com. 25 rooms (none with private bathroom), 5 apts, 30 dorm beds. A/C. $59–$79 single; $79–$99 double; $99–$109 triple or quad; $149–$169 apartment (sleeps up to 4); $820–$980 weekly; $2,800 monthly; $35 per person in dorm (tax included). Extra person $10. AE, DISC, MC, V. Parking about $20 nearby. Subway: A, C, E to 34th St./Penn Station. Guests must be at least 18 years old.

It's hard to argue with the prices at this brand-new Generation Y–targeted place, especially considering the fresh feel and central location. Industrial-chic hallways lead to private rooms that are minuscule and bare-bones basic—more hostel than hotel-like, with nothing more than a firm bed and an open closet. But they're spotless, the mattresses and linens are good quality, and designer Rob Graf has infused them with enough style so they don't feel as dour as most super-cheap sleeps. They're individually dressed in cheeky themes ranging from the Disco Room (graced by a *Fever*-era Travolta in all his white-suited glory) to the Asian mod Madame Butterfly Room (tiny but lovely) to the glow-in-the-dark cosmos of the Orbit Room (complete with black light). Most popular—and the one to grab if you can snare it—is the Madonna Room, a relatively spacious quad where the Material Girl actually lived for a year just before she hit it big. Shoestring travelers who don't mind snoozing with strangers can opt for a single bunk in one of the charm-free but perfectly serviceable dorms. The shared hallway baths have showers only, but they're smart, clean, and new.

For a bit more money, you can even have your own pad: a stylishly retro-modern, fully loaded apartment with an equipped kitchen, private bathroom, and TV in the furnished living room. These babies are quite a deal, so book way ahead. *Tip:* The courtyard-facing apartments are quietest.

The front desk is staffed from 8am to midnight. Pay phones are available, as is a cash- and credit-activated Internet PC. The neighborhood—at the brink of Penn Station, more Midtown than Chelsea—may not be New York's finest, but it's cleaner and safer than ever, and cheap eateries and Irish pubs abound.

The Chelsea Star is a great addition to the budget hotel scene, but a word of warning: It is decidedly youth-oriented; mature travelers looking for standard amenities may be disappointed.

Colonial House Inn. 318 W. 22nd St. (btw. Eighth and Ninth aves.), New York, NY 10011. ☎ **800/689-3779** or 212/243-9669. Fax 212/633-1612. www.colonialhouseinn.com. 20 units (12 with shared bathroom). A/C TV TEL. $80–$99 single or double with shared bathroom, $125–$140 with private bathroom. Rates include expanded continental breakfast. 2-night minimum on weekends. Extra person $15. Weekly rates available. MC, V. Parking $20 nearby. Subway: C, E to 23rd St.

This charming 1850 brownstone, on a pretty residential block in the heart of gay-friendly Chelsea, was the first permanent home of the Gay Men's Health Crisis. The four-story walk-up caters to a largely gay and lesbian clientele, but the friendly staff welcomes everybody equally, and straight couples are a common sight. The whole place is beautifully maintained and professionally run. Rooms are small and basic but clean; all have radios and hair dryers, and those that share a hall bathroom (at a ratio of about three rooms per bathroom) have in-room sinks. Deluxe rooms—those with private bathrooms—also have minifridges, and a few have fireplaces that accommodate Duraflame logs. Both private and shared bathrooms are basic but nice. A terrific, mostly abstract art collection brightens the public spaces. At parlor level is a cute breakfast room where a continental spread is put out from 8am to noon daily, and coffee and tea are available all day. There's a nice roof deck split by a privacy fence; the area behind the fence is clothing optional. The neighborhood is chock-full of great restaurants and shopping, and offers easy access to the rest of the city. Book at least a month in advance for weekend stays.

7 The Flatiron District & Gramercy Park

See the "Midtown Accommodations" map on pp. 102–103 to find the hotels in this section.

EXPENSIVE

✪ **Hotel Giraffe.** 365 Park Ave. So. (at 26th St.), New York, NY 10016. ☎ **212/685-7700.** Fax 212/685-7700. www.hotelgiraffe.com. 73 units. A/C MINIBAR TV TEL. $325–$395 double; $475–$525 suite; from $2,500 penthouse suite. Rates include continental breakfast and weekday afternoon wine and cheese. No extra person charge (maximum of 4 in a room). AE, CB, DC, JCB, MC, V. Valet parking $24. Subway: 6 to 23rd St.

This all-new-in-2000 boutique hotel is poised to dominate the growing Flatiron hotel scene with its smartly designed accommodations and 1930s Moderne-inspired grace. Following the current trend, the refined lobby is as a multipurpose social space, transforming daily from cozy breakfast room to chic evening lounge, complete with pianist coaxing romantic standards out of a baby grand. Soothing, low-lit halls lead to guest rooms that brim with style, comfort, and high-tech functionality. There are no pretensions here—just good design.

All rooms are outfitted in a cushy modern style that suggests '30s deco with its elegant color palette, honey-hued wood, and rich fabrics. Even the smallest (280 sq. ft.) doesn't feel cramped thanks to high ceilings and some of the smartest built-ins I've seen, including huge granite-topped work desks (with high-speed digital and analog data ports), good wardrobes and closets, and lots of drawer space. You'll also find at least three multiline phones with direct-dial numbers, big TVs with VCRs, CD players, and terry robes. Oversize doors with gorgeous fluted glass lead to granite bathrooms with better-than-average counter space. Suites have living rooms with long-legged coffee tables that serve nicely for in-room dining or as additional work space.

Rates are high, but those who book early have a good chance at a king or double/double (the most spacious room configurations) in the "deluxe" category, which have French doors (with bedside-controlled blackout drapes) leading to a small balcony. But even the "superior" rooms have good-size windows that open to let fresh air in and almost magically shut out the street noise when closed.

Dining/Diversions: A stylish subterranean restaurant, Chinoiserie, should be serving cutting-edge French-Chinese cuisine and drawing a chic crowd by the time you arrive.

Amenities: Concierge, limited room service, same-day valet service, turndown (with cute-as-a-button giraffe-shaped cookies, no less), free video library, free access to nearby New York Sports Club. Daily newspapers available in lobby.

Inn at Irving Place. 56 Irving Place (btw. 17th and 18th sts.), New York, NY 10003. ☎ **800/ 685-1447** or 212/533-4600. Fax 212/533-4611. www.innatirving.com. 12 units. A/C MINI-BAR TV TEL. $295–$395 double; $450–$500 suite. Rates include continental breakfast. Extra person $25. AE, CB, DC, JCB, MC, V. Parking $25–$30 nearby. Subway: N, R, 4, 5, 6 to Union Square. Children under 12 not accepted.

Nestled on a charming little street just south of Gramercy Park, this jewel is arguably New York's most intimate, romantic, and historically evocative hotel. Housed in adjoining 1834 Greek Revival town houses, it's a favorite with honeymooners, world travelers, and New York couples on amorous weekend retreats. The decor is lavishly Victorian; each unique room has a fireplace (nonworking) and antiques, period paintings, Oriental rugs, lush Frette linens, and fresh flowers. Additionally, all rooms have VCRs, CD players, hair dryers, and dual-line phones with data port. Some rooms are on the small side and have limited storage space, so ask if you want your space or you're an overpacker like me. The cozy parlor is the perfect place to loll through Edith Wharton's *Age of Innocence*. (The writer was born nearby on 23rd Street, and there's a room here named for Countess Olenska, one of the novel's characters.)

Dining/Diversions: Lady Mendel's Tea Salon serves a supremely elegant five-course afternoon tea; in the evening, the salon becomes a sophisticated fireplace-lit lounge, serving cocktails, select liqueurs, appetizers, and desserts, as well as Lady Mendel's exotic teas and coffees. Fine cigars, cocktails, and appetizers are available at the chic Cibar (see chapter 9).

Amenities: Concierge, limited room service, valet service, free *New York Times,* meeting rooms; light shopping service available. Laptops and fax machines available on request. Nearby health club privileges for a fee.

MODERATE

Gramercy Park Hotel. 2 Lexington Ave. (btw. 21st and 22nd sts.), New York, NY 10010.
☎ **800/221-4083** or 212/475-4320. Fax 212/505-0535. 360 units. A/C TV TEL. $165–$170
single; $180 double; from $210 suite. Extra person $10. Children under 12 stay free in par-
ents' room. AE, CB, DC, DISC, EURO JCB, MC, V. Parking $28 nearby. Subway: 6 to 23rd St.
Pets accepted.

Opened in 1924, this old-world hotel has one of the best settings in the city. It's in
one of New York's loveliest neighborhoods, ideally located on the edge of the private
park—restricted to just a few area residents and to hotel guests, who can also get a
key—that gives Gramercy Park the air of a quiet London square.

Unfortunately, the hotel has been plagued by claims of neglect in recent years, but
management seems to be responding well, and the old place is looking good these
days. You'll still have to overlook the finer details—expect chipped paint here and
there, Brady Bunch–era shag carpeting in some halls, mix-and-match bathrooms that
have been updated haphazardly, and ancient TVs. But rooms are big by city standards,
decently furnished, and comfortable, and the hotel has a surprisingly appealing old
New York vibe. Standard doubles have a king bed or two doubles, and some suites
have pull-out sofas that make them large enough to sleep six; all have big closets,
unstocked minifridges, and hair dryers and fluffy towels in the roomy bathrooms.
Request a park-facing room, which costs no more but features a great view and a small
kitchenette. Off the bustling lobby is a continental restaurant and a smokey, divey
lounge with nightly entertainment that's drawing a young, retro-obsessed crowd;
there's also a beauty salon and newsstand. Valet service and morning room service
(7:30am–11am) are available.

INEXPENSIVE

✪ **Gershwin Hotel.** 7 E. 27th St. (btw. Fifth and Madison aves.), New York, NY 10016.
☎ **212/545-8000.** Fax 212/684-5546. www.gershwinhotel.com. 94 doubles, 31 4-person
dorms. A/C TV TEL (in private rooms only). $109–$139 double; $125–$149 triple; $139–$159
quad; $35 per person in dorm (tax included). Check Web site for seasonal deals. Extra person
$10. AE, CB, EURO, MC, V. Valet parking $20. Subway: N, R, 6 to 28th St.

If you see glowing horns protruding from a lipstick-red facade, you're in the right
place. This budget-conscious, youth-oriented hotel caters to up-and-coming artistic types with its bold modern art collection and wild style. The lobby is a colorful
postmodern cartoon of kitschy furniture and pop art by Lichtenstein, Warhol, de
Koonig, and lesser names. The standard rooms are clean and saved from the budget doldrums by bright colors, Picasso-style wall murals, Phillippe Starck–ish takes
on motel furnishings, and more modern art. All have data ports on the phones and
private bathrooms with hair dryers; none of the bathrooms are bad, but try to nab
yourself one of the cute, colorful new ones. The cheapest accommodations are
four- and eight-bedded dorms: just basic rooms with IKEA bunk beds sharing a
bath, but better than a hostel, especially if you're traveling with a group and can
claim one as your own.

One of the best things about the Gershwin is its great factory-esque vibe, sort of like
an artsy frat or sorority house. The hotel is more service-oriented than you usually see
at this price level—concierge and dry-cleaning/laundry service are even available.
There's always something going on, whether it's live comedy or jazz in the Living
Room or Red Room Bar, a film screening or barbecue on the rooftop garden, or an
opening at the hotel's own art gallery. (The cafe was under renovation at press time.)
An Internet-accessible computer is available for guests' use.

8 Times Square & Midtown West

VERY EXPENSIVE

✪ Le Parker Meridien. 118 W. 57th St. (btw. Sixth and Seventh aves.), New York, NY 10019. ☎ **800/543-4300** or 212/245-5000. Fax 212/708-7471. www.parkermeridien.com. 700 units. A/C MINIBAR TV TEL. $395–$545 double; $435–$575 junior suite; $450–1,050 1-bedroom suite. Special packages and weekend rates are usually on offer (as low as $175 at press time). Extra person $25. Children (12 and under on weekdays, 18 and under on weekends) stay free in parents' room. AE, CB, DC, DISC, ER, EURO, JCB, MC, V. Valet parking $37; self-parking $38. Subway: N, R, B, Q to 57th St. Pets accepted.

This formerly stuffy French luxury hotel has shed its Biedermeier-meets-the-1980s style in favor of a decidedly more modern, laid-back approach that's epitomized in its new slogan: "Uptown. Not Uptight." The airy neoclassical lobby has a new, hipper look that incorporates classic modern furnishings, cool Damien Hirst art above the concierge desk, and a staff fashionably outfitted in Stan Herman–designed black and ecru.

All of the spacious guest rooms should be redone by the time you arrive: Expect comfortable Scandinavian-style decor, sleek granite-and-limestone bathrooms, and the latest high-tech amenities, including built-in work desks with table-level outlets and data ports (both analog and digital); fax machines; 36-inch TVs with VCRs; and CD players. But it's the extensive—and top-notch—facilities that elevate the Parker to a higher level, drawing in a high-profile crowd that ranges from international CEOs to celebs who could afford to stay anywhere. There's no arguing with the value you get for your money here—especially if you get lucky and catch one of the Parker's great package deals.

Dining/Diversions: The Parker has one of the best hotel dining scenes in town. Nowhere is the morning meal treated with such reverence—and decadence—than at Norma's, a soaring, ultramodern ode to breakfast food that *New York* magazine named best in the city, while ultra-charming Seppi's is the uptown version of Prince Street's Raoul's, a classic New York French bistro. Jack's is a cool, Jetsons-style lobby bar with an intimate vibe and a fun menu of signature cocktails.

Amenities: The excellent (if unfortunately named) Gravity has more than 15,000 square feet housing a full-service health club: state-of-the-art equipment, a full menu of classes, squash and racquetball courts, a rooftop sundeck and jogging track, and a fabulous 42nd-floor pool with skyline views; personal trainers, nutrition counseling, and spa services are also on hand. Concierge, 24-hour room service, staffed full-service business center, valet service, turndown, newspaper delivery, baby-sitting, shuttle to Wall Street, express checkout, conference rooms.

✪ The Royalton. 44 W. 44th St. (btw. Fifth and Sixth aves.), New York, NY 10036. ☎ **800/635-9013** or 212/869-4400. Fax 212/575-0012. 205 units. A/C MINIBAR TV TEL. $350–$550 double; from $525 suite. Ask about promotional rates (sometimes as low as $260) and weekend deals. AE, MC, V. Valet parking $35. Subway: B, D, F, Q to 42nd St.

This was the second entry into the hotel market for Ian Schrager and the late Steve Rubell, who first tested the waters with Morgans (see "Midtown East & Murray Hill," later in this chapter) after the glory days of their 1970s disco heaven Studio 54 were a distant memory. More than a decade later, thanks to the pioneering design of French superstar Phillippe Starck, the Royalton is still an ultra-modern show stopper, with lighting fixtures that look like rhinoceros horns, attractive service people dressed in de rigueur black, and furniture—even carpet—with attitude. Even more importantly, Starck and Schrager have reinvented the idea of hotel: This is hotel as public space, as gathering space, as *scene*. Other hotels may have run with the idea, but this is the original, and the best. Never have you seen a lobby quite like this, buzzing with beautiful people and energy. This ain't exactly your average Hilton, baby.

Thankfully, comfort was never sacrificed for style. Beautifully designed with a loose cruise-ship theme in rich mahogany, cool slate, and white cotton duck, even the smallest guest room is spacious enough to have a cushioned banquette for reclining, a good-size work desk, and a roomy bathroom with a 5-foot round tub or an oversize shower stall (request one or the other when you book if it matters to you). All have a VCR, CD player, groovy Kiehl's toiletries, and two two-line speakerphones with direct-dial numbers and conference calling; some even have working fireplaces.

Dining/Diversions: 44 serves reliably good New American cuisine to publishing bigwigs and other power types; service can be lax if you're not one of the in-crowd. The perennially popular lobby features comfy seating nooks, an extensive martini list, a light menu of excellent finger foods, and the Round Bar, a 20-seat circular enclave done in high Jetsons style.

Amenities: Concierge, 24-hour room service, valet service, turndown, newspaper delivery, video rentals, express checkout, conference room, business center, fitness room with personal trainers available.

EXPENSIVE

✪ **The Algonquin.** 59 W. 44th St. (btw. Fifth and Sixth aves.), New York, NY 10036. ☎ **800/ 555-3000** or 212/840-6800. Fax 212/944-1419. www.camberleyhotels.com. 165 units. A/C TV TEL. $259–$379 double; $329–$529 suite. Rates can go as low as $179; check Web site or inquire about discounted rates or special package deals. AE, CB, DC, DISC, EURO, JCB, MC, V. Parking $25 across the street. Subway: B, D, F, Q to 42nd St.

This 1902 hotel is one of the Theater District's best-known landmarks: This is where the *New Yorker* was born, where Lerner and Loewe wrote *My Fair Lady,* and—most famously—where some of the biggest names in 1920s literati, among them Dorothy Parker, met to trade boozy quips at the celebrated Algonquin Round Table. I'm happy to report that the past isn't just a memory here anymore—a complete 1998 restoration returned this venerable hotel to its full Arts-and-Crafts splendor. True to its tradition, the Algonquin is a very social hotel: The splendid oak-paneled lobby is the comfiest and most welcoming in the city, made to linger over afternoon tea or a posttheater cocktail.

While posher than ever, the small rooms are comfortable but on the cramped side—fine for tourists out on the town all day, but not suitable for business travelers who may need to spread out and get some work done. Extras include stocked candy jars (a nice touch). The freshened bathrooms boast short but deep soaking tubs, hair dryers, and bathrobes. Twins are the roomiest doubles. For the ultimate New York vibe, opt for one of the literary-themed suites.

Dining/Diversions: Cocktails, tea, coffee, and an all-day menu are served in the lobby and adjacent Rose Room. The fabulous Oak Room is one of the city's top cabaret rooms, featuring such big names as Andrea Marcovicci. The Monday-night Spoken Word program continues, with speakers as diverse as Spalding Gray, Stanley Tucci, and Paul Theroux. Pub fare is available in the Blue Bar, home to a rotating collection of Hirschfeld drawings that is well worth a look.

Amenities: Well-outfitted fitness and business centers, concierge, room service (daily 7am–midnight), twice-daily maid service, valet service, baby-sitting, newspaper delivery, conference rooms.

Crowne Plaza Manhattan. 1605 Broadway (btw. 48th and 49th sts.), New York, NY 10019. ☎ **800/243-NYNY** or 212/977-4000. Fax 212/333-7393. www.crowneplaza.com. 770 units. A/C MINIBAR TV TEL. $229–$489 double; $479–$1,000 1-bedroom suite; $700–$1,350

Midtown Accommodations

The Algonquin **36**
Americana Inn **32**
The Avalon **26**
Belvedere Hotel **6**
The Benjamin **47**
Best Western Manhattan **29**
Best Western President **7**
Broadway Inn **10**
Casablanca Hotel **15**
Chelsea Lodge **18**
Chelsea Savoy Hotel **20**
Chelsea Star Hotel **16**
Clarion Hotel Fifth Avenue **34**
Colonial House Inn **17**
Comfort Inn Manhattan **31**
Comfort Inn Midtown **14**
Crowne Plaza Manhattan **4**
Crowne Plaza
  at the United Nations **41**
Doubletree Guest Suites **13**
Fitzpatrick Grand Central Hotel **42**
Four Seasons Hotel New York **57**
Gershwin Hotel **27**
The Gorham **51**
Gramercy Park Hotel **23**
Habitat Hotel **58**
Hotel Bedford **40**
Hotel Chelsea **19**
Hotel Edison **11**
Hotel Giraffe **24**
Hotel Metro **30**
Hotel Wolcott **28**
The Inn at Irving Place **22**
The Inn on 23rd **21**
The Kimberly **46**
Le Parker Meridien **52**
The Lowell **56**

continues on
opposite page

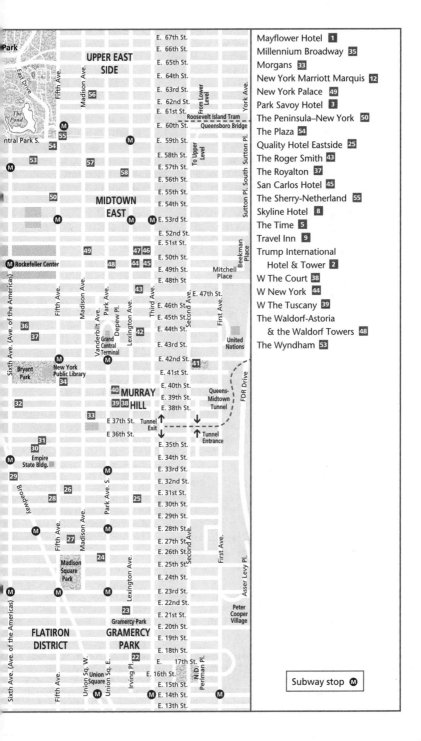

Mayflower Hotel **1**
Millennium Broadway **35**
Morgans **33**
New York Marriott Marquis **12**
New York Palace **49**
Park Savoy Hotel **3**
The Peninsula–New York **50**
The Plaza **54**
Quality Hotel Eastside **25**
The Roger Smith **43**
The Royalton **37**
San Carlos Hotel **45**
The Sherry-Netherland **55**
Skyline Hotel **8**
The Time **5**
Travel Inn **9**
Trump International
  Hotel & Tower **2**
W The Court **38**
W New York **44**
W The Tuscany **39**
The Waldorf-Astoria
  & the Waldorf Towers **48**
The Wyndham **53**

Subway stop **M**

103

2-bedroom suite. Ask about weekend rates, senior rates, and other discounts; check Web site for special deals. Two children under 19 stay free in parents' room using existing bedding. AE, CB, DC, DISC, EURO, JCB, MC, V. Valet parking $37. Subway: 1, 9 to 50th St.; N, R to 49th St.

When Holiday Inn went upscale in 1994 with its new Crowne Plaza line, this Times Square tower became its international flagship. In the neon heart of Broadway, the 46-story glass monolith is as good as a mass-market chain hotel gets—and you couldn't be better located for Midtown's top attractions. The comfortable guest rooms boast contemporary furnishings, marble bathrooms, and all the features you've come to expect, such as in-room safes, plus extras like coffeemakers. Noted designer Adam Tihany gave the public spaces new zest in '99. The top 4 floors are devoted to Crowne Plaza Club rooms, which also feature free continental breakfast, evening hors d'oeuvres, and other extras. Sure, rack rates are high, but discounts are often available, especially for weekend travelers.

Dining/Diversions: There are three satisfactory, if unmemorable, restaurants, including the well-situated Samplings Bar, which serves contemporary pre- and posttheater meals overlooking the lights of Broadway. The Lobby Bar is a comfortable lounge that invites you to sink into a club chair, order up a martini, and stay a while.

Amenities: Excellent fitness center with 50-foot pool and sauna, concierge, 24-hour room service, valet service, newspaper delivery, express checkout, business center, secretarial services, conference rooms, tour desk.

✪ **Doubletree Guest Suites.** 1568 Broadway (47th St. at Seventh Ave.), New York, NY 10036. ☎ **800/222-TREE** or 212/719-1600. Fax 212/921-5212. www.doubletreehotels.com. 400 units. A/C MINIBAR TV TEL. $239–$350 2-room suite; from $400 family or conference suite. Senior, corporate, and AAA discounts available; also inquire about weekend package deals, which included *Lion King* packages at press time. Extra person $20. Children under 12 stay free in parents' suite. AE, DC, DISC, JCB, MC, V. Valet parking $30. Subway: N, R to 49th St.

For less than the cost of a standard room in many hotels, you can have a very nice suite in this 43-story glass monolith, Times Square's only all-suite hotel. Each suite has a separate bedroom and a living room with a pull-out sofa, a dining/work table, a refrigerator, a wet bar, a microwave, a coffeemaker, two TVs, and three phones. For businesspeople, conference suites feature workstations with convenient data ports and outlets to plug in your laptop, and they're large enough for small meetings. What's more, this is a family-friendly hotel with a floor of childproof suites and special amenities for kids, such as the Kids Club, designed by Philadelphia's Please Touch Museum for children 3 to 12, featuring a playroom, an arts-and-crafts center, and computer and video games. Cribs and strollers are available, and there's a kids' room-service menu.

Dining/Diversions: There's a restaurant serving hotel-standard continental and American cuisine, plus a pleasant Broadway-themed piano bar and a free comedy showcase Friday and Saturday evenings.

Amenities: Fitness center, Kids Club with children's programs, concierge, 24-hour room service, valet service, newspaper delivery, express checkout, coin-op laundry room, guest services desk, business center with secretarial services available, newsstand and gift shop, meeting and banquet rooms.

The Gorham. 136 W. 55th St. (btw. Sixth and Seventh aves.), New York, NY 10019. ☎ **800/735-0710** or 212/245-1800. Fax 212/582-8332. www.gorhamhotel.com. 115 units. A/C TV TEL. $205–$400 single or double; $235–$475 suite. Rates can go as low as $205; check Web site for seasonal deals and packages. Extra person $20. Children under 16 stay free in parents' room. AE, CB, DC, EURO, JCB, MC, V. Valet parking $20 next door. Subway: B, D, E to 53rd St.; B, N, R, Q to 57th St.

ⓜ   Family-Friendly Hotels

Doubletree Guest Suites *(p. 104)*   Your young ones will have their very own Kids Club (for ages 3 to 12), with a playroom, an arts-and-crafts center, and computer and video games. For after playtime, there's an entire floor of child-proof suites, complete with kitchenettes and living rooms, for just about the same price you'd pay for a regular room in another Theater District hotel of this high quality.

The Gorham *(p. 104)*   This well-located Midtown choice is another good deal for families, since the large rooms are big enough for two queen beds, and the well-priced suites feature pull-out sofas in the living rooms to accommodate the kids. A fully equipped kitchenette with microwave will make Mom and Dad happy, and Nintendo on the TV will keep Junior occupied for hours.

Gramercy Park Hotel *(p. 99)*   There are no special amenities that make this moderately priced, old-world hotel particularly kid-friendly, but you'll see a lot of youngsters cruising the wood-paneled lobby nonetheless. That's because parents end up with a lot of space for their money here: Standard doubles are big enough for two double beds, still with play space to spare, and some suites have pull-out sofas that make them large enough to sleep six.

Hotel Beacon *(p. 128)*   Ideally located in one of the city's most kid-friendly neighborhoods, the Beacon is one of the best deals in town for families. Fitted with two double beds, virtually all of the spacious standard rooms are big enough for wallet-watching families. The well-outfitted one- and two-bedroom suites are great bargains that give families room to spread out. Every room features a fully equipped kitchenette that makes breakfast and snacktime a cinch, and there's a Laundromat on-site to make Mom and Dad's life easier.

Hotel Olcott *(p. 131)*   Families looking for cheap digs will be happy as clams here. Every big one-bedroom apartment has a kitchenette, a dining table for four, and space to spread out. On the downside, there's TV only in the living room and sofas don't pull out, but most bedrooms have two queens, and the friendly management will lend you a cot or an extra bed for the living room if you prefer. Central Park is just steps away, and there's even a barbecue joint in the building for affordable family meals.

The Milburn *(p. 131)*   This neighbor to the Beacon also offers rooms and suites with kitchenettes, but for even less. The Milburn may not be quite as nice as the Beacon, but it offers equal value for your dollar, and the one-bedroom suites with a pull-out queen sofa are a great bargain for families.

San Carlos Hotel *(p. 124)*   Here's another hotel that will give you the kind of space a family needs. The large suites have pull-out sofas in the living rooms and kitchenettes with microwaves and coffeemakers; some even have full dining-room sets. The junior suites have all the same amenities and are still plenty big enough for wallet-watching families. Coin-op laundry and free breakfast are additional plusses.

Skyline Hotel and **Travel Inn** *(pp. 110–111)*   Hauling the kids to town in the mini-van? You can take advantage of the free parking at these two nice, newly renovated motor hotels. Even if you're not sporting your own wheels, you'll like the family-size rooms, and the kids will love the pools at playtime (a rarity in affordable hotels).

Wonderfully located in the best section of Midtown West—close enough to the Broadway action, yet far enough from the bustle and grime that goes along with it— Gorham is a wonderful, well-priced choice. A 1998 face-lift refreshed an already bright look, and new soft goods (pillows, bedspreads, and so on) in 2000 illustrate management's commitment to maintaining the excellent value. All of the large, pleasingly contemporary rooms have fully equipped kitchenettes with microwaves and coffeemakers; 27-inch TVs with Nintendo; a spacious work desk; three multiline phones with private direct-dial numbers (four in suites); two queen-size or one king bed; and marble bathrooms with makeup mirrors and digital water-temperature controls. The suites feature a separate sitting room with a pull-out sofa and an extra TV, plus whirlpool tubs and velour robes. The location, not far from Times Square and the theme restaurants of 57th Street, makes the Gorham a favorite with kids—don't even get them started on the Nintendo.

At press time, the hotel was offering theater packages that included hard-to-get tickets to *The Lion King;* check the hotel's Web site or inquire whether this or other packages are available when you call.

Dining: There's a northern Italian restaurant site, plus a pleasant breakfast room for the morning meal.

Amenities: Fitness center, concierge, room service (daily 7am–11pm), valet service, newspaper delivery, express checkout, secretarial services, baby-sitting, conference rooms. VCRs available; access to nearby health club.

☉ Millennium Broadway. 145 W. 44th St. (btw. Sixth Ave. and Broadway), New York, NY 10036. ☎ **800/622-5569** or 212/768-0847. Fax 212/768-0847. www.millenniumbroadway. com. 752 units. A/C MINIBAR TV TEL. $305–$345 Millennium double; $395–$495 Premier double. Inquire about special deals and weekend and theater packages, and check for Internet-only rates. Extra person $20 (if rollaway required). Children under 12 stay free in parents' room. AE, CB, DC, DISC, JCB, MC, V. Valet parking $42. Subway: N, R, 1, 2, 3, 9 to Times Square; B, D, F, Q to 42nd St. Pets accepted.

The Millennium Broadway (which, unlike the unaffiliated Millenium downtown, knows how to spell) is one of the top business hotels in the city, but its prime Times Square location and well-priced packages make it a good bet for leisure travelers, too. The spacious rooms have a lovely art deco style, with black-and-white photos, rich red mahogany, and black lacquer details. The fabrics and linens are of excellent quality, the bathrooms have lots of marble counter space, and nice extras include a writing desk, comfy streamline club chairs, a VCR, and multiple two-line phones with all the gadgets. Club rooms, on floors 46 to 52, feature larger-than-normal desks, fax machines, coffeemakers, turndown service, and free continental breakfast and evening cocktails at the top-floor Club Lounge.

New in 1999, an adjoining tower houses the luxurious, high-tech Premier rooms, done in a more contemporary style, with blond ash, green glass, and natural fibers. The Omaha mattresses—the same ones used in the far more expensive Four Seasons— done up in Frette linens just may be the most glorious beds in town. The rooms also feature larger-than-average work space with all the necessary gadgets, a love seat with its own cable-knit throw for curling up, coffeemaker, fax machine, CD player, and oversize bathrooms with soaking tubs and separate showers. The Premier also boasts its own lounge with continental breakfast, cocktails, and large flat-screen TV.

Dining: With very good New American cuisine and a friendly staff, the highly regarded restaurant Charlotte is a classy choice for pre- and postdinner dining as well as cocktails and Sunday brunch.

Amenities: Fitness center with sauna, concierge, room service (6:30am–11pm), valet service, twice-daily maid service, newspaper delivery, video rentals, express checkout, secretarial services, baby-sitting, business center. Five-floor Manhattan Conference Center, with 33 dedicated meeting rooms and 11,000 square feet of exhibition space.

New York Marriott Marquis. 1535 Broadway (btw. 45th and 46th sts.), New York, NY 10036. ☎ **800/843-4898** or 212/398-1900. Fax 212/704-8930. www.marriott.com. 1,946 units. A/C MINIBAR TV TEL. $250–$550 double; $290–$590 concierge-level double; from $500 suite. Ask about AAA, AARP, and corporate discounts. Extra person $20. Children under 18 stay free in parents' room. AE, CB, DC, DISC, JCB, MC, V. Parking $33–$40. Subway: N, R, 1, 2, 3, 9 to Times Square; N, R to 49th St. Pets accepted.

The construction of the 50-story Marriott Marquis was a milestone for Times Square in 1985. Advocates hailed it as a sign of the neighborhood's resurgence, but the Helen Hayes and Morosco theaters were destroyed to make room for it, leading theater lovers to argue that it portended the end of Broadway. Both the hotel and the Great White Way have thrived in ways no one could've predicted. Though many New Yorkers love to hate the pedestrian-unfriendly John Portman–designed hotel, it's a top choice of travelers. Its centerpieces are Portman's signature atrium, rising 37 floors to be the world's tallest, and the glass-enclosed elevators that zip up the atrium's center at knee-buckling speed. The surprisingly large guest rooms have two-line phones, work desks with ergonomic chairs, and coffeemakers. Concierge-level amenities include free continental breakfast and evening hors d'oeuvres. The whole place is in the midst of a $20 million refurbishment, so expect everything to feel fresh. The Marriott frequently hosts conventions and business meetings, so its lobby is often bustling and chaotic.

Dining/Diversions: If it's a clear night, head up to the 3-story revolving rooftop restaurant, aptly named the View, for cocktails and skyline views. There are more restaurants and lounges in the atrium, but the dining gets better just steps outside the hotel (see chapter 6 for recommendations).

Amenities: Health club with whirlpool and sauna, concierge, 24-hour room service, laundry and dry-cleaning service, newspaper delivery, express checkout, business center, conference rooms, gift shop and newsstand, salon, American Express travel desk.

The Time. 224 W. 49th St. (btw. Broadway and Eighth Ave.), New York, NY 10019. ☎ **877/ TIME-NYC** or 212/246-5252. Fax 212/245-2305. www.thetimenyc.com. 192 units. A/C MINIBAR TV TEL. $270–$450 double; from $425 suite. AE, DC, DISC, MC, V. Parking $20. Subway: C, E, 1, 9 to 50th St.; N, R to 49th St.

The design buffs among you are likely to have heard the buzz on this first hotel designed by Adam Tihany, the man behind such incredible spaces as Le Cirque 2000, Jean-Georges, and Wolfgang Puck's Spago restaurants. It's a dazzler, all right, but lacks a few of the extras—like in-room CD players and VCRs—that you get from some of its high-style competitors like the new W Court. Still, it's hard to beat the Theater District location and the cool boutique-chic vibe.

What's more, the guest rooms are inviting, comfortable, and surprisingly practical (much more so than the similarly sized rooms at W New York). They're done in a minimalist style in one of three primary color schemes: your choice of red, yellow, or blue, accented with black and gray. Everything is top quality but understated—think clean lines, low furnishings, and soft backlighting (including the cleverest bedside lighting I've seen). Nicely designed touches like a coffeemaker caddy and built-in valet make the rooms extra efficient (some have double closets instead of drawer space, though, so ask if it matters to you). Still, expect small and you won't be disappointed. Amenities include a printer/copier/fax machine on the big worktable, Web TV, and Bose radios. Things get a bit silly with color-matched scents (yours to invoke only if you wish) and fruits, but the gimmicks don't intrude. Some of the bathrooms are on the smaller side, but all have double-wide showers (suites have whirlpool tubs) and clever cubbyholes that provide additional storage space.

Dining/Diversions: The first New York restaurant from celebrity chef Jean-Louis Palladin, master of nouveau French cooking, hasn't proved to be the tough reservation the hoteliers were hoping for; still, Palladin's inventive bistro-style cooking has garnered two coveted stars from the *New York Times,* and they're well earned. The lobby-level Time Lounge is a futuristic hot spot, with a tapas bar providing an individual twist.

Amenities: Concierge, room service (6:30–10:30am and noon–11pm), valet service, turndown, newspaper delivery, express checkout, gift shop, international newsstand, conference room, access to nearby health club. VCR and videos, CD players, mobile phones, and personal shopper service available.

MODERATE

In addition to the choices below, you might also consider the **Best Western Manhattan,** 17 W. 32nd St. (btw. between Fifth and Sixth aves.; ☎ 800/567-7720 or 212/736-1600; www.applecorehotels.com), where the modest but well-kept rooms range seasonally from $89 to $189, or $129 to $249 for suites. You have a good deal if you can get a room on the lower end of that scale, especially with free continental breakfast, small business and fitness centers, and a rooftop bar with great views of the Empire State Building sweetening the pie.

An even better choice is the **Best Western President Hotel,** 234 W. 48th St. (btw. Broadway and Eighth Ave.; ☎ 800/826-4667 or 212/632-9000; www.bestwesternhotels.com). Rooms are slightly more expensive here—$129 to $229 double, $229 to $499 suite, depending on the season—but the decor is nice, beds are especially comfortable, and the Theater District location is great. Best of all, rates have been known to drop to $89 in the low season, and you might be able to do even better if you qualify for senior or AAA rates.

Belvedere Hotel. 319 W. 48th St. (btw. Eighth and Ninth aves.), New York, NY 10036. ☎ 888/HOTEL58 or 212/245-7000. Fax 212/245-4455. www.newyorkhotel.com. 400 units. A/C TV TEL. $140–$240 double. AAA discounts available; check Web site for special Internet deals (as low as $115 at press time). AE, DC, DISC, MC, V. Parking $17 on next block. Subway: C, E to 50th St.

Here's another great choice from the Empire Hotel Group, the people behind the Upper West Side's Lucerne and Newton. Done with a sharp retro-modern deco flair, the public spaces are much more impressive than you'd expect to find in this price range. They lead to sizable, comfortable, attractive rooms with smallish but very nice bathrooms with hair dryers as well as pantry kitchenettes with fridges, sinks, and microwaves (BYO utensils or go plastic). Beds are nice and firm, fabrics are of high quality, and you'll find voice mail and data ports on the telephones and an iron and ironing board in the closet. The decor is pleasing in all rooms, but ask for a renovated one, where you'll get good-quality cherry-wood furnishings, plus an alarm clock and work desk (in all but a few). Also ask for a high floor (8 and above) for great views; usually they'll cost no more (ask when booking).

Extras that make the Belvedere an excellent value include dry-cleaning and laundry service, a self-serve Laundromat, electronic luggage lockers, fax and Internet-access machines, a stylish breakfast room and light-bites cafe for guests, and the terrific Churrascaria Plataforma Brazilian restaurant (see chapter 6). At press time, a cocktail lounge and meeting rooms were in the works. The Theater District neighborhood is loaded with great restaurants along Ninth Avenue and nearby Restaurant Row.

✪ Broadway Inn. 264 W. 46th St. (at Eighth Ave.), New York, NY 10036. ☎ **800/826-6300** or 212/997-9200. Fax 212/768-2807. www.broadwayinn.com. 40 units. A/C TV TEL. $95–$105 single; $125–$180 double; $205 suite. Rates include continental breakfast. Extra person $10. Children under 12 stay free in parents' room. AE, DC, DISC, JCB, MC, V. Parking $18 3 blocks away. Subway: S, 1, 2, 3, 7, 9 to 42nd St./Times Square; A, C, E to 42nd St.; N, R to 49th St.

More like a San Francisco B&B than a Theater District hotel, this lovely, welcoming inn is a real charmer. The second-floor lobby sets the homey, easygoing tone with stocked bookcases, cushy seating, and cafe tables where breakfast is served. The rooms are basic but comfy, outfitted in an appealing neo-deco style with firm beds, good-quality linens and textiles, and hair dryers in the nice bathrooms. The whole place is impeccably kept—neatniks won't have a quibble. Two rooms have king beds and whirlpool tubs, but the standard doubles are just fine for two if you're looking to save some dough. If there's more than two of you, or you're looking to stay a while, the suites—with pull-out sofa, microwave, minifridge, data ports on the phones, and lots of closet space—are a great deal. The location can be noisy, but double-paned windows keep the rooms surprisingly peaceful; still, ask for a back-facing one if you're extra sensitive.

The inn's biggest asset is its terrific staff, who go above and beyond to make guests happy and at home in New York; service doesn't get any better in this price range. And this corner of the Theater District is now porn-free and gentrifying beautifully; it makes a great home base, especially for theatergoers. The inn has inspired a loyal following, so reserve early. However, there's no elevator in the four-story building, so overpackers and travelers with limited mobility should book elsewhere.

✪ Casablanca Hotel. 147 W. 43rd St. (just east of Broadway), New York, NY 10036. ☎ **888/922-7225** or 212/869-1212. Fax 212/391-7585. www.casablancahotel.com. 48 units. A/C MINIBAR TV TEL. $245–$265 double; $375 suite. Rates include continental breakfast and afternoon snacks. Check Web site for Internet deals ($219 at press time). AE, DC, JCB, MC, V. Parking $18. Subway: N, R, 1, 2, 3, 9 to 42nd St./Times Square.

A wealth of freebies—including breakfast; coffee, tea, and cookies all day; wine, beer, and cheese weekday evenings; complimentary access to a nearby health club (with pool and sauna, no less); and complimentary Internet access—make this stylish Moroccan-themed boutique hotel an excellent value for midrange travelers and earn it a spot in the moderate category, although it's more expensive than the other choices I've included here. With vibrant mosaic tiles, warm woods and rattan, potted palms, and North African–themed art gracing both the public spaces and guest rooms, the vibe is just right—the only thing missing is Bogart and Bergman. The rooms aren't big, but they're nicely outfitted with comfortable platform beds, ceiling fans, VCRs, two-line phones with voice mail and data ports, full-length mirrors, hair dryers, and double-paned windows for quiet. The minibars are stocked with reasonably priced water, sodas, and snacks. The bathrooms are done in gorgeous Andalusian tile, and even the smallest is spacious enough for an oversize shower (request a tub when booking if you want one). Suites have pull-out sofas that convert to single beds, but they're really too small to accommodate families. Everything is high-quality, and beautiful touches like Murano glass sconces and framed Moroccan carpets in the halls add an extra flair.

The small staff is attentive, and the ambitious manager is constantly at work improving the property. Rick's Cyber Cafe is a comfortable second-floor lounge where you can enjoy continental breakfast and all those other goodies; there's a serve-your-self cappuccino machine, an extra-large TV, and PCs with T-1 connectivity. A tiled second-floor courtyard is ideal for summer lounging, and the rooftop deck is a perfect vantage for watching the New Year's ball drop. Dry-cleaning and laundry service, videos, a small high-tech meeting room, and cell phones are also available. And with a sterling Theater District location, who could ask for anything more? Book well ahead, as an increasing number of happy repeat guests and corporate clients fill this place up fast.

Comfort Inn Manhattan. 42 W. 35th St. (Fifth and Sixth aves.), New York, NY 10001. ☎ **800/228-5150** or 212/947-0200. Fax 212/594-3047. www.comfortinnmanhattan.com. 131 units. A/C TV TEL. Jan–July $129–$234 double; Aug–Dec $189–$349 double. Rates include continental breakfast. Ask about senior, AAA, corporate, and promotional discounts; check www.comfortinn.com for online booking discounts (10% off at press time). Extra person $15. Children 18 and under stay free in parents' room. AE, DC, DISC, JCB, MC, V. Parking $16–$18 in nearby garage. Subway: B, D, F, Q, N, R to 34th St.

This centrally located hotel is a good choice, especially for those who prefer to go with a national chain with a familiar profile and a proven reputation. It's on a fine block just a stone's throw from some of Midtown's biggest attractions, including the Empire State Building and Macy's. Don't expect lots of personality: This is a standard, basically characterless chain hotel, but the rooms are clean, well maintained, and remarkably large by Manhattan standards. Nice extras include big closets, hair dryers, in-room safes, on-command movies, and voice mail and data ports on the phones. About 20 rooms have microwaves and minifridges, and about 30 king-bedded rooms come with sleeper sofas. The lobby is attractive enough to invite lounging, and the front desk staff is friendly and helpful. The substantial continental breakfast spread that's included in the rates is a big plus.

○ **Hotel Metro.** 45 W. 35th St. (btw. Fifth and Sixth aves.), New York, NY 10001. ☎ **800/356-3870** or 212/947-2500. Fax 212/279-1310. www.hotelmetronyc.com. 174 units. A/C TV TEL. $150–$225 standard double; $165–$325 deluxe double/quad; $205–$400 suite. Rates include continental breakfast. Check with airlines and other package operators for package deals. Extra person $25. Children under 13 stay free in parents' room. AE, DC, MC, V. Parking $18 nearby. Subway: B, D, F, Q, N, R to 34th St.

The Metro is the hands-down best choice in Midtown for those who don't want to sacrifice either style or comfort for affordability. This lovely art deco–style jewel has larger rooms than you'd expect for the price. They're outfitted with smart retro furnishings, playful fabrics, and extras like voice mail and data port on the phone, hair dryers and huge mirrors in the smallish but well-appointed marble bathrooms, alarm clocks, and irons and ironing boards in the closets. Only about half the bathrooms have tubs, but the others have shower stalls big enough for two (executive rooms have whirlpool tubs). The neo-deco design gives the whole place an air of New York glamour that I've not otherwise seen in this price range. A great collection of black-and-white photos, from Man Ray classics to Garbo and Dietrich portraits, adds to the vibe.

One of the really nice things about this hotel is its welcoming public spaces: The comfy, firelit library/lounge area off the lobby, where buffet breakfast is laid out and the coffeepot's on all day, is a popular hangout, and the well-furnished rooftop terrace boasts one of the most breathtaking views of the Empire State Building I've ever seen (a great place to order up room service from the stylish Metro Grill—see chapter 6). Valet service, a sizable fitness room, and complimentary breakfast add to the great value. One of my all-time favorites—highly recommendable.

Skyline Hotel. 725 Tenth Ave. (at 49th St.), New York, NY 10019. ☎ **800/433-1982** or 212/586-3400. Fax 212/582-4604. www.skylinehotelny.com. 230 units. A/C TV TEL. $149–$179 double; $171–$219 junior or full suite. Extra person $15. Children 14 and under stay free in parents' room. AE, CB, DISC, MC, V. Free storage parking (charge for in/out privileges). Subway: A, C, E to 50th St. Pets accepted with $200 deposit.

This nice, newly renovated motor hotel offers predictable comforts and some uncommon extras—free storage parking (easily worth $25 or more a day) and a lovely indoor pool—that make it an excellent value. A pleasant lobby leads to motel-standard rooms that are a far cry from stylish, but so what? They're bigger than most in this price range and boast decent-size closets; small work desks; and double-paned windows that open to let fresh air in, and shut out a surprising amount of street noise when closed. Some rooms have brand-new bathrooms, but the older ones are still fine. Everything is very well kept, and lots of freshening was in progress during my last visit. The suites have pull-out sofas, making them a great deal for families. (The junior suites are basically one large room, while the full suites have the sitting area and an extra TV in a separate room.) On the downside, some closets are open to the room, there are no bedside alarm clocks or data ports (data ports are scheduled), and hair dryers and irons must be requested from housekeeping.

On site is a pleasing restaurant with a full bar; a Gray Line tour desk; a gift shop; a big, nice ballroom; and a bright rooftop meeting room. Room service is offered from 7am to 11pm, and laundry service is available. The pool has a nicely tiled deck and plush deck chairs, but it's only open in the evenings Monday through Friday (all day Sat and Sun), so don't count on an early-morning swim.

Travel Inn. 515 W. 42nd St. (just west of Tenth Ave.), New York, NY 10036. ☎ **888/HOTEL58,** 800/869-4630, or 212/695-7171. Fax 212/268-3542. www.newyorkhotel.com. 160 units. A/C TV TEL. $150–$200 double; $250 executive suite. AAA discounts available; check Web site for special Internet deals. Extra person $15. Children under 16 stay free in parents' room. AE, DC, DISC, MC, V. Free self-parking. Subway: A, C, E to 42nd St.–Port Authority Bus Terminal.

Extras like a huge outdoor pool and sundeck, an up-to-date fitness room, and free parking (with in and out privileges!) make the Travel Inn another terrific deal, similar to the one offered by the Skyline Hotel (directly above). Like the Skyline, the Travel Inn may not be loaded with personality, but it does offer the clean, bright regularity of a good chain hotel—an attractive trait in a city where "quirky" is the catchword at most affordable hotels. Rooms are oversize and comfortably furnished, with extra-firm beds, work desks, alarm clocks, full-length mirrors, irons and ironing boards, and hair dryers in the bathrooms. (Phones have voice mail, but no data ports yet.) A total renovation had just been completed at press time, and everything feels new and fresh,

How Do I Choose?

The **Skyline Hotel** and **Travel Inn** are similarly outfitted and similarly well-run motor hotels. Which one you should choose depends entirely on your needs.

If you think you'll want to have some laundry or dry cleaning done while you're in residence, only the Skyline will take care of it for you. If working out is your thing, only Travel Inn has a fitness room. Since Travel Inn's outdoor pool is only usable in summer, the Skyline's indoor pool makes it the better choice for swimmers in cooler weather (beware of limited hours, though). Conventioneers will likely prefer Travel Inn's location, just a stone's throw from the Jacob Javits Center.

Attention, drivers—here's the deciding factor for you: The Skyline's free valet parking requires you to leave your car put for the duration of your stay; if you take it out midstay, you're paying full rate from the time you bring it back until the time you leave. So if you think you'll want to use your wheels while you're in residence, free in-and-out privileges make Travel Inn the only way to go (self-parking is a big plus, too).

If none of these factors affect your decision making, simply go for the better rate.

even the nicely tiled bathrooms. Even the smallest double is sizable and has a roomy bathroom. There's an on-site coffee shop, a gift shop run by Gray Line that can book tours and airport transfers, a well-equipped conference room, and a lifeguard on duty at that terrific pool in season. The neighborhood has gentrified nicely and isn't as far-flung as you might think: Off-Broadway theaters and great affordable restaurants are at hand, and it's just a 10-minute walk to the Theater District. A good bet even if you don't have a car.

✪ **The Wyndham.** 42 W. 58th St. (btw. Fifth and Sixth aves.), New York, NY 10019. ☎ **800/257-1111** or 212/753-3500. Fax 212/754-5638. 212 units. AC TV TEL. $160 double; $190–$230 1-bedroom suite; $330–$375 2-bedroom suite (up to 4 guests included in rate). AE, DC, MC, V. Parking $45 next door. Subway: N, R to Fifth Ave.; B, Q to 57th St.

This family-owned charmer is one of Midtown's best hotel deals—and it's perfectly located to boot, on a great block steps away from Fifth Avenue shopping and Central Park. The quirky Wyndham is stuck in the '70s on all fronts, but its guest rooms are enormous by city standards, comfortable, and loaded with character. The entire hotel features a wild collection of wallpaper, from candy stripes to crushed velvets, so some rooms definitely cross the ticky-tacky line. But others are downright lovely, with such details as rich Oriental carpets and well-worn libraries, and the eclectic art collection that lines the walls boasts some real gems. If you're put in a room that's not to your taste, just ask politely to see another one; the staff is usually happy to accommodate.

Most important, you get a lot for your money: The rooms are universally large, and all feature huge walk-in closets (the biggest I've ever seen). The surprisingly affordable suites also have full-fledged living rooms, dressing areas, and cold kitchenettes (fridge only). You'll need a two-bedroom suite if you're bringing the kids (only two guests are allowed in standard rooms or one-bedroom suites), but the rate is a steal considering the space you get. Valet service is available, as is limited room service (the restaurant should be in full swing by the time you arrive). They tell me that the phones have data ports now, but don't expect an alarm clock, a hair dryer, luxury toiletries, or other modern amenities. But so what? At these prices, you can afford to invest in travel sizes.

INEXPENSIVE

Americana Inn. 69 W. 38th St. (at Sixth Ave.), New York, NY 10018. ☎ **888/HOTEL58** or 212/840-2019. Fax 212/840-1830. www.newyorkhotel.com. 50 units (all with shared bathroom). A/C TV TEL. $75–$105 double. Extra person $10. AE, MC, V. Parking $27 nearby. Subway: B, D, F, Q to 42nd St.; N, R to 34th St.

The cheapest hotel from the Empire Hotel Group—the people behind the Belvedere, the Lucerne, and the Newton among other top-notch properties—is a winner in the budget-basic category. Linoleum floors give the rooms an unfortunate institutional quality, but the hotel is professionally run and immaculately kept. Rooms are mostly spacious, with good-size closets and private sinks, and the beds are the most comfortable I've found at this price. Rooms come with a double bed or two twins; a few can accommodate three guests in two twin beds and a pull-out sofa. There's one hall bathroom for every three rooms or so, and all are spacious and spotless. Every floor has a common kitchenette with microwave, stove, and fridge (BYO cooking tools and utensils, or go plastic). The five-story building has an elevator, and four rooms are accessible for disabled travelers. The Garment District location couldn't be more convenient for Midtown sightseeing and shopping. Ask for a back-facing room away from the street noise.

Comfort Inn Midtown. 129 W. 46th St. (btw. Sixth Ave. and Broadway), New York, NY 10036. ☎ **800/567-7720** or 212/221-2600. Fax 212/790-2760. www.applecorehotels.com.

79 units. A/C TV TEL. $89–$219 double, depending on season. Rates include continental break-fast. Ask about senior, AAA, corporate, and promotional discounts; check www.comfortinn.com for online booking discounts. Extra person $10. Children under 14 stay free in parents' room. AE, DC, DISC, MC, V. Parking $24 nearby. Subway: 1, 2, 3, 9 to 42nd St./Times Square; N, R to 49th St.; B, D, F, Q to 47–50th sts./Rockefeller Center.

A major 1998 renovation has turned the formerly dour Hotel Remington into a pleas-ingly value-oriented member of the Comfort Inn chain. Rates can climb higher than they should in autumn or at Christmastime, but low-season rates often make the rooms one of Midtown's best bargains. An attractive mahogany-and-marble lobby leads to the petite but nicely outfitted guest rooms, which boast neo-Shaker furnish-ings and good marble-and-tile bathrooms (a few have showers only, so be sure to request a tub if it matters to you). Everything's fresh and comfortable. In-room extras include hair dryers, coffeemakers (oddly situated in the bathroom, but great for a morning cup o' joe nonetheless), blackout drapes, pay movies, in-room safes, and phones with voice mail and data port. Don't expect much in the way of personal ser-vice, but on-site amenities like a small but satisfying fitness room (stair machine, treadmill, bike) and a business center (with PC, fax, and copier) pick up the slack. The location is excellent, steps from Times Square, Rockefeller Center, and the Theater District. This one's considerably cheerier than the Comfort Inn Manhattan (see above), but stay there if you need your space.

✪ **Hotel Edison.** 228 W. 47th St. (btw. Broadway and Eighth Ave.), New York, NY 10036.
☎ **800/637-7070** or 212/840-5000. Fax 212/596-6850. www.edisonhotelnyc.com.
869 units. A/C TV TEL. $130 single; $150 double; $175 quad; $210 suite. Extra person $15. AE, CB, DC, DISC, MC, V. Valet parking $22. Subway: N, R to 49th St.; 1, 9 to 50th St.

There's no doubt about it—the Edison is one of the Theater District's best hotel bar-gains, if not *the* best. No other area hotel is so consistently value priced. The recently renovated rooms are much nicer than what you'd get for just about the same money at the nearby Ramada Inn Milford Plaza (which ain't exactly the "Lullabuy of Broadway!" these days). Don't expect much more than the basics, but you will find a firm bed (flat pillows, though), motel decor that's more attractive than most I've seen in this category, a phone with data port, and a clean, perfectly adequate tile bathroom. Most double rooms feature two twins or a full bed, but there are some queens; request one at booking and show up early in the day for your best chance at one. Quad rooms are larger, with two doubles.

Off the attractive deco-style lobby is the Cafe Edison, a hoot of an old-style Polish deli that's a favorite among ladder-climbing theater types and downmarket ladies who lunch; Sofia's, an Italian restaurant; a tavern with live entertainment most nights; and a gift shop. Services are kept at a bare minimum to keep rates down, but dry-cleaning/ laundry service and express checkout are available; there is also a beauty salon as well as a guest services desk where you can arrange tours, theater tickets, and transportation. The hotel fills up with tour groups from the world over, but since it has nearly 1,000 rooms, you can carve out some space if you call early enough.

Hotel Wolcott. 4 W. 31st St. (at Fifth Ave.), New York, NY 10001. ☎ **212/268-2900.** Fax 212/563-0096. www.wolcott.com. 250 units. A/C TV TEL. $120 double; $140 triple; $170 suite. Discounted AAA, AARP, and promotional rates may be available. Extra person $20. AE, JCB, MC, V. Parking $17 next door. Subway: B, D, F, Q, N, R to 34th St.

This was one of the grand dames of Manhattan hotels at the start of the 20th century. Its heyday may be over, but the Wolcott has been reinvented as a good-value option for bargain hunters. Only the lobby hints at the hotel's former grandeur; these days, the rooms are motel-standard, but they're well kept and quite serviceable. Plusses

include spacious bathrooms and phones with data ports and voice mail, plus
minifridges in most rooms. On the downside, some of the mattresses aren't as firm as
I might like, and the closets tend to be small. And some of the triples are poorly con-
figured—the front door to one I saw hit up right against a bed—but they're plenty big
enough for three, and come with two TVs to avoid before-bedtime conflicts (as do the
suites). All in all, you get your money's worth here. One of the hotel's most recommendable features is its basement coin-op laundry, a rarity for Manhattan. There's also
a tour desk, plus a decent fitness center, meeting rooms, and a business center that you
can use without additional charge.

Park Savoy Hotel. 158 W. 58th St. (btw. Sixth and Seventh aves.), New York, NY 10019.
☎ **212/245-5755.** Fax 212/765-0668. 70 units. A/C TV TEL. $95–$145 single; $105–$185
double. Rates include tax. AE, MC, V. Parking $20 next door. Subway: A, B, C, D, 1, 9 to
59th St./Columbus Circle; N, R to 57th St.

The Park Savoy isn't quite as nice as its sibling, the Chelsea Savoy (see "Chelsea" earlier in this chapter), but the lower prices reflect the quality difference, making it a good
deal nonetheless. The hotel has been recently renovated so that all rooms have nice
new black-and-white-tiled private bathrooms, which are petite (with showers only)
but attractive and clean. If your budget is tight, two of you can make do in the smallest rooms; the biggest ones can accommodate three or four in two double beds. Rooms
are basic, and a few I saw were in need of a fresh coat of paint, but they do the job.
All have voice mail and alarm clocks, most have walk-in closets, and a few have
minifridges. Services are kept to a minimum to keep rates low, but there's a good Pasta
Lovers restaurant in the building that gives guests 10% off and will deliver to your
room. Best of all is the attractive and convenient location—a block from Central Park
and a stone's throw from Carnegie Hall, Lincoln Center, and the Columbus Circle
subway lines, which give you easy access to the rest of the city.

9 Midtown East & Murray Hill

VERY EXPENSIVE

There's no denying the glamour and recognizability of the **Plaza,** 768 Fifth Ave., at
59th Street (☎ **800/527-4727** or 212/759-3000; www.fairmont.com). Probably the
Big Apple's most famous hotel (remember *North by Northwest? Home Alone 2? Eloise?*),
this 1907 landmark French Renaissance palace has been beautifully refurbished by the
Fairmont chain. Still, inconsistent rooms (some are *small*), tourist hordes crowding the
public spaces, and claims of uneven service mean that you may be better off booking
elsewhere if you're going to spend $500 or more a night. But if your heart's set, check
the Web site for special deals; you may be able to snare a decent rate (or at least a substantial upgrade for your money) in the off-season.

Four Seasons Hotel New York. 57 E. 57th St. (btw. Park and Madison aves.), New York, NY
10022. ☎ **800/819-5053** or 212/758-5700. Fax 212/758-5711. www.fourseasons.com.
370 units. A/C MINIBAR TV TEL. $585–$840 double; from $1,250 suite. Check Web site for
current package deals. Extra person $50. AE, CB, DC, DISC, ER, JCB, MC, V. Valet parking $40.
Subway: N, R, 4, 5, 6 to 60th St.

Hollywood meets Manhattan in the grand but frosty lobby of this ultra-luxury, ultra-
modern hotel. Aging rock stars spice the brew, as can anyone with a generous expense
account or a wad of cash to drop. Designed by überarchitect I. M. Pei in 1993, the
limestone-clad modernist tower rises 52 stories, providing hundreds of rooms with a
view. As soon as you enter the soaring lobby, with its marble floors and backlit onyx

ceiling, you'll immediately know this place is special—even in super-luxe New York, where anything goes. The completely soundproofed guest rooms are among New York's largest, averaging 600 square feet. Each is beautifully furnished in an understated but plush contemporary style and has an entrance foyer, sitting area, a 5-by-3-foot desk with two leather chairs, and a sycamore-paneled dressing area; 23 of the priciest rooms also have terraces. The mammoth Florentine marble bathrooms have soaking tubs and separate showers with pressure controls. Other special touches include bedside-controlled window treatments, fax machine, umbrellas, goose-down pillows, Frette linens, oversize bath towels, and cushy robes, plus multidisk CD players in suites. VCRs are also available. You'd expect less? For this much money, you deserve *more.*

Dining/Diversions: Awarded three stars by the *New York Times,* Fifty-Seven, Fifty-Seven is an excellent New American grill and popular power-breakfast and lunch spot. The snazzy Bar offers an extensive martini menu to wash down light meals. The Lobby Lounge features lunch, afternoon tea, cocktails, and hors d'oeuvres.

Amenities: Luxurious fitness center with whirlpool and sauna, 24-hour concierge, 24-hour room service, valet service with 1-hour pressing, shoe shine, twice-daily maid service with turndown, newspaper delivery, express checkout, baby-sitting, secretarial services, complimentary car drop-off within a 2-mile radius (8am–11pm), business center, conference rooms.

New York Palace. 455 Madison Ave. (btw. 50th and 51st sts.), New York, NY 10022. ☎ **800/NY-PALACE** or 212/888-7000. Fax 212/303-6000. www.newyorkpalace.com. 722 units. A/C MINIBAR TV TEL. $440–$560 double; $900–$1,900 suite. Check Web site or inquire about special weekend packages (as low as $245 at press time). AE, CB, DC, DISC, EURO, JCB, MC, V. Valet parking $47. Subway: 6 to 51st St.

The Sultan of Brunei has restored this convenient Midtown palace with an opulence befitting nouveau royalty. A member of the Leading Hotels of the World organization, the Palace is comprised of the landmark McKim, Mead & White–designed Villard Houses (1882) and a 55-story modern tower. Outfitted with every luxury, all of the rooms are the height of elegance and modern convenience. Which building you choose is all a matter of taste (and the size of your wallet): The main Hotel is rich with old-world style, while the more exclusive Towers, which functions as its own hotel-within-a-hotel, has a sophisticated contemporary-deco style and the added bonus of around-the-clock butler service. The Executive Hotel, housed on the high floors of the Villard Houses, offers upgraded furnishings and extra amenities like a dedicated concierge and continental breakfast and hors d'oeuvres in the exclusive lounge. The views are incredible from the Towers, but they're great from the Hotel too, thanks to the Villard Houses' U-shaped design.

Dining/Diversions: As the new home of the revered Le Cirque, the hotel stars center stage in gourmets' dreams (see chapter 6). Istana, a Mediterranean cafe and restaurant, should not be overlooked: It transcends its hotel-restaurant class with wonderful food, fine ports, a welcoming staff, and even its own olive bar, with more than 30 varieties.

Amenities: There's a new 7,000-square-foot fitness center with all the latest equipment as well as personal trainers, steam rooms, and spa treatments. Concierge, 24-hour room service, turndown, valet service, shoe shine, newspaper delivery, complimentary weekday shuttle to Wall Street, excellent business center with secretarial and translation services, extensive high-tech meeting center.

✪ **The Peninsula–New York.** 700 Fifth Ave. (at 55th St.), New York, NY 10019. ☎ **800/ 262-9467** or 212/956-2888. Fax 212/903-3949. www.peninsula.com. 241 units. A/C

MINIBAR TV TEL. $535–$650 double; from $700 suite. Extra person $50. Children under 12 stay free in parents' room (cribs supplied at no charge). AE, CB, DC, DISC, EURO, JCB, MC, V. Valet parking $38. Subway: E, F to 53rd St./Fifth Ave. Small pets accepted.

After $45 million and 10 months of downtime, the Peninsula reopened in November 1998 as a state-of-the-art stunner. Inside, all that's left of the beaux arts past is the marvelous wedding-cake ceiling in the lobby. Work your way past the redecorated public floors and everything's brand new; the guest room floors were totally gutted and laid out afresh, allowing for high-tech wiring, better room configurations, and what may be the most fabulous bathrooms in the city.

The decor is a rich mix of art nouveau, vibrant Asian elements (including gorgeous silk bedcovers), and contemporary art. Every room boasts lots of storage and counter space, and fabulous linens that include the cushiest bathrobes I've seen. But the real news is the technology, which includes a room-wide speaker system and mood lighting; an executive workstation with desk-level inputs, direct-line fax, and dual-line speakerphones; a bedside panel for everything, from climate controls to the DO NOT DISTURB sign; even a doorside weather display. But wait, there's more: In the huge marble bathrooms, a tub-level panel allows you to control the speaker system, answer the phone, and, if you're in any room above the lowest (superior) level, control the bathroom TV. Simply fabulous—but why go this far and put VCRs and CD players in the suites only?

Dining/Diversions: Freshly contemporary Adrienne serves an admirable eclectic menu with Asian touches, plus lighter meals in the adjoining bistro. With comfortable seating and a wonderful librarylike vibe, the Gotham Lounge offers an excellent afternoon tea, cocktails, and snacks. The Pen-Top Bar & Terrace (see chapter 9) offers rooftop cocktails and some of Midtown's most dramatic views.

Amenities: Three-level rooftop health club and spa (one of New York's best), with heated pool, exercise classes, whirlpool, sauna, and sundeck. Excellent concierge service ("We'll do anything guests ask, as long as it's legal"), 24-hour room service, valet service, newspaper delivery, twice-daily maid service, express checkout, business center, conference rooms, tour desk, salon, secretarial services, baby-sitting, in-room massage.

✪ **The Sherry-Netherland.** 781 Fifth Ave. (at 59th St.). ☎ **800/247-4377** or 212/355-2800. Fax 212/319-4306. www.sherrynetherland.com. 77 units. A/C TV TEL. $310–$495 double; $575–$875 1-bedroom suite; from $885 2-bedroom suite. Rates include continental breakfast at Cipriani's. Children stay free in parents' room. AE, CB, DC, DISC, ER, JCB, MC, V. Valet parking $40. Subway: N, R to Fifth Ave. Pets accepted.

For a taste of genteel New York apartment living, come to the Sherry-Netherland. Housed in a wonderful 1927 neo-Romanesque building overlooking Fifth Avenue and Central Park, the Sherry is one of a kind: both a first-class hotel and a quietly elegant residential building where the guest rooms are privately owned co-ops. As a result, the rooms vary greatly in style, but each is grandly proportioned with high ceilings, big bathrooms, and walk-in closets. These are the largest rooms I've seen in the city, and every one features high-quality furnishings and art, VCR, fax machine, Godiva chocolates upon arrival, and fridge with free soft drinks (voice mail was not in place at this writing, so check before you book if that matters). About half are suites with kitchenettes that have a cooktop or microwave, often both. The hotel is expensive, but at least you get a lot for your dollar here.

The most wonderful thing about the Sherry is its homeyness—even the standard doubles have a residential feel. You'll pay more for a lighter, park- or street-facing room; the views are stunning, but the lower floors can be noisy for light sleepers. Interior-facing rooms are appreciably darker and quieter but no less fabulous, and a lot cheaper. One of my favorite suites is no. 814, an interior one-bedroom done in a playful art deco–contemporary style, with a gorgeous marble bathroom, a terrific kitchen with bar, and a wealth of luxurious space. If you'd prefer a more traditionally styled room, let the excellent staff know. The hotel is old-world formal—there are even attendants in gold-trimmed jackets manning the elevators around the clock—but not the least bit stuffy. A true New York classic.

Dining/Diversions: Packed with Armani-suited moguls, million-dollar models, and East Side denizens, bustling Cipriani's is the ultimate power spot. The wildly expensive food is excellent (especially the pappardelle with in-season mushrooms), as is the tuxedoed service. Well worth the splurge.

Amenities: Concierge, room service (6am–midnight), valet service, newspaper delivery of any paper you choose, twice-daily maid service, fitness room, meeting room, barbershop, beauty salon, newsstand. Free access to library stocked with the *New York Times* best-sellers and a complete catalog of Oscar-winning films.

EXPENSIVE

The Avalon. 16 E. 32nd St. (btw. Fifth and Madison aves.), New York, NY 10016. ☎ **888/ HI-AVALON** or 212/299-7000. Fax 212/299-7001. www.theavalonny.com. 100 units. A/C MINIBAR TV TEL. $225–$380 double; $275–$425 junior suite; $315–$700 deluxe or executive suite. Rates include expanded continental breakfast. Call or check Web site for special offers or packages, as money-saving deals are usually on offer. AE, DC, JCB, MC, V. Valet parking $23. Subway: 6 to 33rd St.

This new-in-1998 boutique hotel is a mostly suite-filled, amenity-laden ode to luxury— I challenge you to find another hotel in the city that offers 5-foot body pillows in every room (Craig Stoltz of the *Washington Post* claimed that one of these gave him his best night's sleep *ever*). The George Patero–designed interiors are attractively done in a muted palette and a sophisticated but comfy Americana style. The basic doubles (there are only 20) are on the small side, but even they come with good work desks with ergonomically correct chairs and easy-access data ports and outlets, double-paned windows to block out noise, 27-inch TVs (VCRs on request), two-line speakerphones with conferencing and their own direct-dial numbers, Egyptian cotton and Irish linens, lighted makeup mirrors in the marble bathrooms, fluffy Frette bathrobes, coffeemakers with free fixin's, and more—even umbrellas. All suites have pull-out sofas and two TVs; expect even more in the most expensive ones, such as whirlpool tubs, cordless phones, and Bose radios. The stylish staff is professional, if a little aloof; still, you can expect to have all your desires met.

Dining/Diversions: The 16–32 Coach House is the domain of star chef Larry Forgione (of An American Place), so come prepared to have your taste buds tantalized. Tea is available in the pleasant library in the afternoons.

Amenities: Concierge, room service (noon–midnight), laundry and dry-cleaning service, turndown, newspaper delivery, high-tech meeting room, free access to nearby Bally's Sports Club. Secretarial services and airport "meet and greet" available.

✪ **The Benjamin.** 125 E. 50th St. (at Lexington Ave.), New York, NY 10022. ☎ **888/ 4-BENJAMIN** or 212/320-8002. Fax 212/465-3697. www.thebenjamin.com. 209 units. A/C MINIBAR TV TEL. $320–$384 standard double; $350–$415 studio double; $420–$550 1-bedroom suite; $775–$931 2-bedroom suite. Extra person $20. AE, CB, DC, DISC, EURO, JCB, MC, V. Parking $35. Subway: 6 to 51st St.; E, F to Lexington Ave. Pets 35 lb. or less accepted.

The former Hotel Beverly is the city's best new hotel. This sophisticated boutique-style hotel boasts soothing, beautifully styled neoclassical-meets-21st-century rooms that are some of the best outfitted in town. Serious planning was put into the design and layout, with one eye to comfort and the other to technology; you'd have to book in at the much pricier Peninsula to guarantee similar quality, service, and high-tech amenities.

First, the bed: a custom-designed Serta bed luxuriously dressed in Frette linens and down duvet, with a cushioned headboard. Order one of 11 custom pillows—ranging from buckwheat to water-filled to classic goose down—for the crowning touch. For the waking hours, you'll have one of the biggest and best workstations I've seen, with desk-level inputs for everything, including digital cable for high-speed Internet access; fax/printer/copier; phones with direct-dial number; an ergonomically correct leather chair; and a movable undertable for in-room dining. The 27-inch TV has Web TV, Sony PlayStation, and front-access inputs for CD players and VCRs (available on request). The white marble bathrooms are on the smallish side, but they're designed to maximum advantage, with good counter and shelf space and ingenious shower caddies with shaving mirrors. But wait—there's more: Every room has a galley kitchenette with stocked minifridge, microwave, coffeemaker, china and utensils, and goodies like popcorn and gummy bears; a Bose Wave radio; and plush Frette robes and laptop-size safes in the big closets. The studios will simply get you a king bed instead of a queen and some additional floor space, while the suites will garner you a CD stereo and a sitting area with a cozy sofa and a cocooning mohair chair that you'll never want to leave.

Dining/Diversions: Larry Forgione's An American Place is one of the city's best contemporary American restaurants (see chapter 6).

Amenities: Concierge, 24-hour room service from An American Place, state-of-the-art fitness center with free weights, full-service spa, valet service, same-day shoe shine, turndown service, choice of six newspapers for delivery, express checkout. PCs, conference rooms, a high-tech executive meeting room, and business services are available.

Crowne Plaza at the United Nations. 304 E. 42nd St. (just east of Second Ave.), New York, NY 10017. ☎ **800/879-8836** or 212/986-8800. Fax 212/986-1758. www.crowneplaza-un.com. 300 units. A/C MINIBAR TV TEL. $229–$379 double; $259–$600 suite. Ask about weekend packages and other discounts, and check online for Internet-only deals. Extra person $25. Children under 17 stay free in parents' room. AE, CB, DC, DISC, JCB, MC, V. Valet parking $30 weekdays, $26 weekends. Subway: S, 4, 5, 6, 7 to Grand Central. Small pets accepted with $500 deposit.

Here's a very nice chain hotel that boasts all the expected comforts, plus a surprising bit of personality. Housed in a lovely neo-Tudor building, the guest rooms are newly renovated and very well done, with excellent-quality linens and fabrics (the towels could be plusher, but the sheets are fabulous) and such extras as two dual-line phones with data ports and voice mail, good work space, bedside control panels for everything from air to lights, double-paned windows to shut out street noise, coffeemakers, irons and ironing boards, trouser presses, safes, and Italian marble bathrooms with hair dryers and makeup mirrors. Executive rooms and suites also feature whirlpool tubs, bidets, and pull-out sofas or love seats; guests in these units have access to the Crowne Plaza Club lounge, with a big-screen TV, Internet access, fax, complimentary continental breakfast, and cocktails. A surprisingly attractive collection of French prints and historic New York City photos gives the entire hotel a nice sense of style. Some may find the far-east location a bit out of the way (Grand Central is a 5-min. walk away), but visitors interested in a quiet, attractive neighborhood will find it fits the bill.

Dining/Diversions: Cecil's Bistro features an expansive breakfast buffet staffed by an omelet maker, plus continental fare at lunch and dinner. The smoke-free Regency Lounge is open for cocktails; there's also a bar that allows smoking adjacent to Cecil's.

Amenities: Fitness center with treadmills, stationary bicycles, stair machine, free weights, saunas, and massage. Clef d'Or concierge, room service (6am–11pm), valet service, newspaper delivery, secretarial services, express checkout, business center.

Fitzpatrick Grand Central Hotel. 141 E. 44th St. (at Lexington Ave.), New York, NY 10017. ☎ **800/367-7701** or 212/351-6800. Fax 212/308-5166. www.fitzpatrickhotels.com. 155 units. A/C TV TEL. $325–$355 double; $425–$1,000 junior suite. Check Web site for weekend rates (sometimes as low as $179) and other special deals. Extra person $30. Children under 12 stay free in parents' room. AE, DC, DISC, JCB, MC, V. Valet parking $30. Subway: S, 4, 5, 6, 7 to 42nd St./Grand Central.

This attractive and intimate Irish-themed hotel is from the Dublin-based Fitzpatrick chain, and it's a terrific choice for those who like the creature comforts a chain hotel can offer but detest the generic blandness that's usually the unavoidable accompaniment. Kelly green–carpeted hallways lead to guest rooms that are pleasingly modern with traditional European accents. Half canopies are a unique and sophisticated touch, and three phones, a coffeemaker, a fridge stocked with Irish spring water and cream for coffee, video games on the TV, a full-length mirror, windows that shut out the street noise and open to let fresh air in, a pants press, terry robes, and sharp white-and navy blue–tiled baths with lots of space and makeup mirrors add to the comfort level. The L-shaped junior suites also have VCRs, CD players, and extra TVs (including one in the giant bathroom), but a sitting room sans pull-out sofa means they're most suited for couples looking for luxury. (Laptop-size safes and in-room PCs were in the plans for all rooms at press time.) The staff is accustomed to catering to U.N. dignitaries, so you can reasonably expect your needs to be well met.

The penthouse level is named for Liam Neeson, a close friend of Mr. Fitzpatrick's. The Garden Suites may not boast the Waterford crystal chandelier and other antiques that the main Penthouse Suite does, but outdoor patios and big, beautifully tiled baths make them a reasonable splurge at $550.

Dining/Diversions: The Wheeltapper Pub is an attractive and comfortable Irish pub serving genuine affordable pub grub as well as Sunday brunch. More sophisticated tastes can opt for the tea menu in the adjacent Infusion Room.

Amenities: Concierge, 24-hour room service, valet service, Irish and American newspapers in lobby, express checkout, baby-sitting, access to nearby health club, limo service.

✪ **The Kimberly.** 145 E. 50th St. (btw. Lexington and Third aves.), New York, NY 10022. ☎ **800/683-0400** or 212/755-0400. Fax 212/750-0113. www.kimberlyhotel.com. 184 units. A/C MINIBAR TV TEL. $229–$339 double; $279–$509 1-bedroom suite; $429–$689 2-bedroom suite; $349–$1,000 specialty suite. Check on deeply discounted off-season and weekend rates as well as package deals. Extra person $25. Children 17 and under stay free in parents' room. AE, CB, DC, DISC, JCB, MC, V. Valet parking $23. Subway: 6 to 51st St.

Surprisingly good rates on suites mean that you could be standing on your private balcony overlooking Manhattan for a lot less than you'd pay for a cell-like room in many other Midtown hotels. Most New Yorkers don't have it this good: These are full apartments with dining areas; living rooms with Oriental rugs; full-size, fully equipped kitchens complete with stove, big fridge, coffeemaker, and a full complement of china and cookware; marble baths; tons of closet space; and private unfurnished balconies (in all but eight suites)—it's all part of the package. The executive suites have larger living space, but the standard one-bedrooms are just fine for most. The two-bedroom suites have two bathrooms, and you can choose between a configuration that adjoins the bedrooms or puts them at opposite ends of the apartment (great for couples traveling together). The 21 regular rooms are handsome and comfortable too, with minifridges and extra-nice bathrooms with deep tubs. Additional in-room amenities include three two-line phones, a fax machine, a shoe-shine machine, and plush robes. The hotel may not be the most stylish place in town, but it's done in an attractive traditional style that's cozy and comfortable, and everything is in very good condition.

I can't promise that the deals will be that attractive when you call, but in winter 2000, one-bedrooms were going for as little as $209—an amazing bargain.

Dining/Diversions: New on the scene is L'Actuel, a beautifully designed modern space serving a moderately priced new French menu that has garnered a precious two (out of four) stars from the *New York Times*. One51 is a chic supper club that turns into a full-fledged nightclub in the later hours. From May through October, there are complimentary 3-hour sunset cruises aboard a 75-foot yacht from Thursday through Sunday (Sunday only in Oct, always weather-dependent).

Amenities: Concierge, room service (6am–11pm), dry-cleaning/laundry service, newspaper delivery, penthouse-level meeting space, express checkout. Free access to the fabulous New York Health & Racquet Club with pool, tennis, squash, and racquetball courts, indoor golf, and any machine you could want. Massages, facials, manicures, and other spa treatments are available at discounted and package rates.

Morgans. 237 Madison Ave. (btw. 37th and 38th sts.), New York, NY 10016. ☎ **800/ 334-3408** or 212/686-0300. Fax 212/779-8352. 154 units. A/C MINIBAR TV TEL. $315–$375 double; $425–$600 1-bedroom suite; penthouse rates upon request. Rates include continental breakfast and afternoon tea. Inquire about discounted weekend rates. AE, DC, DISC, MC, V. Valet parking $36. Subway: 6 to 33rd St.; S, 4, 5, 6, 7 to Grand Central.

Ian Schrager's first boutique hotel opened in 1984 as a low-profile "anti-hotel" without a sign or a staff experienced in hotel management. There's still little to give away its Murray Hill location except for the limos occasionally dropping off some high-profile type, but today the staff is experienced and competent. The hotel's original designer, Andrée Putman, also renovated the stylish interior in 1995; it eschews the over-the-top, hotel-as-theater elements of the Starck-designed Paramount and Royalton hotels for a more low-key, grown-up sensibility and residential style.

The rooms are done with gorgeous fabrics and a soothing color palette. They're not huge, but furnishings designed low to the ground and beautiful custom maple-eye built-ins—including storage and cushioned window seats for both lounging and out-of-sight luggage storage—make them feel very spacious. The beds are luxuriously comfy, with down comforters, Scottish wool blankets, and suede headboards. Other pleasing extras include a VCR, CD player, spacious work desk, and two-line speakerphones with direct-dial telephone number. The small bathrooms are a Putman signature, with black-and-white checkered tile and stainless-steel sinks; most have double-wide stall showers, so request a tub when booking if you require one.

Dining/Diversions: The Philippe Starck–designed Asia de Cuba serves surprisingly good fusion cuisine to a trendsetting crowd, and becomes a white-hot velvet-rope bar scene later in the evening. In the cellar is Morgans Bar, a Rande Gerber (of the Whiskey bars) late-night hot spot for musicians, artists, and models, this time done up as a postmodern salon. The lovely breakfast room is for guests only.

Amenities: 24-hour concierge, 24-hour room service, valet service, newspaper delivery on request, free access to nearby New York Sports Club, meeting space. Fax machines, cell phones, and laptops available for use.

The Roger Smith. 501 Lexington Ave. (btw. 47th and 48th sts.), New York, NY 10017. ☎ **800/445-0277** or 212/755-1400. Fax 212/758-4061. www.rogersmith.com. 130 units. A/C TV TEL. $245–$295 double; $310–$415 1-bedroom suite. Rates include continental breakfast. Corporate and weekend rates may be available; check Web site for seasonal Internet specials. Extra person $20. Children 16 and under stay free in parents' room. AE, DC, DISC, JCB, MC, V. Valet parking $24. Subway: 6 to 51st St.; E, F to Lexington Ave.

Here's a great place for those who want the creature comforts of an upscale Midtown hotel but like the idea of a few artsy twists. Owner James Knowles has a passion for

You Paid What?

47,000 hotels, 700 airlines,
50 rental car companies. And a few
million ways to save money.

Travelocity.com
A Sabre Company

Go Virtually Anywhere.

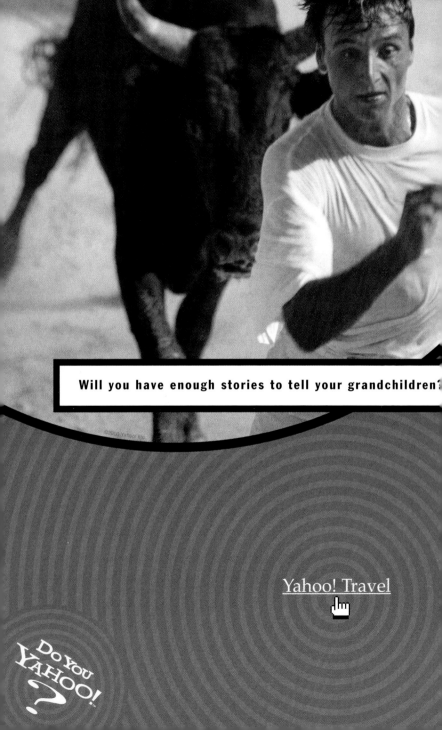

Will you have enough stories to tell your grandchildren?

Yahoo! Travel

DO YOU YAHOO!?

contemporary art, and his hotel is infused with a real independent spirit. Knowles's own bronzes will greet you at the entrance; he even created the main door pulls in his Connecticut foundry. With a regular clientele oddly made up of Swedish business-men, Spanish honeymooners, tennis pros, and low-key rockers (Victoria Williams, Barenaked Ladies, Rufus Wainwright) who like the easygoing vibe, the hotel has a quirky appeal that's a welcome relief from the standard East Side stuffiness, but it's straightforward in its comforts. The rooms, larger than most in the neighborhood, are individually decorated, largely in a classic Americana style. All feature firm beds with good pillows, minifridge, coffeemaker, and writing desk. Suites have well-stocked pantries with microwave and VCRs. Most bathrooms are older but nicely kept; you'll pay about $20 more to stay on the VIP floors, which have brand-new granite baths with a whirlpool tub. Not perfect—a few minor details could use attention—but an appealing choice nonetheless.

Dining/Diversions: A restaurant/bar serves moderately priced American cuisine with a German flair. The hotel hosts an ongoing series of events, including an annual Iberian Festival in February, regular brown-bag lecture lunches, artist suppers, and rotating fine art shows at the Roger Smith Gallery.

Amenities: Valet service, free local calls, iMac in lobby for e-mail access, news-papers at breakfast, free video library, 24-hour delivery from local restaurants (with dishes and utensils provided by housekeeping), conference rooms, rooftop deck, access to nearby health club with pool.

✪ Waldorf=Astoria and the Waldorf Towers. 301 Park Ave. (btw. 49th and 50th sts.), New York, NY 10022. ☎ **800/WALDORF,** 800/774-1500, or 212/355-3000. Fax 212/872-7272 (Astoria) or 212/872-4799 (Towers). www.hilton.com or www.waldorf-towers.com. 1,242 units (159 in the Towers). A/C MINIBAR TV TEL. Waldorf-Astoria: $295–$415 double; $305–$865 suite. Waldorf Towers: $299–$629 double; $374–$3,087 suite. Corporate, senior, seasonal, and weekend discounts may be available, with rates sometimes as low as $199 at the Astoria; also check online or inquire about Hilton's attractive package deals. Extra person $40. Children under 18 stay free in parents' room. AE, CB, DC, DISC, EURO, JCB, MC, V. Valet parking $37. Subway: 6 to 51st St.

If you're looking for legendary New York glamour, there's hardly a more elegant address in town than the Waldorf. Only the Plaza is on equal footing, but you'll get lots more for your money here—and you'll likely spend a lot less.

Hilton Hotels has spent a fortune renovating this legendary art deco masterpiece, and they're committed to keeping the legend in tip-top shape. They deserve extra points for keeping rates comparatively affordable for a property of this stature and quality. No two rooms in the hotel are exactly alike, but all are high-ceilinged and oversize, boasting attractive traditional decor, excellent quality linens and comfy beds, spacious marble bathrooms and closets, and the luxury amenities befitting an old-world hotel of this level. (In a gracious nod to the 21st century, fax machines and high-speed Internet connectivity were in the works for all rooms at press time.)

The exquisite, and quite exclusive, Waldorf Towers occupies floors 27 to 42 and has a separate entrance, away from the pleasant bustle of the main hotel. Many of these big, gorgeous rooms and suites have original art and antiques, full dining rooms and kitchens, and maid's quarters. (These already have fax/printer/copiers, and mobile phones are in the plan.) The Towers is renowned for its excellent butler service and respect for privacy. The Presidential Suite is aptly named, having cosseted many world leaders. It's quite a dramatic scene when the prez is in residence, with paparazzi and Secret Service out front, stopped traffic in the street, and helicopters overhead.

Dining/Diversions: You have a number of very good restaurants to choose from, including the elegant Peacock Alley, a *New York Times* three-star winner thanks to the creative French cooking of Laurent Gras. Inagiku serves exquisite Japanese food and just got a stylish face-lift from Adam Tihany, as did affordable Oscar's, a pleasing American brasserie. Sir Harry's Bar is quiet and clubby, but I prefer the Bull & Bear for stiff drinks around the mahogany bar or a chop in the adjoining dining room. At the Cocktail Terrace, you can sit down to afternoon tea or coddle an evening cocktail while a pianist tinkles the ivories on Cole Porter's very own Steinway Grand.

Amenities: A brand-new 24-hour business center managed by Kinkos, 3,000-square-foot fitness center with massage and personal training services, concierge, theater and transportation desks, boutiques, salon, American Airlines office, 24-hour room service, valet service, conference rooms, express checkout. Tower services include butler service, Clefs d'Or concierge, and newspaper delivery.

W New York. 541 Lexington Ave. (btw. 49th and 50th sts.), New York, NY 10022. ☎ **877/ W-HOTELS** or 212/755-1200. Fax 212/319-8344. www.whotels.com. 717 units. A/C MINI-BAR TV TEL. $279–$425 double; from $525 suite. Senior, corporate, or other discounts may be available, as well as weekend rates; inquire or check online booking. AE, CB, DC, DISC, ER, EURO, JCB, MC, V. Valet parking $34. Subway: 6 to 51st St.

As conceived by David Rockwell (the man behind such dramatic spaces as Nobu and the renovated Grand Central), the W is meant to be an oasis in the urban jungle, a nature-inspired sanctuary from the stresses of city life—a high-falutin' concept, sure, but one that largely works. The hotel is done in a natural palette with exotic touches and an easygoing shabby-chic style. At its heart is a living room–style lobby, designed to draw in hip New Yorkers as well as guests to its social scene. All warmth and light, it's a great place to lounge over a cocktail or a game of chess.

You'll need the lobby to spread out because the guest rooms are *small.* They have a beautiful nature-inspired modern style and feature a heavenly feather bed atop a firm mattress. Other pluses include a 27-inch TV with VCR and Internet service, a CD player, a two-line speakerphone, a safe big enough for a laptop, and a signature box of green wheat grass that implores you, in perfect Smith & Hawken style, to WATER ME. The bathrooms boast plush towels but little counter space. The Signature rooms are in demand thanks to their unique setup, with a bed floating in the middle of the room and a witty desk that's bigger on style than work space; but go for a Standard instead, which gets you a club chair and a bit more space for about the same money.

Dining/Diversions: The brainchild of celebrity restaurateur Drew Nieporent, Heartbeat offers fresh seasonal cuisine with a healthy bent that the *New York Times* lauded as "a pleasure." There's also Cool Juice, a health bar that purportedly counts Sarah, duchess of York, among its fans; the lobby Oasis bar; and Whiskey Blue, a hot spot from nightlife impresario Rande Gerber that's much warmer and more inviting than his Whiskey bar at the Paramount.

Amenities: Excellent 10,000-square-foot spa and health club with tons of equipment, classes, and treatments. Concierge, 24-hour room service, valet service, newspaper delivery, newsstand, business center, high-tech conference facilities, and ballroom.

W The Court/W The Tuscany. 120–130 E. 39th St. (at Lexington Ave.), New York, NY 10016. ☎ **877/W-HOTELS** or 212/685-1100 (The Court), 212/685-1600 (The Tuscany). Fax 212/696-2095. www.whotels.com. 198 units at the Court, 122 at the Tuscany. A/C MINI-BAR TV TEL. The Court $265–$325 double; $650 suite. The Tuscany $325–$425 double; $695 suite. Check online booking for rates as low as $239. AE, CB, DC, DISC, JCB, MC, V. Valet parking $34. Subway: S, 4, 5, 6, 7 to 42nd St./Grand Central. Pets accepted.

Starwood Hotels added this twin set to its rapidly growing W group in 1999, managing to improve its chain-boutique concept in the year since W New York launched. First of all, the bones were better; both the former Doral Court and Doral Tuscany came with bigger guest rooms and bathrooms. Second, W's design group rid themselves of a high-minded concept and just went glam. The results are big, stylish, well-outfitted rooms that are cushy enough to make you want to camp out a while. Taupe sets a soothing palette, deep red accents add sex appeal, and gorgeous linens and fabrics round out the luxe. The overall feeling is more cosmopolitan chic than what you'll find at the playfully nature-minded W New York.

So what's the difference between the Court and the Tuscany? The Court is the social center—where you'll find the restaurant, the lounge, the fitness center, and the buzzy, celeb-heavy scene. The Tuscany is quieter, more low-profile, without its own public space for lounging. The rooms are outfitted exactly the same at both hotels, including a marvelously cozy goose-down feather bed with duvet; a chaise longue with a chenille throw, plus an additional polar-fleece throw on the bed; 27-inch TVs with Internet access; clock radio with CD player; dual-line cordless phone; oversize work desk; waffle-weave robes in the closet; and nice, relatively roomy bathrooms. At the Tuscany, rooms are slightly larger, bathroom shelf space is a tad more generous, and a foyer space with an additional French door separates each guest room from the corridor—well worth the extra dough for light sleepers.

Dining/Diversions: Icon New York is the latest dining hot spot from Drew Nieporent's Myriad Restaurant Group (Nobu, Montrachet, Tribeca Grill, others). The room is plush and sexy, and Chef Paul Sale's light French-American cooking has already garnered $2^{1}/_{2}$ stars from super-critical William Grimes of the *New York Times*. There's also Wetbar, yet another super-hot, ultra-chic lounge from cocktail-hour impresario Rande Gerber (Mr. Cindy Crawford).

Amenities: Concierge, 24-hour room service, dry-cleaning and laundry service, express checkout, meeting space, in-room fax/printer/copier on request, newspaper delivery on request, access to nearby health club, baby-sitting, secretarial services.

MODERATE

Clarion Hotel Fifth Avenue. 3 E. 40th St. (at Fifth Ave.), New York, NY 10016. ☎ **800/ 252-7466** or 212/447-1500. Fax 212/213-0972. www.hotelchoice.com. 189 units. A/C TV TEL. $159–$375 double, depending on season. Ask about senior, AAA, and corporate discounts as well as promotional deals; check Web site for online booking discounts (10% off at press time). Extra person $15. Children under 18 stay free in parents' room. AE, CB, DC, DISC, ER, EURO, JCB, MC, V. Parking $25 two blocks away. Subway: B, D, F, Q to 42nd St.

Location, price, and overall high quality make this newly renovated hotel the best value in Midtown East. Across from Bryant Park and the New York Public Library, near Lord & Taylor, Grand Central, and Rockefeller Center, it's terrifically located in a clean, safe neighborhood that's close to Times Square but a notch down on the hustle-bustle level. What's more, there are only seven rooms per floor, so the property has a pleasing intimacy that's a welcome change from most chain hotels.

The freshly outfitted rooms are attractively decorated with a pleasing natural palette, blond woods, pretty artwork and fabrics, and a hint of smart deco style. They come with either one or two double beds or a queen, a big work desk with convenient desktop data port and laptop outlet, two speakerphones, Nintendo on the 25-inch TV, coffeemaker, alarm, and iron and board in the smallish closet; all rooms have side chairs, but the queens get a comfy club chair. Everything is fresh and spankin' new, from the extra-firm beds to the larger-than-average marble baths (with hair dryer and third phone). For the best view, ask for a high-floor room ending with 5; rates are run-of-house, so you won't pay extra. Amenities include free *USA Today* at the front desk, concierge, laundry and dry-cleaning service, express checkout, and a nice business center with a PC and printer/fax/copier you can use for free (long-distance faxing is extra, of course). An expanded continental breakfast buffet is offered for a nominal charge, and a full-service restaurant (with room service) was in the plans at press time. Complimentary local and 800 calls are a terrific value-added touch.

San Carlos Hotel. 150 E. 50th St. (at Third Ave.), New York, NY 10022. ☎ **800/722-2012** or 212/755-1800. Fax 212/688-9778. www.sancarloshotel.com. 146 units. A/C TV TEL. $195 double; $245 junior suite; $285–$300 1-bedroom suite. Rates include continental breakfast. Check Web site for special seasonal and Internet rates (from $139 double at press time). Monthly rates available. AE, DC, DISC, MC, V. Parking $27 next door. Subway: 6 to 51st St.; E, F to Lexington Ave.

Longtime owner Hy Arbesfeld runs both this hotel and the **Hotel Bedford,** a stone's throw from Grand Central at 118 E. 40th St. (☎ **800/221-6881;** www.bedfordhotel.com). Both hotels are similarly priced and quite recommendable, but I prefer the San Carlos for its big, big rooms and attentive doorman, who adds an air of sophistication to the attractive public spaces (rooms are somewhat smaller and there's no doorman at the Bedford).

All rooms are older and style-free, but each is spacious and boasts new bedspreads and curtains, a hair dryer in the older but very nice bathroom, a safe and iron with board in the big closet, two phones with data port, and a pants press. About 90% also have kitchenettes with microwave, coffeemaker, cooktop, and fridge. The large suites, which have pull-out sofas in the living rooms and at least two big closets, are a particularly good deal for families; some even have full dining room sets. The junior suites only differ in having an archway between the spaces rather than two entirely separate rooms, but they're still plenty big enough for wallet-watching families. Other money-saving pluses include coin-op laundry facilities and complimentary breakfast service in the pleasant breakfast room.

Look for improvements as the hotel embarks on a major renovation that will add a grand new atrium lobby, a fitness center, and more rooms. It has been carefully planned to not interfere with the comfort of guests, but ask for a room away from the action (or book in over at the Bedford) if you're concerned.

INEXPENSIVE

Habitat Hotel. 130 E. 57th St. (at Lexington Ave.), New York, NY 10022. ☎ **800/255-0482** or 212/753-8841. Fax 212/829-9605. www.habitatny.com or www.stayinny.com. 300 units (about 40 with private bathroom). A/C TV TEL. $95–$135 single or double with shared bathroom; $135–$185 single or double with private bathroom; $190–$270 for two single/double rooms with shared bathroom; $285–$350 penthouse deluxe double with private bathroom. Rates include continental breakfast. Check Web site for student rates and seasonal specials as low as $75 double. AE, CB, DC, DISC, JCB, MC, V. Parking $25. Subway: 4, 5, 6 to 59th St.; E, F to Lexington Ave.

This new-in-1999 hotel is marketed as "upscale budget," with rooms dressed to appeal to travelers who are short on funds but big on style. They're well designed in a natural palette accented with black-and-white photos. Everything is better quality and more attractive than I usually see in this price range, from the firm mattresses to the plush towels to the pedestal sinks in every room. (All rooms have voice mail and data ports on the phones, too.) The bathrooms—shared (one for every three to four rooms), semiprivate (two rooms sharing an adjacent bathroom), and private—are all brand new.

The only downside—and it may be a big one for romance-seeking couples—are the sleeping accommodations. A few queens are available (with private bathrooms), but most of the double rooms consist of a twin bed with a pull-out trundle, which takes up most of the width of the narrow room when it's open. The prices are high for the units with private bathrooms considering the setup, and downright exorbitant on the four penthouse deluxe rooms, which have queen beds, private bathrooms, microwaves, and minifridges. Rates are very attractive for the shared-bath rooms, however, especially considering the *Metropolitan Home* mindset and the A-1 location. Two single travelers or couples traveling together can book two rooms that share one private bath (the semiprivate situation) for a very good rate. The neighborhood is safe, chic, and super-convenient—especially for shoppers, since Bloomingdale's is just 2 blocks away.

The public spaces were under renovation when I visited (they should be completed by the time you arrive), but even the temporary lobby was more impressive than most. You'll find a glass-enclosed veranda with great views down Lexington Avenue, a bar, and a library lounge.

Quality Hotel Eastside. 161 Lexington Ave. (at 30th St.), New York, NY 10016. ☎ **800/ 567-7720** or 212/545-1800. Fax 212/790-2760. www.applecorehotels.com. 95 units (59 with private bathroom). A/C TV TEL. $89–$209 double, depending on season. Rates include continental breakfast. Ask about senior, AAA, corporate, and promotional discounts; check www.hotelchoice.com for online booking discounts. Extra person $12. Children under 14 stay free in parents' room. AE, DISC, MC, V. Parking $20 nearby. Subway: 6 to 33rd St.

This hotel is nothing special—just some small, standard rooms done in a vaguely early American style with older bathrooms. Its recommendable features are the location in quiet, residential Murray Hill; the amenities, which include a business center (with copy and fax machines, plus Internet access), and a fitness room (with treadmill and stationary bicycle); and the great low-season rates. In-room extras include coffeemaker, iron and board, alarm clock, hair dryer, and data port and voice mail on the phone; free local phone calls are another plus. There's a meeting room on the premises, and an affordable pasta restaurant next door. Don't expect much in the way of service, or anything in the style department—but considering how expensive an average room has become in this city, this hotel is a pretty good value, particularly when rooms go for as little as $79. Don't bother if rates are higher than $159, as you'll probably find more for your money elsewhere (unless it's holiday time, of course). And skip the shared-bath rooms altogether.

10 The Upper West Side

VERY EXPENSIVE

✪ **Trump International Hotel & Tower.** 1 Central Park West (at 60th St.), New York, NY 10023. ☎ **888/44-TRUMP** or 212/299-1000. Fax 212/299-1150. www.trumpintl.com. 167 units. A/C MINIBAR TV TEL. $495–$575 double; $750–$1,700 1- or 2-bedroom suite. Check Web site for special rates and package deals; also try booking through www.travelweb.com for discounted rates. Children stay free in parents' room. AE, CB, DC, JCB, MC, V. Valet parking $42. Subway: A, B, C, D, 1, 9 to Columbus Circle.

Forget all your preconceptions about The Donald—this is a surprisingly cultivated venture from the ultimate 1980s Bad Boy.

New in 1997, Trump International is housed on 14 lower floors of a freestanding 52-story mirrored monolith at the southwest corner of Central Park, with unobstructed views on all sides. The rooms are on the small side, but high ceilings and smart design make them feel uncluttered. They're beautifully done in an understated contemporary style, with clean-lined furniture, beautiful fabrics, and soothing earth tones. Floor-to-ceiling windows maximize the spectacular views, which are especially breathtaking on the park-facing side. In addition to the standard luxury amenities, each room is equipped with a fax machine, VCR, CD stereo, whirlpool tub in the marble bathroom, excellent bathrobes (light in summer, warm in winter), umbrellas,

Uptown Accommodations

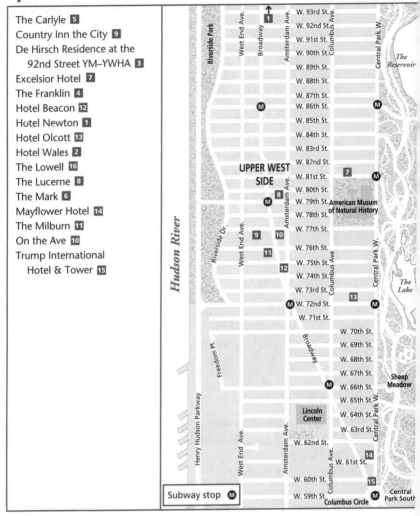

and a telescope for taking in the views. Suites also have a European-style kitchen stocked with china and crystal.

But what really sets this hotel apart is its signature services. Each guest is assigned a Trump attaché who basically functions as your own personal concierge, providing comprehensive business and personal services and, following your stay, recording your preferences to have on hand for your next visit. For the ultimate in romance and convenience, you can arrange in advance to have a chef from Jean Georges cook and prepare a multicourse meal right in your suite's own kitchen.

Dining: Awarded the coveted four stars by the *New York Times,* Jean Georges serves excellent contemporary French cuisine by one of the city's most celebrated chefs (see chapter 6). Unfortunately, word is that not enough reservations are put aside for guests, so be sure to book a table well ahead.

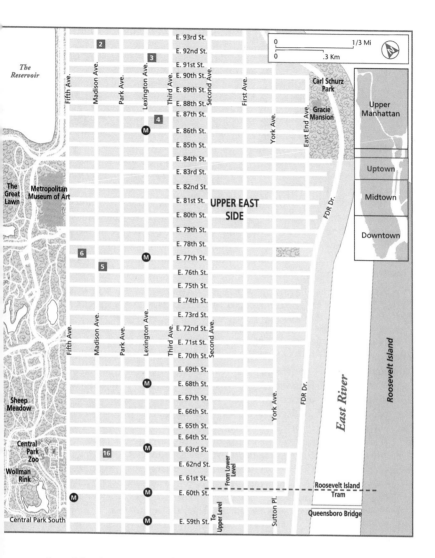

Amenities: Amazing 6,000-foot health and fitness spa with 55-foot lap pool, steam rooms, saunas, personal trainers, and a full slate of spa treatments. Personal attaché service, 24-hour room service, valet service, video rentals, newspaper delivery, business center, conference rooms. Complimentary shoe shine, pressing, local phone calls, cell phones. Baby-sitting, secretarial services, computers, and printers available.

MODERATE

✪ **Country Inn the City.** W. 77th St. (btw. Broadway and West End Ave.), New York, NY 10024. (Exact address omitted by request of owner.) ☎ **212/580-4183.** Fax 212/874-3981. www.countryinnthecity.com. 4 units. A/C TV TEL. $150–$195 double. Rates include continental breakfast. No sales tax added for stays of 7 nights or more. 3-night minimum. Maximum 2 guests per apt. No credit cards. Parking $25 nearby. Subway: 1, 9 to 79th St. No children under 12.

This charming 1891 town house is rich with original details, impeccable Americana-style decor, and more home-style comforts than you'll find anywhere else for the price. Each unit is actually a full studio apartment, with a cozy sofa, table and chairs for two, a private phone with answering machine, an extra phone jack, a safe, and a gorgeous, supremely comfortable queen bed in the large, high-ceilinged bedroom; a big galley kitchenette with a coffeemaker and everything you'll need to prepare a full meal; and a spacious, pretty bathroom. The whole place is bright and elegant, and the appointments, from the Oriental carpets covering the hardwood floors to the (nonworking) fireplaces that grace every room, couldn't be finer. Wonderful portraits in oil, tasteful collectibles, and brandy and fresh fruit on hand enhance the homey atmosphere. My favorite is no. 4, done in soft yellow with a high poster bed and whitewashed floorboards, but which one you'll like best depends on your tastes. No. 6 is the smallest, with a pretty sleigh bed in the corner, a smaller kitchenette, and a shower only in the bathroom, but its fabulous private terrace more than makes up the difference. Everything is immaculate, thanks to a resident housekeeper who provides maid service every other day. A quiet, peaceful air pervades the house, and the neighborhood couldn't be nicer. An excellent choice in every respect; best for travelers of the independent sort, however, since there's no resident innkeeper. No smoking.

✪ **Excelsior Hotel.** 45 W. 81st St. (btw. Columbus Ave. and Central Park West), New York, NY 10024. ☎ **800/368-4575** or 212/362-9200. Fax 212/721-2994. www.excelsiorhotelny.com. 169 units. A/C TV TEL. $179–$279 double; $239–$359 1-bedroom suite; $459–$639 2-bedroom suite. Inquire about seasonal rates and specials (winter rates can go as low as $135, $155 for suites). Extra person $20. Children 12 and under stay free in parents' room. AE, CB, DC, MC, V. Parking $27 two blocks away. Subway: B, C to 81st St./Museum of Natural History.

Now that renovations are complete, the newly elegant Excelsior gives the Lucerne (below) a serious run for its money. Everything is brand new throughout the hotel, from the richly wood-paneled lobby to the supremely comfy guest rooms to the small but state-of-the-art fitness center. The chic residential location, across from the Museum of Natural History and just steps from Central Park, is prime Upper West Side—don't be surprised if you spot a celebrity or two cruising the 'hood.

Freshly done in an attractive traditional style, the guest rooms boast high-quality furnishings, commodious closets (with irons and ironing boards), voice mail and data ports on the two-line phones, Nintendo, thick terry bathrobes, alarms, hair dryers, fax machine on the work desk, free bottled water, and full-length dressing mirrors (a nice touch). The pretty new bathrooms are most impressive. About 120 rooms have PCs with high-definition screens and Internet access ($17.95 per day). The two-bedded rooms are large enough to accommodate budget-minded families (a few even have two queens), and suites feature pull-out sofas and pants presses. The sunny museum-facing rooms are only worth the extra dough if a park view is really important to you, as all rooms are relatively bright and quiet. Housekeeping is impeccable throughout the hotel.

On the second floor is a gorgeous library with books, games, gorgeous leather seating, writing desks, and a large flat-screen TV with VCR and DVD player; an equally well-outfitted breakfast room with a daily breakfast buffet ($14 continental, $18 full); an executive-level conference room; and two furnished open-air decks. Concierge and laundry service are available.

✪ **Hotel Beacon.** 2130 Broadway (at 75th St.), New York, NY 10023. ☎ **800/572-4969** or 212/787-1100. Fax 212/724-0839. www.beaconhotel.com. 200 units. A/C TV TEL. $165–$185 single; $170–$195 double; $225–$295 1-bedroom suite; $450 2-bedroom suite. Extra person $15. Children under 17 stay free in parents' room. AE, CB, DC, DISC, MC, V. Parking $25 nearby. Subway: 1, 2, 3, 9 to 72nd St.

Ideally located in one of the city's most desirable neighborhoods, only a few blocks from Lincoln Center, Central Park, and the Museum of Natural History, the Beacon is one the best deals in town, especially for families. You'll get more style and state-of-the-art comforts at the Excelsior and better service at the Lucerne, but the Beacon will give you *space*. Every generously sized room features a kitchenette (with cooktop, coffeemaker, minifridge, and microwave), roomy closet, alarm, voice mail on the phone (no data port, though), and new marble bathroom with hair dryer. Rooms won't win any personality awards, but they're freshly done in muted florals, and linens are plush. Virtually all standard rooms feature two double beds, and they're plenty big enough to sleep a family on a budget. The large one- and two-bedroom suites are some of the best bargains in the city; each has two closets and a pull-out sofa in the well-furnished living room. The two-bedrooms have a second bathroom, making them well-outfitted enough to house a small army. Another fab family-friendly extra is the self-service Laundromat. There's no room service, but with gourmet markets like Zabar's and Fairway nearby, cooking is an attractive alternative, and there are plenty of restaurants in the immediate area. Concierge and valet service are available, plus access to a terrific nearby health club for a daily fee. All in all, a great place to stay—and a great value to boot.

✪ **The Lucerne.** 201 W. 79th St. (at Amsterdam Ave.), New York, NY 10024. ☎ **800/ 492-8122** or 212/875-1000. Fax 212/579-2408. www.newyorkhotel.com. 250 units. A/C TV TEL. $160–$280 double or junior suite; $230–$500 1-bedroom suite (most less than $400). AAA discounts offered; check Web site for special Internet deals. Extra person $15. Children under 16 stay free in parents' room. AE, DC, DISC, MC, V. Parking $16 nearby. Subway: 1, 9 to 79th St.

Want top-notch comforts and service without paying top-dollar prices? Then book into this Mobil four-star, AAA three-diamond hotel, one of the city's best values. As soon as the morning-suited doorman greets you at the entrance to the 1903 landmark building, you'll know you're getting a lot for your money. The bright marble lobby leads to comfortable guest rooms done in a tasteful Americana style. The standard rooms are big enough for a king, queen, or two doubles (great for those traveling with kids). All rooms have Nintendo, coffeemaker, alarm, two-line phones with voice mail and data port (although not always near the work desk), iron and board, and an attractive bathroom with hair dryer, spacious travertine counters, and good toiletries. Everything is fresh and immaculate. The suites also boast very nice kitchenettes with microwave and stocked minifridge, terry robes, and sitting rooms with sofas and extra TVs and Nintendo sets. The junior suites are a great deal for couples willing to spend a few extra dollars, while the larger suites (with pull-out sofa) give families the room they need (although Mom and Dad might get more space for their money at the Beacon).

The Lucerne prides itself on its excellent service. Amenities include a better-than-average fitness center, a business center, breakfast and dinner room service, dry-cleaning/laundry service, and meeting space with a terrific rooftop sundeck. On site is Wilson's, a neighborhood hot spot featuring good continental fare and even better live jazz 3 or 4 nights a week.

Mayflower Hotel. 15 Central Park West (at 61st St.), New York, NY 10023. ☎ **800/ 223-4164** or 212/265-0060. Fax 212/265-0227. www.mayflowerhotel.com. 365 units. A/C TV TEL. $205–$245 double; $275–$375 suite; from $600 penthouse or 2-bedroom suite. Extra person $20. Children under 16 stay free in parents' room. AE, CB, DC, DISC, ER, JCB, MC, V. Valet parking $28. Subway: A, B, C, D, 1, 9 to Columbus Circle. Small pets accepted.

Set on the edge of Central Park near Lincoln Center, the Mayflower has a spectacular location—in prime Upper West Side territory, but just a stone's throw from the

hustle and bustle of Midtown. The traditionally styled rooms are large (with two doubles, two queens, or a king) and all feature walk-in closets with iron and board, a service pantry with a fridge, and voice mail (most phones have data ports, but request
one if it matters). Bathrooms are fine, although some could use regrouting; all boast
hair dryers. VCRs can be requested, and cell phones are available for rent. You'll pay
more for park views, but they're fabulous.

On site you'll find the good Conservatory restaurant (with bar) and a well-outfitted
fitness center, plus ATM, fax, and currency exchange machines in the lobby. Free newspapers are also available in the lobby (Mon through Sat), as is early morning coffee.
Dry-cleaning and laundry service, limited room service (7am–midnight), conference
rooms, and express checkout are available. All in all, not the neighborhood's best
deal—the Beacon, the Lucerne, and the Excelsior are all better values—but a perfectly
fine place to stay, and much better that most hotels charging the same rates just a few
blocks away in Midtown.

On the Ave. 2178 Broadway (at 77th St.), New York, NY 10024. ☎ **800/509-7598** or
212/362-1100. Fax 212/362-1100. www.ontheave-nyc.com. 250 units. A/C TV TEL.
$175–$235 double; $255 suite. Inquire about seasonal specials. Extra person $20. Children
under 15 stay free in parents' room. AE, CB, DC, JCB, MC, V. Parking $20 next door. Subway:
1, 9 to 79th St.

This stylish, more upscale sister hotel to the Habitat (see "Midtown East," above),
offers designer doubles to midprice travelers. These may not be the best on the Upper
West Side, but the location is first rate and rooms are sleek, chic, and a decent value
despite a few bangs and nicks here and there. Rooms have floating beds, a natural
palette, and eye-catching original art by Alfonso Muñoz. I wish the clean-lined, mod-
ular Scandinavian-reminiscent furnishings were a tad more practical (and less IKEA-
ish), but they're comfortable nonetheless. The nicely renovated white-marble baths
have hair dryers and a good amount of steel counter space; be sure to request a tub if
you want one. The superiors don't offer much more than the standards; back-facing
standards are darker but quieter than Broadway-facing superiors, and you'll get more
space for your money. Splurge on a deluxe room if you really want more space. And
be sure to ask for a no-smoking room if you want one because the textiles really seem
to hold tight to the cigarette smell. Every room has an alarm clock, voice mail and data
port on the telephone, and nice terry robes in the closet. Big Nick's (see chapter 6)
provides 24-hour room service, and guests have access to the high-quality Equinox
health club, 1 block away, for $18 per day. Expect an impressive new lobby by the time
you arrive.

INEXPENSIVE

✪ **Hotel Newton.** 2528 Broadway (btw. 94th and 95th sts.), New York, NY 10025.
☎ **888/HOTEL58** or 212/678-6500. Fax 212/678-6758. www.newyorkhotel.com. 110
units (10 with shared bathroom). A/C TV TEL. $95 double with shared bathroom; $99–$140
double with private bathroom; $170 junior suite. AAA discounts available; check Web site for
special Internet deals. Extra person $20. Children under 15 stay free in parents' room. AE, DC,
DISC, MC, V. Parking $17 nearby. Subway: 1, 2, 3, 9 to 96th St.

Finally—an inexpensive hotel that's actually *nice*. Unlike many of its peers, the
Newton doesn't scream "budget!" at every turn, or require you to have the carefree attitude of a college student to put up with it. As you enter the pretty lobby, you're greeted
by a uniformed staff that's attentive and professional. The rooms are generally large,
with good, firm beds, a work desk (sorry, no voice mail or data ports, though), and a
sizable new bathroom with hair dryer, plus roomy closets in most (a few of the cheapest have wall racks only). Some are big enough to accommodate families with two

doubles or two queen beds. The suites feature two queen beds in the bedroom, a sofa in the sitting room, plus niceties like a microwave, minifridge, and iron and board, making them well worth the few extra dollars. The bigger rooms and suites have been upgraded with cherry-wood furnishings, but even the older laminated furniture is much nicer than I usually see in this price range. The AAA-approved hotel is impeccably kept, and there was lots of sprucing up going on—new drapes here, fresh paint there—during my last visit. The nice neighborhood boasts lots of affordable restaurants, and a cute diner in the same block provides room service from 6am to 2am. The 96th Street express subway stop is just a block away, providing convenient access to the rest of the city. A great bet all the way around.

Hotel Olcott. 27 W. 72nd St. (btw. Columbus Ave. and Central Park West), New York, NY 10023. ☎ **212/877-4200** or 212/877-4600. 200 units. A/C TV TEL. $125 studio double ($805 weekly); $150 suite ($945 weekly). Extra person $15. MC, V. Parking $18 next door. Subway: B, C to 72nd St.

Even as the residential real estate around it soars into the stratosphere, this old dowager remains one of New York's best budget bargains. About half of this residential hotel houses permanent and long-term residents (including a fair number of doctors' offices), but the rest is open to out-of-towners. The studios and suites are an excellent deal for short-term stays, and a downright steal if you take advantage of the weekly rates.

The apartments are about as stylish as Aunt Edna's house—circa 1970, no less—but they're maintained with care and even the studios are bigger than most NYC apartments (the suites are enormous). If only I had this much closet space! The discount furnishings are not pretty, but they're perfectly comfortable. Every apartment has a big bathroom and a kitchenette with minifridge, hot plate with kettle, toaster, and basic dishes and utensils; studios generally have a dining table for two and suites have a four-top. Phones have voice mail and data ports. Suites have TV only in the living room and sofas don't pull out, but the friendly management will lend you a cot (or even an additional bed) if you're bringing the family or sharing with friends. Ask for a renovated room when you book; most of the suites and about half of the studios have brand-new, bright-white kitchenettes and freshly laid tile in the bath.

The Olcott is steps from Central Park on one of Manhattan's most high-class blocks (the famed Dakota apartment building is just doors way). Nearby Columbus Avenue bustles with boutiques and restaurants. Just off the surprisingly sophisticated lobby is Dallas BBQ for decent cheap eats and bathtub-size cocktails.

✪ The Milburn. 242 W. 76th St. (btw. Broadway and West End Ave.), New York, NY 10023. ☎ **800/833-9622** or 212/362-1006. Fax 212/721-5476. www.milburnhotel.com. 112 units. A/C TV TEL. $129–$159 studio double; $149–$180 junior suite; $159–$195 1-bedroom suite. Extra person $10. Children 12 and under stay free in parents' room. AE, CB, DC, MC, V. Self-parking $20. Subway: 1, 9 to 79th St.

On a quiet side street a block from the Beacon, the Milburn also offers reasonably priced rooms and suites with equipped kitchenettes in the same great neighborhood. The Milburn may not be as nice as the Beacon, but it offers equal value for your dollar—arguably better in the less busy seasons, when a double studio goes for just $129. Every room is rife with amenities: dining area, VCR, safe, iron and ironing board, hair dryer, two-line phone with data port, alarm, nice newish bath with hair dryer, and kitchenette with minifridge, microwave, coffeemaker (with free coffee!), and all the necessary equipment. The one-bedroom suites also boast a pull-out queen sofa, an extra TV, and a work desk. Don't expect much from the decor, and the laminated furniture is clearly a cheaper grade than what you'll get at the Beacon, but everything is attractive and in good shape. In fact, the whole place is spotless.

What makes the Milburn a real find is that it's more service-oriented than most hotels in this price range. The friendly staff will do everything from providing free copy, fax, and e-mail services to picking up your laundry at the dry cleaners next door. Additional amenities include a self-serve Laundromat, a new fitness room, free videos, Sony PlayStation on request, newspaper delivery, wheelchair-accessible rooms, and a conference room. All in all, a great choice for bargain-hunters.

11 The Upper East Side

See the "Uptown Accommodations" map on pp. 126–127 to find the hotels in this section.

VERY EXPENSIVE

✪ **The Carlyle.** 35 E. 76th St. (at Madison Ave.), New York, NY 10021. ☎ **800/227-5737** or 212/744-1600. Fax 212/717-4682. 180 units. A/C MINIBAR TV TEL. $450–$695 double; from $650 1-bedroom suite; from $1,200 2-bedroom suite. AE, DC, MC, V. Valet parking $39. Subway: 6 to 77th St. Pets accepted.

If you've ever wondered how the rich and famous live, check into the Carlyle. Countless movie stars and international heads of states (including JFK, who was supposedly once visited by Marilyn here) have lain their heads on the fluffy pillows. Why they choose the Carlyle is clear—its hallmark attention to detail. With a staff-to-guest ratio of about two-to-one, service is simply the best. The English manor–style decor is luxurious but not excessive, creating the comfortably elegant ambience of an Upper East Side apartment. The guest rooms range from singles to seven-room suites, some with terraces and full dining rooms. All have marble bathrooms with whirlpool tubs and all the amenities you'd expect from a hotel of this caliber—even VCR, CD player, fax machine, and serving pantry in every room.

Dining/Diversions: Outfitted with the requisite Chinese screens and English hunting prints, the Carlyle Restaurant features formal French dining in the evening as well as lavish breakfast and lunch buffets. Less stuffy but still dressy is the Cafe Carlyle, the supper club where living legend Bobby Short and other big names entertain, which makes for an expensive but memorable night on the town (see chapter 9). Both rooms serve up a legendary Sunday brunch, à la carte in the restaurant and buffet style in the cafe. Charming Bemelmans Bar (named after children's book illustrator Ludwig Bemelmans, who created the Madeline books and painted the mural here) is a wonderful spot for cocktails; there's live soft jazz Monday through Saturday evenings, with a $10 cover charge. Dressed to resemble Turkey's Topkapi Palace, the Gallery serves breakfast and afternoon tea.

Amenities: High-tech fitness center with sauna and massage room, concierge, 24-hour room service, valet service, twice-daily maid service, banquet rooms. Business and secretarial services—as well as just about anything else you might need—are available.

The Lowell. 28 E. 63rd St. (btw. Park and Madison aves.), New York, NY 10021. ☎ **800/221-4444** or 212/838-1400. Fax 212/605-6808. www.preferredhotels.com. 65 units. A/C MINIBAR TV TEL. $385 single; $485 double; $585–$685 junior suite; $785–$985 1-bedroom suite; from $1,395 2-bedroom suite. Inquire about special packages and weekend and seasonal rates. Extra person $40. AE, DC, ER, JCB, MC, V. Valet parking $45. Subway: B, Q to Lexington Ave. Pets under 15 lb. accepted.

Housed in a historic landmark building on a lovely tree-lined street, this quietly elegant boutique hotel is a real gem. From the moment you enter the refined deco–French Empire lobby with its signed Edgar Brandt console, you know you're in a posh place. The Lowell has a distinct air of exclusivity about it, but without being snobbish. About two-thirds of the rooms are suites. In addition to fine old-world antiques, expect all the luxuries: VCRs, marble-and-brass baths with makeup mirrors, fax machines, windows that open, Scandinavian down comforters, king-size feather pillows, Frette terry robes, bathroom scales, and umbrellas. Each suite has a fully equipped kitchenette but is otherwise unique, with such features as wood-burning fireplaces, full dining rooms, a garden terrace, or even a private gym (this is the one Madonna chose, natch), so be sure to inquire about the available options.

Dining/Diversions: *Wine Spectator* has called the Post House one of the 10 best steak houses in America, but it seems to be resting on its laurels these days. Festooned in English chintz, the Pembroke Room serves breakfast, weekend brunch, and a supremely elegant afternoon tea that's perfect for purists (seasonal, so call ahead).

Amenities: 24-hour concierge, 24-hour room service, fitness center, valet service, newspaper delivery, twice-daily maid service, express checkout, conference rooms, baby-sitting, video rentals, secretarial services.

✪ **The Mark.** 25 E. 77th St. (at Madison Ave.), New York, NY 10021. ☎ **800/ THE-MARK** in the U.S., 800/223-6800 in Canada, or 212/744-4300. Fax 212/744-2749. www.themarkhotel.com. 180 units. A/C MINIBAR TV TEL. $500–$575 double; from $700 suite. Corporate rates available; ask about weekend packages, which can go as low as $299. Extra person $30. Children under 16 stay free in parents' room. AE, CB, DC, DISC, ER, EURO, JCB, MC, V. Valet parking $35. Subway: 6 to 77th St.

After a $35 million renovation, the Mark positioned itself as the Carlyle's chief rival. Located in the heart of a tony neighborhood that makes an ideal base for museum-goers and boutique shoppers, it's superbly elegant and somewhat more contemporary in feeling than the Carlyle. Behind the 1929 building's art deco facade is a neoclassical decor and a wonderful air of tranquility. The lobby's custom-designed Biedermeier furniture and marble floors prepare you for the lovely guest rooms, which are larger than most and feature king-size beds with Frette triple sheeting, overstuffed chairs, upholstered sofas, and museum-quality art. Fresh flowers, two-line phones, fax machines, VCRs, CDs, coffeemakers, terry robes, and even umbrellas are standard, and many rooms have fully outfitted kitchenettes. The marble bathrooms have Italian fixtures, oversize soak tubs, and heated towel racks. The hotel's general manager has been named one of the top 10 in the world, so it comes as no surprise that the service is beyond reproach.

Dining/Diversions: One of the best hotel restaurants in the city, Mark's serves consistently—and deservedly—high-rated New American–fusion cuisine in an elegant wood-paneled setting. The three-course pretheater dinner is an excellent value and the Sunday brunch is one of New York's all-time bests, while afternoon tea is a new institution among Upper East Side ladies. Mark's Bar serves hors d'oeuvres and cocktails.

Amenities: Award-winning Clefs d'Or concierge; 24-hour room service; fitness center with sauna; valet; free newspaper delivery; twice-daily maid service; conference and banquet rooms; complimentary shuttle service to Wall Street weekdays, and to Theater District Friday and Saturday evenings; secretarial services; baby-sitting.

EXPENSIVE

Hotel Wales. 1295 Madison Ave. (at 92nd St.), New York, NY 10128. ☎ **877/847-4444** or 212/876-6000. Fax 212/860-7000. www.waleshotel.com. 86 units. A/C TV TEL. $245–$345 double; $345–$415 suite. Rates include continental breakfast. Check Web site for special seasonal deals (from $225 at press time). Extra person $25. Children 18 and under stay free in parents' room. AE, CB, DC, MC, V. Valet parking $28. Subway: 6 to 96th St. Pets accepted.

This recommendation is built more on promise than anything else. The Wales is just fine but overpriced as it currently stands, considering the worn carpet and mismatched furnishings. But by the time you book in, the rooms are set to be completely renovated, and the models I've seen show a lot of promise: pretty cream and mint walls, gorgeously refinished original woodwork, good-quality carpeting, and accents that add to the Victorian style without unnecessary frill; suites are set to have pull-out chenille sofas, too. The beds are already outfitted in gorgeous Belgian linens and down comforters, and in-room extras include CD player and VCR. The high Victorian lobby, the pleasant halls, and the divine, sun-bright breakfast room/lounge already fulfill the promise of the place. Indeed, the building's bones are great, as is the location: You'll get more for your money on the Upper West Side, even when the place is complete, but the situation is ideal for museum buffs (Muscum Mile is just a stone's throw away) or anybody else who prefers an upscale, comfortingly homogeneous East Side residential location over the madness of Midtown. Still, expect some quirks—older baths, closet sizes that start at teeny and run the gamut—and a hike to the subway.

Dining/Diversions: On premises is Sarabeth's, one of my favorites, offering comforting home-style cooking or afternoon tea (see chapter 6). A harpist accompanies the complimentary morning spread in the wonderful lounge, where help-yourself cappuccino and tea are available around the clock.

Amenities: Room service from Sarabeth's (7am–10pm), dry-cleaning/laundry service, shoe shine, turndown, free video and CD library, free *New York Times* in the lounge, small fitness room (treadmills, bike, free weights), spa services.

MODERATE

The Franklin. 164 E. 87th St. (btw. Lexington and Third aves.), New York, NY 10128. ☎ **877/847-4444** or 212/369-1000. Fax 212/369-8000. www.franklinhotel.com. 48 units. A/C TV TEL. $205–$255 standard double; $225–$275 superior double. Rates include continental breakfast. Extra person $25. Children 18 and under stay free in parents' room. AE, CB, DC, MC, V. Parking $23 next door. Subway: 4, 5, 6, to 86th St.

Here's another Upper East Sider from the Boutique Hotel Group, the people behind the Wales (directly above). If the Wales is Jane Austen's dowager aunt, the Franklin is thoroughly modern Millie. The entire 1931 building has been done in a sleek ultramodern style. The comfy pillow-top beds are dressed with cushioned backlit headboards (clever for bedtime reading), down comforters, Belgian linens, and semisheer white canopies for a romantic touch. Rooms also have built-in cherry wood and steel work tables and night stands; petite TVs with VCRs; in-room safes; CD players; and small but nice black-and-white bathrooms with decent shelf space and hair dryers. The rooms are efficiently designed, but there's no disguising their monklike compactness. Go for a superior if you can afford it, which will give you a decent amount of floor space, a queen bed (instead of a full), and a real cedar-lined closet (as opposed to a foot-long bar hidden behind a full-length mirror); still, don't expect to squeeze more than two in. The standards are only suitable for 1- or 2-night stays—otherwise, you may have a hard time finding a place to put your suitcase.

Again, you'll get more for your money on the Upper West Side—On the Ave. immediately pops to mind for budget-minded style hounds. But the upscale, out-of-the-fray location is great (museum buffs and art dealers particularly love it). Dry-cleaning/laundry service is available, and nice extras like free breakfast, free *New York Times* in the sitting room, free CD and video lending libraries, and help-yourself cappuccino and tea around the clock help to soften the blow.

INEXPENSIVE

De Hirsch Residence at the 92nd Street YM–YWHA. 1395 Lexington Ave. (at 92nd St.), New York, NY 10128. ☎ **888/699-6884** or 212/415-5650. Fax 212/415-5578.

www.92ndsty.org. 300 units (none with private bathroom). A/C. $79 single; $98 double; long-term stays (2 months or more) $895/month single, $1,190–$1,450/month double. AE, MC, V. Parking $20 nearby. Subway: 4, 5, 6 to 86th St.; 6 to 96th St. Guests must be at least 18, and no older than 30 for long-term stays.

Travelers on a tight budget should contact the 92nd Street Y well in advance. The de Hirsch Residence offers basic but comfortable rooms, each with either one or two single beds, a dresser, and bookshelves. Each floor has a large communal bathroom, a fully equipped kitchen/dining room with microwave, and laundry facilities. The building is rather institutional-looking, but it's well kept and secure, the staff is friendly, and the location is terrific. This high-rent Upper East Side neighborhood is just blocks from Central Park and Museum Mile, and there's plenty of cheap eats and places to pick up meal fixings within a few blocks. Daily maid service and use of the Y's state-of-the-art fitness facility (pool, whirlpool, weights, racquetball, aerobics) are included in the daily rates, making this a stellar deal. This is a great bet for lone travelers in particular, since the 92nd Street Y is a community center in the true sense of the word, offering a real sense of kinship and a mind-boggling slate of top-rated cultural events (see chapter 9).

6 Dining

Attention, foodies: Welcome to Mecca. Without a doubt, New York is the best restaurant town in the country, and one of the finest in the world. Other cities might have particular specialties, but no other culinary capital spans the globe so successfully as the Big Apple.

That's due in part to New York's vibrant immigrant mix. Let a newcomer arrive and see that his or her native foods aren't being served and *zap!*—there's a new restaurant, cafe, or grocery to fill the void. Yet we New Yorkers can be fickle: One moment a restaurant is hot; the next it's passé. So restaurants close with a frequency we wish applied to the arrival of subway trains. Always call ahead.

But there's one thing we all have to face sooner or later: Eating in New York just ain't cheap. The primary cause? The high cost of real estate, which is reflected in what you're charged. Wherever you're from, particularly if you hail from the reasonably priced American heartland, New York's restaurants will seem *expensive*. You can't throw a rock in this town without hitting a restaurant charging $20 to $30 for entrees these days. Yet good value abounds, especially if you're willing to eat ethnic, and venture beyond tourist zones into the neighborhoods where budget-challenged New Yorkers eat, like Chinatown and the East Village. But even if you have no intention of venturing beyond Times Square, don't worry: I've included inexpensive restaurants in every neighborhood, including some of the city's best-kept secrets, so you'll know where to get good value for your money no matter where you are in Manhattan.

WHAT'S HAPPENING

Thanks to a booming economy and an optimistic outlook, New York is home to more good restaurants than ever before. Whole new districts have sprouted up: The Flatiron District has grown into a "Restaurant Row" unto itself, sparkling with wonderful splurge-worthy restaurants. The East Village has become ground zero for affordable quality dining, with excellent restaurants at every turn.

In addition to rising prices, there are two major trends that are all products of a thriving dining scene. The first is what I like to call the Big Squeeze: Too many restaurants won't say "no" to diners dying to get in and spend wads of cash, even when they're already packed. As a result, more and more tables are being squeezed into smaller and smaller spaces. Elbow room is a thing of the past, even in some of the city's finer restaurants, where you'd think your money would buy you better. In the listings below, I've tried to consistently mention those restaurants where the tables are on the small side and the seating is tight. As you can see from my reviews, I don't consider this a reason to stay away; some of my favorite restaurants suffer from this problem. However, keep it in mind when you're making your choice. If you want romance and quiet conversation, or simply lots of legroom, choose carefully.

The other big trend that's worth noting is the increasing tendency for waiters to come on like aggressive salespeople. If you're offered a special, feel free to ask how much it is, even in the fanciest restaurant—there's nothing gauche about it. Many waiters will try to push extra starters and sides, but don't feel pressured—if you wanted fries, you would've asked for fries in the first place. The biggest bugaboo in this category is bottled water: Most servers will ask "sparkling or still?" as if perfectly good New York City tap water were not an option. It is. Don't get roped in if plain ol' ice water is all you want; otherwise you can end up with an additional $10 or $15 charge (yep, that's right) for something you didn't really want in the first place.

RESERVATIONS

Reservations are always a good idea in New York, and a virtual necessity if your party is bigger than two. Do yourself a favor and call ahead as a rule of thumb so you won't be disappointed. If you're booking dinner on a weekend night, it's a good idea to call a few days in advance if you can.

For bookings at the city's most popular restaurants, call *far* ahead—a month in advance is a good idea. Most top places start taking reservations exactly 30 days in advance, so if you want to eat at a hot restaurant at a popular hour—Saturday at 8pm, say, at Jean Georges—be sure to mark your calendar and start dialing 30 days prior at 9am. If you're booking a holiday dinner, call even earlier.

But if you didn't call well ahead and your heart's set on dinner at Le Cirque or Gramercy Tavern, don't despair. Often, early or late hours—between 6 and 7pm, or after 10pm—are available, especially on weeknights. And try calling the day before or first thing in the morning, when you may be able to take advantage of a last-minute cancellation. Or go for lunch, which is usually much easier to book without lots of advance notice. And if you're staying at a hotel with a concierge, don't be afraid to use them—they can often get you into hot spots that you couldn't get into on your own.

But What If They Don't *Take* Reservations?   Lots of restaurants, especially at the affordable end of the price continuum, don't take reservations at all. One of the ways they keep prices down is by packing people in as quickly as possible. Thus, the best cheap and midpriced restaurants often have a wait. Again, your best bet is to go early. Often, you can get in more quickly on a weeknight. Or just go knowing that you're going to have to wait if you head to a popular spot; hunker down with a cocktail at the bar and enjoy the festivities around you.

The Best of the Best

For the best of what the city has to offer, take a moment to check out **"Best Dining Bets"** in chapter 1.

THE LOWDOWN ON SMOKING

Following the national trend, New York City enacted strict no-smoking laws a few years back that made most of the city's dining rooms blessedly smoke-free. However, that doesn't mean that smokers are completely prohibited from lighting up. Here's the deal: Restaurants with more than 35 seats cannot allow smoking in their dining rooms. They can, however, allow smoking in their bar or lounge areas, and most do. Restaurants with fewer than 35 seats—and there are more of those in the city than you'd think—can allow or prohibit smoking as they see fit. This ruling has turned some of the city's restaurants into particularly smoker-friendly establishments, which might be a turnoff for nonsmokers.

Your best bet is to call ahead and ask about the smoking policy if it matters to you. If you're hell-bent on enjoying an after-dinner cigarette indoors, make sure that the restaurant has a bar or lounge that allows smoking. Some restaurants, such as Isla and Bar Pitti, even offer dinner tables in their lounges where you can puff away all during the meal if you so choose. And smoking is usually allowed in alfresco dining areas, but never assume—always ask. If you're a nonsmoker who doesn't want to be bothered by secondhand smoke, make sure your seat is well away from the bar.

TIPPING

Tipping is easy in New York. The way to do it: Double the 8.25% sales tax and voilà!, happy waitperson. In fancier venues, another 5.25% is appropriate for the captain. If the wine steward helps, hand him or her 10% of the bottle's price.

In the restaurant reviews below, I've made notes about what you can expect in terms of service. However, keep in mind that it all depends on the luck of the draw, and your waitperson's personality. No matter where you eat, if you get good service, reward your waitperson accordingly. But if you genuinely feel like you were short-shrifted, feel free to let the tip reflect it.

Leave a dollar per item, no matter how small, for the checkroom attendant.

1 Restaurants by Cuisine

AMERICAN

See also "Contemporary American," below.

Big Nick's Burger Joint/
   Pizza Joint (p. 195)
Brooklyn Diner USA (p. 180)
Bubby's (p. 145)
Cafeteria (p. 164)
EJ's Luncheonette (p. 195)
Empire Diner (p. 166)
ESPN Zone (p. 180)
Hard Rock Cafe (p. 180)
Harley-Davidson Cafe (p. 180)
Jekyll & Hyde Club (p. 181)
Joe Allen (p. 178)
Manhattan Chili Co. (p. 182)
Mars 2112 (p. 181)
The Odeon (p. 146)
Official All-Star Cafe (p. 181)

Old Town Bar & Restaurant (p. 170)
Planet Hollywood (p. 181)
Prime Burger (p. 190)
Serendipity 3 (p. 199)
Tavern on the Green (p. 190)
"21" Club (p. 172)
Virgil's Real BBQ (p. 179)
WWF New York (p. 180)

ASIAN FUSION/PAN-ASIAN/ PACIFIC RIM

Junno's (p. 163)
Republic (p. 171)
Roy's New York (p. 141)
Ruby Foo's (p. 194)
Union Pacific (p. 167)
Vong (p. 186)

BELGIAN

Cafe de Bruxelles (p. 160)
Steak Frites (p. 170)

BRAZILIAN

Churrascaria Plataforma (p. 177)

BRITISH

British Open (p. 188)
North Star Pub (p. 142)
Tea & Sympathy (p. 164)

CHINESE

Canton (p. 147)
Grand Sichuan Restaurant (p. 166)
Joe's Shanghai (p. 148)
Mr. Chow (p. 186)
New York Noodletown (p. 148)
Ruby Foo's (p. 194)

CONTEMPORARY AMERICAN

An American Place (p. 184)
Bouley Bakery (p. 144)
Gramercy Tavern (p. 167)
Home (p. 160)
March (p. 185)
Metro Grill (p. 178)
Park View at the Boathouse (p. 197)
Quilty's (p. 151)
Red Cat (p. 165)
River Café (p. 201)
Sarabeth's Kitchen (p. 194)
Savoy (p. 152)
Tavern Room at Gramercy Tavern
 (p. 168)
Time Cafe (p. 156)
Veritas (p. 168)
Wild Blue (p. 141)
Windows on the World (p. 141)

CONTINENTAL

Cité (p. 172)
One If By Land, Two If By Sea
 (p. 159)
Petrossian (p. 173)
Tavern on the Green (p. 190)

FRENCH

Balthazar (p. 149)
Chanterelle (p. 144)
Daniel (p. 196)

Florent (p. 166)
Jean Georges (p. 190)
Jo Jo (p. 197)
La Bonne Soupe (p. 182)
La Grenouille (p. 183)
Le Bernardin (p. 171)
Le Cirque 2000 (p. 184)
Le Gigot (p. 162)
Le Pere Pinard (p. 149)
Pastis (p. 165)
Payard Pâtisserie & Bistro (p. 198)
Steak Frites (p. 170)

GOURMET SANDWICHES/ DELI/TAKEOUT

Barney Greengrass, the Sturgeon King
 (p. 151)
Carnegie Deli (p. 150)
Ess-A-Bagel (p. 188)
Island Burgers & Shakes (p. 181)
Katz's Delicatessen (p. 151)
Mangia (p. 142)
Second Avenue Deli (p. 150)
Stage Deli (p. 150)

GREEK

Estiatorio Milos (p. 173)
Molyvos (p. 179)
Niko's Mediterranean Grill & Bistro
 (p. 195)

INDIAN/INDIAN FUSION

Haveli (p. 155)
Pongal (p. 188)
Salaam Bombay (p. 146)
Tabla (p. 168)

ITALIAN

Babbo (p. 159)
Barbetta (p. 172)
Bar Pitti (p. 162)
Caffe Bondí Ristorante (p. 169)
Caffe Grazie (p. 198)
Carmine's (p. 177)
Follonico (p. 169)
Il Cortile (p. 147)
Lupa (p. 163)
Pietrasanta (p. 183)
Pō (p. 159)
San Domenico (p. 176)

JAPANESE

Blue Ribbon Sushi (p. 150)
BondSt (p. 155)
Haru (p. 191)
Iso (p. 155)
Junno's (p. 163)
Next Door Nobu (p. 145)
Nobu (p. 145)
Shabu Tatsu (p. 158)

JEWISH DELI

Barney Greengrass, the Sturgeon King
   (p. 151)
Carnegie Deli (p. 150)
Katz's Delicatessen (p. 151)
Second Avenue Deli (p. 150)
Stage Deli (p. 150)

KOREAN

Woo Chon (p. 179)

LATIN AMERICAN/ HISPANIC/SOUTH AMERICAN

Boca Chica (p. 157)
Cafe Habana (p. 152)
Calle Ocho (p. 191)
Churrascaria Plataforma (p. 177)
Isla (p. 160)

MEDITERRANEAN

Julian's (p. 178)
Layla (p. 146)
Medusa (p. 170)
Niko's Mediterranean Grill & Bistro
   (p. 195)

MEXICAN

Gabriela's (p. 196)
Zarela (p. 187)

MIDDLE EASTERN

Al Bustan (p. 187)
Layla (p. 146)
Moustache (p. 163)

PIZZA

Grimaldi's Pizzeria (p. 201)
John's Pizzeria (p. 182)
Lombardi's (p. 154)
Pintaile's Pizza (pp. 171, 199)
Serafina Pizza (p. 199)

RUSSIAN/UKRAINIAN

Petrossian (p. 173)
Russian Tea Room (p. 176)
Veselka (p. 158)

SCANDINAVIAN

Cafe at Aquavit (p. 177)

SEAFOOD

Aquagrill (p. 152)
Blue Water Grill (p. 169)
Estiatorio Milos (p. 173)
Le Bernardin (p. 171)
Oyster Bar & Restaurant (p. 187)
Pisces (p. 157)
Union Pacific (p. 167)

SOUL FOOD

Sylvia's (p. 200)

SOUTHERN/BARBECUE

Virgil's Real BBQ (p. 179)

SPANISH

La Paella (p. 156)
Taperia Madrid (p. 199)

STEAKS

Cité (p. 172)
Michael Jordan's–The Steak House
   (p. 185)
Peter Luger Steakhouse (p. 200)
Steak Frites (p. 170)
Wild Blue (p. 141)

SWISS

Roettele A.G. (p. 156)

THAI

Siam Inn Too (p. 183)

TURKISH

Pasha (p. 194)

VEGETARIAN/HEALTH-CONSCIOUS

Angelica Kitchen (p. 157)
Josie's Restaurant & Juice Bar (p. 196)
Pongal (p. 188)
Spring Street Natural Restaurant
   (p. 154)

VIETNAMESE

Nha Trang (p. 148)

2 South Street Seaport & the Financial District

VERY EXPENSIVE

Windows on the World. 1 World Trade Center, 107th Floor (enter on West St., between Liberty and Vesey sts.). ☎ **212/524-7000.** www.windowsontheworld.com. Reservations recommended. Jacket required. Main courses $25–$40; sunset fixed-price (before 6pm) $40; fixed-price brunch $32.50. AE, CB, DC, DISC, MC, V. Mon–Thurs 5–10pm, Fri–Sat 5–11pm, Sun 11am–2pm and 5–10pm. Subway: C, E to World Trade Center; N, R, 1, 9 to Cortlandt St. CONTEMPORARY AMERICAN.

The interior is more hotel dining than high design, but that's just fine: Who needs to look at the inside when all New York's out the window? This formal restaurant boasts the city's most spectacular views, as well as a New American menu that's more than admirable now that Michael Lomonaco, the former executive chef of the "21" Club (you may know him from *Michael's Place* on the Food Network and the Discovery Channel's *Epicurious*), is at the helm. Stick with the simplest, most straightforward-sounding dishes for maximum satisfaction, such as the smoked salmon appetizer, stout-braised Black Angus short ribs, or poached Maine lobster pot pie (all Lomonaco signatures). Windows is home to one of the city's most respected—and most expensive—wine cellars. The sommelier will be happy to point you in the right direction, whether you're a serious oenophile looking for a one-of-a-kind find or a casual wine lover who wants a good-value bottle.

If Windows sounds a tad too stiff or expensive for you, consider **Wild Blue** instead, which I actually prefer over this more formal room (see below).

EXPENSIVE

Roy's New York. 130 Washington St. (at Cedar St., 1 block south of Liberty St.). ☎ **212/266-6262.** www.roysrestaurant.com. Reservations recommended. Dim sum and individual pizzas $7–$13; main courses $18–$34. AE, DISC, MC, V. Mon–Fri 11:30am–2:30pm; Sun–Thurs 5:30–10pm, Fri–Sat 5:30–11pm. Subway: C, E to World Trade Center; N, R, 1, 9 to Cortlandt St. HAWAII/PACIFIC RIM.

Roy Yamaguchi is the Emeril Lagasse of Hawaii, and this is his first East Coast outpost. It's not quite as successful as his stellar island restaurants—is the master spreading himself too thin, perhaps?—but it's still substantially better than most of what's available in the neighborhood. The menu changes daily, but count on such signatures as Szechuan spiced baby-back ribs, a sticky, addictive delight; Maryland blue crab cakes in a spicy sesame beurre blanc; wood-fired pizzas, including a sweet-buttered crab version with brie; and a terrific sake miso marinated butterfish. As you may detect, these are heavy preparations that tend toward sweet; the kitchen here lacks the delicacy of its Pacific island siblings. Some dishes go too far on occasion—the soy-mustard butter on the blackened ahi, normally one of my favorites, was way too spicy on my last visit—but others are downright delectable. The comfortable, spacious room is cheerful, if not overly sophisticated, and the same can be said for the earnest (and improving) servers. The specialty cocktails menu is excellent (especially the divine Big Apple Martini), and wines bottled under Roy's own label are affordable and surprisingly good. All in all, a terrific spot for an upscale lunch or dinner adjoining a day of Financial District sightseeing.

Wild Blue. 1 World Trade Center, 107th Floor (enter on West St., between Liberty and Vesey sts.). ☎ **212/524-7000.** www.windowsontheworld.com. Reservations recommended. Main courses $19–$28. AE, CB, DC, DISC, JCB, MC, V. Mon–Thurs 5:30–10pm, Fri–Sat 5:30–10:30pm. Subway: C, E to World Trade Center; N, R, 1, 9 to Cortlandt St. CONTEMPORARY AMERICAN/STEAKS.

New in 1999 to the World Trade Center's 107th floor is this more intimate, less formal, and less expensive alternative to big sister Windows (see above). The contemporary wood-paneled room is warm and inviting, with big, well-spaced tables and extremely comfortable chairs—and views that are, of course, magnificent. Also the domain of Chef Michael Lomonaco, Wild Blue is at its best when it's acting as the steak house. Both the thick-cut, lamb T-bone chops and char-broiled, prime-aged New York strip steak were better than versions I've had recently at some of the city's best steak houses. Sides are pure steak house fare, too; the fresh creamed spinach, delicately gingered young carrots, and butternut squash hash are models of accompaniment. The more innovative dishes are perfectly passable, but you'll do better elsewhere if that's what you're in the mood for. The wine list is excellent, but designed for big-ticket Windows diners rather than more easygoing Wild Blue patrons; if you're a wine drinker, resign yourself to spending at least $70 on a bottle, or order by the glass. Service is quite attentive. I was presented with a poor excuse for a martini on my last visit, however, so your best bet is to start with a flawlessly mixed cocktail next door, at the Greatest Bar on Earth (see chapter 9).

INEXPENSIVE

Mangia. 40 Wall St. (btw. Nassau and William sts.). ☎ **212/425-4040.** Main courses $5.95–$10.95. AE, CB, DC, DISC, MC, V. Mon–Fri 7am–6pm (delivery 6–10pm). Subway: 4, 5 to Wall St.; J, M, Z to Broad St. GOURMET DELI.

This big, bustling gourmet cafeteria is an ideal place to take a break during your day of Financial District sightseeing. Between the giant salad and soup bars, the sandwich and hot entree counters, and an expansive cappuccino-and-pastry counter at the front of the cavernous room, even the most finicky eater will have a hard time deciding what to eat. Everything is freshly prepared and beautifully presented. The soups and stews are particularly good (there are always a number of daily choices), and a cup goes well with a fresh-baked pizzette (a minipizza). Pay-by-the-pound salad bars don't get any better than this, hot meal choices (such as grilled mahi-mahi or cumin-marinated lamb kabob) are cooked to order, and sandwiches are freshly made as you watch. This place is packed with Wall Streeters between noon and 2pm, but things move quickly and there's enough seating that usually no one has to wait. Come in for a late breakfast or an afternoon snack, and you'll virtually have the place to yourself.

In addition to the Wall Street location, Mangia also has two cafeteria-style cafes in Midtown that offer similar, if not such expansive, menus: at 50 W. 57th St., between Fifth and Sixth avenues (☎ **212/582-5882**); and at 16 E. 48th St., just east of Fifth Avenue (☎ **212/754-7600**).

North Star Pub. At South Street Seaport, 93 South St. (at Fulton St.). ☎ **212/509-6757.** www.northstarpub.com. Main courses $7.50–$12.95. AE, CB, DC, EURO, MC, V. Daily 11:30am–10:30pm (bar open later). Subway: 2, 3, 4, 5 to Fulton St. BRITISH.

This friendly place right at the entrance to the Seaport is a refreshing bit of authenticity in the mollified, almost theme park–like historic district. It's the spitting image of a British pub, down to the chalkboard menus boasting daily specials like kidney pie and strictly British and Irish ales on tap. I love the ale-battered fish-and-chips, good-quality fish deep-fried just right (not too greasy); the excellent golden-browned shepherd's pie (just like Grandma used to make); the bangers 'n' mash, made with grilled Cumberland sausage; and the traditional Ploughman's, including very good pâté, a sizable hunk of cheddar or stilton, fresh bread, and all the accompaniments (even Branston pickle!). In keeping with the theme, there's also a menu of 75 single-malt scotches. All in all, a fun, relaxing place to hang out and eat and drink heartily

Lower Manhattan, TriBeCa & Chinatown Dining

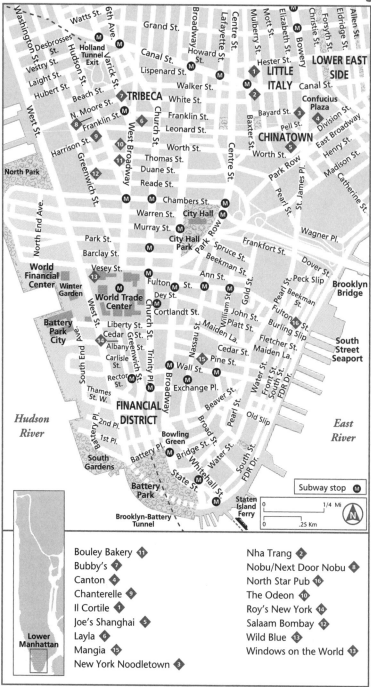

Watts St.
6th Ave.
Washington St.
Desbrosses St.
Grand St.
Broadway
Lafayette St.
Centre St.
Mulberry St.
Mott St.
Elizabeth St.
Bowery
Christie St.
Forsyth St.
Eldridge St.
Allen St.
Holland Tunnel Exit
Howard St.
Hester St.
LOWER EAST SIDE
Vestry St.
Hudson St.
Varick St.
Canal St.
Lispenard St.
LITTLE ITALY
Laight St.
Beach St.
Walker St.
Canal St.
Confucius Plaza
Hubert St.
TRIBECA
White St.
Bayard St.
Baxter St.
Pell St.
Division St.
N. Moore St.
Franklin St.
Franklin St.
CHINATOWN
East Broadway
Harrison St.
Church St.
Leonard St.
Worth St.
Park Row
Henry St.
West St.
Greenwich St.
West Broadway
Worth St.
Thomas St.
Duane St.
St. James Pl.
Madison St.
Catherine St.
North Park
Reade St.
Chambers St.
Warren St.
City Hall
Pearl St.
Wagner Pl.
North End Ave.
Murray St.
City Hall Park
Park Row
Spruce St.
Frankfort St.
Dover St.
Brooklyn Bridge
Park St.
Barclay St.
Beekman St.
Peck Slip
World Financial Center
Vesey St.
Fulton St.
Ann St.
Gold St.
Fulton St.
Beekman St.
Burling Slip
Winter Garden
Dey St.
John St.
South Street Seaport
World Trade Center
Cortlandt St.
William St.
Platt St.
Fletcher St.
Maiden La.
Battery Park City
Liberty St.
Cedar St.
Greenwich St.
Nassau St.
Maiden La.
Cedar St.
Water St.
Front St.
South St.
FDR Dr.
Albany St.
Pine St.
Carlisle St.
Trinity Pl.
Wall St.
Rector St.
Exchange Pl.
Beaver St.
Thames St. W.
FINANCIAL DISTRICT
Broadway
Pearl St.
Old Slip
Hudson River
2nd Pl.
1st Pl.
Bowling Green
Broad St.
Water St.
East River
Battery Pl.
Bridge St.
Whitehall St.
South St.
FDR Dr.
South Gardens
State St.
Battery Park
Staten Island Ferry
Subway stop Ⓜ
Brooklyn-Battery Tunnel
0   1/4 Mi
0   .25 Km

Bouley Bakery ⬥11
Bubby's ⬥7
Canton ⬥4
Chanterelle ⬥9
Il Cortile ⬥1
Joe's Shanghai ⬥5
Layla ⬥6
Mangia ⬥15
New York Noodletown ⬥3

Nha Trang ⬥2
Nobu/Next Door Nobu ⬥8
North Star Pub ⬥16
The Odeon ⬥10
Roy's New York ⬥14
Salaam Bombay ⬥12
Wild Blue ⬥13
Windows on the World ⬥13

Lower Manhattan

(and cheaply). By the time you arrive, look for an expanded menu featuring influences from the former British Empire.

3 TriBeCa

VERY EXPENSIVE

✪ **Bouley Bakery.** 120 W. Broadway (btw. Duane and Reade sts.). ☎ **212/964-2525.** www.bouley.net. Reservations required. Main courses $28–$35; 3-course fixed-price lunch $38; 6- or 7-course fixed-price dinner $75–$90. AE, DC, MC, V. Daily 11:30am–3pm and 5:30–11pm. Subway: 1, 2, 3, 9 to Chambers St. FRENCH-ACCENTED CONTEMPORARY AMERICAN.

The *New York Times*'s newest four-star winner is the ideal choice for gourmands who love fine dining but dislike classic formality. I didn't care for Bouley Bakery when it was new in 1997, and merely intended as a temporary space for Chef David Bouley between bigger projects; it was too small and didn't have a feeling of seriousness or permanence. Since then, it has blossomed into a culinary showcase for the 21st century: The dining room has doubled in size and developed its own brand of self-assured, easygoing refinement. Chanterelle has a similar downtown ease, but you'll never hear Natalie Merchant or Everything But the Girl on the sound system there.

The same poise has taken hold in the kitchen, which creates the city's best contemporary American fare, albeit with a decidedly French accent. Bouley may be the best, most imaginative chef in the city; he has a masterfully light touch and an unfailing sense of culinary balance. His food has a refreshing delicacy, even a sensuality—and his clean, fresh flavors are quite a turn-on. Foie gras with quince purée in Armagnac has a lightness that I didn't think was possible in such a dish; ditto for the beautifully subtle roasted squash soup. Long Island duck is accompanied with organic wheat berries, braised leeks, and a port wine sauce that manages to accent the freshness of the tender breast, rather than smother it. Even roast chicken and Chatham day-boat cod rise to new heights in Bouley's hands. And they don't call this place Bouley Bakery for nothing: The breads and sweets are sublime, too. Excellent through and through.

One word of warning: The restaurant has been known to seat parties at cafe tables in the bakery rather than in the main dining room on busy occasions. Make sure you're guaranteed a table in the main room when you book.

✪ **Chanterelle.** 2 Harrison St. (at Hudson St.). ☎ **212/966-6960.** www.chanterellenyc.com. Reservations recommended well in advance. Fixed-price lunch $20–$35; à la carte lunch $18.50–$25; fixed-price dinner $75; tasting menu $89 ($149 with wines). AE, CB, DC, DISC, MC, V. Mon 5:30–11pm, Tues–Sat noon–2:30pm and 5:30–11pm. Subway: 1, 9 to Franklin St. CONTEMPORARY FRENCH.

Here's my absolute favorite special-occasion restaurant. Chanterelle leaves you saying not only "The food was superb" or "The wine was sublime," but also "Thank you for a marvelous time." Overseen by husband-and-wife co-owners David and Karen Waltuch, the first-rate wait staff—the best in the city—makes sure of it. There's no stuffiness here at all; everyone is encouraged to feel at home and relaxed. The dining room is simple but beautiful, with a pressed-tin ceiling, widely spaced large tables, comfortable chairs, and gorgeous floral displays; there's also a superb modern art collection, featuring works from the likes of Ellsworth Kelly, Cy Twombly, and Cindy Sherman, in the foyer.

Your server will know the handwritten menu in depth and be glad to describe preparations in detail and suggest complementary combinations. The artful cuisine is based on traditional French technique, but Pacific and Pan-European notes sneak into the culinary melodies, and lots of dishes are lighter than you'd expect. The seasonal menu changes every few weeks, but one signature dish appears on almost every menu: a marvelous grilled seafood sausage. Cheese lovers should opt for a cheese course—the presentation and selection can't be beat. The wine list is superlative, but I wish there were more affordable options. Still, you don't come to Chanterelle on the cheap—you come to celebrate. Very expensive, but magnificent.

EXPENSIVE

✪ **Nobu/Next Door Nobu.** 105 Hudson St. (at Franklin St.). ☎ **212/219-0500** for Nobu; ☎ **212/334-4445** for Next Door Nobu. Reservations required far in advance at Nobu; reservations accepted for parties of 6 or more at Next Door Nobu. Main courses $8–$32; sushi $3–$10 per piece; omakase (chef's choice) from $45 at lunch, from $70 at dinner. AE, DC, MC, V. Nobu: Mon–Fri 11:45am–2:15pm; daily 5:45–10:15pm. Next Door Nobu: Mon–Thurs 5:45pm–midnight, Fri–Sat 5:45pm–1am. Subway: 1, 9 to Franklin St. NEW JAPANESE.

Chef Nobuyuki Matsuhisa took New York by storm in 1994 with his innovative, pan-cultural preparations, and Nobu has been flying high ever since. Deeply rooted in Japanese tradition but heavily influenced by Latin American and Western techniques, his cooking bursts with creative spirit. Unusual textures, impulsive combinations, and surprising flavors add up to a first-rate dining adventure that you won't soon forget. Virtually every creation hits its target, whether you opt for the new-style sashimi; light-as-air rock shrimp tempura; or sublime broiled black cod in sweet miso, the best dish in the house. If Kobe beef is available, try this delicacy tataki style (with soy, scallions, and daikon). The knowledgeable staff will be happy to guide you. However, since most dinners are structured as a series of tasting plates, be aware that the bill can soar—wallet-watchers should keep a close eye on the tally. The excitement is heightened by the witty modern decor (check out the chopstick-legged chairs at the sushi bar). The only disappointment is the traditional sushi, which is merely fine; head to BondSt or Blue Ribbon for a full sushi meal.

But you can't get a reservation at Nobu? Take heart, for there's **Next Door Nobu,** the slightly more casual, slightly less expensive (in theory, anyway) version that has a firm no-reservations policy. This is great news in this exclusionary town: Just show up, wait your turn, and you get a table. Since waits can be as long as 90 minutes, the secret is to go early: We walked in at 6:30pm on a weeknight and the place was half empty. This isn't cut-rate Nobu—you get the full treatment here, too. The modern room is highly stylized but comfortable, all the house specialties are available, and the service is equal to the main restaurant. There's also a raw bar. Noodle dishes add a moderately priced dimension to the menu, but it takes a lot of willpower to keep the tab low.

MODERATE

✪ **Bubby's.** 120 Hudson St. (at N. Moore St.). ☎ **212/219-0666.** www.bubbys.com. Reservations recommended for dinner. Main courses $2–$16 at breakfast, brunch, and lunch; $10–$22 at dinner. AE, DC, DISC, MC, V. Mon–Thurs 8am–11pm, Fri 8am–midnight, Sat 9am–midnight, Sun 9am–10pm. Subway: 1, 9 to Franklin St. AMERICAN.

How do I love Bubby's? Let me count the ways. I love Bubby's for the sublime macaroni and cheese, for the divine garlic burger and fries (accompanied by Bubby's own "wup-ass" ketchup), for the homemade meat loaf with warm cider gravy and garlic mashies—better than Ma used to make. I love Bubby's for the roasted rosemary chicken and chipotle-crusted Black Angus steak, and the classic cocktail the bartender will make for me when I'm in the mood. I love Bubby's generous portions, fresh-from-the-field greens, and big home-style breakfasts. I love Bubby's coziness: The high-ceilinged, brick-walled loftlike space is very homey—very TriBeCa—and I love the candlelight that adds a touch of romance to the evening. I love the friendly wait staff that doesn't neglect me, even when Harvey Keitel is sitting two tables over. Best of all, I love Bubby's pies: The core of Bubby's business, baked fresh daily, a half dozen to choose from (along with another half-dozen homemade cakes), and topped with fresh-made whipped cream (pumpkin's my favorite). Yum, yum, Bubby!

Layla. 211 W. Broadway (at Franklin St.). ☎ **212/431-0700.** www.myriadrestaurantgroup.com. Reservations recommended. Appetizers $6–$13; main courses $20–$28; 3-course fixed-price lunch $20; 4-course fixed-price dinner $42; $2 entertainment charge for belly-dancing show. AE, DC, DISC, MC, V. Mon–Thurs 5:30–11pm, Fri noon–2:30pm and 5:30–11:30pm, Sat 5:30–11:30pm, Sun 5:30–9:30pm. Subway: 1, 9 to Franklin St. MEDITERRANEAN/MIDDLE EASTERN.

Here's yet another wonderful TriBeCa restaurant from Drew Nieperont's Robert DeNiro–backed Myriad Group, the brains behind such big names as Nobu, and Heartbeat and Icon (at the W hotels). Unlike the others, though, which generally eschew themes, this one is like a page out of the *Arabian Nights*—there's even a belly dancer to entertain. A stylized take on a sultan's den, the fanciful dining room is the perfect setting for Layla's modern-meets–Middle East cuisine.

Dinner can be expensive, but I wouldn't dream of coming here and ordering a traditional appetizer-and-entree meal. The fun, high-energy setting, and expansive, affordable *meze* (appetizers) menu are made for family-style sharing. In fact, this is such a popular option that there's a $20 per person food minimum in the dining room, which you can circumvent if you wish by eating at the bar. The beautifully presented cuisine has a strong Greek influence, so expect well-prepared hummus, taramasalata, and baba gannoush. But the mezes quickly get more creative, with such excellent specialties as coriander-crusted scallops over chickpeas and grilled flatbread topped with spicy lamb. If you wander over to the entree list, consider the Moroccan couscous with braised lamb and the vegetable pastilla, an ideal dish for sharing.

The Odeon. 145 W. Broadway (at Thomas St.). ☎ **212/233-0507.** www.odeon.citysearch.com. Reservations recommended for parties of 4 or more. Main courses $9–$25. AE, DC, DISC, MC, V. Mon–Thurs noon–2am, Fri noon–3am, Sat 11:30am–3am, Sun 11:30am–2am. Subway: 1, 2, 3, 9 to Chambers St. (walk 3 blocks north). AMERICAN/FRENCH.

The Odeon is always the first place that comes to mind when I crave a late-night meal, but this attractive hot spot is satisfying at any time of day. The striking deco-ish room is perennially trendy but universally welcoming—no velvet ropes here. Sure, De Niro might be a couple of tables away, but it's the food that's the real draw. The restaurant crosses budget and culture lines: It's easy to eat cheap here if you stick to the burgers, vegetarian chili, and sandwiches, or you can spend a little more and go for fresh-off-the-boat Wellfleet oysters, excellent steak frites, roasted free-range chicken, braised lamb shank, and other top-notch brasserie-style dinners. The prices are lower than they have to be for food like this, and the wine list is equally reasonable. With rich wood paneling, Formica-topped tables, leather banquettes, and a sexy bar, the Odeon even manages to be swanky and comfortable at the same time. As proof of its egalitarianism, there's even a kids' menu—and the chocolate pudding is scrumptious.

New on the scene is **Bar Odeon,** across the street from the original at 136 W. Broadway (☎ **212/285-1155**), a little more cafelike than the original, serving a lighter version of Odeon's menu. Worth checking out if the wait's too long at the original.

INEXPENSIVE

Salaam Bombay. 317 Greenwich St. (btw. Duane and Reade sts.). ☎ **212/226-9400.** www.salaambombay.com. Main courses $9–$18; daily all-you-can-eat buffet lunch $10.95. AE, DC, DISC, MC, V. Sun–Fri 11:30am–3pm; Sun–Thurs 5–10:30pm, Fri–Sat 5–11pm. Subway: 1, 2, 3, 9 to Chambers St. PAN-INDIAN.

This Indian restaurant is much more attractive than most curry houses, and the Pan-Indian cuisine is easily a cut above the standard fare. The kitchen roams the subcontinental map, from Punjabi tandooris to Goan spicy fish and back again; all the dishes are confidently prepared with quality ingredients.

The $10.95 all-you-can-eat lunch, offered every day except Saturday, is an extraordinary bargain. I know the notion can be a turnoff (buffet? yuck!), but this is a freshly prepared, top-quality spread—you'll watch the tandoori chef pulling fresh-baked naan from the clay oven as you fill your plate. There are a dozen or so fresh-made meat and vegetarian dishes to choose from, as well as all the traditional accompaniments.

Dinnertime is a real treat: The room is low-lit and formally outfitted, and service is professional and attentive. (My husband and I even celebrated Valentine's Day here a few years back.) The tandoori specialties are succulent, and the sauces generous and delicately spiced. In addition to your familiar favorites, consider trying some of the lesser-known regional specialties, such as *gosht dum pasanda,* a Kasimiri lamb specialty; marinated in yogurt and cooked in a sealed pot, the meat emerges tender and succulent. Terrific!

4 Chinatown & Little Italy

MODERATE

Canton. 45 Division St. (btw. Bowery and Market St.). ☎ **212/226-4441** or 212/966-7492. Reservations recommended. Main courses $11–$22; Peking duck $25. No credit cards. Sun and Wed–Thurs noon–10pm, Fri–Sat noon–11pm. Subway: N, R, 6 to Canal St. CANTONESE.

Eating in Chinatown doesn't have to mean communicating with hand signals to a non-English-speaking waiter under the glare of florescent lights in a dining room that resembles your high-school cafeteria. Canton may be a bit more expensive than most Chinatown restaurants, but the resulting high quality and comforts are well worth the added expense. The room eschews the standard bustle for a simple, subdued atmosphere where the attentive staff speaks Noo Yawk English, you can have a fork if you want one, and the water glasses stay full—but the Americanization stops there. Canton draws uptowners and monied Chinese with what is probably the best, most authentic Cantonese cuisine in the city. Your waiter can help guide you through the menu and design a family-style meal to your tastes, but I recommend starting with the beef and black-bean sauce in crisp lettuce wraps—and save room for the greaseless Peking duck, which comes with pillow-soft pancakes and does not require an advance order. My only complaint is the fried rice: It's excellent, but $14? Come on. Still, a terrific place to dine, and well worth the dough.

Il Cortile. 125 Mulberry St. (btw. Canal and Hester sts.). ☎ **212/226-6060.** www.ilcortile.com. Reservations recommended. Pastas $8–$22; meats and fish $16.50–$32. AE, DC, DISC, MC, V. Sun–Thurs noon–midnight, Fri–Sat noon–1am. Subway: N, R, 6 to Canal St. NORTHERN ITALIAN.

The best restaurant in Little Italy stands out on Mulberry Street thanks to its warm, sophisticated demeanor amid the bright lights and bold decor of its lesser neighbors. The interior has a dramatic skylit atrium; I prefer the cozier front room. There's a certain old-world elegance to the menu: Like a *billet doux* from the chef, it's folded and sealed with gold foil. The second sign that you're out of the Little Italy ordinary arrives with the warm basket of focaccia, crusty small loaves, golden-brown crostini, and crunchy breadsticks. The northern Italian fare is well prepared and pleasing—the greens fresh and crisp, the sauces appropriately seasoned, the pastas perfectly al dente. This is traditional cuisine, but not without a few welcome twists: The filet mignon carpaccio is rolled with onions and parsley, thick cut, and seared; shiitakes give an unexpected flair to the rigatoni. On my last visit, the best dish at our table was the polenta with mushrooms in a savory white wine sauce, a bargain at $11. The wait staff, made up of career neighborhood waiters, is attentive and reserved in an appealing old-world style. The extensive wine cellar, hidden at the front of the restaurant behind a beautiful wooden door that looks as if it may have been liberated from a grand European castle, contains a good number of reasonably priced selections.

INEXPENSIVE

✪ **Joe's Shanghai.** 9 Pell St. (btw. Bowery and Mott sts.). ☎ **212/233-8888.** www.joesshanghai.com. Reservations recommended for 10 or more. Main courses $4.25–$12.95. No credit cards. Daily 11am–11:15pm. Subway: N, R, 6 to Canal St.; B, D, Q to Grand St. SHANGHAI CHINESE.

Tucked away on a little elbow of a side street just off the Bowery is this Chinatown institution, which serves up authentic cuisine to enthusiastic crowds nightly. The stars of the huge menu are the signature soup dumplings, quivering steamed pockets filled with hot broth and your choice of pork or crab, accompanied by a side of seasoned soy. Listed on the menu as "steamed buns" (item numbers 1 and 2), these culinary marvels never disappoint. Neither does the rest of the authentic Shanghai-inspired menu, which boasts such main courses as whole yellowfish bathed in spicy sauce; excellent "mock duck," a saucy bean-curd dish similar to Japanese yuba that's a hit with vegetarians and carnivores alike; and lots of well-prepared staples. The room is set mostly with round tables of 10 or so, and you'll be asked if you're willing to share. I encourage you to do so; it's a great way to watch and learn from your neighbors (many of whom are Chinese), who are usually more than happy to tell you what they're eating. If you want a private table, expect a wait.

Joe's Shanghai now has a second Manhattan location, in Midtown at 24 W. 56th St., between Fifth and Sixth avenues (☎ **212/333-3868**).

✪ **New York Noodletown.** 28¹/₂ Bowery (at Bayard St.). ☎ **212/349-0923.** Reservations accepted. Main courses $4–$12. No credit cards. Daily 9am–4am. Subway: N, R, 6 to Canal St. CHINESE/SEAFOOD.

This just may be the best Chinese food in New York City. Among its fans are Ruth Reichl, former restaurant critic for the *New York Times* and now editor-in-chief of *Gourmet* magazine, who constantly puts it at the top of the heap. So what if the room is reminiscent of a school cafeteria? The food is fabulous. The mushroom soup is a lunch in itself, thick with earthy chunks of shiitakes, vegetables, and thin noodles. Another appetizer that can serve as a meal is the hacked roast duck in noodle soup. The kitchen excels at seafood preparations, so be sure to try at least one: Looking like a snow-dusted plate of meaty fish, the salt-baked squid is sublime. The quick-woked Chinese broccoli or the crisp sautéed baby bok choy make great accompaniments. Other special dishes are various sandy pot casseroles, hearty, flavorful affairs slow-simmered in clay vessels. Unlike most of its neighbors, New York Noodletown keeps very long hours, which makes it the best late-night bet in the neighborhood, too.

Nha Trang. 87 Baxter St. (btw. Canal and Bayard sts.). ☎ **212/233-5948.** Reservations accepted. Main courses $4–$12.50. No credit cards. Daily 10:30am–9:30pm. Subway: N, R, 6 to Canal St. VIETNAMESE.

The decor may be standard-issue, no-atmosphere Chinatown (glass-topped tables, linoleum floors, mirrored walls), but this friendly, bustling place serves up the best Vietnamese in Chinatown. A plate of six crispy, finger-size spring rolls is a nice way to start; the slightly spicy pork-and-shrimp filling is nicely offset by the wrapping of

nd mint. The pho noodle soup comes in a quart-size bowl brim-
█ █etables and various meats and seafood. But my favorite dish is the
si█ █ork chops—sliced paper-thin, soaked in a soy/sugarcane marinade,
and grilled to █ r perfection. Everything is well prepared, though, and your waiter
will be glad to help you design a meal to suit your tastes. If there's a line, stick around;
it won't take long to get a table.

5 The Lower East Side

Deli lovers should also consider **Katz's Delicatessen,** 205 E. Houston St., at Ludlow
Street (☎ 212/254-2246). For details, see "The New York Deli News" below.

MODERATE

✪ **Le Pere Pinard.** 175 Ludlow St. (south of Houston St.). ☎ **212/777-4917.**
Reservations recommended. Main courses $3.50–$14 at lunch (2-course lunch special $9.50),
$11.50–$19.50 at dinner. AE. Sun–Thurs 10am–midnight, Fri–Sat 10am–1am. Subway: F to
Delancey St. FRENCH WINE BAR.

Here's my favorite spot on the Lower East Side's burgeoning dining scene. This little-
known French wine bar and bistro is authentic and charming, with high ceilings, bur-
nished brick walls, well-spaced tables with mix-and-match chairs, and an authentic
come-as-you-are air. Everything is well worn in a good, comfortable way. The kitchen
specializes in the Gallic version of comfort food: steak frites, shell steak with roquefort
sauce, a delectable shepherd's pie with a delightfully cheesy crust, a good brandade,
and a generous charcuterie and cheese plate—the perfect match for the sublime
crusty-on-the-outside, soft-in-the-middle bread that accompanies every meal. Greens
are fresh and well prepared; even a simple mesclun salad wears a just-right vinaigrette.
There are lots of wine choices by both the bottle and glass; I like the restaurant's pro-
tocol, which allows you to taste first even if you're just ordering by the glass. Service is
attentive, but in a casual, easygoing way. Smoking is allowed in the front (bar) room,
while the back room is dedicated to nonsmokers. There's also a pleasant garden in
warm weather. The lunch special is a bargain.

6 SoHo & NoLiTa

EXPENSIVE

Balthazar. 80 Spring St. (at Crosby St., 1 block east of Broadway). ☎ **212/965-1414.**
Reservations recommended well in advance. Main courses $16–$28 at dinner. AE, MC, V.
Mon–Thurs 7:30am–1:30am, Fri–Sat 7:30am–2:30am, Sun 7:30am–12:30am. Subway: C, E
to Spring St. FRENCH BISTRO.

Balthazar has been one of the hottest scenes in town since its doors opened a few years
back, and it shows every sign of remaining high on the hip list (Jerry Seinfeld even
popped the question here). We fully understand why. With all the trappings of an
authentic Parisian brasserie, the space is simply gorgeous. The classic French bistro
fare, ranging from steak frites and grilled calf's liver to a wonderful brook trout with
honey mustard glaze, is surprisingly affordable, and the expansive raw bar offerings are
beautifully displayed and make a worthy splurge. But I have some serious complaints:
The lofty room is so tightly packed and the tables so uncomfortably close that private
conversation is a pipe dream. And this is the loudest restaurant we've ever been in—
my husband and I found ourselves yelling at each other across the tiny table, which
made the whole dining experience less than relaxing. Still, if you're willing to put up
with the discomforts, this is about as exciting as a downtown scene gets. The long

The New York Deli News

There's simply nothing more Noo Yawk than hunkering dow[...]mammoth pastrami sandwich or a lox-and-bagel plate at an authentic Jewish deli, where anything you order comes with a bowl of lip-smacking sour dills and a side of attitude. All of the following are the real deal—you gotta problem wid'dat?

Opened in 1937, the **Stage Deli,** 834 Seventh Ave., between 53rd and 54th streets (☎ 212/245-7850; www.stagedeli.com), may be New York's oldest continuously run deli. The Stage is noisy and crowded and packed with tourists, but it's still as authentic as they come. Connoisseurs line up to sample the 36 famous specialty sandwiches named after many of the stars whose photos adorn the walls. The celebrity sandwiches, ostensibly created by the personalities themselves, are jaw-distending mountains of top-quality fixings: The Tom Hanks is roast beef, chopped liver, onion, and chicken fat, while the Dolly Parton is—drumroll, please—twin rolls of corned beef and pastrami.

For the quintessential New York experience, head to the **Carnegie Deli,** 854 Seventh Ave., at 55th Street (☎ 212/757-2245; www.carnegiedeli.com), where it's worth subjecting yourself to surly service, tourist-targeted overpricing, and elbow-to-elbow seating for the best pastrami and corned beef in town. Even big eaters may be challenged by mammoth sandwiches with names like "fifty ways to love your liver" (chopped liver, hard-boiled egg, lettuce, tomato, and onion). Main courses range from goulash to roasted chicken, and the heavenly blintzes come stuffed with cheese or fruit. Cheesecake can't get more divine, so save room!

The ✪ **Second Avenue Deli,** 156 Second Ave., at 10th Street (☎ 212/677-0606; www.2ndavedeli.com), is the best kosher choice in town (for all you goyim out there, that means no milk, butter, or cheese is served). There's no bowing to tourism here—this is the real deal. The service is brusque, the decor is nondescript, and the sandwiches don't have cute names, but the dishes are true New

---

mirrored bar is a hopping spot unto itself that attracts beautiful people galore, and the boulangerie sells fresh-baked breads, desserts, and sandwiches to go.

Sibling bistro **Pastis** is a spitting image, but wallet-friendlier prices make the annoyances easier to put up with (see "Chelsea & the Meat-Packing District" later in this chapter).

Blue Ribbon Sushi. 119 Sullivan St. (btw. Prince and Spring sts.). ☎ 212/343-0404. Reservations not accepted. A la carte sushi and rolls $2.75–$15.50 (specials may be higher); sushi combos and main courses $11.50–$25. AE, DISC, MC, V. Tues–Sun 4pm–2am. Subway: C, E to Spring St.; N, R to Prince St. SUSHI.

This lovely, almost zenlike closet of a restaurant is a terrific choice for sushi lovers, especially those with adventurous palates. This is hipper-than-thou SoHo, and Blue Ribbon is hot, hot, hot, so don't expect a bargain. But you will get your money's worth here: The fish is as fresh as can be, the top-notch chefs know how to handle it, and the selection is marvelous. Almost evenly split between the Pacific and the Atlantic, the dazzling menu offers up the obvious (ruby-red tuna, meaty yellowtail, creamy sea urchin in the shell) and the out there (blue crab roll, Maine lobster, Japanese mountain yam, even jellyfish). There's a changing array of inventive, Nobu-ish appetizers—we had an incredible, almost foie gras–like monkfish liver last time I was there—and an equally impressive sake list. The staff is a bit harried, but they're very knowledgeable and do a remarkable job keeping up with demand. The biggest downside is that

York classics: gefilte fish, matzo ball soup, chicken livers, potato knishes, nova lox and eggs. And for $16 to $18, you get a monster triple-decker sandwich (try wrapping your gums around the corned beef, tongue, and salami) with a side of fries. The crunchy dills are to die for. Keep an ear tuned to the Catskills-quality banter among crusty wait staff.

If you prefer some cheese on your pastrami or sour cream with your latkes (or just milk in your coffee), the outstanding downtown choice is **Katz's Delicatessen,** 205 E. Houston St., at hipster-hot Ludlow Street on the Lower East Side (☎ **212/254-2246;** www.katzdeli.com). This cavernous, brightly lit place is suitably pre-IPO Noo Yawk, with dill pickles, Dr. Brown's cream soda, and old-world attitude to spare. Half of the space is dedicated to traditional cafeteria-style counter service, while the other half offers waiter service. All of Katz's traditional eats are firstrate, particularly the beloved all-beef hot dogs.

Uptown, it's hard to get more authentic than **Barney Greengrass, the Sturgeon King,** 541 Amsterdam Ave., between 86th and 87th streets on the Upper West Side (☎ **212/724-4707**). This unassuming, daytime-only deli has become legend for its high-quality salmon (sable, gravlax, Nova Scotia, kippered, lox, pastrami—you choose), whitefish, and sturgeon (of course). The terrific chicken liver inspired nothing less than a raging, monthslong debate among city restaurant critics a few years back; purists won't be disappointed.

Sandwiches are priced about the same at all these delis, basically from $12 to $18. You'll get your money's worth, however: They come so stuffed with meat that they're more than most average mortals can consume in one sitting. However, be prepared to pay a $2 to $3 sharing charge if you want to split one with your travel partner (only Katz's and Barney Greengrass are cool enough to let you share gratis).

reservations aren't taken, so come early, come late, or expect a wait. Also, while the booths are very comfortable for two or four, seating can be tight for larger parties.

✪ **Quilty's.** 177 Prince St. (btw. Sullivan and Thompson sts.). ☎ **212/254-1260.** www.quiltysnyc.com. Reservations highly recommended. Main courses $10–$18.50 at lunch (3-course fixed-price $20), $9–$16 at brunch, $22–$29 at dinner. AE, DC, DISC, MC, V. Tues–Fri noon–3pm, Sun 11am–3pm; Mon–Sat 6–11pm, Sun 6–10pm. Subway: C, E to Spring St.; N, R to Prince St. CONTEMPORARY AMERICAN.

No matter how many restaurants I visit in this city, Quilty's remains one of my favorites. Chef Katy Sparks and her crew just get it all right. The subtle, softly lit room is intimate and relaxing, with decently sized and spaced tables, comfortable seating, and an elegantly casual SoHo-goes-pastoral vibe that makes the restaurant feel special without being formal or stuffy. The greeting is warm, and the service professional yet personable. The feisty New American menu changes with the seasons, but you can expect bold, complex flavors that wow without overwhelming. There's always a lot going on in the dishes, but they're always harmonious. Last time I dined here (from the autumn menu), the fresh cèpes baked in parchment and paired with harmony croutons and ricotta salata was a delicate symphony. And a Riesling coriander jus was the ideal twist to the perfect comfort food: roasted organic chicken with buttermilk-battered onion rings. For dessert, the caramelized golden pineapple with vanilla bean–anise sauce was an ideal reinvention of the tropical fruit. The wine list tends toward special vintages and rare labels; lively descriptions make it fun to choose, but the knowledgeable wait staff is happy to suggest pairings if you prefer. Any way you look at it, Quilty's is a winner.

Savoy. 70 Prince St. (at Crosby St.). ☎ **212/219-8570.** Reservations highly recommended. Main courses $10–$14 at lunch, $19–$26 at dinner; fixed-price dinner $48. AE, DISC, MC, V. Mon–Sat noon–3pm; Mon–Thurs 6–10:30pm, Fri–Sat 6–11pm, Sun 6–10pm. Subway: N, R to Prince St.; B, D, F, Q to Broadway–Lafayette St.; 6 to Spring St. CONTEMPORARY AMERICAN.

On a charming brick-paved street, behind a façade with a warm patinalike glow, hides this SoHo treasure. An innovative à la carte menu is served downstairs where, despite the cozy dining room's small size, it's easy to have an intimate conversation. The brilliance of owner/Chef Peter Hoffmann's creative, Mediterranean-accented contemporary cuisine is its subtlety—he wins diners over with gentle flavors and pleasing combinations. The menu changes constantly, but a signature dish is the excellent salt-crusted baked duck. Last time I dined here, cured pork loin with tomatillo sauce, sweet-and-sour cabbage, and butternut squash was also a winner, as was perfectly filleted brook trout on a bed of cornmeal sauce with braised mushrooms and kale. Upstairs there's a cozy bar and a second dining room, seating no more than 15 or so, where the four-course fixed-price dinner is served; almost entirely prepared in the room's brick fireplace, it makes for a memorable evening. The desserts are delectable, and the eclectic wine list offers enough choices under $50 to keep things reasonable. Service is appropriately attentive.

MODERATE

✪ **Aquagrill.** 210 Spring St. (at Sixth Ave.). ☎ **212/274-0505.** Reservations highly recommended. Main courses $14.50–$26. AE, MC, V. Tues–Thurs noon–3pm and 6–10:45pm, Fri noon–3pm and 6–11:45pm, Sat noon–3:45pm and 6–11:45pm, Sun noon–3:45pm and 6–10:45pm. Subway: C, E to Spring St. SEAFOOD.

Attention, seafood lovers: Book now, because this marvelous—and hugely popular— little restaurant serves up some of the city's best fish. The raw bar flies in a phenomenal selection of oysters from around the world daily; the Alaskan Canoe Lagoons were some of the creamiest and dreamiest I've ever had. If you like sea urchin, don't pass on the fresh Maine version if it's available; served in the shell with citrus soy and shaved scallions, it's one of my most memorable taste sensations of the year. Among the entrees, you can keep it cheap and simple with preparations that let the fish's own fresh, clean flavors sing, like poached Atlantic salmon, grilled Maine sea scallops, or roasted Florida swordfish. Or you can spend a little more and opt for one of the more fanciful preparations, such as Atlantic salmon with a falafel crust, cucumbers, tomatoes, and a tart lemon-coriander vinaigrette; or a shellfish-rich bouillabaisse in a garlic saffron tomato broth. On special during my last visit was meaty escolar—so buttery that it was like the foie gras of fish, bathed in a delicate garlic parsley sauce and accompanied by sautéed broccoli rabe, fresh cranberry beans, roasted garlic cloves, and steamed cockles. Service is knowledgeable and efficient, and the wine list boasts a good number of affordable choices.

INEXPENSIVE

✪ **Cafe Habana.** 17 Prince St. (at Elizabeth St.). ☎ **212/625-2001.** Reservations not accepted. Main courses $5–$13. AE, MC, V. Daily 9am–midnight. Subway: B, D, F, Q to Broadway–Lafayette St.; 6 to Spring St. HISPANIC.

I just love this sleek update on a typical Hispanic luncheonette. It manages to be hip without being the least bit pretentious, and what the food may lack in authenticity it

Get Away For Less.

Avis features GM cars.

With great offers and services from Avis, you'll get more out of your vacation! And now you can **save $20 on a weekly rental**. All the information you need is on the coupon below. Plus most rentals come with free unlimited mileage to save you even more.

As an added touch you can count on our famous "We try harder." service for a fast, hassle-free rental. Because speed and personal service is what everyone at Avis is dedicated to delivering.

For more information and reservations, call your travel agent or Avis toll free at **1-800-831-8000**.

AVIS

We try harder.

For You.

Save $20 On A Weekly Rental

It's a Whole New World wit

Frommer's

Frommer's 2000

EUROPE
FROM $60 A DAY

The Ultimate Guide to Low-Cost Comfortable Travel

Frommer's 2000

Italy

The Best of the Cities and the Countryside

NEW!
Spectacular
Color
Photos!

For Travelers Who Want More Than the Official Lin

the
Unofficial
Guide to
Walt Disney
World
2000

Tips and Warnings

Save Time & Money

All Attractions Candidly Ranked & Rated

Frommer's

irreverent
guide to
paris

Frommer's

Grand
Canyon
National Park
2nd Edition

Everything You Need for an
Unforgettable Vacation!

SPECIAL MILLENNIUM EDITION

PLACES
RATED
ALMANAC

Your Guide to Finding the Best Places to
Live in the United States and Canada

All 354 Metropolitan Areas Ranked for:

DAVID SAVAGEAU
with Ralph D'Agostino

Frommer's

washington, d.c.
with kids

Bob Schlinger

Copies Sold!

Born to Shop

LONDON
USA EDITION

THE ULTIMATE GUIDE FOR
TRAVELERS AND FUN TO SHOP

Available at bookstores everywhere.

Lower East Side, East Village & SoHo Area Dining

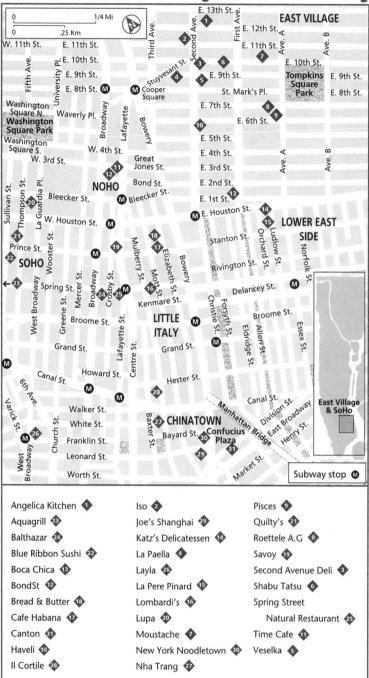

EAST VILLAGE

W. 11th St.   E. 11th St.
Fifth Ave.   University Pl.   E. 10th St.
E. 9th St.
E. 8th St.   Cooper Square
Washington Square N.   Waverly Pl.
Washington Square Park
Washington Square S.
W. 4th St.
W. 3rd St.   Great Jones St.

E. 13th St.
E. 12th St.
E. 11th St.
E. 10th St.
E. 9th St.
St. Mark's Pl.
E. 7th St.
E. 6th St.
E. 5th St.
E. 4th St.
E. 3rd St.
E. 2nd St.
E. 1st St.

Tompkins Square Park
E. 9th St.
E. 8th St.
Ave. A   Ave. B

NOHO
Bleecker St.
Bond St.
Bleecker St.
W. Houston St.

Sullivan St.   Thompson St.   La Guardia Pl.
Prince St.
SOHO
Spring St.
Broome St.
Grand St.
Canal St.
Howard St.
Walker St.
White St.
Franklin St.
Leonard St.
Worth St.

West Broadway   Wooster St.   Greene St.   Mercer St.   Broadway   Crosby St.   Lafayette St.   Centre St.

Mulberry St.   Mott St.   Elizabeth St.   Bowery
Kenmare St.

LITTLE ITALY
Grand St.
Hester St.

CHINATOWN
Bayard St.   Confucius Plaza

E. Houston St.
Stanton St.
Rivington St.
Delancey St.
Broome St.
Grand St.
Canal St.

LOWER EAST SIDE

Orchard St.   Ludlow St.   Norfolk St.   Essex St.
Forsyth St.   Christie St.   Eldridge St.   Allen St.
Division St.   East Broadway   Henry St.   Market St.

Manhattan Bridge

East Village & SoHo

6th Ave.   Varick St.   West Broadway   Church St.   Baxter St.

Subway stop Ⓜ

Angelica Kitchen 1
Aquagrill 23
Balthazar 24
Blue Ribbon Sushi 22
Boca Chica 13
BondSt 12
Bread & Butter 18
Cafe Habana 17
Canton 31
Haveli 10
Il Cortile 28

Iso 2
Joe's Shanghai 29
Katz's Delicatessen 14
La Paella 4
Layla 26
La Pere Pinard 15
Lombardi's 16
Lupa 20
Moustache 7
New York Noodletown 30
Nha Trang 27

Pisces 9
Quilty's 21
Roettele A.G 8
Savoy 19
Second Avenue Deli 3
Shabu Tatsu 6
Spring Street
  Natural Restaurant 25
Time Cafe 11
Veselka 5

153

more than makes up for in quality and flavor: Shrimps are big and hearty; pork is moist and flavorful; cilantro and other spices are fresh and aromatic. Winning starters include *pozole,* hominy corn stew with shredded chicken or pork in a clear broth that you season to taste with oregano, chile, and lime; and the hugely popular Mexican corn on the cob, which is skewered, coated with lime juice and grated cheese, sprinkled with chile powder, and grilled into a messy but sweet popcorny treat. Main courses include the ultra-moist roast pork (perfect with a squeeze of lime) and *camarones al ajillo,* shrimp in spicy garlic sauce. Most everything comes with your choice of red or black beans and rice; go with the yellow rice, as the white rice tends to be a tad anemic. Wine and a handful of Mexican beers are served, but I really enjoyed the not-too-sweet red Hibiscus tea. The room is narrow and tables are petite (especially those for two), but a middle aisle keeps the place from feeling too crowded, and service is easygoing and friendly. Don't be surprised if there's a wait for a table.

There's also a second location, at 11 Abingdon Square (on Eighth Ave. between West 12th and Bleecker streets) in the West Village (☎ 212/989-6883), that tends to be less buzzy and crowded.

✪ Lombardi's. 32 Spring St. (btw. Mott and Mulberry sts.). ☎ **212/941-7994.** Reservations accepted for parties of 6 or more. Small pies $10.50–$16, large pies $12.50–$20; extra charge for additional toppings. No credit cards. Mon–Thurs 11:30am–11pm, Fri–Sat 11:30am–midnight, Sun 11:30am–10pm. Subway: 6 to Spring St.; N, R to Prince St. PIZZA.

Lombardi's is a living gem in the annals of the city's culinary history. First opened in 1905, "America's first licensed pizzeria" cooks Manhattan's best pizza in its original coal brick oven. The wonderfully smoky crust (a generations-old family recipe that Gennaro Lombardi hand-carried from Naples at the turn of the century) is topped with fresh mozzarella, basil, and pecorino romano, and San Marzano tomato sauce. From there, the choice is yours. Topping options are suitably old-world (Citterio pancetta, calamata olives, Esposito sweet Italian sausage, homemade meatballs, beefsteak tomatoes, and the like), but Lombardi's specialty is the fresh clam pie, with hand-shucked clams, oregano, fresh garlic, romano, extra-virgin olive oil, and fresh-ground pepper (no sauce). The main dining room is narrow but very pleasant, with the usual checkered tablecloths and exposed brick walls. A big draw is the garden out back; walk past the kitchen and up a flight of stairs to reach this lovely second-floor deck, where tables sport Cinzano umbrellas and a flowering tree shoots up through the concrete. Another plus: In a city where rudeness is a badge of honor, Lombardi's wait staff is extremely affable.

Spring Street Natural Restaurant. 62 Spring St. (at Lafayette St.) ☎ **212/966-0290.** Reservations accepted for parties of 8 or more. Main courses $8–$16. AE, DC, MC, V. Sun–Thurs 11:30am–midnight, Fri–Sat 11:30am–1am. Subway: 6 to Spring St. HEALTH-CONSCIOUS.

This 28-year-old spot is as comfortable and easygoing as your old college hangout—and just about as affordable, too. The expansive brick-walled room is filled with leafy greenery and anchored by an old oak bar. This is the kind of place where you can sit yourself down at a table and camp for a while, poring over a good book while you nosh on a farm-fresh entree-size salad or a terrific tempeh burger; the staff will happily refill your coffee mug as you relax. But while the food is fresh, all-natural, and unprocessed, and prepared with good health in mind, it's not strictly vegetarian: There's lots of fresh-off-the-boat seafood to choose from, plus free-range chicken and turkey. The menu isn't restricted to soups, sandwiches, and salads, as at many other health-minded restaurants. You can come for a full meal, dining on such entrees as broiled New

England bluefish with shiitake mushrooms, roasted chicken with pommery mustard glaze, or any number of pastas and stir-frys. Everything is well prepared and satisfying. The kitchen can also accommodate sugar, dairy, and other dietary restrictions. There's pleasant outdoor seating along Lafayette Street in good weather.

7 The East Village & NoHo

EXPENSIVE

✪ **BondSt.** 6 Bond St. (2 blocks north of Houston St., btw. Broadway and Lafayette St.). ☎ **212/777-2500.** Reservations highly recommended. A la carte sushi and rolls $6–$18; main courses and sushi combos $14–$26; omakase from $60. AE, MC, V. Mon–Sat 6pm–midnight; lounge Mon–Sat 5pm–2am, Sun 6pm–1am. Subway: 6 to Bleecker St.; B, D, F, Q to Broadway–Lafayette St. SUSHI.

Go to Nobu for the most creative hot Japanese food in the city—but come to BondSt if you want to experience sushi as high art. This super-designed, über-trendy NoHo hot spot does offer some creative cooked dishes, including a beautiful charred Chilean sea bass in Saikyo miso, but BondSt is really all about raw fish. Chef Hiroshi Nakahara has managed to add creative twists to the sushi tradition without skewering it. A number of fishes are flown in from Japan daily, so expect to see choices that don't usually surface on this continent. Purists will love the super-fresh yellowtail, the terrific selection of blue fin and big eye tunas, and the perfectly presented eels, both anago (sea eel) and unagi (freshwater). For the best deal on roes and urchins, go with the Caviar 006 plate, which allows you to sample all of the choices, including herring and mullet roes and Osetra caviar sushi (superfluously topped with gold leaf, but sublime nevertheless), as well as the obvious choices, for a fraction of what it would cost to order them all individually. For the most intriguing selection, start with a few of the creative appetizers, which include fugu sashimi (yep, blowfish) in ponzu sauce—well worth a try for adventurous eaters. The sake selection is excellent. Service is fashionably aloof, but the stick-thin wait staff knows the menu well. Reservations usually require a week's notice, but you might be able to grab a spot at the sushi bar if you stop in (earlier is always better).

MODERATE

Haveli. 100 Second Ave. (at E. 6th St.). ☎ **212/982-0533.** www.haveli.citysearch.com. Reservations accepted. Main courses $8.50–$19; complete dinners $23–$41. AE, DC, JCB, MC, V. Daily noon–12:30am. Subway: F to Second Ave. INDIAN.

The stretch of East 6th Street between First and Second avenues in the East Village is known as "Little India" thanks to the dozen or more Indian restaurants that line the block. Around the corner—and a giant step up in quality—from Little India is Haveli, where the authentically prepared dishes, attractively low-lit dining room, and attentive service are far superior to what you'll find on East 6th Street. All of your favorites are here in top form, including well-stuffed samosas (meat or veggie), first-rate tandooris, and mouthwatering naan. Prices are a little steeper than what you'll find in Little India, but the Haveli experience is worth the extra dough.

Iso. 175 Second Ave. (at 11th St.). ☎ **212/777-0361.** Reservations not accepted. A la carte sushi $2.50–$6; sushi rolls $4.50–$12.50; sushi combos and main courses $13.50–$21. AE, MC, V. Mon–Sat 5:30pm–midnight. Subway: 6 to Astor Place. SUSHI.

Iso is the top choice in town for fresh and beautifully presented sushi at affordable prices. The sushi and sashimi combos make a good-value starting point; supplement with your favorites or a few of the daily special fishes, which may include blue fin toro (tuna belly) or Japanese aji (horse mackerel). The menu also features light, greaseless tempura and entrees like chicken teriyaki and beef negamaki for the sushiphobes in your party. The attractive Keith Haring–themed room is tightly packed but still manages to be relatively comfortable, and service is better than at other sushi joints in this price range. Unless you arrive before 6pm, expect a line—but the high-quality fish and wallet-friendly pricing make Iso worth the wait.

La Paella. 214 E. 9th St. (at Second Ave.). ☎ **212/598-4321.** Reservations accepted for parties of 6 or more. Tapas $4.50–$9; paella for 2 $22–$36. MC, V. Sun–Thurs 5–11pm, Fri–Sat 5pm–12:30am. Subway: 6 to Astor Place. BASQUE/SPANISH.

La Paella's tapas are the best in town, and the paella can hardly be outdone. This is fun eating, the kind of place where patrons return again and again to wash down fish croquettes, chorizos, and green olives with bottles of chilled Negro Modela, a dark Mexican brew that goes well with the flavorful menu of (primarily) grilled delights, or the terrific sangría, served in generous pitchers by the frisky wait staff, many of whom seem as though they just blew in from Madrid. Tapas here are more generously apportioned than at many other places; the grilled calamari is a perfectly sized appetizer without being overwhelming. The tapas and paellas are well priced, but it's easy to run up a tab in the festive setting, which tends to attract large parties after 8pm.

Roettele A.G. 126 E. 7th St. (btw. First Ave. and Ave. A). ☎ **212/674-4140.** Reservations recommended, especially on weekends. Main courses $8–$17; fondue for 2 $32–$36. AE, DC, DISC, MC, V. Tues–Thurs 5:30–10:30pm, Fri 5:30–11:30pm, Sat noon–3pm and 5:30–11:30pm, Sun noon–3pm and 5:30–10pm. Subway: L to First Ave.; 6 to Astor Place. SWISS.

This snug Swiss chalet hideaway is New York's only authentic Swiss restaurant, and it's a winner. The cheese fondue, a hearty dinner for two or a generous appetizer for four, is smooth and beautifully presented with crusty bread and fresh vegetables. Build your meal around it by supplementing with other Alpine and house specialties, such as air-dried beef, classic raclette and Wiener schnitzel, duck liver mousse, and terrific sautéed wild mushrooms over fresh herbs and polenta—plus spaetzle on the side, of course. They stock Swiss and German wines and beers, plus a few French bottles; try the medium-bodied Spatenlager to help wash down all that melted cheese. In keeping with the theme, a wide selection of yummy French and German pastries is available. The only downside used to be harried service, but everything was perfect on my last visit. A real treat!

Time Cafe. 380 Lafayette St. (at Great Jones St.). ☎ **212/533-7000.** www.feznyc.com. Reservations recommended on weekends. Main courses $4–$13.50 at breakfast and brunch, $7.50–$14 at lunch, $8–$22 at dinner; 2- to 3-course fixed-price $16.50–$19.50 at lunch, $27.50–$47.50 at dinner. AE, MC, V. Mon–Thurs 8am–midnight, Fri 8am–1am, Sat 10:30am–1am, Sun 10:30am–midnight. Subway: 6 to Bleecker St.; B, D, F, Q to Broadway–Lafayette St. CONTEMPORARY AMERICAN.

This easygoing, attractive, and affordable spot can provide a night's entertainment or the ideal brunch. The menu features a large selection of contemporary fare with a healthy bent, such as a very good grilled rare tuna sandwich with organic daikon sprouts and sesame wasabi on seven-grain bread; herb-roasted free-range chicken with roasted garlic hominy grits and sautéed spinach; and a host of creative thin-crust pizzas. The food isn't the best in town, but it's perfectly satisfying, and I like the health-minded preparations and the casual, laid-back vibe. I've spotted Michael Stipe here more than once. This branch has a wonderful Moroccan lounge and basement performance space called Fez (see chapter 9).

In addition to this one, there's also the Upper West Side variation, **Time Cafe North,** at 2330 Broadway, at 85th St. (☎ **212/579-5100**), which also has a Fez lounge for cocktails.

INEXPENSIVE

Also consider the all-kosher **Second Avenue Deli,** 156 Second Ave., at 10th Street (☎ **212/677-0606;** www.2ndavedeli.com), for Jewish deli fare extraordinaire; for details, see "The New York Deli News" box earlier in this chapter.

There's also **Moustache** (p. 163) at 265 E. 10th St., between First Avenue and Avenue A (☎ **212/228-2022**), for good, affordable Middle Eastern.

Angelica Kitchen. 300 E. 12th St. (just east of Second Ave.). ☎ **212/228-2909.** Reservations accepted for parties of 6 or more Mon–Thurs. Main courses $5.95–$14.25; lunch deal (Mon–Fri 11:30am–5pm) $6.75. No credit cards. Daily 11:30am–10:30pm. Subway: L, N, R, 4, 5, 6 to 14th St./Union Sq. ORGANIC VEGETARIAN.

If you like to eat healthy, take note: This cheerful restaurant is serious about vegan cuisine. The kitchen prepares everything fresh daily; they guarantee that at least 95% of all ingredients are organically grown, with sustainable agriculture and responsible business practices additionally required before food can cross the kitchen's threshold. But good-for-you (and good-for-the-environment) doesn't have to mean boring—this is flavorful, beautifully prepared cuisine served in a lovely country kitchen–style setting. Salads spill over with sprouts and all kinds of crisp veggies and are crowned with homemade dressings. The Dragon Bowls, a specialty, are heaping portions of rice, beans, tofu, and steamed vegetables. The daily seasonal specials feature the best of what's fresh and in season in such dishes as fiery three-bean chili, slow-simmered with sun-dried tomatoes and a blend of chile peppers; baked tempeh nestled in a sourdough baguette and dressed in mushroom gravy; and lemon-herb baked tofu layered with roasted vegetables and fresh pesto on mixed-grain bread. Breads and desserts are fresh baked and similarly wholesome (and made without eggs, of course).

Boca Chica. 13 First Ave. (at 1st St.). ☎ **212/473-0108.** Reservations accepted for parties of 6 or more Sun–Wed. Main dishes $7.50–$19.75 (most under $13). AE, MC, V. Mon–Thurs 5:30–11pm, Fri–Sat 5:30pm–midnight, Sun noon–4pm and 5:30–11pm. Subway: F to Second Ave. SOUTH AMERICAN.

This lively, colorful joint is always packed with a gleefully mixed crowd working its way through a round of margaritas or a few pitchers of beer. The cuisine is a down-market version of the Pan-Latino favorites that have captivated palates farther uptown, most notably at Patina and Calle Ocho. The food at Boca Chica is a little closer to its hearty South American roots: well-prepared pork, beef, fish, and vegetarian dishes, most pleasingly heavy on the sauce and spice, accompanied by plantains, rice, and beans. There's also a bevy of interesting appetizers, including black-bean soup well seasoned with lime juice and terrific coconut-fried shrimp. While this approach to cooking now tends to be well out of reach of the under-$25 crowd, Boca Chica keeps things at an affordable level, much to the delight of those of us without bottomless wallets. *Be forewarned:* Getting in on weekends is about as hard as sneaking into Havana.

✪ **Pisces.** 95 Ave. A (at 6th St.). ☎ **212/260-6660.** Reservations recommended. Main courses $9–$20; 2-course fixed-price dinner (Mon–Thurs 5:30–7pm, Fri–Sun 5:30–6:30pm) $15. AE, CB, DC, MC, V. Sat–Sun 11:30am–3:30pm; Sun–Thurs 5:30–11:30pm, Fri–Sat 5:30pm–1am. Subway: 6 to Astor Place; F to Second Ave. SEAFOOD.

This excellent fish house serves up the best inexpensive seafood in the city. All the fish is top quality and fresh daily, and all smoked items are prepared in the restaurant's own smoker. But it's the creative kitchen, which shows surprising skill with vegetables as well as fish, that makes Pisces a real winner. The mesquite-smoked whole trout in sherry oyster sauce is sublime, better than trout I've had for twice the price; start with the phyllo-fried shrimp or the tuna ceviche with curried potato chips and roasted pepper coulis, and the world is yours. Other winning dishes include flaky pan-fried skate in a burgundy reduction with garlicky mashed potatoes and roasted pearl onions. There are daily specials in addition to the menu; last time we dined here, I feasted on an excellent grilled mako shark with chard in a cockle stew. The wine list is appealing and very well priced, the decor suitably nautical without being kitschy, and the service friendly and attentive. For wallet-watchers, the early-bird fixed-price makes an already terrific value even better. The Alphabet City locale gives Pisces serious hip, but it's laid-back enough that even Grandma will be comfortable here. Tables spill out onto the sidewalk on warm evenings, giving you a ringside seat for the funky East Village show.

✪ **Shabu Tatsu.** 216 E. 10th St. (btw. First and Second aves.). ☎ **212/477-2972.** Reservations accepted for parties of 4 or more. Full shabu-shabu dinners for 2 $28–$39. AE, DC, DISC, MC, V. Daily 5pm–12:30am. Subway: L to First Ave.; 6 to Astor Place. JAPANESE SHABU-SHABU.

This casual place features shabu-shabu, a dish you prepare yourself in the hotpot of boiling water built into the center of your table. The interactive excitement begins when the waiter brings a plate piled high with raw beef (turkey is also available), tofu, and vegetables and gives an introductory lesson on how to make "shabu." It's lots of fun poking into the pot with your chopsticks, watching your piece of meat or veggies cook to your satisfaction, then dipping them in one of two sauces: one peanuty and the other a tart vinegar, soy, and scallion sauce. After you're done, noodles are piled in and the broth is turned into a yummy after-dinner soup. The food is fresh, high-quality, and appealing even to those who otherwise don't care for Japanese food. The pure entertainment value makes this a great place to take kids or a group, and completely impractical for single diners. Duos can snare a table, but since you can't reserve ahead, don't be surprised if there's a wait; the restaurant is always busy, so it's best to go early or late.

There's another location on the Upper East Side at 1414 York Ave., at 75th Street (☎ **212/472-3322**).

Veselka. 144 Second Ave. (at 9th St.). ☎ **212/228-9682.** Reservations not accepted. Main courses $5–$13. AE, MC, V. Daily 24 hours. Subway: 6 to Astor Place. UKRAINIAN DINER.

Whenever the craving hits for hearty Eastern European fare at old-world prices, Veselka fits the bill with *pierogi* (small doughy envelopes filled with potatoes, cheese, or sauerkraut), *kasha varnishkes* (cracked buckwheat and noodles with mushroom sauce), stuffed cabbage, grilled Polish kielbasa, freshly made potato pancakes, and classic soups like a sublime scarlet borscht, voted best in the city by the *New York Times* and *New York* magazine. Try the buckwheat pancakes for a perfect breakfast or brunch. Despite the authentic fare, the diner is comfortable and appealing, with an artsy slant. It's a favorite after-hours hangout with club kids and other night owls.

8 Greenwich Village

EXPENSIVE

✪ **Babbo.** 110 Waverly Place (just east of Sixth Ave.). ☎ **212/777-0303.** Reservations highly recommended. Pastas $16–$19; meats and fish $19–$29; tasting menus $49–$59 ($85–$89 with wines). AE, DISC, MC, V. Mon–Sat 5:30–11:30pm, Sun 5–11pm. Subway: A, B, C, D, E, F, Q to W. 4th St. (use 8th St. exit). NORTHERN ITALIAN.

Chef Mario Batali's zesty, adventurous cooking has attracted a lot of attention since he began appearing on the Food Network. And justifiably so—Babbo was my pick for 1998's top new restaurant, and I consider it the best Italian restaurant in the city. *Molto Mario* also runs **Pō** on Cornelia Street (☎ 212/645-2189) as well as Lupa (see below), but Babbo is the best forum for enjoying his mind-bogglingly good cuisine.

Tucked away behind an inviting butter-yellow facade, the restaurant is warm and intimate, with well-spaced tables and a relaxed air that makes dining here feel special but comfortable, not formal. The greeting is welcoming and the service smart and friendly. That's a good thing because you may need help choosing from the risk-taking menu. Batali has reinvented the notion of antipasti with such starters as fresh anchovies beautifully marinated in lobster oil, and legendary Faicco soppressata accented with roasted beets, shaved fennel, and Macintosh vinegar. The chef has no equal when it comes to creative pastas; ask anyone who's dined here and they'll wax poetic about the spicy lamb sausage in delicate clouds called mint love letters, quickly becoming Babbo's signature dish. Heavy with offals and game meats, the *secondi* menu features such wonders as tender fennel-dusted sweetbreads; smoky grilled quail in a gamey but heavenly fig and duck liver vinaigrette; and spicy 2-minute calamari, a paragon of culinary simplicity. The knowledgeable sommelier can help you choose from the unusual but excellent wine list, all Italian and well priced.

Reservations are strongly recommended, but there are four nonreserved cafe-style tables and 10 spots at the bar, all serving a full menu to last-minute diners. Still, your best bet is to book ahead for the comfiest seating.

✪ **One If By Land, Two If By Sea.** 17 Barrow St. (btw. W. 4th St. and Seventh Ave. South). ☎ 212/228-0822. Reservations strongly recommended. Jacket recommended; tie optional. Main courses $29–$40; tasting menu $69. AE, DC, DISC, MC, V. Daily 5:30–11:30pm. Subway: 1, 9 to Christopher St. CONTINENTAL.

Ask just about any New Yorker to point you to the city's most romantic restaurant and you'll end up at this candlelit, rose-filled 18th-century carriage house once owned by Aaron Burr. This beautiful, intimate space has been a haven of lovers (and those who hope to be) for nearly 30 years. The fireplace crackles and a pianist fills the room with melody as you are escorted to your table for two by the tuxedoed maître'd. Given the emphasis on romance, it's no wonder that food has always come second here. It has never been bad—just committedly retro in the way that makes food snobs turn up their noses ("Beef Wellington? Ugh!"). But now that Chef David McInerney has taken over the kitchen, even gourmands are giving One If By Land a second look. It's still pleasingly continental-classic, but a few modern touches have given the menu new life. Among the best appetizers are the foie gras terrine with wild field greens and warm brioche, and rosy seared tuna with fresh wasabi, baby fennel, and shiitakes. The pan-roasted duck breast is greaseless and nicely accompanied by cherries and black lentils, and the rack of lamb is lightly smoked and roasted. And, of course, there's the beef Wellington with bordelaise sauce—still a classic, and outstanding. The formal service is attentive without being intrusive. The wine list boasts no bargains, but does have a number of celebratory champagnes.

MODERATE

Cafe de Bruxelles. 118 Greenwich Ave. (at Horatio St.). ☎ **212/206-1830.** Reservations recommended. Main courses $8–$13 at lunch and brunch, $10.95–$19.50 at dinner. AE, DC, MC, V. Tues–Thurs noon–11:30pm, Fri–Sat noon–midnight, Sun–Mon noon–10:30pm. Subway: A, C, E, 1, 2, 3, 9 to 14th St. BELGIAN.

This wonderfully low-key, lace-curtained restaurant is the city's top stop for Belgian-style mussels, frites, and beers. Yummy starters include wild mushrooms in puff pastry, thick-cut country pâté, and escargot in rich roquefort sauce. You might want to follow with the *carbonade flamande* (beef stew made with dark Belgian beer); *boudin blanc* (white pork sausage) with apples and onions; Belgian seafood casserole; or one of eight varieties of mussels, the best of which is the simple mariniere—nothing more than a large bowl of the mollusks cooked in onion, garlic, and white wine. No matter what you choose, your order is accompanied by a metal tin of sublime crispy fries with the traditional accompaniment, mayonnaise. Winning choices from the excellent selection of Trappist ales and lambics include the Affligem Abbey, smooth, rich, and fruity; and my favorite, the Chimay Rouge, a great choice for dark beer lovers.

✪ **Home.** 20 Cornelia St. (btw. Bleecker and W. 4th sts.) ☎ **212/243-9579.** Reservations highly recommended. Main courses $8–$12 at breakfast and lunch, $15–$20 at dinner. AE. Mon–Fri 9am–11pm, Sat 11am–11pm, Sun 11am–10pm. Subway: A, B, C, D, E, F, Q to W. 4th St. (use W. 3rd St. exit). CONTEMPORARY AMERICAN HOME COOKING.

I just love Home. This cozy restaurant is the domain of a husband-and-wife team, Chef David Page and co-owner Barbara Shinn, who have made home-style cooking something to celebrate. Page and Shinn keep things fresh, popularly priced, and welcoming; as a result, their narrow, tin-roofed dining room is always packed. The dinner menu changes regularly, but look for such signature dishes as the rich and creamy blue cheese fondue; an excellent cumin-crusted pork chop on a bed of home-made barbecue sauce; a filleted-at-your-table brook trout accompanied by an apple fig pancake and smoked bacon shallot dressing; and perfectly moist roasted chicken with a side of spicy onion rings. Chocolate lovers should save room for the silky-smooth pudding. Breakfast and weekend brunch are great times to visit, too, with fluffy pancakes and excellent egg dishes. This is a quintessential Village restaurant, loaded with sophisticated charm, but it is tiny. Seating isn't uncomfortable and you won't feel intruded upon by your neighbors, but the tight room isn't built for large parties or those who want to spread out. The lovely garden is heated year-round, but is most charming in warm weather; book an outside table well ahead.

Isla. 39 Downing St. (btw. Bedford and Varick sts.). ☎ **212/352-CUBA.** Reservations highly recommended. Main courses $14–$24. AE, DISC, MC, V. Tues–Thurs 6pm–midnight, Fri 6pm–1am, Sun 11am–3pm and 6–11pm. Subway: 1, 9 to Houston St. NEW CUBAN.

Isla is one of the new standard bearers on New York's super-hot Nuevo Latino scene. The space has a cool '50s Havana diner look, upscaled with white leather banquettes, postmodern materials, and a playfully tropical sensibility. Once the sun goes down, the party vibe is as festive and boisterous as a Miami salsa festival, and the food is excellent. The greeting and service are friendly and unpretentious, a nice change from most spots that are this trendy.

Cast your skepticism aside and start with the Luna Roja, a blend of sauza gold, cointreau, and agua fresca served in a martini glass with a salt and cayenne pepper

Greenwich Village Dining

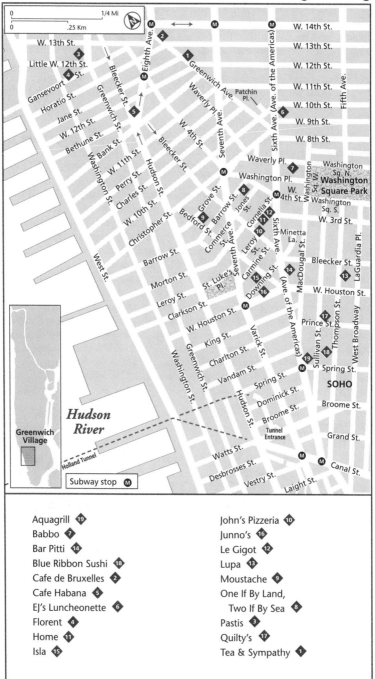

Aquagrill 19
Babbo 7
Bar Pitti 14
Blue Ribbon Sushi 18
Cafe de Bruxelles 2
Cafe Habana 5
EJ's Luncheonette 6
Florent 4
Home 11
Isla 15

John's Pizzeria 10
Junno's 16
Le Gigot 12
Lupa 13
Moustache 9
One If By Land,
  Two If By Sea 8
Pastis 3
Quilty's 17
Tea & Sympathy 1

rim—a wild house invention that makes you beg for more even as your lips go numb. The first-rate New Cuban food is the brainchild of 26-year-old Chef Aaron Sanchez, student of New York's best Latin-American chefs, including his mother Zarela Martinez, of Mexican landmark Zarela (see "Midtown East & Murray Hill"). Flavors are full and simplicity is key in Sanchez's preparations. The fresh ceviches are an excellent way to start. Consider following with the jumbo shrimp in a crisp plantain crust with enchilada sauce and spicy garbanzo rice—yum!—or the luscious roasted chicken breast marinated in spiced rum and citrus and accompanied by smoked black beans. This newcomer is definitely off to the right start.

✪ **Le Gigot.** 18 Cornelia St. (btw. Bleecker and W. 4th sts.). ☎ **212/627-3737.** Reservations highly recommended. Main courses $9–$18 at lunch, $18–$27 at dinner. AE. Tues–Sun noon–3pm; Tues and Sun 5–10pm, Wed–Sat 5–11pm. Subway: A, B, C, D, E, F, Q to W. 4th St. (use W. 3rd St. exit). FRENCH BISTRO.

Conceived as a moderate rather than a special-occasion restaurant, Le Gigot is a bit on the high side, but it's well worth the money. With buttercup walls, white linens, and bentwood cafe chairs, the tiny restaurant is so traditional that it's like a slice of Left Bank Paris transplanted to Greenwich Village. Fittingly, the menu is full of French bistro classics, and they're excellent across the board. There's a nod to the sea with a shellfish-heavy bouillabaisse and a couple of fish preparations, but Le Gigot is really a meat lover's paradise, with prime cuts and creamy sauces. The steak au poivre is aged sirloin flambéed in cognac; free-range chicken is perfectly roasted, dressed in a heavenly Beaujolais shallot and mushroom sauce, and accompanied by crisply crusted gratin potatoes; escargot swims in rich butter and parsley; and traditional cassoulet and steak frites are first-rate realizations. Desserts are as classic and decadent as you'd expect, and there's a small but well-chosen wine list. Brunch is a neighborhood secret, with excellent omelets and crisp fried potatoes. Be aware, though, that the narrow space isn't suitable for large parties or those who need lots of legroom. *Design alert:* The bathrooms are the city's loveliest, with a gorgeous French country style and unusually beautiful brass fixtures.

INEXPENSIVE

Cafe Habana (p. 152) has a second location at 11 Abingdon Square, on Eighth Avenue between West 12th and Bleecker streets (☎ 212/989-6883). There's also a branch of **EJ's Luncheonette** (p. 195), the retro all-American diner, at 432 Sixth Ave., between 9th and 10th streets (☎ 212/473-5555).

Bar Pitti. 268 Sixth Ave. (btw. Bleecker and Houston sts.). ☎ **212/982-3300.** Reservations accepted for parties of 4 or more. Main courses $6–$15 (some specials may be higher). No credit cards. Daily noon–midnight. Subway: A, B, C, D, E, F, Q to W. 4th St. (use 3rd St. exit). TUSCAN ITALIAN.

This indoor/outdoor Tuscan-style trattoria is a perennially hip sidewalk scene, and one of downtown's best dining bargains. Waiting for a table can be a chore (the wait list never seems very organized), but all is forgiven once you take a seat, thanks to authentic, affordably priced cuisine and some of the friendliest waiters in town. Despite the tightly packed seating, Bar Pitti wins you over with its rustic Italian charm—it's the kind of place where the waiter brings over the list of daily specials to your table on a well-worn blackboard, and if you want more cheese, a block of Parmesan and a grater suddenly appear. Peruse the laminated menu, but don't get your heart set on anything until you see the board, which boasts the best of what the kitchen has to offer; the last time we dined here, they wowed us with a fabulous veal meatball special. Winners off the regular menu, which focuses heavily on pastas and panini, include excellent rare beef carpaccio; grilled country bread with prosciutto, garlic, and olive oil; and spinach and ricotta ravioli in a creamy sage and parmesan sauce. The all-Italian wine list is high-priced compared to the menu, but you'll find a few good-value choices.

✪ **Junno's.** 64 Downing St. (btw. Bedford and Varick sts.). ☎ **212/627-7995.** Reservations not accepted. Main courses $8–$14. AE, DC, MC, V. Mon–Thurs 5:30pm–2am (kitchen closes at 11:30pm), Fri–Sat 5:30pm–4am (kitchen closes at midnight). Subway: 1, 9 to Houston St. JAPANESE FUSION.

Junno's is my second-favorite affordable newcomer of the year (behind Lupa, below). The sophisticated industrial moderne space is painted a soothing gray and warmed by retro leather banquettes and a marvelous blue bar. Following the current trend, start with one of the inventive house cocktails, such as the Schoolgirl Martini (Absolut kurant and Japanese plum wine, shaken) or the Tokyo (Maker's Mark, a dash of bitters, Sapporo dry draft). The Japanese fusion cuisine is very good, especially for those (like me) who favor creative Asian fare, and shockingly cheap considering the quality. Korea and France lend the most prominent accents. Among the standout starters are tuna tataki with fennel and gingered ponzu sauce, and scrumptious sweet-shrimp ravioli in miso-mustard sauce. Main courses of note include miso-marinated Spanish mackerel, served napoleon style with shiso rice and pickled cucumbers, and grilled marinated short ribs, served off the bone with a slightly tart sesame and scallion salad. Portions aren't stingy, but they're not huge, either, so you might want to order a starter and an entree even if that's not your normal habit (or three starters between the two of you if it is). Ginger crème brûlée is the best among the so-so desserts. Come early if you want to enjoy a quiet dinner, later in the evening if you want to revel in the party scene.

✪ **Lupa.** 170 Thompson St. (btw. Houston and Bleecker sts.). ☎ **212/982-5089.** Reservations recommended. Pastas $9–$12; main courses $11–$15. AE, DC, MC, V. Tues–Sun noon–3pm and 5:30–11:30pm. Subway: 1, 9 to Houston St. NORTHERN ITALIAN.

God bless Mario Batali, the one big-name chef in the city who thinks you shouldn't have to spend a fortune to eat like a king. *Molto Mario* on TV's Food Network and the man behind Babbo (above) launched this trattoria for regular folks in late 1999, and it's a winner. Reservations are taken for the back room only, and I strongly advise you to arrange for them if you can, since it's quieter and more civilized. The front room is reserved for walk-ins (to avoid the perpetual inaccessibility of Batali's always-packed first restaurant, Pò). It's loud and cramped and you'll probably have to wait for a table unless you come early, but so what? The food is worth it.

Don't be scared off by the all-Italian menu, as a few folks seemed to be on our first visit; the helpful butcher-coated waiter will steer you through the language and preparations. It's a short list, but one that boasts lots of treats. As always with Mario, the pastas stand out: The *bucatini all'Amatriciana,* a classic Italian tube pasta in a smoky tomato sauce made from hog jowl (bacon), is divine, as is the creamy ricotta gnocchi with Italian sausage and fennel. Lupa is also a *salumeria,* so don't miss an opportunity to start with the prosciutto di carpegna with roasted figs, an ideal marriage of salt and sweet. Among the main courses, the classic saltimbocca was a disappointment, but the oven-roasted littleneck clams with sweet soppressata was a joy. Another delight: The wine list is massive and super-affordable.

Moustache. 90 Bedford St. (btw. Barrow and Grove sts.). ☎ **212/229-2220.** Reservations not accepted. Main courses $5–$12. No credit cards. Daily noon–midnight (kitchen closes at 11:30pm). Subway: 1, 9 to Christopher St. MIDDLE EASTERN.

Pizza! Pizza!

In the mood for a slice or two . . . or three? The Village is the perfect place to be. The original location of **John's Pizzeria** (p. 182), 278 Bleecker St. between Sixth and Seventh avenues (☎ **212/243-1680**), is a New York original and still one of the city's best. The pies are thin-crusted, properly sauced, and fresh, and served up piping hot in an authentic old-world setting. Sorry, no slices.

Moustache (pronounced moo-STAH-sh) is the sort of exotic neighborhood spot that's just right. On a quiet side street in the West Village, this charming hole-in-the-wall boasts a cozy Middle Eastern vibe and authentic fare that's both palate-pleasing and wallet-friendly. Delicately seasoned dishes bear little resemblance to the food at your average falafel joint. Expect subtly flavored hummus, tabbouleh, and spinach-chickpea-tomato salad (or a large plate of all three); excellent oven-roasted "pitzas," thin, matzo-like pita crusts topped with spicy minced lamb and other savory ingredients; and—best of all—fluffy, hot-from-the-oven homemade pita bread, which puts any of those store-bought Frisbees to shame. Moustache is hugely and justifiably popular, so don't be surprised if there's a line—but it's well worth the wait.

A second Manhattan location is in the East Village at 265 E. 10th St., between First Avenue and Avenue A (☎ **212/228-2022**).

Tea & Sympathy. 108 Greenwich Ave. (btw. 12th and 13th sts.). ☎ **212/807-8329.** Reservations not accepted. Main courses $5.50–$12 at lunch and brunch, $10.50–$17 at dinner; full afternoon tea $18 ($32 for 2). No credit cards. Mon–Fri 11:30am–10pm, Sat–Sun 10am–10pm. Subway: A, C, E, 1, 2, 3, 9 to 14th St. BRITISH.

When Londoner Nicky Perry moved to New York, she was disappointed to find no proper British tearoom where she could get a decent cup, so she opened her own in the heart of the West Village. Tea & Sympathy seems as if it was transplanted wholesale from Greenwich or Highgate, complete with an oddball collection of creamers and teapots, snappy British wait staff, and plenty of old-time charm. Elbow room is at a minimum and the place is perpetually packed, but it's worth the squeeze for the full afternoon tea, which comes on a tiered tray with crust-off finger sandwiches like hearty chicken salad and egg and 'cress, scones with jam and Devonshire cream, and cakes and cookies for a sugary finish. The menu also features such traditional British comforts as shepherd's pie, bangers and mash, and a savory chicken and leek pie. Anglophiles line up for the Sunday dinner—roast beef and Yorkshire pudding, of course. For dessert, try the treacle pudding, warm ginger cake, or yummy sherry trifle. Next door is a cute shop selling Cadbury Flake bars, Hob Nob biscuits, and other imported English groceries and trinkets.

9 Chelsea & the Meat-Packing District

You'll find the restaurants in this section on the "Midtown Dining" map on p. 174.

MODERATE

Cafeteria. 119 Seventh Ave. (at 17th St.). ☎ **212/414-1717.** Reservations recommended for dinner. Breakfast $5–$10 (served 6am–5pm); sandwiches $7.50–$13; main courses $11–$19 at dinner. AE, DC, MC, V. Daily 24 hours. Subway: 1, 9 to 18th St. AMERICAN.

The greasy spoon goes glam at this round-the-clock Chelsea hot spot. More über-diner than nouvo automat, Cafeteria is all about high style, from the white leather banquettes to the waifish wait staff. Luckily, there's follow-through: Both the food and the service are better than they have to be in this veneer-happy town. The menu features modern takes on the blue-plate classics—meat loaf, chicken pot pie, fried chicken and waffles, and killer mac and cheese made with both cheddar and fontina (yum!)—as well as surprisingly successful neo-American fare, including a well-seared, thick-cut tuna loin. On the downside, seating is tight—but that just puts you that much closer to the latest It-girls and boys, right? A great choice for those who want a dose of downtown's hippest crowd without paying the high tab that accompanies dinner at Moomba. Just put on your best basic black and you'll fit right in. Cafeteria is at its hippest after 10pm or so, but be sure to call ahead or you may be turned away at the door. Daytime has its own advantages, including a mellower vibe and a sidewalk cafe in summer.

Pastis. 9 Ninth Ave. (at Little W. 12th St.). ☎ **212/929-4844.** Reservations accepted for 6–7pm seatings. Salads and sandwiches $9–$14; main courses $12–$18. AE, MC, V. Mon–Fri 9am–5pm, Sat–Sun 9am–4pm; Sun–Thurs 6pm–2am, Fri–Sat 6pm–3am. Subway: A, C, E to 14th St. FRENCH BISTRO.

Pastis is a spitting image of big-sister hot spot Balthazar—complete with straight-from-the–Left Bank decor, classic bistro fare, ridiculously close tables, and the noise level of a Metallica show. Still, I like Pastis a lot better; frankly, the wallet-friendlier prices make the annoyances much easier to put up with. The food is terrific. The *rillettes fermière*, a thick-cut rabbit pâté served with greens and toasts, makes a hearty starter, while the nicely seasoned grilled octopus with white beans is a great choice for lighter tastes. On my last visit, the plat du jour was *poulet à la crème*—a comforting Gallic TV dinner in a crock pot, complete with super-moist roast chicken, veggies, and rice. The steak frites with rich béarnaise is a classic, as it should be in a place like this. There's no massive raw bar as at Balthazar, but the oysters on the half shell are from the same top-quality source. Bottles are pricey, but plenty of good, affordable wines are available by the carafe (don't make the mistake we did and order a half carafe, which was only $4 less than the full). The crêpes Suzette are an appropriately yummy finish.

Your best bet is to dine early, when you can make a reservation (accepted for 6, 6:30, and 7pm seatings). Or come for weekday breakfast or lunch, when things are quieter. Otherwise, expect to pony up to the bar and wait a while; the fashionable crowd makes for great people watching.

The Red Cat. 227 Tenth Ave. (btw. 23rd and 24th sts.). ☎ **212/242-1122.** Reservations recommended. Main courses $17–$24; 5-course tasting menu $45. AE, DC, MC, V. Mon–Thurs 5–11pm, Fri–Sat 5pm–midnight, Sun 5–10pm. Subway: C, E to 23rd St. MEDITERRANEAN-ACCENTED CONTEMPORARY AMERICAN.

This pleasing newcomer symbolizes the renaissance that has taken root in Chelsea. A year or two ago, you could've never envisioned a bistro this mature and refined making a home for itself this far west. Things change quickly in New York, and now the Red Cat seems right at home in this gentrifying, gallery-rich neighborhood. Outfitted like a chic (but still cozy) farmhouse, the long dining room is a pleasing setting for Chef Jimmy Bradley's flavorful, and substantial, Mediterranean-accented cooking. Witness the thick-cut, char-grilled pork chop, accompanied by a savory ragout of roasted shallots, tomatoes, and cracked olives; or the skate wing, pan-crisped in lemon-seasoned brown butter with capers and root vegetables. Bradley diversifies his core ingredients, which I like; in addition to skate, a recent menu boasted balsamic- and thyme-basted quail, toasted orzo with steamed mussels, and calf's liver au poivre. Wines are well chosen and affordable. All in all, a wonderful neighborhood restaurant that offers a good opportunity to break bread with the locals.

INEXPENSIVE

Empire Diner. 210 Tenth Ave. (at 22nd St.). ☎ **212/243-2736.** Reservations not accepted. Main courses $9–$18. AE, CB, DC, DISC, MC, V. Daily 24 hours. Subway: C, E to 23rd St. AMERICAN DINER.

This throwback shrine to the slicked-up all-American diner looks suspiciously like an Airstream camper plunked down on the corner. This classic joint boasts a timeless art deco vibe, honest coffee, and great mashed potatoes. The food is basic diner fare: eggs, omelets, burgers, overstuffed sandwiches, and a very nice turkey platter. Frankly, I think the Empire Diner is overrated—you'll find better breakfast fare elsewhere—but there's no denying its permanent status as a hot-spot fixture on the late-night scene. If you want quiet, go early. If you want an eyeful, wait for the after-hours crowd; 1 to 3am offers the best people watching, when Prada and Gucci meld with Phat Farm and Levi's. There's live music courtesy of a regular pianist. When the weather's warm, a pleasing sidewalk cafe appears, and the limited traffic this far over—mostly aiming for the Lincoln Tunnel—keeps the soot-and-fumes factor down.

✪ **Florent.** 69 Gansevoort St. (2 blocks south of 14th St. and 1 block west of Ninth Ave., btw. Greenwich and Washington sts.). ☎ **212/989-5779.** Reservations recommended for dinner. Main courses $4–$14.50 at brunch and lunch, $8–$19.50 at dinner; 2-course fixed-price lunch $7.25–$11; 3-course fixed-price dinner $17.50 before 7:30pm, $19.50 7:30pm–midnight. No credit cards. Mon–Fri 9am–5am, Sat–Sun 24 hours. Subway: A, C, E, L to 14th St. DINER/FRENCH BISTRO.

So you get a craving at 3am for homemade rillettes, boudin noir, or steak frites and can't decide whether you'd like to eat with club kids, partying celebrities, cross-dressed revelers, truckers from Jersey, or the odd stockbroker? Then get thee down to Florent, the nearly 24-hour French bistro dressed up as a '50s-style diner, where you can have it all. Located in the Meat-Packing District, Florent is a perennial hot spot no matter what the time of day; a kids' menu makes this the perfect place to bring the kids for lunch or early dinner. But it's after the clubs close when the joint really jumps. Tables are tightly packed, almost uncomfortably so in some cases, but it's all part of the late-night festivities. This place has a real sense of humor (check out the menu boards above the bar) and a CD catalog full of the latest indie sounds, all adding to the hipster fun. The food's good, too: The grilled chicken with herbs and mustard sauce is a winner, moist and flavorful, as is the French onion soup crowned with melted gruyère. There are always diner faves like burgers and chili in addition to Gallic standards like moules frites, and the comfort food specialties such as chicken pot pie make regular appearances. The fries are light, crispy, and addictive.

✪ **Grand Sichuan Restaurant.** 229 Ninth Ave. (at 24th St.). ☎ **212/620-5200.** Reservations accepted for parties of 3 or more. Main courses $3.25–$14; lunch special $4.50; dinner special $6.25. AE, DC, MC, V. Daily 11:30am–11pm. Subway: C, E to 23rd St. SZECHUAN CHINESE.

There's no need to head to Chinatown—Grand Sichuan serves up the real thing right here in Chelsea. This comfortable spot has garnered rave reviews for its authentic Szechuan cuisine. Spicy food lovers will be particularly thrilled, as the kitchen excels at dishes that are intensely spiced without being palate-numbing—a brilliant culinary balance that few Chinatown kitchens can achieve. The flavors are complex and strong, especially in such top choices as Szechuan wontons in red oil, Chairman Mao's pork with chestnuts, and my favorite, boneless whole fish with pine nuts in a modified sweet-and-sour sauce. The house bean curd in spicy sauce is another winner, but only for those with a high tolerance for hot. If some in your party shy away from hot and spicy, never fear: The staff will be more than happy to recommend milder dishes.

10 The Flatiron District, Union Square & Gramercy Park

You'll find the restaurants in this section on the "Midtown Dining" map on p. 174.

VERY EXPENSIVE

✪ **Union Pacific.** 111 E. 22nd St. (btw. Park Ave. South and Lexington Ave.). ☎ **212/ 995-8500.** Reservations highly recommended. Fixed-price lunch $29–$59; 3-course fixed-price dinner $65 (plus optional 3-course appetizer flights $22); tasting menus $65–$155. AE, DC, MC, V. Mon–Thurs noon–2pm and 5:30–10:15pm, Fri noon–2pm and 5:15–10:30pm, Sat 5:15–10:30pm. Subway: 6 to 23rd St. ASIAN FUSION/PACIFIC RIM.

This soaring bilevel restaurant is serene and beautiful, with elegant Japanese touches and a lovely wall of water at the entrance (keep an eye out for the low-profile sign). Tables are well spaced and suited to private conversation, but you're best off asking to be seated along one of the banquettes.

The menu may seem contrived at first (young rabbit with glazed turnips and a cane sugar conundrum?), but the combinations are extraordinary. While Chef Rocco DiSpirito has strong French influences, it's the flavors of Japan and the Pacific that give his menu its edge. Still, this is not Nobu. Stellar appetizers include bluefin tuna with yuzu and fresh wasabi, ragout of Maryland blue crab with chanterelles, and caramelized sweetbreads with sorrels and muskmelon. The coldwater fish selections— such as East Coast halibut with cracklin' shallot and young ginger, and Chatham cod with mustard greens and bright lovage broth—also keep the menu firmly rooted: This is a New Yorker's Pacific Rim menu. I've not found anything on the menu that isn't excellent, and the *New York Times* has made the same claim, awarding the restaurant three prestigious stars. Wine pairings are available for both appetizers and entrees, with a surprising number of German and Austrian labels among the selections, adding a whole new dimension to the meal. Expensive, but excellent through and through.

EXPENSIVE

Gramercy Tavern. 42 E. 20th St. (btw. Broadway and Park Ave. South). ☎ **212/477-0777.** Reservations required well in advance. Main courses $18–$25 at lunch; 3-course fixed-price lunch $36; 3-course fixed-price dinner $62. AE, DC, DISC, MC, V. Mon–Thurs noon–2pm and 5:30–10pm, Fri–Sat noon–2pm and 5:30–11pm, Sun 5:30–10pm. Subway: R, 6 to 23rd St. CONTEMPORARY AMERICAN.

Thanks to warm service, a dining room that's an ideal blend of urban sophistication and heartland rusticity, and faultless New American cuisine, owner Danny Meyer and Chef Tom Colicchio's Gramercy Tavern is one of the top dining rooms in the city. At the height of its game these days, it's a cut above big sister Union Square Cafe. It's really hard to go wrong here.

The menu, which changes based on what's fresh and in season, is pleasing from start to finish. The foie gras appetizer exquisitely juxtaposes tender liver with a crunchy, acidic rhubarb relish. The seared pepper-crusted tuna is fanned out on a bed of wilted arugula, white beans, and squash with lemon confit. Saddle of rabbit will wow game lovers, and lowly chicken is elevated to new heights when it's poached and braised with salsify, pistachio, and truffles. The excellent cheese tray features top-notch farmstead selections from New York State, France, Spain, Italy, and England. Desserts, like warm lemon tart soufflé with blueberry compote and ginger ice cream, are divine.

If the main dining room is too rich for your blood, or you simply can't get a reservation, consider the more casual ✪ **Tavern Room,** which has an affordable all-day menu (nothing over $20) featuring salads, a terrific tomato garlic-bread soup, succu-lent roasted baby chicken, and a handful of fish dishes and sandwiches for lighter eaters, plus the restaurant's signature selection of cheeses and desserts. The Tavern Room is smoke-free and ideal for walk-ins, since no reservations are taken. One of the best dining values in town.

Tabla. 11 Madison Ave. (at 25th St.). ☎ **212/889-0667.** Reservations highly recommended. Three-course fixed-price dinner $52; tasting menu $65. AE, DC, DISC, MC, V. Mon–Thurs 5:30–10:30pm, Fri–Sat 5:30–11pm, Sun 5:30–10pm. Subway: 6 to 23rd St. INDIAN FUSION.

Indian fusion, a hybrid cuisine that blends Eastern spices with Western cooking tech-niques, was the trend of 1998—and the bust of 1999. The lone phoenix that rose from the ashes was Tabla, the brainchild of Danny Meyer, the man behind Gramercy Tavern and Union Square Cafe. The bilevel restaurant is strikingly designed: Downstairs is the "Bread Bar," churning out naan, roti, and playful cocktails, while the upstairs dining room boasts well-spaced tables and a relaxed yet convivial atmosphere. It sets a nice tone for Floyd Cardoz's heady, somewhat frenetic cuisine.

The Indian influence is ever present but not overpowering; witness such starters as tandoori shrimp, sharply seasoned with black pepper and drizzled with a maple-lime vinaigrette—seemingly incongruous, but it works. Subtler and more successful is the lobster, baby octopus, and squid with yellow-foot chanterelles, turmeric fettuccine, and jicama. As you might have guessed, the high quality of the ingredients is key; the combinations require more guesswork, but are largely successful. My recommendation is to pair a full-bodied, peppery Spanish Rioja with this strongly spiced cuisine, and follow up with a cooling mango lassi—a dessert rather than a beverage here, with lemon-mint ice and coconut-banana sorbet. All in all, a good bet if you're looking for something completely different.

✪ **Veritas.** 43 E. 20th St. (btw. Fifth Ave. and Park Ave. South). ☎ **212/353-3700.** www.veritas-nyc.com. Reservations recommended. 3-course fixed-price dinner $68. AE, DC, MC, V. Mon–Sat 5:30–11pm, Sun 5–10:30pm. Subway: N, R, 6 to 23rd St. CONTEMPORARY AMERICAN.

This *New York Times* three-star winner (out of a possible four) is my favorite new restaurant of 1999. The simple 65-seat room is the embodiment of clean-lined con-temporary style and unpretentious grace—and the ideal showcase for Scott Bryan's straightforward yet sophisticated cooking, itself a perfect foil for the spectacular 1,300-bottle wine collection. Much of the wine cellar is comprised of full-bodied reds, so Mr. Bryan has created a robust cuisine as accompaniment. There's surprisingly lit-tle red meat on the compact menu, but even a pan-roasted monkfish, dressed with white beans, smoked bacon, roasted tomato, and picholines, bursts with flavors that can stand up to a big, bold red. The menu changes seasonally, but expect such lovely starters as Peekytoe crab ravioli with fines herbes, tomato, and lemon in a delicate shellfish emulsion. Sweetbreads are sublimely roasted and given an Asian slant with marinated shiitakes, a soy glaze, and a peel of ginger. Despite the gravity of the wine list, there are many well-priced choices; the first-rate sommelier will be glad to help you choose, no matter what your budget. Serious oenophiles who want to plan ahead can download the full list in advance, and have their choice opened and waiting at reservation time. Service is mature and attentive.

MODERATE

Also consider the ✪ **Tavern Room at Gramercy Tavern,** 42 E. 20th St. (☎ 212/477-0777), which features a lighter, more affordable take on Chef Tom Colicchio's award-winning New American fare; for details, see the listing for Gramercy Tavern above.

Blue Water Grill. 31 Union Sq. West (at 16th St.). ☎ **212/675-9500.** Reservations recommended. Main courses $12.50–$24.95. AE, MC, V. Mon–Thurs 11:30am–12:30am, Fri–Sat 11:30am–1am, Sun 11am–midnight; Sun brunch 11am–4pm. Subway: L, N, R, 4, 5, 6 to 14th St./Union Sq. SEAFOOD.

This stylish seafooder serves up good-quality fish to an energetic crowd. I prefer Aquagrill (see "SoHo & NoLiTa" earlier in this chapter), but you won't do badly here either—and it's much easier to score a table at Blue Water. You can put together a platter of oysters and littlenecks on the half shell from the extensive raw bar, order up lobster by the pound (steamed, grilled, or broiled—your choice), or go with one of the prepared day's catches. (Sushi platters are available as well, but you're better off at a sushi restaurant if that's what you crave.) Look for both Asian and Mediterranean influences on the menu, which makes the most of what's fresh. The best selections— often Atlantic salmon, wild striped bass, and Pacific mahi—come from the kitchen's wood-burning grill. There's pasta, chicken, and filet mignon for the nonseafooders in your group. If the weather's good, try to sit on the lovely narrow terrace overlooking Union Square. There's a live jazz combo in the art deco–influenced downstairs dining room nightly.

Caffe Bondí Ristorante. 7 W. 20th St. (btw. Fifth and Sixth aves.). ☎ **212/691-8136.** www.bondi-ny.com. Reservations recommended. Pastas $9–$15; meat and fish main courses $16–$25; 4-course fixed-price dinner $29 Sun–Thurs, 5-course fixed-price dinner $39 Fri–Sat. AE, DC, MC, V. Mon–Sat 11:30am–11pm, Sun 11:30am–9pm. Subway: N, R, F to 23rd St. SICILIAN.

This unassuming and charmingly authentic Italian cafe serves Sicilian delicacies with skill and care. The dedication of the Settepani brothers, who own and run the place, shows at every level, from the quality of the food to the friendliness of the staff. You might start with the *conca d'oro,* a lively salad of oranges, fennel, black olives, and red onions in an oil-and-vinegar dressing. The fish soup is from an 11th-century Saracen recipe: sole, grouper, mussels, clams, and shrimp in a sauce of capers, saffron, garlic, pine nuts, and laurel leaves. Among the notable entrees are the shellfish-stuffed brioche (lobster, shrimp, clams, mussels) seasoned with a delicate curry, and an excellent veal scallopini. The biggest reason to dine here, however, is the rear garden, one of the most delightful alfresco spots in the city.

Follonico. 6 W. 24th St. (btw. Fifth and Sixth aves.). ☎ **212/691-6359.** Reservations recommended. Pastas $11.50–$19; meat and fish main courses $19.50–$24. AE, MC, V. Mon–Fri noon–3pm and 6–10:30pm, Sat 5:30–10:30pm. Subway: N, R to 23rd St. TUSCAN ITALIAN.

Follonico is a favorite among Flatiron publishing types for its casually elegant style and Alan Tardi's straightforward, and consistently good, Tuscan cooking. This is comfort food Italian style: a delicately fried *fritto misto* (sampler platter) with a wonderfully simple lemon-caper aioli; hearty, nap-inducing risottos, made fresh daily; osso bucco alla Milanese; and one of the finest spaghetti alla carbonaras around. Tardi is at his best with pastas, and when he's putting the wood-burning oven at the heart of the cozy wood-beamed Tuscan yellow dining room. Wood-roasted calamari—dressed with nothing more than crushed red pepper, extra-virgin olive oil, and a squeeze of lemon—is in top form here, while the deep-fried oysters topped with horseradish cream and Osetra caviar ($4) is a craving that's well worth indulging. The day's whole fish, roasted with potatoes in rock salt, makes an ideal meal ($46 for two). The menu is limited, but there's something for everyone here. Ditto for the wine list, which boasts some very good values.

Medusa. 239 Park Ave. South (btw. 19th and 20th sts). ☎ **212/477-1500.** Reservations recommended. Pastas $10–$15; seafood and meat main courses $15–$24. AE, MC, V. Sun–Thurs noon–1am (kitchen closes at midnight), Fri–Sat noon–3am (kitchen closes at 2am). Subway: L, N, R, 4, 5, 6 to 14th St./Union Sq. MEDITERRANEAN.

If Medusa were just a little more expensive—a few dollars here, a few dollars there—there would be nothing special about it. It would be lost in the sea of overpriced Mediterranean boîtes that regularly come and go in the city. But what Medusa has going for it is value. In the increasingly high-rent, high-profile Flatiron District, Medusa has managed to keep its prices down to earth while still maintaining all the trappings of a downtown see-and-be-seen hot spot. And what's more, the food is good. The grilled octopus with baby greens, tomatoes, and steamed potatoes is a great way to start. All the pastas are fresh and well prepared, as are mostly seafood mains, like oven-roasted Chilean sea bass. I've seen more expressly Mediterranean dishes of late, such as a phyllo-wrapped goat cheese salad and Moroccan chicken accompanied by a fruity couscous. We've always been pleased with our meals at romantic, stylish Medusa; this is a place that manages to feel grown-up without the requisite high tab. There are a few concessions, such as on-the-cheap cafe chairs, but they're all but unnoticeable in the romantically candlelit tomato-red space. Let's hope the people behind Medusa can keep up the good work.

Steak Frites. 9 E. 16th St. (between Fifth Ave. and Union Sq. West). ☎ **212/463-7101.** Reservations recommended. Main courses $8.50–$18 at lunch, $14–$23 at dinner. AE, DC, MC, V. Sun–Tues noon–10:30pm, Wed–Sat noon–midnight. Subway: L, N, R, 4, 5, 6 to 14th St./Union Sq. BELGIAN/FRENCH/STEAKS.

Meat lovers, arm yourselves. The menu offers other choices (pasta, chicken, salads), but order the steak frites for two—certified Black Angus faultlessly grilled, pink inside, blackened outside. Or go with the mussels, which come in a number of presentations, the best of which is the white wine and fresh herbs or the hearty Belgian beer. The frites are better at Cafe de Bruxelles, but they're good here, too, and you'll get good ol' American ketchup on the side rather than Euro-style mayo. The big room is loud and the service isn't quite as attentive as I might like, but the food is well priced and well prepared. And I love the bustling slice-of-St-Germain atmosphere, complete with mahogany-and-brass bar and Toulouse Lautrec–style murals on the walls. There's a good selection of wines and Belgian beers, as you'd expect from a French brasserie. Don't be surprised, however, if you have to wait for your table on busy nights, even with a reservation.

INEXPENSIVE
✪ **Old Town Bar & Restaurant.** 45 E. 18th St. (btw. Broadway and Park Ave. South). ☎ **212/529-6732.** Reservations unnecessary. Main courses $6–$15. AE, MC, V. Mon–Sat 11:30am–1am (kitchen closes at 11:30pm), Sun 11:30am–10:30pm. Subway: L, N, R, 4, 5, 6 to 14th St./Union Sq. AMERICAN.

If you've watched TV at all over the last couple of decades, this place should look familiar: It was featured nightly in the old *Late Night with David Letterman* intro, starred as Riff's Bar in *Mad About You*, and appeared in too many commercials to count, as well as in such movies as *The Devil's Own*, Woody Allen's *Bullets Over Broadway*, and Whit Stillman's *The Last Days of Disco*. But this is no stage set—it's a genuine tin-ceilinged 19th-century bar serving up good pub grub, lots of beers on tap, and a real sense of New York history. Sure, there are healthy salads on the menu, but everybody comes for the burgers. Whether you go low-fat turkey or bacon-chili-cheddar, they're perfect every time. You have your choice of sides, but go with the

Pizza! Pizza!

Pintaile's Pizza, 124 Fourth Ave., between 12th and 13th streets (☎ 212/ 475-4977; www.pintailespizza.com), dresses their daintily crisp organic crusts with layers of plum tomatoes, extra-virgin olive oil, and other fabulously fresh ingredients. This new Union Square–area location of the Upper East Side favorite even has lots of seating for in-house eating.

shoestring fries—what else in a traditional place like this? Other good choices include spicy Buffalo wings with blue cheese, fiery bowls of chili sprinkled with cheddar cheese and dolloped with sour cream, and a Herculean Caesar salad slathered with mayo and topped with anchovies. Food comes up from the basement kitchen courtesy of ancient dumbwaiters behind the bar, where equally crusty bartenders would rather *not* make you a Cosmopolitan, thank you very much. If you want to escape the cigarettes and the predatory singles scene that pulls in on weekends, head upstairs to the blissfully smoke-free dining room.

Republic. 37 Union Sq. West (btw. 16th and 17th sts.). ☎ **212/627-7172.** Reservations accepted for parties of 10 or more. Main courses $6–$9. AE, MC, V. Sun–Wed noon–11pm, Thurs–Sat noon–midnight. Subway: L, N, R, 4, 5, 6 to 14th St./Union Sq. PAN-ASIAN NOODLES.

Proving once and for all that you don't have to sacrifice high style for wallet-friendly prices, this ultra-chic noodle joint serves up affordable fast food in an area where it's getting harder and harder to find a deal. Cushionless, backless benches pulled up to pine-and-steel refectory tables don't encourage lingering, but that's precisely the point: This is the kind of place that knows how to make you feel hip and happy and get you out the door efficiently. The Chinese-, Vietnamese-, and Thai-inspired noodle menu attracts a steady stream of impossibly chic on-the-go customers. For a one-bowl meal, try the spicy coconut chicken (chicken slices in coconut milk, lime juice, lemongrass, and galangal) or spicy beef (rare beef with wheat noodles spiced with chiles, garlic, and lemongrass). The long, curving bar is perfect for solitary diners.

11 Times Square & Midtown West

VERY EXPENSIVE

✪ **Le Bernardin.** 155 W. 51st St. (btw. Sixth and Seventh aves.). ☎ **212/489-1515.** www.le-bernardin.com. Reservations required 1 month in advance. Jacket required/tie optional. Fixed-price lunch $32–$43; fixed-price dinner $75; tasting menu $120. AE, DISC, MC, V. Mon–Fri noon–2:30pm; Mon–Thurs 5:30–10:30pm, Fri–Sat 5:30–11pm. Subway: N, R to 49th St.; 1, 9 to 50th St. FRENCH/SEAFOOD.

If forced to choose, I'd probably peg Le Bernardin as one of my two favorite splurge restaurants (the other being Chanterelle). The seafood at this *New York Times* four-star winner (one of only six in the city) is the best in the Big Apple, if not the world. Food doesn't get better than the flash-marinated black bass ceviche, the freshest fish awash in cilantro, mint, jalapeños, and diced tomatoes. Eric Ripert's tuna tartare always exhilarates, its Asian seasoning a welcome exotic touch. Among lightly cooked dishes that shine are herbed crabmeat in saffron ravioli and shellfish-tarragon reduction; roast baby lobster tail on asparagus-and-cèpe risotto; and an extravagant mix of sea scallops, foie gras, and truffles from the Périgord, wrapped and steamed in a cabbage leaf and splashed with truffle vinaigrette. The crusted cod, served on a bed of haricots verts with potatoes and diced tomatoes, is another favorite. The formal service is impeccable, as is the outrageously pricey wine list, and the room is uptown gorgeous. The fixed-price lunches are a bargain, given the master in the kitchen. The desserts—especially the frozen rum-scented chestnut soufflé or chocolate dome with crème brûlée on a macaroon—end the meal with a flourish.

"21" Club. 21 W. 52nd St. (btw. Fifth and Sixth aves.). ☎ **212/582-7200.** www.21club.com. Reservations required. Jacket and tie required. Main courses $25–$42 (most $30 or more); fixed-price lunch $29; pretheater fixed-price (5:30–6:30pm) $33; tasting menu $70. AE, DC, DISC, JCB, MC, V. Mon–Fri noon–2:30pm; Mon–Thurs 5:30–10pm, Fri–Sat 5:30–11:30pm. Closed Aug or Sept. Subway: B, D, F, Q to 47th–50th sts./Rockefeller Center. AMERICAN.

A former speakeasy in the days of Prohibition, this landmark restaurant is ground zero for New York's old-school business and celebrity power set—and it has recently zoomed its way back onto the list of New York's most interesting dining rooms. After years of being more Ed McMahon than Johnny Carson, the place has a reinvigorated air. And that's due to new owners Orient-Express Hotels, who have made subtle changes in the decor and the menu, while keeping "21" classics like chicken hash, steak tartare prepared tableside, fried oysters, Maine lobster salad, and the famed burger—terribly expensive at $25, but worth it. The historic Bar Room is the best of the dining rooms, with its long mahogany bar, red-checkered tablecloths, and antique toys and other trinkets (many gifts of the celebs who consider "21" their second home) dangling playfully from the ceiling. A real New York classic.

EXPENSIVE

Barbetta. 321 W. 46th St. (btw. Eighth and Ninth aves.). ☎ **212/246-9171.** www.barbettarestaurant.com. Reservations recommended. Main courses $22–$32. AE, DC, DISC, MC, V. Tues–Sat noon–2:30pm and 5pm–midnight. Subway: A, C, E to 42nd St./Port Authority. PIEDMONT ITALIAN.

Open since 1906, this landmark Italian restaurant specializes in the cuisine of Italy's northern Piedmont region. Set in two adjoining town houses, the restaurant is furnished with 18th-century classical antiques (a passion of owner Laura Maioglio, whose father founded the restaurant). An ungainly acoustical-tile ceiling detracts from the main dining room's old-world elegance, but makes it much more pleasant for conversation. This is a real pretheater spot—the room goes from bustling to empty at around 7:45, after which a more sedate crowd settles in. Summer is the best time to come, since you can dine in the marvelous outdoor garden—with wrought-iron furniture, century-old trees, and trickling fountain, it's the most romantic spot in Midtown. But other seasons have their draw, too: From October to Christmas, it's truffle season, and Barbetta's white truffles (hunted by the family's own Piedmontese truffle hounds) are the ultimate decadence.

There have been complaints in past years that the food hasn't quite lived up to the setting, but a new kitchen has revitalized the menu of late, keeping the best of the traditional dishes while adding some new twists. All of the pastas we tried were excellent, especially the handmade agnelotti and the linguine with olives, as was the risotto with wild porcinis. Among the main courses are a number of game dishes, including a wonderful rack of venison with Hudson River Valley apple, and terrific Maine Diver scallops with a Yukon gold crust. Winner of a *Wine Spectator* Award of Excellence, the all-Italian wine list is a phenomenal collection, especially strong in barolos and barbarescos.

✪ **Cité.** 120 W. 51st St. (btw. Sixth and Seventh aves.). ☎ **212/956-7100.** www.citerestaurant.com. Reservations recommended. Main courses $19.75–$29.75; pretheater (5–7:30pm) 3-course fixed-price $43.50; Taste of the Grape 3-course dinner with wine $59.50

(8pm–midnight). AE, MC, V. Mon–Fri 11:30am–11:30pm, Sat–Sun 5–11:30pm. Subway: N, R to 49th St.; B, D, E to Seventh Ave. CONTINENTAL/STEAKS.

This pleasing art deco steak house has the air of a refined Parisian brasserie, making it a sophisticated—and value-wise—choice for a fine Theater District dinner. The standard pretheater fixed-price is a good value unto itself, offering a limited but pleasing number of choices, including the filet mignon steak frites, a mammoth cut that arrives impeccably grilled. But the real deal comes after 8pm, with Cité's fabulous "Taste of the Grape" offer: Choose any appetizer, main course, and dessert from the full dinner menu for $59.50, and enjoy unlimited quantities of the night's four featured wines *at no extra charge*. They're not offering up the cheap stuff—Cité's wine guru Daniel Thames takes this program seriously and has chosen well. Among the wines on recent offer were an '88 Burgess Cellars cabernet sauvignon, a '97 Acacia chardonnay, a Chalone Vineyard pinot noir reserve from '94, and a Nicolas Feuillate brut for celebrating. The full menu features an excellent selection of chops and steaks plus a fine spit-roasted garlic chicken and a stellar swordfish steak au poivre. Consider launching your meal with the creamy sweet corn chowder and wrapping up with the classic Floating Island. The professional wait staff is brisk and attentive, and the overall ambience is much friendlier than at clubbier, more masculine steak houses.

Estiatorio Milos. 125 W. 55th St. (btw. Sixth and Seventh aves.). ☎ **212/245-7400.** Reservations recommended. Main courses $18–$32; fixed-price pre- and posttheater dinner $32. AE, DC, MC, V. Mon–Fri noon–3pm and 5:30pm–midnight, Sat 5:30pm–midnight, Sun 5–11pm. Subway: N, R to 57th St. GREEK/SEAFOOD.

The sea stars center stage at this dazzling Greek seafooder, which managed to earn a terrific rating of "26" for food from Zagat's in just its first full year in the survey. You'll select from the day's catch, seductively displayed on ice and sold by the pound. Appetizers like grilled fresh sardines and charred octopus with onions, capers, and peppers transport you to whitewashed villages overlooking the Mediterranean. Grilled whole fish, whether Arctic char, red snapper, loup de mer, or Dover sole, make the best main-course choice: It's brushed with olive oil and herbs, simply grilled, and then deboned tableside by the wait staff. Watch the bill, though—that by-the-pound pricing can add up quicker than you can say "opa!" To keep expenses down, consider ordering a selection of appetizers—the menu features creatively prepared octopus and baby squid, Greek-inspired salads, and crab cakes that the *New York Times* called "perfect"—and one whole fish to share. The wine list is excellent, and the cheese tray features about 30 farmhouse selections rarely available outside Greece. For dessert, try the tangy homemade yogurt drizzled with honey and dotted with wild blueberries.

✪ **Petrossian.** 182 W. 58th St. (at Seventh Ave.). ☎ **212/245-2214.** www.petrossian.com. Reservations required. Jacket and tie required. Main courses $18–$23 at lunch, $28–$34 at dinner; fixed-price lunch $22 ($39 with caviar); fixed-price dinner $38 ($10–$50 supplement for caviar). AE, DC, DISC, MC, V. Mon–Sat 11:30am–3pm and 5:30–11:30pm, Sun 11:30am–3pm and 5:30–10:30pm. Subway: B, D, E to Seventh Ave.; N, R to 57th St. CONTINENTAL/RUSSIAN.

Petrossian is North America's (and France's) largest importer of Caspian caviar, so they're able to serve high-quality Sevruga, Osetra, and Beluga for no more than you'd pay if you picked it up at the deli counter down at Balducci's. Oh, but this is no deli counter—nowhere in New York is caviar more exquisitely served. Available all evening, the three-course fixed-price dinner is almost an unbelievable deal, and definitely the way to go: For $45, you can start with more than an ounce of high-quality Sevruga (elegantly served in silver with toast points), and follow with a full entree, the best of which is the plate of Petrossian Teasers, a gourmand's delight of smoked eel, trout, cod,

Midtown Dining

Al Bustan 🔶67
An American Place 🔶65
Barbetta 🔶20
Blue Water Grill 🔶36
The British Open 🔶72
Brooklyn Diner USA 🔶6
The Cafe at Aquavit 🔶62
Cafeteria 🔶34
Caffe Bondí Ristorante 🔶45
Carmine's 🔶24
Carnegie Deli 🔶10
Churrascaria Plataforma 🔶19
Cité 🔶53
Daniel 🔶75
Empire Diner 🔶31
ESPN Zone 🔶29
Ess-A-Bagel 🔶40 🔶66
Estiatorio Milos 🔶55
Florent 🔶33
Follonico 🔶46
Gramercy Tavern 🔶43
Grand Sichuan Restaurant 🔶32
Hard Rock Cafe 🔶5
Harley-Davidson Cafe 🔶56
Island Burgers & Shakes 🔶18
Jean Georges 🔶3
Jekyll & Hyde Club 🔶58
Joe Allen 🔶22
Joe's Shanghai 🔶60
John's Pizzeria 🔶1 🔶23
Jo Jo 🔶74
Julian's 🔶17
La Bonne Soupe 🔶61
La Grenouille 🔶63
Le Bernardin 🔶12
Le Cirque 2000 🔶64
Mangia 🔶52 🔶59

continues on
opposite page

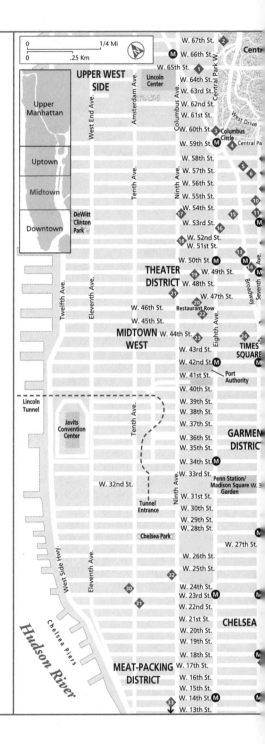

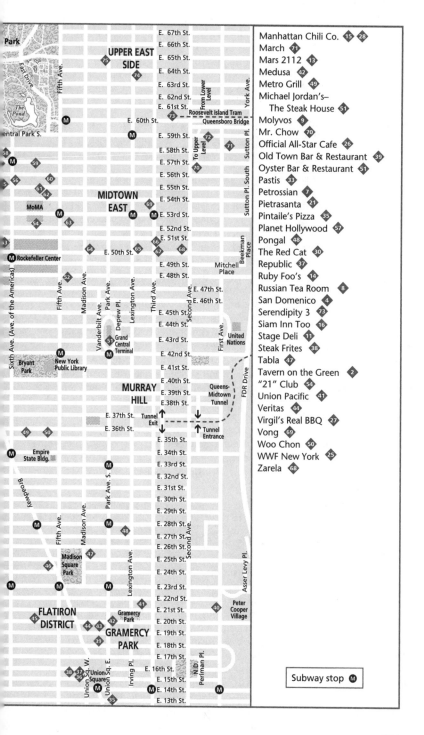

Manhattan Chili Co. 15 28
March 71
Mars 2112 13
Medusa 42
Metro Grill 49
Michael Jordan's–
    The Steak House 51
Molyvos 9
Mr. Chow 70
Official All-Star Cafe 26
Old Town Bar & Restaurant 39
Oyster Bar & Restaurant 51
Pastis 33
Petrossian 7
Pietrasanta 21
Pintaile's Pizza 35
Planet Hollywood 57
Pongal 48
The Red Cat 30
Republic 37
Ruby Foo's 14
Russian Tea Room 8
San Domenico 4
Serendipity 3 73
Siam Inn Too 16
Stage Deli 11
Steak Frites 38
Tabla 47
Tavern on the Green 2
"21" Club 54
Union Pacific 41
Veritas 44
Virgil's Real BBQ 27
Vong 69
Woo Chon 50
WWF New York 25
Zarela 68

Park

UPPER EAST SIDE
75
74

Fifth Ave.
East Ave.

East Drive

The Pond

M

Central Park S.

E. 67th St.
E. 66th St.
E. 65th St.
E. 64th St.
E. 63rd St.
E. 62nd St.
E. 61st St.
E. 60th St.

From Lower Level
Roosevelt Island Tram
Queensboro Bridge

York Ave.

58
M
59
5 56
61
60
62

MoMA
54
63
MIDTOWN EAST
M
69
M

E. 59th St.
E. 58th St.
E. 57th St.
E. 56th St.
E. 55th St.
E. 54th St.
E. 53rd St.
E. 52nd St.
E. 51st St.

72
74
70

To Upper Level

Sutton Pl.
Sutton Pl. South

3
M Rockefeller Center
64
65 66 67 68
E. 50th St.

E. 49th St.
E. 48th St.

Mitchell Place
Beekman Place

Fifth Ave. (Ave. of the Americas)
52

Madison Ave.
Park Ave.
Depew Pl.
Lexington Ave.
Third Ave.
Second Ave.

E. 47th St.
E. 46th St.
E. 45th St.
E. 44th St.
E. 43rd St.
E. 42nd St.
E. 41st St.
E. 40th St.

First Ave.
United Nations

Vanderbilt Ave.
51 Grand Central Terminal
M

Bryant Park
M
New York Public Library

MURRAY HILL

Queens-Midtown Tunnel

FDR Drive

E. 39th St.
E. 38th St.
E. 37th St. Tunnel Exit
E. 36th St.

Tunnel Entrance

E. 35th St.
E. 34th St.
E. 33rd St.
E. 32nd St.
E. 31st St.
E. 30th St.
E. 29th St.
E. 28th St.
E. 27th St.
E. 26th St.
E. 25th St.
E. 24th St.
E. 23rd St.
E. 22nd St.
E. 21st St.
E. 20th St.
E. 19th St.
E. 18th St.
E. 17th St.
E. 16th St.
E. 15th St.
E. 14th St.
E. 13th St.

49 50
M
Empire State Bldg.

Broadway
Fifth Ave.
Madison Ave.
Park Ave. S.
M

48
47
46
Madison Square Park

M M M

41
42 43
44
39
45
FLATIRON DISTRICT

Gramercy Park
GRAMERCY PARK

Peter Cooper Village
40

Asser Levy Pl.

38 37 36
Union Sq. W.
Union Sq. E.
Union Square
M
35
Irving Pl.
N.D. Perlman Pl.
M

Subway stop M

salmon, and sturgeon, accompanied by excellent foie gras and marinated herring. Champagne by the glass ups the tally, but it's the perfect accompaniment. The art deco room may not live up to the promise of the gorgeous beaux arts exterior, but it's impressive nonetheless, and you're bound to be surrounded by big-haired high-society mavens who are a hoot to ogle. Service is aloof but attentive, just as it should be.

Russian Tea Room. 150 W. 57th St. (between Sixth and Seventh aves.). ☎ **212/974-2111.** www.russiantearoom.com. Main courses $13–$24 at lunch, $20–$34 at dinner; 5-course tasting menu $75–$95. AE, CB, DC, DISC, JCB, MC, V. Mon–Fri 11:30am–3pm and 5pm–12:30am, Sat–Sun 10am–12:30am. Subway: B, N, R, Q to 57th St. RUSSIAN.

One of the city's most glamorous restaurants since 1927, the Russian Tea Room has been reborn for the new millennium. The man behind the magic is restaurateur Warner LeRoy of Tavern on the Green (see "The Upper West Side," below). Like Tavern, the new RTR is a mixed bag. LeRoy understands that he's catering to tourists as well as glamour-seeking locals, so understatement didn't figure heavily in his reinvention. The decor can't really be called elegant: The gold is too shiny, the reds too bright. Still, anyone who remembers the garishness of the original will consider this subtle in comparison, and there's no denying the special-occasion appeal. I prefer the old-world first level to the more contemporary second floor, but only the second floor boasts a 37-foot-tall, 20,000-pound glass aquarium shaped like a bear. Wow!

With all this visual stimulation to divert your attention, it almost comes as a surprise that the food is so good. The menu is comprised of traditional Russian dishes, including a decadent tenderloin beef Stroganoff in a mustard cream sauce. The *shashlik Caucasian*—lamb loin skewered, seasoned with Georgian spices (coriander, fenugreek, savory, and the like), and open-flame grilled—is another winning dish. The borscht is a great way to start, but if you're really celebrating, don't miss the caviar show, presented on silver with buckwheat blinis, melted butter, and a flourish. Ask the sommelier to recommend a flight of iced vodkas for you to taste as the perfect accompaniment.

I experienced courteous professional service on my visit, but I've heard complaints to the contrary, and the tourist-targeted prices are too high. Still, I'd choose it over the more touristy Tavern anytime. Definitely a worthwhile dining experience if you're set on experiencing a legend.

San Domenico. 240 Central Park South (btw. Broadway and Seventh Ave.). ☎ **212/ 265-5959.** Reservations required. Jacket requested at dinner. Main courses $18.50–$32.50; pretheater fixed-price $32.50. AE, CB, DC, DISC, JCB, MC, V. Mon–Fri noon–3pm; Mon–Sat 5:30–11pm, Sun 5:30–10:30pm. Subway: N, R to 57th St.; 1, 9 to Columbus Circle. CONTEMPORARY ITALIAN.

Thanks to owner Tony May, San Domenico is one of the few restaurants successful in preserving the best traditions of Italian cooking while adding a modern twist. Inspired by the cuisine of Bologna, San Domenico's menu changes seasonally. Splendid appetizers may include grilled Mediterranean baby octopus with cucumbers and cherry tomatoes, chilled fava bean soup with goat cheese and truffle oil, or a rich mix of lobster, shrimp, king crab, and baby vegetables. Favorite pasta choices: ricotta ravioli with marinated tomatoes and black olives, and the extravagant handmade pasta with chives, caviar, and asparagus. For meat lovers, there's a roasted veal loin with braised radicchio, pearl onions, and creamy bacon sauce. Black sea bass fillet in tomato-herb broth and grilled Norwegian salmon with caviar and sour cream are among the excellent fish offerings. The room is swanky, the service impeccable, and the wine list reads like a grade-A list of Italian vineyards. Wonderful in every way.

MODERATE

In addition to the choices below, there's also the impressive Times Square branch of **Ruby Foo's** (p. 194), 1626 Broadway, at 49th St. (☎ **212/489-5600**), which serves the same creative dim sum and sushi fare as the original Upper West Side location in an even more fanciful space.

☉ The Cafe at Aquavit. 13 W. 54th St. (btw. Fifth and Sixth aves.). ☎ **212/307-7311.** www.aquavit.org. Reservations recommended. Main courses $9–$19; 3-course fixed-price $20 at lunch, $29 at dinner (multicourse menus $48–$75 in main dining room; 3-course pretheater fixed-price $39). AE, DC, JCB, MC, V. Mon–Fri noon–2:30pm, Sun noon–3pm; Mon–Sat 5:30–10:30pm. Subway: E, F to Fifth Ave./53rd St. SCANDINAVIAN.

When Aquavit opened its doors, it opened the eyes of New Yorkers to what fine Scandinavian food could be: Its delicate elegance is reminiscent of Japanese refinement. The main dining room space is soaring and sleek, with birch trees and an indoor waterfall, but I prefer to dine in the more casual upstairs cafe, another sophisticated Scandinavian modern space that also happens to be one of New York's best dining bargains. There's always a good-value fixed-price meal available, but my favorite selections are well-prepared Scandinavian standards from the à la carte cafe menu: the smorgasbord plate, an assortment of delicacies including smoky herring and zesty hot-mustard glazed salmon (which also comes as a full-size entree); and Swedish meatballs, a perfect realization of this traditional dish, accompanied by mashed potatoes and lingonberries (beats IKEA by a mile!). The Arctic char, served with cabbage salad, turkey bacon, and red wine sauce, is another good choice. To help you get Scandinavian sleek, the bar offers a wide selection of aquavits, distilled liquors not unlike vodka flavored with fruit and spices and served Arctic cold, which have a smooth finish and are best accompanied by a full-bodied European brew like Carlsberg.

Carmine's. 200 W. 44th St. (btw. Broadway and Eighth Ave.). ☎ **212/221-3800.** Reservations recommended before 6pm; accepted for 6 or more after 6pm. Family-style main courses $15–$47. AE, DC, MC, V. Tues–Sat 11:30am–midnight, Sun–Mon 11:30am–11pm. Subway: N, R, S, 1, 2, 3, 7, 9 to 42nd St./Times Sq. SOUTHERN ITALIAN FAMILY STYLE.

Everything is done B-I-G at this rollicking, family-style Times Square mainstay. The dining room is vast enough to deserve a map, massive platters of pasta hold Brady Bunch–size portions, and large groups wait to join in the rambunctious atmosphere at this sibling of the original Upper West Sider. This is a value-priced restaurant where the bang for your buck increases for every person you add to your party—but so does the wait, so come early or late to avoid the crowds. Caesar salad and a mound of fried calamari are a perfect beginning, followed by heaping portions of pasta topped with red or white clam sauce, mixed seafood, zesty marinara, and meatballs. The meat entrees include veal parmigiana, broiled porterhouse steak, chicken marsala, and shrimp scampi. The tiramisù is pie-size, thick and creamy, bathed in Kahlúa and marsala. Order half of what you think you'll need.

The original Carmine's at 2450 Broadway, between 90th and 91st streets (☎ **212/ 362-2200**), is the same—but even B-I-G-G-E-R.

☉ Churrascaria Plataforma. 316 W. 49th St. (btw. Eighth and Ninth aves.). ☎ **212/ 245-0505.** www.churrascariaplataforma.com. Reservations recommended. All-you-can-eat fixed-price $28 at lunch, $35 at dinner; half price for children 4–10. AE, DC, DISC, MC, V. Daily noon–midnight. Subway: C, E to 50th St. BRAZILIAN.

It's a carnival for carnivores at this colorful, upscale, all-you-can-eat Brazilian rotisserie. A large selection of teasers like octopus stew, paella, and carpaccio at the phenomenal salad bar may tempt you to fill up too quickly, but hold out for the never-ending parade of meat. Roving servers deliver beef (too many cuts to mention), ham, chicken (the chicken hearts are great, trust me), lamb, and sausage—more than 15 delectable varieties—and traditional sides like fried yucca, plantains, and rice until you cannot eat another bite. The food is excellent, the service friendly and generous, and the cavernous room loud—this is not the place for romance. Instead, it's a fun, festive family affair. The ideal accompaniment is a pitcher of Brazil's signature cocktail, called a *caipirinha:* a margaritalike blend of limes, sugar, crushed ice, and raw sugarcane liquor; those in the know call Plataforma's the best in town.

✪ **Joe Allen.** 326 W. 46th St. (btw. Eighth and Ninth aves.). ☎ **212/581-6464.** Reservations recommended (a must for pretheater dining). Main courses $9–$21 (most less than $17). MC, V. Sun–Tues and Thurs–Fri noon–midnight, Wed and Sat 11:30am–midnight. Subway: A, C, E to 42nd St./Port Authority. AMERICAN PUB.

This upscale Restaurant Row pub is a glorious throwback to the old days of Broadway, when theater types went to places like Sardi's and Lüchow's—and yep, Joe Allen—to toss back a few after the curtain went down. The good news is that Joe Allen is still going strong; in fact, don't be surprised if you spot a stage star or two among the clientele. The uncomplicated American pub food is reliable and well priced, and served at big, comfortable tables (the kind that restaurant managers don't order anymore because they take up too much real estate) covered with red-checked cloths. The meat loaf, in particular, is terrific, but you can't go wrong with the chili, the decent Greek salad, the great burgers, or anything that comes with mashed potatoes. More than 30 beers are available, and some good wines by the glass. You'll thoroughly enjoy perusing the walls covered with posters and other memorabilia from legendary Broadway flops.

Julian's. 802 Ninth Ave. (btw. 53rd and 54th sts.). ☎ **212/262-4800.** Reservations recommended. Main courses $8–$14 at lunch, $15–$24 at dinner; 3-course fixed-price $22–$27 at lunch, $45–$55 at dinner. AE, DC, DISC, MC, V. Tues–Fri noon–midnight, Sat–Mon 11:30am–11pm. Subway: C, E to 50th St. MEDITERRANEAN.

This charming bistro is one of the best-kept secrets on Ninth Avenue's burgeoning restaurant strip. Julian's serves up consistently good midpriced Mediterranean fare in an attractive setting that includes a lovely enclosed garden and alfresco sidewalk seating. I've easily dined here a half-dozen times or more, and the meal has always been pleasing. Seating is comfortable, the brick-walled room is low-lit and never too noisy, the Tuscan tableware is handsome, the service attentive, and the bread addictively crusty. The menu is extensive, always featuring no fewer than 10 pastas and easily another dozen or so meat and fish entrees. You can't go wrong with the roasted rack of lamb with charcoal-grilled asparagus, or the balsamic-glazed roast chicken with lightly sautéed broccoli rabe and garlic mashies. The wine list is affordably priced, and the tiramisù everything it should be. The crowd tends to be more locals than tourists, since most visitors don't make it this far west. A very good bet for a Theater District dinner.

Metro Grill. In the Hotel Metro, 45 W. 35th St. (btw. Fifth and Sixth aves.). ☎ **212/279-3535.** Reservations recommended. Main courses $6–$13 at breakfast, $12–$24 at lunch and dinner (most $18 or less). AE, DC, MC, V. Mon–Fri noon–10pm, Sat–Sun 5–10pm. Subway: B, D, F, Q, N, R to 34th St. CONTEMPORARY AMERICAN.

This stylish restaurant is a Midtown sleeper, serving top-notch, moderately priced contemporary cuisine in a beautifully designed series of colorful, comfortable dining rooms. Fashionable but casual, Metro Grill specializes in uncomplicated Mediterranean-accented fare. The menu changes with the seasons, but expect to find a selection of pizzettes, on grilled semolina flatbread, well-prepared pastas, and a full selection of not-too-fussy entrees. Don't miss the rotisserie chicken, which is always crispy on the outside, juicy on the inside. On my last visit, I thoroughly enjoyed the acorn cornucopia, an acorn squash filled with autumn veggies and porcini mushroom couscous, drizzled with porcini cream. The Atlantic salmon—broiled on the outside, sashimi on the inside—with wasabi dumplings was another winner, as was the Metro burger, a blend of ground beef and lamb accompanied by sweet onions and rosemary fries. If you're two, try to snag one of the deuces in the middle room, which boast wonderfully cushy corner chairs.

✪ **Molyvos.** 871 Seventh Ave. (btw. 55th and 56th sts.). ☎ **212/582-7500.** Reservations recommended. Main courses $12.50–$20 at lunch, $18.50–$24.50 at dinner; fixed-price lunch $22.50; 3-course fixed-price dinner $34.50 (Mon–Fri only). AE, CB, DC, DISC, MC, V. Mon–Thurs noon–3pm and 5:30–11:30pm, Fri–Sat noon–3pm and 5pm–midnight, Sun noon–11pm. Subway: N, R to 57th St.; B, D, E to Seventh Ave. GREEK.

This terrific Greek restaurant is like a cozy upscale taverna. Ruth Reichl of the *New York Times* was so thrilled with its high quality and authenticity that she awarded Molyvos three stars (out of a possible four) a couple of years ago, and I concur wholeheartedly. The menu boasts beautifully prepared favorites—including superb taramasalata, tzatziki, and other traditional spreads—plus a few dishes with contemporary twists. The Greek country salad is generously portioned and as fresh as can be, while the baby octopus starter is grilled over fruit wood to tender, charred perfection. Among the main courses, the lemon- and garlic-seasoned roasted free-range chicken is right on the mark: juicy, tender, and dressed with oven-dried tomatoes, olives, and rustic potatoes. More traditional tastes can opt for excellent moussaka; rosemary-skewered souvlaki; or the day's catch, wood-grilled whole with lemon, oregano, and olive oil in traditional Greek style. Baklava fans shouldn't miss the restaurant's moist, nutty version, which is big enough to share. The room is spacious and comfortable, with a warm Mediterranean appeal that doesn't go overboard on the Hellenic themes, and service that's attentive without being intrusive. The sommelier will be happy to help you choose from the surprisingly good list of Greek wines, making Molyvos a winner on all counts.

Virgil's Real BBQ. 152 W. 44th St. (btw. Sixth and Seventh aves.). ☎ **212/921-9494.** Reservations recommended. Main courses and barbecue platters $6–$25. AE, DC, MC, V. Sun–Mon 11am–11pm, Tues–Sat 11:30am–midnight. Subway: N, R, 1, 2, 3, 7, 9 to 42nd St./Times Sq. BARBECUE/SOUTHERN.

Virgil's may look like a comfy theme-park version of a down-home barbecue joint, but this place takes its barbecue seriously. The meat is house-smoked with a blend of hickory, oak, and fruitwood chips, and most every regional school is represented, from Carolina pulled pork to Texas beef brisket to Memphis ribs. You may not consider this contest-winning chow if you're from barbecue country, but we less-savvy Yankees are thrilled to have Virgil's in the 'hood. I love to start with the barbecued shrimp, accompanied by yummy mustard slaw, and a plate of buttermilk onion rings with blue cheese for dipping. The ribs are lip-smackin' good, but the chicken is moist and tender—go for a combo if you just can't choose. Burgers, sandwiches, and other entrees (chicken-fried steak, anyone?) are also available if you can't face up to all that meat 'n' sauce. And cast that cornbread aside for a full order of buttermilk biscuits, which come with maple butter so good it's like dessert. So hunker down, pig out, and don't worry about making a mess; when you're through eating, you get a hot towel for washing up. The bar offers a huge selection of on-tap and bottled brews.

Woo Chon. 8–10 W. 36th St. (just west of Fifth Ave.). ☎ **212/695-0676.** www.woochon.com. Reservations recommended. Main courses $10–$25. AE, DC, JCB, MC, V. Daily 24 hours. Subway: B, D, F, Q, N, R to 34th St./Herald Sq. KOREAN BARBECUE.

Theme Restaurant Thrills!

The theme-restaurant biz may be on the wane, but the World Wrestling Federation is always happy to buck a trend. Their brand-new **WWF New York** is drawing massive crowds of rabid wrestling fans to 1501 Broadway, at 43rd Street (☎ **212/398-2563**). Don't expect WWF stars to be in residence, but you'll find plenty of memorabilia, high-tech (and low-brow) interactive video exhibits, and perfectly acceptable burger-and-ribs fare—not to mention the WWF's signature raucous atmosphere. There's also a temporary tattoo parlor and plenty to spend your loot on at the WWF store.

Also new on the scene is ✪ **ESPN Zone,** 1472 Broadway, at 42nd Street (☎ 212/921-3776). The mammoth 42,000-square-foot space houses the Studio Grill, with nonstop ESPN programming; the Screening Room, with two giant screens surrounded by a dozen 36-inchers, customized audio and video touch screens, and reclining leather chairs with built-in speakers (the perfect place to watch the game); the Sports Arena, a full floor of sports-related arcade games; set replicas from ESPN's hit shows (including *Sportscenter* and *NBA 2night*); and much more. A sports fan's dream come true.

Always the perennial favorite, New York's ✪ **Hard Rock Cafe,** 221 W. 57th St., between Broadway and Seventh Avenue (☎ **212/459-9320**), is actually one of the originals of the chain, and a terrific realization of the concept. The memorabilia collection is terrific, with lots of great Lennon collectibles. The menu boasts all the Hard Rock standards, including a surprisingly good burger and fajitas, and the comfortable bar mixes up great cocktails.

Harley-Davidson Cafe, 1370 Sixth Ave., at 56th Street (☎ **212/245-6000**), brings out the Hell's Angel in all of us. The just-fine munchies do the trick, and memorabilia documents 90 years of Hog history.

Brooklyn Diner USA, 212 W. 57th St., Broadway and Seventh Avenue (☎ **212/581-8900**), looks like an old-fashioned diner on the outside, but inside you'll find linen tablecloths and mahogany accents instead of coffee-stained Formica tabletops. The food includes better-than-you'd-expect crab cakes, tenderloin steak, and Valrhona chocolate fudge sundaes. To justify the name, there's a 15-bite Brooklyn hot dog and an Avenue U roast beef sandwich.

This round-the-clock authentic Korean barbecue is a good bet for first-timers and purists alike. The menu is massive, but barbecue is the way to go. All the cuts of meat are high-quality, and the jumbo short ribs are better than dessert. This is an interactive meal; you'll cook everything to your taste right at your table's built-in grill. The friendly staff may not speak the best English, but no matter—they're happy to walk novices through all of the steps. A complete barbecue dinner comes with no fewer than 10 sides, including kimchee that puts the Japanese version to shame. It's a feast that's particularly fun with a crowd, but two diners will be well contented, too. Be sure to order up some brews because this deliciously piquant cuisine can really set your taste buds ablaze.

INEXPENSIVE

A branch of **Joe's Shanghai** (p. 148) is at 24 W. 56th St., just west of Fifth Avenue (☎ 212/333-3868), for straight-from-Chinatown soup dumplings and other

The subterranean red planet–themed **Mars 2112,** 1633 Broadway, at 51st Street (☎ **212/582-2112**), is a hoot, from the simulated red-rock rooms to the Martian-costumed wait staff to the silly "Man Eats on Mars!" newspaper-style menu. The eclectic food is better than you might expect, but skip the Star Tours–style simulated spacecraft ride at the entrance if you don't want to lose your appetite before you get to your table. The kids won't mind, though—they'll love it, along with the extensive video arcade.

Something to scare you with, my dear? You'll enter the **Jekyll & Hyde Club,** 1409 Sixth Ave., between 57th and 58th streets (☎ 212/541-9505), through a small, dark room with a sinking ceiling, where a corpse warns you of the oddities to come. There are five floors—grand salon, library, laboratory, mausoleum, observatory—of bizarre artifacts, wall hangings that come to life, and other interactive bone chillers. Kids love it. There's a second, more publike location at 91 Seventh Ave. South, between West 4th and Barrow streets, in Greenwich Village (☎ **212/989-7701**).

At the **Official All-Star Cafe,** 1540 Broadway, at 45th Street (☎ **212/ 840-8326**), center court has a full-size scoreboard, booths shaped like baseball mitts crowd the sidelines, and video monitors guarantee that the great plays in sports history live forever. The food is straight from the ballpark—hot dogs, St. Louis ribs, Philly cheesesteak sandwiches. The All-Star is now facing tough competition from the impressive ESPN Zone, however, and rumors are that Planet Hollywood may move from its 57th Street perch to this space sometime in 2000. Call ahead to avoid disappointment.

The celebrity orbit has dimmed a bit since Ah-nuld left the fold and plans for a Times Square hotel went bust in early 2000, but, at press time, **Planet Hollywood** was still going strong at 140 W. 57th St., between Sixth and Seventh avenues (☎ **212/333-7827**). Frankly, the movie memorabilia doesn't hold the same excitement as the genuine rock-and-roll goods over at the Hard Rock (didn't I see the R2D2 and C3PO robots at three *other* PHs?), but it's still plenty of fun for Hollywood buffs nonetheless. A move to Times Square may be in the offing, so call before you go.

Shanghai fare. There's also cafeteria-style **Mangia** (p. 142) at 50 W. 57th St., between Fifth and Sixth avenues (☎ 212/582-5882).

If you're looking for the quintessential New York Jewish deli, you have your choice between the **Stage Deli,** 834 Seventh Ave., between 53rd and 54th streets (☎ **212/ 245-7850;** www.stagedeli.com), known for its jaw-distending celebrity sandwiches; and the **Carnegie Deli,** 854 Seventh Ave., at 55th Street (☎ **212/757-2245;** www.carnegiedeli.com), for the best pastrami, corned beef, and cheesecake in town. For more, see "The New York Deli News" box earlier in this chapter.

✪ **Island Burgers & Shakes.** 766 Ninth Ave. (btw. 51st and 52nd sts.). ☎ **212/307-7934.** www.island.citysearch.com. Reservations not accepted. Sandwiches and salads $5.25–$9. No credit cards. Sat–Thurs noon–10:30pm, Fri noon–11pm. Subway: C, E to 50th St. GOURMET BURGERS/SANDWICHES.

This excellent aisle-size diner glows with the wild colors of a California surf shop. A small selection of sandwiches and salads are on hand, but as the name implies, folks come here for the Goliath-size burgers—either beef hamburgers or, the specialty of the house, *churascos* (flattened grilled chicken breasts). Innovation strikes with the more than 40 topping combinations: Choose anything from the horseradish, sour cream, and black-pepper burger to the Hobie's (with black-pepper sauce, blue cheese, onion, and bacon). Choose your own bread from a wide selection, ranging from soft sour-dough to crusty ciabatta. Though Island Burgers serves fries now, you're meant to eat these fellows with their tasty dirty potato chips. Terrifically thick shakes and cookies are also available to satisfy your sweet tooth.

✪ John's Pizzeria. 260 W. 44th St. (btw. Broadway and Eighth Ave.). ☎ **212/391-7560.** Reservations accepted for 10 or more. Pizzas $10–$13.50 (plus toppings); pastas $6.50–$11. AE, MC, V. Daily 11:30am–11:30pm. Subway: A, C, E to 42nd St./Port Authority; N, R, S, 1, 2, 3, 7, 9 to 42nd St./Times Sq. PIZZA.

Thin-crusted, properly sauced, and fresh, the pizza at John's has long been one of New York's best—some even consider these *the* best pies New York has to offer. Housed in the century-old Gospel Tabernacle Church, the split-level dining room is vast and pretty, featuring a gorgeous stained-glass ceiling and chefs working at classic brick ovens right in the room. More important, it's big enough to hold pretheater crowds, so the wait's never too long despite the place's popularity. Unlike most pizzerias, at John's you order a whole made-to-order pie rather than by the slice, so come with friends or family. There's also a good selection of traditional pastas to choose from, such as baked ziti and well-stuffed calzones.

This Theater District location is my favorite, but the original Bleecker Street location, at 278 Bleecker St., between Sixth and Seventh avenues (☎ 212/243-1680), is loaded with old-world atmosphere. The location near Lincoln Center, 48 W. 65th St., between Broadway and Central Park West (☎ 212/721-7001), is also worth checking out.

La Bonne Soupe. 48 W. 55th St. (btw. Fifth and Sixth aves.). ☎ **212/586-7650.** www.labonnesoupe.com. Reservations recommended for parties of 3 or more. Main courses $9–$20 (most less than $15); "les bonnes soupes" fixed-price $14; 3-course fixed-price $20 at lunch and dinner. AE, DC, MC, V. Mon–Sat 11:30am–midnight, Sun 11:30am–11pm. Subway: E, F to Fifth Ave.; B, Q to 57th St. FRENCH BISTRO.

This little slice of Paris has been around forever; I remember discovering the magic of fondue here on a high school French Club field trip that took place more years ago than I care to think about. For gourmet at good prices, it's still hard to beat this authentic bistro, where you'll even see French natives seated elbow-to-elbow in the newly renovated dining room. "Les bonnes soupes" are satisfying noontime meals of salad, bread, a big bowl of soup (mushroom and barley with lamb is a favorite), dessert (chocolate mousse, crème caramel, or ice cream), and wine or coffee—a great bargain at just $14. The menu also features entree-size salads (including a good niçoise), high-quality steak burgers, and traditional bistro fare like omelets, quiche Lorraine, croque monsieur, and fancier fare like steak frites and filet mignon au poivre. Rounding out the menu are those very French fondues: emmethal cheese, beef, and yummy, creamy chocolate to finish off the meal in perfect style. Bon appétit!

Manhattan Chili Co. 1500 Broadway (entrance on 43rd St.). ☎ **212/730-8666.** www.manhattanchili.com. Reservations accepted. Main courses $8–$15. AE, DISC, MC, V. Sun–Mon 11:30am–11pm, Tues–Sat 11:30am–midnight. Subway: N, R, S, 1, 2, 3, 7, 9 to 42nd St./Times Sq. AMERICAN SOUTHWESTERN.

This fun, cartoonish Theater District restaurant is a great choice if you have the kids in tow. The big, hearty chili bowls are geared to young palates, which tend to be suspicious of anything unfamiliar. The extensive list of chili choices is clearly marked by spice level, from the traditional Abilene with ground beef, tomatoes, basil, and red wine (mild enough for tenderfeet), to the Texas Chain Gang, which adds jalapeños to the mix for those who prefer hot. In addition, expect familiar favorites like nachos, chicken wings, big salads, and generous burritos and burgers. It's really hard to go wrong here—even vegetarians have lots to choose from.

A second location is next to Dave Letterman's Ed Sullivan Theatre at 1697 Broadway, between 53rd and 54th streets (☎ 212/246-6555), where the expanded menu includes seafood and there's live music, ranging from salsa to reggae to jazz, after 10pm.

Pietrasanta. 683 Ninth Ave. (at 47th St.). ☎ **212/265-9471.** Reservations recommended. Main courses $8–$19. AE, MC, V. Sun–Mon noon–10:30pm, Tues and Thurs noon–11pm, Wed 11am–11pm, Fri noon–midnight, Sat 11:30am–midnight. Subway: C, E to 50th St. TUSCAN ITALIAN.

This charming trattoria is an excellent choice for an affordable pretheater meal. The well-priced pastas are far superior to what you'll get for the same money—or even more—at countless other pasta houses around town. The chef has a deft hand and a fondness for bold flavors, so the dishes are at once refined and appealingly robust. Look for such winning starters as grilled calamari seasoned with fresh basil, white wine, and the perfect squirt of lemon juice; asparagus spears wrapped in imported prosciutto and dressed in a divine lemon-butter sauce; and *fagioli con pancetta,* an unassuming white-bean dish that springs to life with the first bite thanks to flavorful pancetta, rosemary, and lemon. Pasta mains worth seeking out include *agnolotti d'agnello,* hand-formed half-moon pasta filled with hearty lamb in a rosemary, basil, and red wine sauce; and *trenette con calamari,* a simple but gorgeous tricolored dish of black squid-ink pasta, white calamari rings, and roasted red peppers. The kitchen also has an excellent reputation for its time-honored fish, chicken, veal, and pasta preparations. A new waiter made the service a bit awkward on my last visit, but the staff is efficient and well known for keeping an eye on curtain time.

Siam Inn Too. 854 Eighth Ave. (btw. 51st and 52nd sts.). ☎ **212/757-4006.** Reservations accepted. Main courses $7–$16. AE, DC, MC, V. Mon–Fri noon–11:30pm, Sat 4–11:30pm, Sun 4–11pm. Subway: C, E to 50th St. THAI.

Situated on an unremarkable stretch of Eighth Avenue, Siam Inn is an attractive outpost of very good Thai food. All of your Thai favorites are here, well prepared and served by a brightly attired and courteous wait staff. Tom kah gai soup (with chicken, mushrooms, and coconut milk), chicken satay with yummy peanut sauce, and light, flaky curry puffs all make good starters. Among noteworthy entrees are the masaman and red curries (the former rich and peanuty, the latter quite spicy), spicy sautéed squid with fresh basil and chiles, and perfect pad thai. And unlike many of the drab restaurants in this neighborhood, the decor is pretty and pleasing—black deco tables and chairs, cushy rugs underfoot, and soft lighting.

12 Midtown East & Murray Hill

VERY EXPENSIVE

✪ **La Grenouille.** 3 E. 52nd St. (just east of Fifth Ave.). ☎ **212/752-1495.** Reservations required. Jacket and tie required. 3-course fixed-price $45 at lunch, $90 at dinner. AE, CB, DC, MC, V. Tues–Sat noon–2:15pm and 5:30–11pm. CLASSIC FRENCH.

What a gem! They don't get more old school than this jewel of a restaurant, which has been serving New Yorkers in classic French style since 1962. Formerly the domain of the blue-hair-and-blue-blazer set, La Grenouille is now being discovered by a younger crowd. It's quite a find—so utterly retro that it feels like a breath of fresh air. This is a place that's really worth getting dressed up for.

La Grenouille may be classic, but it doesn't feel the least bit stuffy. You'll know it the instant you walk into the elegant dining room, with its gold silk walls, red velvet banquettes, lavish floral arrangements, and tuxedoed waiters. The wait staff is one of the warmest and most attentive in the city, second only to Chanterelle's—and it's a very close second. There's a rare confidence here, in both the food and the service, that sets a tone of comfort and ease.

Nothing comes out of the kitchen that isn't flawlessly prepared and presented. The foie gras is sautéed to perfection and boasts a delicate hint of vanilla; the black truffle–marinated sea scallops roasted in lobster butter are another winningly decadent starter. The spice-rubbed duckling breast with braised salsify was the best duck I've ever had, while the port-glazed veal sweetbreads were fork-tender, not crispy, and beautifully accompanied by a chestnut and walnut cocotte. Order what strikes your fancy—you can't go wrong with any dish here. The wine list is pricey but excellent; your waiter will be happy to point you to the best values. Save room for the soufflé, the ultimate realization of this classic dessert. Simply marvelous!

✪ Le Cirque 2000. In the Villard Houses (next to the New York Palace hotel), 455 Madison Ave. (at 50th St.). ☎ 212/303-7788. www.lecirque.com. Reservations required well in advance. Jacket and tie required. Main courses $28–$39; 3-course fixed-price lunch $42 ($25 in lounge); 5-course fixed-price dinner $90. AE, CB, DC, MC, V. Mon–Sat 11:45am–2:15pm and 5:30–11pm, Sun 5:30–10:30pm. Subway: E, F to Fifth Ave.; 6 to 51st St. FRENCH.

Fine dining goes the way of the big top at Le Cirque 2000, and it's a hit. Iconic restaurateur Sirio Maccioni made a bold move when he relocated his legendary Le Cirque a few years back, but it turned out to be a master stroke. Designer Adam Tihany festooned the gilded-age mansion's almost rococo interiors with jewel-toned circus colors, bright lights, touches of neon, and furniture with such outrageous lines that it looks like Tex Avery drew it for a Bugs Bunny cartoon. And guess what? It works. The fanciful setting is perfect for a magical night on the town. But that's where the reinvention ends—Executive Chef Sottha Khunn's haute French menu is classic Le Cirque. The food is excellently prepared if not innovative: lobster roasted with young artichokes and wild mushrooms; paupiette of black sea bass in crispy potatoes with braised leeks; Black Angus tenderloin in red wine sauce; and roasted rack of lamb. The starters are almost as pricey as the entrees, but we were won over by the flawlessly sautéed foie gras, and seared sea scallops with wild mushrooms and mesclun in a delicate Parmesan basket. The crème brûlée is a perfect realization of the classic dessert, but go with one of the chocolate choices for a suitably decadent finish. The wine list is remarkably well priced, relatively speaking; it seems that Maccioni has thus far avoided the current overcharging trend. There's spectacular courtyard dining in season.

EXPENSIVE

An American Place. 565 Lexington Ave. (at 50th St.). ☎ 212/888-5650. Reservations highly recommended. Main courses $19–$32 at lunch, $26–$36 at dinner. AE, DC, DISC, MC, V. Daily 11:45am–2:30pm and 5–10:30pm. Subway: E, F to Lexington Ave.; 6 to 51st St. CREATIVE AMERICAN REGIONAL.

Other chefs may say that they specialize in creative American cooking, but celebrity Chef Larry Forgione puts his money where his mouth is. This is true American cooking, showing off the best of what the USA has to offer: Maine Belon oysters, Shenandoah Valley lamb, native Buffalo carpaccio, Abermarle fish stew, Hudson Valley foie gras. Forgione is an exceptional talent who excels at creative New American comfort food. This is robust fare served in Hungry Man–sized portions, as it should be. The flavors are bold and well balanced, and the preparations pleasing from start to finish. The Atlantic salmon is roasted as tradition calls, on a fragrant cedar plank, and matched with a smooth and delicious soft corn pudding. The Northeast hot pot is a fisherman's bounty of seafood, simmered with sweet corn in a rich lobster-tomato broth. The aforementioned lamb is pot roasted and served au jus, accompanied by crispy mustard dumplings. The room is handsomely contemporary, with bright colors, deco touches, well-spaced tables, and comfortable seating. Service is warm and without pretensions. In keeping with the all-American theme, there's a winning selection of California wines. The dessert menu features luscious renditions of traditional favorites, including a to-die-for devil's food layer cake (a true slice of Americana, if there ever was one) and double-chocolate pudding complemented with Schrafft's sugar cookies.

✪ **March.** 405 E. 58th St. (btw. First Ave. and Sutton Place). ☎ **212/754-6272.** Reservations required. Jacket and tie requested. 4-course menus $68, $93 with wines; 7-course tasting menu $90, $125 with wines. AE, CB, DC, DISC, JCB, MC, V. Daily 6–11pm. Subway: N, R to Lexington Ave.; 4, 5, 6 to 59th St. CONTEMPORARY AMERICAN.

Here's romantic Manhattan dining as it was meant to be. From start to finish, co-owner/host Joseph Scalice and partner/Chef Wayne Nish do things right. The restaurant is in a beautifully restored town house whose intimate rooms create a perfect setting for Nish's marvelously orchestrated meals. The sophisticated crowd may be nattily dressed, but this isn't a see-and-be-seen kind of place—it's all about the experience, and, for lovers, each other.

March skips the usual appetizers-entrees setup for a new approach: a four-course fixed-price meal that lets you partner smaller portions from vegetarian, seafood, poultry, and meat selections as you wish. Or you can follow four- or seven-course tasting options, in which you follow one of the prescribed menus created by Nish, paired with wines chosen by Wine Director Scalice for best effect. This multicourse approach is terrific because it allows you to fully experience Nish's elegant, excellent cuisine, and adds a beyond-the-ordinary flair that's often missing in special-occasion dining. The menu changes regularly, but expect a host of inventive New American dishes with delicate Pan-Asian, even global, touches: Lobster carpaccio is beautifully married with three roes (Osetra, Mentaiko, and Uni); a confit of duck foie gras gets a savory subcontinental twist from Indian spices, crisped black figs, and persimmon chutney; hot smoked salmon goes transcontinental with German sauerkraut, Irish bacon, and juniper berries. The choices are extensive, so feel free to put yourself in the hands of the first-rate wait staff. A wonderful, special experience. There's now romantic rooftop dining in warm weather.

Michael Jordan's–The Steak House. In Grand Central Terminal (mezzanine level), 23 Vanderbilt Ave. (at 42nd St.). ☎ **212/655-2300.** Reservations recommended. Main courses $17–$33; porterhouse for 2 $62. AE, DC, MC, V. Mon–Sat noon–3pm and 5–11pm, Sun 1–10pm. Subway: S, 4, 5, 6, 7 to 42nd St./Grand Central. STEAKS.

The name may belong to one of sports' greatest heroes, but don't expect an overpriced burger factory with waiters in Bulls jerseys and basketball-shaped plates. Michael Jordan's new restaurant, an elegant steak house and richly appointed cigar lounge, is wholly for grown-ups. This gorgeous art deco space makes a great place to dine thanks to its magnificent location, on the open mezzanine level overlooking the main concourse of newly restored Grand Central Terminal. With a perfect view of the legendary sky ceiling, this is more than just the city's best-looking steak house—it's an incredible only-in-New York dining experience.

And the food? Pure steak-house fare: New York steaks, thick-cut filet mignons, tender rib eyes, and well-marbled sirloins, all prime aged cuts. The star of the show is the porterhouse for two, a whopping 44 ounces of top-quality cow, served suitably charred and salty on the outside. Other choices include buffalo sirloin for two, a pleasing lean cut as long as it's ordered on the rare side, and excellent braised short ribs. We didn't have a problem, but word is that on occasion a steak isn't cooked to order, so don't be shy about sending yours back for another turn on the grill. Skip the more adventuresome starters and sides, such as the disappointing lobster salad, and stick with steakhouse classics like the perfectly creamed spinach, creamy mac and cheese (Mama J's recipe), light-as-air fried onions, and the terrific crimini mushrooms in truffle oil. The wine list is overseen by a helpful sommelier, and service is similarly attentive.

Mr. Chow. 324 E. 57th St. (btw. First and Second aves.). ☎ **212/751-9030.** Reservations recommended. Main courses $24–$35. AE, MC, V. Daily 6–11:45pm. Subway: 4, 5, 6 to 59th St. HAUTE CHINESE.

Mr. Chow may be more than 2 decades old now, but it's hotter than ever. It's a favorite among the celebrity set: Rap star/deejay Ed Lover and his crew were in residence the night we were there, and Jennifer Lopez, rapper Jay-Z, Def Jam chief Russell Simmons, and every Bad Boy Entertainment exec on Puff Daddy's payroll reportedly make regular appearances. But even if you don't spot a famous name, the high-fashion crowd will keep you gloriously entertained—I promise. Michael Chow has been a restaurateur par excellence for three decades now, and his personal style makes this deco dining room extra appealing: This is the kind of place where everyone is treated like a king. I like this egalitarian approach, which says your money is just as good as Puffy's.

The food may not be the best haute Chinese in town, but it's close—and the quality of the dining experience makes Mr. Chow well worth the money. You can have a menu if you insist, but the practice is to let your doting, tuxedoed waiter order for you; just tell him what you like and dislike, and he'll build a suitably harmonious meal. The well-prepared cuisine is more uptown than Chinatown, so this isn't much of a risk. We loved the lightly spicy green prawns, marinated in basil and other herbs; the generously portioned lobster in ginger sauce; and the tandoori-red chicken satay dressed with a sweet butter–peanut sauce that's a pleasing twist on tradition. It's usually pretty easy to get a table if you call ahead—just show up with your sense of humor and you'll have a great time.

Vong. 200 E. 54th St. (at Third Ave.). ☎ **212/486-9592.** www.jean-georges.com. Reservations recommended. Jacket and tie requested. Main courses $20–$36; fixed-price lunch $28; pretheater fixed-price $38; tasting menu $68. AE, DC, MC, V. Mon–Fri noon–2:30pm; Mon–Thurs 6–11pm, Fri–Sat 5:30–11:30pm, Sun 5:30–10pm. Subway: E, F to Lexington/Third aves. and 53rd St.; 6 to 51st St. ASIAN FUSION.

Star Chef Jean-Georges Vongerichten was one of the first to set New York abuzz with imaginative Asian fusion cuisine in the early '90s, and his Vong is still going strong. His brand is a vibrant marriage of Thai spices with French cooking techniques, served up in a room that's as witty and appealing as the exotic cuisine. A Southeast Asian feel is created by salmon and burnt-orange tones, teak wall treatments and bamboo touches throughout, and a pagoda dominating the dining room. This is a proven restaurant used to serving a polished crowd, and the confidence shows in all aspects of preparation, presentation, and service. You really can't go wrong here, whether you opt for the steamed red snapper with mango chutney, cabbage, and watercress; chicken roasted with lemongrass, simply but beautifully paired with sweet rice in a banana leaf;

or crisp squab nesting on an egg noodle pancake with honey-ginger-glazed pearl onions. Don't miss the exotic desserts, such as salad of banana and passion fruit with white-pepper ice cream. The tasting menu presents you with a brilliant cross-section of the menu, while the fixed-price meals are a smokin' deal.

MODERATE

Al Bustan. 827 Third Ave. (btw. 50th and 51st sts.). ☎ **212/759-5933.** www.albustannyc. com. Reservations recommended for dinner. Main courses $14.75–$24.75; 2-course fixed-price lunch $20. AE, CB, DC, DISC, MC, V. Daily noon–3pm and 5:30–10pm. Subway: E, F to Lexington Ave.; 6 to 51st St. LEBANESE.

This pleasing restaurant serves first-rate Middle Eastern cuisine in a simple but pleasing room with a relaxing vibe. It's the ideal place to sit back and indulge in a meze spread. This is where the kitchen excels, and what makes dining at Al Bustan fun. *Time Out New York* calls this the best Middle Eastern fare in the city, and who am I to argue? The creamy hummus benefits from the perfect squirt of lemon; the tart tabbouleh is an ideal blend of parsley, tomato, onion, and cracked wheat; and the lamb kafta is flawlessly grilled and topped with a garlicky yogurt sauce. Food is a tad slow coming out of the kitchen at times, but service is professional and attentive. My only complaint is the lack of a dedicated lunch menu; prices are a bit high for midday, and you can get more for the same money elsewhere. I suggest coming at dinnertime to enjoy the mood and get full value for your dollar.

○ **Oyster Bar & Restaurant.** In Grand Central Terminal (lower level), 23 Vanderbilt Ave. (at 42nd St.). ☎ **212/490-6650.** Reservations recommended. Main courses $10–$35. AE, DC, MC, V. Mon–Fri 11:30am–9:30pm (last seating), Sat 5:30–9:30pm. Subway: S, 4, 5, 6, 7 to 42nd St./Grand Central. SEAFOOD.

Here's one New York institution housed within another: the city's most famous seafood joint in the world's greatest train station, beautifully renovated Grand Central Terminal. The restaurant is looking spiffy, too, with a main dining room sitting under an impressive curved and tiled ceiling, a more casual luncheonette-style section for walk-ins, and a wood-paneled saloon-style room for smokers. If you love seafood, don't miss this place. A new menu is prepared every day, since only the freshest fish is served. The oysters are irresistible: Kumomoto, Bluepoint, Malepeque, Belon—the list goes on and on. The list of daily catches, which can range from Arctic char to mako shark to ono (Hawaiian wahoo), is equally impressive. Most dinners go for between $20 and $25, though it's easy to jack up the tab by ordering live lobster (flown in directly from Maine) or one of the rarer daily specialties. But it's just as easy to keep the tab down by sticking with hearty fare like one of the excellent stews and pan roasts (from about $10 for oyster stew to $20 for a combo pan roast rich with oysters, clams, shrimp, lobster, and scallops) or by pairing the New England clam chowder (at $5, an unbeatable lunch) with a smoked starter to make a great meal.

Zarela. 953 Second Ave. (btw. 50th and 51st sts.). ☎ **212/644-6740.** Reservations recommended. Main courses $11–$16 at lunch, $15–$18 at dinner; 3-course fixed-price dinner $40. AE, DC, MC, V. Mon–Thurs noon–3pm and 5–11pm, Fri noon–3pm and 5–11:30pm, Sat 5–11:30pm, Sun 5–10pm. Subway: E, F to Lexington Ave.; 6 to 51st St. MEXICAN.

Owner and cookbook author Zarela Martinez *(Food from My Heart, The Food and Life of Oaxaca)* draws lively, dedicated crowds with her unsurpassed Mexican food, Manhattan's best margaritas, and a wealth of charm (Zarela herself often greets patrons at the door). Zarela's authentic cooking features the richly flavored specialties of Oaxaca and Veracruz, so don't come expecting standard tacos and combo plates. The *salpicón de pescado,* a snapper hash with tomatoes, scallions, jalapeños, and aromatic spices, is a great way to start, followed by the shrimp braised with poblanos, onions, and queso blanco. The fajitas, grilled marinated skirt steak served with chunky house-made guacamole and flour tortillas, melt in your mouth. Zarela is one Mexican restaurant that prides itself on great desserts, so check out the day's specials. Don't come, however, expecting a relaxing meal; Zarela's has a relentlessly colorful, party-hearty vibe. Also, don't be surprised if you have to wait for a table, even with reservations.

INEXPENSIVE

In addition to the listings below, there's also a cafeteria-style branch of **Mangia** (p. 142) at 16 E. 48th St., just east of Fifth Avenue (☎ 212/754-7600).

The British Open. 320 E. 59th St. (btw. First and Second aves.). ☎ **212/355-8467.** www.britishopen.citysearch.com. Reservations accepted. Main courses $9–$20 (most less than $15). AE, DC, DISC, MC, V. Mon–Sat noon–2am (kitchen closes at midnight), Sun noon–1am (kitchen closes at 11pm). Subway: 4, 5, 6 to 59th St. BRITISH.

Here's the perfect pub for golf lovers, or anybody who pines for a pint and some good English grub. This charmer of an ale house is more sophisticated than most, with a mahogany bar polished to a high sheen, a pretty dining room in back, and friendly, attentive service. Tartan carpet heightens the theme (ah, the Scots would be proud), and little blue lights create a romantic glow. This isn't a copy of a Brit pub—it's the real thing, transplanted from the other side of the Atlantic wholesale, bartender, malt vinegar, and all. The North Star at South Street Seaport is equally genuine, but it's more after-work local than Sunday dinner, if you know what I mean; this is the kind of place you'll be comfortable bringing Grandma to. The extensive menu serves well-prepared versions of the pub staples, plus steaks, chops, and the like. But go for the standards: light, well-battered fish with crispy chips; excellent cottage pie with veggies and mash; plus steak-and-kidney pie, bangers and mash, and so on. You'll find Guinness, Bass, Fullers ESB, and other British imports on tap, and golf and other sports on the telly at any hour.

Ess-A-Bagel. 831 Third Ave. (at 51st St.). ☎ **212/980-1010.** www.ess-a-bagel.com. Reservations unnecessary. Sandwiches $1.35–$8.35. AE, DC, DISC, MC, V. Mon–Fri 6:30am–10pm, Sat–Sun 8am–5pm. Subway: E, F to Lexington Ave.; 6 to 51st St. BAGEL SANDWICHES.

Ess-A-Bagel turns out the city's best bagel, edging out rival H&H, who won't make you a sandwich. Baked daily on-site, the giant hand-rolled delicacies come in 12 flavors—plain, sesame, poppy, onion, garlic, salt, whole wheat, pumpernickel, pumpernickel raisin, cinnamon raisin, oat bran, and everything. They're so plump, chewy, and satisfying that it's hard to believe they contain no fat, cholesterol, or preservatives. Head to the back counter for a baker's dozen or line up for a sandwich over-stuffed with scrumptious salads and spreads. Fillings can range from a generous schmear of cream cheese to smoked Nova salmon or chopped herring salad (both have received national acclaim) to sun-dried tomato tofu spread. There also are lots of deli-style meats to choose from, plus a wide range of cheeses and salads (egg, chicken, light tuna, and so on) and an expanded selection of vegetarian items in 1999. The cheerful dining room has plenty of bistro-style tables.

There's a second, smaller location at 359 First Ave., at 21st Street (☎ 212/260-2252).

✪ **Pongal.** 110 Lexington Ave. (btw. 27th and 28th sts.). ☎ **212/696-9458.** Reservations recommended. Main courses $5–$9.50. DC, DISC, MC, V. Mon–Fri noon–3pm and 5–10pm, Sat–Sun noon–10pm. Subway: 6 to 28th St. VEGETARIAN INDIAN.

One of my favorite finds of 1999 is this Indian spot, a real standout on Curry Hill, the stretch of Lexington in the high 20s that's home to a number of Indian restaurants.

ⓘ   Family-Friendly Restaurants

While it's always a smart move to call ahead to make sure a restaurant has kids' menus and high chairs, you can count on the following restaurants to be especially accommodating.

Carmine's *(p. 177)*   This rollicking family-style Italian restaurant was created with kids in mind. Expect Brady Bunch–size portions of all the favorites, including Caesar salad, veal parmigiana, and pasta topped with zesty marinara and little fist-size meatballs. The bigger the group, the better the bargain.

EJ's Luncheonette *(p. 195)*   These pleasing retro-'50s diners do what they're supposed to do best: serve up great burgers, fries, and blue-plate specials. There's even a kids' menu featuring peanut butter and jelly sandwiches along with downsized versions of the classics. Order up a milk shake on the side, and your kid will be in hog heaven.

John's Pizzeria *(p. 182)*   What kid doesn't love pizza? The Times Square location is particularly well located and kid-friendly, with family-size tables, chefs cooking up pies in brick ovens right before your eyes, and a bustling atmosphere where kids can be kids.

Manhattan Chili Co. *(p. 182)*   These fun Theater District restaurants are geared for all-American tastes and palates—just what a kid wants, right? Expect kid-friendly nachos, chicken wings, not-too-hot bowls of thick and meaty chili, and other faves like burritos and burgers.

Serendipity 3 *(p. 199)*   Kids will love this whimsical restaurant and ice-cream shop, which serves up a huge menu of American favorites, followed up by colossal ice-cream treats. This irony-free charmer even makes grown-ups feel like kids again.

Virgil's Real BBQ *(p. 179)*   This pleasing Times Square barbecue joint welcomes kids with open arms—and Junior will be more than happy, I'm sure, to be *allowed* to eat with his hands.

In addition to these choices, also consider the city's many theme restaurants. Young sci-fi fans shouldn't miss **Mars 2112** *(p. 181),* which boasts its very own theme-park ride and a video arcade that can keep the kids busy for hours (or until you run out of quarters). Little groovy ghoulies will love the thrills and chills of the **Jekyll & Hyde Club** *(p. 181),* while sports-minded kids can drag their baseball dads and soccer moms to the **ESPN Zone** *(p. 180).* For details on these and other choices, see "Theme Restaurant Thrills!" earlier in this chapter.

Pongal specializes in the vegetarian cuisine of southern India, and also happens to be kosher (only in New York!). Trust me—you don't have to be a vegetarian to love this place. The hearty dishes are always freshly prepared to order by the conscientious kitchen (no vats of saag paneer sitting around getting stale in this joint). Ingredients are always top-quality, vegetables and legume dishes are never overcooked, and the well-spiced sauces are particularly divine. The specialty of the house is *dosai,* a large golden crêpe filled with onions, potatoes, and other goodies, accompanied by coconut chutney and flavorful sauce. The food is very cheap, with nothing priced over $9.50, but that doesn't mean you have to put up with a crusty cafeteria to get such a bargain: The restaurant is low-lit and attractive, with professional service and a pleasing ambience, making it a nice choice for a special night on the town.

Prime Burger. 5 E. 51st St. (btw. Fifth and Madison aves.). ☎ **212/759-4729.** Reservations not accepted. Main courses $3.25–$8.50. No credit cards. Mon–Fri 6am–7pm, Sat 6am–5pm. Subway: 6 to 51st St. AMERICAN/HAMBURGERS.

Just across the street from St. Patrick's Cathedral, this no-frills coffee shop is a heavenly find. The burgers and sandwiches are tasty, the fries crispy and generous. The front seats, which might remind you (if you're old enough) of old wooden grammar-school desks, are great fun—especially when business-suited New Yorkers quietly take their places at these oddities. A great quickie stop during a day of Fifth Avenue shopping.

13 The Upper West Side

VERY EXPENSIVE

✪ **Jean Georges.** In the Trump International Hotel & Tower, 1 Central Park West (at 60th St./Columbus Circle). ☎ **212/299-3900.** www.jean-georges.com. Reservations required well in advance. Jacket required; tie optional. Main courses $29–$42 at lunch; 4-course fixed-price lunch $45; 3-course fixed-price dinner $85; tasting menus $95, $115, and $220. AE, DC, MC, V. Mon–Fri noon–2:30pm; Mon–Sat 5:30–11pm. Subway: A, B, C, D, 1, 9 to 59th St./Columbus Circle. FRENCH.

That smarmy Donald Trump can be a very smart guy. When he announced he had secured the services of Jean-Georges Vongerichten (of Vong and Jo Jo) to oversee the restaurant in his new hotel, everyone knew the rave reviews wouldn't be far behind. And they were right—Jean Georges was immediately awarded four coveted stars by the *New York Times*.

Dining here is a sublime experience. In the elegantly restrained Adam Tihany–designed dining room, the menu is the best of Vongerichten's past successes taken one step further. French and Asian touches mingle with a new passion for off-beat harvests, like lamb's quarters, sorrel, yarrow, quince, and chicory. Spring garlic soup with thyme accompanied by a plate of sautéed frog's legs with parsley makes a great beginning. The Muscovy duck steak with Asian spices and sweet-and-sour jus is carved tableside, while the lobster tartine with pumpkin seed, pea shoots, and a broth of fenugreek (one of Jean-Georges's signature aromatic plants) receives a final dash of spices seconds before you dig in. If the chestnut soup is on the menu, don't miss it.

The food is equally excellent but more affordably priced in the cafe **Nougatine,** which serves breakfast, lunch, and dinner; don't expect equally comfy chairs or as much elbow room, however. The professional service is without fault in the main restaurant, and still attentive if not quite as well paced in the cafe. The wine list is also excellent, with a number of unusual choices in every price range. If you're visiting in the warm weather, try to get a table on the lovely outdoor terrace.

EXPENSIVE

Tavern on the Green. In Central Park, Central Park West and W. 67th St. ☎ **212/873-3200.** www.tavernonthegreen.com. Reservations highly recommended, necessary well in advance on holidays. Main courses $20–$40; 3-course pretheater fixed-price (Mon–Fri 5–6:30pm) $26–$40. AE, DC, DISC, MC, V. Mon–Fri 11:30am–3:30pm, Sat 10am–3:30pm, Sun 10am–3:30pm; Mon–Thurs 5:30–11:30pm, Fri–Sat 5–11:30pm, Sun 5:30–10:30pm. Subway: 1, 9 to 66th St./Lincoln Center. AMERICAN/CONTINENTAL.

This legendary Central Park restaurant is a true one of a kind. Warner LeRoy's fantasy palace has one of the city's best settings. Antiques and Tiffany glass fill the space, crystal chandeliers cast a romantic light, tiny twinkling lights glimmer on nearby trees, and the views over the park are wonderful. A festive spirit enlivens the Crystal Room, where you should ask to be seated, especially at Christmas. (A couple of the other dining rooms are so overdone as to cross the line into the realm of tacky, though.) The garden, with its Japanese lanterns and whimsical topiary shrubs, is a lovely place for a drink in summer.

Since the passing of beloved Executive Chef Patrick Clark, the kitchen gets kudos for maintaining his legacy, though it's hard to be completely consistent in an operation this mammoth. The seasonal menus are surprisingly good, particularly if you stick with classic fare. The seared duck foie gras, served with a pear-and-pecan sticky bun and a balsamic-port syrup, is a wonderful beginning to any meal. The superb al dente pasta is made by Pasta Chef Renzo Barcatta. The grilled pork porterhouse is delicious and thick. Salmon is barbecued with Moroccan spices and served with a couscous cake. Despite its big reputation, the Tavern is known for its down-to-earth manner. It can, however, be plagued by uneven service, especially during hectic holiday periods. Book well ahead.

MODERATE

For fun family-style Italian, there's also the original **Carmine's** (p. 177) at 2450 Broadway, between 90th and 91st streets (☎ **212/362-2200**), in addition to the choices below. There's also **Time Cafe North** (p. 157), 2330 Broadway, at 85th St. (☎ **212/579-5100**), for casual, healthy eats and a cool Moroccan-themed lounge for cocktails.

Calle Ocho. 446 Columbus Ave. (btw. 81st and 82nd sts.). ☎ **212/873-5025.** Reservations highly recommended. Main courses $16–$24; Sun brunch $20. AE, DC, MC, V. Mon–Thurs 6–11pm, Fri 6pm–midnight, Sat 5pm–midnight, Sun 11:30am–3pm and 5–10pm. Subway: B, C to 81st St.–Museum of Natural History. PAN-LATIN.

This sleek, chic Nuevo Latino spot is the best thing that happened to the Upper West Side dining scene in 1999. Ask any local: They like Ruby Foo's (below), but they *love* Calle Ocho. For good reason: It's sharply designed in a lively mod style and serves up great cocktails (especially the house drink, the *mojito*, a sweet-tart blend of lime juice, rum, cane sugar, and mint) and exciting New Latin food that knows no borders. Standout dishes include the flamboyant Caribbean lobster ceviche, bursting with passion fruit and other tropical flavors; the fiery *lomo*, adobo-rubbed pork loin accompanied by equally bold chipotle mashed potatoes and a roasted corn salsa; and, for more tender palates, a beautifully grilled beef tenderloin paired with sweet plantain puree and an equally yummy fig-and-onion marmalade. This place is filled to the rafters nightly, yet it doesn't get quite so boisterous as Ruby Foo's; still, you're better off elsewhere if you're looking for quiet contemplation or romance. And don't forget to book ahead if you don't want to dine at 6 or 10:30pm.

Haru. 433 Amsterdam Ave. (btw. 80th and 81st sts.). ☎ **212/579-5655.** Reservations not accepted. A la carte sushi and rolls $2–$12 (special rolls may be higher); sushi combos and main courses $12–$26. AE, DC, MC, V. Mon–Thurs 5–11:30pm, Fri 5pm–midnight, Sat–Sun 12:30pm–midnight. Subway: 1, 9 to 79th St. SUSHI.

This attractive, sophisticated little restaurant serves the Upper West Side's best sushi. Expect generous, super-fresh cuts of all the classics, plus a good number of vegetable choices (shiitake and cucumber, vegetable tempura) and cut rolls. I recommend starting with the seaweed salad, which boasts four kinds of seaweed in vinaigrette, king crab shumai, a couple of grilled kushi yaki skewers, and/or a bowl of miso before launching into your raw meal. The good-looking blond-wood room fills up quickly, so don't be surprised if there's a wait; but we've found that it's rather quiet in the pretheater hour, and Lincoln Center is just a brisk 10- or 15-minute walk away.

Uptown Dining

Barney Greengrass,
  the Sturgeon King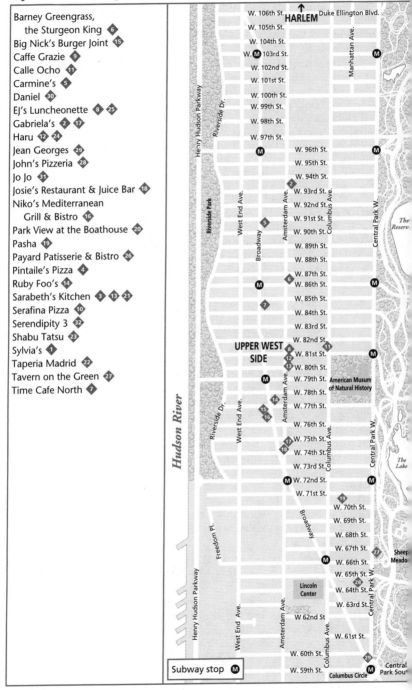
Big Nick's Burger Joint
Caffe Grazie
Calle Ocho
Carmine's
Daniel
EJ's Luncheonette
Gabriela's
Haru
Jean Georges
John's Pizzeria
Jo Jo
Josie's Restaurant & Juice Bar
Niko's Mediterranean
  Grill & Bistro
Park View at the Boathouse
Pasha
Payard Patisserie & Bistro
Pintaile's Pizza
Ruby Foo's
Sarabeth's Kitchen
Serafina Pizza
Serendipity 3
Shabu Tatsu
Sylvia's
Taperia Madrid
Tavern on the Green
Time Cafe North

192

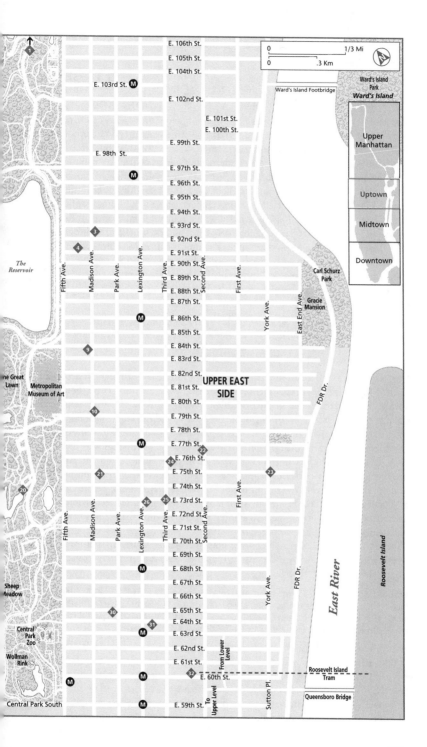

E. 106th St.
E. 105th St.
E. 104th St.
E. 103rd St. Ⓜ
E. 102nd St.
E. 101st St.
E. 100th St.
E. 99th St.
E. 98th St.
Ⓜ
E. 97th St.
E. 96th St.
E. 95th St.
E. 94th St.
E. 93rd St.
E. 92nd St.
E. 91st St.
E. 90th St.
E. 89th St.
E. 88th St.
E. 87th St.
Ⓜ
E. 86th St.
E. 85th St.
E. 84th St.
E. 83rd St.
E. 82nd St.
E. 81st St.
E. 80th St.
E. 79th St.
E. 78th St.
Ⓜ
E. 77th St.
E. 76th St.
E. 75th St.
E. 74th St.
E. 73rd St.
E. 72nd St.
E. 71st St.
E. 70th St.
E. 69th St.
E. 68th St.
Ⓜ
E. 67th St.
E. 66th St.
E. 65th St.
E. 64th St.
E. 63rd St.
Ⓜ
E. 62nd St.
E. 61st St.
E. 60th St.
Ⓜ
E. 59th St.
Ⓜ

Fifth Ave.
Madison Ave.
Park Ave.
Lexington Ave.
Third Ave.
Second Ave.
First Ave.
York Ave.
East End Ave.

UPPER EAST SIDE

The Reservoir

The Great Lawn
Metropolitan Museum of Art

Sheep Meadow

Central Park Zoo

Wollman Rink

Central Park South

Ward's Island Footbridge
Ward's Island Park
Ward's Island

0   1/3 Mi
0   .3 Km

Upper Manhattan

Uptown

Midtown

Downtown

Carl Schurz Park
Gracie Mansion

FDR Dr.

East River

Roosevelt Island

From Lower Level
To Upper Level
Sutton Pl.

Roosevelt Island Tram

Queensboro Bridge

If you're on the east side, Haru has a second location at 1329 Third Ave., at 76th Street (☎ **212/452-2230**).

Pasha. 70 W. 71st St. (btw. Columbus Ave. and Central Park West). ☎ **212/579-8751.** Reservations recommended. Main courses $12–$19. AE, MC, V. Mon–Thurs 5–11pm, Fri–Sat 5pm–midnight, Sun 5–10:30pm. Subway: B, C to 72nd St. TURKISH.

This sexy red-walled restaurant feels posh without being pricey—hence the reason so many Upper West Siders have pegged this as a favorite secret they'd rather not let out of the bag. (Sorry, guys.) The menu may seem exotic at first glance, but anyone familiar with Middle Eastern and Mediterranean fare will recognize the commonalities instantly: lots of lamb (minced, grilled, kabob), eggplant, marinated chicken, and stuffed grape leaves. The meats are excellent cuts, and everything is beautifully prepared. Consider starting with the *manti,* tender steamed dumplings stuffed with ground lamb and mint, and lightly drizzled with a piquant yogurt sauce; or the *patlican salatasi,* eggplant that has been charcoal-grilled and then mashed and tossed with garlic, lemon, and extra-virgin olive oil into a yummy puree. Most impressive among the main courses was the *kagit kabob,* cubed baby lamb delicately cooked in parchment with fresh veggies, potatoes, and herbs. The service is attentive, and the wine list affordable. I dare you to resist a second basket of the soft, grilled pitalike Turkish bread.

Ruby Foo's. 2182 Broadway (at 77th St.). ☎ **212/724-6700.** www.brguestinc.com. Dim sum and sushi rolls $5.50–$8.50; main courses and sushi platters $11–$35 (most less than $22). AE, MC, V. Sun 11:30am–midnight, Mon–Thurs 11:30am–12:30am, Fri–Sat 11:30am–1am. Subway: 1, 9 to 79th St. PAN-ASIAN.

Cross a sushi bar with a dim sum palace, shake with some fanciful modern design and toss in a high-concept cocktail menu, and what do you get? Ruby Foo's. This mammoth tri-level space is filled to the brim nightly with high-spirited (read: loud) folks who just can't get enough of the big menu, bold decor, and fun vibe. The food is much better than you'd expect from a party scene like this. I found the dim sum to be the most pleasing part of the menu: The shrimp and vegetable dumplings were delectably crispy, Malaysian chicken pot stickers were flavorfully curried, and the succulent tamarind-glazed baby-back ribs were a true delight. The sushi is fresh and just fine, although I advise staying away from the more creative preparations—there's a reason the Japanese never rolled up filet mignon, lobster, or mango in seaweed before. I also recommend diverging from traditional ordering patterns and mixing one or two main courses in as part of a family-style meal.

There's a second, equally high-concept branch in Times Square at 1626 Broadway, at 49th Street (☎ **212/489-5600**), where the sound level is surprisingly tolerable considering the bustle.

Sarabeth's Kitchen. 423 Amsterdam Ave. (btw. 80th and 81st sts.). ☎ **212/496-6280.** Reservations accepted for dinner only. Main courses $5–$10 at breakfast, $10.50–$15 at lunch, $12–$26 at dinner. AE, CB, DC, DISC, JCB, MC, V. Mon–Sat 8am–11pm, Sun 8am–9:30pm. Subway: 1, 9 to 79th St. CONTEMPORARY AMERICAN.

Sarabeth's fresh-baked goods, award-winning preserves, and creative American cooking with a European touch keep a loyal following. This charming country restaurant with a distinct Hamptons feel is best known for its breakfast and weekend brunch, when the menu features such treats as porridge with wheatberries, fresh cream, butter, and brown sugar; pumpkin waffles topped with sour cream, raisins, pumpkin seeds, and honey (a sweet tooth's delight); and a whole host of farm-fresh omelets. Expect a *long* wait for weekend brunch; lunch and dinner are just as good and a lot less crowded. Lunch might be a generous Caesar salad with aged Parmesan, brioche crou-tons, and a tangy anchovy dressing, accompanied by velvety cream of tomato soup; a beautifully built country-style sandwich; or a good old-fashioned chicken pot pie. Dinner is more sophisticated, with such specialties as hazelnut-crusted halibut in an aromatic seven-vegetable broth and oven-roasted lamb crusted in black mushrooms, with grilled leeks and Vidalia onion rings on the side. Leave room for the scrumptious desserts.

There's another full-service location at 1295 Madison Ave., at 92nd Street (☎ 212/ 410-7335); a cafe inside the Whitney Museum, 945 Madison Ave., at 75th Street (☎ 212/606-0218); and a bakery at Chelsea Market, 75 Ninth Ave., between 15th and 16th streets (☎ 212/989-2424).

INEXPENSIVE

For breakfast or lunch, also consider **Barney Greengrass, the Sturgeon King,** 541 Amsterdam Ave., between 86th and 87th streets (☎ 212/724-4707), one of the best Jewish delis in town, bar none; see "The New York Deli News" box on p. 150 for fur-ther details.

Near Lincoln Center, **John's Pizzeria,** 48 W. 65th St., between Broadway and Central Park West (☎ 212/721-7001), serves up one of the city's best pies in a nice brick-walled dining room (see p. 182).

Big Nick's Burger Joint/Pizza Joint. 2175 Broadway (at 77th St.). ☎ 212/362-9238. Reservations not necessary. Main courses $3.50–$15. MC, V. Daily 24 hours. Subway: 1, 9 to 79th St. AMERICAN/PIZZA.

A neighborhood legend since 1962, Big Nick's is one of the best spots in the city for a midnight snack. They offer a full menu 24 hours a day, which includes everything from killer French toast and pancakes to Nick's infamous gourmet beef burgers. The classic char-broiled burgers come in a whole host of varieties, from your all-American cheeseburger to the Mediterranean, stuffed with herbs, spices, and onions and topped with anchovies, feta, and tomato. There's also a good selection of Big Nick–style piz-zas, like the Gyromania, topped with well-seasoned gyro meat and onions. As the name suggests, Nick's is a real joint, specializing in homegrown Noo Yawk fare; how-ever, the kitchen gets kudos for developing a diet-watchers menu, with such special-ties as pizzas prepared with skim cheese and lean-ground veal and turkey burgers. There really is something for everyone here—in 1999, the menu grew to more than 1,000 items when Nick added steaks to his repertoire. The atmosphere is suitably lively, with brusque waiters and buspeople scrambling about, cooks calling out orders, and crowded tables full of diners happily chowing down.

If you're in a feta-and-phyllo mood instead, head down the block to the more upscale **Niko's Mediterranean Grill & Bistro,** 2161 Broadway, at 76th Street (☎ 212/873-7000), where the Greek Isles get the Big Nick treatment. The menu is huge, prices are low, and all the standards are up to snuff; don't pass on the flaming saganaki, even if you're only stopping in for lunch.

EJ's Luncheonette. 447 Amsterdam Ave. (btw. 81st and 82nd sts.). ☎ 212/873-3444. Reservations not accepted. Main courses $4–$12. No credit cards. Sun–Thurs 8:30am–11pm, Fri–Sat 8:30am–11:30pm. Subway: 6 to 77th St. AMERICAN DINER.

This retro diner is popular with uptown yups and their kids, who come for hearty American fare in a sleek 1950s setting—turquoise vinyl booths, Formica tabletops, a soda fountain, and a lunch counter with stools that spin. The menu features a large selection of breakfasts so good that you won't be ashamed of indulging in a stack of banana-pecan pancakes for dinner. There's also a terrific selection of burgers (including a great veggie version), well-stuffed sandwiches, hearty green salads, and blue-plate main dishes like meat loaf with mashed potatoes. Everything is well prepared—better than you'd expect from a joint like this, in fact—and service is friendly. Don't miss the amazing sweet potato fries.

Also on the Upper East Side, 1271 Third Ave., at 73rd Street (☎ 212/472-0600); and in Greenwich Village at 432 Sixth Ave., between 9th and 10th streets (☎ 212/473-5555). Weekend brunch is a big deal at all three locations, but expect a wait.

✪ **Gabriela's.** 311 Amsterdam Ave. (at 75th St.). ☎ **212/875-8532.** Reservations accepted for parties of 6 or more. Main courses $7–$13. AE, MC, V. Mon–Thurs noon–11pm, Fri–Sat noon–midnight, Sun noon–10pm. Subway: 1, 2, 3, 9 to 96th St. MEXICAN.

If you love roast chicken, trust me: Gabriela's bird is the best. A blend of Yucatán spices and a slow-roasting rotisserie results in some of the tenderest, juiciest chicken in town—and at $6.95 for a half chicken with two sides (plenty for all but the biggest eaters) and $12.95 for a whole, it's one of the city's best bargains, too. All of the authentic Mexican specialties on the extensive menu are well prepared, generously portioned, and satisfying, from the monster tacos to the well-sauced enchiladas. The fresh, chunky, perfectly limed guacamole should please even Southwest natives. The dining room is large, bright, and pretty, with a pleasing south-of-the-border flair, and the service is quick and attentive. Try one of Gabriela's yummy fruit shakes (both mango and papaya are good bets) or tall agua frescas (fresh fruit drinks), which come in a variety of tropical flavors. A winner!

Gabriela's original location, 685 Amsterdam Ave., at 93rd Street (☎ 212/961-0574), is still going strong, too.

Josie's Restaurant & Juice Bar. 300 Amsterdam Ave. (at 74th St.). ☎ **212/769-1212.** www.josiesnyc.com. Reservations recommended. Main courses $9–$17. AE, DC, MC, V. Mon–Fri noon–midnight, Sat 11:30am–midnight, Sun 11:30am–11pm. Subway: 1, 2, 3, 9 to 72nd St. HEALTH-CONSCIOUS.

You have to admire the sincerity of an organic restaurant that uses chemical-free milk paint on its walls. Chef/owner Louis Lanza doesn't stop there: His adventurous menu shuns dairy, preservatives, and concentrated fats. Free-range and farm-raised meats and poultry augment vegetarian choices like baked sweet potato with tamari brown rice, broccoli, roasted beets, and tahini sauce; eggless Caesar salad; and a great three-grain vegetable burger with homemade ketchup and caramelized onions. The yellowfin tuna wasabi burger with pickled ginger is another signature. Everything is made with organic grains, beans, and flour as well as organic produce when possible. You don't have to be a health nut to enjoy Josie's; Lanza's eclectic cuisine really satisfies. And nobody's gonna actually make you do without: If wheat grass isn't your thing, a full wine and beer list is served in this pleasing modern space, which boasts enough Jetsons-style touches to give the room a playful, relaxed feel.

14 The Upper East Side

Look for the restaurants in this section on the "Uptown Dining" map on p. 192.

VERY EXPENSIVE

✪ **Daniel.** 60 E. 65th St. (btw. Madison and Park aves.). ☎ **212/288-0033.** www.daniel-nyc.com. Reservations required. Jacket and tie required. 2-course fixed-price lunch $36–$49, tasting menus $69–$89; 3-course fixed-price dinner $72, tasting menus $105–$140. AE, MC, V. Tues–Sat noon–2:30pm; Mon–Thurs 5:45–11pm, Fri–Sat 5:45–11:30pm. Subway: 6 to 68th St. FRENCH COUNTRY.

When owner/Chef Daniel Boulud first opened Daniel in 1993, Patricia Wells named it one of the *world's* top 10 restaurants. If Le Cirque 2000 sounds too over the top for your taste, this is the place for you: Gorgeous neo-Renaissance features—rich mahogany doors, sensuous arches, elegant Corinthian columns, and soaring terra-cotta-tiled ceilings—have been beautifully accented with a rich autumn color palette and custom furnishings with subtly playful curves. It's an ideal setting for Boulud's faultless country French cooking.

The menu is heavy with game dishes in elegant but unfussy preparations, plus Daniel signatures like black sea bass in a crisp potato shell, with tender leeks and a light Barolo sauce. Excellent starters include a frisée salad with crisp braised sweetbreads, pistachios, and black truffle. Don't neglect the specials menu; I was the envy of the table with my warm rabbit confit salad with foie gras. Sublime entrees may include braised Chatham cod with cockles and caviar, or chestnut-crusted venison with sweet potato puree. But you can't really go wrong with anything—the kitchen doesn't take a false turn. The wine list is terrific and, divided between seasonal fruits and chocolates, the desserts are uniformly excellent. On the downside, the staff is more formal than I would like, and I've heard the same complaint from others; service at equally classic La Grenouille also stands on ceremony, but I found it to be much warmer.

Daniel is now taking **same-day reservations** for casual light lunches, prepared in the spirit of Lyon (Boulud's hometown) and served in the pleasing lounge from noon to 2pm. The three-course meal is $36, including a glass of wine or a hot beverage. This is a great way to sample the master's marvelous cuisine without laborious advance planning or succumbing to formality.

EXPENSIVE

Jo Jo. 160 E. 64th St. (btw. Lexington and Third aves.). ☎ **212/223-5656.** Reservations strongly recommended. Main courses $19–$35; 3-course fixed-price lunch $28; 4-course fixed-price dinner $45–$65. AE, DC, MC, V. Mon–Sat noon–2:30pm; Mon–Fri 6–11pm, Sat 5:30–11:30pm. Subway: N, R to Lexington Ave.; 6 to 68th St. FRENCH BISTRO.

Owner/Chef Jean-Georges Vongerichten almost single-handedly revolutionized French cooking by replacing butter- and cream-laden sauces with low-fat flavored oils and fresh vegetable juices, and infusing a delicate Asian sensibility. He has drawn crowds at Jo Jo continually since 1991, despite opening higher-profile places like Vong and Jean Georges since then. This breezy yet elegant East Side town house has matured beautifully. It eschews modernism for a warmer, more traditional style that's supremely welcoming: Downstairs, the banquettes are red, the walls a warm yellow; upstairs, parlor-floor windows illuminate the room softly. The compact but inviting menu may offer lighter-than-usual takes on such French staples as goat cheese (in a potato terrine with baby lettuce and arugula juice), foie gras (with quince and warm lentil salad), squab (served rare with warm potato salad in pommery mustard vinaigrette), and duck (roasted with figs, port wine, and glazed turnips). The cuisine—and even the wine—is a value considering the excellence of the cooking, service, and setting. The fixed-prices (including a vegetarian menu at dinner) are downright bargains.

✪ **Park View at the Boathouse.** On the lake in Central Park, near 72nd St. and Park Dr. North (nearest park entrance is 72nd St. and Fifth Ave.). ☎ **212/517-2233.** Reservations highly recommended. Main courses $18–$24 at lunch and brunch, $23–$32 at dinner. AE, DC, DISC, MC, V. Fall/Winter: Wed–Sat 6–10pm, Sat–Sun 11am–3pm. Spring/Summer: Mon–Fri 11:30am–10pm, Sat 11am–11pm, Sun 11am–9pm. Subway: 6 to 77th St. CONTEMPORARY AMERICAN.

Park View is a one-of-a-kind experience—there's no better alfresco dining in the city. What makes it so special? Beautifully set on the edge of the lake and surrounded by great green Central Park, it's quintessentially New York yet magically distant from the urban bustle. And the creative New American cuisine is almost as stellar as the surroundings. Chef John Villa particularly excels at dishes with an Asian flair; Indian-spiced salmon tartare with pappadam and plantain crisps made an appealing Pan-cultural starter, and coriander-spiced tuna loin on a crisp taro cake with mango salsa and cilantro vinaigrette was an ideal marriage of sweet and spice. Not everything works though—red snapper poached in milk?—so ask your waiter to help you steer past the menu's few pitfalls.

Winter features a game menu served in a glass-walled, fireplace-lit dining room, but don't bother. Summer is the time to come; book ahead, since everybody wants to dine here, especially for weekend brunch. Twilight is enchanting, giving Park View the air of a tiny oasis lorded over by the distant twinkling skyline; try to arrive just before sunset, even if it means coming early for a drink at the equally well-situated bar. You've no doubt heard about the dangers of wandering in Central Park after dark, but after 7pm a shuttle runs from Fifth Avenue and 72nd Street (inquire about the current schedule when you reserve).

✪ Payard Pâtisserie & Bistro. 1032 Lexington Ave. (at 73rd St.). ☎ **212/717-5252.** www.payard.com. Reservations recommended. Main courses $11–$24 at lunch, $23–$28 at dinner; fixed-price lunch $28; dinner tasting menu $56. AE, DC, MC, V. Mon–Thurs noon–10:30pm, Fri noon–11pm, Sat noon–4:30pm and 5:45–11pm. Subway: 6 to 77th St. FRENCH BISTRO.

From Daniel Boulud, celebrity chef and owner of the highly acclaimed Daniel, and his former pastry chef, François Payard, comes this grand turn-of-the-century, Parisian-style cafe. Elegant cakes, pastries, and handmade chocolates fill glass cases in the pastry shop up front, while mirrors, mahogany, and straightforward bistro fare entice patrons to the cafe in back. The menu is unabashedly classic, with homemade duck confit, thick slabs of foie gras terrine, sublime steak frites, and fragrant bouillabaisse. The biggest problem with Payard? Choosing among the fabulous, beautifully presented desserts, which rank among the city's best. Everything is house-made, from the signature cakes, breads, and pastries to the delicate candies. Whether you go with the classic crème brûlée or something more decadent (anything chocolate is to die for), you're sure to be wowed. Feel free to come in just for afternoon tea or dessert if the entree prices are too rich for you.

MODERATE

If you're in the mood for sushi, consider the East Side branch of **Haru** (p. 191), at 1329 Third Ave., at 76th Street (☎ **212/452-2230**). If it's a well-prepared contemporary meal or a sweet treat you're after, **Sarabeth's Kitchen** (p. 194) has a pleasing full-service location at 1295 Madison Ave., at 92nd Street (☎ **212/410-7335**), plus a cafe inside the Whitney Museum, 945 Madison Ave., at 75th Street (☎ **212/606-0218**).

Caffe Grazie. 26 E. 84th St. (at Madison Ave.). ☎ **212/717-4407.** Reservations recommended. Main courses $12.50–$19.50. AE, DC, MC, V. Mon–Sat noon–11pm, Sun noon–10pm. Subway: 4, 5, 6 to 86th St. ITALIAN.

This cheery, unpretentious Italian cafe is most notable for its convenient location near the Metropolitan Museum of Art, a neighborhood short of moderately priced, recommendable eats. It's perfect for sipping espresso between museum hops or lingering over an elegant dinner. Appetizers like the bruschetta assortment served with a small

Pizza! Pizza!

Leave it to the chi-chi Upper East Side to specialize in designer pizza. **Serafina Pizza,** 1022 Madison Ave., at 79th Street (☎ 212/734-2676), serves pricey but terrific Tuscan-style pizza, and there's a wonderful alfresco rooftop setting. **Pintaile's Pizza,** at 26 E. 91st St., between Fifth and Madison avenues (☎ 212/722-1967; www.pintailespizza.com), dresses their daintily crisp organic crusts with layers of plum tomatoes, extra-virgin olive oil, and other fabulously fresh ingredients.

---

salad and the warm white-bean salad over prosciutto are generous enough to be a light meal in themselves. The pasta selection mixes staples (satisfying penne pomodoro and linguine pesto) with standouts (lasagne layered with grilled chicken, fresh tomatoes, cheese, and pesto). The entrees, like veal stuffed with prosciutto and spinach and jumbo shrimp with lemon-caper sauce, are fresh and flavorful. All in all, a hidden treasure in a needy neighborhood.

Taperia Madrid. 1471 Second Ave. (btw. 76th and 77th sts.). ☎ **212/794-2923.** Reservations recommended. Tapas $5–$16.50. AE, MC, V. Sun–Thurs 5:30pm–1am, Fri–Sat 5:30pm–3am. Subway: 6 to 77th St. SPANISH.

This authentic Spanish tapas house is a breath of fresh air on the Upper East Side's otherwise bland midpriced dining scene. This place is the real thing: comfortably distressed, with beamed ceilings, mosaic tiles, rough-hewn communal tables attended to by friendly Spanish-accented waiters, and a convivial atmosphere that's suitable for making friends and sharing. Not every one of the 25-plus dishes is successful, but most are simply and appealingly prepared. If you like anchovies like I do, don't miss the *boquerones,* in which the silvery little fishes are marinated in a tart and garlicky extra-virgin olive oil. Another sigh-inducer is the *gambas à la sal de mar,* head-on shrimp pan-fried to perfection in rock sea salt—the winning choice over the shrimp in garlic sauce, if you're trying to decide. In a similar competition, the tender baby squid in sherry vinaigrette beats the bland octopus hands down. I like the paella at La Paella better, but this version is good, too. The sangría is the best in town—not too sweet—and there's a good, affordable selection of Spanish wines. The Spanish and Portuguese cheeses make an ideal finish. Look for live flamenco on Monday from 9:30pm.

INEXPENSIVE

Also consider the local branch of **Shabu Tatsu** (p. 158), at 1414 York Ave., at 75th Street (☎ 212/472-3322), which is well worth the trip to the far east side of town. There's a branch of **EJ's Luncheonette** (p. 195), the retro all-American diner, at 1271 Third Ave., at 73rd Street (☎ 212/472-0600).

Serendipity 3. 225 E. 60th St. (btw. Second and Third aves.). ☎ **212/838-3531.** www.serendipity3.com. Reservations recommended for dinner. Main courses $6–$18; sweets and sundaes $4.50–$10. AE, DC, DISC, MC, V. Sun–Thurs 11:30am–midnight, Fri 11:30am–1am, Sat 11:30am–2am. Subway: N, R to Lexington Ave.; 4, 5, 6 to 59th St. AMERICAN.

You'd never guess that this whimsical place was once a top stop on Andy Warhol's agenda. Wonders never cease—and neither does the confection at this delightful restaurant and sweet shop. Tucked into a cozy brownstone a few steps from Bloomingdale's, Serendipity's small front-room curiosity shop overflows with odd objects, from jigsaw puzzles to silly jewelry. But the real action is behind the shop, where the quintessential American soda fountain still reigns supreme. Remember

Farrell's? This is the better version (complete with candy to tempt the kids on the way out), and it's still going strong. Happy people gather at marble-topped ice-cream parlor tables for burgers and foot-long hot dogs, country meat loaf with mashed potatoes and gravy, and salads and sandwiches with cute names like "The Catcher in the Rye" (their own twist on the BLT, with chicken and Russian dressing—on rye, of course). The food isn't great, but the main courses aren't the point—they're just an excuse to get to the desserts. The restaurant's signature is Frozen Hot Chocolate, a slushie version of everybody's cold-weather favorite, but other crowd pleasers include dark double devil mousse, celestial carrot cake, lemon ice-box pie, and anything with hot fudge. So cast that willpower aside and come on in—Serendipity is an irony-free charmer to be appreciated by adults and kids alike.

15 Harlem

INEXPENSIVE

Sylvia's. 328 Lenox Ave. (btw. 126th and 127th sts.). ☎ **212/996-0660.** Reservations accepted for 10 or more. Main courses $8–$16; Sunday gospel brunch $17. AE, DISC, MC, V. Mon–Thurs 8am–10:30pm, Fri–Sat 7:30am–10:30pm, Sun 11am–8pm. Subway: 2, 3 to 125th St. SOUL FOOD.

South Carolina–born Sylvia Woods is the last word in New York soul food. The place is so popular with both locals and visiting celebs that the dining room has spilled into the building next door. Since 1962, her Harlem institution has dished up the southern-fried goods: turkey with down-home stuffing; smothered chicken and pork chops; fried chicken and baked ham; collard greens and candied yams; and cavity-inducing sweet tea. And then of course there's "Sylvia's World Famous, Talked About, Bar-B-Que Ribs Special"—the sauce is sweet, with a potent afterburn. This Harlem landmark is still presided over by 72-year-old Sylvia, who's likely to greet you at the door herself. Some naysayers say that Sylvia's just isn't what it used to be, but chowing down here is still a one-of-a-kind New York experience. Sunday gospel brunch is a joyous time to go.

16 Brooklyn

EXPENSIVE

✪ **Peter Luger Steakhouse.** 178 Broadway (at Driggs Ave.), Williamsburg, Brooklyn. ☎ **718/387-7400.** www.peterluger.com. Reservations essential; call a month in advance for weekend bookings. Main courses $5–$19 at lunch, $19–$32 at dinner. No credit cards (Peter Luger accounts only). Mon–Thurs 11:45am–9:45pm, Fri–Sat 11:45am–10:45pm, Sun 12:45–9:45pm. Subway: J, M, Z to Marcy Ave. (Or take a cab.) STEAKS.

If you love steak enough to drag yourself out to Brooklyn, then book a table and hop a cab to Williamsburg. Expect loads of attitude and nothing in the way of decor or atmosphere (beer hall is the theme)—but this century-old institution is porterhouse heaven. The first-rate cuts—the only ones this 113-year-old institution serves—are dry-aged on the premises and come off the grill dripping with fat and butter, crusty on the outside and tender pink within. It's the best steak in the five boroughs, bar none. Nonbelievers can order sole or lamb chops, but don't bother if you're not coming for the cow. As sides go, the German fried potatoes are crisp and delicious, and the creamed spinach is everything it should be. Bring wads of cash because this place is expensive, and they don't take credit cards (other than their own house account).

✪ **The River Café.** 1 Water St. (at the East River), Brooklyn Heights. ☎ **718/522-5200.** www.rivercafe.com. Reservations required. Jacket required; tie preferred. A la carte lunch $13–$24; 3-course fixed-price dinner $70; 6-course tasting menu $90. AE, CB, DC, MC, V. Mon–Fri noon–2:30pm, Sat–Sun 11:30am–2:30pm; daily 6–11:30pm. Subway: A to High St./Brooklyn Bridge; 2, 3 to Clark St. Walk downslope, toward the water; it will be on your right in the last block, across from the Eagle Warehouse. (Or take a cab.) CONTEMPORARY AMERICAN.

This magical restaurant is beautifully situated, on a barge festooned with twinkling lights tucked beneath the beautiful Brooklyn Bridge. The view of Lower Manhattan and New York Harbor is simply spectacular—the skyline looks close enough to reach out and touch. Even though lunch and weekend brunch are among the options, go for dinner—that's when the restaurant takes on a celebratory glow and the twinkling lights of the city are most bewitching. The dining room is glamorous, with touches evoking a stylish 1930s supper club (complete with pianist tinkling the ivories), and the beautifully prepared food fresh and seasonal. While there are choices for carnivores, including a wonderful boneless rack of lamb, this is really a seafood lovers' menu. Excellent appetizers may include sashimi-quality tuna and salmon tartare with roe, salmon smoked over fruitwood, or smoked duck foie gras terrine with quince and currant compote. (All smoked items are prepared in the restaurant's own smokehouse.) Entrees include braised Maine lobster with horseradish potatoes and portobellos; quick-seared yellowfin tuna with fennel, glazed cucumber, and 100-year-old balsamic vinegar; and crisp black sea bass in a red wine–butter sauce (as decadent and wonderful as it sounds); as well as the aforementioned rack of lamb and a grilled, aged prime sirloin. Desserts like a miniature Brooklyn Bridge sculpted from Valrhona marquise chocolate provide delightful finales.

INEXPENSIVE

✪ **Grimaldi's Pizzeria.** 19 Old Fulton St. (btw. Front and Water sts.), Brooklyn Heights. ☎ **718/858-4300.** Reservations not accepted. Pies $14 and up, depending on toppings. No credit cards. Mon–Thurs 11:30am–11pm, Fri 11:30am–midnight, Sat–Sun noon–11pm. Subway: A, C to High St.; 2, 3 to Clark St (use Henry St. exit). Walk downslope, toward the water; it will be on your right in the last block, across from the Eagle Warehouse. PIZZA.

Here's New York's best pizza. You don't have to take it from me—just check Zagat's, which gives this Brooklyn classic a whopping 26 (out of 30) for food, a rating usually reserved for the likes of Le Cirque. Thin coal-oven crust, crisp and smoky, is topped with perfectly seasoned red sauce, leafy basil, and only the freshest, whitest mozzarella. Crown this perfect pie with your choice of traditional toppings, including meaty pepperoni and house-roasted red peppers. And you don't have to suffer a greasy pizza joint to enjoy this sublime pizza: Grimaldi's is a surprisingly pleasant place, with red-checked tablecloths, photos of Sinatra covering the walls, and the Chairman of the Board himself crooning from the jukebox. Patsy Grimaldi is likely to greet you himself, warmly, with stogie in hand (despite the no-smoking signs). Otherwise, the service can be gruff, but that's how you'll know you've arrived—in Brooklyn, that is. The best time to come is in summer, when the restaurant sets up tables on the wide sidewalk outside, where you'll have the kind of spectacular views of the Brooklyn Bridge and twinkling lower Manhattan that usually only big money buys.

7

Exploring
New York City

If this is your first trip to New York, face facts: It will be impossible to take in the entire city. Because New York is almost unfathomably big and constantly changing, you could live your whole life here and still make fascinating daily discoveries—we New Yorkers do. This chapter is designed to give you an overview of what's available in this multifaceted place so you can narrow your choices to an itinerary that's digestible for the amount of time you'll be here—be it a day, a week, or something in between.

So don't try to tame New York—you can't. Decide on a few must-see attractions, and then let the city take you on its own ride. Inevitably, as you make your way around the city, you'll be blown off course by unplanned diversions that are just as much fun as what you meant to see. After all, the true New York is in the details. As you dash from sight to sight, take time to admire a lovely cornice on a prewar building, linger over a cup of coffee at a sidewalk cafe, or just idle away a few minutes on a bench watching New Yorkers parade through their daily lives.

GET LOST!
One of the best ways to experience New York is to pick a neighborhood and just stroll it. Bring a map for reference, but put it in your pocket—let yourself get lost. Walk the prime thoroughfares, poke your head into shops, or park yourself on a bench or at an outdoor cafe and just watch the world go by. For tips on where to go, how to get there, and what highlights to be on the lookout for, see **"Manhattan's Neighborhoods in Brief"** in chapter 4.

If getting lost isn't your style—or even if it is—you might consider taking an organized tour. That doesn't have to mean a big bus with an out-of-work actor pointing out the Empire State Building (although general introductory tours are available, too). There are many wonderful walking tours that really let you get to know a neighborhood or a particular aspect of New York. Walking tours are cheap, they're fun, and there's no better way to get to know a neighborhood than with an expert at the helm. For a complete rundown of operators and the kinds of tours they offer, see **"Organized Sightseeing Tours,"** later in this chapter.

1 Sights & Attractions by Neighborhood

MANHATTAN

CHELSEA

Chelsea Piers Sports & Entertainment
Complex (p. 260)

Spirit Cruises (p. 250)

EAST VILLAGE & NOHO

Merchant's House Museum (p. 231)

THE FINANCIAL DISTRICT/LOWER MANHATTAN/NEW YORK HARBOR

Battery Park (p. 259)

Bowling Green Park (p. 218)

Brooklyn Bridge (p. 213)

Double Check (p. 221)

City Hall & City Hall Park (p. 223)

Cunard Building (p. 218)

Ellis Island (p. 212)

Federal Hall National Memorial
(p. 219)

Fraunces Tavern Museum (p. 219)

Group of Four Trees (p. 220)

Kalikow Building (p. 222)

Liberty Plaza (p. 221)

Municipal Building (p. 224)

Museum of American Financial
History (p. 219)

Museum of Jewish Heritage (p. 238)

National Museum of the American
Indian (p. 216 and p. 239)

New York Stock Exchange (p. 214
and p. 219)

The Red Cube (p. 221)

St. Paul's Chapel (p. 222)

South Street Seaport & Museum
(p. 214)

Staten Island Ferry (p. 212)

Statue of Liberty (p. 211)

Surrogate's Court (The Hall of
Records) (p. 223)

Trinity Church (p. 220)

Tweed Courthouse (p. 223)

U.S. Customs House (p. 216)

Wall Street (p. 220)

Woolworth Building (p. 222)

World Trade Center (p. 215 and
p. 221)

THE FLATIRON DISTRICT

Flatiron Building (p. 248)

Theodore Roosevelt Birthplace
(p. 241)

Union Square Park (p. 260)

GREENWICH VILLAGE

Forbes Magazine Galleries (p. 232)

Washington Square Park (p. 260)

HARLEM & UPPER MANHATTAN

Apollo Theatre (p. 268)

Astor Row Houses (p. 268)

The Cloisters (p. 230)

Dyckman Farmhouse Museum
(p. 230)

Morris–Jumel Mansion (p. 231)

Schomburg Center for Research in
Black Culture (p. 240)

Strivers' Row (p. 268)

Studio Museum in Harlem (p. 240)

Sugar Hill (p. 268)

LOWER EAST SIDE

Lower East Side Tenement Museum
(p. 234)

MIDTOWN EAST

Chrysler Building (p. 241)

Dahesh Museum (p. 232)

Empire State Building (p. 242)

Grand Central Terminal (p. 243)

Japan Society (p. 234)

Lever House (p. 247)

Morgan Library (p. 235)

Newseum/NY (p. 239)

New York Public Library (p. 244)

New York Skyride (p. 242)

St. Patrick's Cathedral (p. 248)

Seagram Building (p. 247)

Sony Building (p. 247)

Sony Wonder Technology Lab
(p. 266)

United Nations (p. 246)

Whitney Museum of American Art at
Philip Morris (p. 241)

SOHO

Children's Museum of the Arts
(p. 266)

Downtown Attractions

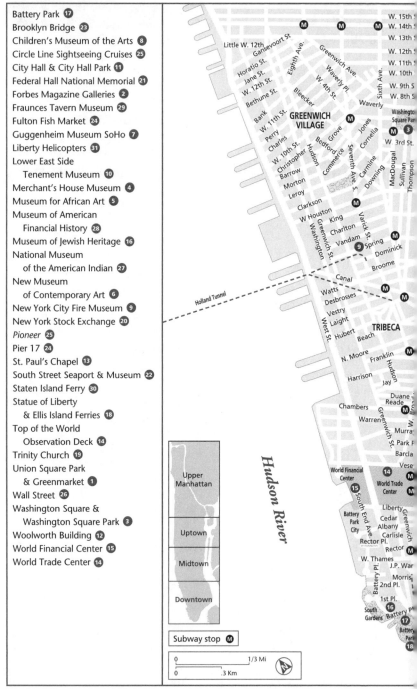

Battery Park **17**
Brooklyn Bridge **23**
Children's Museum of the Arts **8**
Circle Line Sightseeing Cruises **25**
City Hall & City Hall Park **11**
Federal Hall National Memorial **21**
Forbes Magazine Galleries **2**
Fraunces Tavern Museum **29**
Fulton Fish Market **24**
Guggenheim Museum SoHo **7**
Liberty Helicopters **31**
Lower East Side
   Tenement Museum **10**
Merchant's House Museum **4**
Museum for African Art **5**
Museum of American
   Financial History **28**
Museum of Jewish Heritage **16**
National Museum
   of the American Indian **27**
New Museum
   of Contemporary Art **6**
New York City Fire Museum **9**
New York Stock Exchange **20**
Pioneer **25**
Pier 17 **24**
St. Paul's Chapel **13**
South Street Seaport & Museum **22**
Staten Island Ferry **30**
Statue of Liberty
   & Ellis Island Ferries **18**
Top of the World
   Observation Deck **14**
Trinity Church **19**
Union Square Park
   & Greenmarket **1**
Wall Street **26**
Washington Square &
   Washington Square Park **3**
Woolworth Building **12**
World Financial Center **15**
World Trade Center **14**

W. 15th S
W. 14th S
W. 13th S
W. 12th S
W. 11th S
W. 10th
W. 9th S
W. 8th S

Little W. 12th
Gansevoort St
Greenwich Ave.
Waverly Pl.
Horatio St.
Jane St.
W. 4th St.
Eighth Ave.
Sixth Ave.
W. 12th St.
Bethune St.
Bleecker
Waverly
Washingto
Square Par
Bank
W. 11th St.
Perry
Charles
GREENWICH
VILLAGE
Grove
Bedford
Jones
Cornelia
W. 3rd St
W. 10th St.
Christopher
Barrow
Morton
Leroy
Hudson
Commerce
Seventh Ave S
Camine
Downing
MacDougal
Sullivan
Thompson
Clarkson
W Houston
King
Charlton
Vandam
Greenwich St
Washington
Varick St.
Spring
Dominick
Broome
Canal
Watts
Desbrosses
Vestry
Laight
West St.
Hubert
Beach
TRIBECA
N. Moore
Franklin
Hudson
Harrison
Jay
Duane
Reade
Chambers
Warren
Greenwich St.
Murra
Park P
Barcla
Vese
World Financial
Center **14**
World Trade
Center
South End Ave.
Liberty
Battery
Park
City
Cedar
Albany
Carlisle
Rector Pl.
Rector
W. Thames
J.P. War
2nd Pl.
Battery Pl.
Morris
1st Pl.
South
Gardens
Battery
Battery
Park

Holland Tunnel

Hudson River

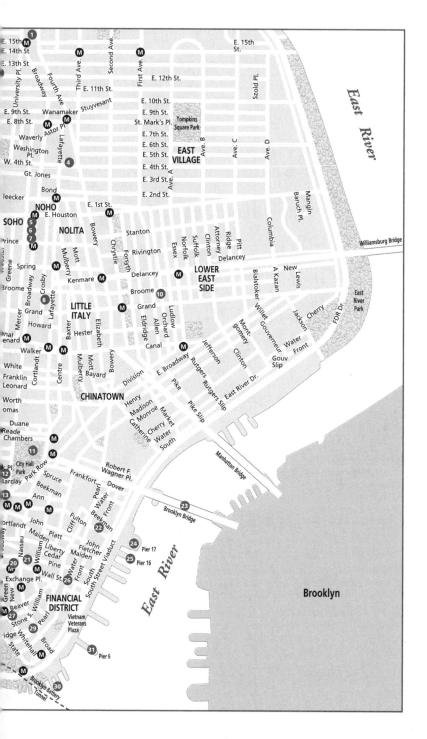

Midtown Attractions

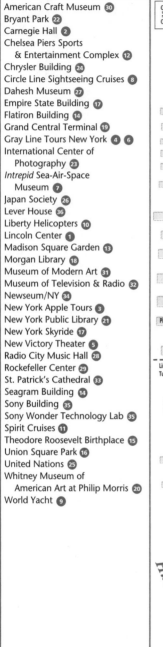

207

Uptown Attractions

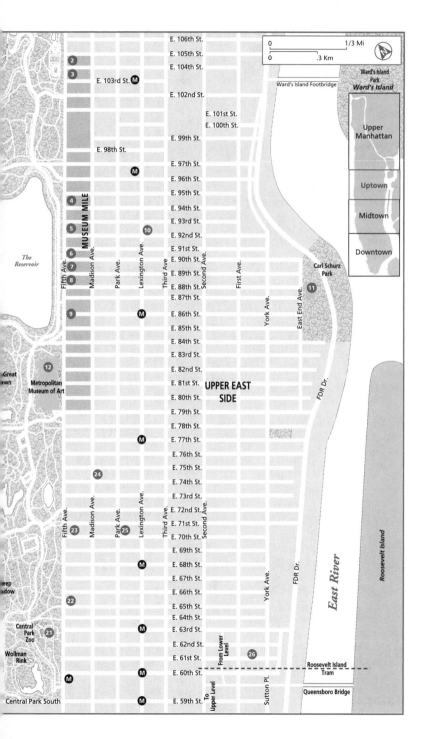

E. 106th St.
E. 105th St.
E. 104th St.
E. 103rd St. Ⓜ
E. 102nd St.
E. 101st St.
E. 100th St.
E. 99th St.
E. 98th St.
E. 97th St.
E. 96th St.
E. 95th St.
E. 94th St.
E. 93rd St.
E. 92nd St.
E. 91st St.
E. 90th St.
E. 89th St.
E. 88th St.
E. 87th St.
E. 86th St.
E. 85th St.
E. 84th St.
E. 83rd St.
E. 82nd St.
E. 81st St.
E. 80th St.
E. 79th St.
E. 78th St.
E. 77th St.
E. 76th St.
E. 75th St.
E. 74th St.
E. 73rd St.
E. 72nd St.
E. 71st St.
E. 70th St.
E. 69th St.
E. 68th St.
E. 67th St.
E. 66th St.
E. 65th St.
E. 64th St.
E. 63rd St.
E. 62nd St.
E. 61st St.
E. 60th St.
E. 59th St.

0   1/3 Mi
0   .3 Km

Ward's Island Footbridge
Ward's Island Park
Ward's Island

Upper Manhattan

Uptown

Midtown

Downtown

The Reservoir

MUSEUM MILE

Fifth Ave.
Madison Ave.
Park Ave.
Lexington Ave.
Third Ave
Second Ave.
First Ave.
York Ave.
East End Ave.
FDR Dr.

Carl Schurz Park

UPPER EAST SIDE

Great Lawn

Metropolitan Museum of Art

Deep Meadow

Central Park Zoo

Wollman Rink

Central Park South

Sutton Pl.

From Lower Level
To Upper Level

East River

Roosevelt Island

Roosevelt Island Tram

Queensboro Bridge

Guggenheim Museum SoHo (p. 233)
Museum for African Art (p. 235)
New Museum of Contemporary Art
(p. 239)
New York City Fire Museum (p. 266)

TIMES SQUARE &
MIDTOWN WEST

American Craft Museum (p. 230)
Bryant Park (p. 259)
Circle Line Cruises (p. 250)
Gray Line Tours (p. 249)
International Center of Photography
(p. 233)
Intrepid Sea-Air-Space Museum
(p. 233)
Lazer Park (p. 267)
Liberty Helicopters (p. 251)
Madison Square Garden (p. 277)
Museum of Modern Art (p. 227)
Museum of Television & Radio
(p. 238)
Radio City Music Hall (p. 245)
Rockefeller Center (p. 244)
Times Square (p. 60, p. 71, p. 318,
and p. 246)
World Yacht (p. 250)

UPPER EAST SIDE

Abigail Adams Smith Museum &
Gardens (p. 229)
Asia Society (p. 230)
Central Park (p. 253)
Central Park Wildlife Center/Tisch
Children's Zoo (p. 257)
Cooper–Hewitt National Design
Museum (p. 230)
El Museo del Barrio (p. 232)
The Frick Collection (p. 232)
Gracie Mansion (p. 231)
Guggenheim Museum (p. 228)
Jewish Museum (p. 234)
Metropolitan Museum of Art (p. 226)
Museum of the City of New York
(p. 238)
National Academy of Design (p. 239)
Neue Gallerie New York (p. 239)
92nd Street Y (p. 251 and p. 332)
Temple Emanu-El (p. 249)
Whitney Museum of American Art
(p. 228)

UPPER WEST SIDE

American Museum of Natural History
(p. 224)
The Ansonia (p. 247)
Cathedral of St. John the Divine
(p. 248)
Central Park (p. 253)
Children's Museum of Manhattan
(p. 265)
The Dakota (p. 247)
Museum of American Folk Art
(p. 236)
New-York Historical Society (p. 240)
Rose Center for Earth and Space
(p. 224)
Wollman Rink (p. 258)

OUTER BOROUGHS
THE BRONX

Bronx Zoo Wildlife Conservation
Park (p. 270)
Edgar Allen Poe Cottage (p. 231)
New York Botanical Garden (p. 271)
Wave Hill (p. 271)
Yankee Stadium (p. 277)

BROOKLYN

Brooklyn Botanic Garden (p. 272)
Brooklyn Heights Historic District
(p. 274)
Brooklyn Museum of Art (p. 272)
Coney Island (p. 273)
Grand Army Plaza (p. 272)
New York Aquarium (p. 273)
New York Transit Museum (p. 273)
Prospect Park (p. 273)

QUEENS

American Museum of the Moving
Image (p. 274)
Flushing Meadows–Corona Park
(p. 266)
Isamu Noguchi Garden Museum
(p. 276)
New York Hall of Science (p. 266)
P.S. 1 Contemporary Art Center
(p. 276)
Queens Museum of Art (p. 276)
Shea Stadium (p. 277)

2 In New York Harbor: The Statue of Liberty, Ellis Island & the Staten Island Ferry

Be sure to budget a full day for the Statue of Liberty and Ellis Island if you intend to explore both attractions thoroughly.

✪ Statue of Liberty. On Liberty Island in New York Harbor. ☎ **212/363-3200** (general info) or 212/269-5755 (ticket/ferry info). www.nps.gov/stli. Ferry ticket/admission to Statue of Liberty and Ellis Island $7 adults, $6 seniors, $3 children under 17. Daily 9am–5pm (last ferry departs around 3:30pm); extended hours in summer. Subway: N, R to Whitehall St./South Ferry; 4, 5 to Bowling Green; 1, 9 to South Ferry (the platform at this station is shorter than the train, so ride in the first 5 cars). Walk south through Battery Park to Castle Clinton, the fort housing the ferry ticket booth.

For the millions who first came by ship to America in the last century—either as privileged tourists or needy, hopeful immigrants—Lady Liberty, standing in the Upper Bay, was their first glimpse of America. No monument so embodies the nation's, and the world's, notion of political freedom and economic potential. Even if you don't make it out to Liberty Island, you can get a spine-tingling glimpse from Battery Park, from the New Jersey side of the bay, or during a free ride on the Staten Island Ferry (see below). It's always reassuring to see her torch lighting the way.

Proposed by French statesman Edouard de Laboulaye as a gift from France to the United States commemorating the two nations' friendship and joint notions of liberty, the statue was designed by sculptor Frédéric-Auguste Bartholdi with the engineering help of Alexandre-Gustave Eiffel (who was responsible for the famed Paris tower), and unveiled on October 28, 1886. Despite the fact that Joseph Pulitzer had to make a mighty effort to attract donations on this side of the Atlantic for her pedestal (designed by American Richard Morris Hunt), more than a million people watched as the French tricolor veil was pulled away. After nearly 100 years of wind, rain, and exposure to the harsh sea air, Lady Liberty received a resoundingly successful $150 million face-lift (including the relandscaping of Liberty Island and the replacement of the torch's flame) in time for its centennial celebration on July 4, 1986. Feted in fireworks, Miss Liberty became more of a city icon than ever before.

Touring Tips: Ferries leave daily every half hour to 45 minutes from 9am to about 3:30pm (their clock), with more frequent ferries in the morning and extended hours in summer. Try to go early on a weekday to avoid the crowds that swarm in the afternoon, on weekends, and on holidays. Be sure to arrive by noon if your heart's set on experiencing everything; go later and you may not have time to make it to the crown (summer visitors should see "Attention: Crown Climbers," below for details on possible restrictions). A stop at Ellis Island (below) is included in the fare, but if you catch the last ferry, you can only visit the statue or Ellis Island, not both.

The ferry ride takes about 20 minutes. Once on Liberty Island, you'll start to get an idea of the statue's immensity: She weighs 225 tons and measures 152 feet from foot to flame. Her nose alone is $4^1/_2$ feet long, and her index finger is 8 feet long. You may have to wait as long as 3 hours to walk up into the crown (the torch is not open to visitors). If it's summer, or if you're just not in shape for it, you may want to skip it: It's a grueling 354 steps (the equivalent of 22 stories) to the crown, or you can cheat and take the elevator the first 10 stories up (a shortcut I wholeheartedly endorse). But even if you take the elevator to get started, the interior is stifling once the temperature starts to climb. However, you don't have to go all the way up to the crown; there are a number of **observation decks** at different levels, including one at the top of the pedestal that's reachable by elevator. Even if you don't go inside, a stroll around the base is an extraordinary experience, and the views of the Manhattan skyline are stellar.

Attention: Crown Climbers

At press time, the park had instituted a special "crown" policy during the peak **summer** season: Visitors who want to walk up to the crown must be on one of the **first two ferries of the day** in order to do so. This policy is subject to change at any time, of course, so your best bet is to call ahead to learn the current policy before you plan your day.

At other times of year, you must be on line to climb to the crown by 2pm; otherwise, you will not be allowed up.

Note: If you're driving into the city to visit Lady Liberty, know that a much less-crowded ferry departs from Liberty State Park in Jersey City, NJ. Ferry fares are the same as from Battery Park. To get there, take the New Jersey Turnpike to exit 14B; parking is available. For more information, call ☎ 201/435-9499.

✪ **Ellis Island.** In New York Harbor. ☎ **212/363-3200** (general info) or 212/269-5755 (ticket/ferry info). www.ellisisland.org. For subway, hours, and ferry ticket details, see the Statue of Liberty, directly above (ferry trip includes stops at both sights).

One of New York's most moving sights, the restored Ellis Island opened in 1990, slightly north of Liberty Island. Roughly 40% of Americans (myself included) can trace their heritage back to an ancestor who came through here. For the 62 years when it was America's main entry point for immigrants (from 1892 to 1954), Ellis Island processed some 12 million people. The greeting was often brusque—especially in the early years of the century, until 1924, when as many as 12,000 came through in a single day. The statistics and their meaning can be overwhelming, but the **Immigration Museum** skillfully relates the story of Ellis Island and immigration in America by placing the emphasis on personal experience.

Today you enter the Main Building's baggage room, just as the immigrants did, and then climb the stairs to the **Registry Room,** with its dramatic vaulted tiled ceiling, where millions waited anxiously for medical and legal processing. A step-by-step account of the immigrants' voyage is detailed in the exhibit, with haunting photos and touching oral histories. What might be the most poignant exhibit is **"Treasures from Home,"** 1,000 objects and photos donated by descendants of immigrants, including family heirlooms, religious articles, and rare clothing and jewelry. Outside, the **American Immigrant Wall of Honor** commemorates the names of more than 500,000 immigrants and their families, from Myles Standish and George Washington's great-grandfather to the forefathers of John F. Kennedy, Jay Leno, and Barbra Streisand. You can even research your own family's history at the interactive **American Family Immigration History Center.** You might also make time to see the award-winning short film **"Trail of Hope, Trail of Tears,"** which plays on a continuous loop in two theaters. Additionally, the museum now stages a 30-minute play five times daily from 10:30am to 3:30pm called **"Ellis Island Stories,"** based on stories from the Ellis Island Oral History Archive ($3 adults, $2.50 seniors and kids 4–17). Whether you make time for this live performance or not, it's difficult to leave the museum unmoved.

Touring Tips: Ferries run daily to Ellis Island and Liberty Island from Battery Park and Liberty State Park at frequent intervals; see the Statue of Liberty listing (directly above) for details.

Staten Island Ferry. Departs from the Whitehall Ferry Terminal at the southern tip of Manhattan. ☎ **718/815-BOAT.** www.SI-Web.com/transportation/dot.htm. Free admission ($3 for car transport on select ferries). 24 hours; every 20–30 min. weekdays, less frequently on off-peak and weekend hours. Subway: N, R to Whitehall St./South Ferry; 1, 9 to South Ferry (ride in the first 5 cars); 4, 5 to Bowling Green.

Here's New York's best freebie—especially if you just want to glimpse the Statue of Liberty and not climb her steps. You get an enthralling hour-long excursion (round-trip) into the world's biggest harbor. This is not strictly a sightseeing ride but commuter transportation to and from Staten Island (remember Melanie Griffith, in big hair and sneakers, heading to the office in *Working Girl*?). As a result, during business hours you'll share the boat with working stiffs reading papers and drinking coffee inside, blissfully unaware of the sights outside.

You, however, should go on deck and enjoy the busy harbor traffic. The old orange-and-green boats usually have open decks along the sides or at the bow and stern; try to catch one of these boats if you can, since the newer white boats don't have decks. Grab a seat on the right side of the boat for the best view. On the way out of Manhattan, you'll pass the Statue of Liberty (the boat comes closest to Lady Liberty on the way to Staten Island), Ellis Island, and from the left side of the boat, Governor's Island; you'll see the Verranzano Narrows Bridge spanning the distance from Brooklyn to Staten Island in the distance.

When the boat arrives at St. George, Staten Island, everyone must disembark. Follow the boat-loading sign on your right as you get off; you'll circle around to the next loading dock, where there's usually another boat waiting to depart for Manhattan. The skyline views are simply awesome on the return trip. Well worth the time spent.

3 Historic Lower Manhattan's Top Attractions

○ **Brooklyn Bridge.** Subway: A, C to High St.; 4, 5, 6 to Brooklyn Bridge–City Hall.

Its Gothic-inspired stone pylons and intricate steel-cable webs have moved poets like Walt Whitman and Hart Crane to sing the praises of this great span, the first to cross the East River and connect Manhattan to Brooklyn. Begun in 1867 and ultimately completed in 1883, the beautiful Brooklyn Bridge is now the city's best-known symbol of the age of growth that seized the city during the late 19th century. Walk across the bridge and imagine the awe that New Yorkers of that age felt at seeing two boroughs joined by this monumental span. It's still astounding.

Designed by John Roebling, this massive engineering feat was plagued by death and disaster at its birth. Roebling was fatally injured in 1869 when a ferry rammed a water-front piling on which he stood. His son, Washington, who was subsequently put in charge, contracted the bends in 1872 while working underwater to construct the bridge's towers, and oversaw the rest of the construction with a telescope from his bed at the edge of the East River in Brooklyn Heights (his wife relayed his instructions to the workers). Washington refused to attend the 1883 opening ceremonies, having had a bitter disagreement with the company that financed the construction. Though it was declared the "eighth wonder of the world" upon its completion, the bridge's troubles were not over: Twelve pedestrians were killed in a stampede when panic about its imminent collapse spread like wildfire on the day it opened to the public. Things are usually calmer now.

Walking the Bridge: Walking the Brooklyn Bridge is one of my all-time favorite New York activities. A wide wood-plank pedestrian walkway is elevated above the traffic, making it a relatively peaceful, and popular, walk. It provides a great vantage point from which to contemplate the New York skyline and the East River.

There's a sidewalk entrance on Park Row, just across from City Hall Park (take the 4, 5, or 6 train to Brooklyn Bridge/City Hall). But why do this walk *away* from

Manhattan, toward the far less impressive Brooklyn skyline? For gorgeous Manhattan skyline views, take an A or C train to High Street, one stop into Brooklyn. From there, you'll be on the bridge in no time: Come above ground, then walk through the little park to Cadman Plaza East and head downslope (left) to the stairwell that will take you up to the footpath. (Following Prospect Place under the bridge, turning right onto Cadman Plaza East, will also take you directly to the stairwell.) It's a 20- to 40-minute stroll over the bridge to Manhattan, depending on your pace, the amount of foot traffic, and the number of stops you make to contemplate the spectacular views (there are benches along the way). The footpath will deposit you right at City Hall Park.

If you'd like to extend this walk a bit, I highly recommend pairing it with a quick tour of Brooklyn Heights and its wonderful Promenade; see "Highlights of the Outer Boroughs," later in this chapter, for exact directions.

New York Stock Exchange. 20 Broad St. (between Wall St. and Exchange Place). ☎ **212/ 656-5165.** www.nyse.com. Free admission. Mon–Fri 9am–4:30pm (ticket booth opens at 8:45am). Subway: J, M, Z to Broad St.; 2, 3, 4, 5 to Wall St.

Wall Street—it's an iconic name, and ground zero for bulls and bears everywhere. This narrow 18th-century lane (you'll be surprised at how little it is) is appropriately monumental, lined with neoclassical towers that reach as far skyward as the dreams and greed of investors who built it into the world's most famous financial market. At the heart of the action is the New York Stock Exchange, the world's largest securities trader, where you can watch the billions change hands and get a fleeting idea of how the money merchants work.

While the NYSE is on Wall Street, the ticket kiosk is around the corner at 20 Broad St., where you'll be issued a ticket with a time on it; you must enter during the 45-minute window of opportunity specified on your ticket. The staff starts handing out tickets at 8:45am, but get in line early if you want to be inside to see all hell break loose at the 9:30am opening bell. The 3,000 tickets issued per day are usually gone by noon; plan on having to return unless you're one of the first in line. Despite the number of visitors, things move pretty quickly.

Don't expect to come out with a full understanding of the market; if you didn't have one going in, you won't leave any more enlightened. Still, it's fun watching the action on the trading floor from the glass-lined, mezzanine-level **observation gallery** (look to the right, and you'll see the Bloomberg people sending their live reports back to the newsroom). You can stay as long as you like, but it doesn't really take more than 20 minutes or so to peruse the other jingoistic exhibits ("NYSE—our hero!"), which include a rather oblique explanation of the floor activities, interactive exhibits, and a short film.

South Street Seaport & Museum. At Water and South sts.; museum is at 12–14 Fulton St. ☎ **212/748-8600** or 212/SEA-PORT. www.southstseaport.org or www.southstreetseaport. com. Museum admission $6 adults, $5 seniors, $3 children. Museum: May–Sept Fri–Wed 10am–6pm, Thurs 10am–8pm; Oct–Apr Wed–Mon 10am–5pm. Subway: 2, 3, 4, 5 to Fulton St. (walk east, or downslope, on Fulton St. to Water St.).

This landmark district on the East River encompasses 11 square blocks of historic buildings, a maritime museum, several piers, shops and restaurants (including the authentically old-world North Star Pub; see chapter 6), and even a Best Western hotel (see chapter 5).

You can explore most of the Seaport on your own. It's an odd place. The 18th- and 19th-century buildings lining the cobbled streets and alleyways are beautifully restored but nevertheless have a theme-park air about them, no doubt due to the J. Crews,

Brookstones, and Body Shops housed within. The height of the Seaport's cheesiness is Pier 17, a historic barge converted into a mall, complete with food court and cheap jewelry kiosks.

Despite its rampant commercialism, the Seaport is worth a look. There's a good amount of history to be discovered here, most of it around the **South Street Seaport Museum,** a fitting tribute to the sea commerce that once thrived here.

In addition to the galleries—which house paintings and prints, ship models, scrimshaw, and nautical designs, as well as frequently changing exhibitions—there are a number of historic ships berthed at the pier to explore, including the 1911 four-masted *Peking* and the 1893 Gloucester fishing schooner *Lettie G. Howard.* A few of the boats are living museums and restoration works in progress; others are available for private charters. You can actually hit the high seas on the 1885 cargo schooner *Pioneer* (☎ 212/748-8786), which offers 2-hour public sails daily from early May through September. Tickets are $20 for adults, $15 for seniors and students, and $12 for children. Advance reservations are recommended, and can be made up to 14 days in advance; always call ahead to confirm sailing times.

Even **Pier 17** has its merits. Head up to the third-level deck overlooking the East River, where the long wooden chairs will have you thinking about what it was like to cross the Atlantic on the *Normandie.* From this level you can see south to the Statue of Liberty, north to the Gothic majesty of the Brooklyn Bridge, and Brooklyn Heights on the opposite shore.

Just to the north of Pier 17 is the famous **Fulton Fish Market,** on Fulton Street at the East River, the nation's largest wholesale fish market. If you're willing to come down here at 4am, you can watch the catch of the day from all over the globe being tossed, traded, and sold the old-fashioned way. The city's great chefs and wholesale buyers from all over the country gather here daily to snap up untold pounds of fish.

At the gateway to the Seaport, at Fulton and Water streets, is the *Titanic* **Memorial Lighthouse,** a monument to those who lost their lives when the ocean liner sank on April 15, 1912. It was erected overlooking the East River in 1913 and moved to this spot in 1968, just after the historic district was so designated.

A variety of events take place year-round, ranging from street performers to concerts to fireworks; check the Web site or dial ☎ **212/SEA-PORT.**

World Trade Center. Bounded by Church, Vesey, Liberty, and West sts. ☎ **212/ 323-2340.** Admission to observation deck $13 adults, $9.50 seniors, $11 students 13–17, $6.50 children 6–12. Observation deck: Sept–May daily 9:30am–9:30pm; June–Aug daily 9:30am–11:30pm. Subway: C, E to World Trade Center; N, R, 1, 9 to Cortlandt St.

Nowhere near as romantic as the Empire State Building, the World Trade Center is nevertheless just as heroic, having withstood a bombing in its basement garage in 1993 without so much as a flinch. Built in 1970, the center is actually an immense complex of seven buildings on 16 acres housing offices, restaurants, a hotel, an underground shopping mall, and an outdoor plaza with fountains, sculpture, and summer concerts and performances. But the parts you'll be interested in are the Twin Towers, which usurped the Empire State to become New York's tallest structures.

The boxlike buildings are so nondescript that the local Channel 11 once used them to represent that number in their commercials. Each is 110 stories and 1,350 feet high. The **Top of the World** observation deck is high atop 2 World Trade Center, to the south. On the 107th floor, it's like a cheesy mini–theme park, offering (besides the views, of course) a 6-minute simulated helicopter tour over Manhattan that's so low-grade it looks like it was filmed in 1978; high-tech kiosks pointing out the sights in every direction; a food court; and a gift shop.

But the reason to come is for those incredible views. The enclosed top floor offers incredible panoramas on all sides, with windows reaching right down to the floor. Go ahead, walk right up to one, and look down—*scaaary.*

If you're lucky and the weather is good, you'll be able to go out on the **rooftop promenade,** the world's highest open-air observation deck. (It's only open under perfect conditions; I've only been able to go out once in a lifetime of visits.) You thought inside was incredible? Wait 'til you see this. While you're up here, look straight down and wonder what Frenchman Philippe Petit could've been thinking when in 1974 he shot a rope across to tower no. 1, grabbed his balancing pole, and walked gingerly across, stopping to lie down for a moment in the center.

You can have a similar view in more convivial conditions by going to the top of 1 World Trade Center, where you can dine at **Windows on the World** or **Wild Blue** (see chapter 6), or linger over a drink and munchies—or put on some dancing shoes and hit the floor—at the **Greatest Bar on Earth** (see chapter 9).

Walking Tour: Wall Street & the Financial District

Start: Battery Park/U.S. Customs House.
Subway: Take the 4 or 5 to Bowling Green, the 1 or 9 to South Ferry, or the N or R to Whitehall St./South Ferry.
Finish: The Municipal Building.
Time: Approximately 3 hours.
Best Time: Any weekday, when the wheels of finance are spinning and lower Manhattan is a maelstrom of frantic activity.
Worst Time: Weekends, when most buildings and all the financial markets are closed.

The narrow winding streets of the Financial District occupy the earliest-settled area of Manhattan, where the Dutch established the colony of Nieuw Amsterdam in the early 17th century. Before their arrival, downtown was part of a vast forest, a lush hunting ground for the Native Americans, inhabited by mountain lions, bobcats, beavers, white-tailed deer, and wild turkeys. A hunting path—which later evolved into Broadway—extended from the Battery to the present City Hall Park.

Today this section of the city, much like Nieuw Amsterdam, centers on commerce. Wall Street is America's most cogent symbol of money and power; bulls and bears have replaced the wild beasts of the forest, and conservatively attired lawyers, stockbrokers, bankers, and businesspeople have supplanted the Native Americans and Dutchmen who once traded otter skins and beaver pelts on these very streets.

A highlight of this tour is the Financial District's architecture, in which the neighborhood's modern manifestations and grand historical structures are dramatically juxtaposed: Colonial, 18th-century Georgian/Federal, and 19th-century neoclassical buildings stand in the shadow of colossal skyscrapers.

The subways all exit in or near **Battery Park,** an expanse of green at Manhattan's tip resting entirely upon landfill—an old strategy of the Dutch to expand their settlement farther into the bay. The original tip of Manhattan ran somewhere right along Battery Place, which borders the north side of the park. State Street flanks the park's east side, and stretched along it, filling the space below Bowling Green, squats the beaux arts bulk of the old:

   1. **Alexander Hamilton U.S. Customs House,** housing the Smithsonian's George Gustav Haye Center of the **National Museum of the American Indian** (☎ 212/668-6624; www.si.edu/nmai) until the museum's new home in

Walking Tour: Wall Street & the Financial District

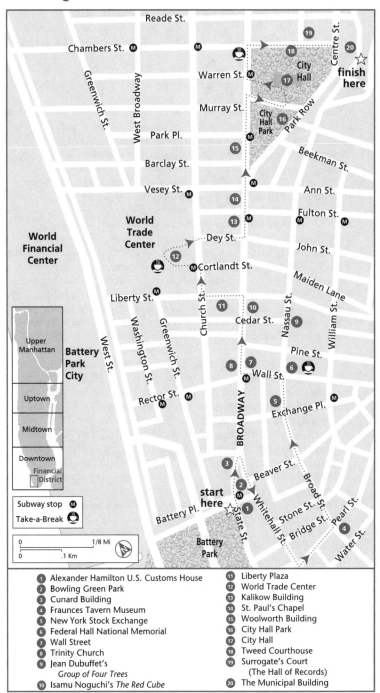

1. Alexander Hamilton U.S. Customs House
2. Bowling Green Park
3. Cunard Building
4. Fraunces Tavern Museum
5. New York Stock Exchange
6. Federal Hall National Memorial
7. Wall Street
8. Trinity Church
9. Jean Dubuffet's
   Group of Four Trees
10. Isamu Noguchi's *The Red Cube*
11. Liberty Plaza
12. World Trade Center
13. Kalikow Building
14. St. Paul's Chapel
15. Woolworth Building
16. City Hall Park
17. City Hall
18. Tweed Courthouse
19. Surrogate's Court
   (The Hall of Records)
20. The Municipal Building

Washington, D.C., is completed in 2002. The giant statues lining the front of this granite 1907 structure personify *Asia* (pondering philosophically), *America* (bright-eyed and bushy-tailed), *Europe* (decadent, whose time has passed), and *Africa* (sleeping), and were carved by Daniel Chester French of Lincoln Memorial fame. The most interesting, if unintentional, sculptural statement—keeping in mind the building's current purpose—is the giant seated woman to the left of the entrance representing America. The young, upstart America is surrounded by references to Native America: Mayan pictographs adorning her throne, Quetzalcoatl under her foot, a shock of corn in her lap, and the generic plains Indian scouting out from over her shoulder. Look behind her throne for the stylized crow figure—an important animal in many native cultures, usually playing a trickster character in myths, which is probably why he's hiding back here.

The airy oval rotunda inside was frescoed by Reginald Marsh to glorify the shipping industry (and, by extension, the Customs office once here). The museum is free and open daily from 10am to 5pm (until 8pm on Thurs). For more information, see "More Manhattan Museums," later in this chapter.

As you exit the building, directly in front of you sits the pretty little oasis of:

2. Bowling Green Park. This is probably the spot, or at least near enough, where in 1626 Dutchman Peter Minuit gave glass beads and other trinkets worth about 60 guilders ($24) to a group of Indians, and then claimed he had thereby bought Manhattan. Now the local Indians didn't consider that they owned this island—not because they didn't believe in property (that's a colonial myth, as they did have their own territories nearby). But Manhattan was considered communal hunting ground, shared by several different groups. So it isn't clear what the Indians thought the trinkets meant. Either (a) they just thought the exchange was a formal way of closing an agreement to extend the shared hunting use of the island to this funny-looking group of pale people with yellow beards; or (b) they were knowingly selling land that they didn't own in the first place, thus performing the first shrewd real-estate deal of the Financial District.

When King George III repealed the hated Stamp Act in 1770, New Yorkers magnanimously raised a statue of him here, although today it's just another lunch spot for stockbrokers. The statue lasted 5 years, until the day the Declaration of Independence was read to the public in front of City Hall (now Federal Hall) and a crowd rushed down Broadway to topple the statue, chop it up, melt it down, and transform it into 42,000 bullets, which they later used to shoot the British.

The park also marks the start of Broadway. Walk up the left side of Broadway; at no. 25 is the:

3. Cunard Building, now a post office but in 1921 the ticketing room for Cunard, one of the world's most glamorous shipping and cruise lines and proprietors of the *QEII.* Cunard established the first passenger steamship between Europe and the Americas, and in this still-impressive Great Hall, you once could book passage on any one of their famous fantastically unfortunate ships, from the *Lusitania* (blown up by the Germans) to the *Titanic* (well, you know how that one ended).

As you exit the building, cross to the traffic island to pat the enormous bronze **bull,** symbol of a strong stock market, ready to charge up Broadway. This instant icon began as a practical joke by Italian sculptor Arturo DiModica, who originally stuck it in front of the New York Stock Exchange building in the middle of the night. The unamused brokers had it promptly removed, and it eventually got placed here.

The Money Museum

Real money buffs (and who among us isn't?) may want to make a brief stop at the **Museum of American Financial History,** 28 Broadway, just north of Bowling Green Park (☎ **212/908-4110** or 212/908-4519; www.financialhistory.org). Exhibits housed in this little museum include numismatic and vintage ticker-tape displays; murals and photos depicting historic Wall Street scenes; and interactive financial news terminals, in partnership with CNNfn, so little bulls and bears can learn how to keep up with the market. Open Tuesday through Saturday from 10am to 4pm; the suggested donation is $2.

Now you're going to backtrack a bit. Head south on Whitehall Street (around the left side of the U.S. Customs House) and turn left onto Pearl Street. Just past Broad Street stretches a historic block lined with (partially rebuilt) 18th- and 19th-century buildings, including:

4. Fraunces Tavern, 54 Pearl St. The restaurant on the main floor is now closed, but the two upper stories still house the **Fraunces Tavern Museum** (☎ **212/ 425-1778**), where you can see the Long Room, in which George Washington made his historic farewell to his soldiers at the end of the American Revolution, and other American history exhibits. Admission is $2.50 for adults, $1 for seniors and students. Open Monday through Friday from 10am to 4:45pm, Saturday from noon to 4pm.

From Fraunces Tavern, head straight up Broad Street. At no. 20, on the left, is the visitor's entrance to the:

5. New York Stock Exchange (☎ **212/656-5165**), which came into being in 1792, when merchants met daily under a nearby buttonwood tree to try and pass off to each other the U.S. bonds that had been sold to fund the Revolutionary War. By 1903, they were trading stocks of publicly held companies in this Corinthian-columned beaux arts "temple" designed by George Post. More than 3,000 companies are listed on the exchange, trading nearly 281 billion shares valued at more than $12 trillion.

Inside you can watch the frenzied action on the trading floor. The observation platform has been glassed in since the 1960s, when Abbie Hoffman and Jerry Rubin created chaos by tossing dollar bills onto the exchange floor. Admission is free; for more information, see "Historic Lower Manhattan's Top Attractions" directly above this walking tour.

After the New York Stock Exchange, continue north (left) up Broad Street. At the end of the block you'll see the Parthenon-inspired:

6. Federal Hall National Memorial, 26 Wall St., at Nassau Street (☎ **212/ 825-6888;** www.nps.gov/feha). Fronted by 32-foot fluted marble Doric columns, this imposing 1842 neoclassical temple is most famous for the history of the old British City Hall building, later called Federal Hall, that once stood here. Peter Zenger, publisher of the outspoken *Weekly Journal,* stood trial in 1735 for "seditious libel" against Royal Gov. William Cosby. Defended brilliantly by Alexander Hamilton, Zenger's eventual acquittal (based on the grounds that anything you printed that was true, even if it wasn't very nice, couldn't be construed as libel) set the precedent for freedom of the press, later guaranteed in the Bill of Rights, which was drafted and signed inside this building.

New York's first major rebellion against British authority occurred here when the Stamp Act Congress met in 1765 to protest King George III's policy of "taxation without representation." J. Q. A. Ward's 1883 statue of George Washington on the steps commemorates the spot of the first presidential inauguration, in 1789. Congress met here after the revolution, when New York was briefly the nation's capital.

Exhibits within (open Mon through Fri from 9am to 5pm, daily in July and Aug) elucidate these events along with other aspects of American history. Admission is free; call ahead if you'd like to hook up with one of the 20- to 30-minute guided tours, which usually take place between 12:30 and 3:30pm.

☕ **TAKE A BREAK**   If you're ready to rest your weary toes for a few minutes, turn left out of Federal Hall and proceed to **Mangia,** at 40 Wall St., between Nassau and William streets (☎ 212/425-4040). This big, bustling gourmet cafeteria is the ideal place to relax over a midmorning snack or a full lunch. Open weekdays from 7am to 6pm; for more information, see chapter 6.

From Federal Hall, or Mangia, turn right up the road that has become the symbol of high finance the world over:

7. **Wall Street.** It is narrow, just a few short blocks long, and started out as a service road that ran along the fortified wall the Dutch erected in 1653 to defend against Indian attack. (Gov. Peter Stuyvesant's settlers had at first played tribes off against each other in order to trick them into more and more land cessation, but the native groups quickly realized that their real enemies were the Dutch.)

Wall Street hits Broadway across the street from:

8. **Trinity Church** (☎ 212/602-0800; www.trinitywallstreet.org). Serving God and Mammon, this Wall Street house of worship—with neo-Gothic flying buttresses, beautiful stained-glass windows, and vaulted ceilings—was designed by Richard Upjohn and consecrated in 1846. At that time, its 280-foot spire dominated the skyline. Its main doors, embellished with biblical scenes, were inspired in part by Ghiberti's famed doors on Florence's Baptistery.

The first church on this site went up in 1697 and burned down in 1776. The church runs a brief tour daily at 2pm. There's a small museum at the end of the left aisle displaying documents (including the 1697 church charter from King William III), photographs, replicas of the Hamilton–Burr duel pistols, and other items.

Surrounding the church is a **churchyard** with monuments that read like an American history book: a tribute to martyrs of the American Revolution, Alexander Hamilton, Robert Fulton, and many more. Lined with benches, this makes a wonderful picnic spot on warm days.

The church is open to the public weekdays 7am to 6pm, Saturday 8am to 4pm, and Sunday 7am to 4pm. Services are held weekdays at 8:15am, 12:05pm, and 5:15, Saturday at 9am, and Sunday at 9 and 11:15am. Trinity holds its **Noonday Concert series** of chamber music and orchestral concerts Thursday at 1pm; a $2 contribution is requested. Call ☎ 212/602-0747 or visit the Web site for details.

Take a left as you leave the church and walk 2 short blocks up Broadway. As you pass Cedar Street, look (don't walk) to your right, across Broadway, and down Cedar and you'll see, at the end of the street:

9. **Jean Dubuffet's** *Group of Four Trees,* installed in 1972 in the artist's patented style: amorphous mushroomlike white shapes traced with undulating black lines.

Dubuffet considered these drawings in three dimensions "which extend and expand into space."

Closer at hand, in front of the tall black HSBC building on Broadway between Cedar and Liberty streets, is:

10. Isamu Noguchi's 1967 *The Red Cube,* another famed outdoor sculpture of downtown Manhattan. Noguchi fancied that this rhomboid "cube"—balancing on its corner and shot through with a cylinder of empty space—represented chance, like the "rolling of the dice." It is appropriately located in the gilt-edged gambling den that is the Financial District.

As you're looking at the *Cube* across Broadway, behind you is the tiny square called:

11. Liberty Plaza, a block off Liberty Street with some benches and shade for lunching CEOs. Turn left and walk through the park, heading east toward Trinity Place. Mingling among the flesh-and-blood office workers seated here is one in bronze, called *Double Check* (1982), by realist American sculptor J. Seward Johnson, Jr.

At Trinity Place, take a right. A short block up on the left will open the grand plaza of the:

12. World Trade Center (WTC), bounded by Vesey, West, Liberty, and Church streets and best known for its famous 110-story twin towers. The WTC is an immense complex. Its 12 million square feet of rentable office space houses more than 350 firms and organizations. About 50,000 people work in its precincts, and some 70,000 others (tourists and businesspeople) visit them each day. The complex occupies 16 acres and includes, in addition to the towers, a 22-story Marriott hotel, a plaza the size of four football fields, an underground shopping mall, and several restaurants.

The plaza, like much of downtown, is rich in **outdoor sculpture,** including the polished black granite miniature mountains (as you enter) crafted by Japanese artist Masayuki Nagare (1972). Fritz Keonig's 25-foot-high bronze morphing sphere (1971) forms the centerpiece of the plaza's wide fountain. Hang a right here between two of the squat black glass buildings to get a glance of Alexander Calder's *Three Wings.* Take particular notice of the curving, metal, winglike flanges, riveted together and painted red.

Do an about-face to return to the central plaza. The left hand of the twin towers is 2 World Trade Center. As you enter on the mezzanine level, to your left, you'll see a 1974 tapestry by Spanish artist Joan Miró and a **TKTS booth** if you want to pick up half-price tickets to one of tonight's Broadway or Off-Broadway shows (for details, see chapter 9). The real thing to do, of course, is head around the elevator banks to the right to buy tickets and whiz up to the 107th-floor **Top of the World Observation Deck,** where you're treated to a 1,377-foot-high perspective of the city and New York Harbor. If it's open, be sure to ascend to the 110th-floor **rooftop promenade,** the world's highest open-air viewing platform, for even more magnificent views. Open daily from 9:30am to 9:30pm (until 11:30pm June through Aug); for more information, see "Historic Lower Manhattan's Top Attractions" directly above this walking tour.

🍵 **TAKE A BREAK**   There are a number of casual choices on the main (street-level) concourse, including **Sbarro Pizza; Menchenko-Tei,** for authentic Japanese bento-box lunches; and **Fine & Shapiro,** for takeout or full-service deli. **Ecce Panis** is an excellent bakery with a small selection of sandwiches, focaccias, breakfast and sweet treats, two daily soups, and an amazing ham and cheese brioche. In summer, you might want to bring your lunches to the tree-shaded tables on the plaza. Once you're done, head over to **Krispy Kreme Doughnuts,** on the plaza at 5 WTC, for a sweet, light-as-air treat (the entrance is outside on the plaza next to Borders, near Church and Vesey sts.).

Walk out the front side of WTC plaza again the way you came in, cross Church Street, and head straight down Dey Street, which is in front of you, back to Broadway. Take a left, and on your left is the:

13. Kalikow Building, at 195 Broadway. This 1915–22 neoclassic tower, formerly AT&T headquarters, has more exterior columns than any other building in the world. The 25-story structure rests on a Doric colonnade, with Ionic colonnades above. The lobby evokes a Greek temple with a forest of massive fluted columns. The building's tower crown is modeled on the Mausoleum of Halicarnassus, the great Greek monument of antiquity. The bronze panels over the entranceway by Paul Manship (sculptor of Rockefeller Center's *Prometheus*) symbolize wind, air, fire, and earth.

Continue south on Broadway. The next block contains the small:

14. St. Paul's Chapel, between Vesey and Fulton streets, New York's only surviving pre-Revolutionary church, and now a transition shelter for homeless men. Under the east portico is a 1789 monument to Gen. Richard Montgomery, one of the first Revolutionary patriots to die in battle. During the 2 years that New York was the nation's capital, George Washington worshiped at this Georgian chapel belonging to Trinity Church and dating from 1766; his "pew" is on the right side of the church. Built by Thomas McBean, with a templelike portico and fluted Ionic columns supporting a massive pediment, the chapel resembles London's St. Martin-in-the-Fields. Explore the small **graveyard** where 18th- and early-19th-century notables rest in peace and modern businesspeople sit for lunch; it's open Monday through Friday 9am to 3pm, Sunday 7am to 3pm. Trinity's **Noonday Concert series** is held here on Monday at noon; the suggested donation is $2. Call the concert hotline at ☎ 212/602-0747 for details, or visit **www.trinitywallstreet.org**.

Continue up Broadway, crossing Vesey and Barclay streets, and at 233 Broadway is the:

15. Woolworth Building. This soaring "Cathedral of Commerce" cost Frank W. Woolworth $13.5 million worth of nickels and dimes in 1913. Designed by Cass Gilbert, it was the world's tallest edifice until 1930, when it was surpassed by the Chrysler Building. At its opening, Pres. Woodrow Wilson pressed a button from the White House that illuminated the building's 80,000 electric lightbulbs. The neo-Gothic architecture is rife with spires, gargoyles, flying buttresses, vaulted ceilings, 16th-century–style stone-as-lace traceries, castlelike turrets, and a churchlike interior.

Step into the lofty marble entrance arcade to view the gleaming mosaic Byzantine-style ceiling and gold-leafed neo-Gothic cornices. The corbels (carved figures under the crossbeams) in the lobby include whimsical portraits of the building's engineer Gunwald Aus measuring a girder (above the staircase to the left of the main door), Gilbert holding a miniature model of the building, and Woolworth counting coins (both above the left-hand corridor of elevators). Stand near the security guard's central podium and crane your neck for a glimpse at Paul Jennewein's murals of *Commerce* and *Labor,* half hidden up on the mezzanine.

To get an overview of the Woolworth's architecture, cross Broadway. On this side of the street, you'll find scurrying city officials and greenery that together make up:

16. **City Hall Park,** a 250-year-old green surrounded by landmark buildings. A Frederick MacMonnies statue near the southwest corner of the park depicts Nathan Hale at age 21, having just uttered his famous words before execution: "I only regret that I have but one life to lose for my country." Northeast of City Hall in the park is a statue of Horace Greeley (seated with newspaper in hand) by J. Q. A. Ward. This small park has been a burial ground for paupers and the site of public executions, parades, and protests.

It is the setting for:

17. **City Hall,** the seat of municipal government, housing the offices of the mayor and his staff, the city council, and other city agencies. City Hall combines Georgian and French Renaissance styles, designed by Joseph F. Mangin and John McComb Jr. in 1803–11. Later additions include the clock and 6,000-pound bell in the cupola tower. The cupola itself is crowned with a stately white-painted copper statue of *Justice* (anonymously produced in a workshop).

☕ **TAKE A BREAK**   Grab a pastry or a diner meal at **Ellen's Cafe and Bake Shop,** 270 Broadway, at Chambers Street (☎ **212/962-1257**). Owner Ellen Hart won the Miss Subways beauty pageant in 1959, and her restaurant walls are lined with her own and other Miss Subways posters, plus photographs of all the politicians who have eaten here: Al D'Amato, Rudy Giuliani, Bella Abzug, Mario Cuomo, and Geraldine Ferraro, to name just a few. Muffins, biscuits, and pastries are all oven-fresh, and full breakfasts of eggs, bacon, pancakes, and Belgian waffles are available. Open weekdays 6am to 7pm, Saturday 8am to 4:30pm.

Along the north edge of City Hall Park, on Chambers Street, sits the:

18. **Tweed Courthouse** (New York County Courthouse, 52 Chambers St.). This 1872 Italianate courthouse was built during the tenure of William Marcy "Boss" Tweed, who, in his post on the board of supervisors, stole millions in construction funds. Originally budgeted as a $250,000 job in 1861, the courthouse project escalated to the staggering sum of $14 million. Bills were padded to an unprecedented extent—Andrew Garvey, who was to become known as the "Prince of Plasterers," was paid $45,966.89 for a single day's work! The ensuing scandal (Tweed and his cronies, it came out, had pocketed at least $10 million) wrecked Tweed's career; he died penniless in jail.

Across Chambers Street and to the right, at the corner of Elk Street, lies the turn-of-the-century:

19. **Surrogate's Court (The Hall of Records),** 31 Chambers St. Housed in this sumptuous beaux arts structure are all the legal records relating to Manhattan real estate deeds and court cases, some dating from the mid-1600s. Heroic statues of distinguished New Yorkers (Peter Stuyvesant, De Witt Clinton, and others) front the mansard roof, and the doorways, surmounted by arched pediments, are flanked by Philip Martiny's sculptural groups portraying *New York in Revolutionary Times* (to your left) and *New York in Its Infancy* (to your right). Above the entrance is a three-story Corinthian colonnade.

Step inside to see the vestibule's beautiful barrel-vaulted mosaic ceiling, embellished with astrological symbols, Egyptian and Greek motifs, and figures representing retribution, justice, sorrow, and labor. Continue back to the two-story skylit neoclassical atrium, clad in honey-colored marble with a colonnaded second-floor loggia and an ornate staircase adapted from the foyer of the Grand Opera House in Paris.

Exiting the Surrogate's Court from the front door, you'll see to your left, at the end of the block, that Chambers Street disappears under:

20. The **Municipal Building,** a grand civic edifice built between 1909 and 1914 to augment City Hall's government office space. It was designed by the famed architectural firm of McKim, Mead, and White (as in Stanford White), who used Greek and Roman design elements such as a massive Corinthian colonnade, ornately embellished vaults and cornices, and allegorical statuary. A triumphal arch, its barrel-vaulted ceiling adorned with relief panels, forms a magnificent arcade over Chambers Street; it has been called the "gate of the city." Sculptor Adolph Weinman created many of the building's bas reliefs, medallions, and allegorical groupings of human figures (they symbolize civic pride, progress, guidance, prudence, and executive power). The heroic hammered-copper statue of *Civic Fame,* Manhattan's largest statue, which tops the structure 582 feet above the street, was also designed by Weinman, holding a crown whose five turrets represent New York's five boroughs.

See many lovey-dovey couples walking in and out? The city's marriage license bureau is on the second floor, and a wedding takes place about every 20 minutes.

4 The Top Museums

✪ **American Museum of Natural History.** Central Park West (btw. 77th and 81st sts.) ☎ **212/769-5100** for information, or 212/769-5200 for tickets (tickets can also be ordered online). www.amnh.org. Suggested admission $9.50 adults, $7.50 seniors and students, $6 children 2–12. Combination packages available that include IMAX films, audio tours, and/or special exhibitions. Space Show tickets (museum admission included) $19 adults, $14 seniors and students, $11.50 children under 12. Sun–Thurs 10am–5:45pm, Fri–Sat 10am–8:45pm. Subway: B, C to 81st St.; 1, 9 to 79th St.

This is the hottest ticket in town as of February 2000, thanks to the grand opening of the new $210 million ✪ **Rose Center for Earth and Space,** home to the brand-new **Hayden Planetarium.** The planetarium's four-story-tall sphere hosts the Tom Hanks–narrated Space Show, the most technologically advanced sky show on the planet—*New York* magazine has called it "the world's largest, most powerful virtual-reality simulator." Prepare to be blown away. The Rose Center is a cutting-edge scientific wonderland that also houses the Big Bang Theater, which re-creates the theoretical birth of the universe; halls chronicling the evolution and history of the cosmos; its own $15^1/_2$-ton meteorite; and much more.

The rest of the 4-square-block museum is nothing to sneeze at, either. It houses the world's greatest natural science collection in a group of buildings made of towers and turrets, pink granite and red brick—a mishmash of architectural styles, but overflowing with neo-Gothic charm. The diversity of the holdings is astounding: some 36 million specimens ranging from microscopic organisms to the world's largest cut gem, the Brazilian Princess Topaz (21,005 carats). It would take all day to see the entire museum, and then you still wouldn't get to everything. If you don't have a lot of time, you can see the best of the best on free **highlights tours** offered daily every hour at 15 minutes after the hour from 10:15am to 3:15pm. Free daily **spotlights tours,** thematic tours that change monthly, are also offered; stop by an information desk for the day's schedule. **Audio Expeditions,** high-tech audio tours that allow you to access narration in the order you choose, are also available to help you make sense of it all.

Money- & Time-Saving Tip

CityPass just may be New York's best sightseeing deal. Pay one price ($31.75) for admission to six top attractions—the Top of the World observation deck at the World Trade Center, the American Museum of Natural History, the Solomon R. Guggenheim Museum, the Museum of Modern Art, the Empire State Building, and the *Intrepid* Sea-Air-Space Museum—which would cost you fully twice as much if you paid for each one separately. More important, CityPass is not a coupon book; it contains actual admission tickets, so you can bypass lengthy ticket lines. CityPass is good for 9 days from the first time you use it. It's sold at all participating attractions, and discounted rates are available for kids and seniors. If you want to avoid that first line, order your CityPass online at **www.citypass.net** or www.ticketweb.com. For phone orders, call Ticketweb at ☎ **212/269-4TIX.** Call CityPass at ☎ **707/256-0490** for further details.

If you only see one exhibit, see the ✪ **dinosaurs,** which take up the entire fourth floor. Start in the **Orientation Room,** where a short video gives an overview of the 500 million years of evolutionary history that led to you. Continue to the **Vertebrate Origins Room,** where huge models of ancient fish and turtles hang overhead, with plenty of interactive exhibits and kid-level displays on hand to keep young minds fascinated. Next come the great **dinosaur halls,** with mammoth, spectacularly reconstructed skeletons and more interactive displays. **Mammals and Their Extinct Relatives** brings what you've learned in the previous halls home, showing how yesterday's prehistoric monsters have evolved into today's modern animals. Simply marvelous—you could spend hours in these halls alone.

Many other areas of the museum pale in comparison. The animal habitat dioramas and halls of peoples seem dated but still have something to teach, especially the Native American halls. Other than peeking in to see the giant whale (viewable from the cafe below), skip the ocean life room altogether; let's hope this is next on the restoration agenda. The new Hall of Biodiversity is an impressive multimedia exhibit, but the doom-and-gloom story it tells about the future of rain forests and other natural habitats may be too much for the little ones. Kids 5 years and older should head to the Discovery Room, with lots of hands-on exhibits and experiments. (Be prepared, Mom and Dad—there seems to be a gift shop overflowing with fuzzy stuffed animals at every turn.)

The museum excels at **special exhibitions,** so I recommend checking to see what will be on while you're in town in case any advance planning is required. Highlights of the past year have included the magical Butterfly Conservatory, a walk-in enclosure housing nearly 500 free-flying tropical butterflies.

In addition, an **IMAX Theater** shows neat films like *Everest* and *Africa's Elephant Kingdom* on a 4-story screen that puts you right in the heart of the action.

Getting Planetarium Tickets: Admission to the Rose Center is included in museum admission, but separate tickets are required to view the planetarium's 30-minute Space Show; don't show up without advance tickets, or you're likely to come away disappointed. At press time, tickets were sold out 6 weeks in advance; demand may slow down by the time you arrive, but placing your order before you leave home is a good idea, so you have your choice of dates and show times. IMAX tickets can also be ordered in advance.

⊙ Metropolitan Museum of Art. Fifth Ave. at 82nd St. ☎ **212/535-7710.** www. metmuseum.org. Suggested admission (includes same-day entrance to the Cloisters) $10 adults, $5 seniors and students, free for children under 12 when accompanied by an adult. Sun and Tues–Thurs 9:30am–5:30pm, Fri–Sat 9:30am–9pm. No strollers allowed Sun (back carriers available at 81st St. entrance coat-check area). Subway: 4, 5, 6 to 86th St.

Home of blockbuster after blockbuster exhibition, the Metropolitan Museum of Art attracts some 5 million people a year, more than any other spot in New York City. And it's no wonder—this place is magnificent. At 1.6 million square feet, this is the largest museum in the Western Hemisphere. Nearly all the world's cultures are on display through the ages—from Egyptian mummies to ancient Greek statuary to Islamic carvings to Renaissance paintings to Native American masks to 20th-century decorative arts—and masterpieces are the rule. You could go once a week for a lifetime and still find something new on each visit.

So unless you plan on spending your entire vacation in the museum (some people do), you cannot see the entire collection. My recommendation is to give it a good day—or better yet, 2 half days so you don't burn out. One good way to get an overview is to take advantage of the little-known **Museum Highlights Tour.** Even some New Yorkers who've spent many hours in the museum could profit from this once-over. Call ☎ **212/570-3711** (Mon–Fri 9am–5pm) or visit the museum's Web site for a schedule of this and subject-specific walking tours (Old Master Paintings, American Period Rooms, Arts of China, and so on); you can also get a schedule of the day's tours at the Visitor Services desk when you arrive.

The least overwhelming way to see the Met on your own is to pick up a map at the round desk in the entry hall and choose to concentrate on what you like, whether it's 17th-century paintings, American furniture, or the art of the South Pacific. Highlights include the American Wing's **Garden Court,** with its 19th-century sculpture, the lower-level **Costume Hall,** and the **Frank Lloyd Wright room.** The beautifully renovated **Roman and Greek galleries** are overwhelming, but in a marvelous way, as is the collection of later **Chinese art.** The highlight of the astounding **Egyptian collection** is the **Temple of Dendur,** in a dramatic, specially built glass-walled gallery with Central Park views. But it all depends on what your interests are. Don't forget the marvelous **special exhibitions,** which can range from "Jade in Ancient Costa Rica" to "Cubism and Fashion." If you'd like to plan your visit ahead of time, the museum's Web site is a useful tool; there's also a list of current exhibitions in the Friday and Sunday editions of the *New York Times.*

Special exhibits and programs abound. To purchase tickets for concerts and lectures, call ☎ **212/570-3949** (Mon–Sat 9:30am–5pm). The museum contains several dining facilities, including a **full-service restaurant** serving continental cuisine (☎ **212/ 570-3964** for reservations). The roof garden is worth visiting if you're here from spring to autumn, offering peaceful views over Central Park and the city.

On **Friday and Saturday evenings,** the Met remains open late not only for art viewing but also for cocktails in the Great Hall Balcony Bar (4–8:30pm) and classical

---

Museum-Going Tip

Many of the city's top museums—including the Natural History Museum, the Met, and MoMA—have late hours on Friday and/or Saturday nights. Take advantage of them. Most visitors run out of steam by dinnertime, so even on jam-packed weekends you'll largely have the place to yourself by 5 or 6pm—which, in most cases, leaves you hours left to explore, unfettered by crowds or screaming kids.

music from a string quintet or trio. A slate of after-hours programs (gallery talks, walking tours, family programs) changes by the week; call for this week's schedule. The restaurant stays open until 10pm (last reservation at 8:30pm), and dinner is usually accompanied by piano music.

The Met's medieval collections are housed in Upper Manhattan at the **Cloisters;** see "More Manhattan Museums," below.

✪ **Museum of Modern Art.** 11 W. 53rd St. (btw. Fifth and Sixth aves.). ☎ **212/708-9400.** www.moma.org. Admission $10 adults ($14 with audio tour), $6.50 seniors and students ($10.50 with audio tour), free for children under 16 accompanied by an adult; pay as you wish Fri 4:30–8:15pm. Sat–Tues and Thurs 10:30am–5:45pm, Fri 10:30am–8:15pm. Subway: E, F to Fifth Ave.; B, D, F, Q to 47th–50th sts./Rockefeller Center.

The Museum of Modern Art (or MoMA, as it's usually called) boasts the world's greatest collection of painting and sculpture ranging from the late 19th century to the present, including everything from van Gogh's *Starry Night,* Picasso's early *Les Demoiselles d'Avignon,* Monet's *Water Lilies,* and Klimt's *The Kiss* to later masterworks by Frida Kahlo, Edward Hopper, Andy Warhol, Robert Rauschenberg, and many others. Top that off with an extensive collection of modern drawings, photography, architectural models and furniture (including the Mies van der Rohe collection), iconic design objects ranging from tableware to sports cars, and film and video (including the world's largest collection of D. W. Griffith films), and you have quite a museum. If you're into modernism, this is the place to be.

While not quite Met-size, MoMA is probably still more than you can see in a day. In true modern style, the museum is efficient and well organized, so it's easy to focus on your primary interests; just grab a museum map after you pay your admission. For an overview, take the **self-guided tour** that stops at the collection's highlights, chosen by the different departments' curators. The **sculpture garden**—an island of trees and fountains in which to enjoy the works of Calder, Moore, and Rodin—is particularly of note. In addition, there's usually at least one beautifully mounted **special exhibition** in house that's worth a special trip, whether it be the works of Finnish master architect Alvar Aalto, Julia Margaret Cameron's remarkable 19th-century photographs of women, or a celebration of sight gags in contemporary art.

Even if you've been to MoMA before, you may want to take another look, especially if your visit falls before March 2001. Conceived as a preliminary experiment in reinstallation (practice for the museum's expansion project, overseen by Japanese architect Yoshio Taniguchi and set to be complete in 2004), **MoMA 2000** sets the museum's old order on end. Organized in three consecutive exhibition cycles, the show is installed throughout the entire museum and juxtaposed with works from other periods to illustrate the relationship between various historical movements. (You're likely to encounter *Open Ends,* focusing on 1960 to the present, running from mid-September 2000. Note that certain works of art that are part of the permanent collection will not be on display during this exhibition, so call ahead if you're coming to see a particular work.) After March 2001, the museum will restore its regular exhibition arrangement.

MoMA also boasts a good number of special programs. There's live jazz Thursday and Saturday evenings at **Sette MoMA** (☎ 212/708-9710), the museum's notable Italian restaurant overlooking the sculpture garden, and Friday evening at the more casual Garden Cafe. A full slate of symposiums, gallery talks by contemporary artists, interactive family programs, and brown-bag lunch lectures are always on offer; call ☎ 212/708-9781 or visit the museum's Web site to see what's on while you're in town. Additionally, there's always a multifaceted film and video program on the schedule; call

Impressions

If you're bored in New York, it's your own fault.

—Myrna Loy

the main number to see what's on. Films are included in the price of admission, but arrive early to make sure you get a seat. Don't miss the marvelous **MoMA Design Store** across the street; see chapter 8 for details.

Solomon R. Guggenheim Museum. 1071 Fifth Ave. (at 88th St.). ☎ **212/423-3500.** www.guggenheim.org. Admission $12 adults, $7 seniors, free for children under 12; pay as you wish Fri 6–8pm. Sun–Wed 9am–6pm, Fri–Sat 9am–8pm. Subway: 4, 5, 6 to 86th St.

It has been called a bun, a snail, a concrete tornado, and even a giant wedding cake; bring your kids, and they'll probably see it as New York's coolest opportunity for skateboarding. Whatever descriptive you choose to apply, Frank Lloyd Wright's only New York building, completed in 1959, is best summed up as a brilliant work of architecture—so consistently brilliant that it competes with the art for your attention. If you're looking for the city's best modern art, head to MoMA or the Whitney first; come to the Guggenheim to see the house.

It's easy to see the bulk of what's on display in 2 to 4 hours. Inside, a spiraling rotunda circles over a slowly inclined ramp that leads you past changing exhibits; scheduled for late 2000 through early 2001 are Amazons of the Avant Garde, focusing on six Russian women who made significant contributions to modern art in the early 20th century, and a Giorgio Armani career retrospective. Usually the progression is counterintuitive: from the first floor up, rather than from the sixth floor down. If you're not sure, ask a guard before you begin. Permanent exhibits of 19th- and 20th-century art, including strong holdings of Kandinsky, Klee, Picasso, and French impressionists, occupy a stark annex called the **Tower Galleries,** an addition accessible at every level that some critics claimed made the original look like a toilet bowl backed by a water tank (judge for yourself—I think there may be something to that view).

The Guggenheim runs some interesting special programs, including free docent tours (there's a 1-hour highlights tour daily at noon), a limited schedule of lectures, free family films, avant-garde screenings for grown-ups, and the World Beat Jazz Series, which resounds through the rotunda on Friday and Saturday evenings from 5 to 8pm.

For details on the **Guggenheim Museum SoHo,** the museum's downtown annex, see "More Manhattan Museums," below.

✪ **Whitney Museum of American Art.** 945 Madison Ave. (at 75th St.). ☎ **877/WHITNEY** or 212/570-3676. www.whitney.org. Admission $10 adults, $8 seniors and students, free for children under 12; pay as you wish Thurs 6–8pm. Tues–Wed and Fri–Sun 11am–6pm, Thurs 1–8pm. Subway: 6 to 77th St.

What is arguably the finest collection of 20th-century American art in the world belongs to the Whitney thanks to the efforts of Gertrude Vanderbilt Whitney. A sculptor herself, she organized exhibitions by American artists shunned by traditional academies, assembled a sizable personal collection, and founded the museum in 1930 in Greenwich Village.

Today's museum is an imposing presence on Madison Avenue—an inverted three-tiered pyramid of concrete and gray granite with seven seemingly random windows designed by Marcel Breuer, a leader of the Bauhaus movement. The rotating permanent collection consists of an intelligent selection of major works by Edward Hopper, George Bellows, Georgia O'Keeffe, Roy Lichtenstein, Jasper Johns, and other significant artists. A pleasing fifth-floor exhibit space is devoted exclusively to works from its permanent collection from 1900 to 1950.

There are usually several simultaneous shows, usually all well curated and more edgy than what you'd see at MoMA or the Guggenheim. Topics range from topical surveys, such as "American Art in the Age of Technology" and "The Warhol Look: Glamour Style Fashion" to in-depth retrospectives of famous or lesser-known movements (such as Fluxus, the movement that spawned Yoko Ono, among others) and artists (Mark Rothko, Keith Haring, Duane Hanson, Bob Thompson). The next Whitney Biennial is scheduled for spring 2002. A major event on the national museum calendar, the Biennials serve as the premier launching pad for new American artists working on the vanguard in every media.

The Whitney is also notable for having the best museum restaurant in town: **Sarabeth's at the Whitney** (☎ **212/606-0218**), worth a visit in its own right (see chapter 6).

Free **gallery tours** are offered daily; call for the current schedule, or check at the information desk when you arrive.

For details on the **Whitney Museum of American Art at Philip Morris,** the petite Midtown annex, see "More Manhattan Museums," below.

5 More Manhattan Museums

In 1978, New York's finest cultural institutions located on Fifth Avenue from 82nd to 104th streets formed a consortium called **Museum Mile,** the name New York City officially gave to the stretch several years later. The "mile" begins at the **Metropolitan Museum of Art** (see "The Top Museums," above) and moves north to **El Museo del Barrio.** However, even the smallest museums along this stretch require some time, so don't plan on just popping into a few as you stroll along, or you'll be sorely disappointed by what you're able to see. Your best bet is to head directly to the museum that's tops on your list first, and then proceed to your second choice along the mile if you have time. If you're heading to the Metropolitan, forget trying to squeeze in anything else—as it is, you'll only see a portion of the collection there in a full day.

For details on Federal Hall National Memorial and Fraunces Tavern Museum, see the walking tour earlier in this chapter. For the Brooklyn Museum of Art, the New York Transit Museum, the American Museum of the Moving Image, the Queens Museum of Art, the Isamu Noguchi Garden Museum, and the P.S. 1 Contemporary Art Center, see "Highlights of the Outer Boroughs," later in this chapter.

If you're traveling with the kids, also consider the museums listed under "Especially for Kids," later in this chapter, which include the **Children's Museum of Manhattan,** the **Sony Wonder Technology Lab,** the **New York Hall of Science,** and the **New York City Fire Museum.**

Also, don't forget to see what's on at the monumental **New York Public Library,** which regularly holds excellent exhibitions; see section 6, "Skyscrapers & Other Architectural Marvels."

Abigail Adams Smith Museum & Gardens. 421 E. 61st St. (btw. First and York aves.). ☎ **212/838-6878.** Admission $4 adults, $3 seniors, free for children under 12. Tues–Sun 11am–4pm (Tues to 9pm in June and July). Closed Aug. Subway: N, R to Lexington Ave.; 4, 5, 6 to 59th St.

It's a shock, a very pleasant one, to find such a little-known jewel on this otherwise thoroughly modern block. This rare survivor from the early American republic was built as a carriage house for Abigail Adams Smith, daughter of President John Adams, and her husband, William Stephens Smith, in 1799. It's been painstakingly restored by the Colonial Dames of America to its early-19th-century condition, when the house served as the Mount Vernon Hotel—a country hotel for bucolic overnights away from the city, if you can believe it. You can explore nine period rooms, outfitted in authentic Federal style, as well as the grounds, planted as a late-18th-century garden would be. By the time you arrive, the new orientation center, offering a scale model of the building as it looked in 1799 and a video on New York City in the early 19th century, will also be open.

American Craft Museum. 40 W. 53rd St. (btw. Fifth and Sixth Aves.). ☎ **212/956-3535.** Admission $5 adults, $2.50 students and seniors, free for children under 12; pay as you wish Thurs 6–8pm. Tues–Sun 10am–6pm (Thurs to 8pm). Subway: E, F to Fifth Ave.

This small but aesthetically pleasing museum is the nation's top showcase for contemporary crafts. The collection focuses on objects that are prime examples of form and function, ranging from jewelry to baskets to vessels to furniture. You'll see a strong emphasis on material as well as craft, whether it be fiber, ceramics, or metal. Special exhibitions can range from handblown glassworks to fine bookbinding. Stop into the gorgeous shop even if you don't make it into the museum.

Asia Society. 725 Park Ave. (at 70th St.). ☎ **212/517-ASIA.** www.asiasociety.org. Gallery admission $4 adults, $2 seniors, free for children under 13; free Thurs 6–8pm. Tues–Sat 11am–6pm (Thurs to 8pm), Sun noon–5pm. Subway: 6 to 68th St./Hunter College.

The Asia Society was founded in 1956 by John D. Rockefeller III with the goal of increasing understanding between Americans and Asians through art exhibits, lectures, films, performances, and international conferences. The society is a leader in presenting contemporary Asian and Asian-American art. Recent exhibits have included "Bamboo Masterworks"; "Monks and Merchants at the Gateway: Silk Road Art from Northwest China, 4th to 7th Centuries C.E.," is on the schedule for fall 2001. The core collection, comprised of Rockefeller's Pan-Asian acquisitions dating from 2000 B.C. to the 19th century, is also worth a peek.

✪ The Cloisters. At the north end of Fort Tryon Park. ☎ **212/923-3700.** www.metmuseum. org. Suggested admission (includes same-day entrance to the Metropolitan Museum of Art) $10 adults, $5 seniors and students, free for children under 12. Nov–Feb Tues–Sun 9:30am–4:45pm; Mar–Oct Tues–Sun 9:30am–5:15pm. Subway: A to 190th St., then a 10-min. walk north along Margaret Corgan Dr., or pick up the M4 bus at the station (one stop to Cloisters). Bus: M4 Madison Ave. (Fort Tryon Park–The Cloisters).

If it weren't for this branch of the Metropolitan Museum of Art, many New Yorkers would never get to this northernmost point in Manhattan. This remote yet lovely spot is devoted to the art and architecture of medieval Europe. Atop a magnificent cliff overlooking the Hudson River, you'll find a 12th-century chapter house, parts of five cloisters from medieval monasteries, a Romanesque chapel, and a 12th-century Spanish apse brought intact from Europe. Surrounded by peaceful gardens, this is the one place on the island that can even approximate the kind of solitude suitable to such a collection. Inside you'll find extraordinary works that include the famed Unicorn tapestries, sculpture, illuminated manuscripts, stained glass, ivory, and precious metal work. Despite its remoteness, the Cloisters are extremely popular, especially in fine weather, so try to schedule your visit during the week rather than on a crowded weekend afternoon. A free guided tour is offered Tuesday through Friday at 3pm and Sunday at noon.

✪ Cooper–Hewitt National Design Museum. 2 E. 91st St. (at Fifth Ave.). ☎ **212/849-8300.** www.si.edu/ndm. Admission $8 adults, $5 seniors and students, free for children

In Search of Historic Homes

New York's voracious appetite for change often means that older residential archi-tecture is torn down so that money-earning high-rises can go up in its place. Sur-prisingly, however, the city maintains a truly fine collection of often-overlooked historic houses that are more than a tale of architecture—they're the stories of the people who passed their ordinary or extraordinary lives in buildings that range from humble to magnificent.

The **Historic House Trust of New York City** preserves 19 houses, located in city parks in all five boroughs. Those particularly worth seeking out include the **Morris–Jumel Mansion,** in Upper Manhattan at 65 Jumel Terrace (at 160th St., east of St. Nicholas Ave.; ☎ **212/923-8008**), built circa 1765 and now Man-hattan's oldest surviving house. The **Dyckman Farmhouse Museum,** farther uptown at 4881 Broadway (at 204th St.; ☎ **212/304-9422**), is the only Dutch Colonial farmhouse remaining in Manhattan, stoically and stylishly surviving the urban development that grew up around it.

The **Edgar Allan Poe Cottage,** 2460 Grand Concourse, at East Kingsbridge Road in the Bronx (☎ **718/881-8900**), was the last home of the brilliant but troubled poet and author, who moved his wife here because he thought the "country air" would be good for her tuberculosis. And the ✪ **Merchant's House Museum,** 29 E. 4th St. between Lafayette Street and the Bowery in the East Vil-lage (☎ **212/777-1089**), is a rare jewel: a perfectly preserved 19th-century home, complete with intact interiors, whose last resident is said to be the inspi-ration for Catherine Sloper in Henry James's *Washington Square.*

Built in 1809, Federal-style **Gracie Mansion,** in Carl Schurz Park, at 89th Street and East End Avenue on the Upper East Side (☎ **212/570-4751**), is now the offi-cial residence of "Hizzoner," the mayor of New York. It's open for guided tours on Wednesday only from late March through mid-November; call for reservations.

Each of the 14 others also has its own fascinating story to tell.

A brochure listing the locations and touring details of all 19 of the historic homes is available by calling ☎ **212/360-8282;** recorded information is avail-able at ☎ **212/360-3448.** You'll also find complete information online at **www.ci.nyc.ny.us/html/dpr/html/nav.html**; click on Historic Houses.

---

under 12; free to all Tues 5–9pm. Tues 10am–9pm, Wed–Sat 10am–5pm, Sun noon–5pm. Subway: 4, 5, 6 to 86th St.

Part of the Smithsonian Institution, the Cooper–Hewitt is housed in the Carnegie Mansion, built by steel magnate Andrew Carnegie in 1901. The museum underwent an ambitious $20 million renovation in 1996 that gave the building a long-overdue refreshening. Some 11,000 square feet of gallery space is devoted to changing exhibits that are invariably well conceived, engaging, and educational. Shows are both historic and contemporary in nature, and topics range from "The Work of Charles and Ray Eames: A Legacy of Invention" to "The Architecture of Reassurance: Designing the Disney Theme Parks." Many installations are drawn from the museum's own vast col-lection of industrial design, drawings, textiles, wall coverings, books, and prints. Exhi-bitions scheduled for 2001 include a retrospective on the modernist glass design of Venetian artist Paolo Venini from the 1920s through the 1980s, and a look at the use of landscape images in wall coverings in the 19th century.

On your way in, note the fabulous art nouveau–style copper-and-glass canopy above the entrance. And be sure to visit the garden, ringed with Central Park benches from various eras.

Dahesh Museum. 601 Fifth Ave. (at 48th St.). ☎ **212/759-0606.** www.daheshmuseum. org. Free admission. Tues–Sat 11am–6pm. Subway: B, D, F, Q to 47–50th sts./Rockefeller Center.

If you consider yourself a classicist, this small museum is for you. It's dedicated to 19th- and early-20th-century European academic art, a continuation of Renaissance, Baroque, and Rococo traditions that were overshadowed by the arrival of Impressionism on the art scene. (If you're not familiar with this academic school, expect lots of painstaking renditions of historical subjects and pastoral life.) Artists represented include Jean-Léon Gérôme, Lord Leighton, and Edwin Long, whose *Love's Labour Lost* is a cornerstone of the permanent collection.

El Museo del Barrio. 1230 Fifth Ave. (at 104th St.). ☎ **212/831-7272.** www.elmuseo.org. Suggested admission $4 adults, $2 seniors and students, free for children under 12. Wed–Sun 11am–5pm. Subway: 6 to 103rd St.

What started in 1969 with a small display in a local school classroom in East Harlem is today the only museum in America dedicated to Puerto Rican, Caribbean, and Latin American art. The northernmost Museum Mile institution has a permanent exhibit ranging from pre-Columbian artifacts to photographic art and video. The display of *santos de palo,* wood-carved religious figurines, is especially worth noting. The well-curated changing exhibitions tend to focus on 20th-century artists and contemporary subjects.

Forbes Magazine Galleries. 62 Fifth Ave. (at 12th St.). ☎ **212/206-5548.** Free admission. Tues–Wed and Fri–Sat 10am–4pm. Subway: L, N, R, 4, 5, 6 to 14th St./Union Sq.

The late publishing magnate Malcolm Forbes may have been a self-described "capitalist tool," but he had esoteric, almost childish, tastes. He also had the altruism to share what he collected with the public for free. With its model boats, toy soldiers, old Monopoly game sets, quirky collection of trophies, miniature rooms, presidential papers and memorabilia, and jewel-encrusted Fabergé eggs, this is a great museum for both you and the kids. Personal anecdotes explain why certain objects attracted Forbes's attention and turn the collection into an oddly interesting biographical portrait.

✪ The Frick Collection. 1 E. 70th St. (at Fifth Ave.). ☎ **212/288-0700.** www.frick.org. Admission $7 adults, $5 seniors and students. Children under 10 not admitted; children under 16 must be accompanied by an adult. Tues–Sat 10am–6pm, Sun 1–6pm. Closed all major holidays. Subway: 6 to 68th St./Hunter College.

Henry Clay Frick could afford to be an avid collector of European art after amassing a fortune as a pioneer in the coke and steel industries at the turn of the 20th century. To house his treasures and himself, he hired architects Carrère & Hastings to build this 18th-century French-style mansion (1914), one of the most beautiful remaining on Fifth Avenue.

Most appealing about the Frick is its intimate size and setting. This is a living testament to New York's vanished Gilded Age—the interior still feels like a private home (albeit a really, really rich guy's home) graced with beautiful paintings, rather than a museum. Come here to see the classics by some of the world's most famous painters: Titian, Bellini, Rembrandt, Turner, Vermeer, El Greco, and Goya, to name only a few. A highlight of the collection is the **Fragonard Room,** graced with the sensual rococo series *The Progress of Love.* The portrait of Montesquieu by Whistler is also stunning.

Sculpture, furniture, Chinese vases, and French enamels complement the paintings and round out the collection. Included in the price of admission, the AcousticGuide audio tour is particularly useful because it allows you to follow your own path rather than a proscribed route. A free video presentation is screened every half hour; starting with this helps to set the tone for what you'll see.

In addition to the permanent collection, the Frick regularly mounts small, well-focused temporary exhibitions. Look for *A Brush with Nature: The Gere Collection of Landscape Oil Sketches* and *The Draftsman's Art: Master Drawings from the National Gallery of Scotland* in late 2000 and early 2001.

Free **chamber music concerts** are held twice a month, generally every other Sunday at 5pm; call or visit the Web site for the current schedule and ticket information.

Guggenheim Museum SoHo. 575 Broadway, at Prince St. ☎ **212/423-3500.** Free admission. Thurs–Mon 11am–6pm. Subway: N, R to Prince St.

Reopened after a lengthy closing, this annex to the Solomon R. Guggenheim Museum (see "The Top Museums," above) now has a considerably lower profile than it enjoyed in past years, but it's worth checking out what's on if you consider yourself a postmodern enthusiast. (And it's easy to combine a stop here with a visit to the New Museum of Contemporary Art and/or the Museum of African Art; see below.) The space generally houses temporary installations of high-tech multimedia works. On an open-ended schedule at press time was Andy Warhol's swan song, *The Last Supper* (1986), his monumental final cycle, comprising more than 60 silkscreens, paintings, and works on paper.

International Center of Photography. 1133 Sixth Ave. (at 43rd St.). ☎ **212/768-4680** or 212/860-1777. www.icp.org. Admission $6 adults, $4 seniors, $1 children under 13; pay as you wish Tues 5–8pm. Tues–Thurs 10am–5pm, Fri 10am–8pm, Sat–Sun 10am–6pm. Subway: B, D, F, Q to 42nd St.

In September 2000, the ICP—one of the world's premier educators, collectors, and exhibitors of photographic art—is scheduled to relocate its museum galleries from its original Museum Mile location (1130 Fifth Ave., at 94th Street) to this expanded Midtown facility. Expect it to be state-of-the-art gallery space—ideal for viewing rotating exhibitions of the museum's 50,000-plus prints as well as visiting shows. The emphasis is on contemporary photographic works, but historically important photographers aren't ignored. It's a must on any photography buff's list.

Call ahead or visit the Web site, though, to check current exhibitions and make sure the move is complete by the time you arrive, as anything can happen to delay a project of this magnitude. Don't be surprised if you find a change in hours and admission fees, too; policies for the new facility were not yet set at press time. Additionally, a limited schedule of exhibitions is set to show at the Museum Mile headquarters through September 2001.

Intrepid **Sea-Air-Space Museum.** Pier 86 (W. 46th St. at Twelfth Ave.). ☎ **212/245-0072** or 212/957-7055. www.intrepidmuseum.org. Admission $12 adults; $9 veterans, seniors, and students; $6 children 6–11; $2 children 2–5. Apr–Sept Mon–Fri 10am–5pm, Sat–Sun 10am–6pm; Oct–Mar Tues–Sun 10am–5pm. Last admission 1 hour before closing. Subway: A, C, E to 42nd St./Port Authority. Bus: M42 crosstown.

The most astonishing thing about the aircraft carrier USS *Intrepid* is how it can be simultaneously so big and so small. It's a few football fields long, weights 40,000 tons, holds 40 aircraft, and sometimes doubles as a ballroom for society functions. But stand there and think about landing an A-12 jet on the deck and suddenly it's minuscule. Furthermore, in the narrow passageways below, you'll find it isn't quite the roomiest of vessels. Now a National Historic Landmark, the entire exhibit also includes the naval destroyer USS *Edson,* and the submarine USS *Growler,* the only intact strategic missile submarine open to the public anywhere in the world, as well as a collection of vintage and modern aircraft, including the A-12 Blackbird, the world's fastest spy plane. Kids just love this place. At least one Saturday a month is dedicated to families as part of the "Seaworthy Saturdays" program; look for such events as "Undersea Exploration," in which kids meet the *Intrepid* Dive Team and examine recovered treasures. New in 2000 are exhibits on defense technology and space exploration in the 21st century, and a grand $5.5 million visitor center, which will be open by the time you arrive. But think twice about going in winter—it's almost impossible to heat an aircraft carrier.

Japan Society. 333 E. 47th St. (btw. First and Second aves.). ☎ **212/832-1155.** www.japansociety.org. Admission $5 adults, $3 seniors and students. Gallery: Tues–Fri 11am–6pm, Sat–Sun 11am–5pm. Subway: E, F to Lexington Ave.; 6 to 51st St.

In a striking modern building by Junzo Yoshimuro (1971), the U.S. headquarters of the Japan Society mounts highly regarded exhibits of Japanese art in a suitably serene gallery. Changing displays have included "Japanese Theater in the World" and "Treasures of Japanese Art from the San Francisco Art Museum." The society also hosts a wide variety of lectures, gallery talks, films, and classes throughout the year; you'll find a list of other Japan-related events and exhibits taking place throughout the city on the Web site.

The Jewish Museum. 1109 Fifth Ave. (at 92nd St.). ☎ **212/423-3200.** www.jewishmuseum.org. Admission $8 adults, $5.50 seniors and students, free for children under 12; pay what you wish Tues 5–8pm. Check Web site for special online admission discounts (50% off at press time). Sun–Mon and Wed–Thurs 11am–5:45pm, Tues 11am–8pm. Subway: 4, 5 to 86th St.; 6 to 96th St.

Housed in a Gothic-style mansion renovated in 1993 by AIA Gold Medal winner Kevin Roche, this wonderful museum now has the world-class space it deserves to showcase its remarkable collections, which chronicle 4,000 years of Jewish history. The 2-floor permanent exhibit, "Culture and Continuity: The Jewish Journey," tells the story of the Jewish experience from ancient times through today, and is the museum's centerpiece. Artifacts include daily objects that might have served the authors of the books of Genesis, Psalms, and Job, and a great assemblage of intricate Torahs. A wonderful collection of classic TV and radio programs is available for viewing through the Goodkind Resource Center (as any fan of television's Golden Age knows, its finest comic moments were Jewish comedy). The scope of the exhibit is phenomenal, and its story an enlightening—and intense—one.

❂ **Lower East Side Tenement Museum.** Visitors' Center at 90 Orchard St. (at Broome St.). ☎ **212/431-0233.** www.tenement.org or www.wnet.org/tenement. Admission $8 adults, $6 seniors and students for tenement tour. Multiple tours available on weekends: $14 adults, $10 seniors and students for any 2 tours; $20 adults, $14 seniors and students for all 3 tours. Tenement tours depart Tues–Fri every half hour 1–4pm and Thurs at 6 and 7pm, Sat–Sun every half hour 11am–4:30pm. Neighborhood Heritage Tour Apr–Dec Sat–Sun 1:30 and 2:30pm. Confino Apartment living history program Sat–Sun hourly noon–3pm. Subway: F to Delancey St.; B, D, Q to Grand St.

This museum is the first-ever National Trust for Historic Preservation site that was not the home of someone rich or famous. It's something quite different: A five-story tenement that 10,000 people from 25 countries called home between 1863 and 1935—people who had come to the United States looking for the American dream and made 97 Orchard St. their first stop. The tenement museum tells the story of the great immigration boom of the late 19th and early 20th centuries, when the Lower East Side was considered the "Gateway to America." A visit here makes a good follow-up to an Ellis Island trip—what happened to all the people who passed through that famous waystation?

The only way to see the museum is by guided tour. The primary tenement tour, held on all open days, offers a satisfying exploration of the museum. A knowledgeable guide leads you into the dingy urban time capsule, where several apartments have been faithfully restored to their exact lived-in condition, and recounts the real-life stories of the families who occupied them in fascinating detail. It's not really for kids, however, who won't enjoy the serious tone and "don't touch" policy. Much better for them is the weekends-only Confino Apartment tour, an interactive living history program geared to families, which allows kids to converse with an interpreter who plays teenage immigrant Victoria Confino circa 1916; kids can also handle whatever they like in the apartment and even try on period clothes. A neighborhood heritage walking tour is also offered on weekends.

All tours are limited in number, so it pays to reserve ahead. The Visitors' Center has several small exhibits, including photos, videos, and a model tenement.

✪ **Morgan Library.** 29 E. 36th St. (at Madison Ave.). ☎ **212/685-0008.** www.morganlibrary. org. Admission $7 adults, $5 seniors, free for children under 12. Tues–Thurs 10:30am–5pm, Fri 10:30am–8pm, Sat 10:30am–6pm, Sun noon–6pm. Subway: 6 to 33rd St.

Here's an undiscovered New York treasure, boasting one of the world's most important collections of original manuscripts, rare books and bindings, master drawings, and personal writings. Among the remarkable artifacts on display under glass are stunning illuminated manuscripts (including Gutenberg bibles), a working draft of the U.S. Constitution bearing copious handwritten notes, Voltaire's personal household account books, and handwritten scores by the likes of Beethoven, Mozart, and Puccini. The collection of mostly 19th-century drawings—featuring works by Seurat, Degas, Rubens, and other great masters—have an excitement of immediacy about them that the artists' more well-known paintings often lack. This rich repository originated as the private collection of turn-of-the-20th-century financier J. Pierpont Morgan and is housed in a landmark Renaissance-style palazzo building (1906) he commissioned from McKim, Mead & White to hold his masterpieces. Morgan's library and study are preserved virtually intact and are worth a look unto themselves for their landmarked architecture (particularly the rotunda) and richly detailed fittings. The special exhibitions are particularly well chosen and curated; subjects can range from medieval bookbinding techniques to the literary genesis of the mystery novel and pulp fiction to a display of treasures from the royal tombs of Ur. A reading room is available by appointment.

Museum for African Art. 593 Broadway (btw. Houston and Prince sts.). ☎ **212/966-1313.** www.africanart.org. Admission $5 adults; $2.50 seniors, students, and children. Tues–Fri 10:30am–5:30pm, Sat–Sun noon–6pm. Subway: N, R to Prince St.

This captivating museum (whose interior was designed by architect Maya Lin, best known for her Vietnam Veterans Memorial in Washington, D.C.) is a leading organizer of temporary exhibits dedicated to historic and contemporary African art and culture. Exhibitions on the calendar for 2001 include "Caravans: Nomads and Traders in Northern Africa," examining the evolution of art through time through immigration, emigration, and diaspora; and "Controlling Power: Gender Roles in African Art," focusing on gender issues as they relate to African masks and statuary. An excellent museum shop showcases contemporary African crafts.

Art for Art's Sake: The Gallery Scene

The biggest news in the art gallery world has been the decreasing importance of SoHo as the capital of contemporary art. As SoHo has become an increasingly commercial, trendy shopping district, major showrooms have fled uptown or to far west Chelsea. But all this commotion may just be the result of natural cycles of change. Now that Broadway has turned into a veritable museum row—with the Museum of African Art, the Guggenheim SoHo, and the increasingly high-profile New Museum of Contemporary Art all calling the stretch between Houston and Prince streets home—it may be just simply that art has taken root in SoHo. So those opposed to such permanence—namely, cutting-edge artists—have fled elsewhere.

All this movement only serves to underline that Manhattan is the undisputed capital of art—or, more significantly, art sales. The island has more than 500 private art galleries, selling everything from old masters to tomorrow's news. Galleries are open free to the public, generally Tuesday through Saturday from 10am to 6pm. Saturday afternoon gallery hopping, in particular, is a favorite pastime—nobody will expect you to buy, so don't worry. The best way to winnow down your choices is by perusing the "Art Guide" in the Friday weekend section of the *New York Times,* or the back of the Sunday "Arts & Leisure" section; the Art section in the weekly *Time Out New York;* the "Cue" section at the back of the weekly *New York* magazine; or the *New Yorker's* weekly "Goings on About Town" section. You can also find the latest exhibition listings online at **www.newyork.citysearch.com** (click on ARTS & ENTERTAINMENT), **www.artnet.com,** and **www.galleryguideonline.com**. An excellent source—more for practicals on the galleries and the artists and genres they represent rather than current shows—is the comprehensive **www.artincontext.org**. The *Gallery Guide* is available at most galleries around town.

I suggest picking a gallery or a show in a neighborhood that seems to suit your taste, and just start browsing from there. I've listed a few good starting points below. This list doesn't even begin to scratch the surface; there are many, many more galleries in each neighborhood, as well as smaller concentrations of galleries in areas like the East Village, TriBeCa, and Brooklyn (www.artincontext.org is a good way to locate them). Keep in mind that uptown galleries tend to be more traditional, downtown galleries more contemporary, and far west Chelsea galleries the most cutting edge. But you'll find that there are constant surprises in all neighborhoods.

UPTOWN   Uptown galleries are clustered in and around the glamorous crossroads of Fifth Avenue and 57th Street as well as on and off stylish Madison Avenue in the 60s, 70s, and 80s. Unlike their upstart Chelsea and SoHo counterparts, these blue-chip galleries maintain their quiet white-glove demeanor. They include **Hirschl & Adler,** 21 E. 70th St. (☎ 212/535-8810; www.hirschlandadler.com), for 18th- to 20th-century European and American painting and decorative arts; art-world powerhouses **Gagosian,** 980 Madison Ave. (☎ 212/744-2313;

Museum of American Folk Art. 2 Lincoln Sq. (Columbus Ave. between 65th and 66th sts., across from Lincoln Center). ☎ **212/977-7298** or 212/595-9533. www.folkartmuseum.org. Free admission; $3 voluntary donation requested. Tues–Sun 11:30am–7:30pm. Subway: 1, 9 to 66th St.

www.gagosian.com), and **PaceWildenstein,** 32 E. 57th St. (☎ 212/421-3292; www.pacewildenstein.com); **Richard Gray,** 1018 Madison Ave. (☎ 212/ 472-8787), focusing on American and European contemporary works; **Mitchell–Innes & Nash,** 1018 Madison Ave. (☎ 212/744-7400); **Knoedler & Company,** 19 E. 70th St. (☎ 212/794-0550), representing such artists as Helen Frankenthaler, Nancy Graves, and Frank Stella; **Mary Boone,** 745 Fifth Ave. (☎ 212/752-2929), known for success with such artists as Ross Bleckner and Eric Fischl; and **Wildenstein,** the classical big brother of PaceWildenstein, 19 E. 64th St. (☎ 212/879-0500; www.wildenstein.com), specializing in big-ticket works: old masters, Impressionism, and Renaissance paintings and drawings.

CHELSEA   The area in the West 20s between Tenth and Eleventh avenues is home to the avant garde of today's New York art scene, with West 26th serving as the unofficial "gallery row." Most galleries are not in storefronts but in the large spaces of multistory former garages and warehouses. Galleries worth seeking out include **Paula Cooper,** 534 W. 21st St. (☎ 212/255-1105), offering a wide range of well-known artists and specializing in conceptual and minimal art; **George Billis,** 526 W. 26th St., 9F (☎ 212/645-2621; www.georgebillis.com), who shows works by talented emerging artists (I saw a marvelous Tom Gregg show here last fall); **Barbara Gladstone,** 515 W. 24th St. (☎ 212/206-9300; www.gladstonegallery.com); powerhouse **Gagosian,** 555 W. 24th St. (☎ 212/ 228-2828; www.gagosian.com), which shows such major artists as Richard Serra; **Cheim & Read,** 521 W. 23rd St. (☎ 212/242-7727), which often shows works by such high-profile pop artists as Diane Arbus, Larry Clark, and Nan Goldin; **DCA Gallery,** 525 W. 22nd St. (☎ 212/255-5511; www.dcagallery.com), specializing in contemporary Danish artists; and **Alexander & Bonin,** 132 Tenth Ave. (☎ 212/367-7474; www.alexanderandbonin.com), which mounts excellent solo exhibitions by select artists from the Americas and Europe.

SOHO   SoHo remains colorful, if less edgy than it used to be, with the action centered around West Broadway and encroaching onto the edge of Chinatown of late. Start with **Bronwyn Keenan,** 3 Crosby St. (☎ 212/431-5083), who's known for a keen eye for spotting emerging talent; **O. K. Harris,** 383 W. Broadway (☎ 212/431-3600; www.okharris.com), which shows a wide and fascinating variety of contemporary painting, sculpture, and photography; **P.P.O.W,** 476 Broome St. (☎ 212/941-8642), known for the high quality of their emerging American artists; the third Manhattan gallery from **Gagosian,** 136 Wooster St. (☎ 212/228-2828; www.gagosian.com), and the second from **PaceWildenstein,** 142 Greene St. (☎ 212/431-9224; www.pacewilden-stein.com); **Louis K. Meisel,** 141 Prince St. (☎ 212/677-1340; www.meisel-gallery.com), specializing in photorealism and American pinup art (yep, Petty and Vargas girls); and **Holly Solomon,** 172 Mercer St. (☎ 212/941-5777), representing such heavyweights as William Wegman and Nam June Paik as well as talented up-and-comers.

This museum displays a wide range of works from the 18th century to the present, reflecting the breadth and vitality of the American folk-art tradition. The textiles collection is the museum's most popular, highlighted by a splendid variety of quilts. The gift shop is filled with one-of-a-kind objects.

Relocation note: In late spring 2001, the museum is scheduled to move to new digs at 45 W. 53rd St., just down the block from the Museum of Modern Art. The new building will quadruple the existing exhibit space.

Museum of Jewish Heritage—A Living Memorial to the Holocaust. 18 First Place (at Battery Place), Battery Park City. ☎ **212/509-6130.** www.mjhnyc.org. Admission $7 adults, $5 seniors and students, free for children under 5. Sun–Wed 9am–5pm, Thurs 9am–8pm, Fri and eves of Jewish holidays 9am–3pm. Last admission 1 hour before closing. Subway: 1, 9 to South Ferry; 4, 5 to Bowling Green.

Located in the south end of Battery Park City, the Museum of Jewish Heritage occupies a strikingly spare six-sided building designed by award-winning architect Kevin Roche, with a six-tier roof alluding to the Star of David and the 6 million murdered in the Holocaust. The permanent exhibits—"Jewish Life a Century Ago," "The War Against the Jews," and "Jewish Renewal"—recount the daily prewar lives, the unforgettable horror that destroyed them, and the tenacious renewal experienced by European and immigrant Jews in the years from the late 19th century to the present. The museum's power derives from the way it tells that story: through the objects, photographs, documents, and, most poignantly, through the videotaped testimonies of Holocaust victims, survivors, and their families, all chronicled by Steven Spielberg's Survivors of the Shoah Visual History Foundation.

Advance tickets are recommended to guarantee admission and can be purchased by calling ☎ **212/945-0039,** or TicketMaster (☎ **800/307-4007** or 212/307-4007; www.ticketmaster.com).

Museum of Television & Radio. 25 W. 52nd St. (btw. Fifth and Sixth aves.). ☎ **212/621-6800** or 212/621-6600. www.mtr.org. Admission $6 adults, $4 seniors and students, $3 children under 13. Tues–Sun noon–6pm (Thurs until 8pm, Fri theater programs until 9pm). Subway: B, D, F, Q to 47–50th sts./Rockefeller Center; N, R to 49th St.

If you can resist the allure of this museum, I'd wager you've spent the last 70 years in a bubble. You can watch and hear all the great personalities of TV and radio—from Uncle Miltie to Johnny Carson to Jerry Seinfeld—at a private console (available for 2 hours). And, amazingly, you can also conduct computer searches to pick out the great moments of history, viewing almost anything that made its way onto the airwaves, from the Beatles' first appearance on *The Ed Sullivan Show* to the crumbling of the Berlin Wall (the collection consists of 75,000 programs and commercials). Selected programs are also presented in two theaters and two screening rooms, which can range from "Barbra Streisand: The Television Performances" to little-seen Monty Python episodes; check to see what's on while you're in town.

Museum of the City of New York. 1220 Fifth Ave. (at 103rd St.). ☎ **212/534-1672.** www.mcny.org. Suggested admission $5 adults; $4 seniors, students, and children; $10 families. Wed–Sat 10am–5pm, Sun noon–5pm. Subway: 6 to 103rd St.

A wide variety of objects—costumes, photographs, prints, maps, dioramas, and memorabilia—trace the history of New York City from its beginnings as a humble Dutch colony in the 16th century to its present-day prominence. Two outstanding permanent exhibits are the re-creation of John D. Rockefeller's master bedroom and dressing room, and the space devoted to "Broadway!" a history of New York theater. The permanent "Furniture of Distinction, 1790–1890" displays 33 elegant pieces representing New York's central role in American cabinetmaking that will have you eyeing your IKEA pieces with new contempt. Kids will love "New York Toy Stories," a permanent exhibit showcasing toys and dolls owned and adored by centuries of New York children. Look for *"Guys and Dolls,"* a tribute to the 50th anniversary of the celebrated musical showcasing costumes and ephemera, from November 2000 to June 2001.

National Academy of Design. 1083 Fifth Ave. (at 89th St.). ☎ **212/369-4880.** www.nationalacademy.org. Admission $8 adults, $5 seniors and students. Wed–Sun 11:45am–5pm (extended Fri hours during annual exhibition). Subway: 4, 5, 6, to 86th St.

Founded in 1825, the National Academy is one of the oldest art institutions in the country and is dedicated to preserving the academic tradition. There are three components: a fine arts school; an honorary professional association of artists; and a museum, which mounts regular exhibits drawn from its large collection on such themes as "Art in the Age of Queen Victoria" and "The Watercolors of Charles Hawthorne." The annual Open Annual Exhibition is the nation's oldest continuing juried show; look for the 176th edition to be held in February and March 2001.

National Museum of the American Indian, George Gustav Heye Center. 1 Bowling Green (btw. State and Whitehall sts.). ☎ **212/668-6624.** www.si.edu/nmai. Free admission. Daily 10am–5pm (Thurs to 8pm). Subway: 1, 9 to South Ferry; 4, 5 to Bowling Green.

Part of the Smithsonian Institution, this collection is the oldest of its kind in the country. It's housed in the beautiful 1907 beaux arts U.S. Customs House (a National Historic Landmark that's worth a look in its own right), but only until its new home is completed on the Mall in Washington, D.C., in 2002. Until then, enjoy items spanning more than 10,000 years of native heritage, collected a century ago mainly by New York banking millionaire George Gustav Heye. About 70% of the collection is dedicated to the natives of the United States and Canada; the rest represents the cultures of Mexico and South and Central Americas. There's a wealth of material here, but it's rather poorly organized. The museum also hosts interpretive programs plus free storytelling, music, and dance presentations; call for a current calendar (☎ **212/514-3888**).

Neue Gallerie New York. 1048 Fifth Ave. (at 86th St.). ☎ **212/628-6200.** www.neuegallerie.org. Admission $10. Fri–Mon 11am–7pm. Subway: 4, 5, 6 to 86th St.

Scheduled to open in fall 2000 is this new museum dedicated to German and Austrian art, with a particular focus on the early 20th century. The emphasis will be works on paper, but will also include decorative arts, painting, and other media. Expect works from such artists as Klimt, Kokoschka, and leaders of the Wiener Werkstätte and Bauhaus movements. Once occupied by Mrs. Cornelius Vanderbilt III, the landmark-designated 1914 Carrèrre & Hastings building is currently being restored and should be worth a look in itself. Be sure to call before you go to guard against unforeseen delays in opening.

New Museum of Contemporary Art. 583 Broadway (btw. Houston and Prince sts.). ☎ **212/219-1222.** www.newmuseum.org. Admission $6; $3 for artists, students, and seniors; free for visitors 18 and under; free to all Thurs 6–8pm. Sun and Wed noon–6pm, Thurs–Sat noon–8pm. Subway: N, R to Prince St.; B, D, F, Q to Broadway–Lafayette St.

With 33,000 square feet of space and the former curator of contemporary art at the Whitney as its brand-new director, the New Museum is now a prime contender on the museum scene. This contemporary arts museum has moved closer to the mainstream in recent years, but it's only a safety margin in from the edge as far as most of us are concerned. Expect adventurous and well-curated exhibitions. Subject matter on the schedule for late 2000–2001 includes "Pierre et Gilles," a survey of the French team's photo-paintings, including their superlative celebrity portraits; and an exhibition of Los Angeles–based artist Paul McCarthy's multimedia architectural installations.

Newseum/NY. 580 Madison Ave. (btw. 56th and 57th sts.). ☎ **212/317-7503.** www.newseum.org/newseumny. Free admission. Mon–Sat 10am–5:30pm. Subway: 4, 5, 6 to 59th St.

An adjunct to the main Newseum in Arlington, VA, Newseum/NY is a photojournalism gallery dedicated to broadening the public's understanding of the press's role and First Amendment issues. It's run by the Freedom Forum (www.freedomforum. org), a nonpartisan foundation dedicated to the support of free speech and free press around the world. This multimedia gallery is only a fraction of the size of the big Newseum, but it's worth checking out nonetheless. You can easily explore it in a half hour or so.

In addition to the rotating mounted exhibit, Newseum/NY hosts a regular free program of evening gallery talks, films, and lectures, such as "Coverage of Poverty in the United States" and "School Violence: A Figment of the Media's Imagination?" Call or visit the Web site to check the current schedule.

New-York Historical Society. 2 W. 77th St. (at Central Park West). ☎ **212/873-3400.** www.nyhistory.org. Admission $5 adults, $3 seniors and students, free for children 12 and under. Tues–Sun 11am–5pm. Subway: B, C to 81st St.; 1, 9 to 79th St.

Launched in 1804, the New-York Historical Society is a major repository of American history, culture, and art, with a special focus on New York and its broader cultural significance. The grand neoclassical edifice near the Museum of Natural History is finally undergoing major renovations. By fall 2000, the fourth floor will be transformed into the new Henry Luce III Center for the Study of American Culture, a state-of-the-art study facility and gallery, and 65% of the society's phenomenal collection will be on permanent display. For the first time, museum-goers will be able to view many large objects stored offsite for decades, including paintings, decorative arts collections, and carriages. Already on display is a small but notable selection of Tiffany lamps and paintings from Hudson River School artists Thomas Cole, Asher Durand, and Frederic Church, including Cole's five-part masterpiece, *The Course of Empire.* Also of note are the society's wide-ranging temporary exhibits; look for "Eye of the Storm: The Odyssey of a Civil War Soldier" and a showcase of Jenny Lind and P. T. Barnum memorabilia in late 2000.

Schomburg Center for Research in Black Culture. 515 Malcolm X Blvd. (Lenox Ave., btw. 135th and 136th sts.). ☎ **212/491-2200,** or 212/491-2265 for program and exhibition information. www.nypl.org. Free admission. Gallery: Mon–Sat 10am–6pm, Sun 1–5pm. Subway: 2, 3 to 135th St.

Arturo Alfonso Schomburg, a black Puerto Rican, set himself to accumulating materials about blacks in America, and his massive collection is now housed and preserved at this research branch of the New York Public Library. The Exhibition Hall and Latimer/Edison Gallery host changing exhibits related to black culture, such as "Black New York Artists of the 20th Century" and "Black New Yorkers/Black New York: 400 Years of African-American History." A rich calendar of talks and performing arts events is also part of the continuing program. Make an appointment to see the 1930s murals by Harlem Renaissance artist Aaron Douglas; it'll be worth your while. Academics and others interested in a more complete look at the center's holding can preview what's available online.

Studio Museum in Harlem. 144 W. 125th St., btw. Malcolm X Blvd. (Lenox Ave.) and Adam Clayton Powell Jr. Blvd. ☎ **212/864-4500.** www.studiomuseuminharlem.org. Admission $5 adults, $3 seniors and students, $1 children under 12. Free to all first Sat of the month. Wed–Fri 10am–5pm, Sat–Sun 1–6pm. Subway: 2, 3 to 125th St.

The small but excellent museum is devoted to presenting 19th- and 20th-century African-American art as well as 20th-century African and Caribbean art and traditional African art and artifacts. Rotating exhibitions are a big part of the museum's focus, such as "Explorations in the City of Light: African-American Artists in Paris, 1945–1965," and an annual exhibition of works by emerging artists as part of its Artists-in-Residence program. There's also a small sculpture garden, a good gift shop, and a full calendar of special events.

Theodore Roosevelt Birthplace. 28 E. 20th St. (btw. Broadway and Park Ave. South). ☎ **212/260-1616.** Admission $2. Hourly tours Wed–Sun 9am–5pm (last tour at 4pm). Subway: N, R to Broadway/23rd St.; 6 to 23rd St.

The present building is a faithful reconstruction, inside and out, on the same site of the brownstone where Theodore Roosevelt was born on October 27, 1858. Period rooms appear as they did in Teddy's youth. The powder-blue parlor is in the rococo revival style popular at the time, the stately green dining room boasts horsehair-covered chairs, and the children's nursery has a window that leads to a small gymnasium built to help the frail young Teddy become more "bully." About 40% of the furniture is original (another 20% belonged to family members). There's also a collection of Roosevelt memorabilia.

Whitney Museum of American Art at Philip Morris. 120 Park Ave. (at 42nd St., opposite Grand Central Terminal). ☎ **917/663-2453.** www.whitney.org. Free admission. Gallery: Mon–Wed and Fri 11am–6pm, Thurs 11am–7:30pm. Sculpture Court: Mon–Sat 7:30am–9:30pm, Sun 11am–7pm. Subway: S, 4, 5, 6, 7 to 42nd St./Grand Central.

This Midtown branch of the Whitney Museum of American Art (see "The Top Museums," earlier in this chapter) features an airy sculpture court and a petite gallery that hosts changing exhibits, usually the works of living contemporary artists. Well worth peeking into if you're in the neighborhood; I just popped in recently and found a wonderful exhibition that juxtaposed the organic-inspired sculptures and drawings of Isamu Noguchi and Ellsworth Kelly. Go to the Web site and click on INFORMATION, then BRANCH MUSEUMS, if you want to see what's on in advance. Free hour-long gallery tours are offered Wednesday and Friday at 1pm

6 Skyscrapers & Other Architectural Marvels

THE TOP STRUCTURES
For details on the **World Trade Center,** see p. 215, and the **Brooklyn Bridge,** p. 213; the **Woolworth Building** is discussed on p. 222.

Chrysler Building. 405 Lexington Ave. (at 42nd St.). Subway: S, 4, 5, 6, 7 to 42nd St./Grand Central.

Built as Chrysler Corporation headquarters in 1930 (they moved out decades ago), this is perhaps the 20th century's most romantic architectural achievement, especially at night, when the lights in its triangular openings play off its steely crown. As you admire its facade, be sure to note the gargoyles reaching out from the upper floors, looking for all the world like streamline-Gothic hood ornaments.

There's a fascinating tale behind this building. While it was under construction, its architect, William Van Alen, hid his final plans for the spire that now tops it. Working at a furious pace in the last days of construction, the workers assembled in secrecy the elegant pointy top—and then they raised it right through what people had assumed was going to be the roof, and for a brief moment it was the world's tallest building (a distinction stolen by the Empire State Building only a few months later). Its exterior chrome sculptures are magnificent and spooky. The observation deck closed long ago, but you can visit its lavish ground-floor interior, which is art deco to the max. The ceiling mural depicting airplanes and other early marvels of the first decades of the 20th century evince the bright promise of technology. The elevators are works of art, masterfully covered in exotic woods (especially note the lotus-shaped marquetry on the doors).

✪ **Empire State Building.** 350 Fifth Ave. (at 34th St.). ☎ **212/736-3100.** www.esbnyc.com. Observatory admission $7 adults, $4 seniors and children 6–12, free for children under 5. Daily 9:30am–midnight (tickets sold until 11:30pm). Subway: B, D, F, Q, N, R to 34th St.; 6 to 33rd St.

King Kong climbed it in 1933. A plane slammed into it in 1945. The World Trade Center superseded it in 1970 as the island's tallest building. And in 1997, a gunman ascended it to stage a deadly shooting. But through it all, the Empire State Building has remained one of the city's favorite landmarks and its signature high-rise. Completed in 1931 on what had been the site of the first Waldorf Astoria, and, before that, Caroline Astor's mansion, it climbs 102 stories (1,454 feet) and now harbors the offices of fashion firms, and, in its upper reaches, a jumble of high-tech broadcast equipment.

Always a conversation piece, the Empire State Building glows every night, bathed in colored floodlights to commemorate events of significance (red, white, and blue for Independence Day; green for St. Patrick's Day; red, black, and green for Martin Luther King Day; blue and white for Hanukkah; even lavender and white for Gay Pride Day). The familiar silver spire can be seen from all over the city. My favorite view of the building is from 23rd Street, where Fifth Avenue and Broadway converge. On a lovely day, stand at the base of the Flatiron Building (see below) and gaze up Fifth; the crisp, gleaming deco tower jumps out, soaring above the sooty office buildings that surround it.

But the views that keep nearly 3 million visitors coming every year are the ones from the 86th- and 102nd-floor **observatories.** The lower one is best—you can walk out on a windy deck and look through coin-operated viewers (bring quarters!) over what, on a clear day, can be as much as an 80-mile visible radius. The citywide panorama is magnificent. One surprise is the flurry of rooftop activity, an aspect of city life that thrives unnoticed from our everyday sidewalk vantage point. The higher observation deck is glass-enclosed and cramped.

Light fog can create an admirably moody effect, but it goes without saying that a clear day is best. Dusk brings the most remarkable views and the biggest crowds. Consider going in the morning, when the light is still low on the horizon, keeping glare to a minimum. Starry nights are pure magic.

In your haste to go up, don't rush through the beautiful 3-story-high marble **lobby** without pausing to admire its features, which include a wonderful streamline mural.

In case you haven't had enough of the real thing, **New York Skyride** (☎ 212/279-9777; www.skyride.com) offers a short motion-flight simulation sightseeing tour of New York (just like a Big Apple version of Disneyland's Star Tours). A high point: It lets you feel what it's like to fall from the building—what fun! Tickets are $11.50 for adults, $8.50 for kids 4–12, and the ride is open daily from 10am to 10pm—but unless the kids insist, skip it.

Impressions

It's the nearest thing to heaven we have in New York.
—Deborah Kerr to Cary Grant in *An Affair to Remember,*
on the Empire State Building

Empire State Building Ticket-Buying Tip

Lines can be horrible at the concourse-level ticket booth, so be prepared to wait—or consider purchasing **advance tickets** online using a credit card at **www.esbnyc.org.** You'll pay a $3 service charge for the privilege, but it's well worth it, especially if you're visiting during busy seasons, when the line can be shockingly long. You're not required to choose a time or date for your tickets in advance; they can be used on any regular open day. However, order them well before you leave home, because they're sent only by regular mail. Expect them to take 7 to 10 days to reach you (longer if you live out of the country). With tickets in hand, you're allowed to proceed directly to the second floor—past everyone who didn't plan as well as you did!

✪ **Grand Central Terminal.** 42nd St. at Park Ave. www.grandcentralterminal.com. Subway: S, 4, 5, 6, 7 to 42nd St./Grand Central.

After more than 2 years and $175 million, Grand Central Terminal has come out from under the tarps and scaffolding. Rededicated with all the appropriate pomp and circumstance on October 1, 1998, the 1913 landmark (originally designed by Warren & Wetmore with Reed & Stem) has been reborn as one of the most magnificent public spaces in the country. The restoration, by the New York firm of Beyer Blinder Belle, is an utter triumph. Their work has reanimated the genius of the station's original intent: to inspire those who pass through this urban meeting point with lofty feelings of civic pride and appreciation for Western architectural traditions. In short, they've put the "grand" back into Grand Central.

By all means, come and visit, even if you're not catching one of the subway lines or Metro North commuter trains that rumble through the bowels of this great place. And even if you arrive and leave by subway, be sure to exit the station, walking a couple of blocks south, to about 40th Street, before you turn around to admire Jules-Alexis Coutan's neoclassical sculpture *Transportation* hovering over the south entrance, with a majestically buff Mercury, the Roman god of commerce and travel, as its central figure.

The greatest visual impact comes when you enter the vast **main concourse.** Cleaned of decades of grime and cheesy advertisements, it boasts renewed majesty. The high windows once again allow sunlight to penetrate the space, glinting off the half-acre Tennessee marble floor. The brass clock over the central kiosk gleams, as do the gold- and nickel-plated chandeliers piercing the side archways. The masterful **sky ceiling,** again a brilliant greenish blue, depicts the constellations of the winter sky above New York. They're lit with 59 stars, surrounded by dazzling 24-carat gold and emitting light fed through fiber-optic cables, their intensities roughly replicating the magnitude of the actual stars as seen from Earth. Look carefully and you'll see a patch near one corner left unrestored as a useful reminder of the neglect once visited on this splendid overhead masterpiece. On the east end of the main concourse is a grand **marble staircase** where there had never been one before, but as the original plans had always intended.

This dramatic beaux arts splendor serves as a hub of social activity as well. New retail shops and restaurants have taken over the mezzanine and lower levels. The highlights of the west mezzanine are **Michael Jordan's—The Steak House,** a gorgeous art deco space that allows you to dine within view of the sky ceiling (see chapter 6), and the gorgeously restored **Campbell Apartment** for cocktails (see chapter 9); on the east mezzanine is **Métrazur** (☎ 212/687-4600), a new restaurant garnering positive reviews for its moderately priced contemporary fare. Off the main concourse at street level, there's a nice mix of specialty shops and national retailers, as well as the grand new **Grand Central Market** for gourmet foods (see chapter 8). The **Transit Museum Store,** in the shuttle passage, houses a gallery annex to the Transit Museum (see "Highlights of the Outer Boroughs") that's worth a look for transit buffs. The **lower concourse** houses newsstands, a food court offering everything from deli sandwiches to caviar, and the famous **Oyster Bar & Restaurant,** also restored to its original old-world glory (see chapter 6).

The **Municipal Art Society** (☎ 212/935-3960; www.mas.org) offers a free walking tour of Grand Central Terminal on Wednesday at 12:30pm; see "Organized Sightseeing Tours," below.

New York Public Library. Fifth Ave. and 42nd St. ☎ **212/869-8089** (exhibits and events) or 212/661-7220 (library hours). www.nypl.org. Free admission to all exhibitions. Rose Main Reading Room and exhibition halls: Mon and Thurs–Sat 10am–6pm, Tues–Wed 11am–7:30pm. Subway: B, D, F, Q to 42nd St.; S, 4, 5, 6, 7 to Grand Central/42nd St.

The New York Public Library, adjacent to Bryant Park (see "Central Park & Other Places to Play," below) and designed by Carrère & Hastings (1911), is one of the country's finest examples of beaux arts architecture, a majestic structure of white Vermont marble with Corinthian columns and allegorical statues. Before climbing the broad flight of steps to the Fifth Avenue entrance, take note of the famous lion sculptures—*Fortitude* on the right, and *Patience* on the left—so dubbed by whip-smart former mayor Fiorello LaGuardia. At Christmastime they don natty wreaths to keep warm.

This library is actually the **Humanities and Social Sciences Library,** only one of the research libraries in the New York Public Library system. The interior is one of the finest in the city and features **Astor Hall,** with high arched marble ceilings and grand staircases. The stupendous **Main Reading Rooms** have now reopened after a massive restoration and modernization that both brought them back to their stately glory and moved them into the computer age (goodbye, card catalogs!).

Even if you don't stop in to peruse the periodicals, you may want to check out one of the excellent rotating **exhibitions;** look for "Utopia: The Search for the Ideal Society in the Western World" from October 14, 2000, through January 27, 2001. There's also a full calendar of **lecture programs,** with past speakers ranging from Tom Stoppard to Cokie Roberts; popular speakers often sell out, so it's a good idea to purchase tickets in advance.

✪ **Rockefeller Center.** Between 48th and 50th sts., from Fifth to Sixth aves. ☎ **212/632-3975.** Subway: B, D, F, Q to 47th–50th sts./Rockefeller Center.

A streamline moderne masterpiece, Rockefeller Center is one of New York's central gathering spots for visitors and New Yorkers alike. A prime example of the city's skyscraper spirit and historic sense of optimism, it was erected mainly in the 1930s, when the city was deep in the Depression as well as its most passionate art deco phase. Designated a National Historic Landmark in 1988, it's now the world's largest privately owned business-and-entertainment center, with 18 buildings on 21 acres.

For a dramatic approach to the entire complex, start at Fifth Avenue between 49th and 50th streets. The builders purposely created the gentle slope of the Promenade, known here as the **Channel Gardens** because it's flanked to the south by La Maison Française and to the north by the British Building (the Channel, get it?). You'll also find a number of attractive shops along here, including a big branch of the **Metropolitan Museum of Art Store,** a good stop for elegant gifts. The Promenade leads to the **Lower Plaza,** home to the famous ice-skating rink in winter (see next paragraph) and alfresco dining in summer in the shadow of Paul Manship's gilded bronze statue *Prometheus,* more notable for its setting than its magnificence as an artwork. All around the flags of the United Nations' member countries flap in the breeze. Just behind *Prometheus,* in December and early January, towers the city's official and majestic Christmas tree.

The **Rink at Rockefeller Plaza** (☎ 212/332-7654), is tiny but positively romantic, especially during the holidays, when the giant Christmas tree's multicolored lights twinkle from above. It's open from mid-October to mid-March, and you'll skate under the magnificent tree for the month of December.

The focal point of this "city within a city" is the **GE Building,** at 30 Rockefeller Plaza, a 70-story showpiece towering over the plaza. It's still one of the city's most impressive buildings; walk through for a look at the granite and marble lobby, lined with monumental sepia-toned murals by José Maria Sert. You can pick up a walking tour brochure highlighting the center's art and architecture at the main information desk in this building.

NBC television maintains studios throughout the complex. *Saturday Night Live,* the *Rosie O'Donnell Show,* and *Late Night with Conan O'Brien* originate in the GE Building (see "Talk of the Town: TV Tapings," later in this chapter, for tips on getting tickets). NBC's *Today* **show** is broadcast live on weekdays from 7 to 9am from the glass-enclosed studio on the southwest corner of 49th Street and Rockefeller Plaza; come early if you want a visible spot, and bring your HI MOM! sign.

The 70-minute **NBC Studio Tour** (☎ 212/664-3700) will take you behind the scenes at the Peacock network. The tour changes daily, but may include the *Today* show, *NBC Nightly News, Dateline NBC,* and/or *Saturday Night Live* sets. Who knows? You may even run into Tom Brokaw in the hall. Tours run throughout the day Monday through Saturday from 8:30am to 5:30pm, Sunday from 9:30am to 4:30pm; of course, you'll have a better chance of encountering some real live action on a weekday. Tickets are $17.50 for adults, $15 for seniors and kids 6 to 16. You can reserve yours in advance or buy them right up to tour time at the grand new **NBC Experience** store, on Rockefeller Plaza at 49th Street. Tour-ticket purchases come with a 15% discount on NBC-themed merchandise in the store, where you can also enjoy some silly interactive features like the virtual reality "Conan O'Brien's Wild Desk Ride" or "Al Roker's Weather Challenge," which lets you do the forecast alongside the jolly meteorologist.

Other notable buildings throughout the complex include the **International Building,** on Fifth Avenue between 50th and 51st streets, worth a look for its Atlas statue out front; and the **McGraw-Hill Building,** on Sixth Avenue between 48th and 49th streets, with its 50-foot sun triangle on the plaza.

The newly restored **Radio City Music Hall,** 1260 Sixth Ave., at 50th Street (☎ 212/247-4777; www.radiocity.com), is perhaps the most impressive architectural feat of the complex. Designed by Donald Deskey, it's one of the largest indoor theaters, with 6,200 seats. But its true grandeur derives from its magnificent art deco appointments. The crowning touch is the stage's great proscenium arch, which from the distant seats evokes a faraway sun setting on the horizon of the sea. The men's and women's lounges are also splendid. The theater hosts the annual **Christmas Spectacular,** starring the Rockettes. The illuminating 1-hour **Stage Door Tour** is offered Monday through Saturday from 10am to 5pm, Sunday from 11am to 5pm; tickets are $15 for adults, $9 for children under 12.

What's New in Times Square

The writer O. Henry once observed that, "New York City will be a great place if they ever finish it." Indeed, no other city is so darn good at reinventing itself: Witness the "new" Times Square. The dust is finally settling on the epic renewal of the crossroads where Broadway meets 42nd Street, and what was once the city's gritty heart is now the hub of its tourist-friendly rebirth.

The neon lights of Broadway are more dazzling than ever, now that ABC's *Good Morning America* has set up a street-facing studio at Broadway and 44th Street, and **Nasdaq's** 8-story billboard—the world's largest video screen, at Broadway and 43rd—has joined the landscape. **WWF New York** and **ESPN Zone** both landed on Broadway in 1999, reinvigorating the whole notion of themed dining (see "Theme Restaurant Thrills!" in chapter 6). Two new hotels—slated to be a Doubletree, at 42nd Street, and a Sheraton, at 47th—are set to join the fleet by late 2000, which means that thousands more visitors can stay right on the Great White Way. Corporate America has even moved in; among the big-name headquarters that have relocated to prime Times Square real estate in '99 and 2000 are Morgan Stanley and Reuters.

In February 2000, the city chose a winning design that will give the **TKTS** discount theater tickets booth at the bustling heart of the area its own brand-new look. The current modified ramshackle trailer will be replaced by a grand red 16-foot staircase, with the new booth tucked underneath. After making your ticket purchase, you'll be able to take a seat on the steps and watch the real-life theater of the absurd taking place around you. Extra ticket windows are set to be added, too, which should speed up the lines. Construction is set to begin in late 2000.

The biggest news for 2000 is 42nd Street. This former porn peddler's paradise is being rebuilt from scratch as a family-oriented amusement mecca—a couple of 'em, in fact. By the end of 2000, the south side of 42nd between Seventh and Eighth avenues will be reinvented as the Forest City Ratner entertainment complex (bound to be christened with a sexier name by the time you arrive), which will include **Madame Tussaud's New York,** a 6-floor fully interactive new-world version of London's famous wax museum; a 26-screen movie complex; and plenty of mall-familiar shopping, including a Disney Store and HMV Records. But wait, there's more: Across the street will be **E-Walk,** where the multilevel **Broadway City** video arcade will be joined in late 2000 by **B.B. King's Blues Room,** a 550-seat music club and restaurant that promises to be a slice of authenticity among the tourist schlock (the legendary Blue Note jazz club is backing the development), plus 13 extra movie screens and more shopping and dining straight from the mall back home.

To quote the great Bart Simpson: Ay caramba!

United Nations. At First Ave. and 46th St. ☎ **212/963-TOUR.** www.un.org. Guided tours $7.50 adults, $6 seniors, $5 students, $4 children (those under 5 not permitted). Daily tours every half hour 9:15am–4:45pm; closed weekends Jan–Feb. Subway: S, 4, 5, 6, 7 to 42nd St./Grand Central.

In the midst of what some consider the world's most cynical city is this working monument to world peace. The U.N. headquarters occupies 18 acres of international territory—neither New York City nor the United States has jurisdiction here—along the East River from 42nd to 48th streets. Designed by an international team of architects (led by American Wallace K. Harrison and including Le Corbusier) and finished in 1952, the complex along the East River weds the 39-story glass slab Secretariat with the free-form General Assembly on beautifully landscaped grounds donated by John D. Rockefeller Jr. One hundred eighty nations use the facilities to arbitrate worldwide disputes.

Guided 1-hour tours take you to the General Assembly Hall and the Security Council Chamber and introduce the history and activities of the United Nations and its related organizations. Along the tour you'll see donated objects and artwork, including charred artifacts that survived the atomic bombs at Hiroshima and Nagasaki, stained-glass windows by Chagall, a replica of the first *Sputnik,* and a colorful mosaic called *The Golden Rule,* based on a Norman Rockwell drawing, which was a gift from the United States in 1985.

If you take the time to wander the beautifully landscaped **grounds,** you'll be rewarded with lovely views and some surprises. The mammoth monument *Good Defeats Evil,* donated by the Soviet Union in 1990, fashioned a contemporary St. George slaying a dragon from parts of a Russian ballistic missile and an American Pershing missile.

The **Delegates' Dining Room** (☎ 212/963-7625), which affords great views of the East River, is open to the public on weekdays for lunch from 11:30am to 2:30pm (reserve in advance). The **gift shop** sells flags and unusual hand-crafted items from all over the world, and the **post office** sells unique United Nations stamps that can be purchased and posted only here.

OTHER NOTABLE STRUCTURES & ENGINEERING FEATS

For **City Hall,** see the walking tour under "Historic Lower Manhattan's Top Attractions," earlier in this chapter.

In addition to the landmarks below, architecture buffs may also want to seek out these notable buildings: The **Lever House,** built in 1952 at 390 Park Ave., between 53rd and 54th streets, and the neighboring **Seagram Building** (1958), at 375 Park Ave., are the city's best examples of the form-follows-function, glass-and-steel International style, with the latter designed by master architect Mies van der Rohe himself. Also in Midtown East is the **Sony Building,** at 550 Madison Ave., designed in 1984 by Philip Johnson with a pretty rose-granite facade and a playful Chippendale-style top that puts it a cut above the rest on the block.

The Upper West Side is home to two of the city's prime examples of residential architecture. On Broadway, taking up the block between 73rd and 74th streets, is the **Ansonia,** looking for all the world like a flamboyant architectural wedding cake. This splendid beaux arts building has been home to the likes of Stravinsky, Toscanini, and Caruso, thanks to its virtually soundproof apartments. It was also the spot where members of the Chicago White Sox plotted to throw the 1919 World Series, a year before Babe Ruth moved in after donning the New York Yankees' pinstripes. Even more notable is the **Dakota,** at 72nd Street and Central Park West. Legend has it that the angular 1884 apartment house—accented with gables, dormers, and oriel windows that give it a brooding appeal—earned its name when its forward-thinking developer, Edward S. Clark, was teased by friends that he was building so far north of the city that he might as well be building in the Dakotas. The building's most famous resident, John Lennon, was gunned down outside the 72nd Street entrance on December 8, 1980; Yoko Ono still lives inside.

◆ **Cathedral of St. John the Divine.** 1047 Amsterdam Ave. (at 112th St.). ☎ **212/ 316-7540** for general information, 212/932-7347 for tour information and reservations, 212/662-2133 for event information and tickets. www.stjohndivine.org. Suggested admission $2; tour $3; tower tour $10. Mon–Sat 8am–6pm, Sun 7am–7:30pm. Tours offered Tues–Sat 11am, Sun 1pm; tower tours 1st and 3rd Sat of the month at noon and 2pm. Services Mon–Sat 8am, 12:15pm, and 5:30pm; Sun 8, 9, and 11am and 7pm. Subway: B, C, 1, 9 to Cathedral Pkwy.

The world's largest Gothic cathedral, St. John the Divine has been a work in progress since 1892. Its sheer size is amazing enough—a nave that stretches two football fields and a seating capacity of 5,000—but keep in mind that there is no steel structural support. The church is being built using traditional Gothic engineering; blocks of granite and limestone are carved out by master masons and their apprentices (some from the surrounding Harlem neighborhood). Perhaps that's why the construction is still going on, more than 100 years after it began, with no end in sight. But what makes this place so wonderful is that finishing isn't necessarily the point.

Though the seat of the Episcopal Diocese of New York, St. John's embraces an interfaith tradition. Internationalism is a theme found throughout the cathedral's iconography; each chapel is dedicated to a different national or ethnic group. You can explore it on the **Public Tour,** offered 6 days a week, or on the twice-monthly **Vertical Tour,** which takes you on a hike up the 11-flight circular staircase to the top, for spectacular views. The cathedral is known for presenting outstanding musical events and important speakers. The free **New Year's Eve concert** draws thousands of New Yorkers; so, too, does its annual **Blessing of the Animals,** held in early October (see the "New York City Calendar of Events" in chapter 2). Call for event information and tickets.

Take a Break: If you need a snack after your tour, stop into the lovely, worn **Hungarian Pastry Shop,** 1030 Amsterdam Ave., between 110th and 111th streets (☎ **212/866-4230**), a favorite among Columbia University students. Order a plateful of crumbly, buttery cookies from the display case up front, then set up camp; this is another place you won't be rushed out of.

Flatiron Building. 175 Fifth Ave. (at 23rd St.). Subway: R to 23rd St.

This triangular masterpiece was one of the first skyscrapers. Its knife-blade wedge shape is the only way the building could fill the triangular property created by the intersection of Fifth Avenue and Broadway, and that happy coincidence created one of the city's most distinctive buildings. Built in 1902 and fronted with limestone and terra cotta (not iron), the Flatiron measures only 6 feet across at its narrow end. So called for its resemblance to the laundry appliance, it was originally named the Fuller Building, then later "Burnham's Folly" (since folks were certain that architect Daniel Burnham's 21-story structure would fall down). It didn't. There's no observation deck, and the building mainly houses publishing offices, but there are a few shops on the ground floor. The building's existence has served to name the neighborhood around it—the Flatiron District, home to a bevy of smart restaurants and shops.

St. Patrick's Cathedral. Fifth Ave. (btw. 50th and 51st sts.). ☎ **212/753-2261.** www.stpatrickscathedral.org. Free admission. Sun–Fri 7am–8:30pm, Sat 8am–8:30pm. Mass: Mon–Fri 7, 7:30, 8, and 8:30am, noon, and 12:30, 1, and 5:30pm; Sat 8 and 8:30am, noon, and 12:30 and 5:30pm; Sun 7, 8, 9, and 10:15am, noon, and 1, 4, and 5:30pm. Subway: B, D, F, Q to 47–50th sts./Rockefeller Center.

The largest Catholic cathedral in the United States is also the seat of the Archdiocese of New York. Designed by James Renwick, begun in 1859, and consecrated in 1879, St. Patrick's wasn't completed until 1906. Strangely, Irish Catholics picked one of the city's WASPiest neighborhoods for this Gothic church, constructed of white marble and stone. Look for Mother Elizabeth Seton, the first American-born saint, among the statues in the nave.

Temple Emanu-El. 1 E. 65th St. (at Fifth Ave.). ☎ **212/744-1400.** www.emanuelnyc.org. Free admission. Museum: Sun–Thurs 10am–4:30pm, Fri–Sat 1–4pm. Services: Sun–Thurs 5:30pm, Fri 5:15pm, Sat 10:30am. Subway: N, R to Fifth Ave.; 6 to 68th St.

Many of New York's most prominent and wealthy families are members of this Reform congregation, housed in the city's most famous synagogue. The largest house of Jewish worship in the world is a blend of Moorish and Romanesque styles, symbolizing the mingling of Eastern and Western cultures. The **Herbert and Eileen Bernard Museum** houses a small but remarkable collection of Judaica, including a collection of Hanukkah lamps with examples ranging from the 14th to the 20th centuries. There are also three galleries telling the story of the congregation Emanu-El from 1845 to the present.

7 Organized Sightseeing Tours

Reservations are required on some of the tours listed below, but even if they're not, it's always best to call ahead to confirm prices, times, and meeting places.

DOUBLE-DECKER BUS TOURS

Taking a narrated sightseeing tour is one of the best ways to see and learn quickly about New York's major sights and neighborhoods. However, keep in mind that the commentary is only as good as the guide, who is seldom an expert. Tour guides tend toward hyperbole and might get a few of the facts wrong. The *New York Times* recently found tour-bus guides spouting the following inaccuracies: 65 people were killed in the World Trade Center blast (it was 6); New York has the oldest subway system in the world (third, behind London's—41 years before New York—and Boston's, which was the first in the U.S.); Frank Sinatra was born in Jersey City (it was Hoboken); and Herald Square was named after the founder of the *New York Herald Tribune* (there was no Mr. Herald). But the idea is to see the highlights, not write a dissertation from this stuff. So enjoy the ride—and take the "facts" you hear along the way with a grain of salt.

Both of these companies offer narrated tours aboard double-decker buses with an alfresco top level. Skip the Brooklyn tours that these guys offer. If you want to see that famous borough, you're better off heading to one or more of the sights I've discussed under "Highlights of the Outer Boroughs," later in this chapter.

Gray Line New York Tours. In the Port Authority Bus Terminal, Eighth Ave. and 42nd St.; also at Times Square Visitors Center, 1560 Broadway (btw. 46th and 47th sts.). Tours depart from 4 additional Manhattan locations. ☎ **212/397-2600.** www.graylinenewyork.com. Hop-on, hop-off bus tours from $25 adults, $16 children 5–11; hop-on, hop-off full-city tour $35 adults, $23 children.

Gray Line offers just about every sightseeing tour option and combination you could want. There are bus tours by day and by night that run uptown, downtown, and all around the town, as well as bus combos with Circle Line cruises, helicopter flights, museum entrances, and guided visits of sights. Two-day options are available, as are some out-of-town day trips (even a full day at Woodbury Commons, if you can't resist an opportunity for outlet shopping).

There's no real point to purchasing some combination tours—you don't need a guide to take you to the top of the World Trade Center or to the Statue of Liberty, and you don't save any money on admission by buying the combo ticket—but others are worth the price, such as the Sunday Harlem Gospel tour, which features a tour of Harlem's top sights and a gospel service for $33 ($24 for kids 5 to 11). I've found Gray Line to put a higher premium on accuracy than the other big tour-bus operators, so this is your best bet among the biggies.

HARBOR CRUISES

If you'd like to sail the New York Harbor aboard the 1885 cargo schooner *Pioneer,* see the listing for South Street Seaport & Museum earlier in this chapter, under "Historic Lower Manhattan's Top Attractions."

Note that some of the lines below may have limited schedules in winter, especially for evening cruises.

✪ **Circle Line Sightseeing Cruises.** Departing from Pier 83, at W. 42nd St. and Twelfth Ave. Also departing from Pier 16 at South St. Seaport, 207 Front St. Sales desk at Times Square Visitors Center, 1560 Broadway (btw. 46th and 47th sts.). ☎ **212/563-3200.** www. circleline.com. Cruises $12–$22 adults, $10–$19 seniors, $6–$12 children 12 and under. Subway to Pier 83: A, C, E to 42nd St. Subway to Pier 16: J, M, Z, 2, 3, 4, 5 to Fulton St.

Circle Line is the only tour company that circumnavigates the entire 35 miles around Manhattan, and I love this ride. The **Full Island** cruise takes 3 hours and passes by the World Trade Center, the Statue of Liberty, Ellis Island, the Brooklyn Bridge, the United Nations, Yankee Stadium, the George Washington Bridge, and more, including Manhattan's wild northern tip. The panorama is riveting, and the commentary isn't bad. The big boats are basic but fine, with lots of deck room for everybody to enjoy the view. Snacks, soft drinks, coffee, and beer are available onboard for purchase.

If 3 hours is more than you or the kids can handle, go for either the 1^1/$_2$-hour **Semi-Circle** or **Sunset/Harbor Lights** cruise, both of which show you the highlights of the skyline. There's also a 1-hour **Seaport Liberty** version that sticks close to the south end of the island. But of all the tours, the kids might like **The Beast** best, a thrill-a-minute speedboat ride offered in summer only.

In addition, a number of adults-only **Live Music & DJ Cruises** sail regularly from the seaport from May through September ($20 to $40 per person). Depending on the night of the week, you can groove to the sounds of jazz, Latin, gospel, dance tunes, or blues as you sail along the skyline. Past performers have included Vicki Sue Robinson, Martha Wash, and Gato Barbieri.

Spirit Cruises. Departing from Pier 61, at Chelsea Piers, W. 23rd St. and Twelfth Ave. ☎ **212/727-2789.** www.spiritcruises.com. 2- to 2^1/$_2$-hour lunch cruises $30–$40; 3-hour dinner cruises $57–$73. Inquire about children's rates. Subway: C, E to 23rd St.

Spirit Cruises' modern ships are floating cabarets that combine sightseeing in New York Harbor with freshly prepared meals, musical revues, and dancing to live bands. The atmosphere is festive and fun, and a touch more relaxed than aboard World Yacht (below). The buffet meals are nothing special, but they're fine.

Spirit cruises also depart from Liberty Landing Marina in Jersey City, NJ; call ☎ **201/333-3603** for details.

✪ **World Yacht.** Departing from Pier 81, at W. 41st St. and Twelfth Ave. ☎ **800/498-4270** or 212/630-8100. www.worldyacht.com. 3-hour dinner cruises $67–$79 Fri–Sat; 2-hour Sun brunch cruise $42. Subway: A, C, E to 42nd St.

If you want a more elegant cruise than what Spirit offers, go with World Yacht. They offer dressy, high-quality cruises with a touch of class and fair-to-middling continental cuisine. Still, come for the experience, which is romantic to the max. There's a 2-hour Sunday brunch cruise with live piano music, and a 3-hour dinner cruise featuring a four-course meal, live entertainment, dancing, and spectacular views. A great way to celebrate a special occasion. You can buy yourself a higher level of food, seating, and service with Ambassador Service ($25 extra per person). A jacket is required at dinner, and sneakers and jeans aren't permitted at any time.

AIR TOURS

Liberty Helicopters. Departing from VIP Heliport at W. 30th St. and Twelfth Ave., or the Downtown Heliport on Pier 6. ☎ **212/967-4550** (VIP Heliport) or 212/487-4777 (Downtown Heliport). www.libertyhelicopters.com. Pilot-narrated tours $52–$190. Subway to VIP: A, C, E, to 34th St. Subway to Downtown: 2, 3 to Wall St.

How about a bird's-eye view of Manhattan? These flight-seeing trips are pricey, so if you only want a taste, choose your heliport carefully: 4¹/₂-minute tours from Midtown's VIP Heliport take in the USS *Intrepid,* Midtown skyscrapers, and Central Park, while those from the Wall Street area's Downtown Heliport focus on the Statue of Liberty and lower Manhattan. Longer tours last 10 or 15 minutes, and the routes are similar no matter which departure point you choose. If you opt for the longest tour, you'll fly far enough uptown to take in the George Washington Bridge and Yankee Stadium. Flights leave every 15 minutes daily from 9am to 9pm, but note that reservations are required for two or more.

SPECIALTY TOURS
MUSEUMS & CULTURAL ORGANIZATIONS

The **Municipal Art Society** (☎ 212/935-3960; www.mas.org) offers excellent historical and architectural walking tours aimed at intelligent, individualistic travelers, not the mass market. Each is led by a highly qualified guide who gives insights into the significance of buildings, neighborhoods, and history. Topics range from the urban history of Greenwich Village to "Money Matters: The Interiors of Wall Street." On Wednesday at 12:30pm, the society sponsors a free tour of **Grand Central Terminal** (call for meeting place; donations accepted). Weekday walking tours are $10, $8 for seniors and students; weekend tours are $15, $12 for seniors and students. Reservations may be required depending on the tour, so it's always best to call ahead. A full schedule is available online.

The ✪ **92nd Street Y** (☎ 212/996-1100; www.92ndsty.org) offers a wonderful variety of walking tours, many featuring funky themes or behind-the-scenes visits. Subjects can range from "Diplomat for a Day at the U.N" to "Secrets of the Chelsea Hotel" to "Artists of the Meat-Packing District" to "Jewish Harlem." Prices range from $15 to $40, but many include ferry rides, afternoon tea, dinner, or whatever suits the program. Guides are well-chosen experts on their subjects, ranging from highly respected historians to an East Village poet, mystic, and art critic (for "Allen Ginsberg's New York" and "East Village Night Spots"), and many routes travel into the outer boroughs. The 92nd Street Y also offers a full range of daylong **bus tours** beyond Manhattan, which are equally as compelling; prices generally range from $50 to $90. Advance registration is required for all walking and bus tours. Schedules are planned a few months in advance, so check the Web site for tours that might interest you.

The **New-York Historical Society** (☎ 212/873-3400; www.nyhistory.org), offers walking tours of various Manhattan neighborhoods on Wednesday and Saturday throughout the year, usually led by an expert guide with special insight into a given area. At press time, author Edward Hayman *(Signs and Wonders: The Spectacular Marketing of America)* was leading guided walks through Times Square, with special emphasis on its neon history. Call or check the Web site to see what's on when you're in town. Tours are generally $12 for adults, $10 for students and seniors.

INDEPENDENT OPERATORS

One of the most highly praised sightseeing organizations in New York is ✪ **Big Onion Walking Tours** (☎ 212/439-1090; www.bigonion.com). Enthusiastic Big Onion guides (all hold an advanced degree in American history from Columbia or New York universities) peel back the layers of history to reveal the city's inner secrets. The 2-hour tours are offered mostly on weekends, and subjects include the "The Bowery," "Presidential New York," "Irish New York," "Central Park," "Greenwich Village in Twilight," "Historic Harlem," and numerous historic takes on Lower Manhattan. One of the most popular programs is the "Multiethnic Eating Tour" of the Lower East Side, where you munch on everything from dim sum and dill pickles to fresh mozzarella. Big Onion also conducts exclusive visits to Ellis Island and Roosevelt Island. Tour prices range from $10 to $16 for adults, $8 to $14 for students and seniors. No reservations are necessary, but Big Onion strongly recommends that you call to verify schedules.

All tours from ✪ **Joyce Gold History Tours of New York** (☎ 212/242-5762; www.nyctours.com) are offered by Joyce Gold herself, an instructor of Manhattan history at New York University and the New School for Social Research, who has been conducting history walks around New York since 1975. Her tours can really cut to the core of this town; Joyce is full of fascinating stories about Manhattan and its people. Tours are arranged around themes like "The Colonial Settlers of Wall Street," "The Genius and Elegance of Gramercy Park," "Downtown Graveyards," "The Old Jewish Lower East Side," "Historic Harlem," and "TriBeCa: The Creative Explosion." Tours are offered most weekends March to December and last from 2 to 4 hours, and the price is $12 per person; no reservations are required. Private tours are available if you're traveling as an individual or with a group.

Now that *Seinfeld* lives only in syndication, Kenny Kramer, former across-the-hall neighbor of *Seinfeld* co-creator Larry David and the real-life inspiration for Cosmo

The Food Lovers' Guide to New York

Addie Tomei (Oscar-winning actress Marisa's mom) offers guided walking tours through her company **Savory Sojurns** (☎ 888/9-SAVORY or 212/691-7314; www.savorysojurns.com) that focus on a subject very near and dear to New York's heart: food. These are 5- to 6-hour events geared to those who want an insider's view of the culinary wonderland that is New York and hands-on experience with its bounty. For instance, on her Chinatown adventure, Addie will take you shopping in Chinatown's best markets, teach you how to identify exotic ingredients, and learn from shop owners how to put them to use. Then you'll proceed to a neighborhood cooking school, where a Chinese chef will teach you how to prepare an Asian feast—which you'll promptly enjoy, of course. The SoHo and Little Italy tour offers a similar shopping experience, followed by a restaurant meal where you can observe the chef in action. Similar tours are offered of Greenwich Village; the Flatiron District and Gramercy Park; Atlantic Avenue, Brooklyn's Middle Eastern enclave; and many other neighborhoods, each with its own unique component. Tours are geared to food lovers, of course, but there's plenty of cultural interest on each tour to keep less food-interested spouses or traveling companions well entertained.

Tour prices are all-inclusive and range from $70 to $250. Reservations should be made as far in advance as possible, at least 3 to 6 months. You'll need to have six or more people to guarantee a tour, but it's also possible to hitch onto another group. Addie is also happy to arrange customized tours for groups of any size.

Kramer ("Giddy-up!"), hopes his 3-hour **Kramer's Reality Tour for Seinfeld Fans** (☎ **800/KRAMERS** or 212/268-5525; www.kennykramer.com) can fill the void. The tour starts out kind of hokey, but really gets going once you board the van (equipped with TV monitors for seeing clips of the show) and hit the road. Among the many stops are the real Monk's, Tom's Restaurant (also immortalized in song by Suzanne Vega); the office building where Elaine worked, Kramer had his coffee-table book published, and George had sex with the cleaning lady on his desk; and the vegetable stand where Kramer was banned for squeezing fruit. Tours are offered Saturday and Sunday at noon, and tickets are $37.50—a little pricey, but fun for die-hard fans and casual viewers alike. Reservations are required.

Would you like to cruise by Monica and Chandler's apartment building? Or Oscar and Felix's? How about the courthouse where the prosecutors of *Law & Order* fight the good fight? **Scene on TV** (☎ **212/410-9830**) offers 1¹/₂-hour narrated mini-bus tours through TV history. Tours depart Saturdays and Sundays from the Times Square Visitor Center, 1560 Broadway, between 46th and 47th streets, at 10am, noon, 2, and 4pm. Tickets are $15 adults, $8 for kids 6 to 12.

Harlem Spirituals (☎ **212/391-0900;** www.harlemspirituals.com) specializes in gospel and jazz tours of Harlem that can be combined with a traditional soul-food meal. A variety of options are available, including a tour of Harlem sights with gospel service, and a soul-food lunch (brunch on Sun) as an add-on ($35 adults, $27 children 12 and under; $65 adults, $55 children with lunch or brunch) that's offered both Wednesday and Sunday. The Harlem jazz tour ($80 per person) includes a neighborhood tour, dinner at a family-style soul-food restaurant, and a visit to a local jazz club; there's also an Apollo Theatre variation on this tour. Additional options include evening tours of Harlem paired with a "behind-the-scenes" gospel choir rehearsal and extended weekday walking tours; Bronx, Queens, and Brooklyn tours are also offered for those who want a taste of the outer boroughs. All tours leave from Harlem Spirituals' Midtown office (690 Eighth Ave., between 43rd and 44th sts.), and all transportation is included.

8 Central Park & Other Places to Play

✪ CENTRAL PARK

Without this miracle of civic planning, Manhattan would be a virtual unbroken block of buildings. Instead, smack in the middle of Gotham, an 843-acre natural retreat provides a daily escape valve and tranquilizer for millions of New Yorkers.

While you're in the city, be sure to take advantage of the park's many charms—not the least of which is its sublime layout. Frederick Law Olmsted and Calvert Vaux won a competition with a plan that marries flowing paths with sinewy bridges, integrating them into the natural rolling landscape with its rocky outcroppings, man-made lakes, and wooded pockets. The park's construction, between 1859 and 1870, provided much-needed employment during an economic depression and drew the city's population into the upper reaches of the island, which at that time were still quite rural. Nevertheless, designers predicted the hustle and bustle to come, and tactfully hid traffic from the eyes and ears of park-goers by building roads that are largely hidden from the bucolic view.

On just about any day, Central Park is crowded with New Yorkers and visitors alike. On nice days, especially weekend days, it's the city's party central. Families come to play in the snow or the sun, depending on the season; in-line skaters come to fly through the crisp air and twirl in front of the band shell; couples come to stroll or paddle the lake; dog people come to hike and throw Frisbees to Bowser; and just about everybody comes to sunbathe at the first sign of summer. On beautiful days, the crowds are part of the appeal—everybody's come here to peel off their urban armor and relax, and the common goal puts a general feeling of camaraderie in the air. On these days, the people-watching is more compelling than anywhere else in the city. But one of Central Park's great appeals is that even on the most crowded days, there's always somewhere to get away from it all, if you just want a little peace and quiet, and a moment to commune with nature.

ORIENTATION & GETTING THERE   Look at your map—that great green swath in the center of Manhattan is Central Park. It runs from 59th Street (also known as Central Park South) at the south end to 110th Street at the north end, and from Fifth Avenue on the east side to Central Park West (the equivalent of Eighth Ave.) on the west side. A 6-mile rolling road, **Central Park Drive,** circles the park, and has a lane set aside for bikers, joggers, and in-line skaters. A number of **transverse** (crosstown) **roads** cross the park at major points—at 65th, 79th, 86th, and 97th streets—but they're built down a level, largely out of view, to minimize intrusion on the bucolic nature of the park.

A number of subway stops and lines serve the park, and which one you take depends on where you want to go. To reach the southernmost entrance on the west side, take an A, B, C, D, 1, or 9 to 59th Street/Columbus Circle. To reach the southeast corner entrance, take the N, R to Fifth Avenue; from this stop, it's an easy walk into the park to the Information Center in the **Dairy** (☎ 212/794-6564; open Tues–Sun 10am–5pm), midpark at about 65th Street. Here you can ask questions, pick up park information, and purchase a good park map.

If your time for exploring is limited, I suggest entering the park at 72nd or 79th streets for maximum exposure (subway: B, C to 72nd St. or 81st St. Museum of Natural History). From here, you can pick up park information at the visitor center at **Belvedere Castle** (☎ 212/772-0210; open Wed–Sun 11am–4pm), midpark at 79th Street. There's also a third visitor center at the **Charles A. Dana Discovery Center** (☎ 212/860-1370; open daily 11am–5pm, to 4pm in winter), at the northeast corner of the park at Harlem Meer, at 110th Street between Fifth and Lenox avenues (subway: 2, 3 to Central Park North/110th St.). The Dana Center is also an environmental education center hosting workshops, exhibits, music programs, and park tours, and lends fishing poles for fishing in Harlem Meer (park policy is catch-and-release).

Food carts and vendors are set up at all of the park's main gathering points, selling hot dogs, pretzels, and ice cream, so finding a bite to eat is never a problem. You'll also find a fixed food counter at the **Conservatory,** on the east side of the park north of the 72nd Street entrance, and both casual snacks and more sophisticated dining at **Park View at the Boathouse** (for details on this and **Tavern on the Green,** see chapter 6).

GUIDED TOURS   **Trolley tours** of the park are offered weekdays from May through November. Tours last 90 minutes and depart from Grand Army Plaza at Fifth Avenue and 59th Street; call ☎ 212/397-3809 for details.

The Dana Center hosts ranger-guided tours on occasion (☎ 212/860-1370). Also consider a private walking tour; many of the companies listed under "Organized Sightseeing Tours," earlier in this chapter, offer guided tours.

FOR FURTHER INFORMATION   Call the main number at ☎ 212/360-3444 for recorded information. Call ☎ 212/360-3456 for special events information. The park also has a comprehensive Web site that's worth checking out before you go at

Central Park

Alice in Wonderland Statue ⑭
Balto Statue ⑳
The Bandshell ⑱
Belvedere Castle ⑥
Bethesda Terrace
 & Bethesda Fountain ⑯
Bow Bridge ⑧
Carousel ㉖
Central Park Wildlife Center ㉓
Charles A. Dana
 Discovery Center ❶
Cleopatra's Needle
 (The Obelisk) ⑨
Conservatory ⑬
Conservatory Garden ❶
The Dairy Information Center ㉕
Delacorte Clock ㉒
Delacorte Theater ❼
Diana Ross Playground ❹
Hans Christian Andersen
 Statue ⑫
Harlem Meer ❶
Hecksher Playground ㉘
Henry Luce
 Nature Observatory ⑥
Imagine Mosaic ⑰
Jacqueline Kennedy Onassis
 Reservoir ❷
Loeb Boathouse ⑮
The Mall ⑲
Pat Hoffman Friedman
 Playground ⑩
Park View at the Boathouse ⑪
Rustic Playground ㉑
Shakespeare Garden ❽
Spector Playground ❸
Swedish Cottage
 Marionette Theatre ❺
Tavern on the Green ㉗
Tisch Children's Zoo ㉓
Wollman Rink ㉔

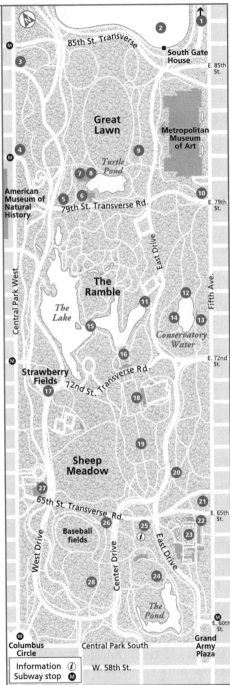

www.centralpark.org. If you have an **emergency** in the park, dial ☎ **800/201-PARK.**

SAFETY TIP   Even though the park has the lowest crime rate of any of the city's precincts, be wary, especially in the more remote northern end. It's a good idea to avoid the park entirely after dark, unless you're heading to one of the restaurants for dinner or to a Summerstage or Shakespeare at the Park event (see chapter 9), when you should stick with the crowds. For more safety tips, see "Playing It Safe" in chapter 4.

EXPLORING THE PARK

The best way to see Central Park is to wander along the park's 58 miles of winding pedestrian paths, keeping in mind the following highlights.

Before starting your stroll, stop by the **Information Center** in the Dairy, midpark in a 19th-century-style building overlooking Wollman Rink at about 65th Street, to get a good park map and other information on sights and events, and to peruse the kid-friendly exhibit on the park's history and design.

The southern part of Central Park is more formally designed and heavily visited than the relatively rugged and remote northern end. Not far from the Dairy is the **carousel** with 58 hand-carved horses (open daily 10:30am– to 6pm, to 5pm in winter; rides are 90¢); the zoo (see "Central Park Wildlife Center," below); and the Wollman Rink for roller- or ice-skating (see "Activities," below).

The **Mall,** a long formal walkway lined with elms shading benches and sculptures of sometimes forgotten writers, leads to the focal point of Central Park, **Bethesda Fountain** (along the 72nd St. transverse road). **Bethesda Terrace** and its grandly sculpted entryway border a large **lake** where dogs fetch sticks, rowboaters glide by, and dedicated early-morning anglers try their luck at catching carp, perch, catfish, and bass. You can rent a rowboat at or take a gondola ride from **Loeb Boathouse,** on the eastern end of the lake (see "Activities," below). Boats of another kind are at **Conservatory Water** (on the east side at 73rd St.), a stone-walled pond flanked by statues of both **Hans Christian Andersen** and **Alice in Wonderland.** On Saturday at 10am, die-hard yachtsmen race remote-controlled sailboats in fierce competitions following Olympic regulations. (Sorry, model boats aren't for rent.)

If the action there is too intense, **Sheep Meadow** on the southwestern side of the park is a designated quiet zone, where Frisbee throwing and kite flying are as energetic as things get. Another respite is **Strawberry Fields,** at 72nd Street on the West Side. This memorial to John Lennon, who was murdered across the street at the Dakota apartment building (72nd St. and Central Park West, northwest corner), is a gorgeous garden centered around an Italian mosaic bearing the title of the lead Beatle's most famous solo song, and his lifelong message: IMAGINE. In keeping with its goal of promoting world peace, the garden has 161 varieties of plants, donated by each of the 161 nations in existence when it was designed in 1985. This is a wonderful place for peaceful contemplation.

Bow Bridge, a graceful lacework of cast iron designed by Calvert Vaux, crosses over the lake and leads to the most bucolic area of Central Park, the **Ramble.** This dense 38-acre woodland with spiraling paths, rocky outcroppings, and a stream is the best spot for bird-watching and feeling as if you've discovered an unimaginably leafy forest right in the middle of the city.

North of the Ramble, **Belvedere Castle** is home to the **Henry Luce Nature Observatory** (☎ 212/772-0210), worth a visit if you're with children. From the castle, set on Vista Rock (the park's highest point at 135 ft.), you can look down on the **Great Lawn,** which has emerged lush and green from renovations, and the **Delacorte Theater,** home to Shakespeare in the Park (see chapter 9). The small **Shakespeare Garden**

Where's Balto?

The people at Central Park say that the question they're asked almost more than any other these days is "Where is the statue of Balto?" The heroic dog is just northwest of the zoo, midpark at about 66th Street.

---

south of the theater is scruffy, but it does have plants, herbs, trees, and other bits of greenery mentioned by the playwright. Behind the Belvedere Castle is the **Swedish Cottage Marionette Theatre** (☎ **212/988-9093**), hosting various marionette plays for children throughout the year; call to see what's on.

Continue north along the east side of the Great Lawn, parallel to East Drive. Near the glass-enclosed back of the **Metropolitan Museum of Art** (see "The Top Museums," earlier in this chapter) is **Cleopatra's Needle,** a 69-foot obelisk originally erected in Heliopolis around 1475 B.C. It was given to the city as a gift from the khedive of Egypt in 1880. (The khedive bestowed a similar obelisk to the city of London, which now sits on the Embankment of the Thames.)

North of the 86th Street Transverse Road is the **Jacqueline Kennedy Onassis Reservoir,** so named after the death of the beloved first lady, who lived nearby and often enjoyed a run along the $1^1/_2$-mile jogging track that circles the reservoir.

At the northeast end of the park is the **Conservatory Garden** (at 105th St. and Fifth Ave.), Central Park's only formal garden, with a magnificent display of flowers and trees reflected in calm pools of water. (The gates to the garden once fronted the Fifth Ave. mansion of Cornelius Vanderbilt II.) **Harlem Meer** and its boathouse were recently renovated and look beautiful. The boathouse now berths the **Dana Discovery Center** (☎ **212/860-1370**), where children learn about the environment and borrow fishing poles at no charge; see "Orientation & Getting There" under "Central Park & Other Places to Play," earlier in this chapter, for further details.

GOING TO THE ZOO

Central Park Wildlife Center/Tisch Children's Zoo. At Fifth Ave. and 64th St. ☎ **212/861-6030.** www.wcs.org/zoos. Admission $3.50 adults, $1.25 seniors, 50¢ children 3–12, free for children under 3. Apr–Oct Mon–Fri 10am–5pm, Sat–Sun 10:30am–5:30pm; Nov–Mar daily 10am–4:30pm. Subway: N, R to Fifth Ave.

It has been nearly a decade since the zoo in Central Park was renovated, making it in the process both more human and more humane. Lithe sea lions frolic in the central pool area with beguiling style. The gigantic but graceful polar bears (one of whom, by the way, made himself a true New Yorker when he began regular visits with a shrink) glide back and forth across a watery pool that has glass walls through which you can observe very large paws doing very smooth strokes. The monkeys seem to regard those on the other side of the fence with knowing disdain. In the hot and humid Tropic Zone, large colorful birds swoop around in freedom, sometimes landing next to nonplussed visitors.

Because of its small size, the zoo is at its best with its displays of smaller animals. The indoor multilevel Tropic Zone is a real highlight, its steamy rain forest home to everything from black-and-white Colobus monkeys to Emerald tree boa constrictors to a leaf-cutter ant farm. So is the large penguin enclosure in the Polar Circle, which is better than the one at San Diego's Sea World. In the Temperate Territory, look for the Asian red pandas (cousins to the big black-and-white ones), which look like the world's most beautiful raccoons. Despite their pool and piles of ice, however, the polar bears still look sad.

The entire zoo is good for short attention spans; you can cover the whole thing in $1^1/_2$ to 3 hours, depending on the size of the crowds and how long you like to linger. It's also very kid-friendly, with lots of well-written and -illustrated placards that older kids can understand. For the littlest ones, there's the $6 million **Tisch Children's Zoo.** With pigs, llamas, potbellied pigs, and more, this petting zoo and playground is a real blast for the 5-and-under set.

ACTIVITIES

The 6-mile rolling road circling the park, **Central Park Drive,** has a lane set aside for bikers, joggers, and in-line skaters. The best time to use it is when the park is closed to traffic: Monday to Friday 10am to 3pm (except Thanksgiving to New Year's) and 7 to 10pm. It's also closed from 7pm Friday to 6am Monday, but when the weather is nice, the crowds can be hellish.

BIKING   Off-road mountain biking isn't permitted; stay on Central Park Drive or your bike may be confiscated by park police.

You can rent 3- and 10-speed bikes as well as tandems in Central Park at the **Loeb Boathouse,** midpark near 72nd Street and East Drive (☎ 212/517-3623), for $8 to $12 a day; at **Metro Bicycles,** 1311 Lexington Ave., at 88th Street (☎ 212/ 427-4450), for $35 a day; at **Pedal Pushers,** 1306 Second Ave., between 68th and 69th streets (☎ 212/288-5592), for about $18 a day; and at **Toga Bike Shop,** 110 West End Ave., at 64th Street (☎ 212/799-9625), for $25 a day.

BOATING   From spring to fall, gondola rides and canoe rentals are available at the **Loeb Boathouse,** midpark near 74th Street and East Drive (☎ 212/517-3623). Rentals are $10 for the first hour, $2.50 every 15 minutes thereafter, and a $30 deposit is required.

HORSE-DRAWN CARRIAGE RIDES   At the entrance to the park at 59th Street and Central Park South, you'll see a line of **horse-drawn carriages** waiting to take passengers on a ride through the park or along certain of the city's streets. Horses belong on city streets as much as chamber pots belong in our homes. You won't need me to tell you how forlorn most of these horses look; if you insist, a ride is about $50 for two for a half hour, but I suggest skipping it.

ICE-SKATING   Central Park's **Wollman Rink,** at 59th Street and Sixth Avenue (☎ 212/396-1010), is the city's best outdoor skating spot, more spacious than the tiny rink at Rockefeller Center. It's open for skating generally from mid-October to mid-April, depending on the weather. Rates are $7 for adults, $3.50 for seniors and kids under 12, and skate rental is $3.50; lockers are available (locks are $6.75).

IN-LINE SKATING   Central Park is the city's most popular place for blading. See the beginning of this section for details on Central Park Drive, the main drag for skaters. On weekends, head to West Drive at 67th Street, behind Tavern on the Green, where you'll find trick skaters weaving through an NYRSA slalom course at full speed, or the Mall in front of the band shell (above Bethesda Fountain) for twirling to tunes. In summer, **Wollman Rink** converts to a hot-shot roller rink, with half-pipes and lessons available (see "Ice-Skating," above).

You can rent skates for $16 a day weekdays and $27 a day weekends from **Blades Board and Skate,** 120 W. 72nd St., between Broadway and Columbus Avenue (☎ 212/787-3911). Wollman Rink (above) also rents in-line skates for park use at similar rates.

PLAYGROUNDS   Nineteen Adventure Playgrounds are scattered throughout the park, perfect for jumping, sliding, tottering, swinging, and digging. At Central Park

West and 81st Street is the **Diana Ross Playground,** voted the city's best by *New York* magazine. Also on the west side is the **Spector Playground,** at 85th Street and Central Park West, and, a little farther north, the **Wild West Playground** at 93rd Street. On the east side is the **Rustic Playground,** at 67th Street and Fifth Avenue, a delightfully landscaped space rife with islands, bridges, and big slides; and the **Pat Hoffman Friedman Playground,** right behind the Metropolitan Museum of Art at East 79th Street, is geared toward older toddlers.

RUNNING   Marathoners and wannabes regularly run in Central Park along the 6-mile **Central Park Drive,** which circles the park (run toward traffic to avoid being mowed down by wayward cyclists and in-line skaters). For a shorter loop, try the midpark 1.58-mile track around the **Jacqueline Kennedy Onassis Reservoir** (keep your eyes ready for spotting Madonna and other famous bodies). It's safest to jog only during daylight hours and where everybody else does. Avoid the small walks in the Ramble and at the north end of the park.

OTHER PARKS

For parks in Brooklyn and Queens, see "Highlights of the Outer Boroughs," later in this chapter. For more information on these and other city parks, go online to **www. ci.nyc.ny.us/html/dpr**.

Battery Park. From State Street to New York Harbor. Subway: N, R to Whitehall St.; 1, 9 to South Ferry; 4, 5 to Bowling Green.

As you traverse Manhattan's concrete canyons, it's sometimes easy to forget you're actually on an island. But here, at Manhattan's southernmost tip, you get the very real sense that just out past Liberty, Ellis, and Staten islands is the vast Atlantic Ocean.

The 21-acre park is named for the cannons built to defend residents after the American Revolution. **Castle Clinton National Monument** (the place to purchase tickets for the Statue of Liberty and Ellis Island ferry; see "In New York Harbor," earlier in this chapter) was built as a fort before the War of 1812, though it was never used as such. You'll most likely recognize Battery Park for the prominent role it played in *Desperately Seeking Susan,* Madonna's first movie. Besides the requisite T-shirt vendors and hot-dog carts, you'll find several statues and memorials scattered throughout the park. This is quite the civilized park, with lots of STAY OFF THE GRASS! signs and Wall Streeters eating deli sandwiches on the many park benches. Pull up your own bench for a good view out across the harbor.

Bryant Park. Behind the New York Public Library, at Sixth Ave. between 40th and 42nd sts. Subway: B, D, F, Q to 42nd St.; 7 to Fifth Ave.

Another success story in the push for urban redevelopment, Bryant Park is the latest incarnation of a 4-acre site that was, at various times in its history, a graveyard and a reservoir. Named for poet and *New York Evening Post* editor William Cullen Bryant (look for his statue on the east end), the park actually rests atop the New York Public Library's many miles of underground stacks. Another statue is also notable: a squat and evocative stone portrait of Gertrude Stein, one of the few outdoor sculptures of women in the city.

This simple green swath, just east of Times Square, is welcome relief from Midtown's concrete, taxi-choked jungle, and good weather attracts brown-baggers from neighboring office buildings. Just behind the library is **Bryant Park Grill** (☎ 212/ 840-6500), an airy bistro with New American food and service that doesn't live up to its fine setting (or high prices). Still, brunch is a good bet, and the grill's two summer alfresco restaurants—**The Terrace,** on the Grill's roof; and the casual **Cafe,** with small tables beneath a canopy of trees—are pleasant on a nice day.

Additionally, the park plays host to New York's **Seventh on Sixth** fashion shows, set up in billowy white tents (open to the trade only) in the spring and fall.

۞ Union Square Park. From 14th to 17th sts., btw. Park Ave. South and Broadway. Subway: L, N, R, 4, 5, 6 to 14th St./Union Sq.

Here's a delightful place to spend an afternoon. Reclaimed from drug dealers and abject ruin in the late '80s, Union Square Park is now one of the city's best assets. The seemingly endless subway work should no longer be disturbing the peace by the time you're here. This patch of green remains, with or without the construction, the focal point of the newly fashionable Flatiron and Gramercy Park neighborhoods. Don't miss the grand equestrian statue of George Washington at the south end or the bronze statue (by Bartholdi, the sculptor of the Statue of Liberty) of the marquis de Lafayette at the eastern end, gracefully glancing toward France.

This charming square is now best known as the site of New York's premier **Greenmarket.** Every Monday, Wednesday, Friday, and Saturday, vendors come down from upstate, Long Island, and as far away as Pennsylvania to hawk fresh veggies and fruits, organic baked goods, cider, wine, and even fresh fish and lobsters in booths that flank the north and west sides of the square. Fresh-cut flowers and plants are also for sale, as are books and postcards. During summer and fall, you can graze the bazaar and easily assemble a cheap and healthy lunch to munch under the trees or at the picnic tables at the park's north end. Musical acts regularly play the small pavilion at the north end of the park, and in-line skaters take over the market space in the after-work hours.

At the north end of the park, a small cafe called **Luna Park** (☎ 212/475-8464) is open in warm weather.

Washington Square Park. At the southern end of Fifth Ave. (where it intersects Waverly Place btw. MacDougal and Wooster sts.). Subway: A, B, C, D, E, F, Q to West 4th St./Washington Sq.

You'll be hard-pressed to find much "park" in this mainly concrete square—a burial ground in the late 18th century—but it's undeniably the focal point of Greenwich Village. Chess players, skateboarders, street musicians, New York University students, gay and straight couples, the occasional film crew, and not a few homeless people compete for attention throughout the day and most of the night. (If anyone issues a friendly challenge to play you in the ancient and complex Chinese game of Go, don't take them up on it—you'll lose money.)

The lively scene belies a macabre past. Once marshland traversed by Minetta Brook, it became in 1797 a potter's field (most green and fertile downtown parks were originally graveyards), and the remains of some 10,000 bodies are buried here. In the early 1800s, the square, or more specifically the infamous Hanging Elm in the northwest corner where MacDougal Street meets the park, was used for public executions. It wasn't until the 1830s that the elegant Greek Revival town houses on Washington Square North known as "The Row" (note especially nos. 21–26) attracted the elite. Stanford White designed Washington Arch (1891–92) to commemorate the centenary of George Washington's inauguration as first president. While in the neighborhood, peek down charming MacDougal Alley and Washington Mews, both lined with delightful old carriage houses.

Despite a city cleanup and increased police presence, it's a good idea to stay out of the park after dark.

CHELSEA PIERS

One of the city's biggest—and most successful—private urban development projects of the last few years has been the 30-acre **Chelsea Piers Sports & Entertainment**

We Can Work It Out

So your hotel doesn't have a gym, and walking around New York just isn't enough of a workout for you? Never fear: The city has a number of health clubs that are open to out-of-towners on a day-to-day basis.

A down-to-earth iron-pumping crowd can be found at **Crunch Fitness,** 404 Lafayette St., between West 4th Street and Astor Place in NoHo (☎ **212/ 614-0120**); 162 W. 83rd St., between Columbus and Amsterdam avenues on the Upper West Side (☎ **212/875-1902**); and at other locations in various neighborhoods throughout Manhattan (check the Yellow Pages). Crunch charges a per-day drop-in fee of $22, and the Lafayette Street location is open 24 hours on weekdays (8am–9pm on weekends).

In Midtown, the **New York Sports Club** has an extensive facility with a 50-foot lap pool and sauna at the Crowne Plaza Manhattan hotel, 1605 Broadway, between 48th and 49th streets (☎ **212/977-8880**); day passes are $25. **Gravity,** the excellent 15,000-square-foot facility at Le Parker Meridien hotel, 118 W. 57th St., between Sixth and Seventh avenues (☎ **212/708-7340**), allows day guests access for $25, $50 if you want access to the glass-enclosed 42nd-floor pool.

And don't forget about the fabulous **Sports Center at Chelsea Piers** (above), the best health club in the city available to day guests for $40.

If you'd rather have others work out your stresses and strains for you—after all, this is vacation, right?—head to the **Stressless Step,** 115 E. 57th St. (between Lexington and Park aves.), 5th Floor (☎ **212/826-6222;** www.stresslessstep. com). This full-service stress-reduction center offers a complete body-work menu, from basic Swedish to nonbrutal shiatsu to hot rock massage, plus facials, wraps, waxing, and more. The rate is $90 for a 55-minute massage. Rates include use of steam room, sauna, whirlpool, and relaxation areas, and no tipping is allowed.

Complex (☎ **212/336-6666;** www.chelseapiers.com). Jutting out into the Hudson River on four huge piers between 17th and 23rd streets, it's a terrific multifunctional recreational facility.

The ✪ **Sports Center** (☎ **212/336-6000**), a three-football-fields-long mega-facility, does health clubs one better. It offers not only the usual cardiovascular training, weights, and aerobics but also a four-lane quarter-mile indoor running track, a boxing ring, basketball courts, a sand volleyball court, a gorgeous 25-yard indoor pool with a whirlpool and sundeck, the world's most challenging rock-climbing wall plus a bouldering wall, and the **Origins Feel-Good Spa** (☎ **212/336-6780**), which offers massage, reflexology, facials, and the like. Day passes to the Sports Center are $40 for nonmembers; spa treatments are extra, of course.

The **Golf Club** (☎ **212/336-6400**), has 52 all-weather fully automated hitting stalls on four levels and a 200-yard net-enclosed artificial-turf fairway jutting out over the water, making it the best place in the city to hit a few. Prepaid ball cards start at $15 for 65 balls, and club rentals are available.

The **Sky Rink** (☎ **212/336-6100**), the city's latest ice spot, has twin around-the-clock indoor rinks for recreational skating and pickup hockey games with Hudson River views. General skating is $11 for adults, $8 for seniors and kids; skate rental is $5.

If wheels are your thing, there are two outdoor **Roller Rinks** (☎ **212/336-6200**) for in-line skating and roller hockey games. Rates for the coming year were not set at press time, but expect to pay about $5 for adults, $3 for kids for general skating; skate rentals are available. The **Skating School** offers instruction if you would like to learn.

The **Field House** (☎ **212/336-6500**) is mainly for team sports, but young rock climbers will enjoy the 30-foot indoor **climbing wall,** designed for kids as well as grown-ups. Open climbs are $17, and children's lessons are available. **Batting cages** are also available ($1 per 10 pitches).

Feeling like a little 10-pin tonight? State-of-the-art **AMF Chelsea Piers Bowl** (☎ **212/835-BOWL**) offers 40 lanes of fun. Games are $6.25 per person, and shoe rental is $4.

Beyond its athletics, the complex is a destination in and of itself. The 1.2-mile esplanade has benches and picnic tables with terrific river views; they serve as the perfect vantage point for watching the *QEII* head out to sea, or the Navy and Coast Guard ships sailing in for Fleet Week each May. For waterfront dining there's New York's largest microbrewery/restaurant, the **Chelsea Brewing Company** (☎ **212/ 336-6440**), on Pier 61, serving up very good brews and okay food on a terrific waterfront terrace.

Getting There: Chelsea Piers is accessible by taxi and the M23 or M14 crosstown buses. The nearest subway is the C and E at 23rd Street and Eighth Avenue, then pick up the M23 and walk 4 long blocks west. Another option is to take the A, C, E to 14th Street or the L train to Eighth Avenue, walk to the river, then follow the walking/riding/running path along the river north.

9 Talk of the Town: TV Tapings

The trick to getting tickets for TV tapings in this city is to be from out of town. You visitors have a much better chance than we New Yorkers; producers are gun-shy about filling their audiences with obnoxious locals and see everybody who's not from New York as being from the heartland—and therefore their target TV audience.

If your heart's set on getting tickets to a show, request them as early as possible—6 months ahead isn't too early, and even earlier is better for the most popular shows. You're usually asked to send a postcard. Always include the number of tickets you want, your preferred dates of attendance (be as flexible as you can with this one), and your address *and* phone number. Tickets are always free. The shows tend to be pretty good about trying to meet your specific date requests, but don't be surprised if Ainsley Harriott is far more responsive than, say, Dave. And even if you send in your request extra early, don't be surprised if tickets don't show up at your house until 1 or 2 weeks before tape date.

If you come to town without any tickets, all hope is not lost. Because they know that every ticket holder won't make it, many studios give out a limited number of standby tickets on the day of taping. If you can just get up a little early and don't mind standing in line for a couple (or a few) hours, you have a good chance of getting one. Now, the bad news: Only one standby ticket per person is allowed, so everybody who wants to get in has to get up at the crack of dawn and stand in line. And even if you get your hands on a standby ticket, it doesn't guarantee admission; they usually only start seating standbys after the regular ticket holders are in. Still, chances are good.

For additional information on getting tickets to tapings, call ☎ **212/484-1222,** the New York Convention and Visitors Bureau's 24-hour hotline. And remember— you don't need a ticket to be on the *Today* show. *Good Morning America* also has a street-facing studio now, in Times Square on Broadway between 43rd and 44th streets, but it's on the second floor (just like the MTV studios across the street, at 1515 Broadway), so you won't be able to peer directly in.

If you do attend a taping, be sure to bring a sweater, even in summer. As anybody who watches Letterman knows, it's an icebox in those studios. And bring ID, as proof of age may be required.

The Ainsley Harriott Show   If you'd like to be in the audience for this British import's cooking and chat fest, call ☎ **212/824-4000** or send a written request to the *Ainsley Harriott Show Ticket Request,* Chelsea Piers, Pier 60—Studio F, New York, NY 10011.

The Daily Show with Jon Stewart   Comedy Central's boldly irreverent, often hilariously funny mock newscast tapes every Monday through Thursday at 5:45pm, at 513 W. 54th St. Make your advance ticket requests by phone at ☎ **212/586-2477,** or check with them for any cancellation tickets for the upcoming week.

Late Night with Conan O'Brien   Conan tix might not quite have the cachet of a Dave ticket, but they're a hot commodity nevertheless—so start planning now. Tapings are Tuesday through Friday at 5:30pm (plan on arriving by 4:45pm if you have tickets), and you must be 16 or older to attend. You can keep trying to get through on the operator line to arrange for tickets by phone, or send your postcard to NBC Studios/*Late Night,* 30 Rockefeller Plaza, New York, NY 10112 (☎ **212/664-3056** or 212/664-3057). Standby tickets are distributed Tuesday through Friday at 9am outside 30 Rockefeller Plaza, on the 49th Street side of the building, on a first-come, first-served basis (read: come early if you actually want to get one).

Later Today   Tickets for this syndicated post-*Today* show hour starring Florence Henderson can be requested by calling ☎ **212/664-3056** or 212/664-3057. Standby tickets are available in the main lobby of NBC Studios, 30 Rockefeller Plaza, at 7:30am on a first-come, first-served basis.

The Late Show with David Letterman   Here's the most in-demand TV ticket in town—so planning 9 months ahead isn't too soon. Tapings are Monday through Thursday at 5:30pm (arrive by 4:15pm), with a second taping Thursday at 8pm (arrive by 6:45pm). You must be 16 or older to attend. Send your postcard at least 6 months early (two tickets max; one request only, or all will be disregarded), to *Late Show* Tickets, Ed Sullivan Theater, 1697 Broadway, New York, NY 10019 (☎ **212/ 975-5853**). On tape days, call ☎ **212/247-6497** at 11am for standby tickets (no in-line standbys anymore); start dialing early because the machine will kick in as soon as all standbys are gone.

Live! with Regis and Kathie Lee   Here's the *other* hottest ticket in town. Tapings with Regis and Kathie Lee's replacement (still unannounced at press time) are Monday to Friday at 9am at the ABC Studios at 7 Lincoln Square (Columbus Ave. and West 67th St.) on the Upper West Side. You must be 10 or older to attend (under 18s must be accompanied by a parent). Send your postcard (four tickets max) at least a *full year* in advance to *Live!* Tickets, Ansonia Station, P.O. Box 777, New York, NY 10023-0777 (☎ **212/456-3054**). Standby tickets are sometimes available. Arrive at the studio no later than 7am and request a standby number; standby tickets are handed out on a first-come, first-served basis, so earlier is better. You might also have a chance at last-minute tickets by calling ☎ **212/456-2410** or 212/456-3055, but this is a longer shot than standby.

Montel Williams Show   Order tickets by calling ☎ **212/989-8101.** You must be 18 or older to attend.

Queen Latifah Show   Requests for tickets can be made by calling ☎ **877/ 485-7144,** by filling out the online request form at **www.latifahshow.com**, or by sending a self-addressed, stamped envelope to *Queen Latifah Tickets,* P.O. Box 2656, G.P.O., New York, NY 10199. You must be 16 or older to attend, and quantities are limited to six per request.

The Ricki Lake Show   Tickets can be requested by calling ☎ **800/GO-RICKI.** You can also use this line to volunteer yourself as a guest for shows such as "I'll Give You My Virginity for a Price" or "I Want to Tell My Girl I Slept with Her Mom." You must be 18 or older to attend.

The Rosie O'Donnell Show   Rosie is so popular that she's one of the toughest tickets in town right now. The schedule varies, but in general Rosie tapings are Monday through Thursday at 10am, and Thursday again at 2pm. No children under 5 are allowed, and under 18s must be accompanied by an adult. Send your postcard as far in advance as possible to NBC Studios/*The Rosie O'Donnell Show,* 30 Rockefeller Plaza, Suite 800E, New York, NY 10112 (☎ **212/506-3288** or 212/664-3056). Call before you send because demand is so great that requests are sometimes suspended or limited to certain months of the year. Standby tickets, if available, are distributed Monday through Thursday at 7:30am outside 30 Rockefeller Plaza, on the 49th Street side of the building; it's a random lottery system, so it doesn't help to show up too early.

The Sally Show   Call ☎ **800/411-7941** or 212/244-3595 for tickets to Sally Jesse Raphaël's talkfest. You must be 18 or older to attend.

Saturday Night Live   Everything about the show may change, but one thing remains the same—SNL's enduring popularity. This is another extremely hard ticket to come by. Tapings are Saturday at 11:30pm (arrival time 10pm); there's also a full dress rehearsal (arrival time 7pm). You must be 16 or older to attend. Send your postcard to arrive *in the month of August only* to NBC Studios/*Saturday Night Live,* 30 Rockefeller Plaza, New York, NY 10112 (☎ **212/664-4000**). Lotteries for pairs of tickets are held during the season; if you're a winner, you'll be notified with only 1 to 2 weeks' advance notice. Standby tickets may be a better bet: They're available at 9:15am on tape day at the 49th Street entrance to 30 Rockefeller Plaza.

The *Today* **Show**   As most of you know, anybody can be on TV with Katie, Matt, and cuddly weatherman Al Roker. All you have to do is show up outside the *Today* show's glass-walled studio at Rockefeller Center, on the southwest corner of 49th Street and Rockefeller Plaza, with your very own HI, MOM! sign. Tapings are Monday through Friday at 7am sharp, but come at the crack of dawn if your heart's set on being in front. Who knows? If it's a nice day, you may even get to chat with Katie, Matt, or Al in a segment.

Total Request Live   The countdown show that made Carson Daly a household name is broadcast live from MTV's second-floor glass-walled studio at 1515 Broadway, at 44th Street in Times Square, weekdays at 3:30pm. Crowds start gathering down below at all hours, depending on the drawing power of the day's guest. Arrive by 2pm at the latest if you want to have a prayer of making it into the in-studio audience (a very long shot). And don't forget to make your WE LOVE YOU, BRITNEY! and MARRY ME, CARSON! signs large enough to be captured on camera.

The View   ABC's girl power gabfest tapes live Monday through Friday at 11am (ticket holders must arrive by 10am). Requests, which should be sent 12 to 16 weeks in advance, can be submitted online (**www.abc.go.com/theview**) or via postcard to

Tickets, *The View,* 320 W. 66th St., New York, NY 10023. Since date requests are not usually accommodated, try standby: Arrive at the studio before 10am and put your name on the standby list; earlier is better, since tickets are handed out on a first-come, first-served basis.

Who Wants to Be a Millionaire   This Regis Philbin–hosted phenomenon is filmed at ABC's Upper West Side studios. To request tickets to be an audience member, send a postcard to *Who Wants to Be a Millionaire,* Columbia University Station, P.O. Box 250225, New York, NY 10025. Ticket requests are limited to four, and you must be 18 or older to attend. If your request can be met, tickets will be sent approximately 2 weeks prior to show time.

10 Especially for Kids

Some of New York's sights and attractions are designed specifically with kids in mind, and I've listed those below. But many of those I've discussed in the rest of this chapter are terrific for kids as well as adults; I've also included cross-references to the best of them below.

For general tips and other resources for visiting the city with the kids, see "For Families" under "Tips for Travelers with Special Needs" in chapter 2.

Probably the best place of all to entertain the kids is in ✪ **Central Park,** which has kid-friendly diversions galore; see "Central Park & Other Places to Play," earlier in this chapter.

MUSEUMS

In addition to the museums designed specifically for kids below, also consider the following, discussed elsewhere in this chapter: The **American Museum of Natural History** (p. 224), whose dinosaur displays are guaranteed to wow both you and the kids; the *Intrepid* **Sea-Air-Space Museum** (p. 233), on a real battleship with an amazing collection of vintage and high-tech airplanes; the **Forbes Magazine Galleries** (p. 232), whose wacky collection includes a number of vintage toys and games; the **Museum of Television & Radio** (p. 238), where you and the kids can pull up episodes of *Sesame Street* and other classic kids' TV shows to watch; the **American Museum of the Moving Image** (p. 274), where you and the kids can learn how movies are actually made; the **Lower East Side Tenement Museum** (p. 234), whose weekend living-history program really intrigues school-age kids; the **New York Transit Museum** (p. 273), where kids can explore vintage subway cars and other hands-on exhibits; and the **South Street Seaport & Museum** (p. 214), which little ones will love for its theme park–like atmosphere and old boats bobbing in the harbor.

✪ **Children's Museum of Manhattan.** 212 W. 83rd St. (btw. Broadway and Amsterdam Ave.). ☎ **212/721-1234.** www.cmom.org. Admission $6 children and adults, $3 seniors. Wed–Sun 10am–5pm. Subway: 1, 9 to 86th St.

Here's a great place to take the kids when they're tired of being told not to touch. Designed for kids 2 to 12, this museum is strictly hands-on. Interactive exhibits and activity centers encourage self-discovery—and a recent expansion means that there's now even more to keep the kids busy and learning. The Time Warner Media Center takes children through the world of animation and helps them produce their own videos. The Body Odyssey is a zany, scientific journey through the human body (just like Will Robinson on *Lost in Space* or *Sabrina the Teenage Witch,* depending what TV generation you belong to). This isn't just a museum for the 5-and-up set—there are exhibits especially designed for babies and toddlers, too. The busy schedule also includes daily art classes and storytellers, and a full slate of entertainment on weekends.

Children's Museum of the Arts. 182 Lafayette St. (btw. Broome and Grand sts.). ☎ **212/941-9198** or 212/274-0986. Admission $5 for everyone 1–65; pay what you wish Wed 5–7pm. Wed noon–7pm, Thurs–Sun noon–5pm. Subway: 6 to Spring St.

Interactive workshop programs for children ages 1 to 12 and their families are the attraction here. Kids dabble in puppet making and computer drawing or join in sing-alongs and live performances. Call for the current schedule.

New York City Fire Museum. 278 Spring St. (btw. Varick and Hudson sts.). ☎ **212/691-1303.** www.nyfd.com/museum.html. Admission $4 adults, $2 seniors and students, $1 children under 12. Tues–Sun 10am–4pm. Subway: C, E to Spring St.; 1, 9 to Houston St.

What's better than fire trucks when you're a little kid? Not much. Housed in a real three-story 1904 firehouse, this museum's displays include vintage fire trucks and equipment all the way back to the horse-drawn days (including the last-known example of a 1921 pumper). Look for the leather hoses, fire boats, poles, bells, Currier & Ives prints, and even a stuffed firehouse dog. Tours with an emphasis on fire safety are available for small groups by calling ahead.

✪ **New York Hall of Science.** 4701 111th St., in Flushing Meadows–Corona Park, Queens. ☎ **718/699-0005.** www.nyhallsci.org. Admission $7.50 adults, $5 children and seniors; free Thurs–Fri 2–5pm. Mon–Wed 9:30am–2pm (Tues–Wed to 5pm in summer), Thurs–Sun 9:30am–5pm. Subway: 7 to 111th St.

Children of all ages will love this huge hands-on museum, which bills itself as New York's only Science Playground. This place is amazing for school-age kids—it's just like Beakman's World come to life. Exhibits let them be engulfed by a giant soap bubble (shades of Veruca Salt, Mom and Dad?), float on air in an antigravity mirror, compose music by dancing in front of light beams, and explore the more-than-miniature world of microbes. There are even video machines that kids can use to retrieve astronomical images, including pictures taken by the *Galileo* in orbit around Jupiter. There's a Preschool Discovery Place for the really little ones. But probably best of all is the summertime Outdoor Science Playground for kids 6 and older—ostensibly lessons in physics, but really just a great excuse to laugh, jump, and play on jungle gyms, slides, seesaws, spinners, and more.

The museum is located in **Flushing Meadows–Corona Park,** where kids can enjoy even more fun beyond the Hall of Science. Not only are there more than 1,200 acres of park and playgrounds but there's a zoo, a carousel, an indoor ice-skating rink, an outdoor pool, and bike and boat rentals. Kids and grown-ups alike will love getting an up-close look at the Unisphere steel globe, which was not really destroyed in *Men in Black.* The park is also home to the **Queens Museum of Art** (see "Highlights of the Outer Boroughs," below) as well as Shea Stadium and the U.S. Open Tennis Center.

Sony Wonder Technology Lab. Sony Plaza, 550 Madison Ave. (at 56th St.). ☎ **212/833-8100.** www.sonywondertechlab.com. Free admission. Tues–Sat 10am–6pm (Thurs to 8pm), Sun noon–6pm (last entrance 30 min. before closing). Subway: E, F, to Fifth Ave.; 4, 5, 6 to 59th St.

Not as much of an infomercial as you'd expect. Both kids and adults love this four-level high-tech science and technology center, which explores communications and information technology. You can experiment with robotics, explore the human body through medical imaging, edit a music video, mix a hit song, design a video game, and save the day at an environmental command center. The lab also features the first high-definition interactive theater in the United States.

THEATER FOR KIDS

The theater scene for kids is flourishing. There's so much going on that it's best to check *New York* magazine, *Time Out New York,* or the Friday *New York Times* for current listings. Besides larger-than-life Broadway shows, the following are some dependable entertainment options.

The ✪ **New Victory Theater,** 209 W. 42nd St., between Seventh and Eighth avenues (☎ 212/382-4020; www.newvictory.org), reopened a few years back as the city's first full-time family-oriented performing arts center and has hosted companies ranging from the Trinity Irish Dance Company to the astounding Flaming Idiots, who juggle everything from fire and swords to bean-bag chairs.

The **Paper Bag Players,** called "the best children's theater in the country" by *Newsweek,* perform funny tales for children 4 to 9 in a set made from bags and boxes, in winter only, at Hunter College's Sylvia and Danny Kaye Playhouse, 68th Street between Park and Lexington avenues (☎ 212/772-4448). If you can't make it to the Kaye, call the players at ☎ 212/362-0431 to inquire whether they'll be staging other performances about town.

TADA! 120 W. 28th St. (☎ 212/627-1732; www.tadatheater.com), is a terrific youth ensemble that performs musicals and plays with a multiethnic perspective for kids and their families.

The **Swedish Cottage Marionette Theatre** (☎ 212/988-9093; www.centralpark. org) puts on marionette shows for kids at its 19th-century Central Park theater throughout the year.

OTHER KID-FRIENDLY DIVERSIONS

In addition to the choices below, don't forget New York's fabulous theme restaurants, which are playgrounds unto themselves for visiting kids. New on the theme-restaurant scene this year is the impressive **ESPN Zone,** and Mom's worst nightmare, **WWF New York.** See "Theme Restaurant Thrills!" in chapter 6.

ZOOS & AQUARIUMS   Bigger kids will love the legendary **Bronx Zoo** (p. 270), while the **Central Park Wildlife Center** with its Tisch Children's Zoo (p. 257) is particularly suitable to younger kids. At the **New York Aquarium** at Coney Island (p. 273), kids can touch starfish and sea urchins and watch bottlenose dolphins and California sea lions stunt-swim in the outdoor aqua theater.

SKY-HIGH VIEWS   Kids of all ages can't help but turn dizzy with delight at incredible views from atop the **Empire State Building** (p. 242) and the **World Trade Center** (pp. 215, 221). The Empire State Building also has the **New York Skyride,** which offers a stomach-churning virtual tour of New York—just in case the real one isn't enough for them.

ARCADES   Lazer Park, in Times Square at 1560 Broadway, at 46th Street (☎ 212/398-3060; www.lazerpark.com), has amusements ranging from good old-fashioned pinball to virtual-reality games and a full-on laser tag arena.

SHOPPING   Everybody loves to shop in New York—even kids. Don't forget to take them to **Books of Wonder,** that temple of sneakerdom **Niketown,** the **NBA Store,** and **FAO Schwarz,** the best toy store in the world—just ask Tom Hanks (remember *Big*?). See chapter 8 for details.

SPECIAL EVENTS   Children's eyes grow wide at the yearlong march of **parades** (especially Macy's Thanksgiving Day Parade), **circuses** (Big Apple, and Ringling Bros. and Barnum & Bailey), and **holiday shows** (the Rockettes' Christmas and Easter performances). See the "Calendar of Events" in chapter 2 for details.

11 Attractions in Upper Manhattan

HARLEM

Over the past several years, the press has heralded Harlem's Second Renaissance, this one with more of an economic emphasis. With all kinds of development projects underway, Central Harlem—from about 110th Street to 155th Street, between St. Nicholas and Fifth avenues—is dispelling its reputation as a symbol of declining urban America. What's more, the revitalized area has become a kind of sleeper hit among outsiders—rediscovered first by visitors (especially Europeans and Japanese) and now by New Yorkers who head up on weekends to its music clubs (see chapter 9), something few would've even considered just a few years ago.

Still, since distances between Harlem's attractions are long and there are some unsafe areas between them, it can be a good idea to join a group tour, especially if it's your first time in New York. See "Organized Sightseeing Tours," earlier in this chapter, for recommendations.

Harlem has always had more than its share of historic treasures. To find them, pay a call on the **Astor Row Houses,** 130th Street between Fifth and Lenox avenues, a fabulous series of 28 redbrick town houses built in the 1880s and graced with wooden porches, generous yards, and ornamental ironwork. Equally impressive is **Strivers' Row,** West 138th and 139th streets, between Adam Clayton Powell Jr. and Frederick Douglass boulevards, a group of 130 houses built in 1891 by developer David H. King Jr., who'd already developed the base of the Statue of Liberty and the original Madison Square Garden. On the north side of 139th Street are neo-Italian Renaissance residences by McKim, Mead & White, while across the street are Georgian-inspired homes. Once the original white owners had moved out, these lovely houses attracted the cream of the Harlem population, the "strivers" (hence the name) like Eubie Blake and W. C. Handy.

Handsome brownstones, limestone town houses, and row houses are sprinkled atop **Sugar Hill,** 145th to 155th streets, between St. Nicholas and Edgecombe avenues, named for the "sweet life" enjoyed by its residents. In the early 20th century, such prominent blacks as W. E. B. DuBois, Thurgood Marshall, and Roy Wilkins lived in the now-landmarked building at 409 Edgecombe Ave.

Besides its bounty of architectural wealth, Harlem has several important cultural institutions. The **Schomburg Center for Research in Black Culture,** 515 Malcolm X Blvd., between 135th and 136th streets (☎ 212/491-2200; www.nypl.org), a research branch of the New York Public Library, hosts changing exhibits related to black culture. For details, see p. 240.

The **Studio Museum in Harlem,** 144 W. 125th St. (☎ 212/864-4500; www.studiomuseum.org), is devoted to the historical and contemporary works for black artists; for details, see p. 240.

The legendary **Apollo Theatre,** 253 W. 125th St. (☎ 212/749-5838), launched or abetted the careers of countless musical icons—including Bessie Smith, Billie Holiday, Dinah Washington, Duke Ellington, Ella Fitzgerald, Sarah Vaughan, Count Basie, and Aretha Franklin—and is in large part responsible for the development and worldwide popularization of African-American music. Since the 1980s, after years of deterioration, it has been revived, especially its famous Wednesday "Amateur Night at the Apollo" show at 7:30pm. For more, see "Major Concert Halls & Landmark Venues" in chapter 9.

In a mixed blessing for the congregations, **Sunday morning gospel services** at Harlem's many churches have become so popular that bus tour groups sometimes outnumber parishioners. At **Abyssinian Baptist Church,** 132 W. 138th St., between

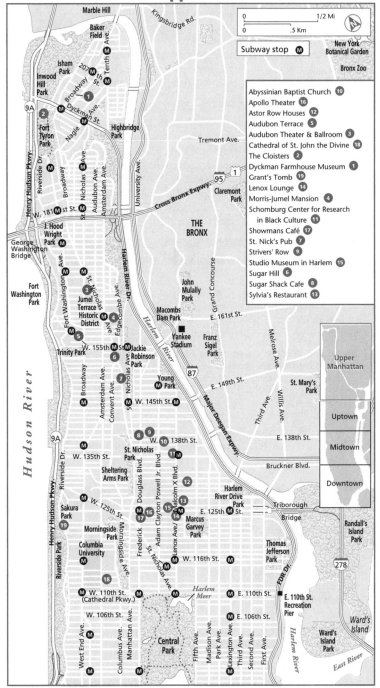

Marble Hill

Baker Field

Isham Park

Inwood Hill Park

Highbridge Park

Fort Tryon Park

Tremont Ave.

THE BRONX

Claremont Park

Fort Washington Park

J. Hood Wright Park

George Washington Bridge

Jumel Terrace Historic District

Trinity Park

John Mulally Park

Macombs Dam Park

Yankee Stadium

Franz Sigel Park

St. Mary's Park

Jackie Robinson Park

Young Park

St. Nicholas Park

Sheltering Arms Park

Harlem River Drive Park

Sakura Park

Morningside Park

Columbia University

Marcus Garvey Park

Thomas Jefferson Park

Randall's Island Park

Harlem Meer

E. 110th St. Recreation Pier

Ward's Island Park

Central Park

Ward's Island

Hudson River

East River

0	1/2 Mi
0	.5 Km

Subway stop Ⓜ

New York Botanical Garden

Bronx Zoo

Abyssinian Baptist Church	10
Apollo Theater	16
Astor Row Houses	12
Audubon Terrace	5
Audubon Theater & Ballroom	3
Cathedral of St. John the Divine	18
The Cloisters	2
Dyckman Farmhouse Museum	1
Grant's Tomb	19
Lenox Lounge	14
Morris-Jumel Mansion	4
Schomburg Center for Research in Black Culture	11
Showmans Café	17
St. Nick's Pub	7
Strivers' Row	9
Studio Museum in Harlem	15
Sugar Hill	6
Sugar Shack Cafe	8
Sylvia's Restaurant	13

Upper Manhattan

Uptown

Midtown

Downtown

Adam Clayton Powell Jr. and Malcolm X boulevards (☎ 212/862-7474), services are at 9 and 11am. Remember that these are religious services first, not gospel shows.

Another essential aspect of Harlem is its food, and it doesn't get any better than what drifts out of the soulful kitchens of **Sylvia's Restaurant** (see chapter 6). If the tourist crowds turn you off, head instead to the **Sugar Shack Cafe,** 2611 Frederick Douglass Blvd. (Eighth Ave.), at 139th Street (☎ 212/491-4422).

IN WASHINGTON HEIGHTS & INWOOD

North of Harlem are these quiet multiethnic residential districts whose main attraction is the **Cloisters** (see "More Manhattan Museums," earlier in this chapter), the Metropolitan Museum of Art's Uptown "castle," beautifully nestled in a bucolic setting with marvelous views and housing a magnificent medieval art collection.

Historic home lovers may want to seek out the **Jumel Terrace Historic District,** west of St. Nicholas Avenue between 160th and 162nd streets, which is centered on the **Morris–Jumel Mansion,** and the Dutch Colonial **Dyckman Farmhouse Museum;** see the "In Search of Historic Homes" box earlier in this chapter.

12 Highlights of the Outer Boroughs

IN THE BRONX

In addition to the choices below, literary buffs might also want to consider the **Edgar Allan Poe Cottage,** the final home for the brilliant but troubled author of *The Raven, The Tell-Tale Heart,* and other masterworks. For details, see the box called "In Search of Historic Homes," earlier in this chapter.

✪ **Bronx Zoo Wildlife Conservation Park.** Fordham Rd. and Bronx River Pkwy., the Bronx. ☎ 718/367-1010. www.wcs.org. Admission $7.75 adults, $4 seniors and children 2–12; discounted admission Nov–Mar; free Wed year-round. There may be nominal additional charges for some exhibits. Nov–Mar daily 10am–4:30pm (extended hours for Holiday Lights late Nov–Jan 2); Apr–Oct Mon–Fri 10am–5pm, Sat–Sun 10am–5:30pm. Transportation: See "Getting There," below.

Founded in 1899, the Bronx Zoo is the largest metropolitan animal park in the United States, with more than 4,000 animals living on 265 acres. Most of the old-fashioned cages have been replaced by more natural settings—this is quite a progressive zoo as zoos go.

One of the most impressive exhibits is the **Wild Asia Complex.** This zoo-within-a-zoo comprises the **Wild Asia Plaza** education center; **Jungle World,** an indoor re-creation of Asian forests with birds, lizards, gibbons, and leopards; and the **Bengali Express Monorail** (open May to Oct), which takes you on a narrated ride high above free-roaming Siberian tigers, Asian elephants, Indian rhinoceroses, and other nonnative New Yorkers (keep your eyes peeled—the animals aren't as interested in seeing you). The **Himalayan Highlands** is home to some 17 extremely rare snow leopards, as well as red pandas and white-naped cranes. The new **Congo Gorilla Forest** is a $6^1/_2$-acre exhibit that's home to Western lowland gorillas, okapi, red river hogs, and other African rain-forest animals.

The **Children's Zoo** (open April to Oct) allows young humans to learn about their wildlife counterparts. Kids can compare their leaps to those of a bullfrog, slide into a turtle shell, climb into a heron's nest, see with the eyes of an owl, and hear with the acute ears of a fox. There's also a petting zoo.

If the natural settings and breeding programs aren't enough to keep zoo residents entertained, they can always choose to ogle the 2 million annual visitors. But there are ways to beat the crowds. Try to visit on a weekday or on a nice winter's day. In summer, come early in the day, before the heat of the day sends the animals back into their enclosures. You can schedule a free guide-led walking tour by calling ☎ 718/220-5141.

Getting There: Liberty Lines' BxM11 express bus, which makes various stops on Madison Avenue, will take you directly to the zoo; call ☎ 718/652-8400. By subway, take the 2 train to Pelham Parkway and then walk 2 blocks west.

New York Botanical Garden. 200th St. and Southern Blvd., the Bronx. ☎ 718/817-8700. www.nybg.org. Admission $3 adults, $2 seniors and students, $1 children 2–12. Extra charges for Everett Children's Adventure Garden, Enid A. Haupt Conservatory, T. H. Everett Rock Garden, Native Plant Garden, and narrated tram tour; entire Garden Passport package is $9.50 adults, $7 seniors and students, $3.50 children 2–12. Apr–Oct Tues–Sun and Mon holidays 10am–6pm; Nov–Mar Tues–Sun and Mon holidays 10am–4pm. Transportation: See "Getting There," below.

A National Historic Landmark, the 250-acre New York Botanical Garden was founded in 1891 and today is one of America's foremost public gardens. The setting is spectacular—a natural terrain of rock outcroppings, a river with cascading waterfall, hills, ponds, and wetlands.

Highlights of the Botanical Garden are the 27 **specialty gardens** (the Peggy Rockefeller formal rose garden, the Nancy Bryan Luce herb garden, and the restored rock garden are my favorites), an exceptional **orchid collection,** and 40 acres of **uncut forest** as close as New York gets to its virgin state before the arrival of Europeans. The **Enid A. Haupt Conservatory,** a stunning series of Victorian glass pavilions that recall London's former Crystal Palace, shelters a rich collection of tropical, subtropical, and desert plants as well as seasonal flower shows. There's also a **Children's Adventure Garden.** Natural exhibits are augmented by year-round educational programs, musical events, bird-watching excursions, lectures, special family programs, and many more activities. Snuff Mill, once used to grind tobacco, has a charming cafe on the banks of the Bronx River.

There are so many ways to see the garden—tram, golf cart, walking tours—that it's best to call or check the Web site for more information.

Getting There: The Garden Shuttle operates weekends from April through October, between Manhattan and the garden ($7); call ☎ 718/817-8700 for reservations and information. Or take Metro North (☎ 212/532-4900) from Grand Central Terminal to the New York Botanical Garden station. By subway, take the D or 4 train to Bedford Park, then take bus Bx26 or walk east 8 long blocks.

Wave Hill. 675 W. 252nd St. (at Independence Ave.), the Bronx. ☎ 718/549-3200. www.wavehill.org. Admission $4 adults, $2 seniors and students; free in winter, and on Sat mornings and Tues in summer. Tues–Sun 9am–4:30pm; extended in summer (check ahead). Transportation: See "Getting There," below.

Formerly a private estate with panoramic views of the Hudson River and the Palisades, Wave Hill has, at various times in its history, been home to a British U.N. ambassador as well as Mark Twain and Theodore Roosevelt. Its 28 acres were bequeathed to the city of New York for use as a public garden that is now one of the most beautiful spots in the city. Programs range from horticulture to environmental education, visual and performing arts, landscape history, and forestry—more than enough to justify a visit.

Getting There: Take the 1 or 9 subway to 231st St., then take the Bx7 or Bx10 bus to the 252nd Street stop; or take the A subway to 207th Street and pick up the Bx7 to 252nd Street. From the 252nd Street stop, walk west across the parkway bridge and turn left; at 249th Street, turn right. Metro North trains (☎ 212/532-4900) travel from Grand Central to the Riverdale station; from there, it's a 5-block walk.

IN BROOKLYN

For details on walking the **Brooklyn Bridge,** see "Historic Lower Manhattan's Top Attractions," earlier in this chapter.

It's easy to link visits to the Brooklyn Botanic Garden, the Brooklyn Museum of Art, and Prospect Park, since they're all an easy walk from one another, just off **Grand Army Plaza.** Designed by Frederick Law Olmsted and Calvert Vaux as a suitably grand entrance to their Prospect Park, it boasts a grand Civil War memorial arch designed by John H. Duncan (1892–1901) and the main **Brooklyn Public Library,** an art deco masterpiece completed in 1941 (the garden and museum are just on the other side of the library, down Eastern Pkwy.). The entire area is a half-hour subway ride from Midtown Manhattan.

✪ **Brooklyn Botanic Garden.** 900 Washington Ave. (at Eastern Pkwy.), Brooklyn. ☎ **718/ 623-7200.** www.bbg.org. Admission $3 adults, $1.50 seniors and students, free for children under 16; free to all Tues–Fri mid-Nov to mid-Mar and Sat 10am–noon year-round. Apr–Sept Tues–Fri 8am–6pm, Sat–Sun 10am–6pm; Oct–Mar Tues–Fri 8am–4:30pm, Sat–Sun 10am–4:30pm. Subway: D, Q to Prospect Park; 2, 3 to Eastern Pkwy./Brooklyn Museum.

Just down the street from the Brooklyn Museum of Art (below) is the most popular botanic garden in the city. This peaceful 52-acre sanctuary is at its most spectacular in May, when thousands of deep pink blossoms of cherry trees are abloom. Well worth seeing is the spectacular **Cranford Rose Garden,** one of the largest and finest in the country; the **Shakespeare Garden,** an English garden featuring plants mentioned in his writings; a **Children's Garden;** the **Osborne Garden,** a 3-acre formal garden; the **Fragrance Garden,** designed for the blind but appreciated by all noses; and the extraordinary **Japanese Hill-and-Pond Garden.** The renowned **C. V. Starr Bonsai Museum** is home to the world's oldest and largest collection of bonsai.

✪ **Brooklyn Museum of Art.** 200 Eastern Pkwy. (at Washington Ave.), Brooklyn. ☎ **718/ 638-5000.** www.brooklynart.org. Suggested admission $4 adults, $1.50 seniors, $2 students, free for children under 12; free first Sat of the month 5–11pm. Wed–Fri 10am–5pm; first Sat of the month 11am–11pm, each Sat thereafter 11am–6pm; Sun 11am–6pm. Subway: 2, 3 to Eastern Pkwy./Brooklyn Museum.

One of the nation's premier art institutions, the Brooklyn Museum of Art rocketed back into the public consciousness in 1999 with the hugely controversial "Sensation: Young British Artists from the Saatchi Collection," which drew international media attention and record crowds who came to see just what an artist—and a few conservative politicians—could make out of a little elephant dung. Indeed, the museum is best known for its consistently remarkable temporary exhibitions, which have included *The Jewels of the Romanovs, Impressionists in Winter,* and *From Hip to Hip Hop: Black Fashion and the Culture of Influence,* as well as its excellent permanent collection. The museum's grand beaux arts building, designed by McKim, Mead & White (1897), befits its outstanding holdings, most notably the Egyptian collection of sculpture, wall reliefs, and mummies. The distinguished decorative arts collection includes 28 American period rooms from 1675 to 1928 (the extravagant Moorish-style smoking room from John D. Rockefeller's 54th St. mansion is my favorite). Other highlights are the African and Asian arts galleries, 58 works by Rodin, and a diverse collection of both American and European painting and sculpture that includes works by Homer, O'Keeffe, Monet, Cézanne, and Degas.

First Saturday is the museum's ambitious—and popular—program that takes place on the first Saturday of each month. It runs from 5 to 11pm and includes free admission and a slate of live music, films, dancing, and other entertainment that can get pretty esoteric (think karaoke, lesbian poetry, silent film, experimental jazz, and disco dancing). Weekly **Insider's Hour Gallery Tours** are offered at 1pm on weekends as well as on select Thursdays and Fridays; call for the schedule.

New York Aquarium. 832 Surf Ave. (at W. 8th St.), Coney Island, Brooklyn. ☎ **718/ 265-3400.** www.nyaquarium.com. Admission $8.75 adults, $4.50 seniors and children 2–12. Daily 10am–5pm. Subway: D, F to W. 8th St., Brooklyn.

Because of the long subway ride (about an hour from Midtown Manhattan) and its proximity to the Coney Island boardwalk, this one is really for summer. The aquarium is home to hundreds of sea creatures. Taking center stage are Atlantic bottlenose dolphins and California sea lions that perform daily during summer at the **Aquatheater.** Also basking in the spotlight are seven beluga whales, gangly Pacific octopuses, and Bertha the sand tiger shark. Black-footed penguins, California sea otters, and a variety of seals live at the **Sea Cliffs exhibit,** a re-creation of a Pacific coastal habitat. Children love the hands-on exhibits at **Discovery Cove.** There's an indoor ocean-view cafeteria and an outdoor snack bar, plus picnic tables.

If you've made the trip out, you simply must check out the human exhibits on nearby **Coney Island's** 2.7-mile-long boardwalk. Not much is left from its heyday, and it can be a little eerie when the crowds aren't around. But you can still use the beach, drop some cash at the boardwalk arcade, and ride the famed wooden **Cyclone** roller coaster (still a terrifying ride, if only because it seems so . . . rickety). You can't leave without treating yourself to a **Nathan's Famous** hot dog, just off the boardwalk at Surf and Stillwell avenues. This is the original—where the term "hot dog" was coined back in 1906.

New York Transit Museum. Boerum Place and Schermerhorn St., Brooklyn. ☎ **718/ 243-8601.** www.mta.nyc.ny.us/museum. Admission $3 adults, $1.50 seniors and children 3–17. Tues–Fri 10am–4pm, Sat–Sun noon–5pm. Subway: C, F to Jay St.; N, R to Court St.; 2, 3, 4, 5 to Borough Hall.

Transit buffs would do well to see if this underground museum, housed in a real (decommissioned) subway station, had reopened at press time (it was closed for renovations in early 2000). It's a wonderful place to spend an hour or so. The museum is small but very well done, with good multimedia exhibits exploring the history of the subway from the first shovelful of dirt scooped up at groundbreaking (Mar 24, 1900) to the present. Kids and parents alike will enjoy the interactive elements and the vintage subway cars, old wooden turnstiles, and beautiful station mosaics of yesteryear. All in all, a minor but remarkable tribute to an important development in the city's history.

Prospect Park. At Grand Army Plaza, bounded by Prospect Park West, Parkside Ave., and Flatbush Ave., Brooklyn. ☎ **718/965-8951,** or 718/965-8999 for events information. www. prospectpark.org. Subway: 2, 3 to Grand Army Plaza (walk down Plaza St. West 3 blocks to Prospect Park West and the entrance) or Eastern Pkwy./Brooklyn Museum.

Designed by Frederick Law Olmsted and Calvert Vaux after their great success with Central Park, this 562 acres of woodland, meadows, bluffs, and ponds is considered by many to be their masterpiece and the pièce de résistance of Brooklyn.

The best approach is from Grand Army Plaza, presided over by the monumental **Soldiers' and Sailors' Memorial Arch** (1892) honoring Union veterans. For the best view of the lush landscape, follow the path to Meadowport Arch, and proceed through to the Long Meadow, following the path that loops around it (it's about an hour's walk). Other park highlights include the 1857 Italianate mansion **Litchfield Villa** on Prospect Park West; the **Friends' Cemetery** Quaker burial ground (where Montgomery Clift is eternally prone—sorry, it's fenced off to browsers); the **carousel** with white wooden horses salvaged from a famous Coney Island merry-go-round; and **Lefferts Homestead** (☎ **718/965-6505**), a 1783 Dutch farmhouse with a museum of period furniture and exhibits geared toward children. There's a map at the park entrance that you can use to get your bearings.

On the east side of the park is the **Prospect Park Wildlife Conservation Center** (☎ **718/399-7339**). This is a thoroughly modern children's zoo where kids can walk among wallabies, explore a prairie-dog town, and much more. Admission is $2.50 for adults, $1.25 for seniors, 50¢ for children 3 to 12. April through October, open Monday through Friday 10am to 5pm, to 5:30pm weekends and holidays; November through March, open daily from 10am to 4:30pm.

✪ BROOKLYN HEIGHTS HISTORIC DISTRICT

Just across the Brooklyn Bridge is a peaceful neighborhood of tree-lined streets, more than 600 historic houses built before 1860, landmark churches, and restaurants. Even with its magnificent promenade providing sweeping views of Lower Manhattan's ragged skyline, it feels more like its own village than part of the larger urban expanse.

This is where Walt Whitman lived and wrote *Leaves of Grass,* one of the great accomplishments in American literature. And in the 19th century, fiery abolitionist Henry Ward Beecher railed against slavery at **Plymouth Church of the Pilgrims** on Orange Street between Henry and Hicks streets (his sister wrote *Uncle Tom's Cabin*). If you walk down **Willow Street** between Clark and Pierrepont, you'll see three houses (nos. 108–112) in the Queen Anne style that was fashionable in the late 19th century, as well as an attractive trio of Federal-style houses (nos. 155–159) built before 1829. Also visit lively **Montague Street,** the main drag of Brooklyn Heights and full of cafes and shops. And don't forget about **Grimaldi's Pizzeria,** near the water on historic Old Fulton Street, serving up the city's best pizza (see chapter 6).

GETTING THERE   Bounded by the East River, Fulton Street, Court Street, and Atlantic Avenue, the Brooklyn Heights Historic District is one of the most outstanding and easily accessible sights beyond Manhattan. The neighborhood is reachable via a number of subway trains: the A, C, F to Jay St.; the 2, 3, 4, 5 to Clark Street or Borough Hall; and the N, R to Court Street.

It's easy to link a walk around Brooklyn Heights and along its Promenade with a walk over the **Brooklyn Bridge** (p. 213), a tour that makes for a lovely afternoon on a nice day. Take a 2 or 3 train to **Clark Street** (the first stop in Brooklyn). Turn right out of the station and walk toward the water, where you'll see the start of the waterfront **Brooklyn Promenade.** Stroll along the promenade admiring both the stellar views of lower Manhattan to the left and the gorgeous multi-million-dollar brownstones to the right, or park yourself on a bench for a while to contemplate the scene.

The promenade ends at Columbia Heights and Orange Street. To head to the bridge from here, turn left and walk toward the Watchtower Building. Before heading downslope, turn right immediately after the playground onto Middagh Street. After 4 or 5 blocks, you'll reach a busy thoroughfare, Cadman Plaza West. Cross the street and follow the walkway through little **Cadman Plaza Park;** veer left at the fork in the walkway. At Cadman Plaza East, turn left (downslope) toward the underpass, where you'll find the stairwell up to the Brooklyn Bridge footpath on your left.

IN QUEENS

For details on the **New York Hall of Science** and **Flushing Meadows–Corona Park** (also home to the Queens Museum of Art, below), see "Especially for Kids," earlier in this chapter.

✪ **American Museum of the Moving Image.** 35th Ave. at 36th St., Astoria, Queens. ☎ **718/784-0077** or 718/784-4777. www.ammi.org. Admission $8.50 adults, $5.50

Brooklyn Heights Attractions

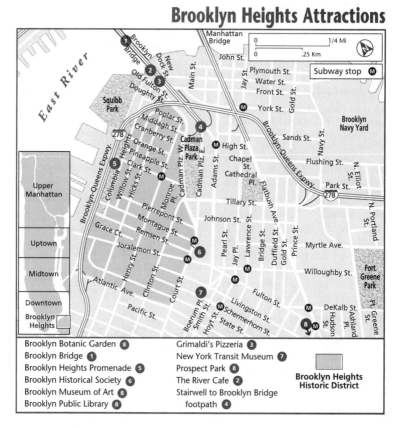

Brooklyn Botanic Garden ⑧
Brooklyn Bridge ①
Brooklyn Heights Promenade ⑤
Brooklyn Historical Society ⑥
Brooklyn Museum of Art ⑧
Brooklyn Public Library ⑧

Grimaldi's Pizzeria ③
New York Transit Museum ⑦
Prospect Park ⑧
The River Cafe ②
Stairwell to Brooklyn Bridge
footpath ④

Brooklyn Heights
Historic District

seniors and college students, $4.50 children 5–18. Tues–Fri noon–5pm, Sat–Sun 11am–6pm. Subway: R to Steinway St.

Head here if you truly love movies. Unlike Manhattan's Museum of Television & Radio (see "More Manhattan Museums" earlier in this chapter), which is more of a library, this is a thought-provoking museum examining how moving images—film, video, and digital—are made, marketed, and shown; it encourages you to consider their impact on society as well. It's housed in part of the Kaufman Astoria Studios, which once were host to W. C. Fields and the Marx Brothers, and more recently have been used by Martin Scorsese (*The Age of Innocence*), Woody Allen (*Radio Days*), Bill Cosby (his *Cosby* TV series), and *Sesame Street*.

The museum's core exhibit, **"Behind the Screen,"** is a thoroughly engaging 2-floor installation that takes you step-by-step through the process of making, marketing, and exhibiting moving images. There are more than 1,000 artifacts on hand, from technological gadgetry to costumes, and interactive exhibits where you can try your own hand at sound-effects editing or create your own animated shorts, among other simulations. Special-effects benchmarks from the mechanical mouth of *Jaws* to the blending of past and present in *Forrest Gump* are explored and explained. And in a nod to Hollywood nostalgia, memorabilia that wasn't swept up by the Planet Hollywood chain is displayed, including a Hopalong Cassidy lunch box, an E.T. doll, celebrity coloring books, and Dean Martin and Jerry Lewis hand puppets. Also on display are sets from *Seinfeld*.

The museum hosts free **film and video screenings,** often accompanied by artist appearances, lectures, or panel discussions. Silent films are presented with live music. The **Pinewood Dialogues** lecture series features renowned film and TV pros discussing their craft; past guests have included Spike Lee, Terry Gilliam, Chuck Jones, and Atom Egoyan, so it's definitely worth seeing if someone's on while you're in town.

✪ **Isamu Noguchi Garden Museum.** 32–37 Vernon Blvd. (at 33rd Rd.), Long Island City, Queens. ☎ **718/721-1932.** www.noguchi.org. Suggested admission $4 adults, $2 seniors and students. Apr–Oct Wed–Fri 10am–5pm, Sat–Sun 11am–6pm. Subway: N to Broadway. Walk west on Broadway toward Manhattan until Broadway ends at Vernon Blvd.; turn left on Vernon and go 2 blocks; the museum is on the left. Shuttle: Sat–Sun, from outside the MoMA bookstore on W. 53rd St. (btw. Fifth and Sixth aves.) to museum hourly 11:30am–4:30pm (return trips noon–5pm); $5 round-trip.

No place in the city is more Zen than this marvelous indoor/outdoor museum show-casing the work of Japanese-American sculptor Isamu Noguchi (1904–88). The beau-tifully installed multigallery exhibit includes more than 250 works in stone, metal, wood, and clay; you'll even see theater sets, furniture, and models for public gardens and playgrounds that Noguchi designed.

A free guided tour is offered at 2pm, and short films about the artist and his work show continuously throughout the day in an intimate theater. A museum shop sells Noguchi's Akari lamps as well as books, cards, posters, and the like.

P.S. 1 Contemporary Art Center. 22–25 Jackson Ave. (at 46th Ave.), Long Island City, Queens. ☎ **718/784-2084.** www.queensmuse.org. Suggested admission $4 adults, $2 seniors and students. Wed–Sun noon–6pm. (Hours vary in summer, so call ahead.) Subway: E, F to 23rd St./Ely Ave. (walk 2 blocks south); 7 to 45th Rd./Court House Sq. (walk 1 block south).

If you're interested in contemporary art that's too cutting-edge for most museums, don't miss P.S. 1. Reinaugurated in 1997 after a 3-year $8.5 million renovation of the Renaissance Revival building that was originally a public school, this is the world's largest institution exhibiting contemporary art from America and abroad. You can expect to see a kaleidoscopic array of works from artists ranging from Jack Smith to Julian Schnabel; the museum is particularly well known for large-scale exhibitions by artists such as James Turrell.

Queens Museum of Art. Next to the Unisphere in Flushing Meadows–Corona Park, Queens. ☎ **718/592-9700.** www.ps1.org. Suggested admission $4 adults, $2 seniors and children, free for children under 5. Wed–Fri 10am–5pm, Sat–Sun noon–5pm. Subway: 7 to Willets Point/Shea Stadium.

One way to see New York in the shortest time (albeit without the street life) is to visit the Panorama, an enormous building-for-building architectural model of New York City complete with an airplane that takes off from LaGuardia Airport. The 9,335-square-foot Gotham City is the largest model of its kind in the world, with 895,000 individual structures built on a scale of 1 inch = 100 feet. Also on permanent display is a collection of Tiffany glass manufactured at Tiffany Studios in Queens between 1893 and 1938.

13 Spectator Sports

For details on the **New York City Marathon** and the **U.S. Open Tennis Championships,** see the "New York City Calendar of Events," in chapter 2.

BASEBALL　With two baseball teams in town, you can catch a game almost any day from opening day in April to beginning of playoffs in October. (Don't bother trying to get subway series tix, though—they're the hottest seats in town. Ditto for Opening Day or any playoff game.)

Year-Round Yankee Tour

For a taste of Yankee glory at any time of year, take the **Babe Ruth Tour of Yankee Stadium** (☎ **718/579-4531**). This official tour of the House That Ruth Built will take you onto the field, to Monument Park, into the dugout. You'll even visit the press box and—if you're lucky—take a peek inside the clubhouse. The guide peppers the tour with lots of Yankee history and anecdotes as you go. And who knows? You might even spot that cutie Derek Jeter as you make the rounds. Tours are offered Monday through Saturday at noon (other times are available for groups of 12 or larger). **Note:** *There are no Saturday tours when the team is in town.* Tickets are $8 for adults, $4 for seniors and kids 14 and under. No reservations are required; all you need to do is show up at the ballpark's press gate just before tour time, but it's still a good idea to call and confirm.

Star catcher Mike Piazza and the Amazin' **Mets** play at **Shea Stadium** in Queens (Subway: 7 to Willets Point/Shea Stadium). For tickets and information, call the **Mets Ticket Office** at ☎ **718/507-TIXX,** or visit **www.mets.com**.

The **Yankees,** who won a mind-blowing 25th World Championship in 1999, play at the House That Ruth Built, otherwise known as Yankee Stadium (Subway: C, D, 4 to 161st St./Yankee Stadium). For tickets, call **TicketMaster** (☎ **212/307-1212** or 212/307-7171; www.ticketmaster.com) or **Yankee Stadium** (☎ **718/293-6000;** www.yankees.com). After the game, check into one of the rowdy sports bars across the street to down a brew and relive the action with fellow fans. Serious baseball fans might check the schedule well in advance and try to catch **Old Timers' Day,** usually held in July, when pinstriped stars of years past return to the stadium to take a bow. This is your chance to cheer for legends like Whitey Ford and Reggie Jackson in person.

At Yankee Stadium, upper tier box seats, especially those behind home plate, give you a great view of all the action. Upper tier reserve seats are directly behind the box seats and are significantly cheaper. Bleacher seats are even cheaper, and the rowdy commentary from that section's roughneck bleacher creatures is absolutely free. Most of the expensive seats (field boxes) are sold out in advance to season ticket holders. You can often purchase these very same seats from scalpers, but you'll pay a premium for them. Tickets can be purchased at the teams' **clubhouse shops** in Manhattan; see p. 309.

BASKETBALL   Two pro teams call **Madison Square Garden,** Seventh Avenue between 31st and 33rd streets (☎ **212/465-6741** or www.thegarden.com; **212/307-7171** or www.ticketmaster.com for tickets; Subway: A, C, E, 1, 2, 3, 9 to 34th St.), home court: Patrick Ewing, Latrell Sprewell, Allen Houston, Marcus Camby, and the rest of the **New York Knicks** (☎ **212/465-JUMP;** www.nyknicks. com); and the **New York Liberty** (☎ **212/564-WNBA;** www.wnba.com/liberty), who electrify fans with their tough-playing defense and star players like Rebecca Lobo and Teresa Weatherspoon. Knicks tickets are hard to come by, so plan ahead if you want a front-row seat near first fan Spike Lee.

ICE HOCKEY   The **New York Rangers** play at Madison Square Garden, Seventh Avenue between 31st and 33rd streets (☎ **212/465-6741** or 212/308-NYRS; www.newyorkrangers.com; Subway: A, C, E, 1, 2, 3, 9 to 34th St.). The memories of the Mark Messier–led 1994 Stanley Cup team linger on, much to the chagrin of the present underachieving team, which suffered another serious blow when Wayne Gretzky retired in April 1999. Tickets are hard to get nevertheless, so plan well ahead; call ☎ **212/307-7171,** or visit www.ticketmaster.com for online orders.

8 Shopping

Calling New York a shopper's delight is like saying you caught a little flick last night called *Lawrence of Arabia*. An understatement, to say the least.

At first glance, the size and breadth of the city's shopping scene seems more overwhelming than anything else. The range of possibilities could test the limits of the most die-hard shopaholic. Even as more and more big chains lay down roots in the city (what New Yorkers like to refer to as the "mallification" of Manhattan), the world's most unique crop of specialty shops continues to thrive right alongside them. From dinosaur fossils to duck eggs, platform shoes to Chanel suits, love potions to love seats—you'll find a world's worth of merchandise in the Big Apple.

1 The Top Shopping Streets & Neighborhoods

Here's a rundown of New York's most interesting shopping areas, with some highlights of each to give you a feel for the neighborhood. **If addresses and phone numbers are *not* given here,** refer to the store's expanded listing by category under **"Shopping A to Z,"** later in this chapter.

DOWNTOWN
LOWER MANHATTAN & THE FINANCIAL DISTRICT
The Financial District and environs are home to two kinds of shopping: discount shopping à la **Century 21** department store and **J&R** for electronics galore; and mall-style retail shopping.

National chains and standard mall stores are housed in **South Street Seaport** (☎ 212/732-7678; subway: 2, 3, 4, 5 to Fulton St.) on Pier 17 and on Fulton Street, the Seaport's main cobbled drag; in the **World Financial Center** across the West Side Highway from the World Trade Center in Battery Park City (☎ 212/945-0505); and on the ground level of the **World Trade Center** (☎ 212/435-2728; www.panynj.gov/wtc; subway: 1, 9, N, R to Cortlandt St.; C, E to World Trade Center). The World Trade Center makes a good bet for standards like the **Gap, Banana Republic,** and **J. Crew,** the **Body Shop, Nine West,** the **Limited,** plus a terrific branch of **Borders Books & Music.**

CHINATOWN

Don't expect to find the purchase of a lifetime on Chinatown's streets, but there's some fun browsing to be had. The fish markets along Canal, Mott, Mulberry, and Elizabeth streets are fun to browse for their bustle and exotica. Dispersed among them (especially along **Canal**), you'll find a mind-boggling collection of knock-offs: sunglasses, designer bags, and watches. **Mott Street,** between Pell Street and Chatham Square, boasts the most interesting of Chinatown's off-Canal shopping, with an antiques shop or two dispersed among the tiny storefronts selling blue-and-white Chinese dinnerware.

The definite highlight of Chinatown shopping is ✪ **Pearl River Mart,** 277 Canal St., at Broadway (☎ **212/431-4770;** subway: N, R to Canal St.), a 3-floor Chinese mall overflowing with affordable Asian exotica, from paper lanterns to Chinese snack foods to Mandarin-collared silk pajamas to mah-jongg sets to Hong Kong action videos. This fascinating place can keep you occupied for hours. The sibling **Pearl River Department Store,** 200 Grand St., between Mott and Mulberry streets (☎ **212/966-1010**), is equally enchanting. You can preview the bounty online at **www.pearlriver.com**.

The stretch of **the Bowery** (Third Ave.) from Houston to Canal streets is considered the "light-fixture district" for its huge selections and great bargains on light fixtures, lamps, and ceiling fans. The best of the bunch is **Lighting by Gregory,** 158 Bowery, between Delancey and Broome (☎ **212/226-1276;** www.lightingbygregory.com).

THE LOWER EAST SIDE

The bargains aren't quite what they used to be in the **Historic Orchard Street Shopping District**—which basically runs from Houston to Canal along Allen, Orchard, and Ludlow streets, spreading outward along both sides of Delancey Street—but prices on leather bags, shoes, luggage, fabrics on the bolt, and men's and women's clothes are still quite good. Be aware, though, that the hard sell on Orchard Street can be pretty hard to take. Still, the Orchard Street Bargain District is a nice place to discover a part of New York that's disappearing. Come during the week, since most stores are Jewish-owned, and therefore close Friday afternoon and all day Saturday. Sunday tends to be a madhouse. Stop in first at the **Lower East Side Visitor Center,** 261 Broome St., between Orchard and Allen streets (☎ **888/825-8374** or 212/226-9010; subway: F to Delancey St.) for a shopping guide.

The artists and other trendsetters who have been turning this neighborhood into a hopping club scene have also added a cutting edge to its shopping scene in recent years, too. You'll find a growing handful of alterna-shops in the area south of Houston between Allen and Clinton streets. In addition to **Foley & Corinna** (see "Fashions" in "Shopping A to Z," later in this chapter), highlights include high-style **Zao[ma],** 175 Orchard St. (☎ **212/505-0500**), for Japanese housewares and cutting-edge clothes; **Cherry,** 185 Orchard St. (☎ **212/358-7131;** www.erols.com/hotcherry), for modernist home accessories and retro-cool apparel; **TG-170,** 170 Ludlow St.

Sales Tax

New York City sales tax is 8.25%, but it was eliminated on clothing and footwear items under $110 as of March 1, 2000.

If you're visiting from out of state, consider having your purchases shipped directly home to avoid paying sales tax.

(☎ **212/955-8660**), for new designs in club-kid clothes; and **Have a Seat,** 37 Clinton St. (☎ **212/353-9550**), a groovy modern furnishings store featuring wild '50s, '60s, and '70s designs.

SoHo

People love to complain about super-fashionable SoHo—it's become too trendy, too tony, too Mall of America. True, **J. Crew,** 99 Prince St. (☎ **212/966-2739**), is only one of many big names that have supplanted the artists and galleries that used to inhabit its historic cast-iron buildings. But SoHo is still one of the best shopping 'hoods in the city—and few are more fun to browse. It's the epicenter of cutting-edge fashion and still boasts plenty of unique boutiques. The streets are chock-full of tempting stores, so your best bet is to just come and browse.

SoHo's prime shopping grid is from Broadway east to Sullivan Street, and from Houston down to Broome, although Grand Street, 1 block south of Broome, has been sprouting shops of late. **Broadway** is the most commercial strip, with such recognizable names as **Pottery Barn, Victoria's Secret, Old Navy,** and **A/X Armani Exchange.**

Among the designers in residence in SoHo are **Anna Sui,** 113 Greene St. (☎ **212/941-8406**), whose slinky fashions have a glammy edge; wild, colorful retro-inspired designs from golden boy **Todd Oldham,** 123 Wooster St. (☎ **212/219-3531;** www.toddoldham.com); **Marc Jacobs,** 163 Mercer St. (☎ **212/343-1490**), who excels at modern takes on classic cuts; trend-busting British designs from the legendary **Vivienne Westwood,** 71 Greene St. (☎ **212/334-5200**); austerely beautiful Japanese design from **Yohji Yamamoto,** 103 Grand St. (☎ **212/966-9066**); pretty and playful Asian motifs from **Vivienne Tam,** 99 Greene St. (☎ **212/966-2398**); Prada offshoot **Miu Miu,** 100 Prince St. (☎ **212/334-5156**); plus sleek-chic from **Cynthia Rowley** and wild club clothes at Patricia Field's **Hotel Venus.**

If you're more interested in affordable everyday wearables, consider **Harriet Love,** the incomparable **Eileen Fisher,** and **Phat Farm** for upscale hip-hop wear (see "Fashions" in "Shopping A to Z," later in this chapter).

SoHo is also fabulous for accessories. The cobbled streets boast stores galore, from chic **Calvin Klein Shoes,** 133 Prince St. (☎ **212/505-3549**), and **Omari,** 132 Prince St. (☎ **212/219-0619**), to chunkier styles at **John Fluevog,** 104 Prince St. (☎ **212/431-4484;** www.fluevog.com). The wonderful **Hat Shop,** 120 Thompson St. (☎ **212/219-1445**), is a full-service milliner for women that also features plenty of off-the-rack toppers, while **Kirna Zabête,** 96 Greene St. (☎ **212/941-9656**), is all feminine delight, with girly accessories ranging from scented travel pillows to leopard-print rain boots.

Fashion is only half the story at **Anthropologie,** 375 W. Broadway (☎ **212/343-7070;** www.anthropologie.com), whose funky-chic affordable wearables mix with fun gifts and home decorating items—much like Urban Outfitters for grown-ups.

High-end home stores are another huge part of the SoHo scene, from **Smith & Hawken,** at 394 W. Broadway (☎ **212/925-1190**), to hot potter **Jonathan Adler's** cool shop at 465 Broome St. (☎ **212/941-8950**)—anybody who has been reading interior design magazines over the last couple of years will recognize his bold vases instantly. **Global Table,** 107 Sullivan St. (☎ **212/431-5839**), is a great source for beautiful tableware from around the world.

NoLiTa

Just a few years ago, **Elizabeth Street** was a nondescript adjunct to Little Italy and the no-man's-land east of SoHo. Today it's the grooviest shopping strip in town, star of the neighborhood known as NoLiTa. Elizabeth and neighboring Mott and Mulberry streets are dotted with an increasing number of shops between Houston and Spring streets, with a few pushing 1 more block south to Kenmare. It's an easy walk from the Broadway/Lafayette stop on the B, D, F, Q line to the neighborhood, since it starts just east of Lafayette Street.

This may be a burgeoning neighborhood, but don't expect cheap—NoLiTa is clearly the stepchild of SoHo. Its boutiques are largely the provence of sophisticated shop-keepers specializing in high-quality fashion-forward products and design. Highlights include **Calypso Enfants,** 284 Mulberry St. (☎ 212/965-8910), for stylish kidswear with a tropical flair. At no. 280 is **Jade** (☎ 212/925-6544), for reinterpretations of traditional Asian and Indian fashions in sumptuous jewel-toned silks (gorgeous accessories, too).

Mott Street is an accessories bonanza, with **Jamin Puech** at no. 252 (☎ 212/334-9730), for some of the most beautiful and unusual daytime and evening bags I've ever seen, all handmade in France by a husband-and-wife design team; **Sigerson Morrison** for eye-popping shoe designs (see "Shoes," later in this chapter); and **Calypso,** no. 280 (☎ 212/965-0990), for grown-up haute island style.

On **Prince Street,** there's **Gates of Morocco,** at no. 8 (☎ 212/925-2650), for traditional Moroccan imports, and ✪ **kar'ikter,** at no. 19 (☎ 212/274-1966), which stocks New York's biggest collection of sleek and playful Alessi housewares from Italy as well as Tin-Tin animation cells and toys.

The boutique density is most intense on Elizabeth. Offerings range from gorgeous contemporary jewelry at **Elma Blint et al,** no. 245 (☎ 212/965-0494), to **Shì,** no. 233 (☎ 212/334-4330), dedicated to new artists with an eye for innovation in home decor. **Area I.D.** (☎ 212/219-9903) and **Ace** (☎ 212/226-5123), vintage modern furniture neighbors at no. 262 and no. 269, both have a predisposition for sleek Danish design.

THE EAST VILLAGE

The East Village remains the international standard of bohemian hip. **Kmart,** 770 Broadway (☎ 212/673-1540), between 8th and 9th streets, is so out of place that it's marvelous camp: Japanese kids stare and marvel at gargantuan boxes of laundry detergent as if they were Warhol designed, while multipierced and mohawked locals navigate the name-brand maze alongside stroller-pushing housewives. The easiest subway access is the 6 train to Astor Place, which lets you right out at Kmart and **Astor Wines & Spirits;** from here, it's just a couple blocks east to the prime hunting grounds.

East 9th Street between Second Avenue and Avenue A has become one of my favorite shopping strips in the entire city. Lined with an increasingly smart collection of boutiques, it proves that the East Village isn't just for kids anymore. Up-and-coming designers sell good-quality and affordably priced original fashions for women along here, including **Lisa Tsai,** 436 E. 9th St. (☎ 212/529-8231), a bright, cheery shop with wonderful retro-inspired designs and accessories; and **Mark Montano,** at no. 434 (☎ 212/505-0325), who harkens back to styles from Victoria to Jackie O as inspiration for his line of wonderful wearables and handbags; plus Meghan Kinney Studio and the utterly fabulous Jill Anderson. Kitschy collectibles can be had at the charming **Cha Cha Tchatchka,** 437 E. 9th St. (☎ 212/674-9242) and Atomic Passion, at no. 430 (☎ 212/533-0718).

For stylish gifts and little luxuries, there's **Paper Rock Scissors,** 436 E. 9th St. (☎ 212/358-1555), for handmade treasures; **Mascot Studio,** whose remarkable one-of-a-kind picture frames are sold at no. 328 (☎ 212/228-9090); and ✪ **H,** at no. 335 (☎ 212/477-2631), with wonderful Japanese-inspired and other collectibles,

Additional Sources for Serious Shoppers

If you're looking for a specific item, check the online shopping listings at **www. newyork.citysearch.com** or **www.timeoutny.com** before you go. The Time Out shopping site is much more limited, but it's unsullied by advertising like the more extensive CitySearch site. (CitySearch takes payment for Web space from shops, and lists advertisers first in any given shopping category, such as "Antiques" or "Children's Clothing.")

For the latest sales, visit **www.inshop.com**, where you can search for sales by merchandise type, store name, or designer name. The information is extremely detailed, such as, "Kate Spade is having a 2-day sale at her SoHo store. All her fab handbags from the Fall/Winter collection will be 40% off. For example, her classic tote handbags in winter's wool fabrics are now $120 to $150, regularly $200 to $250." This tip is accompanied by exact dates and store location and hours—an excellent source for bargain hunters, as is **www.nysale.com**, a free registration site that can let you in on unadvertised sales taking place throughout the city. Another source for sale info in New York and other cities is **www.styleshop.com**.

Hard information about current sales, new shops, and special art, craft, and antiques shows is best found in the "Check Out" section of *Time Out New York* or the "Sales & Bargains," "Best Bets," and "Smart City" sections of *New York* magazine.

---

from slinky vases to rice-paper coasters. If you're really enjoying this neighborhood, check out the offerings on surrounding blocks, too, which aren't quite as mature yet, but are on their way.

If it's strange, illegal, or funky, it's probably available on **St. Marks Place,** which takes over for 8th Street, running east from Third Avenue to Avenue A. This skanky strip is a permanent street market, with countless T-shirt and boho jewelry stands. The height of the action is between Second and Third avenues, which is prime hunting grounds for used-record collectors (see "Music," later in this chapter).

LAFAYETTE STREET FROM SOHO TO NOHO

Lafayette Street has a retail character all its own, distinct from the rest of SoHo. It has grown into a full-fledged Antiques Row, especially strong in midcentury furniture. Prices are high, but so is quality. Dispersed among the furniture and design stores are a number of cutting-edge clothiers—this is where skateboard fashion got its start down the catwalks.

The stretch to stroll is between 8th Street to the north and Spring Street to the south. Either take the 6 train to Astor Place and work your way south; get off at Spring Street and walk north; or take the B, D, F, or Q to Broadway–Lafayette and get dropped off in the heart of the action. Highlights include **Art & Industrial Design,** 399 Lafayette St. (☎ **212/477-0116**), for sculptural furniture, Italian glass, and movie props (the mechanical penguins from the second *Batman* movie were on sale here for a while). **Guéridon,** no. 359 (☎ **212/677-7740;** www.gueridon.com), features sophisticated 20th-century European pieces, mainly French. **Lost City Arts,** at no. 275 (☎ **212/941-8025;** www.lostcityarts.com), offers vintage furnishings and a quirky selection of accessories (station signs, 3-D photos, and the like), plus their own three lines of midcenturyish furnishings and accessories, including one inspired by the otherwise forbiddingly expensive custom designs of Machine Age genius Warren MacArthur. **City Barn Antiques,** at no. 269 (☎ **212/941-5757**), is one of the nation's foremost specialists in Heywood–Wakefield. There's much, much more—

furniture hunters and design lovers will be enthralled for hours. Most dealers are well versed in shipping worldwide.

Among the fashion outlets worth noting are **Bond 07,** just off Lafayette at 7 Bond St. (☎ 212/677-8487), and **Spooly D's,** 51 Bleecker St., at Lafayette (☎ 212/598-4415), both featuring artfully displayed collections of classic vintage fashions and accessories (Bond 07 often features homewares, too); **Daryl K.,** 21 Bond St. (☎ 212/777-0713), for sleek, sexy wear for men and women; and **Screaming Mimi's,** the city's most famous vintage clothing outlet. South of Houston is **X-Large,** 267 Lafayette St. (☎ 212/334-4480; www.xlarge.com), for upscale hip-hop wear (the Beasties' Mike D is a co-owner). And don't forget the wonderful **Pop Shop,** which sells cool casual wear emblazoned with Keith Haring's distinctive modern art (see "Logo Stores," later in this chapter).

GREENWICH VILLAGE

The West Village is great for browsing and gift shopping. Specialty book- and record stores, antiques and craft shops, and gourmet food markets dominate. (Attention gourmands: Don't miss **Balducci's** if you can help it.) The best **Tower Records** in the country is at West 4th Street and Broadway. Except for NYU territory—8th Street between Broadway and Sixth Avenue for trendy footwear and affordable fashions, and Broadway from 8th Street south to Houston, anchored by **Urban Outfitters** at 628 Broadway (☎ 212/475-0009; www.urbanoutfitters.com) and dotted with skate and sneaker shops—the Village isn't much of a destination for fashion hunters. Clothes hounds looking for volume shopping are better off elsewhere.

The prime drag for strolling is bustling **Bleecker Street,** where you'll find lots of leather shops and record stores interspersed with a good number of interesting and artsy boutiques. Just a few of the highlights include **Old Japan,** 382 Bleecker St. (☎ 212/633-0922), for vintage silk kimonos and Japanese collectibles, including cool scarves and handbags fashioned out of kimonos, as well as buckwheat pillows made of kimono cotton; **Barr–Magill,** at no. 333 (☎ 212/741-0656), whose black-and-white photography—much of it featuring the city as subject—makes a great souvenir; **Davis & Gardner,** at no. 318 (☎ 212/229-0660), for an eclectic mix of antiques with a real romantic bent; and **Condomania,** at no. 351 (☎ 212/691-9442), everybody's favorite creative condom store. **Sleek on Bleecker,** at no. 361 (☎ 212/243-0284), features fashionable but affordable fashions for working women with style.

Narrow **Christopher Street** is another fun street to browse, because it's loaded with genuine Village character. Those who really love to browse should also wander **west of Seventh Avenue,** where charming boutiques are tucked among the brownstones. Highlights include **Vass–Ludacer,** 43 Eighth Ave. (☎ 212/255-6565), for unique jewelry designs inspired by past centuries; **House of Cards and Curiosities,** 23 Eighth Ave. (☎ 212/675-6178), the Village's own funky take on an old-fashioned nickel-and-dime; and any number of boutiques along Hudson Street.

MIDTOWN
THE FLATIRON DISTRICT & UNION SQUARE

When 23rd Street was the epitome of New York Uptown fashion more than a hundred years ago, the major department stores stretched along **Sixth Avenue** for about a mile from 14th Street up. These elegant stores stood in huge cast-iron buildings that were long ago abandoned and left to rust. In the last few years, however, the area has grown into the city's discount shopping center, with superstores and off-pricers filling up the renovated spaces: **Filene's Basement, TJ Maxx,** and **Bed Bath & Beyond** are all at 620 Sixth Ave., while witty **Old Navy** is next door, and **Barnes & Noble** is just a couple of blocks away at Sixth Avenue near 22nd Street.

On Broadway just a few blocks north of Union Square is **ABC Carpet & Home,** a magnet for aspiring Martha Stewarts. If it's actually a rug you're looking for, you'll find a whole slew of imported carpet dealers lining Broadway from ABC north to about 25th Street.

Upscale retailers who have rediscovered the architectural majesty of **lower Fifth Avenue** include **Restoration Hardware,** at 22nd Street (☎ 212/260-9479; www.restorationhardware.com), plus mainstays like **Kenneth Cole** and **Victoria's Secret.** You won't find much that's new along here, but it's a pleasing stretch nonetheless. SoHo's **Anthropologie,** with a fun mix of affordable wearables and home decor, has a second home at 85 Fifth Ave., at 15th Street (☎ 212/627-5885).

HERALD SQUARE & THE GARMENT DISTRICT

Herald Square—where 34th Street, Sixth Avenue, and Broadway converge—is dominated by **Macy's,** the self-proclaimed world's biggest department store, and other famous-name shopping, like **Toys 'R' Us** at 34th Street and Broadway and **Old Navy** across from Macy's on 34th Street. At Sixth Avenue and 33rd Street is the **Manhattan Mall** (☎ 212/465-0500), anchored by an unremarkable Stern's department store and home to mall standards like Foot Locker and Radio Shack.

A long block over on Seventh Avenue, not much goes on in the grimy, heavily industrial Garment District. This is, however, where you'll find that quintessential New York experience, the **sample sale.**

TIMES SQUARE & THE THEATER DISTRICT

This neighborhood has become increasingly family-oriented: hence, **Warner Bros.** at the crossroads of Times Square; Richard Branson's rollicking **Virgin Megastore; The Gap** at 42nd and Broadway; and the mammoth new **E-Walk** retail and entertainment complex on 42nd Street between Seventh and Eighth avenues, which should be overflowing with mall-style retail shops by the time you read this.

But there's also some only–in–New York substance behind the Disneyfied, Mall-of-America glitz. **West 48th Street** between Sixth and Seventh avenues is the place to shop if you want to make your own music. You'll find friendly **Sam Ash,** 160 W. 48th St. (☎ 212/719-2299; www.samash.com), **Manny's Music,** 156 W. 48th St. (☎ 212/819-0576; www.mannysmusic.com), and **48th Street Custom Guitars,** no. 170 (☎ 212/764-1364; www.48thstguitar.com) like ducks in a row.

West 47th Street between Fifth and Sixth avenues is the city's famous **Diamond District.** Apparently, more than 90% of the diamonds sold in the United States come through this neighborhood first, so there are some great deals to be had if you're in the market for a nice rock or another piece of fine jewelry. Be ready to wheel and deal with the largely Hasidic dealers, who offer quite a juxtaposition to the crowds. For a complete introduction to the district, including smart buying tips, point your Web browser to **www.47th-street.com.** For semiprecious stones, head 1 block over to the **New York Jewelry Mart,** 26 W. 46th St. (☎ 212/575-9701). Virtually all of these dealers are open Monday through Friday only.

You'll also notice a wealth of electronics stores throughout the neighborhood, many suspiciously trumpeting GOING OUT OF BUSINESS sales. These guys have been going out of business since the Stone Age. That's the bait and switch; pretty soon you've spent too much money for not enough stereo. If you want to check out what they have to offer, go in knowing what going prices are on that PDA or digital camera you're interested in. You can make a good deal if you know exactly what the market is, but these guys will be happy to suck you dry given half a chance.

FIFTH AVENUE & 57TH STREET

The heart of Manhattan retail is the corner of Fifth Avenue and 57th Street. Time was, only the very rich could make this sacred crossroads their ground-zero shopping site. Not anymore, now that **Tiffany & Co.,** which has long reigned supreme here, sits a stone's throw from a huge **Original Levi's Store** and a **Warner Bros. Studio Store,** with **Niketown** and the **NBA Store** just down the street. In addition, a good number of mainstream retailers, like **Banana Republic** and **Liz Claiborne,** have set up their flagships along Fifth, further democratizing the avenue.

Fifth Avenue has only a few big-name designer boutiques left in the 50s, although the opening of the **Gianni Versace** shop at 647 Fifth Ave. (☎ 212/317-0224; www. versace.com) just before his death has heralded a new era of respect for the avenue. Other deluxe designer tenants are **Fendi,** at no. 720 (☎ 212/767-0100), and **Ferragamo,** no. 661 (☎ 212/759-3822; www.ferragamo.com). You'll also find big-name jewelers along here, as well as chi-chi department stores like **Bergdorf Goodman, Henri Bendel,** and **Saks Fifth Avenue,** all of which have helped the avenue maintain its classy cachet.

While 57th Street has similarly changed in the last few years, many big names are still hanging on. Italian knit queen **Laura Biagiotti** is at 4 W. 57th St. (☎ 212/399-2533); Tom Ford's stellar **Gucci** is at 10 W. 57th St. (☎ 212/826-2600; www. gucci.com); **Chanel** is at 15 E. 57th St. (☎ 212/355-5050); and **Christian Dior** is at 19 E. 57th St. (☎ 212/931-2950); as well as **Prada, Hermès,** and **Louis Vuitton** (see "Leather Goods, Handbags & Luggage," later in this chapter) and others.

UPTOWN
MADISON AVENUE

Madison Avenue from 57th to 79th streets has usurped Fifth Avenue as *the* tony shopping street in the city. In fact, in 1998, it vaulted ahead of Hong Kong's Causeway Bay to become the most expensive retail real estate in the world. Bring lots of plastic.

This strip of Madison is home to the most luxurious designer boutiques in the world—particularly in the high 60s—with **Barneys New York** as the anchor. **Calvin Klein** is all chrome and clean edges at 654 Madison, at 60th Street (☎ 212/292-9000), hawking magnificent threads for men and women, plus home furnishings. **Giorgio Armani** holds minimalist court at 760 Madison Ave., at 65th Street (☎ 212/988-9191). Glamorous **Valentino** is at 747 Madison Ave. (☎ 212/772-6969), while Italian super-chic is at home at **Dolce & Gabanna,** no. 825 (☎ 212/249-4100). Other sophisticated names lining the strip are **Ungaro** at no. 792 (☎ 212/249-4090) for body-conscious sophisticates; **Max Mara** at no. 813 (☎ 212/879-6100) for luxurious understatement; **Marina Rinaldi,** at no. 800 (☎ 212/734-4333), a Max Mara offshoot with beautiful clothes for size 10s and up; **Givenchy** at no. 710, at 63rd St. (☎ 212/772-1040) for the ultimate in haute Parisian style; plus **Vera Wang** for chic bridal wear and **Ralph Lauren's** stunner of a store for the ultimate in all-American style. Donna Karan has her **DKNY** flagship store at 655 Madison Ave., at 60th Street (☎ 212/223-3569).

For those of us without unlimited budgets, the good news is that stores like **Crate & Barrel** and the fabulous **Ann Taylor** flagship make the untouchable Madison Avenue seem approachable and affordable. Shoe freaks should be on the lookout for wallet-friendly **Unisa,** 701 Madison Ave. (☎ 212/753-7474); **Joan & David** at no. 816 (☎ 212/772-3970), where style triumphs over trendiness; **Timberland,** at no. 709 (☎ 212/754-0434), for the best in rugged footwear; and **Sergio Rossi,** no. 835 (☎ 212/396-4814), for glamorous mules, sexy slingbacks, and classic pointy-toe pumps.

Open Hours

Keep in mind that open hours can vary significantly from store to store—even different branches of the Gap can keep different schedules depending on location and management. As a rule of thumb, stores open at 10 or 11am on Monday through Saturday, and 7pm is the most common closing hour (although sometimes it's 6pm). Both opening and closing hours tend to get later as you move downtown; stores in the East Village often don't open until 1 or 2pm, and they stay open until 8pm or later.

All of the big department stores are open 7 days a week. However, unlike department stores in suburban malls, most of these stores don't keep a regular 10am to 9pm schedule. The department stores, and shops along major strips like Fifth Avenue, usually stay open later 1 night a week (often Thurs), although not all shops may comply. Sunday hours are usually noon to 5 or 6pm. Most shops are open 7 days a week, but smaller boutiques may close 1 day a week, and some neighborhoods virtually shut down on a particular day—namely the Lower East Side on Saturday, the East Village on Monday, and most of the Financial District for the weekend. But at holiday time, anything goes: Macy's often stays open until midnight for the last couple of weeks before Christmas!

Your best bet is to **call ahead** if your heart's set on visiting a particular store.

Upper Madison, from about 72nd to 86th streets, has become the domain of cozy-chic home stores for the uptown Martha Stewart set. Between 80th and 82nd streets, look for beautiful all-cotton fabrics on the bolt at **Maison Decor,** no. 1094 (☎ 212/744-7079), and sophisticated country French imports at **A La Maison,** no. 1078 (☎ 212/396-1020).

THE UPPER WEST SIDE

The Upper West Side's best shopping street is **Columbus Avenue.** Small shops catering to the neighborhood's white-collar mix of young hipsters and families line both sides of the pleasant avenue from 66th Street (where you'll find an excellent branch of **Barnes & Noble**) to about 86th Street. For comfort over style (these city streets can be murder on the feet!), try **Aerosoles,** 310 Columbus Ave. (☎ 212/579-8659), or **Sacco** for women's shoes that offer a bit of both. Other highlights include **La Belle Epoque,** at no. 280 (☎ 212/362-1770), for vintage posters, mostly prewar European advertisements; **Robert Marc Opticians,** at no. 190 (☎ 212/799-4600), for fashionable eyewear; **Elma Blint et al.** at no. 453 (☎ 212/501-9577), for terrific contemporary jewelry designs; and **Maxilla & Mandible** for groovy museum-quality natural science–based gifts (see "Museum Stores," later in this chapter).

Boutiques also dot Amsterdam Avenue, but main-drag Broadway is most notable for its terrific gourmet edibles at **Zabar's** and **Fairway** markets, both legends in their own right (see "Edibles," later in this chapter).

2 The Big Department Stores

Barneys New York. 660 Madison Ave. (at 61st St.). ☎ **212/826-8900.** Subway: N, R to Fifth Ave.

After financial woes that forced the closure of the original Chelsea store a few years back, New York's self-made temple of chic is back on top. This Madison Avenue store exudes impeccable high style—and a frostiness that I can't seem to overcome, but Elsa Klensch fans probably won't mind. While the store focuses on hot-off-the-runway womenswear, its menswear runs the gamut from classic to cutting edge. The fragrance department works hard to offer offbeat and unusual scents as well as the classics. Chelsea Passage is one of the world's best gift and tabletop departments. Bring your platinum card because nothing comes cheap here.

Bergdorf Goodman. 754 Fifth Ave. (at 57th St.). ☎ **212/753-7300.** Subway: E, F to Fifth Ave.

Once the fanciest specialty store in New York, Bergdorf's is a museum of haute couture. The store is beautifully designed on an intimate scale, and many claim that it lacks the nouveaux-riche feel of Bendel's, but its formality and quiet just makes me feel uncomfortable (or maybe it's just that I can't afford anything here?). The customer base is primarily composed of ladies who lunch and businesswomen with gobs of money but little time for nonsense. Still, there's an unparalleled gift and tabletop floor, worth a browse alone, as well as some finely tuned designer salons. Just across the street is **Bergdorf Goodman Man,** a palace of fine men's fashion.

✪ **Bloomingdale's.** 1000 Third Ave. (Lexington Ave. at 59th St.). ☎ **212/705-2000.** Subway: 4, 5, 6 to 59th St.

This is my favorite of New York's big department stores. It's more accessible than Barneys or Bergdorf's and more affordable than Saks, but still has the New York pizzazz that Macy's and Lord and Taylor now largely lack. Taking up the space of a city block, Bloomie's has just about anything you could want, from clothing (both designer and everyday basics) and fragrances to housewares and furniture. It pays to make a reconnaissance trip to get the overview, then move in for the kill. The main entrance is on Third Avenue, but pop up to street level from the 59th Street station and you'll be right at the Lexington Avenue entrance.

✪ **Century 21.** 22 Cortlandt St. (btw. Broadway and Church St.). ☎ **212/227-9092.** Subway: N, R, 1, 9 to Cortlandt St.; C, E to World Trade Center.

Just across from the World Trade Center, Century 21 long ago achieved legend status as *the* designer discount store. If you don't mind wrestling with the aggressive, ever-present throngs, this is where you'll find those $20 Todd Oldham pants or the $50 Bally loafers you've been dreaming of—not to mention underwear, hosiery, and ties so cheap that they're almost free. Don't think that $250 Armani blazer is a bargain? Look again at the tag—the retail price on it is upward of $800.

✪ **Henri Bendel.** 712 Fifth Ave. (btw. 55th and 56th sts.). ☎ **212/247-1100.** Subway: N, R to Fifth Ave.

This beautiful Fifth Avenue store is a lot of fun to browse. It feels like you're shopping in the town house of a confident, monied old lady who doesn't think twice about throwing on a little something by Anna Sui and an outrageously wide-brimmed hat to go out shopping for the day—and she's got the panache to pull it off. It's a super-stylish, high-ticket collection, but the sales are good, and there's always some one-of-a-kind accessories that make affordable souvenirs (and earn you one of the black-and-white striped shopping bags, the best in town). The interior is so divine that you should remember to take a break from perusing the racks to look up, down, and around every once in a while. The pretty tearoom looks out on Fifth Avenue through Lalique windows.

Lord & Taylor. 424 Fifth Ave. (at 39th St.). ☎ **212/391-3344.** Subway: B, D, F, Q to 42nd St.

Okay, so maybe Lord & Taylor isn't the first place you'd go for a vinyl miniskirt. But I like Lord & Taylor's understated, elegant mien. Long known as an excellent source for women's dresses and coats, L&T stocks all the major labels for men and women, with a special emphasis on American designers. Their house-brand clothes (khakis, blazers, turtlenecks, and summer sportswear) are well made and a great bargain. Sales, especially around holidays, can be stellar. The store is big enough to have a good selection (especially for petites), but doesn't overwhelm—I wish the lighting were better, though, but it's a minor complaint. The Christmas window displays are an annual delight.

Macy's. At Herald Square, W. 34th St. and Broadway. ☎ **212/695-4400.** Subway: B, D, F, N, Q, R, 1, 2, 3, 9 to 34th St.

A 4-story sign on the side of the building trumpets, "MACY'S, THE WORLD'S LARGEST STORE"—a hard fact to dispute, since the 10-story behemoth covers an entire city block, even dwarfing Bloomie's on the other side of town. Macy's is a hard place to shop: The size is unmanageable, the service is dreadful, and the incessant din from the crowds on the ground floor alone will kick your migraine into action. But they do sell *everything*. Massive renovation over the past few years has redesigned many departments into more manageable "ministores"—there's a Metropolitan Museum Gift Shop, a Swatch boutique, and cafes and makeup counters on several floors—but the store's one-of-a-kind flair that I remember so well from my childhood is just a memory now. Still, sales run constantly, holiday or no (1-day sales are popular on Wed and Sat), so bargains are guaranteed. And because so many feel adrift in this retail sea, the store provides personal guides/shoppers at absolutely no charge. My advice: Get the floor plan, and consult it often to avoid wandering off into the sportswear nether-world. At Christmastime, come as late as you can manage (the store is usually open until midnight in the final shopping days).

Saks Fifth Avenue. 611 Fifth Ave. (btw. 49th and 50th sts.). ☎ **212/753-4000.** Subway: B, D, F, Q to 47th–50th sts./Rockefeller Center; E, F to Fifth Ave.

There are branches of Saks all over the country now, but this is it: the Saks *Fifth Avenue.* This legendary flagship store is well worth an hour or two of your time, and the smaller-than-most size makes it manageable in that amount of time. Saks carries a wide range of clothing; departments err on the pricey designer side (stay out of the lingerie department if you're looking for basics) but run the gamut to affordable house-brand basics. As department stores go, there's something for everyone here. Some call this men's department the finest in the city. The cosmetics and fragrance departments on the main floor are justifiably noteworthy, since they carry many hard-to-find and brand-new brands. And the store's location, right across from Rockefeller Center, makes it a convenient stop for those on the sightseeing circuit. Don't miss the holiday windows.

Takashimaya. 693 Fifth Ave. (btw. 54th and 55th sts.). ☎ **212/350-0100.** Subway: E, F to Fifth Ave.

This petite branch of Japan's most famous department store chain doesn't resemble the domestic branches. Rather, this Fifth Avenue outpost exudes an appealingly austere, Japanese-tinged French country charm. Paris's most famous florist, Christian Tortu, has a main-floor boutique that's a work of art in its own right. The serenely elegant Tea Box specializes in delicate bento lunches and beautiful sweets. Aesthetes shouldn't miss this place.

3 Shopping A to Z

ANTIQUES & COLLECTIBLES

Looking for glass? Then don't miss **Galileo,** which boasts a small but stellar collection of vintage glassware; see "Home Fashions & Housewares," below. Midcentury furniture lovers should be sure to browse **Lafayette Street;** see "The Top Shopping Streets & Neighborhoods," earlier in this chapter.

Most call it the 26th Street flea market; the famous **Annex Antiques Fair and Flea Market** (☎ 212/243-5343) is an outdoor emporium of nostalgia, filling a few parking lots along Sixth Avenue between 24th and 27th streets on weekends year-round. The assemblage is hit or miss—some days you'll find treasures galore, and others it seems like there's nothing but junk. A few quality vendors are almost always on hand, though. The truly dedicated arrive at 6:30am, but the browsing's still plenty good as late as 4pm. Sunday is always best, since there's double the booty on hand. The Web site, **www.annexantiques.citysearch.com,** will also link you to other flea markets around the city. Another popular market is the **SoHo Antiques and Collectibles Market,** at Broadway and Grand Street (☎ 212/682-6200; www.sohoantiques.citysearch.com), Saturday and Sunday from 9am.

Alphaville. 226 W. Houston St. (btw. Sixth Ave. and Varick St.). ☎ **212/675-6850.** www.alphaville.com. Subway: 1, 9 to Houston St.

This gallery specializes in 1940s, '50s, and '60s toys and movie posters, all in mint condition and beautifully displayed. Space toys are an emphasis. Well worth a look for nostalgic baby boomers, even if you have no intention of buying.

Chelsea Antiques Building. 110 W. 25th St. (btw. Sixth and Seventh aves.). ☎ **212/929-0909.** www.chelseaantiques.com. Subway: F to 23rd St.

Right around the corner from New York's best flea market (above), 100 dealers occupy this 12-floor building, open daily. Prices are so good that it's known as a dealer's source, and shoppers are the type who love to prowl, touch everything, and sniff out a bargain. Highlights include **Waves** (☎ 212/989-9284; www.wavesradio.com) for antique radios and phonographs, including a good selection of 78s and Edison cylinders; **Julian's Books** (☎ 212/929-3620; www.julianbook.com) for first, signed, and rare editions; **Retro-Metro/The Missing Link** (☎ 212/645-6928) for cufflinks, handbags, and other vintage jewelry and accessories; and **Toys from the 50s** (☎ 212/352-9182; www.toys-50s.com), specializing in classic TV show toys and memorabilia.

Chisolm Gallery. 55 W. 17th St. (just east of Sixth Ave.), 6th Floor. ☎ **212/243-8834.** www.vintagepostersnyc.com. Subway: F to 14th St.

Here's the city's best source for collectible-quality vintage travel and advertising posters. Every piece in the collection, which spans the last 100 years, is well chosen and beautifully restored; expect lots of French adverts in the mix. With top quality comes steep prices, so expect to dig deep if you fall in love with a piece.

✪ **The End of History.** 548^1/$_2$ Hudson St. (btw. Perry and Charles sts.). ☎ **212/647-7598.** Subway: 1, 9 to Christopher St.

This marvelous shop specializes in Murano, Blenko, Holmegaard, and other European glass, with a strong emphasis on the '60s. The constantly changing collection features lots of dazzling shapes and colors, all fetchingly displayed on select pieces of for-sale furnishings, which often have a Scandinavian or mod flair. This shop is so creatively put together that you'll have a blast browsing even if their collectibles aren't your thing.

Form & Function. 95 Vandam St. (1 block north of Spring St., btw. Hudson and Greenwich sts.). ☎ **212/414-1800.** Subway: 1, 9 to Houston St.

Co-owned by Fred Schneider of the B-52s, this gallery specializes in lesser-known designers and design trends from 1945 to 1975—a boon to those of us who have seen enough Heywood–Wakefield to last a lifetime. This is a serious gallery, not a midcentury kitschfest, so come for the high quality of the home designs. Vintage electronics are featured, too.

J. Fields Studio & Gallery. 55 W. 17th St. (just east of Sixth Ave.), 6th Floor. ☎ **212/989-4520.** Subway: F to 14th St.

Right next door to Chisolm (above), this terrific gallery is the place for vintage and contemporary film posters, both foreign and domestic. A limited supply of music posters is on hand, too (including a good selection of psychedelic "Bill Graham Presents" posters from the '60s). J. Fields is considered the best vintage-poster restorer in the city, so quality is first-rate. Prices are high, but with vintage lobby cards starting at $15, even those with small budgets can own a bit of movie history.

Kentshire Galleries. 37 E. 12th St. (btw. University Place and Broadway). ☎ **212/673-6644.** Subway: N, R, L, 4, 5, 6 to 14th St./Union Sq.

Here's the city's prime stop for 18th- and 19th-century English antiques, ranging from jewelry and tabletop items to formal furnishings.

Manhattan Art & Antiques Center. 1050 Second Ave. (btw. 55th and 56th sts.). ☎ **212/355-4400.** www.the-maac.com. Subway: N, R to Lexington Ave.

This 3-floor antiques center represents just about every genre of collecting on the map, from perfume bottles and porcelain to arms and armor. Once you've toured the more than 100 stalls, stroll along 60th Street, where about 2 dozen dealers selling higher-end goods line both sides of the street.

Mood Indigo. 181 Prince St. (btw. Sullivan and Thompson sts.). ☎ **212/254-1176.** Subway: C, E to Spring St.; N, R to Prince St.

Looking for the perfect vintage cocktail shaker? How about some hip martini glasses for those Cosmopolitans you just learned to make? Maybe a certain piece of Jadite or Fiestaware to complete your collection? Then come to this dandy of a shop, the city's top dealer in glassware, dishware, and kitchen accessories from the 1930s through the 1950s. The charming shopkeepers also specialize in bakelite jewelry and 1939 World's Fair memorabilia, and boast a whopping collection of '50s novelty salt-and-pepper shakers. Everything is pristine, so expect to pay accordingly.

Going . . . Going . . . Sold!

Auctions specialize in anything collectible, from animation cels to fine wines to Chinese ceramics to Academy Awards fashions. The two major auction houses are **Christie's,** at 20 Rockefeller Plaza, 49th Street between Fifth and Sixth avenues (☎ **212/636-2000;** www.christies.com), and 219 E. 67th St., between Second and Third avenues (☎ **212/606-0400**); and **Sotheby's,** 1334 York Ave., at 72nd Street (☎ **212/606-7000;** www.sothebys.com). Every now and then a celebrity estate (like Jackie O's and the Duke and Duchess of Windsor's so famously did) goes up for auction. No matter what the auction, viewings are free and open to the public; full calendars are available online. If you plan to participate, be sure to review the catalog for price estimates beforehand, and attend the sale preview for an advance look at the merchandise.

Newel Art Galleries. 425 E. 53rd St. (btw. First Ave. and Sutton Place). ☎ **212/758-1970.** www.newel.com. Subway: 6 to 51st St.

This wonderful gallery houses six floors of the best furniture from ages past—be it a throne that would make King Arthur proud or an art deco vanity that Carole Lombard might've loved. Browsing hardly gets better.

ART
See the box titled "Art for Art's Sake: The Gallery Scene" in chapter 7.

BEAUTY
Floris of London. 703 Madison Ave. (btw. 62nd and 63rd sts.). ☎ **212/935-9100.** www.florisoflondon.com. Subway: N, R to Fifth Ave.; B, Q to Lexington Ave.

Fragrance lovers shouldn't miss this gorgeous new-world outpost of the marvelous British fragrance house (since 1730). Princess Di was a big fan, and who could blame her? These scents epitomize English botanical splendor and elegance. Floris now sells scented candles and home fragrances, too.

♦ **Kiehl's.** 109 Third Ave. (at 13th St.). ☎ **212/677-3171.** Subway: L, N, R, 4, 5, 6 to 14th St.–Union Sq.

Kiehl's is more than a store: It's a virtual cult. Models, stockbrokers, foreign visitors, and just about everyone else stops by this always-packed old-time apothecary for its simply packaged, wonderfully formulated products for women and men. Lip Balm no. 1 is the perfect antidote for the biting winds of city or slope. It's now sold at Saks, too, but come to the original.

MAC. 113 Spring St. (btw. Mercer and Greene sts.). ☎ **212/334-4641.** www.maccosmetics. com. Subway: N, R to Prince St.

What began as a Canadian-based, custom-designed modeling makeup line has become a super-successful retail operation thanks to a chic color line, eco-friendly packaging, and decent prices (considering the quality). Lighter and more sheer than most, the lipsticks are particularly popular; I buy redwood practically by the gross. The downtown-chic, don't-hate-me-because-I'm-beautiful unisex staff is surprisingly helpful. Another, smaller branch is in the Village at 14 Christopher St. (☎ **212/243-4150**), plus counters at Saks, Bloomingdale's, and Henri Bendel.

Sephora. 1500 Broadway (btw. 43rd and 44th sts.). ☎ **212/944-6789.** www.sephora. com. Subway: N, R, S, 1, 2, 3, 7, 9 to Times Sq./42nd St.

This French beauty superstore took Manhattan by storm in 1999. You'll find everything you could want here, from scents to nail color to cleansers to bath salts to makeup brushes to hair accessories . . . you get the picture. In addition to their own exclusive brand, they carry an extensive number of upscale lines, including Shu Uemura, Urban Decay, Bliss, Clarins, and Elizabeth Arden. Testers galore. Also at Rockefeller Center, 636 Fifth Ave., at 51st St. (☎ **212/245-1633**); in SoHo at 555 Broadway, between Prince and Spring streets (☎ **212/625-1309**); and at the World Trade Center (☎ **212/432-1311**).

BOOKS
THE BIG CHAINS
Barnes & Noble Booksellers. On Union Square, 33 E. 17th St. ☎ **212/253-0810.** www.bn.com. Subway: L, N, R, 4, 5, 6 to 14th St./Union Sq.

With locations throughout the city, B&N is the undisputed king of city bookstores. The Union Square location is my favorite: The selection is huge and well organized, the store is comfortable and never feels too crowded, and you're welcome to browse—or nab a comfy chair and read—for as long as you like. There's a cafe, of course, and an extensive magazine stand.

There's another superstore at 1972 Broadway, at 66th Street (☎ 212/595-6859), plus additional good-size locations at 4 Astor Place, between Broadway and Lafayette Street (☎ 212/420-1322); 675 Sixth Ave., near 22nd Street (☎ 212/727-1227); 160 E. 54th St., at Third Avenue (☎ 212/750-8033); at Rockefeller Center, 600 Fifth Ave., at 48th St. (☎ 212/765-0590); 2289 Broadway, at 82nd St. (☎ 212/362-8835); and 240 E. 86th St., at Second Avenue (☎ 212/794-1962).

Call ☎ 212/727-4810 for the latest schedule of readings; the calendar is extensive, and featured luminaries have included Martin Amis, Peter Jennings, David Byrne, and Elmore Leonard.

Borders Books & Music. 5 World Trade Center (at Church and Vesey sts.). ☎ 212/839-8049. www.borders.com. Subway: N, R, 1, 9 to Cortlandt St.; C, E to World Trade Center.

Borders is a welcome addition to the Financial District. The selection of both books and music is extensive, service is great, and the store hosts a wealth of in-store events, including appearances from best-selling authors to musicians like Lou Reed and Jonatha Brooke. Also at 461 Park Ave., at 57th Street (☎ 212/980-6785), and 550 Second Ave., at 32nd Street (☎ 212/685-3938).

SPECIALTY BOOKSTORES

New York has more terrific specialty bookstores than I can possibly list here. These are just *some* of the best. Also consider **Tower Books,** a branch of the mega-music chain (see "Music," below).

Archivia. 944 Madison Ave. (btw. 74th and 75th sts.). ☎ 212/439-9194. Subway: 6 to 77th St.

Here you'll find new, imported, and rare books on architecture, the decorative arts, gardening, and interior design. A book and design lover's dream.

Argosy Books. 116 E. 59th St. (btw. Park and Lexington aves.). ☎ 212/753-4455. www.argosybooks.com. Subway: 4, 5, 6 to 59th St.

Antiquarian-book hounds should check out this stately 75-year-old store, with high ceilings, packed shelves, a quietly intellectual air, and an outstanding collection of rarities, including 18th- and 19th-century prints, maps, and autographs.

Books of Wonder. 16 W. 18th St. (btw. Fifth and Sixth aves.). ☎ 212/989-3270. www.booksofwonder.com. Subway: L, N, R, 4, 5, 6 to 14th St./Union Square.

You don't have to be a kid to fall in love with this charming bookstore, which served as the model for Meg Ryan's shop in *You've Got Mail* (Meg even worked here for a spell to train for the role). Kids will love BOW's story readings; call for a schedule.

✪ **Coliseum Books.** 1771 Broadway (at 57th St.). ☎ 212/757-8381. www.coliseumbooks. com. Subway: A, B, C, D, 1, 9 to 59th St./Columbus Circle.

This big, well-stocked independent is a must on any book lover's list—and it's well located for visitors, right on the edge of the Theater District, a stone's throw from Central Park. It may not be Barnes & Noble cozy, but you'll find an excellent selection of fiction and literature (both contemporary and the classics), along with great travel, art, and coffee-table books. Staff, poised atop a raised platform in the middle of the store, are on hand to answer questions or proffer a literary opinion.

Complete Traveller. 199 Madison Ave. (at 35th St.). ☎ 212/685-9007. Subway: 6 to 33rd St.

Whether your destination is Texas or Tibet, you'll find what you need in this, possibly the world's best travel bookstore. There are maps and travel accessories as well, plus a rare collection of antiquarian travel books whose facts may be outdated but whose writers' perceptions continue to shine. The staff is attentive.

A Different Light Bookstore. 151 W. 19th St. (btw. Sixth and Seventh aves.). ☎ **212/ 989-4850.** www.adlbooks.com. Subway: 1, 9 to 18th St.

The city's largest gay and lesbian bookstore stocks just about every category—fiction, nonfiction, biography, travel, gay/lesbian studies, and more—plus cassettes, calendars, you name it. There's also a cafe. Check the Web site for a full calendar of readings and video nights.

Forbidden Planet. 840 Broadway (at 13th St.). ☎ **212/473-1576.** Subway: L, N, R, 4, 5, 6 to 14th St./Union Sq.

Here's the city's largest collection of sci-fi, comics, and graphic-illustration books. The range of products can't be beat, and the proudly geeky staff really knows what's what. Great sci-fi-themed toys, too.

✪ **Gotham Book Mart.** 41 W. 47th St. (btw. Fifth and Sixth aves.). ☎ **212/719-4448.** Subway: B, D, F, Q to 47th–50th sts./Rockefeller Center.

Paris may have had its Sylvia Beach, but New York was lucky enough to have Frances Steloff. She opened Gotham Book Mart in 1920, and quickly became a defender of the First Amendment rights of authors. She championed such once-banned works as Henry Miller's *Tropic of Cancer,* and numbered among her admirers Ezra Pound, Saul Bellow, and Jackie Kennedy Onassis. Frances has since passed on, but her aura lives. As always, the emphasis is on poetry, literature, and the arts. This is New York's undisputed literary landmark; look for the sign that says WISE MEN FISH HERE.

Hagstrom Map & Travel Center. 57 W. 43rd St. (btw. Fifth and Sixth aves.). ☎ **212/ 398-1222.** Subway: B, D, F, Q to 42nd St.

This bookstore sells travel guides and an incredible selection of cartography to meet just about any map need. Also in lower Manhattan at 125 Maiden Lane, between Pearl and Water streets (☎ **212/785-5343**).

Kitchen Arts & Letters. 1435 Lexington Ave. (btw. 93rd and 94th sts.). ☎ **212/ 876-5550.** www.kitchenartsandletters.com. Subway: 6 to 96th St.

Foodies take note: Here's the ultimate cook's and food-lover's bookstore. You'll be wowed by the depth of the selection, which includes rare and out-of-print cookbooks. The staff will conduct free searches for hard-to-find titles. The shop is an overstuffed jumble, but if this is your bag, you'll be browsing for hours.

Murder Ink. 2486 Broadway (btw. 92nd and 93rd sts.). ☎ **212/362-8905** or 800/488-8123. www.murderink.com. Subway: 1, 9 to 96th St.

Murder, she wrote, he wrote, they wrote. This is the ultimate specialty bookstore—as much fun as a good mystery. They claim to sell every mystery in print, and also carry a huge selection of out-of-print paperbacks, hard-to-find imported titles, and rare signed first editions.

Mysterious Book Shop. 129 W. 56th St. (btw. Sixth and Seventh aves). ☎ **212/ 765-0900.** www.mysteriousbookshop.com. Subway: B, D, E to Seventh Ave.

Mystery and true-crime fans will also enjoy this Midtown bookshop, specializing in current and rare whodunits.

Oscar Wilde Bookshop. 15 Christopher St. (btw. Sixth and Seventh aves.) ☎ **212/ 255-8097.** www.OscarWildeBooks.com. Subway: 1, 9 to Christopher St./Sheridan Sq.

The world's oldest gay and lesbian bookstore is still going strong. It's much smaller than A Different Light (above), but the nice staff makes this landmark a pleasure.

Posman Books. In Grand Central Terminal (at the base of the Vanderbilt Ramp), Vanderbilt Ave. and 42nd St. ☎ **212/983-1111.** www.posmanbooks.com. Subway: S, 4, 5, 6, 7 to 42nd St./Grand Central.

This big, new store is a browser's delight, with smart and well-displayed fiction and nonfiction collections as well as a terrific art and cookbook inventory. Also at NYU, 1 University Place, across from Washington Square Park (☎ **212/533-2665**), where the emphasis is on literature and philosophy; and at the New School, 70 Fifth Ave., at 13th St. (☎ **212/633-2525**), specializing in art, architecture, fashion, and design.

Rand McNally Travel Store. 150 E. 52nd St. (btw. Lexington and Third aves.). ☎ **212/ 758-7488.** www.randmcnally.com. Subway: E, F to Lexington Ave.; 6 to 51st St.

Sheet maps, globes, city maps, international maps, laminated maps—so many maps, in fact, you might never get lost again. A wide range of travel guides, atlases, and such travelers' aids as voltage converters and inflatable pillows, too. Also at 555 Seventh Ave., between 39th and 40th streets (☎ **212/944-4477**).

Rizzoli. 31 W. 57th St. (btw. Fifth and Sixth aves.). ☎ **212/759-2424.** Subway: N, R to Fifth Ave.

This clubby Italian bookstore is the classiest—and most relaxing—spot in town to browse for visual art and design books, plus quality fiction, gourmet cookbooks, and other upscale reading. There's a decent selection of foreign-language, music, and dance titles as well. Also in SoHo at 454 W. Broadway, between Houston and Prince streets (☎ **212/674-1616**), and at 3 World Financial Center (☎ **212/385-1400**).

✪ **St. Mark's Bookshop.** 31 Third Ave. (at 9th St.). ☎ **212/260-7853.** Subway: 6 to Astor Place.

Established in 1977, this left-of-center East Village bookshop is a great place to browse. You'll find lots of terrific alternative and small-press fiction and poetry, plus cultural criticism, Eastern philosophy, and mainstream literature with an edge. You'll also find art, photography, and design books as well as an alternative 'zine rack. Lots of spoken-work CDs and cassettes, too.

Shakespeare & Co. 716 Broadway (just north of 4th St.). ☎ **212/529-1330.** Subway: N, R to 8th St.

A boutiquelike bookstore in the Village stocks the latest fiction (and non-) best-sellers, and has a generally well-rounded inventory. The displays are quite enticing if you're looking for something new to read. Another branch is uptown, at 939 Lexington Ave., between 68th and 69th streets (☎ **212/570-0201**).

✪ **The Strand.** 828 Broadway (at 12th St.). ☎ **212/473-1452.** Subway: L, N, R, 4, 5, 6 to 14th St./Union Sq.

Something of a New York legend, The Strand is worth a visit for its staggering "8 miles of books" as well as its extensive inventory of review copies and bargain titles at up to 85% off list price. It's unquestionably the city's best book deal—there's almost nothing marked at list—and the selection is phenomenal in all categories (there's even a rare book department on the third floor). Still, you'll work for it: The narrow aisles mean you're always getting bumped; the books are only roughly alphabetized; and there's no air-conditioning in summer. Nevertheless, a used-book lover's paradise. There's a smaller Strand downtown, at 95 Fulton St., between William and Gold streets (☎ **212/732-6070**).

Urban Center Books. In the Villard Houses, 457 Madison Ave. (at 51st St.). ☎ **212/935-3592.** www.urbancenterbooks.com. Subway: 6 to 51st St.

The Municipal Art Society's bookstore boasts a terrific selection of books on architecture, design, and urban planning.

CLOTHING
RETAIL FASHIONS
The Top Designers
You'll find the classic designer names—**Chanel, Hermès, Alfred Dunhill, Gucci, Prada,** and friends—lined up like haute couture soldiers along Fifth Avenue and 57th Street. The biggest names in clean-lined modern design—**Calvin Klein, Donna Karan, Armani, Dolce & Gabbana**—call super-chic Madison Avenue home. Established avant-garde designers—**Anna Sui, Yohji Yamamoto, Vivienne Westwood, Todd Oldham**—hang out in SoHo, while talented up-and-comers have set up shop in NoHo, NoLiTa, and along 9th Street in the East Village. See "The Top Shopping Streets & Neighborhoods," earlier in this chapter.

Fashion Flagships
Some New York flagship stores of the major brands are an experience you won't catch in your nearest mall. These stores are display cases for the complete line of fashions, so you'll often find much more to choose from than in your at-home branch. You'll find other locations throughout the city, but these are meant to be the biggest and best: Check out the gorgeous **Ann Taylor** at 645 Madison Ave., at 60th Street (☎ 212/832-2010); the brand-new **Banana Republic** flagship at Rockefeller Center, 626 Fifth Ave., at 52nd Street (☎ 212/644-6678; www.bananarepublic.com); **Eddie Bauer,** 1960 Broadway, at 68th Street (☎ 212/877-7629; www.eddiebauer.com), which also carries the AKA Eddie Bauer line and the sports and mountaineering line; **Liz Claiborne,** 650 Fifth Ave., at 52nd Street (☎ 212/956-6505; www.lizclaiborne.com), which carries all of Liz's lines; the **Original Levi's Store** at 3 E. 57th St., between Fifth and Madison avenues (☎ 212/838-2125); and **Victoria's Secret,** 34 E. 57th St., between Madison and Park avenues (☎ 212/758-5592; www.victoriassecret.com). **Old Navy** has a huge flagship featuring its affordable basics and signature sense of humor at 610 Sixth Ave., at 18th Street (☎ 212/645-0663; www.oldnavy.com). **Diesel** sells its casual, youthful streetwear at 770 Lexington Ave., at 60th Street (☎ 212/308-0055). **J. Crew** has a big bilevel SoHo store at 100 Prince St., between Mercer and Greene streets (☎ 212/966-2739).

For Men & Women
agnès b. 116–118 Prince St. (btw. Wooster and Greene sts.). ☎ **212/925-4649.** Subway: N, R to Prince St.

Wanna look like Catherine Deneuve in *The Umbrellas of Cherbourg* or Belmondo in *Breathless*? Then look no further than agnès b, whose French fashions are at once super-stylish and classically cool. The emphasis is on breezy, silky styles for women here, at 13 E. 16th St., between Fifth Avenue and Union Square West (☎ 212/741-2585), and at 1063 Madison Ave., between 80th and 81st streets (☎ 212/570-9333). The men's store, **agnès b homme,** is at 79 Greene St., at Spring Street (☎ 212/219-6000). The striped shirts are timeless, and the leather car coat is thoroughly mod.

Brooks Brothers. 346 Madison Ave. (at 44th St.). ☎ **212/682-8800.** www.brooksbrothers.com. Subway: S, 4, 5, 6, 7 to 42nd St./Grand Central.

The perfect definition of all that is preppy lies behind this clubby storefront. The label is synonymous with quality, quiet taste, and classic tailoring. The cut of the man's suit is a tad boxy, making it great for the full American body but not quite right for the skinny European guy. Also in the Financial District (appropriately enough) at 1 Church St., at Liberty Street (☎ **212/267-2400**).

Canal Jean Co. 504 Broadway (btw. Spring and Broome sts.). ☎ **212/226-1130.** www.canaljean.com. Subway: N, R to Prince St.; 6 to Spring St.

This big, bright store almost single-handedly started the SoHo shopping revolution nearly 2 decades ago. You'll find scads of well-priced jeans (low-riders, bell-bottoms, and just plain regular), midriff-baring T-shirts, and flannels, with the requisite vinyl purses/backpacks, and clunky costume jewelry thrown in. A new 15,000-square-foot juniors department adds even more of the same. Go downstairs for vintage wear, but know that the stuff they have is geared to the skateboard set and tends to be a tad shopworn.

Cynthia Rowley. 112 Wooster St. (btw. Prince and Spring sts.). ☎ **212/334-1144.** Subway: N, R to Prince St.

Rowley has become one of downtown's big fashion guns. Once you see her dynamite slim-cut designs for men and women, you'll sing her praises too. Modern without being super-trendy, her clothes are beautifully made, witty, sophisticated, and cool.

✪ **Jeffrey New York.** 449 W. 14th St. (near Tenth Ave.). ☎ **212/206-1272.** Subway: A, C, E, L to 14th St.

At the end of a deserted street in the still-industrial Meat-Packing District is this oasis of cutting-edge haute couture. Jeffrey New York caters to the Barney's crowd, but this new outpost of the famed Atlanta mega-boutique is much more accessible and user-friendly. Great accessories and shoes galore. The collection is mostly geared to women, but there's a notable men's department, too, and a deejay to keep tag-alongs entertained. A worthy schlep for style hounds.

Nicole Fahri. 10 E. 60th St. (just east of Fifth Ave.). ☎ **212/223-8811** (or ☎ 212/223-2288 for reservations at Nicole's). Subway: N, R to Fifth Ave.

This cool-chic British import specializes in the same kind of simple, clean-lined casual urban wear that Banana Republic does, but it's for those who can afford better. Great cuts, neutral colors, and natural fabrics. There's a stylish home store and Modern British cuisine at **Nicole's** (☎ **212/223-2288**), a *New York Times* two-star winner worth a visit in its own right.

Patricia Field. 10 E. 8th St. (btw. Fifth Ave. and University Place). ☎ **212/254-1699.** www.patriciafield.com. Subway: 6 to Astor Place.

The wildest club kids and trendiest trendsetters know Patricia Field as *the* place to shop. Pat Field has been the leading doyenne of cutting-edge chic and downtown cool for more than 2 decades now, and she still reigns. Her shop sports the city's grooviest, most outrageous men's and women's clubwear. The store's wild makeup counter will appear tame once you see the outlandish 'dos in the wacky wig and hair salon. There is nothing understated about this place—it's a hoot to browse. Pat Field's SoHo location, **Hotel Venus,** 382 W. Broadway, between Spring and Broome streets (☎ **212/966-4066**), is a bit more upscale, but no less funky.

Phat Farm. 129 Prince St. (btw. W. Broadway and Wooster St.). ☎ **212/533-PHAT.** www.phatfarm.com. Subway: N, R to Prince St.

For the most stylish hip-hop clothes on the market, head to music impresario Russell Simmons's SoHo boutique. Extra-puffy down jackets, extra-baggy pants, logo Ts—you'll find it all here.

Polo/Ralph Lauren. 867 Madison Ave. (at 72nd St.). ☎ **212/606-2100.** Subway: 6 to 68th St.

Among all the high-ticket designers whose shops line Madison Avenue (see "The Top Shopping Streets & Neighborhoods," earlier in this chapter), Ralph Lauren deserves special mention for the stunning beauty of this shop, housed in a landmark Rhinelander mansion. While **Polo Sport,** his store across the street at 888 Madison Ave. (☎ **212/434-8000**), is also snazzy and worth a look, this particular mansion was one of New York's first important freestanding American designer shops and has continued to wear as well as the classics Ralph churns out. Housewares and infants' clothing as well as women's and men's clothes are for sale. The activewear and sporty country looks are across the street.

Shanghai Tang. 714 Madison Ave. (btw. 63rd and 64th sts.). ☎ **212/888-0111.** Subway: N, R to Fifth Ave.; 4, 5, 6 to 59th St.

This Hong Kong clothier boasts one of the loveliest, wittiest stores on Madison Avenue. The designs are irreverent takes on Chinese classics—Mandarin-collared jackets, ankle-length cheung sams—done in shimmering silks, lustrous velvets, and rich jacquards, and a vibrant palette that runs the gamut from the hot pink to electric blue (plus black, for those of us who prefer to tone down rather than up).

Tristan & America. 1230 Sixth Ave. (at 49th St.). ☎ **212/246-2354.** Subway: B, D, F, Q to 47th–50th sts./Rockefeller Center.

This Canadian retailer sells affordable, nicely tailored clothing in muted palettes to men and women who love Banana Republic's clothes, but need a break from the high prices there. Look for great men's sweaters, affordable women's suits, and nicely cut trousers and A-line skirts. Also in SoHo at 560 Broadway, between Prince and Spring streets (☎ **212/965-1810**).

Just Women

○ **Eileen Fisher.** 395 W. Broadway (btw. Spring and Broome sts.). ☎ **212/431-4567.** www.eileenfisher.com. Subway: C, E to Spring St.

Slowly making their way around the nation in her own shops and through outlets like Saks and the Garnet Hill catalog, Eileen Fisher's separates are a dream come true for stylish women looking for easy-to-wear classic pieces that transcend the latest fads. She designs fluid clothes in a pleasing neutral palette and uses natural fibers that don't sacrifice comfort for chic. The A-line styles look a bit droopy on shorter women, but otherwise suit all figure types well. The superior quality, fabrics, and style make these clothes worth every penny. This beautifully austere SoHo location is Fisher's prime showcase. Also at 103 Fifth Ave., near 18th Street (☎ **212/924-4777**); 521 Madison Ave., at 53rd Street (☎ **212/759-9888**); 341 Columbus Ave., near 77th Street (☎ **212/362-3000**); 1039 Madison Ave., between 79th and 80th streets (☎ **212/ 879-7799**). The closet-size location at 314 E. 9th St., between First and Second avenues (☎ **212/529-5715**), basically functions as an outlet store, with lots of sale merchandise and seconds on hand.

Foley & Corinna. 108 Stanton St. (at Essex St.). ☎ **212/529-2338.** Subway: F to Delancey St.

The Lower East Side's best boutique specializes in affordable original designs with a distinctly '70s flair that's beautifully retro in a wasn't-Pucci-cool way, not kitschy. You'll find a few reconstructed vintage pieces mixed in (such as pristine vintage Ts with added lace for a sexier look), plus an excellent handbag collection.

Harriet Love. 126 Prince St. (between Greene and Wooster sts.). ☎ **212/966-2280.** Subway: N, R to Prince St.

Harriet Love is for women who prefer flowing lines and comfy fabrics over the slinky couture duds that threaten to overrun SoHo's boutiques. Harriet's clothes are stylish without being trendy; you'll be able to wear them well after the season ends. Expect beautiful sweaters and accessories galore from an eclectic mix of American and European designers.

✪ **Jill Anderson.** 331 E. 9th St. (btw. First and Second aves.). ☎ **212/253-1747.** Subway: 6 to Astor Place.

Finally, a New York designer who designs affordable clothes for real women to wear for real life—not just for 22-year-old size-2s to match with a pair of Pradas and wear out club-hopping. This narrow, peaceful shop and studio is lined on both sides with Jill's simple, clean-lined designs, which drape beautifully and accentuate a woman's form without clinging. They're wearable for all ages and many figure types (her small sizes are small enough to fit petites, and her larges generally fit a full-figured size 14). Her clothes are feminine without being frilly, retro-reminiscent but completely modern, understated but utterly stylish. If Jill's clothes sound appealing to you, don't miss her shop—you won't regret it.

Meghan Kinney Studio. 312 E. 9th St. (btw. First and Second aves.). ☎ **212/260-6329.** Subway: 6 to Astor Place.

If Audrey Hepburn were alive today, this is probably where she'd shop. Meghan Kinney specializes in gorgeous, figure-flattering separates with elegantly straight lines in fabrics that cling just a bit, but not too much. Her well-priced clothes transcend constantly changing trends—pieces you buy today are likely to become wardrobe basics for years to come.

Nicolina. 247 W. 46th St. (btw. Broadway and Eighth Ave.). ☎ **212/302-NICO.** Subway: N, R, S, 1, 2, 3, 9 to 42nd St./Times Sq.

This charming and sophisticated shop is a Theater District anomaly. Come for fashionable basics in high-quality natural materials: wide-legged linen pants, flowing A-line and princess-cut dresses in silk and cotton, sweaters from labels like Beyond Threads and Sarah Arizona in fine wools, cotton, and silk. Great accessories, too, plus a small selection of contemporary and vintage gifts. A joy to browse.

Vera Wang. 991 Madison Ave. (at 77th St.). ☎ **212/628-3400.** Subway: 6 to 77th St.

The lady who designed that white frock for Nancy Kerrigan to wear in the 1994 Olympics is still the hottest name in bridal fashions. Vera clothes scads of top stars (particularly petite ones with great figures) on their big day or for the Oscars in her simple, elegant designs. Vera's studio is open by appointment only, so brides-to-be looking for the best should call ahead. If you don't have big bucks, ask about the annual warehouse sale, usually in September.

Attention, ladies: Vera has opened a separate bridesmaids store at 980 Madison Ave., 3rd Floor (☎ **212/628-9898**).

Just Men

Paul Smith. 108 Fifth Ave. (at 16th St.). ☎ **212/627-9770.** Subway: F to 14th St.

This temple of new English fashion is a can't miss. When it comes to menswear that's at once of-the-moment and undisputedly classic, Paul Smith wins the prize. Jackets, suits, pants, shoes (among the handsomest in town), sportswear, and accessories that are super-pricey but worth every cent.

Paul Stuart. Madison Ave. at 45th St. ☎ **212/682-0320.** Subway: S, 4, 5, 6, 7 to 42nd St./Grand Central.

Paul Stuart is a touch more hip and a touch more expensive than Brooks Brothers. Stuart is the quintessential European men's haberdasher—gorgeous fabrics, impeccable tailoring, and high price tags. You'll find everything from suits to weekend wear; there's womenswear too, but I find Paul Stuart to be all about men. This is a way-of-life store for those who subscribe.

Thomas Pink. 520 Madison Ave. (at 53rd St.). ☎ **212/838-1928.** Subway: E, F to Fifth Ave.; 6 to 51st St.

One of London's most revered shirtmakers has set up camp on a prime Madison Avenue corner. This shop specializes in beautifully made presized cotton shirts, crafted from the finest quality twofold pure cotton poplin. While the name Thomas Pink bespeaks tradition to anyone who knows fine shirtmaking, don't expect stuffy: The tailors work in a broad and lively palette, in both classic and modern styles. The huge selection of ties is equally eye-catching, with some of the richest jewel tones I've seen.

Just Kids

If you need the basics, you'll find branches of **Gap Kids** and **Baby Gap** all over town—it's harder to avoid one than to find one. The department stores are also great sources, of course.

Greenstones et Cie. 442 Columbus Ave. (between 81st and 82nd sts.). ☎ **212/580-4322.** Subway: 1, 9 to 79th St.

This store specializes in funky, cute upscale sportswear from such European lines as Kenzo, Miniman, Clayeux, and Petit Boy. Many of the clothes are one-of-a-kind or hand-crafted items, so expect to pay accordingly. Also at 1184 Madison Ave., between 86th and 87th streets (☎ **212/427-1665**).

OshKosh B'Gosh. 586 Fifth Ave. (btw. 47th and 48th sts.). ☎ **212/827-0098.** www.oshkoshbgosh.com. Subway: E, F to Fifth Ave.

Wisconsin's most famous name in fashion has a store decked out with train compartments to display the clothes: infants in the rear, boys on the left, and girls on the right. Prices are affordable, especially for European shoppers who pay upward of $100 for overalls at home. The store gives away size-conversion charts at the center desk/cashier.

Shoofly. 465 Amsterdam Ave. (at 82nd St.). ☎ **212/580-4390.** www.shooflynyc.com. Subway: 1, 9 to 79th St.

This pleasing shop specializes in top-quality clothing, footwear, and accessories for kids from newborns through teens. You'll find lots of distinctive stuff here, including imported lines. The shoe selection, in particular, is terrific, and not too pricey. Also at 42 Hudson St., between Duane and Thomas streets, in TriBeCa (☎ **212/406-3270**).

✪ **Stork Club.** 142 Sullivan St. (btw. Houston and Prince sts.). ☎ **212/505-1927.** Subway: C, E to Spring St.

This super-charming SoHo store overflows with gorgeous one-of-a-kind children's wear from both new designers and the store's own "Stork Club" label. You'll find a wonderful collection of vintage toys, too.

Vintage Clothing

✪ **Allan & Suzi.** 416 Amsterdam Ave. (at 80th St.). ☎ **212/724-7445.** Subway: 1, 9 to 79th St.

Make it past the freaky windows and inside you'll find one of the best consignment shops in the city. Allan and Suzi have specialized in gently worn 20th-century designer wear for well more than a decade now, and their selection is marvelous. Their extensive vintage and contemporary couture collection—which ranges from conservative Chanel to over-the-top Halston, Mackie, and Versace—is so well priced that it's well within reach of the average shopper looking for something extra-glamorous to wear. The wild one-of-a-kind pieces (for ogling only) are worth a look unto themselves.

Argosy. 428 E. 9th St. (btw. First Ave. and Ave. A). ☎ **212/982-7918.** Subway: 6 to Astor Place.

This narrow shop offers a small but utterly pristine collection of '60s and '70s fashions, including an excellent collection of stylish leather jackets. Prices are reasonable considering the quality.

Love Saves the Day. 119 Second Ave. (at 7th St.). ☎ **212/228-3802.** Subway: 6 to Astor Place.

This is the store made famous in Madonna's big film break, *Desperately Seeking Susan* (she bought those groovy boots here). LSD hasn't changed much since, except the prices keep going up. In addition to the big and entertaining collection of tacky vintage clothes, there's another good reason to come: the impressive assortment of Donny and Marie memorabilia and other collectible kitsch.

Metropolis. 43 Third Ave. (btw. 9th and 10th sts.). ☎ 212/358-0795. www.metropolisapparel. com. Subway: 6 to Astor Place.

It's rumored that some of the biggest names in the fashion world scout this clean, orderly vintage shop for street fashion ideas. With good reason, too: Some of the coolest old clothes in the world turn up here, from skater pants and micro-cords to gingham-checked Western shirts perfect for your very own hoedown or hullabaloo.

✪ **Screaming Mimi's.** 382 Lafayette St. (btw. 4th and Great Jones sts.). ☎ **212/ 677-6464.** www.screamingmimisnyc.com. Subway: 6 to Astor Place.

Think you hate vintage shopping? Think again: Screaming Mimi's is as neat and well organized as any high-priced boutique. The clothes are a little pricier than in some competing shops, but it's worth paying for the well-chosen selection and top-notch display. The vintage housewares department offers a cornucopia of kitschy old stuff, and the selection of New York memorabilia is a real hoot. Good accessories, too.

EDIBLES

New York boasts the finest gourmet markets in the world. Below are my favorites, but foodies will also have a ball at **Chelsea Market,** a big, dazzling food mall at 75 Ninth Ave., between 15th and 16th streets (☎ 212/243-5678); and **Fairway,** 2127 Broadway, at 74th Street (☎ **212/595-1888**), an excellent and completely unpretentious gourmet food market down the street from Zabar's (see below). Grand Central now has its own gourmet food hall, **Grand Central Market,** with such pleasing vendors as **Adriana's Caravan** (☎ **212/972-8804;** www.adrianascaravan.com) for exotic spices and **Corrado Bread & Pastry** (☎ **212/599-4321**), carrying loaves and pastries from Bouley Bakery. There's also the **Vinegar Factory,** 431 E. 91st St., between First and York avenues (☎ **212/987-0885**), another high-end food emporium from the Zabar family, this time with a chic uptown vibe.

✪ **Balducci's.** 424 Sixth Ave. (at 9th St.). ☎ **212/673-2600.** www.balducci.com. Subway: A, B, C, D, E, F, Q to W. 4th St. (use 8th St. exit).

Though you'll need a yuppified income to afford anything here, this gourmet grocery is a foodie's dream come true. It's relatively small (the shopping carts are even scaled down) and always packed, but the store overflows with imported foodstuffs; the best and freshest meats, fish, and breads; picture-perfect fruits and veggies, including international exotica like hard-to-find starfruit and enoki mushrooms; and deli, cheese, and dessert counters to die for. The knowledgeable staff manages to keep its collective cool even at the height of the holiday bustle. You can put together a gourmet take-out meal at the prepared foods counter, but I suggest heading to the new **Cafe Balducci,** at Sixth Avenue and West 10th Street (☎ 212/673-6369), where you can order from the extensive selection of sandwiches, salads, and other prepared foods and enjoy your meal at one of the pleasant cafe tables. Balducci is scheduled to open a second market on the Upper West Side in the Phillips Club hotel, 155 W. 66th St., between Broadway and Amsterdam Avenue (☎ 212/835-8800), in mid-2000.

Dean & Deluca. 560 Broadway (at Prince St.). ☎ **212/431-1691.** www.dean-deluca.com. Subway: N, R to Prince St.

This gourmet supermarket is a little too self-consciously hip, but it's hard to argue with quality. In addition to the excellent butcher, fish, cheese, and dessert counters (check out the stunning cakes and the great character cookies) and beautiful fruits and veggies, you'll find a dried fruit and nut bar, a huge coffee bean selection, a gorgeous cut-flower selection, lots of imported waters and beers in the refrigerator case, and a limited but quality selection of kitchenware in back. There's a small cafe up front, too.

Other **cafe-only** locations include a roomy branch at 9 Rockefeller Center, across from the *Today* show studio (☎ 212/664-1363); in the Theater District at the Paramount hotel, 235 W. 46th St., between Broadway and Eighth Avenue (☎ 212/869-6890); and in the Village at 11th Street and University Place (☎ 212/473-1908).

✪ **Zabar's.** 2245 Broadway (at 80th St.). ☎ **212/787-2000.** Subway: 1, 9 to 79th St.

More than any other of New York's gourmet food stores, Zabar's is an institution. This giant deli sells prepared foods, packaged goods from around the world, coffee beans, excellent fresh breads, and much more (no fresh veggies, though). This is the place for lox, and the rice pudding is the best I've ever tasted. You'll also find an excellent selection of cooking and kitchen gadgets on the second floor, and a never-ending flow of Woody Allen film stock characters who shop here daily. Prepare yourself for serious crowds.

BAGELS

No one should visit New York without tasting a real New York bagel. H&H, below, is my (and most New Yorkers') favorite, but for excellent bagels and sit-down service, head to **Ess-A-Bagel** (p. 188) instead.

H&H Bagel. 2239 Broadway (at 80th St.). ☎ **212/595-8003.** www.hhbagels.com. Subway: 1, 9 to 79th St.

H&H is the king of New York bagel makers. Stop in to this bare-bones shop for a piping-hot bagel, so good it needs no accompaniment. If you prefer the traditional toppings—cream cheese, lox, and the like—they're sold in refrigerator cases for take-home use. Other locations: 639 W. 46th St., at Twelfth Avenue, across from the *Intrepid* (☎ 212/595-8000); and 1551 Second Ave., between 80th and 81st streets (☎ 212/734-7441). All locations are open around the clock, so come by for a bagel fix anytime. If you crave more H&H when you get home, call ☎ 800/NY-BAGEL to order; they ship almost anywhere.

CHOCOLATES

Li-Lac Chocolates. 120 Christopher St. (btw. Bleecker and Hudson sts.). ☎ **800/ 624-4784** or 212/242-7374. www.lilacchocolates.com. Subway: 1, 9 to Christopher St.

Li-Lac is one of the few chocolatiers anywhere still making sweets by hand. In business in the same location since 1923, this supremely charming Village shop whips up its chocolate and maple-walnut fudge fresh every day, and it's a fudge-lover's dream come true. If fudge isn't your bag, they also make pralines, caramels, and other hand-dipped chocolates, including specialty sweets for the holidays (hollow bunnies and chocolate eggs for Easter, chocolate Santas for Christmas, and so on). Also at Grand Central Market in Grand Central Terminal (☎ **212/370-4866**).

Richart Design et Chocolat. 7 E. 55th St. (btw. Fifth and Madison aves.). ☎ **212/ 371-9369.** www.richartusa.com. Subway: E, F to Fifth Ave.

Vogue called these sophisticated Lyonnaise sweets "the most beautiful chocolates in the world." Dark-chocolate lovers, in particular, will find themselves in heaven in this jewel box of a store, where the chocolates are displayed like the precious gems they are. They're made from the finest ingredients—Venezuelan Criollo cocoa, Normandy creams, Piedmontese hazelnuts—and flown in from France weekly (daily in busy seasons). Extremely expensive, but per-piece pricing means that everybody can afford to indulge in these marvelous treats.

Teuscher Chocolates of Switzerland. 620 Fifth Ave. (at the Channel Gardens in Rocke-feller Center). www.teuscher.com. ☎ **800/554-0924** or 212/246-4416. Subway: B, D, F, Q to 47th–50th sts./Rockefeller Center.

At $50 a pound, you'd think they were selling gold bouillon. Teuscher makes mints, pralines, and wondrous marzipan, but it's the truffles that folks write home about. Splurge on one or two justifiably famous champagne truffles, and you'll weep with joy. Also at 25 E. 61st St., just east of Madison Avenue (☎ **212/751-8482**).

ELECTRONICS

J&R Music World/Computer World. Park Row (at Ann St., opposite City Hall Park). ☎ **800/221-8180** or 212/238-9100. www.jandr.com. Subway: 2, 3 to Park Place; 4, 5, 6 to Brooklyn Bridge/City Hall.

Midtown may be overrun with electronics dealers, but it's the Financial District's J&R that's the city's top discount computer, electronics, small appliance, and office equipment retailer. The sales staff is knowledgeable but can get pushy if you don't buy at once or know exactly what you want. Don't succumb—take your time and find exactly what you need. Or better yet, peruse the store's copious catalog or extensive Web site, both of which make advance research, mail order, and comparison shopping easy.

Sony Style. 550 Madison Ave. (btw. 55th and 56th sts.). ☎ **212/833-8000.** Subway: E, F to Fifth Ave.

This all-Sony retail store doesn't offer any bargains, but electronics buffs will enjoy perusing the full line of company products. On street level is the gadget store, full of small electronics from Sony PlayStations to bookshelf stereo systems. Downstairs is the "Home Entertainment Lounge," a stylish setting for the complete line of audio components and home-entertainment systems.

GIFTS

If you're looking for a special gift for a creative spirit, be sure to check out the shops that line **East 9th Street** in the East Village; the side streets of **SoHo,** where a good number of unusual boutiques still survive; new **NoLiTa;** and Greenwich Village, especially in the wonderful cadre of one-of-a-kind shops in the **West Village.** See "The Top Shopping Streets & Neighborhoods," earlier in this chapter.

For first-rate Fifth Avenue gifts, don't forget **Tiffany & Co.,** whose upper level boasts wonderful small gifts like money clips, key rings, picture frames, and more, all crafted in signature Tiffany silver or crystal and wrapped in the unmistakable blue box; see "Jewelry & Accessories," below.

An American Craftsman. 790 Seventh Ave. (at 52nd St.) ☎ **212/399-2555.** Subway: 1, 9 to 50th St.

This pleasing shop sells exotic wood bowls and furniture, hand-blown glassware, silver jewelry, and other fine-quality gift items—all, as the name implies, hand-crafted by American artists. Their wooden jewelry box and humidor collection is stunning. Other branches: In the Village at 317 Bleecker St., at Grove St. (☎ 212/727-0841); and 478 Sixth Ave., between 11th and 12th streets (☎ 212/243-0245); and uptown at 1222 Second Ave., at 64th Street (☎ 212/794-3440).

✪ **Avventura.** 463 Amsterdam Ave. (at 82nd St.). ☎ **212/769-2510.** Subway: 1, 9 to 79th St.

Here's the finest outlet for art glass, Italian pottery, and creative tableware in the city. Prices are high, but deservedly so. A delight for gift shoppers and collectors alike.

✪ **Extraordinary.** 251 E. 57th St. (just west of Second Ave.). ☎ **212/223-9151.** Subway: 4, 5, 6 to 59th St.

This warm, friendly gallery–cum–gift shop is well worth going out of your way to discover. Owner J. R. Sanders, an interior designer who has created lauded exhibits at many city museums, has directed his copious talents to assembling a gorgeous and beautifully displayed collection of gifts from around the world. Lacquered crackle–egg shell trays from Vietnam, carved mango bowls from the Philippines, clever rosewood serving utensils camouflaged as tree branches from Africa, creative cheese servers and wine goblets by American glassblowers—all eye candy for those who thrive on whimsy and good design. Best of all, prices are shockingly reasonable—you'd pay twice as much at any other gallery or boutique. Truly extraordinary! *Tip:* Pair your visit with a stop at the Terence Conran Shop (p. 306) or a pint at the British Open pub (p. 352).

✪ **Felissimo.** 10 W. 56th St. (just west of Fifth Ave.). ☎ **800/565-6785** or 212/247-5656. www.felissimo.com. Subway: E, F to Fifth Ave.

This five-floor emporium is the spot for those who love beautiful things. Despite the Italian name, this is the only U.S. outpost of one of Japan's largest mail-order companies. The aesthetic is distinctively Asian, but far from exclusively so—rather, more in the simple, clean-lined, Zenlike display of the gorgeous housewares, accessories, and jewelry. Goods run the gamut from leather-bound picture frames to Moroccan slippers to organic cotton sheets to the perfect pet accessories. Sure, lots of items are pricey, but on my last visit I walked out with a $14 barrette and a $30 set of sake cups, and I was in heaven. Simply fabulous, and a must for shoppers looking for gifts of distinction. There's a wonderful Japanese tearoom on the fourth floor.

Jack Spade. 56 Greene St. (btw. Spring and Broome sts.). ☎ **212/625-1820.** Subway: C, E to Spring St.; N, R to Prince St.

Looking for a gift for the man who has everything? Then head to Jack Spade, which specializes in vintage and new "guy toys." The inventory changes constantly, but expect goodies along the lines of vintage phonographs and microscopes, old maps and globes, cool desk accessories, and the like. This new shop was launched by the husband of Kate Spade, she of chic handbags and paper goods, so you can expect a smart, upmarket collection. Well worth a look.

La Maison Moderne. 144 W. 19th St. (btw. Sixth and Seventh aves.). ☎ **212/691-9603.** Subway: 1, 9 to 18th St.

This lovely little shop is filled with a beautiful, affordable mix of both vintage and contemporary gift items. Lots of care went into assembling this charming Parisian-inspired store, and it shows. My favorite part of the store is the basement, where you'll find one-of-a-kind homewares like hand-crafted velvet pillows and the cutest collection of teapots in town.

Mxyplyzyk. 125 Greenwich Ave. (at 13th St., near Eighth Ave.). ☎ **212/989-4300.** www.mxyplyzyk.com. Subway: A, C, E, 1, 2, 3, 9 to 14th St.

Come to this unpronounceable Village shop for one of the city's coolest and most creative collections of one-of-a-kind housewares, officeware, and gifts. A blast to browse.

HOME FASHIONS & HOUSEWARES

There's a mammoth **Crate & Barrel** at Madison Avenue and 59th Street (☎ **212/308-0011**), and discount superstore **Bed Bath & Beyond** at Sixth Avenue and 18th Street (☎ **212/255-3550**).

The second floor of **Zabar's** (see "Edibles" above) is an excellent source for high-end kitchenware galore, as is **Broadway Panhandler,** at 477 Broome St., between Greene and Wooster in SoHo (☎ **212/966-3434**).

Other excellent bets for home fashions are **Felissimo** (see "Gifts" above), with wonderful tableware and glassware on the third floor; and **Nicole Fahri** (see "Fashions" above), whose basement level has a fabulous home collection with a high-end hunting-lodge-goes-to-Asia look. **Tiffany & Co.** (see "Jewelry," below) stocks classic crystal stemware.

✪ **ABC Carpet & Home.** 888 Broadway (at 19th St.). ☎ **212/473-3000.** www.abccarpet. com. Subway: L, N, R, 4, 5, 6 to 14th St./Union Sq.

This two-building emporium is the ultimate home fashions and furnishings department store. On the west side of the street is the 10-floor home emporium, which is a dream come true for aspiring Martha Stewarts. Shopping ABC has often been compared to taking a fantasy tour of your ancestor's attic: The goods run the gamut from Moroccan mosaic-tile end tables to hand-painted Tuscan pottery to Tiffanyish lamps to distressed bed frames made up with Frette linens to much, much more, all carefully chosen and exquisitely displayed. There's a whole floor of on-the-bolt upholstery fabrics to die for. Prices aren't bad comparatively speaking, but these are high-end goods. Some of the smaller items are quite affordable, though, and their occasional sales yield substantial discounts. In back is the **ABC Parlour Cafe,** serving lunch fare, weekend brunch, tea, and elegant desserts. Across the street is the multifloor carpet store, which boasts a remarkable collection of area rugs in particular.

Fishs Eddy. 889 Broadway (at 19th St.). ☎ **212/420-9020.** www.fishseddy.com. Subway: L, N, R, 4, 5, 6 to 14th St./Union Sq.

What a great idea—selling remainders of kitschy, custom-designed china left over from yesteryear. Ever wanted a dish that *really* says "Blue Plate Special"? Or how about a coffee mug with the terse logo "Cup o' Joe to Go"? The store is Browse Heaven, and prices are low enough. Other items for sale include basic vintage and retro-inspired flatware, heavy crockery bowls, and classic restaurant-supply glassware that can be

Street Shopping

New York has a very active street culture. Along main thoroughfares throughout the city, you'll see street merchants selling everything from fresh fruit to knapsacks to art books to baseball cards. Many are legitimate, licensed vendors, but some aren't. Chances are, if there's a suitcase involved or a blanket that can be rolled up and carted away quickly, or the collection of stuff for sale is a little too eclectic (like it could be the contents of somebody's apartment or a traveler's bag, say), the vendor shouldn't be there.

The museum streets of **West 53rd and 54th** are peppered with vendors selling their own art. Book vendors line Broadway on the **Upper West Side,** especially on weekends. If you encounter a vendor selling just-published hardcover books on the street, chances are they've been stolen. And paperback books sold without covers are considered returned goods and aren't meant for resale. Hawkers with faux Chanel and Prada handbags and "designer" watches are most prolific in **Times Square** and in the **Flatiron District,** particularly along lower Fifth Avenue. The quality is questionable, so don't even think about shelling out more than $20 for a counterfeit watch. **SoHo** is popular with high-end street peddlers, mostly legitimate, hawking hand-crafted silver jewelry, coffee-table books, and their own art, mainly along Prince Street. **St. Marks Place** (8th St.) in the East Village is big on cheap sunglasses and the kind of chunky silver jewelry Marilyn Manson would love.

At the city's immensely popular weekly **outdoor flea markets,** particularly those along 26th Street and Sixth Avenue, you'll find all kinds of stuff, from trash-worthy junk to highly collectible antiques. (See "Antiques & Collectibles" earlier in this section.) Most flea-market vendors are perfectly legitimate, but on occasion you'll run across one that's clearly hawking stolen goods.

When it comes to this type of alternative retail, the best rule of thumb is this: Use your best judgment, and let your conscience be your guide. But if you choose to buy what are clearly stolen goods, keep in mind that you're encouraging this kind of resale with your wallet—and the next set of stuff for sale on the street could be yours.

hard to find in regular stores, like soda-fountain and pint glasses. Also at 2176 Broadway, at 77th Street (☎ **212/873-8819**).

✪ **Galileo.** 37 Seventh Ave. (at 13th St.). ☎ **212/243-1629.** Subway: 1, 2, 3, 9 to 14th St.

This eclectic shop features an excellent mix of contemporary wares and 20th-century vintage pieces. The selection of fine-quality linens and kitchen towels is small but smart. There are usually a few pieces of furniture scattered about, often blond-wood postwar pieces from the likes of Heywood–Wakefield or Paul McCobb. Gorgeous accessories galore, as well as the most pristine selection of vintage glassware I've seen—an excellent collection of tumblers, highballs, cocktails, and more. Registry is available.

Leader Restaurant Equipment & Supplies. 191 Bowery (at Spring St.). ☎ **800/ 666-6888** or 212/677-1982. Subway: 6 to Spring St.

The Bowery is the place to find restaurant-supply-quality kitchenware, and Leader is the best dealer on the block. This big, bustling, friendly shop is a particularly good source for Chinese and Japanese wares—chopsticks, rice and noodle bowls, sushi plates, sake cups, and the like. You'll see a lot of the same styles you'd find at the high-end home stores in SoHo or the Village, but at a fraction of the prices (this is where they buy, too).

Moss. 146 & 150 Greene St. (btw. Houston and Prince sts.). ☎ **212/226-2190.** Subway: N, R to Prince St.

If you have any interest in modern industrial design, don't miss this sleek, brightly lit store. All kinds of everyday objects are reinvented by cutting-edge European designers, from staplers to flatware to shelving units. The products (mostly by European designers) were designed with 21st-century homes in mind, so they're surprisingly utilitarian and space-efficient.

Portico Bed & Bath. 139 Spring St. (btw. Wooster and Greene sts.). ☎ **212/941-7722.** Subway: C, E to Spring St.

After ABC, Portico is my favorite outlet for luxurious linens, ultra-plush towels, waffle-weave robes, and well-designed bath accessories. Also at 584 Broadway at 20th Street in the Flatiron District (☎ **212/473-6662**), and on the Upper West Side at 450 Columbus Ave., between 81st and 82nd streets (☎ **212/579-9500**). There's also a hit-or-miss outlet store at 233 Tenth Ave., at 24th Street (☎ **212/807-8807**).

Pratesi. 829 Madison Ave. (at 69th St.). ☎ **212/288-2315.** www.pratesi.com. Subway: 6 to 68th St./Hunter College.

This excellent Italian linenmaker claims that most of the crowned heads of Europe were conceived on Pratesi linens, so it's bound to be good enough for you and yours. Excellent bathrobes, too.

Terence Conran Shop. 415 E. 59th St. (at First Ave.). ☎ **212/755-9079.** www.conran. com. Subway: 4, 5, 6 to 59th St.

Sir Terence Conran rules the London design and restaurant world, and now he's looking to make new inroads in America with the bold new Bridgemarket complex, housing restaurants (still in the works at press time) and this sleek home shop. It's like an upscale—and, frankly, overpriced—version of IKEA, with lots of sleek contemporary lines and lightweight materials (chrome, blond woods, colorful plastic). Still, he set the tone for affordable contemporary design, and that alone makes this bright, browseable multilevel shop worth a look.

Totem Design Group. 71 Franklin St. (btw. Church St. and Broadway). ☎ **212/925-5506.** www.totemdesign.com. Subway: 1, 9 to Franklin St.

Totem is dedicated to manufacturing and distributing furniture and objects by talented young domestic and international designers. Designs range from minimalist to whimsical to super-swanky, but the threefold theme of form, function, and affordability is common throughout.

JEWELRY & ACCESSORIES

Every big-name international jewelry merchant has a shop on Fifth Avenue in the 50s: **Bulgari,** at no. 730 (☎ **212/315-9000;** www.bulgari.com); royal jeweler **Asprey,** at no. 725 (☎ **212/688-1811**) and in the Carlyle Hotel; ultra-glamorous **Harry Winston,** at no. 718 (☎ **212/245-2000;** www.harrywinston.com); **Cartier,** at no. 653 (☎ **212/753-0111;** www.cartier.com), which also has a new store on Madison Avenue and 69th Street (☎ **212/472-6400**); and, best of all, **Van Cleef & Arpels,** at no. 744 (☎ **212/644-9500**), which also has a boutique at Bergdorf's. Some of the smaller boutique names are on Madison Avenue in the '60s; **Fred Leighton,**

773 Madison Ave., at 66th Street (☎ **212/288-1872**), specializes in magnificent estate jewelry.

Bargain hunters shouldn't miss the **Diamond District,** the nation's leading wholesale gem and jewelry center, on West 47th Street; see "The Top Shopping Streets & Neighborhoods," earlier in this chapter.

Fortunoff. 681 Fifth Ave. (btw. 53rd and 54th sts.). ☎ **800/FORTUNOFF** or 212/758-6660. www.fortunoff.com. Subway: E, F to Fifth Ave.

Despite the high-ticket facade, Fortunoff is a good resource for Swatch watches and a nice place to start pricing classic pieces: gold earrings, necklaces, bracelets, and the like. The styles aren't innovative, but the store tries to keep up an image as a discounter, and prices are low. Great for silver and wedding gifts, too.

Reinstein/Ross. 29 E. 73rd St. (btw. Fifth and Madison aves.). ☎ **212/772-1901.** Subway: 6 to 77th St.

If you're looking for an engagement ring or another piece of finely crafted jewelry but find yourself thoroughly bored with standard settings, check out the unusual designs here. Many of their gold and silver pieces are done with beautiful matte finishes, and they also specialize in uncommon gems. Also at 122 Prince St., between Greene and Wooster, in SoHo (☎ **212/226-4513**).

Robert Lee Morris. 400 W. Broadway (btw. Spring and Broome sts.). ☎ **212/431-9405.** Subway: C, E to Spring St.

Sculptural silver jewelry is this renowned designer's thing, but he's always got something new and original in his SoHo store. He's now working extensively with South Sea pearls in beautiful hues (cream, pink, peach, gray) and other delicate waterstones.

✪ **Stuart Moore.** 128 Prince St. (at Wooster St.). ☎ **212/941-1023.** Subway: N, R to Prince St.

Those interested in sleek, minimal, angular modern design should head for this sizable store, which showcases the works of Stuart Moore and other supremely talented contemporary designers. Ultra-modern, elegant, and simply terrific—I could browse here for hours.

✪ **Tiffany & Co.** 727 Fifth Ave. (at 57th St.). ☎ **212/755-8000.** www.tiffany.com. Subway: N, R to Fifth Ave.

The most famous jewelry store in New York—and maybe the world—deserves all the kudos. This wonderful multilevel store offers a breathtaking selection of jewelry, signature watches, table and stemware, and a handful of surprisingly affordable gift items. I particularly like the whimsical designs, like butterfly brooches and other playful shapes. The store is so full of tourists at all times that it's easy to browse without having any intention of buying. If you do indulge, anything you buy—even a $50 silver bookmark or key chain—comes wrapped in that unmistakable blue box and presented with flair.

Tourneau Time Machine. 12 E. 57th St. (at Madison Ave.). ☎ **212/758-7300.** www.tourneau.com. Subway: N, R to Fifth Ave.

This snazzy three-floor emporium is the one to visit. It's the world's largest watch store, carrying more than 90 brands and 8,000 different styles. The mind-boggling selection runs the gamut from Swatch to Rolex.

LEATHER GOODS, HANDBAGS & LUGGAGE

The big names of European luxury leather goods have their stores on Fifth Avenue in the '50s or Madison Avenue in the '60s. **Hermès,** 11 E. 57th St. (☎ **212/751-3181**), begins a parade of big-name purveyors of luxury leathers from Fifth Avenue to Park Avenue that includes **Prada,** 45 E. 57th St. (☎ 212/308-2332; www.prada.com), and **Louis Vuitton,** 49 E. 57th St. (☎ 212/371-6111; www.vuitton.com). Prada is also at 724 Fifth Ave., between 56th and 57th streets (☎ 212/664-0010), and uptown at 824 Madison Ave. (☎ 212/327-4200); **Prada Sport** is in SoHo at 116 Wooster St. (☎ 212/925-2221). Louis Vuitton is also in SoHo at 114–116 Greene St., at Prince Street (☎ 212/274-9090).

Greenwich Village is the place to go for funkier and more affordable leather looks, especially along Christopher and Bleecker streets in the West Village. Worth seeking out are **Bleecker House,** at 182 Bleecker St., between MacDougal and Sullivan streets (☎ 212/358-1440), for jackets, and the **Village Tannery,** a few doors down at no. 173 (☎ 212/673-5444), for bags, wallets, and organizers.

Coach. 595 Madison Ave. (at 57th St.). ☎ **212/754-0041.** www.coach.com. Subway: N, R to Lexington Ave.; 4, 5, 6 to 59th St.

Traditionally super-preppy, this New York–based bag manufacturer has become more highstyle of late, and the line is all the better for it. Pricey, but the quality is top-notch—these bags last almost forever. Great men's briefcases and new accessory lines, too. Also at 5 World Trade Center (☎ 212/488-0080), and other locations throughout the city.

Crouch & Fitzgerald. 400 Madison Ave. (at 48th St.). ☎ **212/755-5888.** www. corporategifts.com. Subway: 4, 5, 6 to 42nd St.

This long-time specialist in leather goods is an excellent source for the big names in luggage as well as its own top-quality house brands.

kate spade. 454 Broome St. (at Mercer St.). ☎ **212/274-1991.** Subway: N, R to Prince St.

Kate Spade revolutionized the high-end handbag market with her practical yet chic rectangular handbags. They come in a wide range of fabrics and sizes, from pretty seer-suckers to groovy prints to fashionable flannel to basic black, plus a wide range of solids. The daintier evening line is charming, particularly the grosgrain silks.

Manhattan Portage Ltd. Store. 333 E. 9th St. (btw. First and Second aves.). ☎ **212/995-1949.** www.manhattanportageltd.com. Subway: 6 to Astor Place.

Come here for the hippest nylon and canvas carry-alls in town. True to its name, Manhattan Portage manufactures all its bags right in the city, and they're made from hard-wearing materials that can stand up to an urban lifestyle. Popular styles include all-purpose messenger bags, deejay bags, and backpacks in a range of colors from iridescent yellow to camouflage. Manhattan Portage bags are also sold through other outlets, but you're unlikely to find such a complete selection elsewhere.

LOGO STORES

Coca-Cola Fifth Ave. 711 Fifth Ave. (btw. 55th and 56th sts.). ☎ **212/418-9261.** Subway: E, F, N, R to Fifth Ave.

The one that began the Fifth Avenue theme-store invasion. T-shirts, jackets, baseball caps, key chains, glassware—if they can slap a Coke logo on it, it's probably for sale here. You'll also find vintage vending machines—and, of course, Coke.

The Disney Store. 711 Fifth Ave. (at 55th St.). ☎ **212/702-0702.** Subway: E, F to Fifth Ave.

Disney burst onto Manhattan's retail scene with this monster 3-story emporium. You'll find another big branch on 34th Street between Fifth and Sixth avenues (☎ 212/279-9890). The Upper West Side store at Columbus Avenue and 66th Street

(☎ **212/362-2386**) is worth mentioning for its collection of ABC TV souvenirs (the studio is right next door), from Regis and Kathie Lee Ts to goodies spouting those wry black-on-yellow TV IS GOOD messages. Look for a new Times Square location in 2000, too.

Mets Clubhouse Shop. 143 E. 54th St. (btw. Lexington and Third aves.). ☎ **212/ 888-7508.** www.mets.com. Subway: E, F to Lexington Ave.

New York's other favorite baseball team has its very own logo store in Midtown. Stop in for goods galore—baseball caps, T-shirts, posters, Piazza jerseys, '69 Miracle Mets memorabilia, and much more. You can buy regular season game tix here, too.

NBA Store. 666 Fifth Ave. (at 52nd St.). ☎ **212/515-NBA1.** www.nbastore.com. Subway: B, D, F, Q to 47th–50th sts./Rockefeller Center.

For all things NBA and WNBA, head to this three-level mega-store, a multimedia celebration of pro basketball, complete with a bleacher-seated arena for player appearances and signings.

Niketown. 6 E. 57th St. (btw. Fifth and Madison aves.). ☎ **212/891-6453.** Subway: N, R to Fifth Ave.

More multimedia advertorial than sportswear store, Niketown is surprisingly low-key and attractive, with 5 floors of shoes and athletic wear displayed in stark Lucite and polished metal surroundings. "Museum" cases display Sneakers of the Rich and Famous, and everywhere you're assailed by images of celebrity pitchmen and women, with His Airness prevalent above all others, of course (retirement? what retirement?). No sales or bargains here—plan on paying top dollar for the high-style athletic wear. Somebody's gotta pay for this place!

✪ The Pop Shop. 292 Lafayette St. (btw. Houston and Prince sts.). ☎ **212/219-2784.** www.haring.com. Subway: B, D, F, Q to Broadway/Lafayette St.

For affordable and wearable art that makes supercool souvenirs, come to the Pop Shop. This groovy store is chock-full of items based on designs by artist Keith Haring, who died in 1990. T-shirts, posters, calendars, stationery, toys, notebooks, neat transparent backpacks—all sport the vivid primary colors and loopy stick-figure drawings that Haring made famous. Best of all, the Pop Shop is a nonprofit organization, offering continued support to the AIDS-related and children's charities that the young artist championed in life.

Warner Bros. Studio Store. 1 E. 57th St. (at Fifth Ave.). ☎ **212/754-0300.** Subway: N, R to Fifth Ave.

This mega–theme store sits right near both Van Cleef & Arpels and Tiffany—wouldn't Bugs have a field day in those joints! Another three-story shop with cartoon-character everything, including animation cels for sale. There's an equally monolithic branch at 1 Times Square, at 42nd Street and Broadway (☎ **212/840-4040**) as well as one in the World Trade Center (☎ **212/775-1442**).

Yankees Clubhouse Shop. 393 Fifth Ave. (btw. 36th and 37th sts.). ☎ **212/685-4693.** www.yankees.com. Subway: 6 to 33rd St.

For all your Bronx Bombers needs—hats, jerseys, jackets, and so on. Tickets for regular-season home games are also for sale, and there's a limited selection of other New York team jerseys. Also at 110 E. 59th St., between Park and Lexington avenues (☎ **212/758-7844**); and at 8 Fulton St. in the South Street Seaport (☎ **212/ 514-7182**).

MUSEUM STORES

In addition to these standouts, other noteworthy museum shops worth seeking out include the **New York Public Library,** the **Museum for African Art,** the **Jewish Museum,** and the **Museum of American Folk Art;** see chapter 7. There's also a terrific **New York Transit Museum Store,** with lots of nifty transportation-themed gifts, at Grand Central Terminal, in the shuttle passage next to the Station Masters' office (☎ 212/878-0106); the cufflinks made out of vintage subway tokens are just great.

American Craft Museum. 40 W. 53rd St. (btw. Fifth and Sixth aves.). ☎ **212/956-3535.** Subway: E, F to Fifth Ave.

The nation's top showcase for contemporary crafts boasts an impressive collection of crafts in its museum store, too. Come for exquisite handblown glassware, one-of-a-kind jewelry, original pottery, and other artistic treasures, all beautifully displayed.

✪ **Maxilla & Mandible.** 451 Columbus Ave. (btw. 81st and 82nd sts.). ☎ **212/724-6173.** www.maxillaandmandible.com. Subway: B, C to 81st St.

This shop is not affiliated with the American Museum of Natural History, but a visit here makes a good adjunct to your trip to the museum (which is right around the corner). It may look like a freak shop at first glance, but it's really a fascinating natural history emporium. Inside you'll find unusual rocks and shells from around the world, luminescent butterflies in display boxes, even surprisingly affordable real fossils containing prehistoric fish and insects that come with details on their history and where they were excavated. There's also a good variety of natural history–themed toys for the kids.

Metropolitan Museum of Art Store. Fifth Ave. at 82nd St. ☎ **212/570-3894.** www.metmuseum.org. Subway: 4, 5, 6 to 86th St.

Given the scope of the museum itself, it's no wonder that the gift shop is outstanding. Many treasures from the museum's collection have been reproduced as jewelry, china, and other objets d'art. The range of art books is dizzying, and upstairs is an equally comprehensive selection of posters and inventive children's toys. And you don't even have to go uptown to indulge: Other branches can be found on the plaza at Rockefeller Center, 15 W. 49th St. (☎ 212/332-1360); in SoHo at 113 Prince St. (☎ 212/614-3000); and on the mezzanine level at Macy's (☎ 212/268-7266).

✪ **MoMA Design Store.** 44 W. 53rd St. (btw. Fifth and Sixth aves.). ☎ **212/767-1050.** www.moma.org. Subway: E, F to Fifth Ave.; B, D, F, Q to 47th–50th sts./Rockefeller Center.

Across the street from the Museum of Modern Art is this terrific shop, whose stock ranges from museum posters and clever toys for kids to fully licensed reproductions of many of the classics of modern design, including free-form Alvar Aalto vases, Frank Lloyd Wright chairs, and Eames recliners. If these high-design items are out of your reach, there are plenty of more affordable outré home accessories to choose from.

Across the street at the museum, the main gift shop has a stellar collection of gift books, artsy notecards, and the like, all with a modern twist.

MUSIC

Music buffs will find a wealth of new-and-used shops in the West Village. Standouts include **Rebel Rebel,** 319 Bleecker St. (☎ 212/989-0770), for British and Japanese imports and New Wave and glam classics; and **Rockit Scientist,** just off Bleecker at 43 Carmine St. (☎ 212/242-0066), a tiny place with a huge folk and psych collection. **Vinyl Mania,** 60 Carmine St. (☎ 212/924-7223; www.vinylmania.com), and **Sonic Groove,** 41 Carmine St. (☎ 212/675-5172; www.sonicgroove.com), supply the sounds for many of the city's major raves. **Sam Goody,** 390 Sixth Ave. at 8th Street (☎ 212/674-7131), diverges from the mall-store norm with its cutting-edge in-house performance series. Unfortunately, **Bleecker Bob's Golden Oldies,** 118 W. 3rd St. (☎ 212/475-9677), has outlived its legend; it's now a dirty little hole-in-the-wall with lots of worn, badly organized vinyl and a rude staff.

Grungy **St. Marks Place** between Third and Second avenues in the East Village is another great bet. **Smash Records** (☎ 212/473-2200) is a standout, as are **Sounds** (☎ 212/677-3444), the dirt-cheap granddaddy of the St. Marks shops, and **Mondo Kim's** (☎ 212/598-9985; www.kimsvideo.com) for indie music, video, and 'zines.

In the Financial District, **J&R Music World** has a big selection of classical, jazz, and rock, and brand-new releases are almost always on sale; see "Electronics," above, for details.

For musical instruments, see "Times Square & the Theater District" under "The Top Shopping Streets & Neighborhoods," earlier in this chapter.

Academy Records & CDs. 12 W. 18th St. (btw. Fifth and Sixth aves.). ☎ **212/242-3000.** www.academy-records.com. Subway: L, N, R, 4, 5, 6 to 14th St./Union Sq.

This Flatiron District shop has a cool intellectual air that's more reminiscent of a good used-book store than your average used-record store. Academy is always filled with classical, opera, and jazz junkies perusing the extensive and well-priced collection of used CDs and vinyl. In addition to the extensive classical and jazz collection is a variety of other audiophile favorites, from rare '60s pop songsters to spoken word.

✪ **Bleecker St. Records.** 239 Bleecker St. (near Carmine St., just west of Sixth Ave.). ☎ **212/255-7899.** Subway: A, B, C, D, E, F, Q to W. 4th St.

This sizable, well-lit space is great for one-stop shopping. The clean, well-organized CD and LP collections run the gamut from rock, oldies, jazz, folk, and blues to Oi! punk. You'll find lots of imports, collectible, and out-of-print records (including singles), a terrific collection of used CDs, and a mix of casual listeners and serious collectors cruising the bins.

✪ **Colony Record & Tape Center.** 1619 Broadway (at 49th St.). ☎ **212/265-2050.** www.colonymusic.com. Subway: N, R to 49th St.; 1, 9 to 50th St.

This long-lived Theater District shop is housed in the legendary Brill Building, basically the Tin Pan Alley of '50s and '60s pop, where legendary songwriters like Goffin and King and producers like Don Kirschner and Phil Spector crafted the soundtrack for a generation. It's the perfect home for Colony, a nostalgia emporium filled with a pricey but excellent collection of vintage vinyl and new CDs. You'll find a great collection of Broadway scores and cast recordings, plus decades worth of recordings by pop song stylists both legendary and obscure. There's also one of the best collections of sheet music in the city (including some hard-to-find international stuff), and a great selection of original theater and movie posters. You can stock up your in-home karaoke machine here, too.

Footlight. 113 E. 12th St. (btw. Third and Fourth aves.). ☎ **212/533-1572.** www.foot-light.com. Subway: L, N, R, 4, 5, 6 to 14th St./Union Sq.

If you like Colony (above), also check out this dreamy collection of vintage vinyl, strong in jazz and pop vocalists, soundtracks, and show tunes.

Generation Records. 210 Thompson St. (btw. Bleecker and 3rd sts.). ☎ **212/254-1100.** Subway: A, B, C, D, E, F, Q to W. 4th St.

This tidy little store sells mostly CDs and is an excellent source for "import" live recordings. Originally specializing in hardcore, punk, and heavy metal, the new collection upstairs still has a heavy edge but has since diversified appreciably. Downstairs is a well-organized and well-priced used CD selection that's not as picked over as most and runs the genre gamut; there's also a good selection of used LPs. Despite the help's tough look, they're actually quite friendly and helpful.

Jazz Record Center. 236 W. 26th St. (btw. Seventh and Eighth aves.), 8th Floor. ☎ **212/675-4480.** Subway: 1, 9 to 28th St.

Jazz Record Center is *the* place to find rare and out-of-print jazz records. In addition to the extensive selection of CDs and vinyl (including 78s), videos, books, posters, and other memorabilia are available. Prices can be high, as befits the rarity of the stock. Owner Frederick Cohen is extremely knowledgeable, so come here if you're trying to track down something obscure (Cohen does mail-order business as well).

NYCD. 426 Amsterdam Ave. (btw. 80th and 81st sts.). ☎ **212/724-4466.** www.nycd.com. Subway: 1, 9 to 79th St.

This neat, narrow little store is home to one of the city's best collections of used rock CDs thanks to its off-the-beaten-track Upper West Side location. Downtown trollers simply don't make it this far uptown to prune the selection, so it's easy to find lots of top titles among the pickings.

✪ **Other Music.** 15 E. 4th St. (btw. Broadway and Lafayette St.). ☎ **212/477-8150.** www.othermusic.com. Subway: B, D, F, Q to Broadway/Lafayette St.; 6 to Astor Place.

Head to Other Music for the wildest sounds in town. You won't find a major label here (that's what Tower, across the street, is for). This shop focuses exclusively on small international labels, especially those on the cutting edge (you can find records on the Knitting Factory label here). The bizarro runs the gamut from underground Japanese spin doctors to obscure Irish folk; needless to say, the world music selection is terrific. Fascinating and bound to be filled with music you've never heard of. The sales staff really knows their stuff, so ask away.

Throb. 211 E. 14th (btw. Second and Third aves.). ☎ **212/533-2328.** www.throb.com. Subway: L to Third Ave.

Throb is home to CDs and 12-inch vinyls of not-even-close-to-mainstream genres: house, ambient, jungle, drum-and-bass, trance, trip hop. Imports are also big business here. A popular stop for dance-club deejays. Test drive the trippy sounds in a listening booth. You'll also find record bags and T-shirts.

Tower Records. 692 Broadway (at W. 4th St.). ☎ **212/505-1500.** www.towerrecords.com. Subway: N, R to 8th St.; 6 to Astor Place.

As mighty of a chain as it may be, it's hard to complain about Tower. Both the Village location and the Upper West Side branch (2107 Broadway, at 66th St.; ☎ 212/799-2500) are huge multimedia superstores brimming with an encyclopedic collection of music—classical, jazz, rock, world, you name it. The Village location also stocks a very good selection of indie and alternative labels. Just behind it at West 4th and Lafayette is **Tower Books** (☎ 212/228-5100), where you'll find videos, books, and magazines; and the **Tower Clearance Outlet** (☎ 212/228-7317), selling cut-out CDs for a song. Look for in-stores by big names in music, usually advertised in the *Time Out New York* and *Village Voice*.

Virgin Megastore. 1540 Broadway (at 45th St.). ☎ **212/921-1020.** www.virgin.com. Subway: N, R, 1, 2, 3, 7, 9 to Times Sq./42nd St.

Right in the heart of Times Square, this superstore bustles day and night. For the size of it, the selection isn't as wide as you'd think; still, you're likely to find what you're looking for among the two levels of domestic and imported CDs and cassettes. Other plusses are an extensive singles department, a phenomenal number of listening posts, plus a huge video department. There's also a bookstore, a cafe, and a multiplex movie theater, and you can even arrange airfare on Virgin Atlantic with the on-site travel agent. The Union Square location, 52 E. 14th St., at Broadway (☎ **212/598-4666**), is equally hopping. As at Tower, look for a busy schedule of in-stores at both locations.

PAPER & STATIONERY

kate spade paper. 59 Thompson St. (btw. Broome and Spring sts.). ☎ **212/965-8654.** Subway: C, E to Spring St.

The très hip SoHo bag-maker (see "Leather Goods, Handbags & Luggage," above) now sells her own elegantly charming line of preprinted notecards, stationery, organizers, journals, datebooks, photo albums, and the like in this smart little store. Products are covered in the same leathers, nylons, canvases, and silk shantung that her trademark bags wear, and styles change with the season. Great for the stylish gal who hasn't sacrificed pen and paper for a Palm Pilot.

Kate's Paperie. 561 Broadway (btw. Prince and Spring sts.). ☎ **212/941-9816.** www.katespaperie.com. Subway: N, R to Prince St.

Three cheers to Kate's for keeping the art of letter writing alive in our computer age. I could browse for hours among this delightful shop's handmade stationery and wrap, innovative invitations and thank you's, imported notebooks, writing tools, and other creative paper products, including cool paper lampshades. Lovely art cards, too—perfect for writing the folks back home. A joy! The SoHo location is best, but also at 8 W. 13th St., between Fifth and Sixth avenues in the Village (☎ **212/633-0570**), and 1282 Third Ave., between 73rd and 74th streets on the Upper East Side (☎ **212/396-3670**).

SHOES

Designer shoe shops start on **East 57th Street** and amble up **Madison Avenue,** becoming pricier as you move uptown. **SoHo** is an excellent place to search for the latest styles; the streets are overrun with terrific shoe stores. Cheaper copies of the trendiest styles are sold along **8th Street** between Broadway and Sixth Avenue in the Village, which some people call Shoe Row. Most department stores have two sizable shoe departments—one for designer stuff and one for daily wearables. See "The Top Shopping Streets & Neighborhoods" and "The Big Department Stores," earlier in this chapter. For **Niketown,** see "Logo Stores," above.

✪ **Giraudon New York.** 152 Eighth Ave. (btw. 17th and 18th sts.). ☎ **212/633-0999.** www.giraudonnewyork.com. Subway: A, C, E, L to 14th St.

This French designer makes fashionable, well-made street shoes for hip men and women who want something cleanlined and stylish but not too chunky or trendy. Not cheap, but not overpriced—these shoes last forever. Prices run $115 to $200, and sales are excellent.

Kenneth Cole. 95 Fifth Ave. (at 17th St.). ☎ **212/675-2550.** www.kencole.com. Subway: N, R to 23rd St.

Kenneth Cole may be hitting the runway these days with a complete line of stylish clothing, but he'll always be most famous for footwear. An ideal blend of comfort and glamour for both men and women. Great leather jackets and accessories, too. Also at 353 Columbus Ave., near 77th Street (☎ **212/873-2061**); 597 Broadway, just off Houston in SoHo (☎ **212/965-0283**); and street level at Grand Central Terminal, 107 E. 42nd St. (☎ **212/949-8079**).

Jimmy Choo. 645 Fifth Ave. (at 51st St.). ☎ **212/593-0800.** Subway: E, F to Fifth Ave.

Manolo fans should also check out the similarly sexy but slightly trendier styles at this sophisticated three-floor emporium. I've hardly seen shoes displayed more beautifully.

Manolo Blahnik. 31 W. 54th St. (btw. Fifth and Sixth aves.). ☎ **212/582-3007.** Subway: E, F to Fifth Ave.

If you make only one wild and crazy purchase in your life, it may well be a pair of Manolos—wildly sexy women's shoes notorious for the cut and sway of the shoe and the way they shape the leg. Most famous are the catch-me-if-you-can high heels, but there are plenty of flats and low heels, too. Custom shoes in your own fabric are also a possibility. Cinderella never had it so good.

Sacco. 324 Columbus Ave. (btw. 75th and 76th sts.). ☎ **212/799-5229.** www. saccoshoes.com. Subway: B, C to 81st St.

This city chain specializes in mostly Italian-made women's shoes that cross style with supreme comfort. I especially love their fall and winter boots, comfortable enough to carry me around the city on even the most arduous of research days. Lots of terrific basic blacks and browns. Good prices and sales, too. Also at 111 Thompson St., at Prince, in SoHo (☎ **212/925-8010**); 94 Seventh Ave., at 16th, in Chelsea (☎ **212/ 675-5180**); and 2355 Broadway, at 86th (☎ **212/874-8362**).

✪ **Sigerson Morrison.** 242 Mott St. (btw. Houston and Prince sts.). ☎ **212/219-3893.** www.sigersonmorrison.com. Subway: B, D, F, Q to Broadway/Lafayette St.; N, R to Prince St.

Women who love shoes and are willing to pay in the neighborhood of $200 or $250 for something really special should make a beeline for this NoLiTa shop. These fashion-forward originals wow with their immaculate details, bright color palette, and sexy, strappy retro appeal. Worth every penny. You'll also find some of their styles at Bergdorf Goodman and Saks if you don't want to go downtown.

Stapleton Shoe Company. 68 Trinity Place (at Rector St., 3 blocks south of the World Trade Center). ☎ **212/964-6329.** Subway: N, R to Rector St.

If Imelda Marcos had been a man, her first stop would have been this shoe store, right near the American Stock Exchange. Stapleton sells men's brands like Bally, Timberland, and Johnston & Murphy, all at discounts so deep it'll feel like insider trading. The women's branch is **Anbar Shoes,** 93 Reade St., between Church Street and West Broadway (☎ **212/227-0253**).

SPORTING GOODS
For **Niketown,** see "Logo Stores," above.

Eastern Mountain Sports. 611 Broadway (at Houston St.). ☎ **212/505-9860.** Subway: B, D, F, Q to Broadway/Lafayette St.

This one-stop sporting shop is famous for all-weather, high-tech camping, hiking, and climbing gear. This is an excellent, affordable source for Polartec pullovers, waterproof shells, and the like. You'll also find hardware like compasses, cookwear, and Swiss Army knives. Also at 20 W. 61st St., between Broadway and Columbus on the Upper West Side (☎ **212/397-4860**).

Paragon Sporting Goods. 867 Broadway (at 18th St.). ☎ **212/255-8036.** www.paragonsports.com. Subway: L, N, R, 4, 5, 6 to 14th St./Union Sq.

Paragon is an excellent all-purpose sporting goods store. The emphasis here is on equipment and athletic wear for virtually every sport, from tennis to biking to mountain climbing. End-of-the-season sales, especially on sneakers and outdoor clothing, bring serious discounts.

Patagonia. 101 Wooster St. (btw. Prince and Spring sts.). ☎ **212/343-1776.** www.patagonia. com. Subway: N, R to Prince St.; C, E to Spring St.

Expensive though it may be, Patagonia deserves kudos for its commitment to producing efficient and eco-friendly sports and adventure wear—fleece pullovers made from recycled plastic soda bottles, shell jackets in ultra-light weatherproof materials, organic cotton T-shirts. Also on the Upper West Side at 426 Columbus Ave., between 80th and 81st streets (☎ **917/441-0011**).

TOYS

If your kids love to read, don't miss **Books of Wonder** under "Books," above. Vintage collectors should see **Alphaville** and the **Chelsea Antiques Building** under "Antiques & Collectibles."

FAO Schwarz. 767 Fifth Ave. (at 58th St.). ☎ **212/644-9400.** www.fao.com. Subway: N, R to Fifth Ave.

The best-loved toy store in America was designed with an eye for fun: The elevator is shaped like a huge toy soldier, and there are plenty of hands-on displays to keep the little ones occupied for hours. Entire areas are devoted to specific toy makers (Lego, Fisher Price, *Star Wars* action figures, Barbie). You and the kids will find plenty of affordable little gifts to take home as souvenirs (the front-left corner specializes in prewrapped gifts for moms and dads on business trips).

Kidding Around. 60 W. 15th St. (btw. Fifth and Sixth aves.). ☎ **212/645-6337.** Subway: F to 14th St.

This boutique stocks pricey high-quality toys, many imported from Europe. The emphasis is on the old-fashioned—low-tech goodies like puzzles, rocking horses, and tops. One wall is devoted exclusively to tub toys, windups, and other stocking stuffers. Also at 68 Bleecker St., between Broadway and Lafayette (☎ **212/598-0228**).

Penny Whistle. 448 Columbus Ave. (btw. 81st and 82nd sts.). ☎ **800/PWT-TOYS** or 212/873-9090. www.pwt-toys.com. Subway: B, C to 81st St.

The merchandise at this upscale shop is geared toward slightly older kids, and there's a brace of silly doodads that adults will get a kick out of, too. Also at 1283 Madison Ave., at 91st Street (☎ **212/369-3868**).

WINE & SPIRITS

Acker Merrall & Condit Co. 160 W. 72nd St. (btw. Broadway and Columbus aves.). ☎ **212/787-1700.** Subway: 1, 2, 3, 9 to 72nd St.

This attractive little store is the Upper West Side's best wine source. There are no bad bottles here. The careful selection is well displayed, with opinionated cards attached to each bin to help you choose. A supremely knowledgeable staff is on hand for additional assistance.

Astor Wines & Spirits. 12 Astor Place (at Lafayette St.). ☎ **212/674-7500.** www. astoruncorked.com. Subway: 6 to Astor Place.

This large store is the source for excellent values on liquor and wine; their stock is deep, and ranges far and wide. The staff is always willing to recommend a vintage. Astor hosts an excellent slate of regular wine tastings Thursday and Friday from 5 to 8pm and Saturday from 3 to 6pm, often paired with edibles from local restaurants and gourmet shops.

Morrell & Company. 1 Rockefeller Plaza (at 49th St.). ☎ **212/688-9370.** www. winesbymorrell.com. Subway: B, D, F, Q to 47th–50th sts./Rockefeller Center.

One of the leading stockists in America boasts a friendly, helpful staff, and their Fine Wine Division hosts high-profile auctions. Adjacent is the new **Morrell Wine Bar & Cafe** (☎ 212/262-7700), an ideal place to sample the goods in comfort.

Sherry-Lehmann. 679 Madison Ave. (btw. 61st and 62nd sts.). ☎ **212/838-7500.** www.sherry-lehmann.com. Subway: N, R to Lexington Ave.; 4, 5, 6 to 59th St.

Zagat's has called Sherry-Lehmann "the Rolls-Royce" of wine shops, and the readers of *Decanter* magazine just named it best wine merchant in the United States. Their vast inventory is mind-boggling and includes ritzy gift baskets that make luxurious gifts. Service is excellent and free wine tastings are often on hand. Expensive, but the place to come if you're looking for a special bottle.

New York City After Dark

New York's nightlife scene is an embarrassment of riches. There's so much to see and do in this city after the sun goes down that your biggest problem is probably going to be choosing among the many temptations.

There's no way that I can tell you in these pages what's going to be on the calendar while you're in town. So for the latest, most comprehensive nightlife listings, from classic and cutting-edge theater and performing arts to live rock, jazz, and dance club coverage, *Time Out New York* is my favorite weekly source; a new issue hits newsstands every Thursday. The free weekly *Village Voice,* the city's legendary alterna-paper, is available late Tuesday downtown and early Wednesday in the rest of the city. The arts and entertainment coverage couldn't be more extensive, and just about every live music venue advertises its shows here. Another great weekly is *New York* magazine; flip to the "Cue" section at the back for the latest happenings. The *New York Times* features terrific entertainment coverage, particularly in the two-part Friday "Weekend" section. The cabaret, classical music, and theater guides are particularly useful.

Sponsored by the Theatre Development Fund, **NYC/Onstage** (☎ 212/768-1818; www.tdf.org) is a recorded service providing complete schedules, descriptions, and other details on theater and the performing arts. The bias is toward Broadway and Off-Broadway plays, but NYC/Onstage is a good source for chamber and orchestral music (including all Lincoln Center events), dance, opera, cabaret, and family entertainment, too.

Some of your best, most comprehensive and up-to-date information sources for what's going on about town are in cyberspace, of course. For a complete rundown of Web sources, see pp. 38–48 **"Planning Your Trip: An Online Directory."**

In addition to the wealth of choices below, you might want to consider one of the sunset or dinner cruises that circle Manhattan, taking in the twinkling lights of the skyline from all sides. The cruises offered by World Yacht are particularly romantic. See "Harbor Cruises" under "Organized Sightseeing Tours" in chapter 7.

1 All the City's a Stage: The Theater Scene

Nobody does theater better than New York. No other city—not even London—has a theater scene with so much breadth and depth, with so many wide-open alternatives. Broadway, of course, gets the most ink and the most airplay, and deservedly so: Broadway is where you'll find the big stage productions and the moneymakers, from crowd-pleasing warhorses like *Phantom of the Opera* and *Miss Saigon* to phenomenal newer successes like *Cabaret, Chicago,* and *The Lion King.* But today's scene is thriving beyond the bounds of just Broadway—smaller, "alternative" theater has taken hold of the popular imagination, too. With bankable stars on stage, crowds lining up for hot tickets, and hits popular enough to generate major-label cast albums, Off-Broadway isn't just for culture vultures anymore.

Despite this vitality, plays and musicals close all the time, often with little warning—witness the widespread shock (and the huge push to grab up the remaining tickets) that accompanied the announcement of the closing of *Cats,* the longest-running musical on Broadway, in mid-2000. Even the most basic production is expensive to mount, and ticket sales must be robust to keep it in business. So I can't tell you precisely what will be on while you're in town. Before you arrive, or even once you reach town, check the **publications** listed at the start of this chapter or the **Web sites** listed in "Planning Your Trip: An Online Directory" to get an idea of what you might like to see. A useful source is the **Broadway Line** (☎ **888/BROADWAY** or 212/302-4111; www.broadway.org), where you can obtain details and descriptions on current Broadway shows, hear about special offers and discounts, and choose to be transferred to TeleCharge or TicketMaster to buy tickets. There's also **NYC/Onstage** (☎ **212/768-1818;** www.tdf.org), providing the same kind of service for both Broadway and Off-Broadway productions.

Even though I can't guarantee what'll be on stage when you're visiting, the likelihood is good that you'll find lots of large-scale musicals and revivals on Broadway, and more original drama and offbeat musicals on the Off-Broadway stage. If you find new drama on Broadway, it's likely to be the transcontinental transfer of a London stage hit, similar to Yasmina Reza's for-thinking-theatergoers-only *Art* in 1998, and Michael Frayn's Bohr and Heisenberg atomic-science fantasy *Copenhagen* in 2000. If you're coming to see the big hits, chances are extremely good that you'll still find *Les Misérables* at the Imperial and *Phantom* at the Majestic. Kids will be enchanted by Disney's one-two punch of *Beauty and the Beast,* and, if you can get tickets (call now!), *The Lion King.* Off-Broadway is more volatile, but you're likely to still find the ridiculously fun *Blue Man Group: Tubes* at the Astor Place Theatre and the percussion sensation *Stomp!* at the Orpheum Theatre; both are performance art pieces that are more palatable than you'd expect, and have been pleasing kids and grown-ups alike for years now. And I'd pretty much stake my life on the fact that the legendary show *The Fantasticks* will still be alive and kicking at the Sullivan Street Playhouse—it opened on May 3, 1960, and is now the longest-running musical in the world.

Helping to assure the recent success of the New York theater scene has been the presence of A-list Hollywood stars. Kevin Spacey, Whoopi Goldberg, Glenn Close, Holly Hunter, Christian Slater, Patrick Stewart, Quentin Tarantino, Natasha Richardson, Nicole Kidman, Dame Judi Densch, and Liam Neeson are just some of the famous names that have appeared on Broadway marquees in the last few years. In 2000, Jack Wagner made his stage debut in *Jekyll & Hyde,* while Kathie Lee Gifford filled in for Bernadette Peters in *Annie Get Your Gun* (a task Susan Lucci also took on in late '99). And Broadway hasn't been the only call to stage: Uma Thurman, William

Map labels:

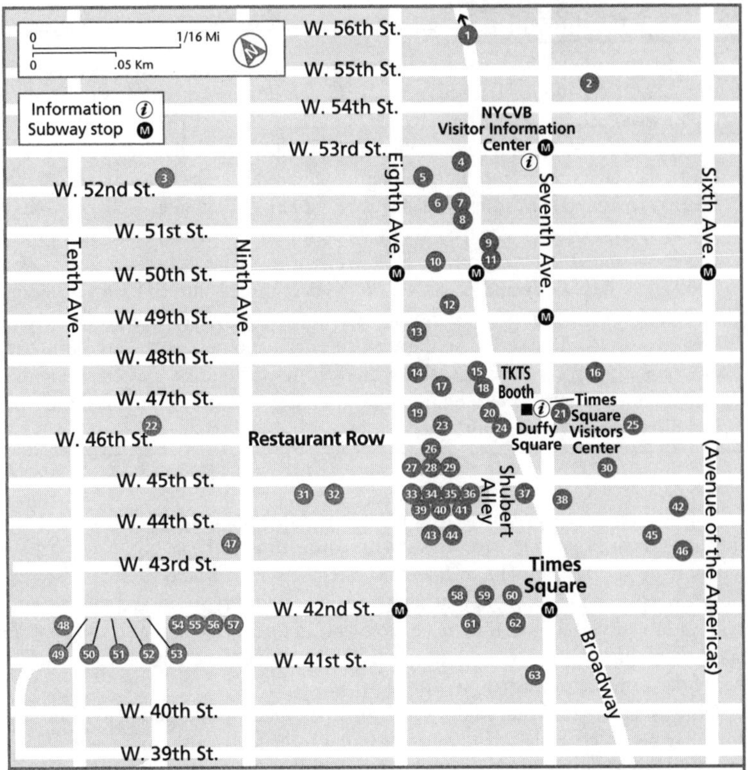

0 — 1/16 Mi
0 — .05 Km

Information ⓘ
Subway stop Ⓜ

W. 56th St.
W. 55th St.
W. 54th St.
W. 53rd St.
W. 52nd St. ③
W. 51st St.
W. 50th St.
W. 49th St.
W. 48th St.
W. 47th St.
W. 46th St. ㉒
W. 45th St.
W. 44th St.
W. 43rd St.
W. 42nd St.
W. 41st St.
W. 40th St.
W. 39th St.

Tenth Ave.
Ninth Ave.
Eighth Ave.
Seventh Ave.
Sixth Ave.
(Avenue of the Americas)
Broadway

NYCVB
Visitor Information
Center Ⓜ ⓘ

TKTS
Booth ⓘ
Times Square Visitors Center
Duffy Square

Restaurant Row
Shubert Alley
Times Square

Ambassador ⑫
American Place ㉕
Belasco ㊷
Biltmore ⑰
Booth ㊱
Broadhurst ㊵
Broadway ④
Brooks Atkinson ⑲
Circle in the Square ⑩
Cort ⑯
Douglas Fairbanks ㊼
Duffy ㉔
Edison ⑳
Ensemble Studio ③
Ethel Barrymore ⑱
Eugene O'Neill ⑬
45th Street ㉛
Ford Center for the Performing Arts ㊺
Gershwin ⑩
Golden ㉝
Harold Clurman ㊷

Helen Hayes ㊹
Intar ㊴
Imperial ㉗
John Houseman ㊾
Judith Anderson �51
Kaufman ㊽
Lamb's ㊺
Longacre ⑭
Lunt-Fontanne ㉓
Lyceum ㉚
Lyric ㊾
Majestic ㊴
Manhattan Theatre Club ②
Mark Hellinger ⑧
Marquis ㉙
Martin Beck ㉜
Minskoff ㊲
Mitzi Newhouse ①
Music Box ㉘
Nat Horne ㊿
Nederlander ㊽
Neil Simon ⑥

New Amsterdam �62
New Victory ㊻
Palace ㉑
Playwright's Horizons �55
Plymouth ㉟
Richard Rodgers ㉖
Roundabout ㊳
Royale ㉞
Samuel Beckett �56
Selwyn �61
South Street �52
St. Clement's ㉒
St. James ㊸
Shubert ㊶
Stardust ⑨
Town Hall ㊻
Village Gate ⑦
Virginia ⑤
Vivian Beaumont ①
Walter Kerr ⑮
WestSide ㊼
Winter Garden ⑪

Worth Seeking Out

Legendary among Off-Broadway theaters is the **Public Theater,** 425 Lafayette St. (☎ **212/260-2400,** or TeleCharge at 212/239-6200 for tickets; www.publictheater. org or www.telecharge.com), the legacy of the late visionary theater producer Joseph Papp. Now under the direction of George C. Wolfe, the Public always draws top talent to the stage with its groundbreaking stagings of Shakespeare's plays—past schedules have featured F. Murray Abraham as Lear and Liev Schreiber as Hamlet—as well as new plays, classical dramas, and solo performances. The Public also produces Broadway shows on occasion, such as *Bring in 'Da Noise, Bring in 'Da Funk* and 2000's *The Wild Party,* and hosts New York's best annual alfresco event, Shakespeare in the Park, each summer (see the "Park It! Shakespeare, Music & Other Free Fun" box, later in this chapter). The theater also offers "Free at Three," a monthly series of free performances, readings, and symposia showcasing new and emerging talent. If that's not enough, it's also home to Joe's Pub (see "Cabaret," later in this chapter). Definitely worth seeking out!

H. Macy, Frances MacDormand, Judith Light, Molly Ringwald, Toni Collette, and Taye Diggs have all earned raves for Off-Broadway runs in the last couple of years. All this star power has brought in lots of theatergoers who would've otherwise stayed home. Keep in mind, though, that stars' runs are often very short, and tickets tend to sell out fast. If you hear that there's a celeb you'd like to see coming to the New York stage, don't put off your travel and ticket-buying plans. (The box office can tell you how long a star is contracted for a role.)

Lastly, keep in mind that while "Off-Broadway" may mean experimental and therefore may be riskier, it doesn't have to mean lower quality in any way. These days, the best Off-Broadway shows don't need to move to Broadway to be legitimized. In fact, in many ways, especially with dramas, being away from Broadway can mean they're freer to be hits without being huge draws. Witness such recent powerhouse hits as Margaret Edson's *Wit; Hedwig and the Angry Inch* (step aside, *Rent*—here's a musical that really rocks!); and the interactive performance-art hit *De La Guarda,* plus the aforementioned long-runners *Blue Man Group* and *Stomp!* And remember—*Rent* is just one of many phenomenons that made its debut Off-Broadway.

THE BASICS

The terms **Broadway, Off-Broadway,** and **Off-Off-Broadway** refer to theater size, pay scales, and other arcane details, not location—or, these days, even star wattage. Most of the Broadway theaters are in Times Square, huddled around the thoroughfare the scene is named for, but not directly on it: Instead, you'll find them dotting the side streets that intersect Broadway, mostly in the mid-40s between Sixth and Eighth avenues (44th and 45th sts. in particular) but running north as far as 53rd Street. There's even a Broadway theater outside Times Square: the Vivian Beaumont in Lincoln Center, at Broadway and 65th Street.

Off-Broadway, on the other hand, is not that exacting an expression. With the increasing popularization of off-the-beaten-track productions, the distinction between Off- and Off-Off-Broadway productions has become fuzzier. Off-Off-Broadway shows tend to be more avant-garde, experimental, and/or nomadic. Off- and Off-Off-Broadway productions tend to be based downtown, but pockets show up in Midtown and on the Upper West Side. Broadway shows tend to keep pretty regular **schedules.**

There are usually eight performances a week: evening shows Tuesday through Saturday, plus matinees on Wednesday, Saturday, and Sunday. Evening shows are usually at 8pm, while matinees are usually at 2pm on Wednesday and Saturday, and 3pm on Sunday. Schedules do vary, however; *Les Misérables,* for instance, also stages a Monday show to accommodate the seemingly endless tourist demand. And times often vary depending on the show's length; the 1999 staging of *The Iceman Cometh* started nightly at 7pm to accommodate the marathon $4^1/_4$-hour running time. Shows usually start right on the dot, or within a few minutes of starting time; if you arrive late, you may have to wait until after the first act to take your seat, which can really be a drag.

Off-Broadway shows tend to follow a similar daily schedule and time clock, but you'll find more variations. Off-Broadway theaters usually stage an additional Sunday evening show. Some, such as the rock musical *Hedwig and the Angry Inch,* also stage 11:30pm shows on Friday and Saturday to accommodate the downtown crowds who could care less about the late hour (this is the exception, not the rule).

Ticket prices for Broadway shows vary dramatically. Expect to pay for good seats; the high end for any given show is likely to be between $60 and $100. The cheapest end of the price range can be as low as $20 or as high as $50, depending on the theater configuration. If you're buying tickets at the very low end of a wide available range, be aware that you may be buying obstructed-view seats. If all tickets are the same price or the range is small, you can pretty much count on all of the seats being pretty good. Otherwise, price is your barometer. Note that legroom can be tight in these old theaters, and you'll usually get more in the orchestra seats.

Off-Broadway and Off-Off-Broadway shows tend to be cheaper, with tickets often as low as $10 or $15. However, seats for the most established shows and those with star power can command prices as high as $50.

Don't let price be a deterrent to enjoying the theater. There are ways to pay less if you're willing to make the effort and be flexible, with a few choices at hand as to what you'd like to see. Read on.

TOP TICKET-BUYING TIPS
BEFORE YOU LEAVE HOME

Phone ahead or go online for tickets to the most successful or popular shows as far in advance as you can—in the case of shows like *The Lion King,* it's never too early.

Buying tickets can be simple, if the show you want to see isn't sold out. You need only call such general numbers as **TeleCharge** (☎ **212/239-6200;** www.telecharge.com), which handles most Broadway and Off-Broadway shows and some concerts; or **TicketMaster** (☎ **212/307-4100;** www.ticketmaster.com), which also handles Broadway and Off-Broadway shows and most concerts. If you're an American Express gold or platinum cardholder, check to see if tickets are being sold through **American Express Gold Card Events** (☎ **800/448-TIKS;** www.americanexpress.com/gce). You'll pay full price just as you would through TeleCharge or TicketMaster, but AmEx has access to blocks of preferred seating that are specifically set aside for gold cardholders, so you may be able to get tickets to a show that's otherwise sold out, or better seats than you would be able to buy through other outlets.

Owned by Cameron Mackintosh (producer behind such megahits as *Cats, Phantom of the Opera, Les Misérables,* and *Miss Saigon*), **Theatre Direct International (TDI)** is a ticket broker that sells tickets to select Broadway and Off-Broadway shows direct to individuals and travel agents. Check to see if they have seats to the shows you're interested in by calling ☎ **800/334-8457** or pointing your Web browser to **www.theatredirect.com**. (Disregard the discounted prices, unless you're buying for a group of 20 or more; tickets are full price for smaller quantities.) Because there's a service charge of $15 per ticket, you'll do a bit better by trying TicketMaster or TeleCharge first; but because they act as a consolidator, TDI may have tickets left for a specific show even if the major outlets don't.

Other reputable ticket brokers include **Keith Prowse & Co. (☎ 800/669-8687** or 914/328-2357; www.keithprowse.com) and **Global Tickets Edwards & Edwards (☎ 800/223-6108)**. For a list of other licensed ticket brokers recommended by the New York Convention & Visitors Bureau, get a copy of the Official NYC Visitor Kit (see "Visitor Information" in chapter 2 for details). All kinds of ticket brokers list ads in the Sunday *New York Times* and other publications, but don't take the risk. Stick with a licensed broker recommended by the NYCVB.

If you don't want to pay a service charge, try calling the **box office** directly. Broadway theaters don't sell tickets over the telephone, but a good number of Off-Broadway theaters do.

Also, before you resort to calling broker after broker to snag tickets to a hot show, consider calling the **concierge** at the hotel where you'll be staying. If you've chosen a hotel with a well-connected concierge, he or she may be able to have tickets waiting for you when you check in—for a premium, of course. For more on this, see "When You Arrive," below.

For details on how to obtain advance-purchase theater tickets at a discount, see **"Reduced-Price Ticket Deals,"** below, or p. 41 of **"Planning Your Trip: An Online Directory."**

WHEN YOU ARRIVE

Once you arrive in the city, getting your hands on tickets can take some street smarts—and failing those, cold hard cash. Even if it seems unlikely that seats are available, always **call the box office** before attempting any other route. Single seats are often easiest to obtain, so people willing to sit apart may find themselves in luck.

You should also try the **Broadway Ticket Center,** run by the League of American Theaters and Producers (the same people behind the Broadway Line, above) at the Times Square Visitors Center, 1560 Broadway, between 46th and 47th streets (open daily from 8am to 8pm). They often have tickets available for otherwise sold-out shows and only charge $4.50 extra per ticket.

Even if saving money isn't an issue for you, check the boards at the **TKTS Booth** in Times Square; more on that under "Reduced-Price Ticket Deals," below.

In addition, your **hotel concierge** may be able to arrange tickets for you. These are usually purchased through a broker and a premium will be attached, but they're usually good seats and you can count on them being legitimate. (A $20 tip to the concierge for this service is reasonable—perhaps even more if the tickets are for an extremely hot show, like *The Lion King*. By the time you've paid this tip, you might come out better by contacting a broker or ticket agency yourself.) If you want to deal with a licensed broker direct, **Global Tickets Edwards & Edwards** has a local office that accommodates drop-ins at 234 W. 44th St., between Seventh and Eighth avenues (☎ 212/398-1432; open Mon–Sat 9am–8pm).

If you buy from one of the **scalpers** selling tickets in front of the theater doors, you're taking a risk. They may be perfectly legitimate—a couple from the 'burbs whose companions couldn't make it for the evening, say—but they could be swindlers passing off fakes for big money. It's a risk that's not worth taking.

One preferred **insiders' trick** is to make the rounds of Broadway theaters at about 6pm, when unclaimed house seats are made available to the public. These tickets—

Good Tickets for a Good Deed

One option for finding hard-to-get tickets is more expensive than most, but good for your self-esteem. **Broadway Cares/Equity Fights AIDS CareTix** program gets producers, theater owners, celebrities, and other Broadway types to donate their coveted house seats to Broadway and Off-Broadway shows. They sell these tickets for double the face value ($120 for a $60 ticket, for example), with the proceeds donated to people living with the disease. Not only do you get what are probably the best seats in the house but 50% of your purchase is tax deductible. Call ☎ **212/ 840-0770,** ext. 229 or 230, for ticket choices, which are limited in number. Ticket requests are taken the month prior to the dates you're interested in on the first day of the month (starting Mar 1 if you're interested in seeing a show in Apr, for instance); mark your calendar if you're trying to snag coveted tix like *The Lion King.* For other shows, call at least 48 hours in advance.

reserved for VIPs, friends of the cast, the press, or other hangers-on—offer great locations and are sold at face value.

Also, note that **Mondays** are often good days to cop big-name show tickets. Though most theaters are dark on that day, some of the most sought-after choices aren't. Locals are at home on the first night of the work week, so all the odds are in your favor. Your chances will always be better on weeknights, or for Wednesday matinees, rather than weekends.

REDUCED-PRICE TICKET DEALS

Your best bet is to try before you go. You may be able to purchase **reduced-price theater tickets** in advance over the phone (or in person at the box office) by joining one or more of the online theater clubs. Membership is free and can garner you discounts of up to 50% on select Broadway and Off-Broadway shows. I like the extensive list of offers that's always available from the **Playbill Club (www.playbillclub.com)** best, but there's no harm in joining more than one. For further details, see p. 38 **"Planning Your Trip: An Online Directory."**

The Theatre Development Fund runs a Student Mailing List that offers deep discounts—up to 75%—on theater tickets to college students, as well as a Student Voucher Program that allows students to attend four programs at participating Off-Broadway theaters and dance and music groups for $28. Visit the Web site (www.tdf.org) for details and to sign up.

Broadway shows—even blockbusters—sometimes have a limited number of cheaper tickets set aside for students and seniors, and they may even be available at the last minute; call the box office direct to inquire. *Rent* has offered all kinds of bargains to keep younger theatergoers coming.

The best deal in town on same-day tickets for both Broadway and Off-Broadway shows is at the ✪ **Times Square Theatre Centre,** better known as the **TKTS booth** run by the nonprofit Theatre Development Fund in the heart of the Theater District at Duffy Square, 47th Street and Broadway (open 3 to 8pm for evening performances, 10am to 2pm for Wed and Sat matinees, from 11am on Sun for all performances). Tickets for that day's performances are usually offered at half price, with a few reduced only 25%, plus a $2.50 per ticket service charge. Boards outside the ticket windows list available shows; you're unlikely to find certain perennial or outsize smashes, but most other shows turn up. Only cash and traveler's checks are accepted (no credit cards). There's often a huge line, so show up early for the best availability and be prepared to wait—but frankly, the crowd is all part of the fun. If you don't care much what you see and you'd just like to go to a show, you can walk right up to the window later in the day and something's always available.

Run by the same group and offering the same discounts is the **TKTS Lower Manhattan Theatre Centre,** on the mezzanine of 2 World Trade Center (open Mon–Fri 11am–5pm, Sat 11am–3:30pm). All the same policies apply. The advantages to coming down here are that the lines are generally shorter, your wait is sheltered indoors, and matinee tickets are available the day before, so you can plan ahead.

Note: Reconstruction is set to begin on the Duffy Square booth in mid-2000. It's a good idea to call NYC/Onstage at ☎ **212/768-1818** and press "8" for the latest TKTS information, as there may be a temporary relocation or other news you should be aware of before you head to the booth.

Many theater shows, particularly long-running shows like *Miss Saigon* and *Cats,* offer special coupons that allow you to buy two-fers—two tickets for the price of one certain nights of the week. You can find these coupons at many places in the city: hotel lobbies, in banks, even at restaurant cash registers. A guaranteed bet is the Times Square Visitors Center, 1560 Broadway, between 46th and 47th streets. They're also likely to be available at the new NYCVB Visitor Information Center at 810 Seventh Avenue, between 52nd and 53rd streets.

2 Opera, Classical Music & Dance

While Broadway is the Big Apple's greatest hit, many other performing arts also flourish in this culturally rich and entertainment-hungry town.

In addition to the listings below, check out what's happening at **Carnegie Hall** and the **Brooklyn Academy of Music,** two of the most respected—and enjoyable—multifunctional performing arts venues in the city. The marvelous **92nd Street Y** also regularly hosts events that are worth considering. I've listed the operatic and symphonic companies housed at **Lincoln Center** below; also check the center's full calendar for all offerings. See "Major Concert Halls & Landmark Venues," later in this chapter.

OPERA

New York has grown into one of the world's major opera centers. The season generally runs from September to May, but there's usually something going on at any time of year.

In addition to the choices below, serious fans might want to see what's on from the **New York Grand Opera** (☎ 212/245-8837; www.csis.pace.edu/newyorkgrandopera), which often puts on free productions at Central Park's Summerstage in July and August as well as workshop programs throughout the year at Carnegie Hall's Weill Recital Hall and the company's own hall.

Amato Opera Theatre. 319 Bowery (at 2nd St.). ☎ **212/228-8200.** www.amato.org. Subway: F to Second Ave.; 6 to Bleecker St.

This cozy, off-the-beaten-track venue is run by husband-and-wife team Anthony and Sally Amato and functions as a showcase for talented young American singers. The intimate 100-plus-seat house celebrated its 50th season last year amid a rising reputation and increasing ticket sales. The staple is full productions of Italian classics—Verdi's *La Traviata,* Puccini's *Madame Butterfly,* Bizet's *Carmen,* with an occasional Mozart tossed in—at great prices ($25). Performances, usually held on Saturday and Sunday, now regularly sell out, so it's a good idea to reserve 3 weeks in advance.

Note for parents: Once a month at 11:30am on Saturday, "Opera in Brief" offers fully costumed, kid-length versions of the classics interwoven with narration so Mom and Dad have a palatable forum in which to introduce the little ones to opera. At $15 or so per ticket, these matinee performances are wallet-friendly, too.

Metropolitan Opera. At the Metropolitan Opera House, Lincoln Center, Broadway and 64th St. ☎ **212/362-6000.** www.metopera.org. Subway: 1, 9 to 66th St.

Tickets can cost a small fortune (anywhere from $25 to $275), but for its full productions of the classic repertory and schedule packed with world-class grand sopranos and tenors, the Metropolitan Opera ranks first in the world. Millions are spent on fabulous stagings, and the venue itself is a wonder of acoustics. Among the notable events of the 2000–01 calendar are the Met Opera premiere of Busoni's *Doktor Faust;* new productions of Beethoven's *Fidelio* and Verdi's *Il Trovatore;* and revivals of such crowd-pleasers as Bizet's *Carmen,* Verdi's *Aida* and *La Traviata,* Puccini's *La Bohème,* and Wagner's *Parsifal.*

To guarantee that its audience understands the words, the Met has outfitted the back of each row of seats with screens for subtitles—translation help for those who want it, minimum intrusion for those who don't. James Levine continues his role as the brilliant and popular conductor of the orchestra.

New York City Opera. At the New York State Theater, Lincoln Center, Broadway and 64th St. ☎ **212/870-5570** (information or box office), or 212/307-4100 for TicketMaster. www.nycopera.com or www.ticketmaster.com. Subway: 1, 9 to 66th St.

The New York City Opera is a superb company, with a delightful duality to its approach: It not only attempts to reach a wider audience than the Metropolitan with its more "human" scale and significantly lower prices ($20 to $95) but it's also committed to adventurous premieres, newly composed operas, the occasional avant-garde work, American musicals presented as operettas (Stephen Sondheim's *Sweeney Todd* is an example), and even obscure works by mainstream or lesser-known composers. Its mix stretches from the "easy" works of Puccini and Verdi and Gilbert & Sullivan to the more challenging oeuvres of the likes of Arnold Schönberg and Philip Glass.

New York Gilbert and Sullivan Players. At Symphony Space, Broadway and 95th St. ☎ **212/864-5400** or 212/769-1000. www.nygasp.org. Subway: 1, 2, 3, 9 to 96th St.

If you're in the mood for light-hearted operetta, try this lively company, which specializes in Gilbert and Sullivan's 19th-century English comic works. Tickets are affordable, in the $25 to $50 range. The annual calendar generally runs from October through April and includes four shows a year.

CLASSICAL MUSIC

Just about any grand interpreter of the classics comes through New York. The many concert halls throughout the city—ranging from the expected, like **Carnegie Hall,** to the surprising, like the **92nd Street Y**—book the best of the best (see "Major Concert Halls & Landmark Venues," later in this chapter).

Bargemusic. At the Fulton Ferry Landing (just south of the Brooklyn Bridge), Brooklyn. ☎ **718/624-2083** or 718/624-4061. www.bargemusic.org. Subway: 2, 3 to Clark St.

Many thought Olga Bloom peculiar, if not deranged, when she transformed a 40-year-old barge into a chamber music concert hall. More than 20 years later, Bargemusic is an internationally renowned recital room boasting more than 100 first-rate chamber music performances a year. Olga trawls from the pool of visiting musicians who love the chance to play in such an intimate setting, so the roster regularly includes highly respected international musicians as well as local stars like violinist Cynthia Phelps.

There are three shows per week, on Thursday and Friday evenings at 7:30pm and Sunday afternoon at 4pm. The musicians perform on a small stage in a cherry-paneled, fireplace-lit room accommodating 130. Bloom herself places name cards on the red-velvet cushions of the folding chairs, and there's bread and cheese, cakes and cookies, and wine and coffee. The barge may creak a bit and an occasional boat may speed by, but the music rivals what you'll find in almost any other New York concert hall—and the panoramic view through the glass wall behind the stage can't be beat. Neither can the price: Tickets are just $23 ($20 seniors, $15 students). Reserve well in advance.

The Juilliard School. 60 Lincoln Center Plaza (Broadway at 65th St.). ☎ **212/769-7406.** www.juilliard.edu. Subway: 1, 9 to 66th St.

During its school year, the nation's premier music education institution sponsors about 550 performances of the highest quality—at the lowest prices. With most concerts free and $15 as a maximum ticket price, Juilliard is one of New York's greatest cultural bargains. Though most would assume that the school presents only classical music concerts, Juilliard also offers other music as well as drama, dance, opera, and interdisciplinary works. The best way to find out about the wide array of productions is to call, visit the school's Web site (click on CALENDAR OF EVENTS), or consult the bulletin board in the building's lobby. Note that tickets are required even for free performances. Watch for master classes and discussions open to the public featuring celebrity guest teachers.

✪ **New York Philharmonic.** At Avery Fisher Hall, Lincoln Center, Broadway at 65th St. ☎ **212/875-5030,** or Center Charge at 212/721-6500 for tickets. www.newyorkphilharmonic. org. Subway: 1, 9 to 66th St.

Symphony-wise, you'd be hard-pressed to do better than the New York Philharmonic.

Last-Minute Ticket-Buying Tips

Most seats at New York Philharmonic performances are sold to subscribers, with just a few left for the rest of us. But there are still ways to get tickets. Periodically, a number of same-day orchestra tickets are set aside at the philharmonic, and sold first thing in the morning for $25 a pop (maximum 2). They usually go on sale at 10am weekdays, 1pm Saturday (noon if there's a matinee). And when subscribers can't attend, they may turn their tickets back to the theaters, which then resell them at the last moment. These can be in the most coveted rows of the orchestra. Ticket holders can donate unwanted tickets until curtain time, so tickets that are not available first thing in the morning may become available later in the day. The hopeful form "cancellation lines" 2 hours or more before curtain time for a crack at returned tickets on a first-come, first-served basis. Senior/student/disabled rush tickets may be available for $10 (maximum 2) on concert day, but never at Friday matinees or Saturday evening performances. To check availability for all performances, call Audience Services at ☎ **212/875-5656.**

Note that Lincoln Center's **Alice Tully Hall** (where the Chamber Music Society performs and other concerts are held), the **Metropolitan Opera,** the **New York City Opera,** and **Carnegie Hall** offer similar last-minute and discount programs (the **New York City Ballet** offers Student Rush tickets only). It makes sense to call the box office first to check on same-day availability before heading to the theater—or, if you're willing to risk coming away empty-handed, be there at opening time for first crack.

The country's oldest orchestra is under the strict but ebullient guidance of music director Kurt Masur. Since he has announced that he'll retire in 2002, don't miss this final chance to see the master conductor leading his orchestra. Highlights of the 2000–01 season include the Mendelssohn Festival in October; Bach's *Christmas* oratorio performed by the Choir of St. Thomas Church, the Leipzig choir Bach himself once directed; and Dame Felicity Lott singing an all-Strauss program conducted by Mazur to close the season in June. Other celebrity soloists scheduled throughout the year include violinist Sarah Chang, pianist Helen Huang, and world-renowned cellist Yo-Yo Ma. There's a summer season in July, when themed classics brighten the hall, as well as summer concerts in Central Park that are worth checking into.

Tickets range from $13 to $110; opt for a rush-hour concert or a matinee for the lowest across-the-board prices. If you can afford it—and if the tickets are available—it's well worth it to pay for prime seats. The acoustics of the hall are such that, at the midrange price points, I prefer the second tier (especially the boxes) over the more expensive rear orchestra seats. Go cheap if you have to; you're sure to enjoy the program from any vantage.

DANCE

In general, dance seasons run September to February and then March to June, but there's almost always something going on. In addition to the major troupes below, some other names to keep in mind are the **Brooklyn Academy of Music,** the **92nd Street Y Tisch Center for the Arts, Radio City Music Hall,** and **Town Hall** (see "Major Concert Halls & Landmark Venues," below).

For particularly innovative works, see what's on at the **Merce Cunningham Studio,** 55 Bethune St. (☎ 212/691-9751; www.merce.org); the **Dance Theater Workshop,** in the Bessie Schönberg Theater, 219 W. 19th St. (☎ 212/691-8500 or 212/924-0077; www.dtw.org), a first-rate launching pad for nearly a quarter-century; and **Danspace Project,** at St. Mark's Church, 131 E. 10th St. (☎ 212/674-8194), whose performances lean toward the seriously avant-garde.

Also see if Pilar Rioja is performing at the **Repertorio Español,** Gramercy Arts Theater, 138 E. 27th St. (☎ 212/889-2850; www.repertorio.org). She introduces new works as well as performing flamenco favorites, and her classic Spanish movements mix awesome restraint with explosive passion.

In addition to regular appearances at City Center (below), the **American Ballet Theatre** (www.abt.org) takes up residence at Lincoln Center's Metropolitan Opera House (☎ 212/362-6000) for 8 weeks each spring; their recent reinterpretation of *Swan Lake* caused quite a stir. The same venue also hosts such visiting companies as the Kirov, Royal, and Paris Opéra ballets.

City Center. 131 W. 55th St. (btw. Sixth and Seventh aves.). ☎ 877/581-1212 or 212/581-1212. www.citycenter.org. Subway: B, N, Q, R to 57th St.; B, D, E to Seventh Ave.

Modern dance usually takes center stage in this Moorish dome-topped performing arts palace. The companies of Merce Cunningham, Martha Graham, Paul Taylor, Alvin Ailey, Twyla Tharp, the Dance Theatre of Harlem (celebrating its 30th year this season), and the American Ballet Theatre are often on the calendar. Don't expect cutting edge—but do expect excellence. Sight lines are terrific from all corners, and a new acoustical shell means the sound is pitch-perfect.

✪ **Joyce Theater.** 175 Eighth Ave. (at 19th St.). ☎ 212/242-0800. www.joyce.org. Subway: C, E to 23rd St.; 1, 9 to 18th St.

Housed in an old art deco movie house, the Joyce has grown into one of the world's greatest modern dance institutions. You can see everything from Native American ceremonial dance to Maria Benites Teatro Flamenco to the innovative works of Pilobolus to the Martha Graham Dance Company. In residence annually is Eliot Feld's ballet company, Ballet Tech, which WQXR radio's Francis Mason called "better than a whole month of namby-pamby classical ballets." The Joyce now has a second space, **Joyce SoHo,** at 155 Mercer St., between Houston and Prince streets (☎ 212/431-9233), where you can see rising young dancers and experimental works in the intimacy of a 70-seat performance space.

✪ **New York City Ballet.** At the New York State Theater at Lincoln Center, Broadway and 64th St. ☎ **212/870-5570.** www.nycballet.com. Subway: 1, 9 to 66th St.

Highly regarded for its unsurpassed technique, the New York City Ballet is the world's best. The company renders with happy regularity the works of two of America's most important choreographers: George Balanchine, its founder, and Jerome Robbins. Under the direction of Ballet Master in Chief Peter Martins, the troupe continues to expand its repertoire and performs to a wide variety of classical and modern music. The cornerstone of the annual season is the Christmastime production of *The Nutcracker,* for which tickets usually become available in early October. Ticket prices for most events run $16 to $72.

3 Major Concert Halls & Landmark Venues

Apollo Theatre. 253 W. 125th St. (btw. Adam Clayton Powell and Frederick Douglass blvds.). ☎ **212/749-5838.** Subway: 1, 9 to 125th St.

Built in 1914, the Apollo had its heyday in the 1930s, when Count Basie, Duke Ellington, Ella Fitzgerald, and Billie Holiday were on the bill. By the 1970s, it had fallen on hard times, but a 1986 restoration breathed new life into the historic Harlem landmark. Today the Apollo is again internationally renowned for its African-American acts of all musical genres, from hip-hop acts to B.B. King to Wynton Marsalis's "Jazz for Young People" events. Wednesday's "Amateur Night at the Apollo" is a loud, fun-filled night that draws in young talents from all over the country with high hopes of making it big (a very young Lauryn Hill started out here—and didn't win!).

✪ **Brooklyn Academy of Music.** 30 Lafayette Ave., Brooklyn. ☎ **718/636-4100.** www. bam.org. Subway: B, M, N, R to Pacific Ave.; D, Q, 2, 3, 4, 5 to Atlantic Ave.

BAM is the city's most renowned contemporary arts institution, presenting cutting-edge theater, opera, dance, and music. Offerings have included historically informed presentations of baroque opera by William Christie and Les Arts Florissants; pop opera from Lou Reed; Marianne Faithfull singing the music of Kurt Weill; dance by Mark Morris and Mikhail Baryshnikov; the Philip Glass ensemble accompanying screenings of *Koyannisqatsi* and Lugosi's original *Dracula;* the Royal Dramatic Theater of Sweden directed by Ingmar Bergman; and many more experimental works by both renowned and lesser-known international artists as well as visiting companies from all over the world.

Of particular note is the **Next Wave Festival,** from September through December, this country's foremost showcase for new experimental works (see the "New York City Calendar of Events" in chapter 2). The new **BAM Rose Cinemas** show first-run independent films, and there's free live music every Thursday, Friday, and Saturday night at **BAMcafé,** which can range from atmospheric electronica from coronetist Graham Haynes to radical jazz from the Harold Rubin Trio to the tango band Tanguardia! ($10 food minimum).

There's no need to take the subway if you're coming from Manhattan's East Side. Shuttle service departs from the Whitney Museum at Philip Morris, 120 Park Ave. (at

42nd St.), 1 hour prior to curtain; the fare is $5 each way. Call for details.

✪ **Carnegie Hall.** 881 Seventh Ave. (at 57th St.). ☎ **212/247-7800.** www.carnegiehall. org. Subway: B, N, Q, R to 57th St.

Perhaps the world's most famous performance space, Carnegie Hall offers everything from grand classics to the music of Ravi Shankar. The 2,804-seat main hall welcomes visiting orchestras from across the country and the world. Many of the world's premier soloists and ensembles give recitals. The legendary hall is both visually and acoustically brilliant; don't miss an opportunity to experience it if there's something on that interests you.

There's also the intimate 284-seat **Weill Recital Hall,** usually used to showcase chamber music and vocal and instrumental recitals. Carnegie Hall has also reclaimed an ornate underground concert hall, occupied by a movie theater for 38 years, and is in the process of turning it into an intermediate-size third stage. For last-minute ticket-buying tips, see the feature on p. 326.

✪ **Lincoln Center for the Performing Arts.** 70 Lincoln Center Plaza (at Broadway and 64th St.). ☎ **212/546-2656.** www.lincolncenter.org. Subway: 1, 9 to 66th St.

New York is the world's premier performing arts city, and Lincoln Center is its premier institution. Whenever you're planning an evening's entertainment, check the offerings here—which can include opera, dance, symphonies, jazz, theater, film, and more, from the classics to the contemporary. Lincoln Center's many buildings serve as permanent homes to their own companies as well as major stops for world-class performance troupes from around the globe.

Resident companies include the following: The **Chamber Music Society of Lincoln Center** (☎ 212/875-5788; www.chamberlinc.org), performs at Alice Tully Hall or the Daniel and Joanna S. Rose Rehearsal Studio, often in the company of such high-caliber guests as Anne Sofie Von Otter and Midori. The **Film Society of Lincoln Center** (☎ 212/875-5600; www.filmlinc.com) screens a daily schedule of movies at the Walter Reade Theater, and hosts a number of important annual film and video festivals as well as the Reel to Real program for kids, pairing silent screen classics with live performance. **Jazz at Lincoln Center** (☎ 212/875-5299; www. jazzatlincolncenter.org) is led by the incomparable Wynton Marsalis, with the orchestra usually performing at Alice Tully Hall; the new "Jazz at the Penthouse" program, where great jazz pianists like Ellis Marsalis and Tommy Flanagan play in a spectacular candlelit setting overlooking the Hudson River, is the hottest ticket in town. **Lincoln Center Theater** (☎ 212/362-7600; www.lct.org) consists of the Vivian Beaumont Theater, a modern and comfortable venue with great sight lines that has been home to much good Broadway drama, and the Mitzi E. Newhouse Theater, a well-respected Off-Broadway house that has also boasted numerous theatrical triumphs. Past seasons have included excellent productions of Tom Stoppard's *Arcadia, Carousel* in revival, and David Hare's one-man show, *Via Dolorosa.* For details on the **Metropolitan Opera,** the **New York City Opera,** the **New York City Ballet,** the **Juilliard School,** the phenomenal **New York Philharmonic,** and the **American Ballet Theatre,** which takes up residence here every spring, see "Opera, Classical Music & Dance," earlier in this chapter.

Most of the companies' **major seasons** run from about September or October to April, May, or June. **Special series** like Great Performers and the new American Songbook, showcasing classic American show tunes, help round out the calendar. Indoor and outdoor events are held in warmer months: Spring blooms with the **JVC Jazz Festival;** July sees **Midsummer Night's Swing** with partner dancing, lessons, and music on the plaza; **Mostly Mozart** attracts talents like Alicia de Larrocha and André Watts; the 3-year-old **Lincoln Center Festival** celebrates the best of the performing arts;

Park It! Shakespeare, Music & Other Free Fun

As the weather warms, New York culture comes outdoors to play.

Shakespeare in the Park, held at Central Park's Delacorte Theater, is by far the city's most famous alfresco arts event. Organized by the late Joseph Papp's Public Theater, the schedule consists of two summertime productions, usually one of the Bard's plays and a revival (such as 1997's restaging of the 1944 musical *On the Town*). Productions usually feature big names and range from traditional interpretations (Andre Braugher as an armor-clad *Henry V*) to avant-garde presentations (Morgan Freeman, Tracey Ullman, and David Alan Grier in *Taming of the Shrew* as a Wild West showdown). Patrick Stewart's role as Prospero in *The Tempest* a few years back was so popular that the show was propelled onto Broadway for an award-winning run. The theater itself, next to Belvedere Castle near 79th Street and West Drive, is a dream—on a beautiful starry night, there's no better stage in town. Tickets are given out free on a first-come, first-served basis (two per person), at 1pm on the day of the performance at the theater. The Delacorte might have 1,881 seats, but each is a hot commodity, so people generally line up on the baseball field next to the theater about 2 to 3 hours in advance (even earlier if a big box-office name is involved). You can also pick up same-day tickets between 1 and 3pm at the Public Theater, at 425 Lafayette St., where the Shakespeare Festival continues throughout the year. For more information, call the Public Theater at ☎ **212/539-8500** or the Delacorte at ☎ **212/861-7277,** or go online at **www.publictheater.org**.

With summer also comes the sound of music to Central Park, where the **New York Philharmonic** and the **Metropolitan Opera** regularly entertain beneath the stars; for the current schedule, call ☎ **212/360-3444,** 212/875-5709, or 212/362-6000, or visit **www.lincolncenter.org**.

The most active music stage in the park is **SummerStage,** at Rumsey Playfield, midpark around 72nd Street, which has featured everyone from the Godfather of

Lincoln Center Out-of-Doors is a series of free alfresco music and dance performances in August and September; the **New York Film Festival,** and more. Check the "Calendar of Events" in chapter 2 or Lincoln Center's Web site to see what special events will be on while you're in town.

Tickets for all performances at Avery Fisher and Alice Tully halls can be purchased through **CenterCharge** (☎ **212/721-6500**) or online at www.lincolncenter.org (click on BOX OFFICE & SCHEDULE in the upper-right corner). Tickets for all Lincoln Center Theater performances can be purchased thorough **TeleCharge** (☎ **212/239-6200;** www.telecharge.com). Tickets for New York State Theater productions (New York City Opera and Ballet companies) are available through **Ticket-Master** (☎ **212/307-4100;** www.ticketmaster.com), while tickets for films showing at the Walter Reade Theater can be bought via **Movie Phone** (☎ **212/777-FILM;** www.777film.com; the theater code is 954). For last-minute ticket-buying tips, see the feature on p. 326.

Lincoln Center is normally home to the **New York Public Library for the Performing Arts** (☎ **212/870-1630**), but the collection is currently pieced out to disparate locations as the library undergoes renovations; call or check **www.nypl.org** for location information.

Soul, James Brown, to the angel poet of punk, Patti Smith. Recent offerings have included concerts by Hugh Masekela, Sugarhill Gang, the Jon Spencer Blues Explosion, and Marianne Faithfull; and "Viva, Verdi!" festival performances by the New York Grand Opera; cabaret nights; and more. The season usually lasts from mid-June to early August. Tickets aren't usually required (some big-name shows charge for admission, such as Lyle Lovett in the summer of '99); however, donations are warmly accepted. For the latest performance info, call the SummerStage hotline at ☎ **212/360-2777** or visit **www. summerstage.org**.

Central Park may be the most happening park in town, but the calendar of free events heats up throughout the city's parks in summertime. You can find out what's happening by calling ☎ **888/NY-PARKS** or 212/360-3456, or pointing your Web browser to **www.ci.nyc.ny.us/html/dpr**.

A full slate of free concerts (Philip Glass and Robert Fripp have been among recent performers), modern and classical dance performances, family events, and more are regularly offered year-round in Winter Garden and on the Plaza of the **World Financial Center** (☎ **212/945-0505;** www.worldfinancialcenter.com) in Battery Park City. Events are regularly held at the **South Street Seaport** (☎ **212/732-7678;** www.southstseaport.org) indoors at Pier 17 in winter, outdoors on Pier 16 in summer.

Additionally, most of the city's top museums offer free music and other programs after regular hours on select nights. The **Metropolitan Museum of Art** has an extensive slate of offerings each week, including live classical music and cocktails on Friday and Saturday evenings. There's lots of fun to be had at others as well, including the **Museum of Modern Art** and the **Brooklyn Museum of Art,** which hosts the remarkably eclectic **First Saturday** program monthly. For details, see the museum listings in chapter 7.

Offered daily, 1-hour **guided tours** of Lincoln Center tell the story of the great performing arts complex, and even offer glimpses of rehearsals; call ☎ 212/875-5350.

Madison Square Garden. On Seventh Ave. from 31st to 33rd sts. ☎ **212/465-MSG1.** www.thegarden.com. Subway: A, C, E, 1, 2, 3, 9 to 34th St.; B, D, F, G, N, R to Herald Square.

Kiss, The Who, Springsteen, Tina Turner, Lauryn Hill, and other monsters of rock and pop regularly fill this 20,000-seat arena, which is also home to the Knicks, the Rangers, and the WNBA's Liberty. A cavernous concrete hulk, it's better suited to sports than to concerts, or in-the-round events such as the Ice Capades, Ringling Bros. Barnum & Bailey Circus, or the International Cat Show. End up in the back for the Smashing Pumpkins, and you'd better bring binoculars.

You'll find far better sight lines at the **Theater at Madison Square Garden,** an amphitheater-style auditorium with 5,600 seats that has also played host to some major pop stars, from Barbra Streisand to Oasis. Watch for possible annual stagings of *The Wizard of Oz,* which has starred Roseanne and Eartha Kitt in past productions; *A Christmas Carol,* with Roger Daltrey as Scrooge; and family shows such as *Sesame Street Live.*

The box office is located at Seventh Avenue and 32nd Street. Or you can purchase tickets through **TicketMaster** (☎ 212/307-7171; www.ticketmaster.com).

◯ 92nd Street Y Tisch Center for the Arts. 1395 Lexington Ave. (at 92nd St.). ☎ **212/ 996-1100.** www.92ndsty.org. Subway: 4, 5, 6 to 86th St.; 6 to 96th St.

This generously endowed community center offers a phenomenal slate of top-rated cultural happenings, from classical to folk to jazz to world music to cabaret to lyric theater and literary readings. Just because it's the "Y," don't think this place is small potatoes: Great classical performers—Isaac Stern, Janos Starker, Nadja Salerno-Sonnenberg—give recitals here. In addition, the full concert calendar often includes luminaries such as Max Roach, John Williams, and Judy Collins; Jazz at the Y from Dick Hyman and guests; the longstanding Chamber Music at the Y series; the classical Music from the Jewish Spirit series; and regular cabaret programs. The lectures and literary readings calendar is unparalleled, with featured speakers ranging from Lorne Michaels to David Halberstam to Tim Koogle (CEO of Yahoo!) to Katie Couric to Susan Sontag to Charles Frazier to the Reverend Jesse Jackson to . . . the list goes on and on. The poetry center calendar has included V. S. Naipaul, E. L. Doctorow, and James Earl Jones reading from *American Slave Narratives*. There's a regular schedule of modern dance, too, through the Harkness Dance Project. Best of all, readings and lectures are usually priced between $12 and $20 for nonmembers (although select lectures can be priced as high as $30), dance is usually $15 to $20, and concert tickets generally go for $25 to $35—half or a third of what you'd pay at comparable venues.

Radio City Music Hall. 1260 Sixth Ave. (at 50th St.). ☎ **212/247-4777,** or 212/307-7171 for TicketMaster. www.radiocity.com or www.ticketmaster.com. Subway: B, D, F, Q to 49th–50th sts./Rockefeller Center.

This stunning 6,200-seat art deco theater, with interior design by Donald Deskey, opened in 1932. After an extensive renovation in 1999, legendary Radio City continues to be a choice venue, where the theater alone adds a dash of panache to any performance. Star of the Christmas season is the **Radio City Music Hall Christmas Spectacular,** starring the legendary Rockettes. Visiting pop chart-toppers, from Luis Miguel to Radiohead, also perform here. Thanks to perfect acoustics and uninterrupted sight lines, there's hardly a bad seat in the house. The theater also hosts dance performances, family entertainment, and a number of annual awards shows—such as the Essence Awards, the GQ Man of the Year Awards, and anything MTV is holding in town—so this is a good place to celeb-spot on show nights.

Town Hall. 123 W. 43rd St. (btw. Sixth and Seventh aves.). ☎ **212/840-2824,** or 212/307-4100 for TicketMaster. www.the-townhall-nyc.org or www.ticketmaster.com. Subway: N, R, S, 1, 2, 3, 7, 9 to 42nd St./Times Sq.; B, D, F, Q to 42nd St.

This intimate landmark theater—a National Historic Site designed by McKim, Mead & White—is blessed with outstanding acoustics, making it an ideal place to enjoy many kinds of performances, including theater, dance, lectures, drama, comedy, film, and pop and world music. The calendar regularly includes such offerings as American tap and Brazilian tango exhibitions; Native American music and global rhythms; comedy from the Kids in the Hall Reunion Tour or Bill Maher; live tapings of "A Prairie Home Companion" with Garrison Keillor; lectures by luminaries such as Marianne Williamson and Frank Gehry; concerts by the likes of Martina McBride, David Sandborn, or the reunited Blondie; symphony, opera, and ballet companies from around the world; and much more. The grade is extremely steep, so unless Lurch sits in front of you, fellow audience members shouldn't block your view.

4 Live Rock, Jazz, Blues & More

I discuss the top venues, both large and small, below. But there are far more than these, and new ones are popping up all the time. For the latest, be sure to check the publications discussed at the opening of this chapter as well as the online sources outlined in **"Planning Your Trip: An Online Directory."**

LARGER VENUES

For coverage of **Madison Square Garden,** the **Theater at MSG,** and **Town Hall,** see "Major Concert Halls & Landmark Venues," above.

Beacon Theatre. 2124 Broadway (at 74th St.). ☎ **212/496-7070.** www.livetonight.com. Subway: 1, 2, 3, 9 to 72nd St.

This pleasing midsize Upper West Side venue—a 1928 art deco movie palace with an impressive lobby, stairway, and auditorium seating about 2,700—hosts mainly pop music performances. Featured acts have ranged from street-smart pop diva Sheryl Crow to befuddled Beach Boy Brian Wilson. You'll also find such special events as the bodybuilding "Night of Champions" on the mix-and-match calendar.

Hammerstein Ballroom. At the Manhattan Center, 311 W. 34th St. (btw. Eighth and Ninth aves.). ☎ **212/564-4882.** Subway: A, C, E to 34th St./Penn Station.

In the past couple of years, this midsize venue has become one of the city's most popular rock stages, hosting such acts as Sonic Youth, Everything But the Girl, Robbie Williams, and Jonny Lang and Chris Whitley on a double bill. Oasis and Marilyn Manson both debuted their last American tours here, and Fatboy Slim hosted a fabulous deejay party on his first American tour. The sound system is very good, and the stage is mounted high enough that sight lines are decent even from the main floor. The side balconies are always reserved for VIPs, but the main balcony level, graded for good views and boasting comfortable theater-style seating, is usually open to regular Joes and Janes like us. However, you have to have a mezzanine-level ticket to gain access, so request one when you're buying if you want one (there's usually no cost difference). Otherwise, you'll end up on the general-admission, standing-room-only floor, which some (not me!) prefer.

Roseland. 239 W. 52nd St. (btw. Broadway and Eighth Ave.). ☎ **212/777-6800** or 212/247-0200. www.roselandballroom.com or www.livetonight.com. Subway: C, E, 1, 9 to 50th St.

This old warhorse of a venue, a 1919 ballroom gone to seed, has been under threat of the wrecking ball for years now. Everybody has played at this too-huge-for-its-own-good general-admission hall, from Marc Anthony to Fiona Apple to Busta Rhymes to Smashmouth to Rage Against the Machine to Jeff Beck. Bands who tend to inspire mosh pits like to book here (think Nine Inch Nails, the Offspring), since there's plenty of space for slamming and surfing at the front of the stage. Thankfully, there's also lots of room to steer clear and still enjoy the show. Advance tickets can be purchased at the Irving Plaza box office (see p. 334) without a service charge. Take a moment on your way through the lobby to check out the cases memorializing Roseland's postwar heydays as the city's premier dance hall. Ballroom dancing still takes place Sunday from 2:30 to 11pm; admission is $11.

MID-SIZE & MULTIGENRE VENUES

Also see what's on at the stellar **Joe's Pub** (p. 340), a top-flight cabaret that hosts intimate shows by pop acts.

Ticket-Buying Tips

Tickets for events at all larger theaters as well as at Hammerstein Ballroom, Roseland, Irving Plaza, S.O.B.'s, and Tramps can be purchased through **TicketMaster** (☎ 212/307-7171; www.ticketmaster.com).

Advance tickets for an increasing number of shows at smaller venues—including CBGB's (and CB's 313 Gallery), Bowery Ballroom, Mercury Lounge, and the Knitting Factory—can be purchased through **Ticketweb** (☎ 212/269-4TIX; www. ticketweb.com). Do note, however, that Ticketweb sells out in advance of actual ticket availability. Just because Ticketweb doesn't have tickets left for an event doesn't mean it's completely sold out, so be sure and check with the venue directly.

Even if a show is sold out doesn't mean you're out of luck. There's usually a number of people hanging around at show time trying to get rid of extra tickets for friends who didn't show, and they're usually happy to pass them off for face value. You'll also see professional scalpers, who are best avoided—it doesn't take a rocket scientist to tell the difference. Be aware, of course, that all forms of resale are illegal.

The Bottom Line. 15 W. 4th St. (at Mercer St.). ☎ **212/228-7880** or 212/228-6300. www.bottomlinecabaret.com. Subway: N, R to Astor Place; A, B, C, D, E, F, Q to W. 4th St.

The Bottom Line built its reputation by serving as a showcase for the likes of Bruce Springsteen and the Ramones, and it remains one of the city's most well-respected venues. With table seating, wait service, decent burgers and fries, and a no-smoking policy, it's one of the city's most comfortable, too. The Bottom Line is renowned for its excellent sound and bookings of the best rock and folk singer/songwriters in the business. Loudon Wainwright, Marshall Crenshaw, Robyn Hitchcock, Lucinda Williams, June Carter Cash, Jimmy Webb, Emmylou Harris, Tower of Power, and David Johansen (and alter-ego Buster Poindexter, natch) are among the many artists who make this their favored venue for area appearances. There are usually two shows nightly.

✪ Bowery Ballroom. 6 Delancey St. (at Bowery). ☎ **212/533-2111.** www.boweryballroom. com. Subway: F, J, M, Z to Delancey St.

New in 1998, this marvelous space is run by the same people behind the pleasing Mercury Lounge (see below). The Bowery space is bigger, accommodating a crowd of 500 or so, and even better. The stage is big and raised to allow good sight lines from every corner. The sound couldn't be better, and art deco details give the place a sophistication that doesn't come easy to general-admission halls. My favorite spot is on the balcony, which has its own bar and seating alcoves. This place is quickly becoming a favorite with alt-rockers like Vic Chesnutt, Travis, Cracker, Shudder to Think, and the marvelous Toshi Reagon, as well as more established acts (Warren Zevon, Neil Finn, Patti Smith), who thrive in an intimate setting. Save on the service charge by buying advance tickets at Mercury's box office.

Irving Plaza. 17 Irving Place (1 block west of Third Ave. at 15th St.). ☎ **212/777-1224** or 212/777-6800. www.irvingplaza.com. Subway: L, N, R, 4, 5, 6 to 14th St./Union Sq.

This high-profile midsize music hall is the prime stop for national-name rock bands that aren't quite big enough yet (or anymore) to sell out Hammerstein, Roseland, or the Beacon. Think Shawn Mullins ("Lullaby"), Lit, the Reverend Horton Heat, Kenny Wayne Shepherd, Cowboy Junkies, Cheap Trick. From time to time, big-name artists also perform—Bob Dylan and Trent Reznor have both played "secret" shows here. All in all, a very nice place to see a show, with a well-elevated stage and lots of open space even on sold-out nights. There's an upstairs balcony that offers unparalleled views, but come early for a spot.

The Knitting Factory. 74 Leonard St. (btw. Broadway and Church St.). ☎ **212/ 219-3006.** www.knittingfactory.com. Subway: 1, 9 to Franklin St.

New York's premier avant-garde music venue has four separate spaces, each showcasing performances ranging from experimental jazz and acoustic folk to spoken-word and poetry readings to out-there multimedia works. Regulars who use the Knitting Factory as their lab of choice include former Lounge Lizard John Lurie; around-the-bend experimentalist John Zorn; guitar gods Vernon Reid, Eliot Sharp, and David Torn; innovative sideman (to Tom Waits and Elvis Costello, among others) Marc Ribot; and television's Richard Lloyd. (If these names mean nothing to you, chances are good that the Knitting Factory is not for you.) The schedule is peppered with edgy star turns from the likes of Yoko Ono, Taj Mahal, Faith No More's Mike Patton, and Lou Reed. There are often two show times a night in the remarkably pleasing main performance space, so it's easy to work a show around other activities. The Tap Bar offers an extensive list of microbrews and free live music, often soundtracking obscure silent films.

(MOSTLY) ROCK CLUBS

In addition to the choices below, rock fans on the hunt for diamonds in the rough might also want to see what's on at folk rock's legendary **Bitter End,** 147 Bleecker St. in the Village (☎ 212/673-7030; www.bitterend.com); **Brownie's,** in the East Village at 169 Ave. A, between 10th and 11th streets (☎ 212/420-8392; www.browniesnyc. com), which gets points for quantity with its nightly jam-packed lineup; punk rock's **Continental,** 25 Third Ave., at St. Mark's Place (☎ 212/529-6924; www. nytrash.com/continental), where artists like Joey Ramone and Spacehog occasionally surface among the unknowns; and, from former Dictators frontman Dick Manitoba, **Manitoba's,** 99 Ave. B., between 6th and 7th streets (☎ 212/982-2511), an easygoing East Village hangout where country-pop faves Beat Rodeo have a steady Monday gig that's well worth checking out.

✪ **Arlene Grocery.** 95 Stanton St. (btw. Ludlow and Orchard sts.). ☎ **212/358-1633.** www.arlene-grocery.com. Subway: F to Second Ave.

Live music is always free at this Lower East Side club, which boasts a friendly bar and a good sound system. Arlene Grocery primarily serves as a showcase for hot bands looking for a deal or promoting their self-pressed record. On occasion, bigger names like Mark Eitzel and Milla Jovovich take the stage to exercise their chops, but it's far more likely that the act on stage will be brand new to you. Still, there's little risk involved thanks to the no-cover policy and bookers who know what they're doing. The crowd is an easygoing mix of club-hoppers, rock fans looking for a new fix, and industry scouts looking for new blood.

Cafe Wha? 115 MacDougal St. (btw. Bleecker and 3rd sts.). ☎ 212/254-3706. Subway: A, B, C, D, E, F, Q to W. 4th St.

You'll find a carefree crowd dancing in the aisles of this casual basement club just about any night of the week. From Wednesday through Sunday, the stage features the house's own Wha Band, which does an excellent job of cranking out crowd-pleasing covers of familiar rock-and-roll hits from the '70s, '80s, and '90s; comedians from sister club the Comedy Cellar warm the crowd on Friday and Saturday. Monday night is the hugely popular Brazilian Dance Party, while Tuesday night is Vintage Funk

Night. Expect to be surrounded by lots of Jersey kids and out-of-towners on the weekends, but so what? You'll be having as much fun as they are. Reservations are accepted.

CBGB. 315 Bowery (at Bleecker St.). ☎ **212/982-4052,** or 212/677-0455 for CB's 313 Gallery. www.cbgb.com. Subway: F to Second Ave.; 6 to Bleecker St.

Don basic black, not because you'll be doing the right thing fashionwise but because you'll leave without visible residue. The original downtown rock club has seen better days, but no other spot is so rich with rock-and-roll history. This was the launching pad for New York punk and New Wave: the Ramones, Blondie, the Talking Heads, Television, the Cramps, Patti Smith, Stiv Bators and the Dead Boys—everybody got started here. These days, you've probably never heard of most acts performing here. Never mind—CB's still rocks. Expect loud and cynical, and you're unlikely to come away disappointed. Come early if you have hopes of actually seeing the stage.

More today than yesterday is **CB's 313 Gallery,** a welcome spin-off that showcases alternative art on the walls and mostly acoustic singer/songwriters on stage. Same goes for CB's new **downstairs lounge,** which has a more cerebral alt edge to its sounds. Within striking distance of the history, but much more pleasant all the way around.

The Cooler. 416 W. 14th St. (btw. Ninth Ave. and Washington St.). ☎ **212/229-0785.** www.thecooler.com. Subway: A, C, E to 14th St.; L to Eighth Ave.

A former meat locker in the heart of the Meat-Packing District has been transformed into this marvelously moody alt music club with a discriminating taste for the experimental—anything goes, as long as it's good. Offerings run the gamut from reggae, roots, and punk rock to club parties, electronica, and video art; artists can range from Afrika Bambaataa to the acid-jazz Groove Collective to proto-hippies Royal Trux to astrological crooner Harvey Sid Fisher (as seen on *The Daily Show*) to any number of local boy Thurston Moore's numerous side projects (when he isn't busy with Sonic Youth, of course). Deejay nights range from ambient to 100% hip-hop. There's no sign, so look for the metal doors and the staircase leading to the subterranean entrance. Advance tickets can be purchased at X-Large, 267 Lafayette St. (at Prince Street) in SoHo.

Fez Under Time Cafe. 380 Lafayette St. (at Great Jones St.). ☎ **212/533-2680.** www.feznyc.com. Subway: 6 to Bleecker St.

You have to reserve a seat a few days ahead for the wildly popular Thursday night Mingus Big Band, when the low-ceilinged basement performance space is filled with the cool sounds of jazz. The rest of the week brings an eclectic live music-and-performance art mix, which can range from Combustible Edison to esoteric local acts to fun lounge-lizardy tributes to acts like Queen, ABBA, and the Monkees from Loser's Lounge. The stage is fronted by tightly packed picnic-style tables and a few coveted booths. Time Cafe's pleasing, well-priced menu is served during performances (see chapter 6). I would love this sophisticated space if it were just better ventilated; if you need to escape the rampant cigarette smoke, head upstairs to the relaxing lounge and bar with an *Arabian Nights* ambience.

☻ Mercury Lounge. 217 E. Houston St. (at Essex St./Ave. A). ☎ **212/260-4700.** www.mercuryloungenyc.com. Subway: F to Second Ave.

The Merc is everything a top-notch live music venue should be: unpretentious, extremely civilized, and outfitted with a killer sound system. The rooms themselves are nothing special: a front bar and an intimate back-room performance space with a low stage and a few tables along the wall. The calendar is filled with a mix of accomplished local rockers and national acts like P.O.D. and Art Alexakis from Everclear. The crowd is grown-up and easygoing. The only downside is that it's consistently packed thanks to the high quality of the entertainment and all-around pleasing nature of the experience.

Rodeo Bar. 375 Third Ave. (at 27th St.). ☎ **212/683-6500.** www.rodeobar.com. Subway: 6 to 28th St.

Here's New York's oldest—and finest—honky-tonk. Hike up your Wranglers and head those Fryes inside, where you'll find longhorns on the walls, peanut shells underfoot, and Tex-Mex on the menu. But this place is really about the music: urban-tinged country, foot-stompin' bluegrass, swinging rockabilly, Southern-flavored rock. Bigger names like Brian Setzer and up-and-comers on the tour circuit like Hank Williams III occasionally grace the stage, but regular acts like Dixieland swingers the Flying Neutrinos and the retro-rocking Camaros usually supply free music, keeping the urban cowboys plenty happy. A 10-gallon hat full o' fun.

Wetlands. 161 Hudson St. (at Laight St.). ☎ **212/386-3600,** or 212/978-0838 for upcoming show info. www.wetlands-preserve.org. Subway: A, C, E, 1, 9 to Canal St.

Now celebrating its 11th year, this environmentally conscious club isn't just for Deadheads anymore. Sure, Phish is worshiped by most of the crowd and you'll still find Haight–Ashbury scenesters like Jorma Kaukonen on the schedule every once in a while, but the club's musical focus has really broadened in recent years. Wetlands regularly offers hip-hop, soul, global funk, ska, and other groovy world music in addition to mind-bending jazz, indie, and roots rock. A terrific venue.

JAZZ, BLUES, LATIN & WORLD MUSIC

Be aware that a night at a top-flight jazz club can be expensive. Cover charges can vary dramatically—from as little as $10 to as high as $65, depending on who's taking the stage—and there's likely to be an additional two-drink minimum (or a dinner requirement, if you choose an early show). Call ahead so you know what you're getting into; reservations are also an excellent idea at top spots.

For those of you who like your jazz with an edge, see what's on at the **Knitting Factory** (p. 335). Trad fans should also consider the Thursday Mingus Big Band Workshop at **Fez Under Time Cafe** (p. 336). Those wearing their dancing shoes should check out the Brazilian Mondays and Vintage Funk Tuesdays at **Cafe Wha?** (p. 335) and the nightly parties at the **Greatest Bar on Earth,** where Monday is dedicated to funk, Thursday to Latin music, and Friday and Saturday nights to swing (p. 00). There's also world-beat jazz every Friday and Saturday from 5 to 8pm in the rotunda at the **Guggenheim Museum;** see chapter 7.

Additionally, the Lower East Side's **Tonic,** 107 Norfolk St., between Delancey and Rivington (☎ 212/358-7503), has a downstairs lounge that has blossomed into quite the avant-garde jazzerie. Swing is a nightly affair at **Swing 46,** a jazz and supper club on the Theater District's Restaurant Row at 349 W. 46th St. (☎ **212/262-9554**), where even first-timers can join in the fun; free swing lessons are offered nightly at 9:15pm. Blues fans should also look into the new **Tribeca Blues,** 16 Warren St., between Broadway and Church Street (☎ **212/766-1070**). What's more, look for the massive (550-seat) **B.B. King Blues Room** to open up in the new E-Walk complex, on 42nd Street between Seventh and Eighth avenues, just before the end of 2000.

And don't forget **Jazz at Lincoln Center,** the nation's premier forum for the traditional and developing jazz canon; see "Major Concert Halls & Landmark Venues," earlier in this chapter.

Birdland. 315 W. 44th St. (btw. Eighth and Ninth aves.). ☎ **212/581-3080.** www. birdlandjazz.com. Subway: A, C, E to 42nd St.

This legendary club abandoned its distant uptown roost in 1996 for a more convenient Midtown nest, where it has established itself once again as one of the city's premier jazz spots. While the legend of Parker, Monk, Gillespie, and other bebop pioneers still holds sway, this isn't a crowded, smoky joint of yesteryear. The big room is spacious, comfy, and classy, with an excellent sound system and top-notch talent roster any night of the week. Expect lots of accomplished big bands and jazz trios, plus occasional appearances by stars like Tito Puente, Pat Metheny, and Dave Brubeck. You can't go wrong with the regular Sunday night show, starring Chico O'Farrell's smokin' Afro-Cuban Jazz Big Band. The Southern-style food is even pretty good.

✪ **Blue Note.** 131 W. 3rd St. (at Sixth Ave.). ☎ **212/475-8592.** www.bluenote.net. Subway: A, B, C, D, E, F, Q to W. 4th St.

The Blue Note attracts the biggest names in jazz to its intimate setting. Those who've played here include just about everyone of note: Lionel Hampton, Dave Brubeck, Ray Charles, B.B. King, Manhattan Transfer, Dr. John, George Duke, Roberta Flack, Chaka Khan, and the superb Oscar Peterson. Dizzy Gillespie even celebrated his 81st birthday here. The sound system is excellent, and every seat in the house has a sight line to the stage. A night here can get expensive, but how often do you get to enjoy jazz of this caliber? There are two shows per night, and dinner is served; also consider a Sunday brunch or matinee show.

Chicago B.L.U.E.S. 73 Eighth Ave. (btw. 13th and 14th sts.). ☎ **212/924-9755.** Subway: A, C, E, L to 14th St.

Here's the best blues joint in the city, with a genuine Windy City flair. The contrived decor makes the place feel more theme park than roadhouse, but the music is the real thing. Kick back on the comfortable couches for some of the best unadulterated blues around, which can include big names like Buddy Miles and Lonnie Brooks.

✪ **Iridium.** 44 W. 63rd St. (at Columbus Ave., below the Merlot Bar & Grill). ☎ **212/582-2121.** www.iridiumjazz.com. Subway: A, B, C, D, 1, 9 to Columbus Circle; 1, 9 to 66th St.

This well-respected and snazzily designed basement boîte across from Lincoln Center books accomplished acts that play crowd-pleasing standards and transfixing new compositions. The Les Paul Trio still plays every Monday night, and other top-notch performers who often appear include the Nicholas Payton Quintet, McCoy Tyner and Bobby Hutcherson, and the excellent Jazz Messengers. In addition to just-fine cuisine from the upstairs restaurant, there's an extensive wine list.

The Jazz Standard. 116 E. 27th St. (btw. Park Ave. South and Lexington Ave.). ☎ **212/576-2232.** www.jazzstandard.com. Subway: 6 to 28th St.

Kudos to the Jazz Standard, where both the food and music meet all expectations: This is the only combination restaurant/jazz club to be awarded two stars by the *New York Times.* You can order the highly regarded New American cuisine in both the airy street-level dining room (known as 27 Standard) and the spacious basement jazz lounge. Boasting a sophisticated retro-speakeasy vibe, the Jazz Standard is one of the city's largest jazz clubs, with well-spaced tables seating 150. The rule is straightforward, mainstream jazz by new and established musicians. You really can't go wrong here.

Small's. 183 W. 10th St. (at Seventh Ave.). ☎ **212/929-7565.** www.smallsjazz.com. Subway: 1, 9 to Christopher St.

Here's a great destination for committed jazzophiles: If you just don't want to stop grooving after the other clubs close, head to this cozy basement hideaway, which stays open all night. Scheduled performers, which often include cutting-edge unsigned acts

Take the A Train

Harlem's jazz scene has taken on new energy in recent years, serving up top-notch music without the high cover charges and drink/food minimums that downtown clubs often require.

Showmans Cafe, 375 W. 125th St., between St. Nicholas and Morningside avenues (☎ 212/864-8941; subway: A, B, C, D to 125th St.), hosts nightly music ranging from soulful jazz to funky bebop. Said to be a favorite of Billie Holliday's, the art deco–cool **Lenox Lounge,** 288 Lenox Ave., between 124th and 125th streets (☎ 212/427-0253; subway: 2, 3 to 125th St.), hosts top-flight live jazz in the back room for a crowd that comes to listen and be wowed.

St. Nick's Pub, 773 St. Nicholas Ave., at 149th Street (☎ 212/283-9728; subway: A, B, C, D to 145th St.), is an older Sugar Hill closet that has been rediscovered by a younger crowd, drawn in by its great jazz every night of the week except Tuesday. The Monday jazz jams with Patience Higgins and the Sugar Hill Quartet attract music lovers and players from all walks of life, and the service is just as friendly whether you come from the neighborhood, downtown, or out of town.

And if you want to pair your Harlem jazz experience with a first-rate soul-food meal, check to see if **Wells,** 2247 Adam Clayton Powell Blvd., between 132nd and 133rd streets (☎ 212/234-0930; subway: 2, 3 to 135th St.), is still hosting the Harlem Renaissance Orchestra on Monday night. Good jazz is also served up a few other nights a week—along with legendary chicken and waffles—but it's this swingin' 16-piece band that really rocks the house.

or overlooked talents, play from around 10pm to 2am, followed by a nightly jam session until dawn (and often beyond). No alcohol is served, but that doesn't keep the crowds away—they're happy to come just for the music. Drinks are free with the $10 cover, and all ages are welcome.

✪ **S.O.B.'s.** 204 Varick St. (at Houston St.). ☎ **212/243-4940.** www.sobs.com. Subway: 1, 9 to Houston St.

If you like your music hot, hot, hot, S.O.B.'s is the place for you. This is the city's top world-music venue, specializing in Brazilian, Caribbean, and Latin sounds. The packed house dances and sings along nightly to calypso, samba, mambo, African drums, reggae, or other global grooves, united in the high-energy, feel-good vibe. Bookings include top-flight performers from around the globe; Astrud Gilberto, Ruben Blades, King Sunny Ade, Tito Puente, Eddie Palmieri, Buckwheat Zydeco, Beausoleil, and the unsurpassed Celia Cruz are only a few of the names who have graced this lively stage. The room's Tropicana Club style has island pizzazz that carries through to the Caribbean-influenced cooking and extensive tropical drinks menu. This place is so popular that it's an excellent idea to book in advance, especially if you'd like table seating. At press time, Latin dance lessons were offered before Monday's La Tropica party so you could be ready to strut your stuff once the band takes the stage. Friday features a late-night French Caribbean dance party, while Saturday is reserved for Brazilian samba.

Sweet Basil. 88 Seventh Ave. South (btw. Grove and Bleecker sts.). ☎ **212/242-1785.** www.sweetbasil.com. Subway: 1, 9 to Christopher St.

The choice runs from fusion to traditional at this intimate but excellent jazz club. You can count on finding top names playing top-notch music. Pricey, but you'll get your money's worth. The Sunday brunch is so popular that they've added a Saturday version as well. Reservations are a must on weekends.

✪ **The Village Vanguard.** 178 Seventh Ave. South (just below 11th St.). ☎ **212/255-4037.** www.villagevanguard.net. Subway: 1, 2, 3, 9 to 14th St.

What CBGB's is to rock, the Village Vanguard is to jazz. One look at the photos on the walls will show you who's been through, from Coltrane, Miles, and Monk to recent appearances by Wynton Marsalis and Joshua Redman. Expect a mix of established names and high-quality local talent, including the Vanguard's own jazz orchestra. The sound is great, but sight lines are terrible, so come early for a front table. The crowd can seem either overly serious or overly touristy, but don't let that stop you—you'll always find great music.

5 Cabaret

An evening spent at a sophisticated cabaret just might be the quintessential New York night on the town. It isn't cheap: Covers can range from $10 to $60, depending on the showroom and the act, and also require two-drink or dinner-check minimums. Always reserve ahead, and get the complete lowdown when you do.

In addition to the top-flight choices below, you might also wish to see what's on at **Danny's Skylight Room** at the Grand Sea Palace Thai restaurant, 346 W. 46th St., between Eighth and Ninth avenues (☎ 212/265-8133), which offers a surprisingly strong lineup as well as dinner/show packages; the **Firebird Cafe,** 363 W. 46th St. (☎ 212/586-0244), which hosts excellent singers in an intimate and luxurious setting, with elegant Russian eats from the adjoining restaurant; and yet another Restaurant Row favorite, friendly and affordable **Don't Tell Mama,** 343 W. 46th St. (☎ 212/757-0788), where you'll find an evening of torch songs, comedy, and more, including a lively piano bar (drinks only, no dinner). In the Village is **Duplex Cabaret,** 61 Christopher St., at Seventh Ave. South (☎ 212/255-5438; www.duplex.citysearch.com), where you can expect a high camp factor and lots of good-natured fun that runs the gamut from minimusicals to drag revues to stand-up comedy.

✪ **Cafe Carlyle.** In the Carlyle hotel, 781 Madison Ave. (at 76th St.). ☎ **212/570-7189.** Closed July–Aug. Subway: 6 to 77th St.

Cabaret doesn't get any better than this. First of all, this is where you'll find Bobby Short—and that's all those who know cabaret need to know. Nothing evokes the essence of Manhattan more than an evening with this quintessential interpreter of Porter and the Gershwins. When he's not in residence, you'll find such rarefied talents as Eartha Kitt, Betty Buckley, and Michael Feinstein. The room is intimate and as swanky as they come. Expect a high tab—admission is $60 with no minimum, but add dinner and two people could easily spend $300—but if you're looking for the best of the best, look no further. On most Mondays, Woody Allen joins the Eddy Davis New Orleans Jazz Band on clarinet to swing Dixie style.

Joe's Pub. At the Joseph Papp Public Theater, 425 Lafayette St. (btw. Astor Place and 4th St.). ☎ **212/539-8777** or TeleCharge at 212/239-6200 (for advance tickets). www. joespub. com. Subway: 6 to Astor Place.

This beautiful—and hugely popular—cabaret and supper club, eloquently named for the legendary Joseph Papp, is everything a New York cabaret should be. All elegant retro-style, the multilevel space serves up a classic American menu (think burgers, shrimp cocktail, baked Alaska) and top-notch entertainment from a more eclectic mix of talent than you'll find on any other cabaret calendar. The sophisticated crowd comes for music and spoken word that ranges from legendary Broadway duo Betty Comden and Adolph Green to Brazilian vocal sensation Virginia Rodrigues to pop from husband-and-wife singer/songwriters Michael Penn and Aimee Mann. There's always jazz on the calendar, and don't be surprised if Broadway actors show up on off-nights to exercise their substantial chops.

The Oak Room. At the Algonquin hotel, 59 W. 44th St. (btw. Fifth and Sixth aves.). ☎ **212/840-6800.** Subway: B, D, F, Q to 42nd St.

Recently refurbished to recall its glory days, the Oak Room is one of the city's most intimate, elegant, and sophisticated spots for cabaret. Headliners include such first-rate talents as Andrea Marcovicci, Steve Ross, the marvelous Julie Wilson, and cool-cat jazz guitarist John Pizzarelli, plus occasional lesser names that are destined for greatness.

6 Stand-Up & Sketch Comedy

Cover charges are generally in the $8 to $15 range, with Dangerfield's at $20 for the Saturday late show and all-star Caroline's going as high as $26 on occasion. Many clubs also have a two-drink minimum. Be sure to ask about the night's cover when you make reservations.

   In addition to the choices below, you might also want to see what's on at **Don't Tell Mama** and **Duplex,** cabarets that tend to tickle the funny bone on a regular basis; see directly above.

✪ **Carolines on Broadway.** 1626 Broadway (btw. 49th and 50th sts.). ☎ **212/757-4100.** www.carolines.com. Subway: N, R to 49th St.; 1, 9 to 50th St.

Caroline Hirsch presents today's hottest headliners in her upscale Theater District showroom, which doesn't have a bad seat in the house. You're bound to recognize at least one or two of the established names and hot up-and-comers on the bill in any given week, like Dave Chapelle, Colin Quinn, Kathy Griffin, Robert Wuhl, Jimmie Walker ("Dyn-o-mite!"), Pauly Shore, the *Daily Show*'s Lewis Black, or Caroline Rhea *(Sabrina, the Teenage Witch)*. Monday is New Talent Night, while HOT97 radio hosts up-and-coming black comedians on most Wednesdays.

✪ **Comedy Cellar.** 117 MacDougal St. (btw. Bleecker and W. 3rd sts.). ☎ **212/254-3480.** www.comedycellar.com. Subway: A, B, C, D, E, F, Q to W. 4th St. (use 3rd St. exit).

This intimate subterranean club is the club of choice for stand-up fans in the know, thanks to the best, most consistently impressive lineups in the business. I'll always love the Comedy Cellar for introducing an uproariously funny unknown comic named Ray Romano to me a few years back.

Dangerfield's. 1118 First Ave. (btw. 61st and 62nd sts.). ☎ **212/593-1650.** Subway: N, R to 60th St.; 4, 5, 6, to 59th St.

Dangerfield's is the nightclub version of the comedy club, with a mature crowd and a straight-outta-Vegas atmosphere. The comedians are all veterans of the comedy-club and late-night talk-show circuit.

✪ **Gotham Comedy Club.** 34 W. 22nd St. (btw. Fifth and Sixth aves.). ☎ **212/367-9000.** www.gothamcomedy.com. Subway: F, N, R to 23rd St.

Here's the city's trendiest and most sophisticated comedy club. The young talent—Tom Rhodes, Jeff Ross, Lewis Schaeffer, Lynn Harris—is redhot. Look for theme nights like the lovelorn laugh riot "Breakup Girl Live!" and "A Very Jewish Thursday."

New York Comedy Club. 241 E. 24th St. (btw. Second and Third aves.). ☎ **212/696-5233.** www.newyorkcomedyclub.com. Subway: 6 to 23rd St.

With a $5 cover charge on weekdays ($10 Fri and Sat), this small club offers the best laugh value for your money. Despite what the owners call their "Wal-Mart approach" to comedy, the club has presented Damon Wayans, Chris Rock, and Brett Butler, among others, in its two showrooms. Weekends set aside time for African-American and Hispanic comics. Come early for a good seat.

Stand-Up New York. 236 W. 78th St. (at Broadway). ☎ **212/595-0850.** www.standupny.com. Subway: 1, 9 to 79th St.

The Upper West Side's premier stand-up comedy club hosts some of the brightest young comics in the business, such as Joe DiResta and Paul Mercurio. Drop-in guests have included Dennis Leary, Robin Williams, and Mr. Upper West Side himself, Jerry Seinfeld.

Upright Citizens Brigade Theater. 161 W. 22nd St. (btw. Sixth and Seventh aves.) ☎ **212/366-9176.** www.uprightcitizens.com. Subway: 1, 9 to 23rd St.

You've seen their twisted, highly original sketch comedy on Comedy Central—now you can see the Upright Citizens Brigade, New York's premier sketch comedy troupe, live. The biggest success to come out of New York's late '90s alternative comedy explosion, the UCB now has its very own showcase. The best of the nonstop hilarity is *A.S.S.S.C.A.T.*, the troupe's extremely popular long-form improv show. You won't pay more than $5 for any show; phone reservations are a must.

7 Bars & Cocktail Lounges

SOUTH STREET SEAPORT & THE FINANCIAL DISTRICT

Also consider the **North Star Pub,** at South Street Seaport, 93 South St., at Fulton Street (☎ **212/509-6757**), a genuine British pub boasting one of the finest single-malt scotch menus in the city in addition to hand-pulled British and Irish pints. And **Roy's New York,** 130 Washington St., at Cedar Street, 1 block south of the World Trade Center (☎ **212/266-6262**), serves terrific cocktails with a tropical twist in its adjacent bar. See chapter 6.

✪ **The Greatest Bar on Earth.** 1 World Trade Center, 107th Floor (on West St., btw. Liberty and Vesey sts.) ☎ **212/524-7000.** www.windowsontheworld.com. Subway: A, C, E to Chambers St.; N, R, 1, 9 to Cortlandt St.

High atop the World Trade Center sits the Greatest Bar on Earth, whose name is only a slight exaggeration. This is a magical spot for cocktails, decent à la carte dining (finger foods and gourmet munchies mostly), and dancing. No matter how many times I come up here, I'm wowed by the incredible views. The place is huge, but intimate nooks and a separate back room bring the scale down to comfortable proportions. The crowd is a lively mix of in-the-know locals and stylish out-of-towners. This is a great place to come with a group; the music is loud, and the joint really jumps as the night goes on. Quintessentially—and spectacularly—New York. Look for swing on Friday and Saturday, plus mambo, funk, and R&B other nights of the week. Wednesday is home to the hip Mondo 107 strato-lounge deejay party.

Wall St. Kitchen & Bar. 70 Broad St. (btw. Beaver and S. William sts., about 1¹/₂ blocks south of New York Stock Exchange). ☎ **212/797-7070.** www.wallstkitchen.citysearch.com. Subway: J, M, Z to Broad St.; 4, 5 to Bowling Green.

Want to rub elbows with some genuine bulls and bears after a hard day of downtown sightseeing? Head to this surprisingly appealing and affordable bar, housed in a spectacular former bank in the heart of the Financial District. Like its sister hangout, Soho Kitchen & Bar (below), Wall St. Kitchen specializes in on-tap beers (around 50 are on offer at any given time) and "flight" menus of wines and microbrews for tasting. The familiar bar food is well prepared and reasonably priced. Come on a weekday to enjoy the crowd.

TRIBECA

Bubble Lounge. 228 W. Broadway (btw. Franklin and White sts.). ☎ **212/431-3443.** Subway: 1, 9 to Franklin St.

From the first cork that popped, this wine bar dedicated to the bubbly was an effervescent hit. Hundreds of champagnes and sparkling wines are served in this glamorous living-room setting, 25 of them by the glass, to pair with caviar, foie gras, and elegant sweets. The crowd is appropriately sophisticated, but you don't have to spend a fortune to enjoy this swanky place: Champagne starts at $8 a glass.

El Teddy's. 219 W. Broadway (btw. Franklin and White sts.). ☎ **212/941-7070.** Subway: 1, 9 to Franklin St.

This upscale South-of-the-Border restaurant is a great place to pony up to the bar for a cocktail. The food's a bit pricey for what you get, but the bathtub-size margaritas are terrific, and you have about 2 dozen to choose from. All the fashionistas left years ago, but the kitschy decor is still retro-hip. You can't miss this place—just look for the enormous Statue of Liberty crown suspended over the sidewalk.

✪ The Sporting Club. 99 Hudson St. (btw. Franklin and Leonard sts.). ☎ **212/219-0900.** www.thesportingclub.net. Subway: 1, 9 to Franklin St.

The city's best sports bar (rated no. 1 in the *Daily News*) is a guy's joint if there ever was one. The space is as big as a linebacker, with giant TV screens at every turn tuned to just about every game on the planet. (Wall Streeters bring their international cohorts here to catch everything from English football to Japanese sumo.) The menu is what you'd expect: wings, burgers, club sandwiches, and *lots* of beer. There's no better place for sports fans to get crazy at Super Bowl time and during March Madness. When the big games are over, this turns into a surprisingly popular singles place.

Walker's. 16 No. Moore St. (at Varick St.). ☎ **212/941-0142.** Subway: 1, 9 to Franklin St.

Walker's is an old holdout from prefabulous TriBeCa. It's surprisingly charming, with a tin ceiling, a long wooden bar, oldies on the sound system, and cozy tables where you can dine on affordable meat-and-potatoes fare. The bartenders are a friendly bunch, but do yourself a favor and don't get fancy with your drink orders; stick with Guinness or one of the other drafts.

CHINATOWN & LITTLE ITALY

✪ Double Happiness. 173 Mott St. (btw. Grand and Broome sts.). ☎ **212/941-1282.** Subway: B, D, Q to Grand St.; 6 to Spring St.

Thanks to its stylish speakeasy aura and low-key vibe, last year's new kid in town has outlived its initial buzz. The only indicator to the subterranean entrance is a vertical WATCH YOUR STEP sign. Once through the door, you'll find a beautifully designed lounge with artistic nods to the neighborhood throughout. The space is large, but a low ceiling and intimate nooks add a hint of romance (although the loud funkified music mix may deter true wooing). Don't miss the green tea martini, an inspired house creation.

Mare Chiaro. $176^1/_2$ Mulberry St. (at Broome St.). ☎ **212/226-9345.** Subway: 6 to Spring St.

This authentic corner of Little Italy now hosts a bizarro mix of slumming NoLiTa hipsters, uptown singles, and neighborhood holdovers from an age when this was just a drinking man's bar. But Mare Chiaro still works its crusty magic, transporting you back to another era with its gentrification-resistant vibe. A great place for a cheap beer at a crossroads of city life.

THE LOWER EAST SIDE

Also consider French bistro **Le Pere Pinard,** 175 Ludlow St., south of Houston (☎ 212/777-4917), which has a terrific—and thoroughly French—wine bar; see chapter 6.

Butcher Bar. 93 Stanton St. (btw. Ludlow and Orchard sts.). ☎ **212/358-1633.** www.arlene-grocery.com. Subway: F to Second Ave.

With brick walls, a cozy open fireplace, and the same unpretentious atmosphere as its sister space, Arlene Grocery (see "(Mostly) Rock Clubs," above), this is the ideal place to nurse a brew between bands. Sandwiches are served in daytime.

✪ **Idlewild.** 145 E. Houston St. (btw. First and Second aves., on the south side of Houston). ☎ 212/477-5005. Subway: F to Second Ave.

It may look unapproachable from the street, with nothing but an unmarked stainless-steel facade, but inside you'll find a fun, easygoing bar that's perfect for lovers of retro-kitsch. The interior is a larger-scale repro of a jet airplane, complete with reclining seats, tray tables, and too-small bathrooms that will transport you back to your favorite midair moments in no time. There are booths in back for larger crowds, and an Austin Powers–style bar to gather around at center stage. The deejay spins a listener-friendly mix of light techno, groovy disco in the funkadelic vein, and '80s tunes from the likes of the Smiths and the Cure.

Lansky Lounge. 138 Delancey St. (entrance on Norfolk St., between Rivington and Delancey sts.). ☎ 212/677-9489. Subway: F to Delancey St.

A doorman stands on the sidewalk to point patrons down a flight of stairs, through an alley, and back up a staircase into this faux speakeasy. It's still one of the Lower East Side's coolest scenes, with a cool-as-a-cucumber zoot-suit vibe that has outlived New York's flirtation with neo-swing. The special martinis and infused vodkas are terrific. Come on a weeknight, when the crowd is more local than bridge-and-tunnel. The food is kosher and comes from neighboring Ratner's. *Note:* The bar is closed on Friday night in observance of the Jewish Sabbath.

Ludlow Bar. 165 Ludlow St. (btw. Stanton and Houston sts.). ☎ **212/353-0536.** Subway: F to Second Ave.

This friendly little lounge manages to avoid the pretensions of its hipper-than-thou neighbors. Still, in keeping with the lounge trend, you'll find cozy furniture, a purple-felt pool table, and a deejay spinning jazzy house, drum-and-bass, trip-hop, and funk for an artsy crowd that's slightly older than neighboring Max Fish's.

SOHO

Ice Bar. 528 Canal St. (at Washington St.). ☎ **212/226-2602.** Subway: 1, 9 to Houston St.

Here's a cutting-edge spot for those who don't mind going out of their way—really out of their way—for something completely different. Ice Bar is managing to draw a scene way out west (almost to the West Side Highway) by crossing an outrageously cool white-on-white retro-futuristic interior (blue-lit for ultimate effect) with an everybody's-welcome egalitarian attitude. Expect an electronica soundtrack (what else?). Don't go too early in the week, or early in the evening, unless you want to be alone.

○ **Merc Bar.** 151 Mercer St. (btw. Prince and Houston sts.). ☎ **212/966-2727.** Subway: N, R to Prince St.; B, D, F, Q to Broadway/Lafayette St.

Notable for its long tenure in the fickle world of beautiful-people bars, upscale Merc Bar has mellowed nicely. You'll still find a good-looking crowd in the a superbly appointed lounge, but now they're confident rather than trend-happy. The decor bespeaks civilized rusticity with warm woods, a canoe over the bar, copper-top tables, and butter-leather banquettes—think SoHo goes to Yosemite. A great place to nestle into a comfortable couch with your honey and enjoy the scene. The European martini (Stoli raspberry and Chambord) is divine. Look carefully, because there's no sign.

Ñ. 33 Crosby St. (btw. Grand and Broome sts.). ☎ **212/219-8856.** Subway: N, R to Prince St.; 6 to Spring St.

On a charming cobbled street that somehow escaped gentrification, Ñ (pronounced like the Spanish letter, *enyay*) is long, narrow, candlelit, and hip. Despite its cool, the staff is warm, and the extensive, award-winning sherry list is excellent. There's also a nice, fruity sangría, plus a full bar for non-Spanish tastes. You can order some of the city's best tapas, which come out of a very tiny kitchen in back. Flamenco dancers heighten the appeal on Wednesday night at 9pm.

Pravda. 281 Lafayette St. (btw. Prince and Houston sts.). ☎ **212/226-4944** or 212/334-5015. www.pravda.citysearch.com. Subway: B, D, F, Q to Broadway/Lafayette St.

If you were prowling New York's watering holes looking for Boris and Natasha, this is where you'd most likely find them. This Soviet-chic lounge makes pricey but perfect martinis for a classy crowd drawn in by the romantic pre-Gorbachev revolutionary vibe. More than 70 vodkas are on hand from 18 countries. There's plenty of Russian caviar on hand to wash down with those pricey cocktails, plus a full humidor for the cigar-bar crowd. There's no sign, so look for the light that says "281" on the east side of the street and walk down the stairwell.

Soho Kitchen & Bar. 103 Greene St. (btw. Spring and Prince sts.). ☎ **212/925-1866.** Subway: N, R to Prince St.

This fun, easygoing bar and restaurant is a nice antidote to the standard SoHo pretensions. The large, lofty space attracts an animated after-work and late-night crowd to its central bar, which dispenses more than 21 beers on tap, a whole slew of microbrews by the bottle, and more than 100 wines by the glass, either individually or in "flights" for comparative tastings. The menu offers predictable but affordable bar fare: buffalo wings, oversize salads, good burgers, and a variety of sandwiches and thin-crust pizzas.

THE EAST VILLAGE & NOHO

In addition to the choices below, also consider the magical **Fez,** 380 Lafayette St., at Great Jones St. (☎ 212/533-2680), a dimly lit Moroccan-themed bar and lounge that I much prefer to the downstairs performance space; see p. 336.

B Bar & Grill. 40 E. 4th St. (at Bowery). ☎ **212/475-2220.** www.bbarandgrill.com. Subway: 6 to Bleecker St.

As Bowery Bar, this place was *the* celebrity hot spot a few years back. Reincarnated a couple of years ago as B Bar, it has managed to survive the limelight. Its physical features are the key to its enduring appeal: Originally a Gulf gas station, the cavernous bar/dining room is '60s modern and attractive, with high ceilings, comfy booths, retro-style mood lighting, a large central bar, and the latest alterna-hits on the sound system. But the 6,500-square-foot tree-filled courtyard—alfresco space that's otherwise unheard of in this city—is the biggest draw. The bar offers a regular selection of signature drinks, including a Ketel One martini that even Bond could love. The reasonably priced food is better than you'd expect. Come early for quiet, later for a chic party (don't be surprised to find a velvet rope).

Burp Castle. 41 E. 7th St. (btw. Second and Third aves.). ☎ **212/982-4576.** Subway: 6 to Astor Place.

This oddball theme bar is a must for serious beer lovers. It's styled as a "Temple of Beer Worship," complete with medieval-inspired decor, choral music on the sound system, and soft-spoken waiters in monkish garb. Before you have time to let the weirdness of it all sink in, you'll be distracted by the incomparable beer list. There are more than 500 bottled and on-tap beers to choose from—including a phenomenal collection of Trappist ales, of course. The staff is courteous but a bit too studiedly monkish in its behavior; I couldn't wrest an actual recommendation out of them. Be prepared to choose, or head elsewhere if you think you'll just throw your hands in the air and order a Bud.

✪ **dba.** 41 First Ave. (btw. 2nd and 3rd sts.). ☎ **212/475-5097.** Subway: F to Second Ave.

Along with Temple Bar (below), this is my other favorite New York bar. It has completely bucked the loungey trend that has taken over the city, instead remaining firmly and resolutely an unpretentious neighborhood bar that's as comfy as your favorite shirt, where everyone is welcome and at home. Most important, dba is a beer- and scotch-lover's paradise, with a massive drink menu on the giant chalkboards behind the bar. Owner Ray Deter specializes in British-style cask-conditioned ales (the kind that you pump by hand) and stocks a phenomenal collection of 90 single-malt scotches. The relaxed crowd is a pleasing mix of connoisseurs and casual drinkers who like the unlimited choices and egalitarian vibe. Excellent jukebox, too.

Decibel. 240 E. 9th St. (btw. Second and Third aves.). ☎ **212/979-2733.** www.sakebar. com. Subway: 6 to Astor Place.

This subterranean sake bar is a genuine Japanese refuge. The warren of little, dimly lit rooms draws a hip crowd with its long, excellent list of sakes (about 70 are on hand) and affordable Japanese nibbles. The menu explains everything you ever wanted to know about sake and then some; feel free to ask the bar's wise and tolerant staff for suggestions. Japanese beers and saketinis (martinis made with sake—an excellent invention) are also available.

Drinkland. 339 E. 10th St. (btw. aves. A and B). ☎ **212/228-2435.** www.drinkland.com. Subway: L to First Ave.

Serious electronica, drum-and-bass, and trip-hop fans should head to this Alphabet City boîte, which boasts a pop-art interior by the set designer for *Austin Powers,* and a committed legion of deejays spinning the latest for a crowd that really comes to listen.

✪ **Temple Bar.** 332 Lafayette St. (just north of Houston St., on the west side of the street). ☎ **212/925-4242.** Subway: B, D, F, Q to Broadway/Lafayette St.; 6 to Bleecker St.

Here's my favorite lounge in the city. Members of the It crowd will tell you it's passé, which only serves to increase its appeal as far as I'm concerned—it's easy to get in now, and, on weeknights at least, you can usually manage to find a comfy seat. One of the first comers to New York's lounge scene, Temple Bar is still a gorgeous art deco hangout, with a long L-shaped bar leading to a lovely seating area with velvet drapes, romantic backlighting, and Sinatra softly crooning in the background. Cocktails simply don't get any better than the classic martini (with just a kiss of vermouth, of course) or the smooth-as-penoir silk Rob Roy (Johnnie Walker Black, sweet vermouth, bitters). Elegant finger foods provide a reason to never leave. Bring a date—and feel free to invite me along anytime. A Sunday night readings series hosts acclaimed writers like Colin Harrison *(Afterburn)* and Katherine Russell Rich *(The Red Devil: To Hell with Cancer and Back).* The entrance is a little inconspicuous, so look for the petroglyphlike lizards on the facade.

Tom & Jerry's (288 Bar). 288 Elizabeth St. ☎ **212/260-5045.** Subway: B, D, F, Q to Broadway/Lafayette St.; 6 to Bleecker St.

Here's an extremely pleasing neighborhood bar minus the grunge factor that usually plagues such joints. The place has an authentic local vibe, and the youngish, artsy crowd is unpretentious and chatty. The beer selection is very good and the mixed drinks are better than average. Flea-market hounds will enjoy the vintage collection of "Tom & Jerry" punchbowl sets behind the bar, and creative types will enjoy the rotating collection of works from local artists. There's no sign, but you'll spy the action through the plate-glass window on the east side of Elizabeth Street just north of Houston.

GREENWICH VILLAGE

Also consider the cheap-chic **Junno's,** 64 Downing St., between Bedford and Varick streets (☎ 212/627-7995), a sophisticated industrial-moderne restaurant that also hosts a red-hot bar scene until 4am on weekends; see chapter 6.

Bar d'O. 29 Bedford St. (at Downing St.). ☎ **212/627-1580.** Subway: A, B, C, D, E, F, Q to W. 4th St. (use 3rd St. exit).

This intimate space is home to the Village's best lounge scene—which unfortunately makes it crowded, but still cozy and appealing. A different deejay sets the scene for the mixed gay/straight crowd nightly in this low-slung, candlelit space; best is the exotic lounge music from In Hi-Fi on Thursday. Drag diva Joey Arias wows the crowd three times weekly (Tues, Sat, and Sun at press time) with her spot-on Billie Holiday renditions.

✪ **Chumley's.** 86 Bedford St. (at Barrow St.). ☎ **212/675-4449.** Subway: 1, 9 to Christopher St.

A classic. Many bars in New York date their beginnings to Prohibition, but Chumley's still has the vibe. The circa college-age crowd doesn't date back nearly as far, however. Come to warm yourself by the fire and indulge in a once-forbidden pleasure: beer. The door is unmarked, with a metal grille on the small window; another entrance is at 58 Barrow St., which takes you in through a back courtyard.

Clementine. 1 Fifth Ave. (at 8th St.). ☎ **212/253-0003.** Subway: A, B, C, D, E, F, Q to W. 4th St.

Reminiscent of an elegant art deco ocean liner, this chic restaurant sports a swanky but comfortable front-room lounge that's worth seeking out if you'd like a sophisticated cocktail and a late-night bite to eat. It's very popular among a sleek, cell-phone-toting crowd thanks to its terrific New American food and full card of Clementine-only cocktails.

Late-Night Bites

All this bar-hopping and clubbing really works up an appetite. Where to eat?

Open until 4am nightly, **Blue Ribbon,** 97 Sullivan St., between Prince and Spring streets in SoHo (☎ 212/274-0404), is where the city's top chefs come to unwind after they close their own kitchens for the night. Thanks to a top-drawer oyster bar and excellent comfort food, this cozy bistro is always packed, so expect a wait.

Newest on the late-night dining scene is **Leshko's,** 111 Ave. A, at 7th Street (☎ 212/777-2111), a Ukrainian diner that has been given a chic makeover by the owners of gay hot-spot Barracuda (see "The Gay & Lesbian Scene," below) and transformed into a hip restaurant-cum-club serving new twists on pierogies and other affordable Eastern European diner fare. Particularly popular among gay scenesters. Open until 1am on weeknights, 2am on weekends.

In addition to Blue Ribbon, Leshko's, and **Clementine** (above), other great choices for after-hours eats include the funky Francophile diner **Florent** (p. 166), and authentic bistro **Pastis** (p. 165), both in the red-hot Meat-Packing District. TriBeCa has the **Odeon** (p. 146), an attractive and affordable art deco bistro that's one of the top after-hours eateries in town. The West Village boasts **Cafeteria** (p. 164), the glam version of a 24-hour greasy spoon. A quintessential late-night choice in far west Chelsea is the **Empire Diner** (p. 166), a throwback shrine to the slicked-up all-American diner where the after-hours crowd may be the best people-watching in town. In the East Village, head to **Veselka** (p. 158), a comfortable and appealing diner offering authentic Eastern European fare at rock-bottom prices. In Midtown, Korean barbecue is an option around the clock at **Woo Chon** (p. 179).

Also, remember that many of the bars and cocktail lounges listed in this chapter—like **Bongo, Decibel, Lot 61, Old Town,** and **Heartland Brewery**—serve food, from full meals to munchies, well into the wee hours.

White Horse Tavern. 567 Hudson St. (at 11th St.). ☎ **212/989-3956.** Subway: 1, 9 to Christopher St.

Poets and literary buffs pop into this 1880 pub to pay their respects to Dylan Thomas, who tipped his last jar here before shuffling off this mortal coil. Best enjoyed in the warm weather when there's outdoor drinking, or at happy hour for the cheap drafts that draw in a big frat-boy and postfrat yuppie crowd.

CHELSEA & THE MEAT-PACKING DISTRICT

Additionally, retro-glam greasy spoon **Cafeteria,** 119 Seventh Ave. at 17th Street (☎ 212/414-1717), boasts a red-hot basement lounge scene.

✪ **Bongo.** 299 Tenth Ave. (btw. 27th and 28th sts.). ☎ **212/947-3654.** Subway: C, E to 23rd St.

This casual, comfortable mid-century-modern lounge is the place to come for cocktails that are well made and a great value considering their extra-large size. Don't miss the French martini, made with Vox vodka and Lillet—yum! Even better: Bongo boasts a full raw-bar menu—a half-dozen varieties of oysters, cherrystones and littlenecks, even lobster and caviar—and an excellent lobster roll. The crowd is hip, but, happily, not too trendy. Come early if you want to have space to sit and eat.

Ciel Rouge. 176 Seventh Ave. (btw. 20th and 21st sts.). ☎ **212/929-5542.** Subway: 1, 9 to 23rd St.

This is a haven for hip Francophiles in need of a shot of Left Bank lounging. Completing the red-hued scene are well-mixed drinks, decent food, and live jazz on Tuesday. The plush space converts to a piano bar the rest of the week.

Justin's. 31 W. 21st St. (btw. Fifth and Sixth aves.. ☎ **212/352-0599.** Subway: F, N, R to 23rd St.

Surprise, surprise—Sean "Puffy" Combs's tony soul fooder is the hangout of choice for hip-hop stars and music industry execs. You can dine here on upscale Caribbean soul food (reservations suggested), but come instead for the late-night scene in the sophisticated lounge if you're up for some top-notch people-watching. Be prepared for the velvet rope on busy nights.

Lot 61. 550 W. 21st St. (near 11th Ave.). ☎ **212/243-6555.** www.lot61.com. Subway: C, E to 23rd St.

This cavernous hot spot in far west Chelsea is my favorite of the shallow fashionista hangouts, and it's hotter than ever. The fabulous warehouse-meets-*Wallpaper* design is so humorously high style that you just gotta love it—where else are you going to recline on rubber sofas rescued from upstate mental hospitals surrounded by oversize art from contemporary bad boys like Damien Hirst and Sean Landers? Nowhere else but Lot 61. So as not to find yourself cramped into the front bar, make a reservation in the lounge, where you can sip Cosmopolitans and graze from a surprisingly terrific menu of finger foods and other light dishes. Earlier is better; let the celebs and Kate Mosses in training fill up the room around you. Dress well, take a taxi, look carefully for the door (the logo is faint), and brush off the withering looks from the help. It's easy to catch a cab on the way out, as there's a garage on the same block.

Merchant's New York. 112 Seventh Ave. So. (at 17th St.). ☎ **212/366-7267.** Subway: 1, 9 to 18th St.

New York's young working crowd just loves this place. For good reason: It's attractive, comfortable, and mixes a great martini. On the ground floor is a stylish living room–like bar, with a mezzanine for dinner. In the downstairs lounge a fireplace roars even in a heat wave, while air-conditioning delivers a polar blast. The crowd is a pleasing mix: yuppies looking for love, smart folks on dates, gays and straights, friends chatting on the couches and chairs downstairs. The food is pretty good, too.

✪ **Serena.** In the basement level of the Hotel Chelsea, 222 W. 23rd St. (btw. Seventh and Eighth aves.). ☎ **212/255-4646.** Subway: C, E, 1, 9 to 23rd St.

This plush new basement boîte is as hip as can be—I've even spotted mix-master Moby here. It's relatively unpretentious considering its hot-spot-of-the-moment status; still, dress the part if you want to make it past the doorman, especially on weekends. The crowd is young and pretty, and the music mix is a blast—think Fatboy Slim meets ABBA meets Foghat, and you'll get the picture.

THE FLATIRON DISTRICT, UNION SQUARE & GRAMERCY PARK

Also consider the ✪ **Old Town Bar & Restaurant,** 45 E. 18th St., between Broadway and Park Avenue South (☎ 212/529-6732), a genuine tin-ceilinged 19th-century bar that's a terrific place to soak up some old New York atmosphere; see chapter 6.

Cibar. At the Inn at Irving Place, 56 Irving Place (btw. 17th and 18th sts.). ☎ **212/ 460-5656.** Subway: N, R, 4, 5, 6 to 14th St./Union Sq.

This stylish, amber-lit, art nouveau–accented lounge, Gramercy Park's bid for the cocktail crowd, is decidedly a bar for grown-ups. A romantic place to enjoy pricey but terrific martinis and cigars, all served by aspiring models who haven't realized their calling yet.

Dusk Lounge. 147 W. 24th St. (btw. Sixth and Seventh aves.). ☎ **212/924-4490.** Subway: F to 23rd St.

This casual, artsy lounge is a great choice for Anglophiles who relish the rise of Cool Britannia. There's a fab mirrored mosaic wall, comfortable banquettes opposite, a friendly bar serving affordable drinks, a pool table, and British tunes—from drum-and-bass to Manic Street Preachers and Blur—on the sound system. Expect an easy-going, youngish crowd that stays relaxed and unpretentious into the evening.

Heartland Brewery. 35 Union Sq. West (at 16th St.). ☎ **212/645-3400.** www.heartland-brewery.com. Subway: L, N, R, 4, 5, 6 to 14th St./Union Sq.

The food leaves a bit to be desired, but the house-brewed beers are first-rate. Great American Beer Festival three-time award-winner Farmer Jon's Oatmeal Stout is always on hand, as are three or four hand-crafted ales and a lager or two. A good selection of single malts and tequilas, too. The wood-paneled two-level bar is big and appealing, but expect a loud, boisterous after-work crowd, plus a good number of Germans and Brits (testament to the quality of the brew). There's now a second location, in Midtown at 1285 Sixth Ave., across from Radio City (☎ 212/582-8244).

Park Avenue Country Club. 381 Park Ave. So. (at 27th St.). ☎ **212/685-3636.** Subway: 6 to 28th St.

This place bills itself as a "sports cafe," and it is indeed more polished than your average beer-and-pretzels sports bar. That said, it's a very comfortable place to hunker down over a club sandwich and a beer to watch the game. There are TVs at every turn, and a nice mahogany central bar serves up an extensive list of bottled and on-tap brews.

Pete's Tavern. 129 E. 18th St. (at Irving Place). ☎ **212/473-7676.** www.petestavern.com. Subway: L, N, R, 4, 5, 6 to 14th St./Union Sq.

The oldest continually operating establishment in the city, Pete's opened in 1864—while Lincoln was still president! It reeks of genuine history—and, more importantly, there's Guinness on tap, a terrific happy hour, and a St. Patrick's Day party that makes the neighbors crazy. The crowd is a mix of locals from ritzy Gramercy Park and more down-to-earth types.

TIMES SQUARE & MIDTOWN WEST

In addition to the choices below, also consider the genuinely terrific bar at the original theme restaurant, the **Hard Rock Cafe,** 221 W. 57th St., between Broadway and Seventh Avenue (☎ 212/459-9320), where you can groove to classic rock while you peruse a truly astounding collection of memorabilia. There's also **ESPN Zone,** the ultimate sports bar. See "Theme Restaurant Thrills!" in chapter 6. A second branch of **Heartland Brewery** (see above) is across from Radio City at 1285 Sixth Ave., at 51st Street (☎ 212/582-8244).

And don't forget terrific ✪ **Joe Allen,** the legendary Broadway pub on Restaurant Row, 326 W. 46th St., between Eighth and Ninth avenues (☎ 212/581-6464), great for an after-theater cocktail even if you don't dine here; see chapter 6.

✪ **The Algonquin.** 59 W. 44th St. (btw. Fifth and Sixth aves.), New York, NY 10036. ☎ **212/840-6800.** Subway: B, D, F, Q to 42nd St.

The past isn't just a memory anymore at this venerable literary landmark—a complete 1998 restoration returned it to its full Arts-and-Crafts splendor. The splendid oak-paneled lobby is the comfiest and most welcoming in the city, made to linger over pre- or posttheater cocktails. You'll feel the spirit of Dorothy Parker and the legendary Algonquin Round Table that pervades the room. Adjacent is the pubby, clubby **Blue Bar,** home to a rotating collection of Hirschfeld drawings that's well worth checking out.

Flute. 205 W. 54th St. (btw. Seventh Ave. and Broadway). ☎ **212/265-5169.** www. flutebar.com. Subway: B, D, E to Seventh Ave.; 1, 9 to 50th St.

This swanky subterranean champagne lounge is a terrific place to linger over a glass of the bubbly and fancy finger foods, from affordable light bites to foie gras and Petrossian caviar. The sexy, intimate space is punctuated with cozy seating nooks and sofas that are ideal for nuzzling. A deejay spins a funky dance mix later in the evening that makes conversation difficult, but that gives you a perfect excuse to cuddle even closer (there's live jazz on Wed). A much-needed addition to the Theater District. Look carefully for the stairs leading to the entrance; they're on the north side of the street, about midblock. And call ahead because Flute hosts guest list–only parties twice a month.

Mickey Mantle's. 42 Central Park South (btw. Fifth and Sixth aves). ☎ **212/688-7777.** www.mickeymantles.com. Subway: B, Q to 57th St.

Of course, it's terribly sad that the Mick, who gave his life to the bottle, should have his name on a bar. But if you're a fan, it's definitely worth a visit to his classic mahogany-and-brass sports bar and restaurant, which chronicles his life and career in photos. The crowd is a laid-back mix of white-collar after-workers and interested tourists. Classic moderately priced burger fare is available, plus the requisite souvenirs. A great place to watch the game.

✪ **The Royalton.** 44 W. 44th St. (btw. Fifth and Sixth aves.). ☎ **212/869-4400.** Subway: B, D, F, Q to 42nd St.

After all these years, the arch Philippe Starck–designed lobby of this Ian Schrager hotel is still a major hangout for the fashionable crowd. The Starck–Schrager team really knows how to generate a social scene: The sunken lounge space features comfy seating nooks, an extensive martini list, and a light menu of excellent finger foods. In the back is restaurant 44, filled with editorial powerhouses from nearby Condé Nast, which is just about as glam as the publishing world gets. Come early to nab a seat in the marvelous Round Bar, a 20-seat circular enclave done in high Jetsons style (on your right just past the invariably cute doorman).

✪ **Russian Vodka Room.** 265 W. 52nd St. (btw. Broadway and Eighth Ave.). ☎ **212/ 307-5835.** Subway: C, E, 1, 9 to 50th St.

This terrific old-school lounge is a real Theater District find. It's not going to win any style awards, but it's extremely comfortable and knows what's what when it comes to vodkas. There's more than 50 on hand, plus the RVR's own miraculous infusions; you can order an iced rack of six if you can't decide between such yummy flavors as cranberry, apple cinnamon, ginger, horseradish, and more (the raspberry makes a perfect Cosmo). The thirtysomething-and-up crowd is peopled with post-Soviet imports as well as New Yorkers in the know about this best-kept secret. The Russian nibbles are top flight, too, and you can reserve a table for full dinner in the back dining room. Come early if you want to snag a bar table.

Tír Na Nóg. 5 Penn Plaza (Eighth Ave. between 33rd and 34th sts.). ☎ **212/630-0249.** Subway: 1, 2, 3, 9 to 34th St./Penn Station.

Tír Na Nóg is a standout among the Irish pubs that line Eighth Avenue in the shadow of Penn Station. The handsome decor lends the place a genuine Celtic vibe, as does the Murphy's on tap and the lilt of the friendly bartender. The bar has quickly established itself among both locals and bridge-and-tunnel types for its unpretentious, lively air. There's good pub grub, a small dance floor, and live foot-stompin' Irish music Friday and Saturday nights.

The View Lounge. On the 48th floor of the New York Marriott Marquis, 1535 Broadway (btw. 45th and 46th sts.). ☎ **212/398-1900.** Subway: N, R, 1, 2, 3, 9 to Times Square; N, R to 49th St.

If it's a clear night, head up to this aptly named three-story revolving rooftop bar and restaurant for great views and decent cocktails. Grab a window seat if you can; it takes about an hour to see the 360-degree view of Times Square go by.

Whiskey Park. 100 Central Park South (at Sixth Ave.). ☎ **212/307-9222.** www.midnightoilbars.com. Subway: B, Q to 57th St.

Here's a social scene extraordinaire, courtesy of Mr. Cindy Crawford, bar-and-lounge impresario Rande Gerber. This sleek cocktail lounge is a terrific addition to a chic neighborhood that needed some updating in the nightlife department. The space is gorgeous in a retro-moderne way, featuring all dark woods, mohair upholstery, and mood lighting. This isn't the place to show up in jeans and tennies—the beautiful crowd is super-successful and super-stylish. Come early in the week to really enjoy the place. *Be forewarned, however:* The attitude can swing unpredictably between friendly and condescending.

MIDTOWN EAST & MURRAY HILL

Also consider the **British Open,** 320 E. 59th St., between First and Second avenues (☎ 212/355-8467), a perfect pub for anybody who pines for a well-pulled pint and an easygoing vibe straight outta London; see chapter 6. There's also a comfy, and popular, bar underneath Grand Central's sky ceiling at **Michael Jordan's–The Steak House,** on the mezzanine level (☎ 212/655-2300).

Bull & Bear. At the Waldorf=Astoria. 301 Park Ave. (btw. 49th and 50th sts.). ☎ **212/872-4900.** Subway: 6 to 51st St.

The name speaks to its business-minded clientele; in fact, there's even an LED stock ticker in constant service for those three-martini lunches. The Bull & Bear is like a gentlemen's pub, with brass-studded red leather chairs, a waistcoated staff, and a grand troika-shaped mahogany bar polished to a high sheen at the center of the room. Still, it's plenty comfy for casual drinkers. Ask Oscar, who's been here for more than 30 years, or one of the other accomplished bartenders to blend you a classic cocktail. An ideal place to kick back after a hard day of sightseeing.

The Campbell Apartment. In Grand Central Terminal, 15 Vanderbilt Ave. ☎ **212/953-0409.** Subway: S, 4, 5, 6, 7 to 42nd St./Grand Central.

Additional Sources for Bar- & Club-Hoppers

If you want even more bars and clubs to choose from, pick up the pocket-size *Shecky's Bar, Club & Lounge Guide* or the annual *Time Out New York Eating & Drinking* guide, both available in most city bookstores. Hipster monthly *Paper* boasts opinionated coverage of the downtown bar scene online (**www.papermag.com**). You'll find additional online recommendations at **www.newyork.citysearch.com** and **www.digitalcity.com/newyork.**

This swank new lounge has been created out of the former business office of prewar businessman John W. Campbell, who transformed the space into a pre-Renaissance palace worthy of a Medici. The high-ceilinged room has been restored to its full Florentine glory, and serves wines and champagnes by the glass, single-malt scotches, fine stogies, and haute noshies to a well-heeled commuting crowd. Architecturally impeccable, and well worth seeking out; be prepared for a crowd, however. (*Tip:* Try to snag a seat in the little-used upstairs room if you want some quiet.)

Divine Bar. 244 E. 51st St. (btw. Second and Third aves.). ☎ **212/319-9463.** Subway: E, F to Lexington Ave.; 6 to 51st St.

This glowing hacienda-style wine bar is a big hit with a cute and sophisticated under-40 crowd (think up-and-coming media types and you'll get the picture), with a few older patrons in the mix who come for the excellent selection of wines and microbrews rather than the pickup scene. I prefer the second, fireplace-lit level over the first floor. The deejay plays a familiar, radio-friendly mix, and there's live acoustic music on Sunday. Good tapas and an extensive humidor round out the appeal.

The Ginger Man. 11 E. 36th St. (btw. Fifth and Madison aves.). ☎ **212/532-3740.** Subway: 6 to 33rd St.

The big bait at this appealing and cigar-friendly beer bar is the 66 gleaming tap handles lining the wood-and-brass bar, dispensing everything from Sierra Nevada and Hoegaarden to cask-conditioned ales. The cavernous space has a clubby feel, as Cohiba-toking Wall Streeters and the young men and women they flirt with lounge on sofas and chairs. The limited menu is well prepared, and prices are better than you'd expect from an upmarket place like this.

✪ **King Cole Room.** At the St. Regis hotel, 2 E. 55th St. (at Fifth Ave.). ☎ **212/339-6721.** Subway: E, F to 53rd St.

The birthplace of the Bloody Mary, this theatrical spot may just be New York's best hotel bar. The Maxfield Parrish mural alone is worth the price of a classic cocktail (ask the bartender to tell you about the "hidden" meaning of the painting). The sophisticated setting demands proper attire, so be sure to dress for the occasion. The *New York Times* calls the bar nuts "the best in town," but there's an elegant bar-food menu if you'd like something more substantial.

Mica Bar. 252 E. 51st St. (btw. Second and Third aves.). ☎ **212/888-2453.** Subway: E, F to Lexington Ave.; 6 to 51st St.

This cool Japanese-inspired bar is an ideal spot for a romantic cocktail, or relaxed drinks with a small group of friends. You'll find comfortable low-slung furniture and votives throughout the intimate bilevel space, with petite bonsai tucked into wall niches. The friendly staff serves up a terrific cocktail menu; try the saketini (Finlandia, sake, dry vermouth, cucumber) for a neat twist on the original. Good selections of beer, wine, sake, single malts, and brandies, plus Pan-Asian finger foods are available. A bamboo open-air terrace adds extra appeal in warm weather.

Oak Bar. At the Plaza hotel, 768 Fifth Ave. (at 59th St.). ☎ **212/546-5330.** Subway: N, R to 60th St.

And they do mean oak! The warm wood sets an elegant tone throughout this clubby beer hall. Sumptuous red chairs and old-time waiters set the right mood for the after-work power crowd. The bar gets very crowded after 5pm, but the atmosphere always remains sophisticated and old world.

⚫ **Pen-Top Bar & Terrace.** On the 23rd floor of the Peninsula hotel, 700 Fifth Ave. (at 55th St.). ☎ **212/956-2888.** Subway: E, F to Fifth Ave.

This petite penthouse bar offers some of Midtown's most dramatic views, straight down fabulous Fifth Avenue in both directions. Best of all is the huge rooftop patio, Midtown's best open-air spot on warm evenings—it's much bigger than the bar itself. Expect an extremely well-heeled crowd that doesn't mind the big tab that follows cock-tails here. The Pen-Top is extremely popular, so don't be surprised if you can't get in, especially on nights when the weather isn't accommodating to alfresco revelers.

Top of the Tower. On the 26th floor of Beekman Tower, 3 Mitchell Place (First Ave. at 49th St.). ☎ **212/355-7300.** Subway: 6 to 51st St.

Location is everything, and this lounge has a great one from which to preside over glo-rious Manhattan. The art deco room sets the mood for the view, which includes the romantic Empire State Building. A simply wonderful place to escape the urban bustle for a quiet, elegant drink. A pianist keeps the tone hushed and romantic after 9pm. Pricey but well-respected continental cuisine is served if you'd like to stay for dinner.

THE UPPER WEST SIDE

Amsterdam Avenue from 72nd to 86th streets has evolved into a major bar-hopping strip, dotted with yuppified bars and an ever-growing list of trendy lounges, plus long-standing neighborhood joints like the **Hi-Life Bar & Grill,** at 83rd Street (☎ 212/787-7199), which has a pleasant alfresco patio and makes a great martini; and **Wilson's,** just west of Amsterdam at 201 W. 79th St. (☎ 212/769-0100; www.wilsonsgrill.com), an attractive bar and restaurant, presents good-quality live jazz and blues. I suggest just strolling the avenue on a nice night and popping into the spots that suit your fancy.

All State Cafe. 250 W. 72nd St. (btw. Broadway and West End Ave.). ☎ **212/874-1883.** Subway: 1, 2, 3, 9 to 72nd St.

Despite its proximity to Broadway, this subterranean pub is one of Manhattan's undis-covered treasures. It's easy to miss from the street, and the regulars like it that way. The All State attracts a grown-up neighborhood crowd drawn in by the casual ambience, the great burgers, and an outstanding jukebox. A fireplace makes it even more homey and inviting in cold weather.

Evelyn Lounge. 380 Columbus Ave. (at 78th St.). ☎ **212/724-2363.** Subway: B, C to 81st St./Museum of Natural History.

This basement bar is one of the more chic spots on the Upper West Side. Expect an attractive Victorian-modern space outfitted with velveteen sofas and a stylishly dressed yuppie crowd on the make. There's the requisite cigar room, plus live music a few nights a week.

O'Neal's. 49 W. 64th St. (btw. Broadway and Central Park West). ☎ **212/787-4663.** Sub-way: 1, 9 to 66th St.

O'Neal's easygoing, old-time atmosphere makes it a favorite among a grown-up neigh-borhood crowd as well as students from nearby Juilliard. Lincoln Center is a stone's throw away, making this a great place for a pretheater cocktail or a reasonably priced, if unremarkable, bite to eat.

Shark Bar. 307 Amsterdam Ave. (btw. 74th and 75th sts.). ☎ **212/874-8500.** Subway: 1, 2, 3, 9 to 72nd St.

This perennially popular upscale spot is well known for its good soul food and even better singles' scene. It's also a favorite hangout for sports celebs, so don't be surprised if you spot a New York Knick or two.

THE UPPER EAST SIDE

✪ **Bemelmans Bar.** At the Carlyle hotel, 35 E. 76th St. (at Madison Ave.). ☎ **212/744-1600.** Subway: 6 to 77th St.

Named after children's book illustrator Ludwig Bemelmans, who created the Madeline books after he painted the whimsical mural here, is a supremely luxurious spot for cocktails. Tuck into a dark, romantic corner and nurse a classic martini (both house bartenders have been on the job for more than 40 years) as you eye the best-heeled crowd in town. Jazz vocalist Barbara Carroll has been singing here for 14 years; expect to find her or other relaxing live entertainment Monday through Saturday from 9:30am to 1am ($10 cover).

Brandy's Piano Bar. 235 E. 84th St. (btw. Second and Third aves.). ☎ **212/650-1944.** Subway: 4, 5, 6 to 86th St.

A mixed crowd—Upper East Side locals, waiters off work, gays, straights, all ages—comes to this intimate, old-school piano bar for the friendly atmosphere and nightly entertainment. The talented wait staff does most of the singing while waiting for their big break, but enthusiastic patrons join in on occasion. An appealing and affordable night on the town.

Elaine's. 1703 Second Ave. (btw. 88th and 89th sts.). ☎ **212/534-8103.** Subway: 4, 5, 6 to 86th St.

The Big Chill claimed that Elaine's was over and done with way back when. They were dreaming. Glittering literati still come here for dinner and book parties. Look for such regulars as Norman Mailer, Woody Allen, and other A-list types. If you can't get a table, you can always scan the room from the upfront bar.

Mark's Bar. In the Mark hotel, 25 E. 77th St. (at Madison Ave.). ☎ **212/744-4300.** Subway: 6 to 77th St.

If the more high-profile luxe hotel bars like Bemelmans or the King Cole are just too full, head to this lesser-known but equally appealing compatriot. The space is outfitted like an elegant living room with a romantic flair. The crowd tends to be older and quite used to sipping expensive cocktails like the house Bloody Mary, a worthy challenger to the King Cole's original. Sophisticated nibbles are also served.

8 Dance Clubs & Party Scenes

Nothing in New York nightlife is as mutable as the club scene. In this world, hot spots don't even get 15 minutes of fame—their time in the limelight is usually more like a commercial break.

First things first: Finding and going to the latest hot spot is not worth agonizing over. Clubbers spend their lives obsessing over the scene. My rule of thumb is that if I know about a place, it must not be hip anymore. Even if I could tell you where the hippest club kids hang out today, they'll have moved on by the time you arrive in town.

One big trend in recent years that makes the scene so hard to chart is that "clubs" as actual, physical spaces don't mean much anymore. The hungry-for-nightlife crowd now follows events of certain party "producers" who switch venues and times each week. As the scene becomes more and more amorphous, venues become less and less traditional. Lots of the bars and lounges listed in the previous section host "club" scenes on various nights of the week, such as—at press time, at least—the loungey Beige on Tuesdays at **B Bar,** Testpress Sundays at **Drinkland,** and Mondo-107 Strato-Lounge on Wednesdays at the **Greatest Bar on Earth.**

The tracking game is best left to the perennial party crowd who know the rest of the crowd as well as the guy at the door (who lets them in for free) and someone at the bar (who comps them drinks). You're just not likely to get that well connected in your week of vacation. Just find someplace that amuses you, and enjoy the crowd that enjoys it with you.

In the listings below, I've concentrated on a wide variety of club scenes, from performance artsy to perennially popular discos, most of which are generally easy to make your way into. You can find listings for the most current hot spots and movable parties in the publications and online sources listed in **"Planning Your Trip: An Online Directory"** and in the note called "Additional Sources for Bar- & Club-Hoppers," above. Another good bet is to cruise hip boutiques in SoHo, the East Village, and the Lower East Side, where party planners usually leave flyers advertising the latest goings-on. No matter what, **always call ahead,** because schedules change constantly and can do so at the last minute. Even better: You also may be able to put your name on a guest list that will save you a few bucks at the door.

Keep in mind that New York nightlife starts late. With the exception of places that have scheduled performances, clubs stay almost empty until about 11pm. Don't depend on plastic—bring cash, and plan on dropping a wad at most places. Cover charges often start out high—anywhere from $10 to $30—and often get more expensive as the night wears on.

In addition to the choices below, lovers of Brazilian, Afro-Caribbean, and other world music should seriously consider ✪ **S.O.B.'s** (p. 339), where top-notch live bands keep the dance party sizzling nightly; **Cafe Wha?** (p. 335) isn't quite so high quality, but it also steams up the dance floor. On the other side of the coin, certain bars, like **Lot 61** and **Serena,** evolve into some of the hottest dance-free party scenes in town as the night wears on.

Baktun. 418 W. 14th St. (btw. Ninth Ave. and Washington St.). ☎ **212/206-1590.** www.baktun.com. Subway: A, C, E, L to 14th St.

This newish club, upstairs neighbor to the Cooler (see "Live Rock, Jazz, Blues & More," above), has been hot, hot, hot since the word go. Sleek Baktun was conceived as a multimedia lounge, and as such incorporates avant-garde video projections (shown on a clever double-sided video screen) into its raging dance parties as well as live cybercasts. The music tends toward electronica, with some live acts in the mix. Best among the top-quality parties is N'Ice, a big, unpretentious, Friday night house party.

Centro-Fly. 45 W. 21st St. (btw. Fifth and Sixth aves.). ☎ **212/627-7770.** Subway: F to 23rd St.; N, R to 23rd St.

Anyone who remembers the old rock-and-roll joint Tramps won't believe the swank Op Art club that fills the space now. It's so fab, in fact, that Mary J. Blige used it as a video set. The sunken bar must be the coolest in town. Despite the fabulousness of the place, Centro-Fly is quite welcoming. Two mondo sound systems and a four-turntable booth are luring in top-notch deejay talent. Depending on the night, look for deep house, hip-hop, or another edgy music mix.

Cheetah. 12 W. 21st St. (btw. Fifth and Sixth aves.). ☎ **212/206-7770.** Subway: F, N, R to 23rd St.

With ultrasuede on the walls and cheetah prints everywhere, this outrageously glam club is reminiscent of Studio 54. The Euro-trash crowd loves it. In the words of owner Robert Shalom, "Anyone who wants to have a good time and has $100 to spend will feel welcome." Glitzy Cheetah seems to be experiencing a hip resurgence of late.

Getting Beyond the Velvet Rope

If your heart's set on getting into an exclusive club or lounge, here are a few pointers that may help to tip the scale in your favor:

- **Dress well and fashionably.** Like it or not, the doorman is sizing you up to decide if you're hip enough to make the scene. If you want to get in, you have to play along.
- **Arrive early.** This is an especially good tip for getting into bars like Lot 61. Frankly, the bouncers are just not as vigilant at 9pm, when the place is half empty, as they are at 11pm—and once you're inside, you're in for the night if you wish.
- **Be polite.** No matter how obnoxious the doorman may be, giving attitude back won't help. And who knows? You might just charm him with your winning personality.
- **Don't try to talk your way in.** Don't drop names or make up some story to get in the door. These guys have heard it all. If you're not wanted, why bother? Take your business to a friendlier establishment, where you'll be happier in the long run.

Parties worth seeking out include GBH—"Great British House"—complete with deejays imported from across the pond; and Twelve West, as close to the old 54 as a club gets these days, with a huge crowd partying to a mix that runs the gamut from classic rock to drum-and-bass beats.

Copacabana. 617 W. 57th St. (btw. Eleventh and Twelfth aves.). ☎ **212/582-2672.** www.copacabanany.com. Subway: A, B, C, D, 1, 9 to 59th St./Columbus Circle.

Riding the wave of 1999's Latin Explosion, the Copa once again elicits images of retro-glamour among a grown-up crowd that likes to groove to the hottest Latin music in town. There's a high cheese factor in the glittery Big '80s vibe, but it's all part of the fun. Take a cab to the far-west location.

Culture Club. 179 Varick St. (btw. King and Charlton sts.) ☎ **212/243-1999.** Subway: 1, 9 to Houston St.

Attention Karma Chameleons: This is where the Regan '80s come to life in their full, big-haired glory. This silly dance club attracts a big bridge-and-tunnel and tourist crowd looking for some good, clean fun. Decidedly unhip, very accessible, and lots of retro enjoyment for those with a touch of nostalgia for Duran Duran, Pac Man, Boy Toy–era Madonna, Lita Ford, and *Miami Vice*. On occasion, the tides change and locals move in, as when deejay Grandmaster Flash himself takes to the turntables.

Decade. 1117 First Ave. (at 61st St.). ☎ **212/835-5979.** www.decadeny.com. Subway: N, R to Lexington Ave.; 4, 5, 6 to 59th St.

Finally—somewhere to dance until nearly dawn for the baby boomers. This hybrid supper club/dance club attracts well-dressed, well-heeled thirty-, forty-, and fiftysomethings who lounge in the cigar and champagne bars in between boogie downs to a fun mix of tunes from the '70s, '80s, and '90s. There's live music a few nights a week, including the Monday night All-Star Jam, starring session musicians who've played with the likes of Santana and Aretha Franklin, and live R&B, light jazz, and swing on Tuesday. The service is top-notch, too, making this an all-around terrific (if expensive) place to spend an evening.

Exit. 610 W. 56th St. (btw. Eleventh and Twelfth aves.). ☎ **212/582-8282.** Subway: A, B, C, D, 1, 9 to 59th St./Columbus Circle.

If you want the biggest party in town, read no further. This behemoth club made a big splash when it joined the scene in late '99. It's a doozy—and since it covers 45,000 square feet and is able to accommodate more than 5,000 partiers, any velvet rope scene is pure posturing. The main floor is a mammoth atrium with a deejay booth—usually housing the top talent of the moment spinning tunes—suspended above. The space was made for crazy carnival acts like Antigravity, a bizarre club-land take on the Flying Wallendas. Upstairs is a warren of ultra-plush VIP rooms—each with its own deejay—that has already drawn in celebs like Sandra Bullock and Puffy, who love being on the receiving end of all this fuss. With capacity this big, expect club-goers of all stripes to show up on any given night.

✪ **Mother.** 432 W. 14th St. (at Washington St.). ☎ **212/366-5680.** www.mothernyc. com. Subway: A, C, E to 14th St.

A diverse crowd, both gay and straight, descends on this friendly, long-lived club for a variety of hugely popular events, thanks to the untiring talents of husband and wife Chi-Chi Valenti and Johnny Dynell (she's the hostess; he's the deejay). Saturday's Click + Drag, a futuristic techno-fetish party, is probably the most out-there of the regular events, but just about any night at Mother is a wild one. Now that the legendary 10-year party Jackie 60 has ended, Tuesday's Queen Mother, a campy dress-up drag party (named for the Queen Mum, of course), is a tad mellower but filling the void nicely. Friday's lesbian Clit Club is a club circuit institution. Performance art, poetry readings, and multimedia fun round out the goings-on.

✪ **Nell's.** 246 W. 14th St. (btw. Seventh and Eighth aves.). ☎ **212/675-1567.** www. nells.com. Subway: A, C, E, 1, 2, 3, 9 to 14th St.

After Freud came Nell's in the popularization of the couch in modern life. Nell's was the first to establish a loungelike atmosphere years ago. It has been endlessly copied by restaurateurs and nightclub owners, who have since realized that if people wanted to stay home, why not make "out" just as comfy as "in"? Nell's attracts everyone from homies to Wall Streeters, and it's as marvelous as ever. Most of the parties have a soulful edge. Look for the hugely popular laid-back Voices on Tuesday, sort of a sophisticated weekly *Star Search* that's a showcase for a surprising number of new talents as well as big names looking for an intimate moment (celebs from Brian McKnight to Madonna have exercised their chops here).

Roxy. 515 W. 18th St. (at Tenth Ave.). ☎ **212/645-5156.** www.roxynyc.com. Subway: A, C, E, L to 14th St.; 1, 9 to 18th St.

This megaclub is still going strong, with lights, sound, and action continually drawing a mix of city clubbers, wide-eyed kids from the 'burbs, and straights and gays of every color (including a fair share of divas in drag). There's in-line roller disco on Wednesday and an accessible mix of disco, salsa, and hip-hop on Friday. But the reason to come is Saturday, when Roxy is home to the biggest gay dance party in the city, with legendary deejay Victor Calderone at the helm, spinning a terrific tribal house mix. Live acts on occasion (Joan Jett was on the schedule at press time).

Shine. 285 W. Broadway (at Canal St.). ☎ **212/941-0900.** Subway: A, C, E, 1, 9 to Canal St.

Let's Do the Time Warp

The owner of Nell's, Nell Campbell, was once known as Little Nell, the name under which she appeared as Columbia in *The Rocky Horror Picture Show.*

This new(ish) club draws a well-dressed crowd to TriBeCa with a loungey vibe and a few well-placed 21st-century twists—most notably, great cocktails and terrific deejay talent. The biggest club night is Thursday's Shag, when those uptown yups loosen up and get down to a groovelicious mix; a committed hip-hop crowd takes over after hours. Don't overlook Giant Step Mondays, a new weekly party that has seen such top-flight international deejay talent as Ben Watt (Everything But the Girl). You'll also find cabaret and performance art that runs the gamut from classic to kooky.

Supper Club. 240 W. 47th St. (btw. Broadway and Eighth Ave.). ☎ **212/921-1940.** www. thesupperclub.com. Subway: N, R to 49th St.

This ultra-plush dance hall and supper club has been dressed and waiting for the big-band swing trend to come along for a few years now. The 17-piece house band plays old-school swing every Friday and Saturday night early on for an older supper crowd, with the Supper Club Dancers entertaining with show-stopping dance numbers. Later in the evening, around 11pm, the tables are cleared and the young neo-swingers show up dressed to the nines to strut their stuff to an ultra-hot visiting jump band like the Jumpin' Gigolos or Harlem's fabulous Yallopin' Hounds.

2i's. 248 W. 14th St. (btw. Seventh and Eighth aves.). ☎ **212/807-1775.** Subway: A, C, E, L, 1, 2, 3, 9 to 14th St.

This loungey club is finally getting the attention it deserves, thanks to its unique global spin on the party calendar. The place to come if you're looking for reggae, hip-hop, Latin, R&B, and other soulful sounds.

Twilo. 530 W. 27th St. (btw. Tenth and Eleventh aves.). ☎ **212/268-1600.** www. twilo.com. Subway: C, E to 23rd St.

Go west—way west—to this mega-size dance factory, on the site of the legendary Sound Factory. Superstar deejay Junior Vasquez still spins pulsating dance music marathons, called Juniorverse, for an adoring, mostly gay crowd on Saturday. Twilo Fridays draws an energized straight crowd with imported international deejays. The well-received new Wednesday party hosts live local and international talent for a dance crowd.

○ **Vinyl.** 6 Hubert St. (btw. Hudson and Greenwich sts.). ☎ **212/343-1379.** Subway: A, C, E to Canal St.; 1, 9 to Franklin St.

This commodious TriBeCa club welcomes a big, mixed black/white, gay/straight crowd to hip-hop- and house-flavored party nights ruled by a first-rate crop of deejays. Best of all on an unimpeachable party calendar is the long-lived Body and Soul, a Sunday afternoon acid-garage-house party that's on its way to becoming a legend. Also look at the weekly Dance Ritual, when deejay "Little Louie" Vega spins a house mix flavored with Latin, soul, and gospel for a committed crowd that comes to dance, not pose.

Webster Hall. 125 E. 11th St. (btw. Third and Fourth aves.). ☎ **212/353-1600.** www. webster-hall.com. Subway: 6 to Astor Place.

Five floors and a seemingly endless warren of rooms mean that there's something for everyone at this old warhorse of a nightclub. Weekends are a great time to come if you're just looking for a straightforward crowd and music mix. Even though it's dominated by a bridge-and-tunnel crowd, Webster Hall is still a plenty interesting place to hang, especially if you're with a group. Expect to wait in line to get in.

9 The Gay & Lesbian Scene

To get a thorough, up-to-date take on what's happening in gay and lesbian nightlife, pick up a free copy of *Homo Xtra (HX)* or *HX for Her,* by far the best guides to the gay scene. They're available for free in bars and clubs or at the Lesbian and Gay Community Center (see "Tips for Travelers with Special Needs" in chapter 2). *Time Out New York* also boasts a terrific gay and lesbian section. Always remember that asking people in one bar can lead you to discover another that fits your tastes.

These days, many bars, clubs, cabarets, and cocktail lounges are neither gay nor straight but a bit of both, either catering to a mixed crowd or to varying orientations on different nights of the week. In addition to the choices below, most of the clubs listed under "Dance Clubs & Party Scenes," above, cater to a gay crowd, some predominantly so. Be sure to see what's happening at **Mother, Roxy, Twilo, Exit, Cheetah,** and **Vinyl,** all of which regularly cater to gay and/or gay/straight mixed crowds. The **Duplex** is at the heart of the gay cabaret scene (see "Supper Clubs & Cabarets," above). Among the bars and cocktail lounges, consider **Bar d'O,** particularly on nights when the phenomenal Joey Arias is performing.

✪ **Barracuda.** 275 W. 22nd St. (btw. Seventh and Eighth aves.). ☎ **212/645-8613.** Subway: C, E, 1, 9 to 23rd St.

Chelsea is now central to gay life—and gay bars. This trendy, loungey place is a continuing favorite, voted "Best Bar" by *HX* and *New York Press* magazines, while *Paper* singles out the hunky bartenders. There's a sexy bar for cruising out front and a comfy lounge in back. Look for the regular drag shows.

Big Cup. 228 Eighth Ave. (btw. 21st and 22nd sts.). ☎ **212/206-0059.** Subway: C, E to 23rd St.

Big Cup isn't a bar but a coffeehouse. Still, you'd be hard-pressed to find a cooler, comfier pickup joint, or a more preening crowd. This is where all the Chelsea boys hang; just think of it as a living room-y lounge without the alcohol. By the way, it also happens to be a fab coffeehouse.

Boiler Room. 86 E. 4th St. (btw. First and Second aves.). ☎ **212/254-7536.** Subway: F to Second Ave.

This East Village bar is everybody's favorite gay dive. Despite the mixed guy-girl crowd, it's a serious cruising scene for well-sculpted beautiful boys who just love to pose, and a perfectly fine hangout for those who'd rather play pool.

✪ **The Cock.** 188 Ave. A (at 12th St.). ☎ **212/777-6254.** Subway: L to First Ave.

This gleefully seedy East Village joint is the most envelope-pushing gay club in town. A self-proclaimed "rock and sleaze fag bar" is dedicated to good, sleazy fun: Witness Foxy, a hugely popular regular game show–style party in which the participants compete for "Foxy dollars" from the crowd in increasingly creative ways; needless to say, there's a good deal of hard-bodied nudity involved, and a few Ping-Pong balls among the myriad accessories. Other outrageous antics spice the weekly brew. Head elsewhere if you're the retiring type.

✪ **Crazy Nanny's.** 21 Seventh Ave. South (at Leroy St.). ☎ **212/366-6312.** Subway: 1, 9 to Houston St.

This longstanding lesbian bar is huge, friendly, hugely popular, and perpetually trendy. There's two floors, two bars, a groovy jukebox, dancing, video games, and a variety of theme nights, including Drag Kings and Queens on Thursday, and no-cover Kasual Karaoke on Sunday and Wednesday. Out-of-towners are welcome.

Don Hill's. 511 Greenwich St. (at Spring St.). ☎ **212/219-2850** or 212/334-1390. Subway: C, E to Spring St.; 1, 9 to Canal St.

This big, eclectic place draws a heavily integrated gay-lesbian/straight crowd that comes for top-notch local rock, glam, and punk talent some nights, campy parties on others. The best of the party nights is Squeezebox on Friday, a rollicking gay/straight party with a drag edge. Ultimate groupie (and Liv Tyler's mom) Bebe Buell shows up on the bill occasionally.

✪ **g.** 223 W. 19th St. (btw. Seventh and Eighth aves.). ☎ **212/929-1085.** Subway: 1, 9 to 18th St.

Big crowds of muscular, designer-dressed men have made this lovely, relaxed lounge a popular style scene for meeting dream dates. There's a juice bar, too, and magazines that invite early-hours lounging.

Hell. 59 Gansevoort St. (btw. Washington and Greenwich sts.). ☎ **212/727-1666.** Subway: A, C, E to 14th St.

This glamorous lounge is a sexy haven for a predominantly gay weekend crowd in the hipper-than-hell Meat-Packing District. The cocktails are well mixed, and plenty of comfy sofas are on hand for getting cozy. Ahead of its time in the 'hood, Hell is not quite as ultra-hot as it used to be, but that just means there's more room for you.

Henrietta Hudson. 438 Hudson St. (at Morton St.). ☎ **212/924-3347.** Subway: 1, 9 to Houston St.

This friendly and extremely popular women's bar is known for drawing in an attractive, upmarket lipstick lesbian crowd that comes for the great jukebox and videos as well as the pleasingly low-key atmosphere.

Meow Mix. 269 E. Houston St. (at Suffolk St.) ☎ **212/254-0688.** Subway: F to Second Ave.

This funky East Villager is a great lesbian hangout. It draws in a young, attractive, artsy crowd with nightly diversions like groovy deejays and the hugely popular Xena Night.

Stonewall Bar. 53 Christopher St. (at Seventh Ave. So.). ☎ 212/463-0950. Subway: 1, 9 to Christopher St.

A new bar at the spot where it all started. A mixed gay and lesbian crowd—old and young, beautiful and great personalities—makes this an easy place to begin. At least pop in to relive a defining moment in queer history.

Ty's Bar. 114 Christopher St. (at Bedford St.). ☎ **212/741-9641.** www.tys.citysearch.com. Subway: 1, 9 to Christopher St.

This very friendly, unassuming gay bar has been a part of the Village men's cruise scene for about a million years.

Wonder Bar. 505 E. 6th St. (btw. Avenues A and B). ☎ **212/777-9105.** Subway: 6 to Astor Place.

The "sofa look" has lent a loungier, more stylish tone to this packed-on-weekends East Village hangout. There's some male cruising, but fun, hip, and friendly Wonder Bar gets points for making straights feel welcome, too. Deejays spin a listener-friendly mix in the back room nightly.

Index

See also Accommodations and Restaurant indexes, below.

FROMMER'S® COMPLETE TRAVEL GUIDES

Alaska
Amsterdam
Arizona
Atlanta
Australia
Austria
Bahamas
Barcelona, Madrid &
  Seville
Beijing
Belgium, Holland &
  Luxembourg
Bermuda
Boston
British Columbia & the
  Canadian Rockies
Budapest & the Best of
  Hungary
California
Canada
Cancún, Cozumel &
  the Yucatán
Cape Cod, Nantucket &
  Martha's Vineyard
Caribbean
Caribbean Cruises & Ports
  of Call
Caribbean Ports of Call
Carolinas & Georgia
Chicago
China
Colorado
Costa Rica
Denmark
Denver, Boulder & Colorado
  Springs
England
Europe

European Cruises & Ports
  of Call
Florida
France
Germany
Greece
Greek Islands
Hawaii
Hong Kong
Honolulu, Waikiki &
  Oahu
Ireland
Israel
Italy
Jamaica
Japan
Las Vegas
London
Los Angeles
Maryland & Delaware
Maui
Mexico
Miami & the Keys
Montana & Wyoming
Montréal & Québec City
Munich & the Bavarian
  Alps
Nashville & Memphis
Nepal
New England
New Mexico
New Orleans
New York City
New Zealand
Nova Scotia, New Brunswick
  & Prince Edward Island
Oregon
Paris

Philadelphia & the
  Amish Country
Portugal
Prague & the Best of the
  Czech Republic
Provence & the Riviera
Puerto Rico
Rome
San Antonio & Austin
San Diego
San Francisco
Santa Fe, Taos & Albuquerque
Scandinavia
Scotland
Seattle & Portland
Singapore & Malaysia
South Africa
Southeast Asia
South Pacific
Spain
Sweden
Switzerland
Thailand
Tokyo
Toronto
Tuscany & Umbria
USA
Utah
Vancouver & Victoria
Vermont, New Hampshire
  & Maine
Vienna & the Danube Valley
Virgin Islands
Virginia
Walt Disney World &
  Orlando
Washington, D.C.
Washington State

FROMMER'S® DOLLAR-A-DAY GUIDES

Australia from $50 a Day
California from $60 a Day
Caribbean from $70 a Day
England from $70 a Day
Europe from $60 a Day

Florida from $60 a Day
Hawaii from $70 a Day
Ireland from $60 a Day
Italy from $70 a Day
London from $85 a Day

New York from $80 a Day
Paris from $85 a Day
San Francisco from $60 a Day
Washington, D.C.,
  from $60 a Day

FROMMER'S® PORTABLE GUIDES

Acapulco, Ixtapa &
  Zihuatanejo
Alaska Cruises & Ports of Call
Bahamas
Baja & Los Cabos
Berlin
California Wine Country
Charleston & Savannah
Chicago

Dublin
Hawaii: The Big Island
Las Vegas
London
Maine Coast
Maui
New Orleans
New York City
Paris

Puerto Vallarta, Manzanillo
  & Guadalajara
San Diego
San Francisco
Sydney
Tampa & St. Petersburg
Venice
Washington, D.C.

FROMMER'S® NATIONAL PARK GUIDES

Family Vacations in the
National Parks
Grand Canyon

National Parks of the
American West
Rocky Mountain

Yellowstone & Grand Teton
Yosemite & Sequoia/
Kings Canyon
Zion & Bryce Canyon

FROMMER'S® MEMORABLE WALKS

Chicago
London

New York
Paris

San Francisco
Washington D.C.

FROMMER'S® GREAT OUTDOOR GUIDES

New England
Northern California

Southern California & Baja
Southern New England

Washington & Oregon

FROMMER'S® BORN TO SHOP GUIDES

Born to Shop: China
Born to Shop: France

Born to Shop: Italy
Born to Shop: London

Born to Shop: New York
Born to Shop: Paris

FROMMER'S® IRREVERENT GUIDES

Amsterdam
Boston
Chicago
Las Vegas

London
Los Angeles
Manhattan
New Orleans

Paris
San Francisco
Seattle & Portland
Vancouver

Walt Disney World
Washington, D.C.

FROMMER'S® BEST-LOVED DRIVING TOURS

America
Britain
California

Florida
France
Germany

Ireland
Italy
New England

Scotland
Spain
Western Europe

THE UNOFFICIAL GUIDES®

Bed & Breakfasts in
California
Bed & Breakfasts in
New England
Bed & Breakfasts in
the Northwest
Beyond Disney
Branson, Missouri
California with Kids
Chicago

Cruises
Disneyland
Florida with Kids
Golf Vacations in the
Eastern U.S.
The Great Smoky &
Blue Ridge
Mountains
Inside Disney

Hawaii
Las Vegas
London
Miami & the Keys
Mini Las Vegas
Mini-Mickey
New Orleans
New York City
Paris

Safaris
San Francisco
Skiing in the West
Walt Disney World
Walt Disney World
for Grown-ups
Walt Disney World
for Kids
Washington, D.C.

SPECIAL-INTEREST TITLES

Frommer's Britain's Best Bed & Breakfasts and
Country Inns
Frommer's Britain's Best Bike Rides
The Civil War Trust's Official Guide
to the Civil War Discovery Trail
Frommer's Caribbean Hideaways
Frommer's Food Lover's Companion to France
Frommer's Food Lover's Companion to Italy
Frommer's Gay & Lesbian Europe
Frommer's Exploring America by RV
Hanging Out in Europe
Israel Past & Present

Mad Monks' Guide to California
Mad Monks' Guide to New York City
Frommer's The Moon
Frommer's New York City with Kids
The New York Times' Unforgettable
Weekends
Places Rated Almanac
Retirement Places Rated
Frommer's Road Atlas Britain
Frommer's Road Atlas Europe
Frommer's Washington, D.C., with Kids
Frommer's What the Airlines Never Tell You